OVERCOME BY MODERNITY

OVERCOME BY MODERNITY

HISTORY, CULTURE, AND COMMUNITY IN INTERWAR JAPAN

Harry Harootunian

PRINCETON UNIVERSITY PRESS   PRINCETON AND OXFORD

Library of Congress Cataloging-in-Publication Data
Harootunian, Harry D., 1929–
Overcome by modernity : history, culture, and community in interwar Japan /
Harry Harootunian.
p. cm.
Includes bibliographical references and index
ISBN 0-691-00650-4 (cloth : alk. paper)
1. Japan—Civilization—1912–1945. 2. Japan—Civilization–Western influences.
3. Japan—Relations—Foreign countries. 4. Civilization, Modern—20th century. I. Title.
DS822.4 . H36 2000
952.03'3—dc21   00-022857

This book has been composed in Sabon

The paper used in this publication meets the minimum requirements
of ANSI/NISO Z39.48-1992 (R1997) (*Permanence of Paper*)

www.pup.princeton.edu

Printed in the United States of America
1   3   5   7   9   10   8   6   4   2

For Kristin Ross

Contents

Preface

All the Names of History

WHATEVER else Friederich Nietzsche might have meant when he declared, eponymously, "I am all the names of history" (Letter to Jacob Burckhardt, Turin, January 1889), it is conceivable that despite the different historical routes taken, all, invariably, have arrived at modernity.[1] One of the more widely agreed upon characteristics of modernity, where none practically exists, is the fact that modernism—the ideology of the modern—has subsumed all preceding histories as prefigurations of moments that now have been surpassed. In fact, modernism was so powerful a force that it managed to show how all preceding history was nothing more than its antecedent, a view articulated by Marx, who saw the past of precapitalist formations as a prelude to the establishment of the capitalist mode of production.[2] Under this view, history was simply the overdetermined precedents leading to modernity, whereas modernity became "all the names of history." For Nietzsche, modernity appeared as the cure to the "historical sickness" that was plaguing nineteenth-century Europe, a solution to that "excess of historical consciousness" which inhibited creativity and forced society to enlist its culture from the "vast store house of theatrical masks and costumes" that the past has become for it.[3] Even before Nietzsche, we should recall Marx's withering judgment on the political revolutionaries of the late eighteenth century, who stopped short of "revolutionizing themselves and things, in creating something entirely new" to "anxiously conjure up the spirits of the past to their service and borrow from them names, battle slogans and costumes in order to present the new scene of world history in this time-honored disguise and borrowed language. Thus Luther donned the mask of the Apostle Paul, the Revolution of 1789 to 1814 draped itself alternatively as the Roman Republic and the Roman Empire, and the Revolution of 1848 knew nothing better to do than to parody, in turn, 1789 and the revolutionary tradition of 1793 and 1795."[4]

With Nietzsche, however, the solution was to find "suprahistorical" or "eternalizing" forces within culture that would both staunch the excess of history stifling creativity and signal the "recurrence" of a new beginning. It is not surprising that the pioneer spokesman of this modernist antipathy for history and the counterfeit civilization it authorized in Japan was Takayama Chogyū, who, in his essay "On the Aesthetic Life" (*Biteki seikatsu no ronzu*, 1902), excoriated the civilization of Meiji in the idiom of Nietzsche's withering critique of Europe's bourgeois culture.[5] Like many of his contemporaries, living at the end of the Meiji period, Takayama targeted the shallowness of Japan's new civilization, its commitment to the machine, money, and materiality, and Japan's addiction to a derivative culture, art, architecture, fashion that clearly belonged to another's historical experience. Takayama's prescient denunciation of mediocrity, impoverished creativity, and cultural imitation prefigured the later defense of cultural spirit (*bunka seishin*) and wide-scale rejection of Meiji civilization in the 1930s which, ultimately, contributed to organizing a social discourse devoted to fixing the ground of cultural authenticity and the source of originality and creativity. But it was also a signification of a modernism that would seek to stabilize values, eternalize them, by "overcoming history," by ridding society of the ceaseless fascination with the new and the novel and the succession of change (the ever new in the ever same) that motored modern society, and the specter of unrelieved uncertainty that marked the domination of historical culture.

If Nietzsche called attention to how Europe's cultural creativity had reached an impasse, owing to the excess of historical consciousness that dutifully recorded the temporal passage of the same, and denounced his contemporaries for drawing upon masks and costumes offered by the past, Japanese critics could recognize that their adopted culture was an imitation of an imitation, a reification of a reification, a mask covering a mask. This was the problem inevitably faced by so-called industrial latecomers, who always came too late to a capitalist culture that already was in process of emptying progress of value and moving toward the logic of overcoming. While I will discuss the problematic status of envisaging Japan as a "latecomer" or "late-developing" society below, it is important to say here that the narrative that dominated Japanese sensibility between the wars was distinguished by a consciousness that oscillated furiously between recognizing the peril of being overcome by modernity and the impossible imperative of overcoming it. Between the two world wars, Japanese society underwent a massive industrial transformation, introducing a whole panoply of new technologies driven by new sources of electric power and machine production. By 1918 its cities were showing the formation of large, industrial sites, recruiting its labor force from the countryside (a migration that must surely have established a record for swiftness), and the country was perched to embark upon the production of commodities for mass consumption. This experience, which established what Japanese called "modern life" in the short space of roughly two decades, was positively described as the moment Japan was overwhelmed by modernity. Yet the same period of time also saw Japan commit itself to a war with those very industrial societies it had earlier joined in World War I, and its most prominent thinkers, critics, and artists inaugurate a symposium in 1942 at Kyoto that systematically tried to assess the meaning of the recent experience of modernization and how best to overcome the modern.

This book is concerned with Japan's entry into the heroic phase of capitalist expansion—what the critic Uchida Roan described in 1918 as the "essential something that has captured the public spirit"—and with how Japanese reflected on the experience of "modern life" in the crucial decades between the two world wars. It is not concerned with retrieving the experience of modernity as lived by Japanese during this period, as if the real, as such, could be transparently presented in the narrative of social history, but rather with how that experience was thought about and discussed, and how contemporaries recalled what they lived through.

This historical moment was marked by the intensification of the process of capitalist modernization which, as is well known, had begun earlier in the nineteenth century under the impetus of the new, reformist Meiji government. But it was only at the time of World War I, and because of Japan's decision to enter the war on the Allied side, that the process of modernization, originally characterized by a commitment to developing light industries and installing the necessary infrastructure, moved to heavy and capital industries driven by new sources of power. As a result of the war and the shift to a new productive register, Japan was transformed into an industrial power equal to most European nations like France, England, and even Germany, according to leading indices of development, ahead of societies like Italy and the Soviet Union but trailing the United States. According to Sawada Ken, in an article appearing in 1923 in *Chūō kōron*, Japan's urbanization, reflecting the industrial transformation, compared favorably and significantly with that of the world's principal countries. Appealing to demographic data and the movement of populations as criteria, Sawada proposed that Japan possessed an economy of scale that already was beginning to match other, more mature industrial societies. What differed was merely the modality of expansion, as Japan's urbanization assumed a more horizontal trajectory, while the growth of cities in Western societies seemed to show a penchant for verticality. People who visit and look at the "forest of skyscrapers standing in a row in Manhattan remark: "The cities of Europe and the United States have developed vertically. But the cities of Japan have developed horizontally.' "[6]

Supported by a general common sense expressed by a number of contemporary observers, Sawada's view contrasts sharply with later historical and social scientific accounts that have depended upon the category of "late developer" to explain Japan's eventual turn to militarism and fascism in the late 1930s, aping the experience of Germany and Italy, yet contrasted to France and England, which supposedly had developed mature, liberal, and democratic institutions because modernization had taken place earlier and over a longer period of time. Both Marxists and non-Marxists explain the experience of latecomer or late-developing societies as instances of how the economic time-lag caused "politically" deformed development (including both fascism and "actually existing socialism") and produced what has come to be called "alternative modernities" that seem to lack (according to the congratulatory conceit of so much liberal social science) the necessary institutions capable of avoiding and braking the slide into political totalism, transmuting quantitative temporality into qualitative difference. But what the late-developer explanation always neglects to make clear is that during the 1920s and 1930s, virtually every country in the West (including the United States) experienced either a fascist movement or powerful intellectual and cultural impulses that clearly displayed recognizable characteristics associated with fascism.[7] It is interesting to note that a significant sector of Marxism and non-Marxists both emphasized the dominant and privileged role of economic forces, hence promoting an economism that excluded other factors. In the case of Marxists of the Third International this argument was carried over to an assessment of imperialism itself. Among non-Marxists, notably supporters of modernization and neomodernization (currently called globalization), the theory of a time lag has led to promoting a model of economic and political development according to which the Western historical experience (United States, France, and England) appears as normative and the route to modernity these societies putatively followed becomes the one most capable of evolving those institutions of state and civil society that would avoid large-scale revolutionary upheaval. Marxists, on their part (and I wouldn't exclude variations like "world-systems" theory) saw late development as a consequence of an "imperialist chain" (the phrase is from Nicos Poulantzas) that put the periphery (Asia, Africa, Latin America) at the mercy of the center, the core, as it were, comprised of the major industrial powers, whose expansion depended upon the availability of new markets, abundant raw materials, and cheap and plentiful labor. But Marxists of the Third International deviated from a Leninist conception of imperialism by envisaging it as simply an economistic phenomenon—the stage of monopoly and finance capitalism. Others, however, like Poulantzas, returning to a modified Leninist understanding, have sought to show that fascism actually belongs to the imperialist stage of capitalism and that its primary causes stem neither from the experience of late development nor from economic crises. While these factors are important in accounting for the entire ensemble of imperialism, "as elements of *one of the possible conjunctures* of this stage," fascism is not exclusively reducible to them.[8] "Imperialism . . . is not in fact just a question of modifications in the economic domain, such as monopoly concentration, the fusion of banking and industrial capital into finance capital, the export of capital, and the search for colonies for purely 'economic' reasons, etc. These 'economic' factors actually determine a new articulation of the capitalist system, thereby producing profound changes in *politics* and *ideology*."[9] In this view, fascism develops not as the linear successor to the bourgeois-liberal state (as Tosaka Jun observed long before Poulantzas), but rather from complex and often shifting class alliances, the ambiguous character of popular support it has enlisted in the initial stages, a willingness to make "compromise measures" to support diverse class aspirations and illusions, and, ultimately, fascism's move to purge itself of its class origins, and indeed class itself, even as it realigns with big business.[10] With this move, fascism, as we shall see, produced an ideology that corresponded to petty bourgeois yearnings, as Aono Suekichi presciently observed in 1930 (the fetishism of power, strong state, intensive concerns for national culture, corporatism and authoritarianism, technocracy, not to forget militarism), that was compatible with imperialism.[11]

By privileging economism, both Marxian and non-Marxian narratives, in any case, agreed that late development prompted rapid economic development in countries like Germany, Italy, and Japan, state sponsored at the expense of developing mediating social and political institutions—civil society and the usual separation of public and private spheres that would curb the excesses of the state. For modernizers, the realignment of capitalist development and individual rights according to a model of evolutionary, linear "growth" would lead to the establishment of a liberal-democratic order. This narrative of evolutionary growth would show the persistence of older, cultural values as they were enlisted to assist the seemingly natural transition to a new social formation. In this scenario, traditional values were therefore measured by their capacity to adapt to new and evolving conditions, thus demonstrating their fitness for survival or their inability to make the necessary adjustment, which would guarantee their disappearance as society moved to a higher stage. By contrast, Marxists, regardless of internal differences, saw unevenness—the survival of feudal residues in a modernizing society—as the calamitous sign of social contradictions filled with revolutionary potential. By emphasizing the centrality of the time lag, virtually fetishized in the social sciences since the 1950s, based on the presumption of a single and thus normative temporality, both narratives could call attention to the uniqueness of each national experience. What I mean by this is that a single and normative temporality would show where a society was located on the developmental trajectory and how far it needed to go to catch up. Yet this distance would also encourage a search for those cultural values in the late-developing society that could be analogously matched to Western values, which were seen to have already assisted the development of England, France, and the United States as mature, modern societies. This meant that a single, normative temporality constantly demanded a comparative perspective in which the latecomer that closed the distance was seen as unique and exceptional, whereas others that had not shown a capacity to develop lacked the necessary cultural means to catch up and were locked in a zone of timelessness. Hence, modernizers who privileged evolutionary growth invariably highlighted the importance played by "traditional" cultural values, institutions, and practices that had survived from the past to now negotiate new directions and orientations. In the 1960s and 1970s, there was, in the study of Japan, a powerful intellectual consensus that was convinced that Japan had, in fact, avoided the route of revolutionary violence taken by societies like China and Russia precisely because of the mediating and ameliorating role played by enduring values that could peacefully adapt to new exigencies. This elastic capacity for adaptations by older values in new situations was, of course, the mark of their fitness.[12]

Marxists, on their part, unfailingly called these surviving residues feudal hangovers, whose presence in the midst of modernizing societies constituted instances of serious social contradictions that the contemporary arrangement of authority, consisting of persisting elements of the old order combined with new, political forms, would not be able to contain in the near future.[13] But no less than modernizers, they claimed that the coexistence of traditional and modern forms meant that the modern experience was exceptional and not bound to models derived from other histories. The trouble with this view is that it conformed precisely to what Marxists like Walter Benjamin and Ernst Bloch were saying of the modern and modernizing experience in Europe during the interwar period, which Bloch saw, presciently, as the sign of capitalism's inevitable propensity to produce unevenness, even though it promised eventual even development everywhere it prevailed. Japanese Marxist explanations of Japan's modernity in the 1930s often risked resembling the interpretations of more strident ultranationalists who were busily trying to represent the nation's character as unique and exceptional, despite the shadow of absolutism inscribed in contemporary political culture. Instead of concentrating on the development of capitalism as a global process, they focused on the formation of capitalism within Japan, thus implying the existence of a state prior to the introduction of capitalism, which was its most recent historical form, and privileging the race nation as the principal unit of analysis.

While these two narratives have jointly contributed immensely to our understanding of Japan's modernity, it has been at a price of privileging certain forms of historical inquiry, economistically driven social/political history, and marginalizing others. It has been accomplished by emphasizing the primacy of structures, institutions, and movements over thought and experience, as if they were lived separately. In this book I focus explicitly on the problem of politics and culture and their often mutual imbrication during the interwar period. I want to explain why thinkers as different as Walter Benjamin and Miki Kiyoshi and Georges Bataille, writing from entirely different locations, converged on the task of trying to account for the aporetic relationship between politics and culture, experience and possibility, modernism and fascism as the condition for properly understanding their moment and how they might best act in the current situation. From Benjamin's all too familiar call for a reversal of the contemporary fascist tendency to "aestheticize politics" to Miki's announcement at virtually the same time that the most important problem of the day confronting the world was the steady "politicization of culture," we have, I think, a disclosure of an experience that a good deal of historiography has simply ignored or failed to see.

With this problematic in view, I have tried, in any case, to avoid the logic of the prevailing received narratives that have persistently appealed to the comparative experience of late economic development as the invariant element in explaining Japan's modern history and its difference from Western industrial societies. It is important to understand the assumptions made by that logic. The modernizing strategy, as I have suggested, has seen development comparatively according to a baseline experience attributed to Western societies, tracking the variable locations of latecomers like Japan, and assessing the political and social costs incurred from starting later. In this scenario, it is assumed that capitalism, despite when and where a society starts, will eventually lead to even development within society, the establishment of an even ground sometime in the indeterminate future. Hence, the thrust of this explanatory strategy is to focus almost exclusively on the unevenness *between* societies as the marker of relative development, not on its appearance *within* societies. By doing so, it effectively displaces the vast structural imbalance that always accompanies capitalism, its "innermost antagonistic character," and its inevitable propensity for constant crises.[14] Moreover, this strategy often bypassed the visible signs of unevenness in the cultural domain altogether in order to account for the inequalities in the political economic realm.

In fact, capitalism has no really normal state but one of constant expansion; and expansion requires the permanent production of excess, surplus, in order for it to survive. Part of the price paid for continual expansion is the production of permanent unevenness, permanent imbalance between various sectors of the social formations, the process by which some areas must be sacrificed for the development of others, such as the countryside for the city in the early days of Japan's transformation, as noted by Yanagita Kunio, the colony for the metropole, or even one city for another.

Capitalism, in the language of DeLeuze and Guattari, is "continuously reterritorializing with one hand what it has deterritorialized with the other." It is at this point where the necessary illusion of eventual even development is conceptualized, constituting a kind of promissory note on the future that is never delivered, even in the last instance. While Marxists have shown more sensitivity toward the specter of unevenness within societies, articulated in class antagonism and the scandal of social contradiction, too often they have, like non-Marxian modernizers, displaced it to the global scene as a marker of comparative development that will ultimately be eliminated by full and even development, whether socialistic or capitalistic. Without throwing out the baby with the bathwater, it will be the effort of this book to resituate unevenness back to domestic society in order to assess its effects on the production of culture in its interaction with a modernizing political economy.

But the really crucial consequence of the time-lag strategy has been the projection of an image of different temporalities in different climes or longitudes. In this script, temporality was always measured from one, base time line since, it was believed, true time was kept by the modern West. What this has meant is that so-called global late developers like Japan, and indeed any colonized society, exist in a temporality different from the modern, in a suspended state of growth that still lacks full maturity and thus timeliness. It is precisely this time lag that produces the scandal of imagining modernities that are not quite modern—usually a euphemism for being "not quite white"—and new, often outrageous classifications like "alternative modernities" or retroactive modernities differentiated from the temporality of the modern West which, then, allow us to safely situate societies like Japan in a historical trajectory derived from another's development.

In this book, I am interested in showing that Japan's modernity, far from moving toward the achievement of true time, as if there were a developmental archimedean point (after all, what else is modernization theory?), was rather an inflection of a larger global process that constituted what might be called co-existing or co-eval modernity, inasmuch as it shared the same historical temporality of modernity (as a form of historical totalizing) found elsewhere in Europe and the United States. Where my conception differs from the more recent appeals to "alternative" and "retroactive" modernities is in the recognition that co-eval modernity simply calls attention to the experience of sharing the same temporality, that whatever and however a society develops, it is simply taking place at the same time as other modernities. But the experience also, and necessarily, marks a difference. The problem raised by the formulation of an "alternative" modernity is the unstated presumption of exceptionalism and uniqueness. The appeal to the adjectival "alternative" implies not just difference but one that constitutes a better choice. What co-eval suggests is contemporaneity yet the possibility of difference.[15] This sense of difference characterized the experience of modernity elsewhere—in China, with its semi-imperialist status, among late developers like Brazil, in colonized societies like India—and reflected the negotiation between the local and received cultural habits—the culture of reference—and the requirements of the new global processes of capitalist expansion. In many ways, the interwar experience of Japan's "modern life" constituted a doubling and thereby a reworking through the logic of historical repetition of the modernizing process that undoubtedly was occurring in places like Brazil, India, and China. Thinkers and writers responded to Japan's modernity by describing it as a *doubling* that imprinted a difference between the new demands of capitalism and the market and the force of received forms of history and cultural patterns. Although this conception of doubling was frequently seen as a unique emblem of Japan's modern experience, its logic showed that modernity everywhere would always result in what the philosopher Watsuji Tetsurō, and others who figure prominently in this book, called a "double life" (*nijū seikatsu*), and what Ernst Bloch, commenting on German life in the early 1930s, described as the "synchronicity of the non-synchronous, the simultaneity of the non-contemporaneous." Both writers point to the jarring coexistence of several pasts and the present in the now of everydayness, often in a relationship of unevenness.[16] Among a number of thinkers in the interwar period, this form of cultural analysis supplied the optic through which to see the spectacle of modern life taking place before them. Yet, they could have been describing any cultural experience marked by the penetration of capital and its conception of social formation into the received system of reference.

If we can agree that Japanese society was physically changed by the end of World War I, or on its way to a progressively qualitative and quantitative transformation as a result of the consequent move to heavy and capital industries capable of producing commodities for large-scale consumption, we are in a position to read its effects on the formation of "modern life" in Japan differently. What this entails is seeing modernity as a particular mode of experience that is not necessarily and only reducible to the empirical domain, as many historians have believed. Instead of examining the material transformation of Japanese society as an instance of some hypostatized conception of the social—the very subject and substance of social and political history—we need to read this episode not for the familiar story lines authorized by such historical narratives but rather as the production of experience that tried to catch hold of the moving present ("fleeting and fragmentary," as Baudelaire described the modern present) and thus give it meaning and direction. By the same measure, we need to account for the reason why Japanese produced so much thought during this period that sought to grasp this experience of material transformation philosophically rather than merely sociologically or empirically; why, in fact, the terms for understanding and interpreting were overwhelmingly philosophic and only secondarily sociocultural; and why, as Tosaka Jun put it, "everydayness" (*nichijōsei*) had to be seen as a philosophic concept in order to understand the "modern life" of the present. However much Tosaka condemned the contemporary practice of hermeneutics (especially his old teacher Nishida Kitarō) as a bourgeois philosophy, his own approach to the modern experience was just as philosophic and interpretative.

Nevertheless, before we turn to this question, it is still important to provide an idea of the historical conjuncture that marked Japan's passage into accelerated capitalist modernization and the force of the context it produced. During the decade of the 1920s and into the 1930s (usually referred to by their reign names, Taishō, 1912–1926, and Shōwa, 1926–1988), Japanese society witnessed a heightened urbanization, the expansion of industrialization, capital accumulation, and thus a significant increase of leading indices to put the country proximally close to most industrial societies.[17] Historically, Japanese society was changed by the war and the swift move to heavier forms of industrialization. War and vast industrial growth signaled, according to both Arno Mayer and Perry Anderson, the installation of a global historical conjuncture where "differing historical temporalities gathered to constitute a field of overdetermination."[18] This conjuncture was undoubtedly prompted by the war (accelerated in countries like Germany and Japan, which stayed on the sidelines but served as a major supplier to the Allies) and its subsequent peacetime transformation to commodity production for mass consumption. Politically, it was distinguished by what Mayer has identified as the "persistence" of the old order—the rule of semi-aristocratic political classes rooted in the land—despite the pace of capitalist modernization and the formation of new classes like the *zaikai* in Japan. During and after the war, the emergence of new social constituencies (gender, status groupings, sexual identities) and classes, fueled by a growing consciousness of disenfranchisement, began actively to challenge the received arrangements of authority and order by demanding reform and revolution. In Japan, this upheaval coincided with the period of "Taishō Democracy," and the organization of a labor movement and tenant unions in the countryside and new, radical, and not so radical political movements led by socialists, Marxian communists, anarchists, and social democrats calling for a widening of the political franchise, broader participation, and social reconstruction (*kaizō*). But what distinguished this conjuncture most in Japan, and undoubtedly elsewhere, was the co-existence of the place between precapitalist pasts that had not yet disappeared with capitalism, industrialization in an indeterminate present being lived by large numbers of people in the cities, and, finally, an unenvisaged future that thinkers were trying to imagine on the basis of what had already changed.[19]

Accordingly, the coordinates of this global conjuncture were the persistence of a predominately agrarian political order rapidly in the process of becoming industrialized, with its semi-aristocratic ruling class (in Japan marked by the entrenchment of the emperor, the court, and those oligarchs who could claim the right domainal credentials), and an emergent industrial capitalist system with its incipient labor movement. What marked this moment in Japan and elsewhere, especially in the expanding metropolitan cities like Tokyo and Osaka (not to forget Berlin, London, Paris, New York), was a discernible production of "modern life," often identified as the experience of everydayness, that was made possible by the massive transformation of the political economy from the time of World War I and after. In Japan and elsewhere, modernity was seen as a spectacle of ceaseless change (the narrative of historical progress and the law of capitalist expansion) and the specter of unrelieved uncertainty introduced by a dominant historical culture no longer anchored in fixed values but in fantasy and desire. This observation was as true of Germany, as refracted first by thinkers like Georg Simmel and Seigfried Kracauer, and France, with its own interwar fascination with "Americanization," as it was of Japan, where the concern for modern life was even more overdetermined as a generation of perceptive thinkers, writers, and scholars tried to make sense of the spectacle of modernity—the experience of the new in the ceaseless flow of change—and calculate the meaning of its destabilizing force. What immediately captured the attention of thinkers and writers was this experience of the new and its consequences for settled social relationships, new classes, subjectivities, gender, and sexuality and how the production of desire was threatening to undermine the received culture of reference. Just as Kracauer completed an account of the German "white-collar class" in his *Die Angestellten* (1930) that charted their sagging aspirations and growing anxieties, provoked by a growing sense of homelessness and the search for "shelter," the Japanese writer and critic Aono Suekichi (1890–1961) published, at the same time, his *Sarariman: kyōfu no jidai*. Even though Aono's text appeared at the same moment as Kracauer's book and addressed similar themes, as both shared a common sympathy for Marxism, it owed nothing to it. What Aono aimed to show was the panic lived by Japan's middle-class workers.

Ultimately, the concern for laying hold of an experience capable of resisting the erosions of change and supplying a stable identity—difference—in a world dominated by increasing homogeneity and sameness was the way discourse recoded the historical problem of the interwar period. By focusing on the spectacle of historical surplus and excess and the need to find an authentic and stable ground in the ceaselessly shifting scene, discourse pointed to the emergent regime of "modern life" and its production of an experience rooted in the mass consumption of commodity culture. In other words, the very conditions the postwar world welcomed and even "toasted," according to Theodore Adorno, the very means to celebrate the heady promise of the 1920s, also produced the phenomena of "atrophy," "neutralism," and the "guilt of death" that resulted in abdicating the responsibility to stem the general terror and oppression that would appear later. "These phenomena," Adorno observed, "were formed within the societies of a liberalist Europe. . . ."[20] But the same could be said of Japan during these years, which saw the Great Kantō Earthquake, the murder of countless Korean workers and anarchists, the plunge into continental imperialism and the appearance of militarism masquerading behind imperial legitimacy. In Japan, the acceleration of industrial capitalism and the momentary surge of liberalism combined to make up for the deficit in social revolution left by the Meiji Restoration. But according to Tosaka Jun, the failure to complete such a social revolution was already inscribed in the structure of capitalism (the regime of private property) Meiji Japan installed and the liberalism it authorized, which naturally opened the flood gates and thus accommodated every kind of jingoism and fascism under its protective, pluralistic umbrella.[21] Hence the very context of capitalist modernization that accounts for the explosion of a modernist response was also the preparatory ground for the "gathering of fascism."[22]

When I refer to modernism and modernists in this book, I am using the term not as a limited aesthetic marker but as a broad signifier that includes art and literature, to be sure, but also philosophy, religion, and social and political thought. I am also using modernism as an ideologization of the process of capitalist modernization and transformation Japanese were experiencing and trying to grasp. Although Japanese modernism conformed to the broader global conjuncture, it also decisively inflected it into patterns of difference that marked, as elsewhere, the distinct place where a regional past co-existed with industrialization. In this sense, it is probably more accurate to refer to modernisms rather than a singular modernism, just as it is more useful to designate fascisms rather than a single, all-encompassing model. But like fascism, there are as many definitions and explanations of modernism as there are people willing to speak about it. While older cultural models, usually identified as "academic," associated with a still available past constituted a target for modernism and its recognition that the stability of forms was being undermined by ceaseless change, they also continued to supply an arsenal of resources that could be mobilized to withstand the ruin and reification caused by capitalist modernization and the market, which already had begun to serve as an organizing principle for new social relationships, identities, and value. Arno Mayer, writing about the appearance of modernism in late nineteenth-century Europe, noted an interesting contradiction between an emergent bourgeoisie that favored collecting "classical" art, "buying or building 'historical' country manors or city mansions, and patronizing the traditional performing arts" rather than "encouraging" and "appropriating" the modern quest. The effect of this appropriation of older cultural models was to reaffirm "ruling classes and official cultures that were disproportionately oriented to the preindustrial and prebourgeois world."[23] Despite the usual association of avant garde dismissal and contempt for history, as such, the past, especially precapitalist past, offered a storehouse of tropes for modernist rearticulation that could be deployed against the ruin of reification. In a paradoxical way, these modernists against modernity, as Raymond Williams has called them, sought in historical representations a refuge against the alienating effects of everyday modern life and thus attributed to art and culture, in the broadest sense, absolute value that remained immune from the changing valuations of the market and the political world. Modernism in Japan sought, therefore, to resist the culture of capitalism (Anderson reminds us how most modernists shared an antipathy for the market, even though he fails to add that many embraced a capitalism without its periodic crises and social effects) and an emerging modern life that itself was constantly being buffeted by a process of revolutionizing production, chronic civil strife, and social and economic uncertainty. Above all else, modernism in Japan's interwar period was produced in a conjuncture that prompted the recognition of a vast field of economic and cultural unevenness that it sought to resolve, overcome, and even repress. That is, modernism sought to flee history at the same time that it appealed to older historical representations of the authentic cultural object as a way to replace abstraction and fragmentation with concreteness and wholeness.

Modernism was the historical watermark of uneven development, its signature, even though it sought to efface and repress this historical condition of production. I have already suggested that capitalism has no really normal, balanced state, even though it claims one in an indeterminate future. Japanese capitalism was no exception, despite the early Meiji effort to avoid the free play of the market by privileging state control over the fair market price as the governing engine of the economy, favoring political regulation over the economy to regulate business cycles. Yet, despite this substitution of state over market, politics from the top over economics from below (the market), Japanese society was not able to completely circumvent the effects of an inherent structural imbalance built into the system. This was especially true of the period after World War I, which experienced a sustained roller coaster ride in the economy that came to a crashing climax with the world depression.[24] Because capitalism was devoted to the realization of infinite expansion and the production of excess, it was faced with the constant crisis of accumulation, the constant revolutionizing of its conditions of existence, and thus the constant manufacturing of unevenness. Growth, after all, depends upon recognizing that some areas will always be sacrificed for the development of others. To be sure, this experience of unevenness was seen in Japan, and elsewhere, as simply an inevitable but temporary stage in a trajectory that would eventually lead to even development in all sectors and societies. But this was a necessary ideological claim to justify unlimited expansion and the production of surplus and excessive desire, if not to explain the periodic crises as blips in the larger narrative of capitalism. The presumption of a normal, balanced state was a necessary fiction, in other words, whose promise would finally be reached in the indeterminate future. In this way, more advanced countries—those designated as the center of the industrial world in the interwar period—could export their own domestic unevenness abroad, knowing that unevenness was the permanent, normal state of capitalism and not simply a passing historical stage. They could thus displace their domestic unevenness to the colonies and countries on the periphery like Japan and Latin America, where the process of industrialization had begun later than it had in Western Europe and the United States. (Some writers, today, see in the Third World the specter of permanent and unrelieved unevenness, but they could look closer to home for its signs.)

It was the spectacle of lived unevenness in both the political economic and sociocultural domains that enabled the formation of a modernism capable not only of repressing all of the signs of this experience but of looking forward to the accomplishment of a progressive, modern society where all the remnants, residues of the archaic, even the "sense of history," have been swept away or effectively effaced. Fredric Jameson, who entertains this relationship between modernism and the unevenness of "simultaneous non-simultaneity" (Bloch), has seen modernism as a stage that is historically overcome with the establishment of postmodernity, which he characterizes as more modern than modernism.[25] But this affirmation relies on seeing an earlier modernism congruent with uneven development as a temporary historical stage that will soon be succeeded by a fuller and, presumably, more even development. In Japan, this form of modernism was early formulated to repress the marks of unevenness in both political economic (temporal) and sociocultural (spatial) realms and was ultimately transmuted, by the end of the 1930s, into a call to overcome the modern—precisely the "historical stage" of uneven modernity that had enabled the production of an ideology of modernism in the first place. Yet if it sought to conceal the calamitous signs of unevenness everywhere by pointing to its eventual elimination in a truly modern society, it also revealed the persistence of unevenness in the way it related the cultural/aesthetic realm to the political economic. What I mean is that modernism in Japan valorized culture in such a way as to declare its removal or semi-autonomy from the political economic domain and thus its immunity from commodification. With this move, it announced a different kind of uneven relationship between the cultural (spatial) and the political economic (temporal), and the establishment of a sphere free from the commodity form and a space from which to mount a critique against the prevailing political and social order. But this appeal to culture and communitarianism was, as I show later, simply the inverse of the commodity form itself. At one level, this move to the spatial-cultural/aesthetic represented a utopian aspiration, in the effort to mark out a zone not yet infected by the commodity; at another, it was simply the utopian shadow of what was already ideological-social abstraction. In this way, fascism provided a kind of inner lining to modernism.

Yet the appeal to culture and community also derived from the process of social fragmentation introduced by the division of the labor, alienation, and the establishment of "semi-autonomous" and "compartmentalized" domains that the 1942 symposium on overcoming the modern would locate in the momentous division of knowledge and the specialization of spheres. The progressive fragmentation of social life also dramatized the difference between "lived time" and commodified clock time or a temporality measured by money, the recalling of the archaic which was often still visible against the routines of everyday life, and the separation of the senses, especially as Yanagita Kunio (1875–1962) observed in *Meiji Taishōshi, sesōhen* when he conceded the importance of the "eye that sees society."[26] In this account, Yanagita reported that the actor Ueyama Sojin, returning after a long stay in Hollywood, noted how the look or gaze of Tokyoites had become "very fearsome." What this referred to was the practice of living in the city that constantly demanded looking at reality "repeatedly" because the position of the individual was always changing. This shift to the eye contrasted with village life where people rarely ever looked at one another or made eye contact as they passed each other on the street because they knew who they were passing. To this end, Yanagita advised rethinking older colors and even sounds that had once been taken for granted.[27] In this regard, Jameson has argued that recognition of the new was possible only in circumstances characterized by the constant contrast of modern practices and older customs, where the new was easily identified as something that was not old, received, customary (a view that informs Yanagita's book on Meiji and Taishō society), where past mixed uneasily with the present, the ever changing with the static.[28] Georg Simmel, in his penetrating essay on "The Ruin," pointed to how the landscape housed the residues of different pasts next to new, modern buildings, streets, and sites, and how the contrast forged an acute awareness and sorting out of the new and the old. The new is experienced as modern because the old and archaic are still around. At the level of social relationships, Edogawa Rampo's detective stories, written in the 1920s and 1930s, constantly hammered on the theme of triangulated love affairs ending badly for the woman, who usually was made to pay for exceeding the role assigned to her by the Civil Code and popular ideology. In this world women are forced to remain as reminders of the old and traditional, even though modern life has made it possible for them to live more autonomously, while men are always permitted to live the new as if it was natural to them.[29] Yet it was the novelist Tokunaga Sunao who best described the dilemma of unevenness lived by Japanese in the 1920s and how social contradiction had become a permanent imprint of "modern life." In his novel *Taiyō no nai machi* (Streets without sun), Tokunaga stages a scene that clearly demonstrates the profound mix of the new and old at both the material and ideological levels. Portraying the importance of the street—the durable sign of Japanese modern life in the 1920s—he captured a moment of lived unevenness and the clash of different temporalities that lay at the heart of Japan's modern experience:

> The streetcars, automobiles, trucks and bicycles all stop; even the side cars, which come flying impetuously, chained to each other, come to a halt. What's happened? What has occurred? The pale November sun brings out swarms of people as if they were rough knobs in a sand storm. The human wave, like a cluster of beads in a pool, shove against each other and begin to sway. What has happened is the "Imperial Passing Through," the visitation of an important personage to the Prince Regent. Whispers that begin at the front [of the stalled crowd] spread, in an instant, to the rear. The motor cars stop their buzzing; people remove their hats.

Tokunaga's scene shows how the intense movement on the streets—the sign of the modern—and the incessant crowds of people, noise, and chaos suddenly come to a screeching halt because an imperial retinue is passing through to immediately reveal the powerful co-existence of the old in the form of the emperor system, an archaic residue from a distant agrarian society deposited now in the center of the modern street intersection.[30] In other words, the new was constantly buffeting against the old, often demanding a mode of accommodation between their separate claims. Yet such encounters seemed immediately to call attention to the problem of time, the market's capacity to effectively freeze the moment of history, replacing lived time with the procession of the timeless commodity. Circumstances such as these prompted Walter Benjamin, in another place, to observe that "fashion is the eternal recurrence of the new."[31]

In carrying out the modernist project, Japanese often appropriated the diverse pasts signified by remnants and residues, standing as mute reminders of different times and experience, dramatically contrasted to the ever-changing new as points of "involuntary" recall of a lived moment that, they believed, was both whole and coherent, and thereby free from the erosions of the market and the "flair for fashion." The past signaled by surviving residues, like Simmel's "ruins," offered the prospect of a life and experience that was located in a different formation. The presence of the past in artifacts, practices, temples testified to both precapitalist origins and its capacity to resist the instability of the "eternal recurrence of the new," the world of the commodity form and the regime of social abstraction necessitated by the capitalist system of exchange value. At the same time, the memory of a prior time and lived experience supplied the material for the construction of an image of national culture seemingly devoid of all marks of unevenness in which the life of the nation is portrayed as fully achieved and enduring, decisively formed before the transformations of capitalist modernization. If modernism, as a broad signifier, was symptomatic of the presence of unevenness, the construction of memory thus became one of its most principal and enduring forms of cognition. This privileging of memory was a corollary of the valorization of the cultural/aesthetic domain over the political economic. While this recourse to memory appeared to privilege the content of a cultural imaginary, it really disclosed that the problem faced by modernism was one of form and representation.

What modernist discourse in Japan, and elsewhere, confronted was the crisis of modernity over the stability and reliability of forms of representation. While this crisis was manifested throughout the modernizing world (including colonies like India and struggling national societies like China and Brazil), in Japan it was inflected in discussions over the form best suited to represent lived experience in social circumstances dominated by the ever new in the ever same (Kobayashi Hideo, Kon Wajirō, Tosaka Jun), the auratic endowment of culture-memory (Watsuji Tetsurō, Kuki Shūzō, Miki Kiyoshi), and the experience of the communal body (Yanagita Kunio, Orikuchi Shinobu, folkists like Takada Yasuma, but Miki could also be included here). This crisis, then, was over the forms most capable of relaying and communicating the lived experience—the experience of genuine difference—and securing accessibility to a memory that was being shattered into splinters by speed, shock, and sensation. The present was seen as the foreground, often as the place where traditions were being crushed, provoking a crisis in the communication of experience itself, in memory and the operation of the very possibility of historical recall. The recognition of this problem invariably meant that writing which ordinarily depended upon developmental dispositions was seen as no longer adequate. In Japan and throughout the modernizing world, this distrust for narrative form (and materials) resulted in an immense effort to recall older cultural practices (religious, aesthetic, literary, linguistic) that derived from a remote past before the establishment of modern, capitalist society, and that were believed to be still capable of communicating an authentic experience of the people (Miki's "foundational experience" [*kisoteki keiken*])—race or folk that historical change could not disturb. Efforts to rescue a submerged authenticity invariably aimed at restoring origin and making present the auratic. This move echoes Walter Benjamin's valorization of the storyteller and his rejection of historical narrative for the anecdote. We can see a similar response in Kobayashi Hideo's elevation of the *shi shōsetsu* (a hybrid form of novelization that reached maturation, at least for him, in Shiga Naoya) and its capacity to communicate the singularity of lived everyday experience and his denunciation of historical narratives for failing to represent the sense of commonness and endurance in the experiential. Orikuchi Shinobu's resuscitation of the archaic chanters of prayers as the source for all subsequent art sought to remind his contemporaries of the auratic still inscribed in the production of literature even in the present. (This gesture also explains why discovery of the everyday in modern life or its identity was usually situated in space rather than the temporality of narrative.) Both the so-called I-novel (*shi shōsetsu*) and various discursive efforts to displace history dramatized how historical narrative—the developmental form it relied on—had lost its living relationship to the present—the place of modern life—as the form of memorative communication. Some writers, like Kon Wajirō, Gonda Yasunosuke, Tosaka Jun, and Aono Suekichi, resorted to a strategy that distanced the memorative past, as such, and its demand for narrating conditions of existence in fixed periods for a vigorous engagement of a performative present. In this regard, the abstract space of capitalism became the site for the performing present, against the specificity of place that increasingly belonged to an indeterminate past. Others, by contrast, like Kuki Shūzō, Watsuji Tetsurō, Miki Kiyoshi, Tanizaki Junichirō, and a regiment of native ethnologists, looked longingly to some moment in the past, or simply the past itself as an indefinite moment, as the place of community or culture, that would serve as the primordial and originary condition of the Japanese folk. It is important to suggest here that this image of culture and community was as timeless and frozen as the commodity form itself.

In this way, the crisis was inflected into claims of cultural authenticity and diverse efforts to recall the eternal forms of community outside of history (and thus immune to the social abstractions of capitalism). Yet this particular inflection of the crisis of representation invariably worked to yoke modernism (seeking to solve the question of representation) to

fascism (aiming to resolve the problem of political representation), combining ideologemes the state subsequently but selectively appropriated for
national mobilization and war in the late 1930s. I think it is important to
return to the question of fascism in the interwar period and its location
in the cultural discussions of the time. Any consideration of the cultural
analysis of modernity will lead to the limited political possibilities available to a historical moment marked by a global economic crisis and incipient political struggle. What I mean is that the cultural analysis prompted
by the wrenching modern experience—the desire to lay hold of it—and
the attempt to resolve its crisis would predictably result in a political resolution consistent with the nature of the analysis itself. If some modernists
were committed to progressive forms of expression and looked to the
future as a self-styled avant garde announcing the shape of things to come,
it was also likely that they would, like the surrealists, opt for some form
of "cultural bolshevism," just as "modernists who opposed modernity"
would favor a set of political arrangements based on cultural conservation
and communitarianism. We need not side either with Benjamin, who
wanted to realign politics to aesthetics, or Miki Kiyoshi, who worried
about the increasing politicization of culture and its apparent "loss" of
autonomy (even though we must all surely choose a mode of relating
culture and politics), since in the overheated atmosphere of the 1930s it
was often difficult actually to differentiate the two claims historically.
Both solutions were programmatic overstatements of the problem and
tended to simplify their specific historical complexity. But that both sides
of the formula were concerned with trying to align culture and politics in
modernizing societies in a new and lasting configuration capable of resolving the question of representation as a condition for knowing how to act
in a critical time suggests that we no longer can simply ignore the question
of fascism and its many inflections during the 1930s.

We need not go so far, however, as to simply ignore the testimony and
experience of contemporaries who actually believed they were facing a
cultural and political crisis and that fascism was one of the prevailing attempts to resolve it on a global scale. This view, still persistent in
"social scientific" accounts (and Japanese disavowals), strikes me as taking Pierre Bourdieu's advice to "never trust the native informant" further
than imagined. We must, in any case, take seriously contemporary observations like Tsukui Tatsuo's conviction that the "emperor, for Japanese,
is the beginning and end. If one leaves from the emperor he must return
to it."[32] Although Tsukui was an extreme Japanist during the late 1930s,
there were many who would agree with his sentiment that even though
"fascism is the politics of Mussolini in Italy, the imperial polity is the
correct adaptation of the theory of fascism [in Japan]."[33] There are other,
prominent social thinkers, like Takada Yasuma, Toda Teizō, and Suzuki

Eitarō, who submitted to quite recognizable forms of fascism and even defended this move by appealing to the name of the folk. By the same measure, we also have to avoid easy and completely indefensible arguments that seek to distinguish between real fascism as found in Germany and Italy and militarism as developed by the Japanese. There has been a continuing effort, in Japan and outside, to argue that whatever else Japanese developed in the 1930s, it was not fascism but rather something closer to militarism, as if this distinction would have made any sense to anybody living in Nazi Germany, where the interweave of fascism and militarism was a tightly knotted textile, or in Italy, where "fascist virility" was bonded to forms of violence and militarism. (In fact, this distinction is simply an exhausted echo of Jean Kirkpatrick's astonishing effort some years ago to distinguish between totalitarian and authoritarian regimes.) Perhaps it would be possible to split the difference and classify states like Germany as fascist militarism and Japan as militaristic fascism, but qualifying distinctions would prove meaningless. DeLeuze and Guattari put it best when they equated fascism with a micropolitics and located its force in a form of molecularity. While fascism invented the totalitarian state, they argue, it exceeded its limits to proliferate "molecular focuses in interaction. . . .What makes fascism dangerous is its molecular or micropolitical power."[34] It was like a spreading cancer. Moreover, it is a mass movement precisely in the sense that a thinker like Seki Sakayoshi could propose that the emperor was the whole body, not simply a part, that encompassed all of society. Finally, we need not go as far as historians like Gilbert Allardyce who, years ago, triumphantly announced that fascism had no real meaning outside of specific, historical experiences like Italy and that it was a deflated concept that meant virtually nothing.[35] But Allardyce, and those who have continued to hoe this row, have missed seeing the complex relationship between fascism and modernism, politics and culture altogether, as have countless other historians who have, in their own nominalist way, in and out of Japan, tried to restrict its utility to a narrow political range or define it out of existence. This view has, of course, led to confident declarations reassuring us that we need not fear the return of fascism. Some years ago, Ernst Nolte, who later went on to become a principal participant in the *historikerstreit* controversy, pronounced the definite death of fascism because the same set of conditions he designated as enabling it would never return. In more recent years, he has put forth the idea that German fascism was a last-ditch stand against the spread of communism, an inflection of an earlier idea circulating in the late 1930s that was employed by a number of states, including Japan, to suppress the left. And more recently, the left historian Perry Anderson has warned against the effort to "conjure up renewed dangers of fascism, a lazy exercise of right and left alike today."[36]

One of the problems that has inhibited historians is the failure to draw a distinction between fascist movements and regimes, on the one hand, and ideology, on the other, between cultural and political impulses and institutions and performatives. The cultural analyses that configure conceptions of political order are not always the same as the forces that mobilize movements and establish regimes, even though they might share a fund of common ideologemes. While cultural and communitarian theorists in Japan were not always committed or card-carrying fascists or even jack-booted militarists, all fascists need not wear brown shirts (or be ranking members of the military high command). Much of the thinking produced by cultural and communitarian theorists was appropriated by a state bent on preserving capitalism, without all of its consequences for class conflict, its alienating effects, instability, and cultural and economic unevenness—without, in short, the accompanying institutions of civil society. In this regard, it is important to revisit texts by Tosaka Jun, for example, or Herbert Marcuse, and indeed all of those interwar thinkers who forged the equation among capitalism, liberalism, and fascism. Tosaka believed it was liberalism that opened the way to degraded forms of "Japanism," invariably based upon the same obsessions for grounded authenticity motivating more serious thinkers like Watsuji, Miki, and Yanagita. His arguments recall what Marcuse explained as its (liberalism's) rejection of history for "affirmative culture" that ultimately resulted in a "depravation of history." Both of these thinkers were involved in trying to show how the totalitarian state, despite its obvious tactic to divert its own struggle against liberalism into one over world views, bypassed the social structure basic to liberalism and was largely in accord with it. Both also recognized, as did Miki Kiyoshi, who sledded into fascism, the intimate kinship between the claims of folkism and the primacy of technology, despite the overt denunciations of "enlightenment" and rationality. Fascism, according to Slavoj Žižek, far from constituting an external opposite and thus opponent to liberal democracy, derives its force and relevance from liberal democracy's own internal antagonisms. When confronted with prospects of its own failure and impending dissolution, capitalism must negate itself from "within" if it is to survive, which means pass into fascism. "Is not fascism," Žižek asks rhetorically, "a kind of inherent self-negation of capitalism, an attempt to change something so that nothing really changes by means of an ideology which subordinates the economy to the ideological-political domain?"[37] This sense of negation and the subordination of the economy, which remains intact with its commitment to advanced technology, to an ideological/cultural order calling for authenticity, folkism, and communitarianism, is very close to the critique Tosaka mounted in his *Nihon ideorogiron* of 1935. Tosaka's important critique has largely been ignored by historians in any subse-

quent analysis of the current situation in Japan during the crucial decade
of the thirties; it has been discounted altogether in postwar discussions
rushing to forget the war and modernity and establish a new liberal political subject (and consensus) consistent with the modernizing reforms of
the American Occupation. In a certain sense, my book is an attempt to
retrieve Tosaka's powerful critique of fascism and how its ideological appeal to culture and community was sanctioned by a liberal endowment.
Tosaka's book, a self-conscious effort to rewrite Marx's *German Ideology*, demonstrated how idealism was bonded to liberalism and was expressed in the condensed trope of archaism, which sought to repress the
materiality of historical practice. One of the goals of this book is to rescue
this powerful critique from oblivion, cover the same ground from the
different perspective of another time and place, and place it in a larger
context of both Japanese and Western thinkers who were struggling with
the question of modernism and fascism in the 1930s. While I do not concentrate on analyzing this particular text of Tosaka's, even though I de-
vote a long section to his philosophy of everydayness and spatiality, my
aim has been to imagine how the text on the Japanese ideology might
have been written from the perspective of our present.

Fascism in Japan, and elsewhere, appeared under the guise of what
might be called gemeinschaft capitalism and the claims of a social order
free from the uncertainties and indeterminacies of an alienated civil society, where an eternalized and unchanging cultural or communal order
was put into the service of the capitalist mode of production to establish
a "capitalism without capitalism." When a thinker like Yanagita Kunio
exulted in the "hybridity" produced as a result of a mixing of Japan's
past and its modern present, he was also ratifying the permanence of unevenness itself and thus the necessity of finding stable forms of representation that would anchor the changing present. The quest for a "capitalism
without capitalism," at the heart of his project, was driven by a desire to
return to a fixed moment in an indefinite past (in the present) and the
singularity of experience by taking away class, gender, or even regional
identifications, in order to reunite, through things, customs, "living culture" (*seikatsu bunka*), religious belief, without content, much like
Adorno's "frozen emanations," with an aura impossible to reach. In the
discourses of the 1930s, there was a widespread effort to imagine some
sort of corporate structure capable of eliminating excess and unevenness
to establish a stable social organism whose parts formed a communal
body. Under such an arrangement, everybody would thus once more occupy their own place directed by the figure of what Žižek has called the
"mastering agency." Paradoxically, what these "frozen emanations"
thinkers sought to resuscitate were the products of a disintegrated aura,
rescued by cultural and communitarian theory grappling with everyday

modernity that now constituted a form of action without agents. Yet, the specular indeterminacy of a factual present—the site of performance— and an absent past—the object of memorative desire—constituted not so much a resistance to modernity in Japan (and elsewhere) but one of the principal conditions of what it meant to become modern. In prewar Japan, contemporaneity and the appeal to the timelessness of memory disclosed a structure of deferral and desire which the appeal to repetition sought to resolve (in actuality, "overcome") while only managing to stimulate even greater anxiety. The very incompleteness marked by the appeal to an absent past and a vanished communal order in the present was, in fact, the sign of modernity itself. As Benjamin would observe and Japanese confirm, it is "precisely the modern which conjures up prehistory."

Finally, I should like to say that in writing this book I have been guided by three considerations. First, despite the appearance of a linear narrative that starts with modernism and ends with fascism, my intention has been to argue that modernism and fascism were contemporary to each other, sharing the temporality of simultaneity and constantly imbricating each other in such a way as to constitute a network of thick intertexts. Because of this, I have seen the various chapters as autonomous studies loosely connected with each other because they share a temporal horizon of modernity and occupy the same space. Second, in an effort to orchestrate a continuing conversation, I have sought to juxtapose writers and texts to each other that until now have not been put into such relationships, even though they were all contemporaries, in either Japanese or non-Japanese writing. More often than not, they have been treated as if they occupied different spaces and even temporalities, restricted to narrow discursive and disciplinary domains. By placing them into direct relationship with each other because of their concerns for the question of modernity, they reaffirm the premise that modernity itself is our primary temporalizing category. Third, I have resorted to long expositions of positions, based on a reading of strategic texts, not simply to show the rich texture of thinking but because these thinkers and their texts have not been translated (there are a few isolated exceptions) and are not being read, again with a few exceptions, by either Japanese or people who know Japanese. Yet, as I hope these studies show, the production of texts about modernity in Japan's interwar period resonated with concerns and sentiments found elsewhere throughout the industrial world to disclose, not the operation of the one-way street of influence, but intensities inflecting a common historical conjuncture. In chapter 1 I supply an account of the political-economic conditions accompanying Japan's accelerated modernization during the interwar period. The purpose is to show the circumstances under which Japanese began to figure and fantasize modern life in the 1920s and 1930s, to talk and write about it more ubiquitously than actually live it. Chapter

2 considers the future of the past, which is the subject of discourse and discussion, that is, it constitutes a form of future anteriority, inasmuch as I concentrate on analyzing the famous (or infamous) Conference on Overcoming Modernity, held in July 1942, six months after the war with the United States began. The conference, as we shall see, was concerned with the experience of the last two decades and beyond and tried to assess the meaning of Japan's modernity in light of a war that many believed was an assault on the West. In chapter 3 I return to the site of modern life in the 1920s and early 1930s—the past of the future represented by the Conference on Modernity—and examine a number of thinkers who began to respond to the challenge of modern life by seeking to understand it and its promise for the future. While many of these writers and thinkers were progressives, they all shared a commitment to the primacy of the performative present. In chapters 4 and 5 I examine what I have called the discourse on the social, a kind of secondary discussion that responded to the challenges posed by modern life and those who promoted its promise for the future. This discourse invariably turned toward an indefinite past to envisage a cultural and communitarian endowment that anchored Japanese identity to constitute the sign of genuine authenticity and fixity in an environment of ceaseless temporal change. In chapter 6, which must, in part, be seen as a conclusion, I consider some of the texts of Miki Kiyoshi, who, as the consummate modernist thinker, sought often to bring together the various claims of modernity and its critics, to unify folk with a modernist culture devoted to making and technology, politics and culture. Miki often skirted with forms of fascist totalizing, even though he also sought to distance himself and Japan from an identity with it. Nevertheless, there is a good deal of folkic totalism in Miki's thinking, which in lesser hands or more determined thinkers like Takada Yasuma easily slipped into fascism. While the war and defeat brought an end to this particular experience, it would be wrong to say that they terminated either modernism or fascism, which would reappear in different forms and registers in Japan and elsewhere in the years after the war. Because of this, it would be premature to conclude what clearly in Japan, and elsewhere, has not yet played itself out.

Acknowledgments

THIS BOOK grew out of a collaboration with Tetsuo Najita at the University of Chicago that produced a long article for the *Cambridge History of Japan* called "The Revolt against the West." I thank him for that collaboration and for his prompt and penetrating reading of this manuscript and his incisive comments, which I have not always managed to successfully incorporate.

I thank William Haver and Carol Gluck for their thorough readings of the manuscript and their countless suggestions, which, again, I have tried to incorporate, hopefully to their satisfaction. I also thank Masao Miyoshi and my colleague Xudong Zhang for their respective readings of the manuscript, which I have found invaluable.

I am indebted to the Stanford Humanities Center for giving me a year of solid research time. The cordiality of the center's director and staff made my stay there pleasant. I want to express my appreciation to the staff of Columbia University's Starr Library who made their resources available to me, and to Katsuhiko Endo and Ken Kawashima for reading and discussing with me a number of texts that have been important to my account. I would like also to note publicly my gratitude to my editor Brigitta van Rheinberg of Princeton University Press for her encouragement, support, and kindness in seeing the manuscript through to print. Thanks also to Bill Mihalopoulos for the index and Judy Geib and Sabu Kosho, again, for their cover design.

Finally, I thank Kristin Ross, again, for her tireless work in helping me unknot complex and often unintelligible arguments of my own making and corralling unruly sentences that often tried to take on a life of their own. I dedicate this book to her.

OVERCOME BY MODERNITY

CHAPTER 1

The Fantasy of Modern Life

ALTHOUGH the Meiji state put into place the infrastructure of a modern capitalist political economy, the economy itself did not grow at a constant speed between the years 1887 and 1920. The time span was punctuated by business cycles and variations produced by the growth process itself and by specific events like the Sino-Japanese War of 1894–1895 and the Russo-Japanese War of 1904–1905. This meant a rather shaky round of spurts and retrenchments, the deflation of the 1880s, subsequent recovery based mainly on the development of textile and traditional handicrafts industries, railway construction, and the stimulus supplied by the Sino-Japanese War. But the decision to switch over to the gold standard in 1897 braked serious expansion, while the Russo-Japanese War boosted the development of heavy engineering industries. The end of the war drove the country into recession and then into a pattern of slow growth again. World War I removed most of Japan's advanced, industrial competitors from both domestic and world markets and thus provided the country with the opportunity to substitute domestically produced goods for imports and to increase exports of manufactures despite the relative backwardness of this sector. The war also signaled the transformation of the industrial base from light to concentrated heavy industries and the ceaseless migration of rural populations to the urban sites of industrial production.

The result of Japan's participation in the war was an unprecedented stimulus in all sectors of the economy, but especially those involving engineering, shipbuilding, machine tools, and electrical engineering. Despite the continuation of growth and slumps in the postwar period, the expansion stimulated by the war lifted the economy to the status of a modern industry. Even though traditional sectors such as agriculture and small businesses would continue to be responsible for producing the bulk of the output and providing employment, by the 1920s the economy's future was firmly rooted in expanding industrial and financial sectors. Critics, along the way, noted the sharp lines of unevenness between newer, modern capital industries and the so-called traditional sectors, which, in the Meiji period, had grown concurrently and even complementarily rather than competitively. But by 1920 and the succeeding years, the sharply silhouetted contrast was widely observed in the uneven relationship between the large metropolitan sites like Tokyo/Yokohama and Osaka/

Kobe, which literally had been transformed overnight, and a countryside that supplied the cities with a labor force and capital but, according to Yanagita Kunio, received nothing in return. By the time of the war, the modern sector had increased so rapidly that it began to conflict with the demands of the traditional economy, which was still supplying most of the consumer's needs. Hence, the relationship was less symbiotic than parasitic, producing the conditions of permanent unevenness and unequal development that were necessary for the continuing expansion of capital industries. Accordingly, the establishment of what economists called a "dual" or "differential" economic structure (euphemisms for unevenness) included a wide range of new technology, productivity, wages, scales of production, profit rates and margins, managerial practices, and forms of industrial manufacturing. Moreover, it brought new classes and an awareness of new identities and subject positions, and it expanded the possibilities for women in the labor market. The sites of modern capital industries required the expansion of the cities, with its migrant armies of new arrivals from the countryside, looking for work and the prospects of new life. The process produced differences in the nature of markets in which products were sold and also supplied much needed capital, labor, new technologies, and managerial skills.

After the early Meiji period, governments employed all powers at their disposal to promote growth in modern capital industries as a national necessity. Yet the program required sacrificing traditional areas of economic activity. By favoring armaments, investment goods, and exports over consumption goods, state policy kept the standard of living lower than they might have been. Between 1885 and 1920, the rise in personal consumption per capita, a rough measure to be sure, was only 67 percent. This very slow increase in the standard of living resulted in political and social strains in the early 1920s and the explosive conflict among expectation, desire, and capability. In the fantasy of everyday modern life, as it was figured in the popular media, the contest was played out in a struggle between desire and value, between the promise of excess and the fear of scarcity.[1]

Over the thirty years between 1883 and 1913, agricultural production contributed about 20 percent and other associated traditional activities about 40% to the net national product. By the same token, the modern sector was growing at about two or three times as fast as these sectors but remained at a relatively small scale. Agricultural production after 1900 expanded principally because of the increased land utilization—reclamation, labor, machinery, better fertilizers. But the farm population began to fall slightly but steadily in these years, even though the availability of arable land was increasing. It has been observed, in this connection, that the scale of farming landholders was small. Once legal obstacles to land transfer were removed, ownership moved toward more concentrated, surplus landowners who found it more beneficial to lease land they could not work to tenants rather than hire agricultural day laborers when needed. As a result, the estimated figures attesting to accelerated tenancy increased to about 45 percent of the farming population by the time of World War I. By 1900 landowners were collecting rents equivalent to almost a quarter of Japan's rice crop. Until the beginning of the war, the share steadily increased to heighten the power of landowners, who could invest their capital (rents) in local enterprises, and whose growing financial status permitted them to enhance their political standing to become a force in national politics. Between 1900 and 1913, the average rate of agricultural production rose to 1.8 percent a year as the farm population fell. As for the putative modern sector before the war, its narrative consisted of showing an order of development inaugurated by light industries, principally textiles, accompanied by mining, attention to the establishment of metallurgical industries, and railways; with the conversion from steam to electric power, it was possible to introduce new, heavy engineering and chemical industries and the mass production of automobiles and other consumer appliances. In the thirty years between 1883 and 1913, the labor force increased from twenty-two to twenty-six million. Even though agriculture employment decreased slightly, the workforce in the modern sector increased fourfold in these years from a modest base of 200,000 in the early 1880s. At the same time, the number of people working in traditional occupations increased by 60 percent and absorbed over three quarters of the increase in the workforce, owing to the preponderant role played by the traditional sector in the overall economy.[2]

By all accounts, World War I rescued Japan from fiscal collapse and balance-of-trade payments. Until 1913 capital industries such as branches of heavy industry were not profitable in the world market, and Japan was in no position to compete with more developed industrial societies. Moreover, the country had not yet recovered from the expenses of the earlier Russo-Japanese War. But all of this was to change as Japan became a member of the allied coalition but was spared any active involvement in the theater of fighting (excepting small operations in North China and the Pacific Islands). During the war, the economy enjoyed a positive boom and relative prosperity because of its role as a supplier to the allied cause. In Asia, Japan was liberated from trade competitors as its own domestic market was freed from the importation of foreign goods. Similarly, the growth rate was matched by a significant reorganization of international trade and payments, not to mention a spurt in investments. Because Japanese industries were diverted from producing consumer goods, consumption rates were low throughout the war years and wages remained depressed. At the same time, some people profited immeasurably from the wartime boom, especially investors and speculators. A sign of the new independence of private enterprise from government was the formation of the *zaikai*—a modern business establishment—and the founding of the Industrial Club of Japan in 1917. War's end reintroduced economic normalcy by the 1920s, and the years following witnessed both growth and severe business cycles. Yet, the foundations of modern industry had been firmly implanted; despite the recessionary cycles that plagued Japan in the 1920s, the labor force continued to grow, with women entering new industries in large numbers, and the traditional sector, producing consumer goods for the domestic market, continued at a much slower pace. One of the interesting aspects of the 1920s is that the decade was inaugurated by an economic crash that ended in an even worse one. The decade was punctuated by the Great Kantō Earthquake of 1923, occurring just as the country was climbing out of its economic slump, a disaster that affected seventeen prefectures and principally the city of Tokyo. Approximately 554,000 out of 2.3 million households lost their homes, 105,000 people died, 30,000 were injured, and 250,000 lost their jobs. In the wake of the quake, the gross annual wealth decreased, which meant Japan could not return to the gold standard. Four years later, the nation was confronted by a major financial panic (1927) that resulted in a run on the banks, which had made loans to companies that were not able to repay, prefiguring what was to come in 1929 and 1930. In 1929 Japan was drawn into the grips of a worldwide depression from which it slowly emerged by the middle of the 1930s, when it began its move on China.

By the end of the 1920s, half of the nation's population was agricultural. Since the pace of agricultural productivity was locked in what seemed like a permanent recession, especially after 1925, the quality and standard of living associated with farm life decreased throughout the decade and beyond. Agricultural prices continued a steady decline after 1920, farm incomes remained low relative to other workers, and farms carried an average of 800-900 yen in loans, even though the interests rates were usually quite low. At the same time, the prices of products were also falling. The nonfarming population, in the cities and the countryside, constituted the major segment of the employed population during the 1920s and was involved in traditional and secondary sectors of economic activity. According to Nakamura Takafusa, Japan, because of this differential between modern and traditional sectors, had become a large capitalist nation, with big companies and industries commanding immense power, but according to the population ratio between modern workers and nonmodern workers, "the impact of the traditional society remained strong."[3]

What was striking about these years was the massive urbanization experienced in Tokyo and other cities like Osaka. As an emblem of the new power of cities, the Tokyo Taishō Exhibition Hall was opened in March

1914 in Ueno. The aim of the exhibition hall was to encourage industry and to "confer blessings on the new government." On the first day the exhibition opened, the Tokyo *Asahi shinbun* reported that "once the exhibition was opened and the public admitted through the front gate . . . fifteen minutes earlier because of the violent crush of spectators, the countless people who had been eagerly waiting were transformed into a tidal wave when they heard that police guards were trying to control entry and surged forward like an avalanche."[4] Over six hundred geisha from the city were employed to serve as welcomers at the exhibition booths, and over half of the booths had tags indicating they were sold out. Anyone who turned around the great exhibition hall could not fail to be impressed with its "total image" of economy, culture, and power in Japan at the beginning of the new Taishō era. The head of Tokyo City Assembly and Chamber of Commerce encapsulated this new image of power when he remarked, "In our business world, there are no differences among the human species, no national barriers. We have many people throughout the country, possessing the will, who expect to promote the true spirit, correct society's wrongs, and reach the citadel of true wealth and power. The economic men occasioned by the great exhibition hall of Taishō are not clan cliques but [are driven by] a free spirit. They endeavor mightily to make a state of true wealth and power."[5] The reference to "wealth and power" obviously echoed the earlier Meiji slogan, but the criticism of clan government clearly dramatized how far the state was from actually realizing "true wealth and power." Plainly, the promoter of the exhibition hall was not the state but rather the city of Tokyo, which already envisaged a different image for Japan.

The Great Exhibition Hall not only symbolized vast changes taking place in economy and politics; it also signified the city as the site of the new political economy. This was materially evident in the shift of population. The Japanese population in the 1880s was approximately thirty-four million; by 1910 it had grown to almost fifty-six million. Among the working population in these years, the number increased from roughly twenty million to about twenty-seven million. The total population grew at an annual rate of 1.6 percent, while the workforce expanded at a slightly lower pace. From the first decade of the twentieth century into the 1920s, the rapid rate of industrialization brought a virtual demographic revolution. But the concomitant growth in the population in heavier and capital industries and the service sectors was also marked and was mainly concentrated in the cities. Those people who migrated to the cities during these years were usually second and third sons of farming families, who had no access to family inheritance, women, and those who were looking for higher wages. (This element became more pronounced when the more or less even development between traditional and modern sectors began to break down and wages among the latter began to overtake the former.) Despite the steady march of farm migrants to the cities, by 1919 two out of three Japanese still lived in village communities of under ten thousand people or less.[6]

In 1920 the population of Tokyo had reached 3.35 million, more than doubling its size in a little more than two decades; Osaka jumped from 820,000 to 1.25 million; Kyoto, from 350,000 to 700,000; Kobe, from 210,000 to 640,000. Nagoya's 240,000 grew to 610,000, and Yokohama lurched from 190,000 to 570,000. Excluding these six cities, only two cities had a population of more than 100,000 in 1898—Hiroshima and Nagasaki; by 1920 Nagasaki had a population of 180,000, Hiroshima 160,000, Hakodate 140,000, Kure 130,000, Kanazawa 130,000, Sendai 120,000, Otaru 110,000, and Sapporo, Yawata, and Kagoshima 100,000 each, totaling ten. Among cities numbering more than 50,000 people in 1898, six had already reached the 100,000 level by 1920 (Sendai, Otaru, Hakodate, Kanazawa, Kagoshima, and Kure), while others following in suit were Sakai, Niigata, Toyama, Wakayama, Okayama, Fukushima, Fukuoka, and Kumamoto. This narrative was followed down the scale of smaller cities with populations under 30,000. These figures impressed contemporary urbanologists like Sawada Ken, who in 1923 published the essay "Toshi to Hangyaku," which signaled the formation of a discourse on cities aimed at liberating them and their development from the state. But in this essay, Sawada was already prepared to show how the current of history had plainly reflected the intense concentration of population in the cities which, for him, represented an incontestable sign of advancement. What seemed to attract him was the observation that Japan's urbanization compared favorably with that of the world's industrial societies. The United States possessed three cities with populations exceeding one million people—New York, Chicago, and Philadelphia—but Japan was evenly matched in this sector.[7] Germany only had Berlin; France, only Paris; and England, the "ancestral country of industrialism," no more than the two cities of London and Glasgow. "That Japan has the two cities of Tokyo and Osaka clearly tells the story that it was never behind the civilized countries in population concentration."[8] Even when looking at large cities with more than 500,000 people, Sawada continued, you will discover the same fact. The five cities of Tokyo, Osaka, Kyoto, Kobe, and Nagoya all exceeded 500,000 people. When compared to European nations like England, there was only London, Glasgow, Birmingham, Liverpool, and Manchester; in France, only Paris and Marseilles, in Germany, Berlin, Hamburg, Munich, and Dresden. Sawada dismissed a prevailing observation that contended that Japan's modern cities were "inferior" in population size and that, as a result, "Japan should not be judged according to European standards. Because the density is different, despite

the similarity of population size, there is a different look among them."⁹
Sawada contested claims that the density of Japan's cities was greater
than that found elsewhere and went on to show, in detail, that Tokyo was
less compact than cities like New York, Paris, and London. Although he
complained about the nature of Japan's cities, he provided forceful evidence and argumentation to demonstrate that Japan's cities, by 1920,
compared favorably with the demographics of other, world-class cities.
The same comparative argument could have been made concerning the
ratio of rural to urban populations (excepting the United States and possibly England) and the relative similarities in gross national output. What
the meteoric growth of cities symbolized was the construction of a modern labor force in Japan (and its concomitant recruitment of women into
the labor market) and the relative decline of the agricultural sector, farm
labor, and attempts to reinforce rural solidarity and link communities
more closely to the state. Even though the Japanese population remained
more agrarian than urban through the 1930s, the division between city
and countryside was vastly overdetermined in the cultural realm, where
the metropolis produced an image of itself as universal while farm life
was made to appear as a backwater, languishing in a different temporality.

There were, for our purposes, two factors that stamped the character
of the accelerated growth of Japan's cities: massive migration and the
formation of a women's labor force. The demographic development was
supplemented by an accounting of people who had actually left their place
of household registration (*koseki*). What these figures show is the effect
of mass migration from the countryside to the cities and the consequences
it held for the family system as it had been defined by the Meiji Civil
Code. Qualitatively, urbanization in the 1920s undermined the political
and social solidarity of the family. Yanagita Kunio early observed, in his
Meiji Taishōshi, sesōhen, that the incessant flow of people into the cities
produced an estranged life. "The loneliness of life in the early days of the
city," he wrote, "depended on making people into travelers, yearning for
families long absent. But the effect of too much importance on one's home
village was that the cities were filled with residents that were not attached
to anything, anywhere."¹⁰ His contemporary, the detective story writer
Edogawa Rampo, made these alienated strangers of the city the subject
of a number of his stories and attributed the commission of bizarre crimes
to their socially anomic experience. The story *"Dzaka no satsujin jiken"*
(Murder in D Hill) showed both the centrality of the streets and the loneliness of recent arrivals to the great city. The opening of the story has the
protagonist meditating on his new, unfamiliar surroundings:

> It was a hot, steamy night in early September and I was sipping ice coffee in
> a favorite cafe called the White Plum on a broad street in D Hill. At the time,
> I had only recently left school and had not yet found a job. I laid around the

boarding house and even read some books. When I lost interest in reading, I went on aimless walks. Sometimes I made the round of coffee shops that weren't too pricey and this became a daily routine. The White Plum was close to the boarding house and whenever I went out for a walk it was usually the first place I'd go into. Somehow I got into the bad habit of overstaying whenever I entered this coffee shop.[11]

With nothing to do and no friends, the protagonist of this story, like many others, is cast afloat in the urban flow of strangers who simply wander the streets with no explicit purpose. In this story, it is interesting to note that Rampo has his protagonist suddenly spot somebody he knew from a former life.

If writers like Yanagita and Rampo reported the qualitative effects of the mass migration into the cities (and the former's *Meiji Taishōshi, sesōhen* and more analytic *Toshi to Nōson* [1929] are filled with such observations), its quantitative dimensions were analyzed by a variety of social researchers, like Kagawa Toyohiko and Andō Masayoshi in their *Nihon dōtoku tōkei yōran* (Statistical survey Japanese morality, 1934) and Toda Teizō, who in 1938 published his analysis of the first national census, taken in 1920. With Kagawa, a social gospel Christian, and Andō, we have a mix of statistics and moral judgments: the marshaling of figures and data showing the large number of farm women who had migrated to the cities in the preceding decade to service their pleasure zones, and stinging moral condemnation of the government for having encouraged the unregulated expansion of prostitution and the destruction of traditional rural life. Toda's work was less moralistic but nevertheless pointed to the social consequences of the immense numbers of people who had left their place of registration. Even by 1920, the status of population distribution had already captured the attention of the state as a problem that needed to be understood. Within a total population of nearly 56 million, approximately 10 percent lived apart from their families in 1920. But if seen in the light of the working population of approximately 27 million, the figure for those who had left their families was even larger. What seemed difficult for Toda to gauge was the observation that the figure for large cities like Tokyo and Osaka was probably larger than the national ratio. Assuming that if two out of every three Japanese still lived in the countryside in 1920, most of these people would have been registered in *koseki*. If one-third of the population was living in the cities, say 18 million people, and if 10 percent of the national population were now outside of their registered households, then it was possible to assume that most of these people were probably residing in the cities. This would mean that the majority of the 5,747,000 (the 10 percent) were occupants of the cities, approximately a third of the urban population. According to Toda, even a tenth of the total population was considerable, and one could only guess at the pace of subsequent migrations and departures from places of registration. In a population of a thousand, 108 people lived outside their family life. In Tokyo, 630,000 city folk, or 27 percent, were separated from their ancestral households.[12] These people lived as service employees, domestic servants, and so forth. As for ages, the majority were in their late teens and early twenties.

Still another measure of this phenomenon was the average size of ordinary households that excluded separated members: 4.5 people nationally, 3.7 for Tokyo, and 3.5 for Osaka. In provinces like Aomori and Iwate, Toda found that 60 percent of households had at least five members. For cities like Tokyo and Osaka, this figure was lower, and households rarely exceeded three members. Hence, the trend, even by 1920, was toward smaller households with fewer personnel, as attested by the media blitz promoting new forms of consumption and new commodities for the nuclear family of the "culture houses" (*bunka jūtaku*). What emerged from Toda's analysis was the beginning of the dismantling process of large households and the progressive installation of the nuclear family in Japan's large cities. By the same measure, his analysis pointed to greater possibilities for isolation and alienation, what Rampo described as a "thinning out" of social relationships. What sustained growth after the postwar boom were poor farming families who supplied a seemingly inexhaustible reservoir of cheap labor to feed industry's desiring machine. The migration of second and third sons and daughters, as already suggested, contracted the size of households in the countryside and led to the formation of smaller units in the cities. If this pattern of migration legitimated the patriarchal system by limiting inheritance, the new life in the cities, for both men and women, constantly flew in the face of these constraints and practices to create ceaseless social strain and lived contradictions.

In this respect, women entered the workforce in large numbers in the postwar years. Until 1930 factory hands were predominately women, whereas workers in the nonmanufacturing sector were largely male. Yet, if the figures of Kagawa and Andō are to be believed, tens of thousands of young women streamed into the "pleasure zones" to staff their large entertainment quarters, cafes, coffee shops, bars, dance halls, and theaters, and to service the sex trade. The Marxist critic Hirabayashi Hatsunosuke was close to the truth when, in the mid 1920s, he pointed to the progressive "feminization of culture." Aware that large numbers of women had already become factory workers, many actively involved in left-wing labor activity, Hirabayashi observed that women could be seen and heard everywhere in Tokyo, as office workers, phone operators, bank tellers, bus conductors, and so forth.[13] Kagawa and Andō estimated that in 1924 there were a little more than 50,000 prostitutes throughout the country servicing an average of two to three men daily. The total number of yearly revelers was approximately 22 million, and the yearly average of clients for a prostitute was about 441 in 1933. This figure referred to licensed or registered prostitutes but did not include the vast army of unlicensed and informal sex workers who worked in cafes, bars, and restaurants, which would have made the numbers higher, especially in the larger cities where most of this activity was concentrated. To add weight to this assumption, Kagawa and Andō pointed out that the existence of "special restaurants" (*tokushu inshokuten*) increased exponentially after the middle 1920s and replicated the pattern of growth in cafe bars and coffee shops that recruited large numbers of women from both countryside and the city, including "children of the fallen middle class," the group Aono Suekichi was to eulogize.[14] All of these businesses simply "hastened . . . the supply to satisfy the requirements of those who pursue sexual desire."[15]

Women accounted for almost 35 percent of Japan's total employment in all industries. Between 1920 and 1930, more than half of all factory workers were women, even though the ratio was reversed in the succeeding decade with the establishment of newer industries that demanded higher-skilled workers. Koji Taira has argued significantly, and persuasively, that Japan's economic modernization, which meant the implementation of the factory system after the war, was "manned by women."[16] In his thinking, the economic and technological advances in the process of capitalist modernization were sustained by the relative backwardness of the labor force, numerically dominated by women and girls, and the retention of low wages. Factories, representing the newer, modern sector of the economy, were promoted as the sign of capitalist progress, and this privilege linked factory employment to the gendered composition of the workforce. But, as Taira reminds us, women workers did not enjoy any special advantages by participating in the industrialization process, apart from winning some economic independence and social autonomy. Like they were for the scores of women and girls that poured into the service sectors, low wages were apparently the price for independence. These women suffered from long working days, without rest and holidays, depressed wages, and a wide variety of health hazards. (Kagawa and Andō pointed to the relationship between the social evils of prostitution and health risks among sex workers, which paralleled a comparable experience among female factory workers.) Despite the implementation of legislation from 1911 on, designed to improve the working conditions of women and children, progress came slowly, and the major problems of depressed wages and unhealthy conditions continued to plague women factory workers. By the middle 1920s, when Japanese industrialism was beginning to move to a new stage of development characterized by the establishment of firms requiring higher technical proficiency from workers, the demand for skilled male labor increased as the wage differential between men and women widened. According to Taira, new employment practices were instituted that prefigured a "Japanese Employment System" and the effort to stabilize the relationship between capital and labor, management and workers in a historical conjuncture marked by incessant labor disputes, strikes, and mobilization in both the cities and the countryside.[17] It was at this point that the increasing demand for male workers began to drive large numbers of women into the informal and service sectors, such as small shops, stores, and cafes. But this numerical preponderance of women in the modernization process and the life they lived in the cities— financially independent, socially autonomous, and politically active— overdetermined in discourse the figure of the *modan garū* (modern girl), and the exaggerated threat to the settled conceptions of patriarchically dominated relationships (authorized by law) as well as the effort of mass media to reassert the integrity and stability of the household unit by enforcing the traditional role ascribed to wife and mother (however modernized they were materially). These "modern girls" became the heroes of this new, feminized culture announced by Hirabayashi. The new modern life was figured first in discourse, as fantasy, before it was ubiquitously lived as experience, and its major elements were independent women, commodities, and mass consumption. What this fantasizing discourse inadvertently inspired was not only the fear of progressive social disorder and conflict but also the growing sense that the processes guaranteeing cultural reproduction (not to forget biological reproduction) were in danger of disappearing altogether. If the formation of mass culture produced overdetermination as the historical sign of the crisis of social indeterminacy, the modern girl was its contemporary trope.

The expanding metropolitan sites like Tokyo and Osaka supplied a vast space for discourse to imagine and figure a new form of life, a place for fantasizing what had not yet become a lived reality for all. Yet even as a fantasy of "modern life," it was able to dramatize the production of desire inspired by a new life promising new commodities for consumption, new social relationships, identities, and experience. What the metropolis produced first, then, was a social discourse of everyday modern life, often called *bunka seikatsu* (cultural living) by contemporaries, that constantly announced itself in mass media like popular magazines, newspapers, advertisements, radio, and movies, pointing to the ceaseless changes in material life introduced by new consumer products and a conception of life vastly different from the rhythms of received, routine practices. Discourse continuously pointed to the succession of events and looked to the future, as the making of constant eventfulness became the principal commodity of newspapers and popular magazines, not to forget radio, and the progressive fragmentation and destabilization of cultural forms. Yet this reflexive discourse, formulated in the immediate postwar period and linked to the prospect of international peace and peacetime industrial production and consumption provoked by the appearance of new forms of everyday life, was more important than the actual ubiquity of the new modern life itself. It pointed to an evolving historical situation—something that was occurring in social practice and would continue to do so— and often prefigured and preceded the widespread establishment of commodity culture in Japan and its regime of new subjectivities and social relationships. In other words, more than reflecting a historical reality already in place in the 1920s, it figured a fantasy life that demanded to be fulfilled.[18] As such, this discourse on everyday "modern life" (*modan raifu*, as it was sounded out in Japanese), what the Marxist philosopher Tosaka renamed, at the time, as the "quotidianization of thought" because he was convinced its message emanated from the lived experience of a new constituency called the "people" (*minshū*) and the "masses" (*taishū*), was more futuristic and anticipatory of a different kind of society, fascinated yet capable of prompting dread and anxiety. Others, as we shall see, saw the shape of even worse things to come in the commodified inscriptions of the new life as they fled to the safety of traditional cultural shelter. It was the dread of mass culture and consumption in the 1920s (not to mention the specter of mass politics) and its threat to unhinge older, fixed social relationships and subjectivities that led to the formation of a secondary discourse on the social aimed at representing the essence of society and performing a virtual poeticizing or aestheticizing of everydayness in order to negate the divisions, fragmentation, and conflict that had instituted society in Japan.

If, as Max Weber observed immediately after World War I, bureaucratic rationality would dominate everyday life to form a seamless fit between political power and the social lifeworld, Japanese thinkers and critics tried to offset this eventuality by returning to the older equation that identified life with art and culture. Both the left and the right participated in this secondary discourse on the social and pressed their respective claims for defining the meaning of everyday life: the left seeking to construct a conception of modernity rooted in an analysis of the phenomenological present that would avoid reducing all historical epochs to capital but still be capable of retaining it as a moment in a larger historical process not yet completed and whose outcome lay in the future; while conservatives, Japan's version of "modernists against modernity," anxiously looked to locate a space whose recovery would fulfill historic cultural models outside of history itself. This move entailed finding a refuge from what many perceived as an inauthentic social life of capitalism for a ground of authentic knowledge capable of establishing a society without history within the heart of historical society, or, as Slavoj Žižek described it later, "capitalism without capitalism."

The new "cultural living" advertising the advent of new forms of consumption, living, and experience seized hold of society immediately after World War I. Countless new journals, newspapers, and films presented this new conception of life as it unfolded in the space of the streets—streets that were beginning to become more important than the things they actually linked together. Recognition of the establishment of a new everydayness was, in part, dramatized by the government itself, which soon after the war began to promote what was called a "daily life reform movement" (seikatsu kaizen undō) or the "simple life movement" (shinpuru raifu undō) inspired by a French best-seller, La vie simple (1917), a translation of an American book. The purpose of this movement was to insure the government's control over the new modern life that was being imagined in popular media and to implement a program that would emphasize efficiency and economies yet encourage people to avoid excess and immersing themselves too deeply in the new commodity culture. The opening of the Peace Exhibition Hall in 1923 not only linked its celebration of the virtues of global peace and harmony to the encouragement of industry, it offered a living display of the new cultural living. Its meaning was even more important as it emphasized the importance of a culture of peaceful consumption against a tradition of militaristic production.[19] Prefixing life and living with the word for culture—bunka—pointed to how life itself was now identified with culture, when before it had not been, and the extent to which production and lived experience were decoupled.

What lay behind this official recognition of a transformation exclusively promoting commodity production and new possibilities for consumption—at least for the middle classes—was a widely shared conviction about the necessity of encouraging the adoption of rationality, efficiency, and economies in the conduct of social life. The Ministry of Education in 1920, apparently still reeling from the recent "rice riots" and now attempting to avoid comparable conflict in the future, issued a proclamation calling for greater diversity in food consumption and proposing the importance of ending the centrality of rice in the Japanese diet.[20] Yet this call was expanded to include new regulations regarding housing and the consumption of utilities that would lead to the protection of lower-class families. The "simple life" enunciated by the state referred to rationalization, and a new culturally lived experience was identified with Western style. Although cultural life targeted the city "salaryman" and his family, it was concentrated first on the production and consumption of commodities for family use. The forum for these commodities was the department store, which developed rapidly in these years and made available the permanent display of household consumer goods. Not always restricted to the presentation of expensive, high-quality goods, department stores like Mitsukoshi offered cheaper goods in annexes in Marunouchi, like "Cotton Day."[21] While this rationalization of household life had been encouraged from the top, the desire for consumption quickly spread beyond any possible control or regulation to reach all sectors of Japanese society and ultimately exceeded the constraints of marginal utility (rationality and economies) envisaged by its promoters. If department stores offered a permanent display of "modern life," popular discourse (and advertisements) kept the spectacle of endless consumption constantly before the population. Cultural living, however limited politically and socially at the time of its inception, became a cultural unconsciousness for Japanese living in the cities. More than anything else, it dramatized the immense difference between the old and the new. "The economy of the older period privileged production," intoned a contemporary explanation, "and the worker was compelled to sacrifice his life because of this. In the new age, it is clear that consumption now accompanies production and is opposed to the sacrifices the worker was forced to make. We have to take the advancement of life seriously."[22]

The house and the household were at the heart of this transformation. It was in the household, according to a later account (1924), that health, morality, peace and harmony, activity and mental serenity of the whole family were managed. It must progress as society progresses. "Feudal houses," as such, "were not only difficult to situate in contemporary life but were tremendously injurious to the progress of society today. . . . A house unifies inasmuch as it simplifies life."[23] But we should note that the central thrust of "cultural living" and its emphasis on the consumption of household commodities disclosed the degree to which the state, in its inaugural efforts to move from mere (military) production to (commodity) consumption, targeted women as the principal subject. Indeed, consumption, from the very beginning, was closely identified with women and was thus gendered to a degree that explains why the primary figure and ideologeme of the 1920s and early 1930s was the *modan garū*. This gendering of consumption worked in such a way as not simply to overdetermine the figure of the modern woman and the putative dangers she posed to settled forms of patriarchal order and reproduction but, strangely, to equate the promotion of scientific knowledge and rationality with the feminization of culture. The move to "cultural living" seemed to identify modernity itself with the status of women consumers who were being enjoined, in new magazines like *Shufu no tomo* (Housewife's friend) and *Kagaku chishiki* (Scientific knowledge), not to mention more middle-brow periodicals like *Josei* (Woman) and *Fujin kōron* (Women's opinion), to name only the better know publications, to become rational and informed consumers of products that would enhance and improve the life and health of the household. Even though the major goal was to make women into rational custodians of the household political economy, the effects of this process could not simply be limited to preserving the family as the primary, solidary social unit. This gendering of consumption in the early 1920s meshed quickly with the phenomenon of large numbers of women who were entering the labor force and undoubtedly contributed to contemporary descriptions announcing the establishment of a "feminine culture."[24]

The marks of this new culture were Western clothing, cosmetics, and the beauty salon. What the rationalization of household life required, as a concretization of "cultural living," was a change of the position of women in the household political economy. It not only announced the end of the seclusion and isolation women had experienced as virtual prisoners of the household, it had consequences for their status outside of family life, as larger numbers began pouring into the labor force, especially in those areas like learning, education, and sports that had been male preserves. In this sense, the experience of rationalizing everyday life with efficient and cheaply made consumer items, promoted to encourage greater solidification of family life, especially in the new environment of the cities where its size diminished, led to a transformation of the role occupied by women and a reorganization of the relationship between their private (enclosed) and public (open) worlds. In the process of assuming responsibility for reorganizing everyday life according to new standards of efficiency and economies, women acquired a new sense of subjectivity (when before it had been exceedingly weak) that took them outside of the household to become principal actors in the drama of modernity. The figure of the "modern girl" and "kissing girl," represented as a flapper, portrayed by Tanizaki's Naomi (*Chijin no ai*), who was made to resemble the movie actress Mary Pickford, an exaggerated personification of the independent female flapper projected by the Hollywood dream factory, was the overdetermined figure that signified both the changes women had already experienced and the aspirations they sought to realize. But this figure also disclosed both fear of the threat she posed to settled conceptions of civil order and the possibility of a gender war. In Japan during the 1920s and early 1930s, the true other of modernity was not so much the worker but woman. The surfacing of sharp gender distinctions and the claims associated with them constituted, along with the recognition of class divisions constantly kept alive by the left, a threat to order of such magnitude that it became an unstated spur to the production of cultural theory that sought to uphold received practices of reproduction (both cultural and biological) that were made to appear gender neutral. Despite

Kuki Shūzō's celebration of feminine design and articles of clothing in the late Edo period, there is nothing about his theory of culture to suggest that he had embraced the prevailing view that characterized the 1920s as the time of a feminization of culture. By the same measure, Orikuchi's female chanters of archaic rituals did not signify acceptance of the new role played by women in the interwar period. In fact, most cultural theory seemed to be purposely mute on questions of gender, as well as class, and sought to present an image of Japan that was marked neither by social divisions nor by gender difference and sexual differentiation. Precisely because most cultural and communitarian theory remained silent on gender especially, which I suspect was seen as an even greater threat to social order than the specter of class conflict because it struck at the heart of a conception of reproduction, the fear of new gendered aspirations was the driving force behind the effort to present a view of national life that was whole, unblemished by division and harmonious, where, as Yanagita proposed, there was only the "ordinary and abiding folk," *jōmin*.

For Japanese, modernity was speed, shock, and the spectacle of constant sensation. These qualities were often exaggeratedly symbolized in the discourse of the popular media as new subjectivities like the modern girl, the "Marxist boy," the kissing girl, and the cafe waitress; the force of its ubiquity was conveyed by advertisements proclaiming new household products like irons, phonographs, radios, and kitchen-labor devices. According to the contemporary *Kokumin nichijō ōkagami* (Great mirror of national everyday life), a publication constantly admonishing people to consume the new, the "economics of the family was centered in the kitchen and its high economies had great influence."[25] Moreover, the list of consumer items was almost endless, privileging Western-style skirts and trousers, new, Western foods and modes of preparation, the new "culture houses," toys for middle-class children, and so on, all promising "convenience," "utility," and "economies." With these commodities, and the necessity of consuming them, came the acquisition of new identities that traversed class, gender, and sexuality, even though it seems evident that women were originally targeted as the subject of commodity consumption. In the post–World War I period, the site of this explosion of modern life was the metropolitan center, and its primary constituencies, especially after the earthquake of 1923, were the masses who worked in the urban industries, consumed its products, and played on its streets. In fact, the discourse on everyday modern life was really about life on the streets where, as the urban ethnographer Kon Wajirō observed in countless studies conducted in the 1920s and early 1930s, innumerable identities were being played out daily on every street corner where people could assume different subject positions by the way they held and smoked cigarettes, dressed, styled their hair, and walked, and by the choices they made for

play and consumption in the Ginza. Life on the streets constantly external-
ized the power of desire and the way people enacted their innermost fantasies as if they were on a large and endless theater stage. The Iwanami
publishing house, announcing a forthcoming series of cheaply priced
books aimed at the consuming "people" (minshū), declared its hope to
"liberate immortal books which have been the life of study and research
of the few and put them in the hands of the people who stand in every
nook and cranny of the streets."[26]

This linking of the streets and the new constituency of the people emblematized Japan's new modern life. People who poured into the streets
were made conscious that they, in fact, were the people, the minshū, and,
as Tosaka perceptively observed, their activities had "quotidianized" all
thinking. The word for street, gaitō, surfaced in the 1920s and was immediately identified with city folk who were colonizing and consuming its
offerings. For Japanese living in the cities during the 1920s, words like
gaitō and minshū entered into the lexicon of commonly uttered buzz-
words that were used everywhere in speech and the writing of the popular,
mass media, called ryūkōgo, and came to be associated with dynamically
progressive and fast-moving people on the streets, consuming new products and forms of entertainment. As one writer put it, the Oriental tradition of sacrifice and struggle was getting weaker, and people were turning
increasingly to the "pleasuring of daily life. . . . Like eating cooked rice
when famished, drinking water when thirsty, pleasure has become an important part of the real and actual life of the people."[27]

In Japan, no less than in industrializing societies like France, Germany,
and Italy, as memory of the war receded and the harsh sacrifices exacted
by two earlier wars with China and Russia faded, the heroism of production was being replaced by heroic consumption. What resulted was not
so much a clash between newer and established values as a struggle
of desire against values in general. For ordinary people in the 1920s, the
"pluck of Meiji" and the obsession with "rising in the world" (risshin
shusse) (as Earl Kinmonth has so aptly described this earlier petit bourgeois ideology, "making it") that seemed to encapsulate so much of the
Meiji march to realize "wealth and power" and encourage endless depri-
vation gave way to the search for comfort and pleasure, leisure and
play. The pleasures offered by a new consumption culture—the "philosophy of fun" (goraku no tetsugaku) coined and celebrated by the social
critic Gonda Yasunosuke—and the production of a social discourse defining everyday modern life on the streets may have overstated its reach as
a widespread reality and concealed the observable fact that it was restricted to the urban middle class (at least before the earthquake). Nevertheless, it still attested to social practices and a lived history that would
trouble critics searching for meaning as they confronted signs of social

indeterminacy, fragmentation, and conflict. Many early recognized that in the power of desire to inspire endless consumption and to offset fixed values lay a challenge to settled relationships. Almost immediately, criticism surfaced to call attention to the baleful consequences of the quest for materiality, its ostentation and self-indulgence, and especially its effects on work and reproduction, and to demand the reinstatement of "spiritual values" in everyday life. In the wake of the earthquake, the idea of "heaven's punishment" (*tenkan*) circulated to indicate how opulence and frivolity needed to be reconsidered and how modern customs constituted an "omen" of catastrophe. Elegant goods and expensive products were "valueless before heaven's punishment" as life must be lived simply and the venerable classic *I ching* consulted for the reading of signs.[28] From Tsubouchi Shōyō's early (1906) anticipation of a daily life suffused with spiritual values of the highest order to Abe Jirō's reworking of *allgemein bildung*—personal moral and cultural cultivation—there was no lack of thoughtful and anxious concern for the growing importance of desire (materiality) and the eclipsing of spirituality. Others, in this vein, were reminded of the unevenness of development between city and countryside, how even in the cities people were living in mixed cultural registers, and how the past still interacted with the new in the present—how past, as William Faulkner once said, was not yet past.

Hence, the streets, which had existed earlier in Edo and other cities, were now transformed into public spaces to stage acts of consumption and realize new identities. When juxtaposed to the household, the street was the place of activity and independence. The household, for men, was seen as a sanctuary of retreat and relaxation, the seat of patriarchy that protected and nourished children. Opposed to this sense of privacy, seeking to make invisible the wife/mother, as well, was the workplace, which represented the site of business and production. As a public place, it incorporated men into its machinery and made them aware of the necessity of working for wages to continue to maintain the household refuge. Only the streets were truly open and offered the stage for people to become free, to realize their desire. In this regard, the "dance place" (*odoriba*) was a platform between the household and the workplace and consciously seen as the place of freedom.[29] Once large-scale business and industrial sites were established, it became increasingly difficult to combine workplace and household. Large numbers of people were thus thrown daily into the streets, shuffling between home and firm or factory, as wage earners. But this daily mixing of large numbers of people using the streets to get to one place or another instilled the idea of street life that combined both the mixed and the different.[30] Moreover, only social discourse, as we shall see, was able to totalize the scene of the streets and see it as the whole of what was happening in the modern lives of the people. The streets, accordingly, offered the opportunity to constantly defamiliarize and refamiliarize a scene that people took for granted. Once resituated in a conception of a totality, or social whole, the familiar gave way to new and different conceptions of the lived experience. That is to say, the street led to envisioning the social. Yet it is important to add that the street, in an entirely opposing direction, was the place dominated by the commodity form, which worked to homogenize and standardize life into a customized existence, seeking constantly to dissolve the very difference and heterogeneity it made possible.

Nevertheless, like the quiet and familiar street scene portrayed by the Portuguese poet Fernando Pessoa, which suddenly and unexpectedly explodes to show its difference, or even Tokunaga's noisy and chaotic avenue that comes to a screeching halt because of the entry of an imperial personage, what was a moment ago familiar is now changed, disclosing its "disquiet." When the countless passers-by of the streets of Tokyo are looked at as students preparing for jobs, salarymen returning home, the unemployed constantly looking for something, the lumpen who seem to have no fixed location, revelers, housewives, and so on, the scene changes into something unfamiliar. In a certain sense, it is precisely this difference and heterogeneity of class, gender, and sexuality that marked the streets that Yanagita Kunio tried to efface with his conception of *jōmin*, the indefinite and unmarked "ordinary and abiding folk."

It is interesting to note that the later discussants of modernity disparagingly looked back on the preceding two decades and the formation of mass culture as the time of Americanization, the film, and Fordist processes of production. Often they dismissed it as "hedonistic" and "crass" materialism, hopelessly superficial when contrasted to the historical culture of Europe, even though it had derived from it—a materialism that had no other purpose than the circulation of commodities and the reproduction of consumption. Contemporaries, like the Marxist critic Ōya Sōichi, condemned "modern custom" (*modansō*) as superficial and diluted, while others acknowledged its vitality and promise. As early as 1918, the influential opinion journal *Chūō kōron* ran a special issue on modernity that sought to identify the "symbolic currents of the new age" and found them in the "image of the automobile," the "moving pictures," and the "cafe." A decade later, the playwright Kikuchi Kan declared that "true modernity, made in Japan, was just beginning," and proof of this lay in the appearance of what he called "new women and men" announcing the "birth of a new human being." In this historical conjuncture, Uchida Roan, a critic, reported that "after the war, the cream of milk skimmed off in department stores and movie pictures was American capitalism," which he later described as an "essential something that had caught the public spirit."[31] It is important to note here that the whole spectacle of

American life entering Japan was grasped by the eye and was made to appeal directly to vision, as attested to by the popularity of American film.[32] The Marxist literary critic Hirabayashi Hatsunosuke observed that

> even Japan had become a complete vassal state of Hollywood. Even if you go to a rural cinema, at least one American film will be on the program. In the cities we can see movie houses that specialize in featuring Western films, the majority of them being American, and observe large numbers of fans who do not view anything but Western cinema. . . . Comedy and action, which are the principal forms of American cinema, have rapidly changed the life of Japan today. From the outfit of the cafe waitress to the uniform of the boy scout, there is nothing that has not been influenced by the film. Harold Lloyd spectacles and striped trousers are directly related to fashions in hair cutting and the movies. But its most extreme product was undoubtedly the modern girl and modern boy. It can't be said they were unrelated to Western whiskey and the cafe, the dance hall and the movies.[33]

While the older imports of European culture had been channeled though print media, American life style, which became the cultural dominant after the war, and especially the earthquake, signaling the quickening of quantitative production and consumption, was displayed directly in film and centered on the pleasures of buying, entertainment, and sports. What caught Uchida's attention was how American capitalism, through its leading products, had come to dominate everyday life in Japan by offering a powerful image of how it was being lived elsewhere. The poet Satō Haruo in 1919 advised contemporaries that the West was genuinely important and that the film was equal to the "opening of the country" in the "cultural history of Japan," especially the "action film."[34] It was this image of "American life style," as it was increasingly called, that found its way into newspapers and magazines. Kikuchi Kan, participating in a roundtable discussion published by *Modan Nippon* (Modern Japan) in 1930, asserted that the "modern of our young era will be intellectual. It is because we will call as the now the modern with respect to life style."[35] Here, "intellectually modern" undoubtedly referred to utopianism, new forms of representation, abstract art, and functionalism, but it was manifestly evident that what momentarily constituted modern life was an Americanism that overwhelmed the claims of high art and thought. Ideas were being replaced by things, as the arc of consumption swung widely to accommodate the masses. Some, like Yanagisawa Ken, however, were convinced that motion pictures had great cultural influence on Japanese society because they "imposed a Westernization of depth rather than one of surfaces," inverting the worries of the novelist Natsume Sōseki's seething denunciation of the surface culture of the West that Japanese had hurriedly imported and that threatened the country with the prospect of a nervous breakdown in the near future.[36] But, now, according to another observer of the scene, the people might spend a lot of time laughing in movie houses, but "they still understood well the thing called the West."[37] "My favorite among the symbols of modernity," wrote Satō Haruo, "is the motion pictures. When I reflect on them, I feel duty bound to live in the present."[38] And Kikuchi Kan, perhaps the most astute recorder of the contemporary scene, confessed that "even though one watches continuously for four or five hours a day, one always does so cheerfully."[39] He would gladly watch anything with a Western content rather than sit through a film dealing with Japan. The film critic Tsumura Hideo observed that the American film had swept through Asia and reached even the "natives" of Southeast Asia, not to forget the backlands of Kyushu and Shikoku. What accounted for this sweeping success was both its presentation of a world of commodities—"cultural life"—and the observable fact that American films were usually westerns and slapstick comedies that had little dialogue and could easily be understood by large numbers of people. As a leading industry exporting a product, film was not just a sign of capitalism; it also put on display commodity culture produced by American capitalism, lived and experienced by its principal subjects, modern men and women.

In its capacity to deterritorialize, capitalism simply "undermined every fixed social identity" and produced innumerable new subject positions all challenging the fixity of received traditional roles.[40] Novelists like Tanazaki Junichirō, Kawabata Yasunari (particularly in *Asakusa kurenaiden*), and especially Edogawa Rampo explored new sexual identities and their consequences for settled social relationships. In discourse, "all seemed captivated by the modern girl, and were drawn to her hairstyle, clothing, attitudes, facial and bodily movements, and the way of walking."[41] The figure of the modern girl was symbolized by the short skirt worn above the knees, Louise Brooks haircut, rouge, and lipstick; she appeared as a woman who "struts through the throngs" signifying both sexual and financial independence. A vastly exaggerated image, to be sure, but one that worked to dramatize the limits or extremities of new behavior and the excitement and danger it elicited. A special issue of *Fujin kōron* ("Miscellaneous Views of the Modern Girl," January 1928) proposed that the image of the modern girl was a complete copy influenced by American action films. "The modern girl is not intellectually modern," one participant announced, "but only modern from the standpoint of feeling."[42] Others denounced this image as a sign of decline, a "poisonous vapor," the "thick falsehood of cosmetics." But despite the consensual clamor portraying the modern girl as a danger, writers like Kikuchi Kan pointed to these "new women" as representatives of a new sexual awakening and declared that their appearance announced the beginning of modernity in

1927. "Young women," he wrote "have become unusually empowered at this time and they . . . are able to 'cross swords' with men in matters of love." Kikuchi, who had already written about such women in his fiction, was attesting to the prominence of these liberated women in areas such as work and sexuality, which had once been in the grip of the patriarchal system. Uchida Roan recognized the genuinely erotic behavior of the modern girl in her bodily movements and language, in the manner of "pouting" and even "scowling" that "elicited widespread emulation" and imitation. He also observed that "it would be difficult to understand the modern girl and boy without seeing American movies." Kitazawa Hideichi, writing in *Josei* (August 1925), asserted that the "younger generation respects women who are spiritually independent, aware that they are humans equal to males, rather than women who misuse the power of the weak and are defeated. If the young people of the new age pursue femaleness that possesses such a tendency and attitude, they will not have to look outside the group of modern girls."[43] In this statement, Kitazawa listed the special qualities of these modern girls: (1) respect for the self or a consciousness that they were equal to men, a sense of femaleness liberated from the idea of traditional morality and causality; (2) they are born free in nature and need not got through any special process of intellectual awakening. For this reason, they are already empowered to act and thus transcend established morality.

Despite the idealized nature of this overdetermined figure of the girl, it was not all fantasy. Critics like Hirabayashi and Chiba Kameo perceived in this idealized discussion the signs of genuine material social forces and change that undergirded the emergence of the modern girl. Chiba, for example, who looked at the temperament of change of not only the modern girl but also contemporary women as a whole, saw in the transformations of women's life style prompted by the acquisition of personal income and economic independence a momentous social event that already pointed to fundamental structural mutation. "The numbers of young women who were already drawing salaries from employment had suddenly increased to over seven million. Because these [women] draw pay checks by themselves, they now can be seen freely [attending] even plays. As for what the modern girl is or whether she is a luxury, whether they are people signifying a trend that is deteriorating or one that is luxurious, it is because they have increased so much." [44] The view that there are followers of the modern girl among the daughters of the bourgeoisie is the "priceless indication" that attaches the growth of the modern girl to the increase of women in the labor force. In this regard, Hirabayashi, envisaged the progress of mechanization and the revolutionizing of technology as the context for the formation of the modern girl. A champion of technological progress, Hirabayashi believed that cinema imparted the most significant influence on the development of "modernism" and constituted the sign of a new technology. But, he continued, the machine not only broadened the possibility for cultural production and made life more convenient, it also caused the spiritual level of people to be transformed. One of its principal results was the emergence of the modern girl. The speed symbolized by technology rapidly replaced the learning and experience of people even at the spiritual level. "Elderly people today are not limited to the knowledge and experience in proportion to the length of the time they have lived. It is natural to not respect a person just because they were born first. Looking at the newspapers and magazines, listening to the discussions in the streets, it is no longer an age that generally respects the aged today . They have become the targets of ridicule, antipathy, and pity. The youth are emancipated from the authority of the aged and we can discover here the social basis of the modern girl."[45]

While there was probably more anticipation than reality in this observation, more desire than actuality, Hirabayashi was, I believe, more right than wrong when he concluded that the "emergence of the modern girl marked the special characteristic of women in an age of declining authority."[46] What is important about these observations is the recognition that the figure of the modern girl was not simply an empty symbol, an imaginary construction of the movies and popular discourse, but was the signification of more deeply rooted social and material processes that were threatening to alter the social structure of Japanese society and throw into question the status of traditional forms of morality and claims of authority. Embedded in the seductive imaging of the modern girl was the formation of a new women's consciousness that the prevailing system of authority had not anticipated and which cultural ideology would seek to efface, displace, and even repress as the calamitous sign of social contradiction and uneven development.

After the earthquake, material changes simply affirmed the image and power of this figure. While film culture was favored as the route to grasping the new everyday life in its textured materiality, others saw how it could be understood concretely and holistically in newspapers and mass circulation magazines and in new forms of popular music imported from the United States. Publications like *Modan Nippon* (Modern Japan), in its inaugural edition (10/30), celebrated a litany of modern and new customs and images of things people would soon be seeing, such as "flush toilets," "pavements," "Western clothes," "chairs," "apartments," and "business suits." Moreover, life, it was announced, would be more "sporty" and "speedy," "there would be more respect for women and a downgrading of men," and people would be hearing more "jazz," seeing more "women's legs" and "breasts." Another edition, along with the Kodansha popular magazine *Kingu* (King), praised the "Yankee spirit" and welcomed it and "American daily life" to Japan. Other publications reported on a culture of glimmering neon lights and the steady march of people from dance halls to jazz joints and cafes, crowds of people drinking hard in bars and scurrying off in one-yen taxi cabs on "broadened thoroughfares" constructed after the earthquake of 1923. Social discourse in magazines like *Shufu no tomo* described the new "culture houses" of salarymen, the appearance of nuclear families living in the cities, their household economies and outdoor recreation such as excursions to parks and miniature golf links and leisure time spent with the family, milling through department stores stocked with affordable commodities like cameras, radios, and irons.

The women's magazine *Fujin kōron* in the 1930s ran transcripts of discussions in which Japan's leading male and female critics assessed the status of the new cultural living. One particular discussion concentrated on the utility of the bed and the bedroom in contrast to the tatami room and the futon. At about the same time, the poet Hagiwara Sakutarō confessed he preferred the comforts of a Western-style bed, even though he announced his own desire to "return to Japan" in a poem that condensed all of the anxieties a whole generation expressed concerning the price paid for modernization and Westernization. The decade of the 1920s also saw a veritable explosion of a kid's culture consisting of new products targeting children of the middle class: phonograph records, toys like miniature trains and telescopes, and new candies such as Meiji and Morinaga. The use of the term "mama" apparently began sometime in 1929.[47] Children even had their own magazine, which imitated the more popular women's journals like *Shufu no tomo* and *Josei* and aimed to distribute useful information concerning health and education. Although much of the glitter of this material culture was aimed at the middle classes, with the working class still embedded in more received forms of everyday life, it did trickle down and permeate the various social strata of the cities, if not the more remote villages of the countryside.

But because the discourse on everyday life was concerned with surface descriptions, literally advertising the establishment of a new reality, tracking it and figuring it, it also began to reveal doubts about the consequences of this conquest of commodity culture and complain of the effects of the unevenness and social contradictions people were living. By the time the army was forcibly occupying Manchuria and the first effects of the world depression were reaching Japan, the social critic Aono Suekichi, as we shall see, was reporting that salarymen in the early 1930s were beginning to show signs of "psychological unhappiness" because they could not satisfy their desire for consumption and fulfill their aspirations as a social class. Magazines like *King* tried to promote upbeat messages that sanitized "street life" in advertisements that extolled beauty and discussions advising ways to maintain healthy households and living within one's means. Virtually every issue promised new knowledge and the virtues of what Kodansha named "commonsense science" (which Tosaka Jun would see as the ideology of the status quo) that reached a mass readership through direct mailing. One of the paradoxes of the period is how mass circulation magazines dispersed an ideology of the recovered family and established social relationships yet continued to introduce new possibilities for consumption capable of eroding the bonds of social solidarity. The newspapers went even further with both advertisements targeting consumers and lurid tales of scandals that invariably kept the image of new kinds of (sexual) relationships before the reading public.

What enthusiasm for the modern conceded was the recognition that so many of the changes were restricted to urban areas, and only their rumor reached the countryside. This image of the metropolitan city as universal was constantly affirmed by writers like Kikuchi Kan who celebrated the birth of a new human. "Modern thought that has come to Japan is beginning today to give birth to the modern masses," he wrote enthusiastically and optimistically in *Bungei shunjū* (February 1927).[48] It is important to acknowledge that his optimism failed to take into account, four years later, the army's imperial seizure of Manchuria and its subsequent closing down of journals like *Kindai shisō* (Modern thought). In fact, writers like Kikuchi rarely fastened their attention on Japan as a whole and merely assumed that Tokyo, the part, stood in for the whole, repressing the very unevenness that the city/countryside division dramatized and, by extension, that existed between the metropole and the colony. While his attention was entirely riveted to street life and the changes in life style and attitudes found in the cities, his silence obscured the existence of the other half of Japan, the place of the villages where the majority of the population still lived and the small businessman—the "reliable" backbone of the middle classes, who remained ambivalently outside of the benefits of new forms of consumption. Modernism, celebrating the birth of new human, a "modernism without pretension," as Kikuchi put it, effectively repressed the vast unevenness signified by cities like Tokyo, just as effectively as the appeals to culture and community, as we shall see, worked to efface the divisions introduced by modern life by freezing both in eternity. The monthly *Ie no hikari* (Light of the household), distributed widely throughout the countryside, rarely advertised new products or offered articles describing the superiority of Western clothing and foods. Instead, it provided information on how to get along with what people had and regularly offered useful tips on such things as the preparation of "joyful egg dishes for guests" and "how to make *shōyu* for household use" rather than buying it. Avoiding, at all times, the glamorous side of women's culture, it ran ads for "immediate employment" in jobs like "maids," "store clerks," "bus conductors," "inn servants," and "factory" (small rural shops). Yamakawa Hitoshi in 1934 surveyed living conditions in the North (admittedly already affected by the depression) and reported that most households did not even possess one futon to sleep on, often using piles of trash for bedding, while another survey of Osaka Prefecture in the same year showed that that there was an average of no more than 1.8 lamps for lighting per household and that the light bulbs used had the power of sixteen candles. The critic Ikuta Aoyama dismissed modern men and women (Kikuchi's new humans) as a "parade of goblins that have no substance" and called for a termination of all further discussion of "Tokyo tastes and gemeutlich."[49] The small towns and villages of the countryside were left behind the capitalization of the cities, even as they were expected to sustain the engines of capitalism's desiring machine.

This sense of alienation, recorded brilliantly by Yanagita Kunio and confirmed by the historian Hani Gorō in his denunciation of "community studies," opened the way for the development of communitarianism, rural cooperation, and the advocacy of self-reliance. In an article in *Ie no hikari* in February 1931, for example, a writer proposed that agriculture, fishing, and forestry were the bases of a country's industry and the "kernel of the economy." If these basic economic activities were allowed to collapse, sacrificed to industrialization and consumption, the country itself would collapse. "The life and death of one industry manages the life and death of all others." To avoid this unhappy fate, the writer recommended a moratorium on consuming luxury items and renewed moral discipline capable of overcoming "the lewdness and dissipation of town and country." As a result of "frivolous Western influence, young men and women put on airs and rampantly swagger 'newness.' " What he called for was a return to the spiritual foundations of society and a rearticulation of the "principles of the mutual splendor of coexistence (*kyōzon dōei*)": maintaining harmonious relations with neighbors and promoting cooperation within communities and between villages.[50] To this end, the writer recommended (1) the establishment of a regime of frugality; (2) greater efforts to increase capital accumulation in the countryside; (3) encouraging increased efficiency in agricultural production; and (4) cutting down production costs and a cautious expansion of the market as the only solution to rural relief. It is important to suggest, at this point, that the idea of village cooperation was envisioned as an alternative to the consumption culture identified with the cities. The villages were seen, in time, as a refuge against the profligacy of the cities, and the cities were envisaged as the cause of rural impoverishment and grief. Ikuta Aoyama saw no reason for the coexistence of the old and new, since the latter was superficial while the former was not. Kagawa and Andō, as already suggested, quantified the mass recruitment of young women conscripted to staff the vast pleasure quarters of the cities. A new religion, Hitonomichi Kyōdan, appeared in the cities to minister to those Aono had identified as "psychologically unhappy." Enlisting its members widely from among city classes, the new religion was organized to offer counseling to unhappy men and women and to emphasize the importance of "spousal harmony" as the work of the gods. Although it provided the prospect of stoicism of the spirit, less sex at home, it also promoted the possibility of realizing the good life in the customs and commodities of modern life because the new life-styles required money and expenditure. The magazine *Shufu no tomo* in 1931 addressed the issue of disharmony prompted by a dissatisfactory sex life among couples and how its continuation could be "injurious to nature." The magazine advised greater cooperation between couples, which meant that women should suppress their needs in the interest of saving the family. These frank discussions on modern sexuality conveyed a mixed or contradictory message that acknowledged a relationship between women's new liberated status and an awareness of their own sexual needs at the same time that they counseled them to cooperate in the interest of preserving the family and affirming a patriarchal order that cared more for men's needs. The appearance of a number of journals devoted to exploring modern sexuality may well have reflected simply the success of the mass media in titillating a readership already hardened to the discipline of daily scandals, but it also revealed, again, the existence of the changing circumstances women were experiencing and the identification of new needs that required serious attention.[51]

What this surface discussion on the everyday life of new commodities, custom, and social relationships revealed, albeit inadvertently, was the historical role of unequal development in the subsequent production of a modernist discourse that would seek to repress and efface its signs. It raised the spectacle of disunity, division, and difference, which it did not know how to resolve; it conveyed this message of unevenness through juxtaposition and propinquity. Its image of an implied disunity collided with the consensual conviction upheld by the state that society must be made to show that no real divisions exist, that life corresponds perfectly to the very categories employed to provide the social unit with its representation of unity. This unit, as the discourse on everydayness was showing, was threatened by the separation of activities of social agents and the changeability of social relations; it could be restored only if the divisions that had actually constituted society—capital and labor—are negated, concealed, or resolved in the future.[52] What is important, for my purposes, is how this discussion on modern life ultimately produced a secondary discourse on the social, culminating in the wartime conference on overcoming modernity, devoted to displacing the doubts provoked by the spectacle of unevenness that challenged the metropolitan interpretation of its own experience as universal. Native ethnologists like Yanagita Kunio early recognized the presence of unequal development in the policy to sacrifice the countryside for the city, while the sociologist Takada Yasuma, a translator of Simmel and a proponent of interactionist social theory, declared his allegiance to gemeinschaft, as he put it, and a reaffirmation of the principles of harmony and consensus as the essential forms of social relationships in Japan. By the early 1930s, there were attempts to rein in the culture of consumption and eliminate its excesses in calls for "regulating custom." Shigeta Tadamasa wrote an influential book called *Fūzoku keisatsu no riron to jissai* (The theory and reality of policing custom, 1934) in which he sought to explain the reasons for policing contemporary custom. Policing, he claimed, was necessary to limit and even prohibit acts and conduct injurious to society in order to preserve the social good.[53] Moreover, systems devoted to regulating public places like dance halls were inaugurated in the mid-1920s to prevent admittance of geisha and students who were minors. Ordinances were promulgated to prevent children from going to the cinema because, as Gonda Yasunosuke observed, their heads were emptied out. In the 1930s films considered "harmful to the customs of contemporary society" were increasingly censored, and showing them incurred risks.[54] This was especially true of Western imports, which invariably featured scenes portraying the kiss and associated emotions that ended up on the floor of the cutting room. Women's fashions, especially Western apparel, and popular songs were also subjected to regulations in the interest of preserving public morality.

In contrast to the discussions on everyday life, preoccupied with the surface and the present—hence marking its own historicity—the discourse on the social was concerned with depth, searching for fixed essences beneath the visible skin of contemporary life. It fastened on those traces that would reveal an existence prior to capitalism and modernity. Seeking to repress signs of its own historicity, this discourse pursued the task of constructing a vast synchronic drama that, because it was posited upon forgetting the instituting moment, could not allow into it any diachronic reflection or reference. When Marxists and progressives turned to critique, they projected an image of culture which, based on the existence of an everydayness of the present, would complete modernity in the future. Yet for both the left and the right, the task was still to overcome the division, disunity, and fragmentation that contemporary society was experiencing. This folding back and retracing ultimately made the discourse on the social ideological, inasmuch as its purpose was to remove, conceal divisions, naturalize historical relationships, and eternalize them by attributing to them coherence based on an essence outside of time. Instead of attending to the place of production, it resorted to the production of place. The temporal process was incorporated into space. This discursive activity, split off from one derived from social practice, was less a simulation of the real, as Marx once believed, than a dissimulation of it. It was for this reason that thinkers and writers sought to install in the present a moment of recall or recovered experience, a memory *of* rather than *from* a time before time (as the ethnologist Orikuchi Shinobu might have put it), whether it was an aesthetic principle, a religious practice, a communitarian ideal, or a cultural imaginary.

In the writings of Yanagita Kunio, we have the example of how the recognition of cultural unevenness, what he called *ainoko bunmei* (mixed civilization), was not a temporary stage in an evolutionary narrative but a permanently entrenched condition that could be found throughout East Asia. His program endeavored, with others trying to account for the speed of modernization, to supply the figure of a palimpsistic imaginary where the earlier and essential layers of national life, in the form of custom, practice, and beliefs, were still able to filter through the modern overlays and provide a map for the present. The philosopher Watsuji Tetsurō, a former student of Martin Heidegger, called this stratigraphic layering *jusōsei* and envisioned history as a spatial stockpiling of strategic epochs in the itinerary of the spirit, each laying on top of each other yet somehow transparent. Yanagita appealed to the trope of a nonlinear history of custom by employing the vivid imagery of a stalactitic formation that grows unobserved into the shape of a large icicle. Others, like Kuki Shūzō, looked to an essential experience such as *iki* that had reached its maturation in the late eighteenth century and was therefore prior to capitalism and free from Western metaphysics yet fully capable of anchoring the Japanese of the present, even though it called attention to a way of life of a particular past era. On a closer look, his hermeneutic meditation on the form of late Edo culture, as encapsulated in the elusive term *iki*, was more an imagined recalling of something that never quite existed, an originary experience that came from the future rather than the past that stood-in for the genius of the race. In this regard, Miki Kiyoshi's powerful conception of a "foundational experience," a rereading of both Marx and Nishida Kitarō, provided a whole generation with the necessary conceptual apparatus to undertake the arduous task of trying to think their way to overcoming the modern. The native ethnologist Orikuchi saw in folkloric traces—what Yanagita had identified as living "vestiges," the figure of a primordial everyday life that would reveal another place of difference outside of history and remind contemporaries of its production of enduring values such as "constancy," "eternity," and "absoluteness." But all of these, and more, were simply constructions that came into existence precisely and suddenly at the moment when older conceptions of life were beginning to disappear. Hence, thought and literature turned increasingly to locating a metaphorical space whose discovery would fulfill ageless models outside of society itself. This move entailed finding a refuge from what many believed to be an inauthentic social life (based on inauthentic knowledge) in which the process of capitalist modernization was integrating people into larger impersonal units of organization and enforcing greater dependence on them. What this discourse on the social disclosed was an immense struggle to catch hold of an everydayness—modern life—that always escapes because it lacks a true subject yet manages, at the same time, to routinize every aspect of social life. It aimed, therefore, to redefine daily life itself enduringly as something that was neither always escaping nor rooted in routine, to give it a stable and fixed form and meaning in order to overcome an indeterminate public space—the streets—where culture was being lived and alienations, fetishisms, and reifications were producing their effects.[55]

By rejecting an outer and objective domain already in process of becoming reified, discourse began to identify the place of creativity that produced enduring meaning and cultural values capable of fixing stable social relationships such as the family, village, and communal cooperative. In this transaction, the empirical was often abandoned, the performative present dismissed, to make place for an essentialized entity to occupy. As an interpretive mode aimed at unearthing the ground of authenticity, the new cultural discourse favored a hermeneutics that promised to probe beneath the surface and thereby locate a fixed "existence," a timeless everydayness, as imagined by native ethnologists, a paradigmatic moment revealing the genius of the race in a historical time/style, an eternal aesthetics or poetics now made visible by the glaring contrast posed by Western culture (Tanizaki Junichirō, Kobayashi Hideo), a spatially privileged climate and history free from change, authorizing an entirely different ethic of social relationships unaccountable to time (Watsuji Tetsurō), in the scene of speaking (Tokieda Motoki), the countryside (Yanagita), or in the auratic experience of the "other place" (Orikuchi). Although Marxists and progressive thinkers rejected this method, they nonetheless imagined the possibility of realizing a more evenly developed modern society by starting with the present and its performative dimension, through the exercise of critique, science, and rationality. As late as 1941, the philosopher Miki Kiyoshi, who traveled an intellectual route from Marxism to phenomenology, sought to resolve the apparent fragmentations and divisions marking modernity by uniting culture and life (*seikatsu*). Miki appealed to an older Asian tradition that had always insisted upon the integration of culture into everyday life. "The philosophy of everyday culture," he wrote, "starts from the basic idea that culture and daily life are unified, that daily life is culture." If pursued from below culture is reached, but if one begins with culture one reaches daily life. What Miki hoped to unify was a conception of "cultural life" (*bunka seikatsu*) that had, until recently, characterized modern everydayness in the interwar period with one derived from the actual experience of the social lifeworld of the people, yoking essence to a form of existence, poetics, and history, without ever proposing a specific agenda. Yet we must read his proposal as a sign of the very fragmentation of everyday life and culture that the discourse on the social was seeking to resolve. Where he departed from so many of his contemporaries was in his belief that "living culture" (*seikatsu bunka*) was movement, making, transforming, not fixed, static, "things as they are," or simple negativity toward the given. In the end, this effort to negate or conceal the social divisions that instituted society in modern Japan, the immense task of repressing the vast unevenness that had gripped both political economy and culture, gave way to a frenzied attempt to "overcome the modern." If, as we shall see, the discourse on the social and the conference on overcoming sought to eternalize forces in a fixed "spirit," "essence," and "existence," it could only do so by dissolving the modern and appealing to myth and national poetics and aestheticism. But because modernity itself constituted a constant overcoming, Japanese found themselves facing the impossible task of temporally overcoming what was already an overcoming. This dilemma could only remind them of the inevitable succession of historical phenomena, the excess of historical consciousness, and a common destiny that they would always remain overcome by modernity.

CHAPTER 2

Overcoming Modernity

EVENT AND EVENTFULNESS

In July 1942 a prominent group of Japanese critics, thinkers, scholars, and writers met in the old imperial capital city of Kyoto during what was described as two very hot summer days to discuss the question of how to "overcome the modern" (*kindai no chōkoku*) and the meaning of the war for the nation. Six months into the war, Japan had virtually swept across Southeast Asia, where its troops were initially welcomed as deliverers of Asians from white man's colonialism, and had occupied most of the islands of the western Pacific. As a member of the Axis Powers, Japan was committed to a global conflict that had begun earlier in Europe, despite its own subsequent claims that it was only waging a war in East Asia or the Pacific. Because the war was global, its meaning for the country and its recent history of capitalist modernization could not be seen as merely a local experience but rather had to be considered within the broader context of a "world-historical" mission and destiny. The war, in other words, provided the occasion for evaluating the meaning of modernity, as such, and Japan's role in taking it to its next stage.

The symposium was sponsored by the Literary Society (Bungakkai), which subsequently published the proceedings, and its participants came from the major intellectual-cultural constituencies of the period, such as the Kyoto School of Philosophy, the Japan Romantic Group (Nihon Romanha), and members of the Literary Society.[1] The discussion was undoubtedly prompted by Japan's recent decision to wage war in Southeast Asia and on the Pacific islands, for the initial and probably unanticipated swiftness of military success realized by July 1942 persuaded even the most skeptical that the nation would play a leading role in shaping the new world order after the war. Yet this delusion was possible only by resorting to the paradox of accepting the global dimensions of the conflict—its "world-historical mission"—while misrecognizing the state's more limited aim of solidifying Japanese hegemony in East Asia and waging a war that the military saw as a regional intervention. The resulting blindness to this contradiction risked making all of the heady discussions about "world-historical meaning" into an elaborate alibi for Japanese imperialism. According to the preamble delivered by one of the conference's organizers, Kawakami Tetsutarō, the purpose of the symposium was not to reach a definitive solution of the problem of how to overcome the modern but to explore the meaning of Japan's war in light of its modernizing experience. "I do not know yet," he announced, "whether the conference will or will not be successful. Still, it should not be disputed that it was organized during the first year of the war. Certainly, our intellectuals have not yet individually accounted for the blood of the Japanese that has been the true, original moving spirit of our spiritual life until recently and its rivalry with Western intelligence which has been clumsily systematized in the present." A strange confusion and breakdown, he added, presided over the conference.[2] But the war he was referring to here had been continuously waged since the Meiji Restoration of 1868 and was an enormous struggle to become modern without forfeiting either the nation to Western imperialism or its spirit to slavish imitation. In fact, it was the same war that the writer Hayashi Fusao, one of the participants representing the Nihon Romanha, would later call the "one hundred year war in Asia." Another member of the Romantic faction, Kamei Katsui-chirō, saw the war as a profound spiritual crisis that finally would give Japan the opportunity to rid itself of the "sickness" of Westernization. "From the day we received the deathbed culture of the West," he wrote in one of the supplementary essays accompanying the symposium's transcript ("Gendai seishin ni kansuru oboegaki"), "it is the mode of civilization that has violated the deepest regions of the spirit. To me, daydreams and chatter, while becoming rapidly fashionable, are the greatest enemy. No matter how we talk about thought, it is permeated by this poison and I fear it is easy to become homogenized and mechanized. This is within us and is not a symptom we are aware of ourselves. Men become its joyful sacrifice." When compared to this "magical power," he continued, it is simply not enough to only grasp the thinking of the American and British enemy today (6). Kamei believed that it was a primary task of his generation to grasp the idea that people who fall under the impression that it is possible to wage "intellectual war" according to slogans, propaganda, and sermons are simply "puppets" (kairai). How modernity has weakened and distorted "our spirit" resembled the way disease attacks the body and lays it to waste. Kamei's appeal to the trope of disease inflicted by modern civilization necessitated a proper medical treatment which all of the participants of the symposium were pledged to finding in the course of discussion. "The war we wage today is externally an overthrow of Anglo-American power but internally it involves [finding] the fundamental medical treatment for . . . a spirit filled with modern civilization"(15).[3]

The Kyoto philosopher Nishitani Keiji proposed, in his supplementary essay " 'Kindai no chōkoku' shiron," that the "modern thing" was a "European thing," even though all the participants would recognize in

"Americanism" a baneful inflection of this Europeanization. What characterized this episode of massive cultural importation since the Meiji period, which he compared to Japan's earlier encounter with continental Chinese civilization, was the fact that the import meant accepting a culture driven by "progress" and the ceaseless differentiation and specialization within the spheres of knowledge. Even foreigners, who have produced the spectacle of a specialized knowledge, have forfeited understanding the connections between the different spheres (19). The immediate consequence of this "progressive specialization of knowledge" and the loss of connection was the elimination of cultural "wholeness" and its unifying principle.

Originating in Europe's early modern epoch, with the religious Reformation, Renaissance, and the growth of natural science, Nishitani saw in this historical conjuncture the "breakup of foundations" and the dissolution of the putative unity of Europe's world view. "Early modern humanity," he wrote, "was one that confronted a basic difficulty with respect to how it should grasp the self itself, according to having been situated within a course split between three world views"(20) The religious Reformation fixed on a deity as an absolute other with respect to the world and humanity contained a rejection toward both; humans could realize relief only through acts of submission and belief in God. But science, on the other hand, was empowered to grasp the natural world through mathematical and physical laws and thereby manifested an indifference or unconcern for the religious denial of humanity, owing to its disposition to comprehend humans similarly as all living things. The Renaissance, an opposing gesture, constituted a complete affirmation of humanity and thus promoted its cultivation (kyōyō) toward completion and perfection. Accordingly, the differentiation of spheres that corresponded to God, the world and the spirit resulted in further specialization into religion, science, culture, history, ethics, and so forth, which Nishitani described as a "descent" that could not be reversed (20).

The triangulation was intertwined with the problem of politics as well, a problem that invariably centered on the status of the individual and individualism. When the authority of individual existence in the world is promoted, individualism and cosmopolitanism become one and the same thing, producing a "completed nationalism" opposed to both a "completed cosmopolitanism or socialism" that can only result in a profound conflict among the individual, the state, and the world (23). At the time the Meiji Restoration enthusiastically imported this culture, it also took on board the "separation of knowledges" that risked dividing the unified world view in Japan and introducing unrelieved conflict once Japanese became concerned with the needs of the self. Nishitani proposed that the problem of a common modernity lay in the formation of a new awareness of the self and self-awareness of a new humanity that demanded "reconstituting the foundation of a world view." The solution was to return to "Oriental religious" practice, which, through its own conception of "freedom," was vastly different from the freedom of Western individualism, avoided the differentiation between culture and science, and supplied an awareness of a "subjective nothingness" capable of redirecting people back to a disposition where they would voluntarily "dissolve the self and serve the public" (*messhi hōkō*). The problem of overcoming the modern required getting around the modern ego and its pursuit of private interest in order to restore a prior religiosity that had been lost in the Japanese embrace of modern culture. Nishitani was convinced that this prior religiosity would reunite "daily life" with "actuality."[4] It is important to recognize that Nishitani described this religious view as "an actual Way" and thus called attention to the real over an apparent or putative reality currently dominating daily life. Throughout the 1930s, a variety of differing outlooks contested the meaning of what constituted the actual (*genjitsu*), usually in an effort to lay claim to defining daily life, and either located it outside of contemporary phenomenal life, as in the writings of Kuki Shūzō or Nishitani, or tried to reunite it with the lived reality of daily life, like Tosaka Jun and the aesthetician Nakai Masakazu. For Nishitani, the argument for an "actual Way" was based on the conviction that it was "energetically practiced in the coming and going of real daily life and in the work of a variety of occupations" (26). This particular observation revealed how discourse, in the interwar period, constantly tried to lay sole claim to defining the content of daily life and how, despite even the immense changes introduced by industrial capitalism, it became the site of competing strategies seeking to identify cultural purpose and meaning.

In this regard, the symposium on modernity constituted a culmination of and, perhaps, a closure to the interwar attempt to grasp daily life in its "actuality" rather than its mere virtuality. I shall have more to say of this contest over the meaning of everyday life, which, after all, was often the enabling condition for discourse in the interwar period. But it is sufficient here to say that the symposium put into question the status of daily life by rejecting the experience of modernity itself, as Kamei Katsuichirō frequently put it, because it had distorted the "spirit" of the people.

It was this effort to reject the modern and its spiritual distortions that prompted the call for an overcoming. The concept of overcoming obviously derived from European philosophic antecedents that went back to Hegel, who first posited the possibility of an overcoming that would lead to the end of history. But the idea was reworked by Nietzsche, who posed the problem of an excess or surplus of historical consciousness that already was stalking European life in the nineteenth century and thus marking the beginnings of humanity's late modernity.[5] What Nietzsche was referring to was the growing reliance on a historical culture that prevented European civilization from developing its own sense of style. This immersion in a historical culture that constantly called up the styles of the past as models for the present undermined both creativity and originality and prompted Nietzsche to call it a "historical sickness" that could only be corrected by appealing to "eternalizing forces."[6] According to Gianni Vattimo, Nietzsche never used the term for "overcoming" (*Verwindung*), even though he was convinced that cultural degeneration—slavish imitation—could be overcome through art and religion. Hence, modernity was seen as the moment of overcoming, the time that would, in effect, destroy timeliness, the regime of the ever new that immediately grows old to be replaced by a newer fashion. This seemingly interminable process, virtually unstoppable, undermined any chance for genuine creativity, which, for Nietzsche, constituted the only worthwhile form of life. The tyranny of time could only be ended by a radical eternalization, the timeless itself. In Japan, this sense of an overcoming was appropriated by the critic Takayama Chogyū, who, in his last major text, *Biteki no seikatsu ronzu* (On the aesthetic life, 1902), excoriated Japanese for producing an imitative culture, shallow, mediocre, uncreative for the life offered by the "overman" (*chōjin*) who was able to "overcome the present" (*gendai no chō-koku*). By the time the conception of overcoming began to circulate in the 1930s, it undoubtedly carried with it these Nietzschean meanings even as it was generalized to apply to Japan's contemporary circumstances. In the end, most people could agree that the call referred to overcoming Japan's dependence upon the modern West.

The Kyoto historian Suzuki Shigetaka, a participant who more or less represented the Kyoto School of Philosophy at the symposium, proposed that overcoming meant an "overcoming of democracy in politics," an "overcoming of capitalism in economics," and an "overcoming of liberalism in thought."[7] Suzuki reasoned that the idea of overcoming referred first or was equal to "overcoming the world domination of Europe." But neither was this its principal meaning nor did it resolve the crucial question of which modernity Japanese were obliged to overcome—the modernity of nineteenth-century Europe or indeed everything since the Renaissance. Germans like Hans Freyer and the French sociologist Emile Durkheim have situated the problem of the modern more within recent history, while the Russian philosopher Nicholas Berdeyev and the English historian Christopher Dawson pushed its boundaries back to the fifteenth century. If the development of the modern spirit since the Renaissance necessarily concludes in the nineteenth century, the views of these latter writers, he believed, must have sufficient foundation. Suzuki obviously agreed with Dawson and Berdeyev and the long duration of modernity, even though he acknowledged that this larger view sanctioned the construction of a topography that not all of the participants were prepared to accept.[8] Suzuki was convinced that grasping the original meaning of the modern was necessary for "clarifying its European meaning"; then it was equally important to understand what this problem meant for the Japanese, and whether the modern that should be overthrown required investigating the nineteenth century or the Renaissance. But because overcoming the modern is related to the problem of "humanity," it is important to consider the future of Christianity. Since the appearance of machine civilization and a new image of humanity is related to the emergence and development of science, it was therefore necessary to problematize the relationship between the position and limits of scientific studies in reaching a solution to the crisis of civilization. By the same measure, historical studies sees the overcoming of the "idea of progress as a deep problem of all relationships and thus fixes the overcoming of historicism . . . as a primary necessity. Hence the overcoming of historicism is the overcoming of modern historiography."[9] This "cognitive mapping," as Fredric Jameson has called it, this effort to negotiate the uniquely local experience of Japan's modernity within a contemporary global process, nevertheless set down the boundaries within which discourse would take place. Even if all of the participants did not always agree with each other—and it must be remembered that the symposium was composed of three major intellectual constituents—we can see how all connected with the central themes figured by Suzuki's topography.

The importance of Suzuki's mapping is that it revealed what was the characteristic modernist dimension of the *kindai no chōkoku* symposium and its kinship with subsequent modernist discussions in the interwar period. This was especially evident in the attack on history and historicism as a code for capitalist modernization whose itinerary, its "progress," even its *Ratio*, as Sigfried Kracauer has called it, was devoted to narrating a particular story line. One of the enduring marks of modernist discourse in Japan and elsewhere was its rejection of the market, commodity relationships, and a system of historical representation that testified to the inexorable laws of capitalist motion and the progress of its development. More will be said of this later, but it is important to suggest here that for people like Suzuki, "modern" meant the period of capitalism that had been inaugurated in the Meiji period. When he and others called for an overcoming, they invariably identified those aspects of capitalism that had already been firmly established in Japanese society—the primacy of private property, liberalism, the idea of democracy (not the fact as such, since nobody then or now could seriously think Japan was democratic, but only the ubiquity of a fearful image that was greater than the reality), the singular importance of exchange value, production for mass consumption, and the commodification of social relationships. But while history and historicism were the signs under which a critique of capitalism was undertaken, it was not so much the social order that was being put into question but rather the consequences for settled social relationships and cultural production of a particular economic system. Just as social relationships no longer cohered to a fixed order of the world, so representations of the social totality were always in danger of being undermined by a system of development driven by ceaseless change. In fact, it was value itself that was put into crisis, and, with it, the problematizing of representation under capitalism, which many saw in the appearance of social abstraction and commodification and the elimination of concreteness and referentiality. Social thinkers like Tosaka Jun and Shimmi Masamichi had already seen in the early 1930s how fascism had sought to distance its claims from capitalism in the apparent interest of mounting a critique against it by appealing to an "unhistorical history" and the eternality of the folk. But this move never entailed rejecting the structure of capitalism as such and its foundational commitment to private property. Rather, fascism sought to eliminate its social consequences like class conflict and the clamor for greater political representation from new industrial classes by altering the nature of representation itself and mapping both the market and the principle of private ownership onto communitarian and corporate representations. While the symposium on modernity never went so far, it is still possible to discern in the discussions a dangerous kinship with fascism in its desire to bracket history and hence the development that had propelled the country to its present in order to represent Japan as fixed and eternal. In all of those discussions about an ineluctable "spirit," the symposium shared with the prevailing discourse on cultural authenticity the fantasy that neither history nor techno-economic development had managed to change what was essentially and eternally Japanese. What representation promised to accomplish was, in fact, a reinforcement of capitalist productive modes by ridding them of political excesses demanding democratization.

Suzuki's mapping gave precise definition to the historical epoch of capitalism that critique was supposed to overcome through an act of dehistoricization. Once history was cleared away, it would be possible to envisage a stage or time that was exclusively Japanese, which meant installing an order that was both capitalist and Japanese yet no longer subject to the laws of historical motion that had brought capitalist modernity to its current state in Japan. Notwithstanding Takeuchi Yoshimi's desire to show that the symposium never managed to construct an ideology of fascism or war, it nevertheless was implicated in configuring interwar fascism. It was nurtured in the hothouse environment of the 1930s and represented an effort to bring a moratorium to the "crisis" of the decade, what the philosopher Miki Kiyoshi theorized as the "current situation" (*jimu*) that was manifest progressively in a series of domestic and foreign episodes which ultimately transformed Japanese society into a mobilized war machine by the end of the decade.[10] Kamei Katsuichirō, following the lead set by Suzuki Shigetaka, put it most bluntly when he wrote that after

> listening to the various explanations concerning the meaning of the modern, I feel that it is nothing other than the conflict we have been experiencing during the last decade or so. . . . In a word the Japanese who have lived through the 1920s and 1930s . . . have lived in a time without belief. Since the Meiji period there has always been a diversity of responses to the question that asks what kind of prospects have been produced by this disorder and misery. Whether it is the influence of foreign thought or the diffusion of science, for me it is only the intention that pursues the inexpressible truth in the words *Kami* and Buddha. However vague my hope, if there is strength to ride over the modern it is in this belief in the gods. Indeed, the resurrection of the gods is, I believe, the central problem of contemporary thought.[11]

A political dead end that sought resolution in a series of domestic and foreign adventures leading to total mobilization and war was matched by a spiritual confusion that looked to the return of the gods and, indeed, the return of an original possibility that, paradoxically, would inaugurate a new start. But it was spiritual confusion that led to the "disorder" and "misery" of modernization, not the other way around.

The "current situation" that prompted the description of crisis in Japan stemmed, as Suzuki proclaimed, from a global destiny. "The problem of today," he insisted, "is far more important than the rise and fall of a few states. If we fail to reach an understanding of what kind of fundamental things contemporary changes are pointing to, we will never settle the posture toward our period."[12] What he could only have had in mind was a broader assessment that went beyond the immediacy of events such as the Pacific War in order to grasp the larger movement of culture. It was not simply Japan's local experience of modernity that needed to be understood, but rather the larger cultural configurations whose effects were being recorded locally in Japan. Miki Kiyoshi, who did not attend the symposium but who clearly was associated with Kyoto philosophy, had, a few years earlier (1939) proposed in a position paper prepared for the Konoe brain trust—Shōwa Kenkyūkai—that it was vitally important to grasp the "development of the 'China Incident' " and the relationship between the problem of domestic reform and the "incident" from the perspective of thought and culture. As for new philosophic principles," he urged, "they must overcome (*chōkoku*) the modernism which is the distinct sign of ruin from a still higher perspective."[13] Miki looked to what he named "cooperativism" (*kyōdōshugi*), which closely resembled the communitarianism inspired by contemporary native ethnologists and social thinkers, as one of those new philosophic principles that must "systematically surpass" the variety of established modernisms, as he took it upon himself to outline this new solution. By discerning the reason of history inhering in the event called the China Incident, he demonstrated how the temporal solution of the problem of capitalism—"the most important result for all the countries of the world"—was linked to securing the spatial "unification of East Asia." The China Incident as an event "revealed" the meaning of what to many was simply an arbitrary act of military adventurism and imperial expansion. Yet if the episode was seen from the larger perspective Miki designated, its real meaning would disclose how Japan was in a position to assist the "modernization of China" that was a necessary condition for revealing the "world historical meaning" of the event leading to the seizure. This world historical meaning was the unification of Asia. The move into North China was simply the beginning of the establishment of a new cultural, read as economic, bloc that would soon become part of a new, global division of nation states (here, Miki's prescience remains uncontested) that was already occurring in the 1930s and thus represented a ratification of the current situation. Under the authority of history's reason, the task for Japan was to imagine its destiny in the formation of an "East Asian Cooperative Union that would include Japan, Manchuria and China," "founded on Oriental humanism" and synthesizing "gemeinschaft and gesellschaft" as the only way to "overcome" the aporias of "subjectivism" (*shukanshugi*) and "objectivism."[14] Ever faithful to the problematic of Kyoto philosophy, Miki was convinced that Japan was on its way to "overcoming" the curse of Western philosophy and its unbending and baneful devotion to maintaining the subject/object dualism and its consequences for knowledge and power.

If, as Miki argued, great events are always occurring but "transcending" their local character by demanding an interrogation of "whatever reason of history that is already embedded in them," then the event of the war with the United States provided the occasion for both the convening of the *kindai no chōkoku* symposium and a sanction for fully appraising the cultural meaning many believed inherent in the struggle with the United States. While the war with the United States was caused by a clash of political and economic interests in the Pacific, the war revealed a surplus of cultural meaning that was not always readily apparent in the immediate reasons prompting the coming of hostilities. To be sure, many thoughtful Japanese, even among the participants in the symposium, were already disposed to seeing the war as a sign filled with "world historical meaning," as proposed by Nishida Kitarō's students Kōsaka Masaaki, Kōyama Iwao, Nishitani Keiji, and Miki Kiyoshi (though he remained peripheral to the discourse of the Kyoto school). This group organized its own symposium early in the war (July 1942) called "The World Historical Position and Japan" (*Sekaishiteki tachiba to Nihon*), which was devoted to discussing the world historical meaning of the war and Japan's unique role in it. Where this discussion departed from the symposium on modernity was in the decision to concentrate on the centrality of the state and its destiny as the singular subject of history. "The state," Kōyama wrote (1943), "overcomes national boundaries as we have understood them and progresses to a stage of conditions where it pursues [its] destiny."[15] What he meant was that the state was reaching a new level of development—a "unique worldly" configuration called "co-prosperity spheres" (*kyōeiken*) or "wider regional spheres" (*kōikiken*), whose "meaning and structure" differed from empire and "leagues of states" but rather revealed an entirely new arrangement produced from a variety of states that "pursued intimate political unity based on geographical, historical, and economic solidarity and human, ethnic, and cultural kinship."[16] These new worldly configurations would seek "new moral principles different from those that had governed Europe." The discourse on "The World Historical Position and Japan" departed from the earlier symposium (only Suzuki and Nishitani attended both) in its inordinate effort to explain the decision for war within the broader context of the movement of world history, and to analyze what this meant for the Japanese state in a future world order once the Anglo-American alliance was destroyed. Too easily and too readily this symposium and the supporting texts of Kōsaka and Kōyama (and even the elliptical religio-philosophic outpourings of Nishitani) supplied ideological rationalization for the Axis war effort, the Pacific War, and Japan's representation of its colonial aspirations in Asia as a new and advanced stage in the development of world history. Kōyama, perhaps the leading ideologue of this inflection of Kyoto philosophy, even proposed that the establishment of a new configuration of capitalist spheres constituted a higher level of rationality. In this regard, it was less a discussion of overcoming, even though it called for an "overcoming of national boundaries," than an elaborate justification of the war in Hegelian philosophic language.

But the critic Odagiri Hideo later proposed that the symposium on modernity was an "intellectual war" that was functionally analogous to the "total war" being waged by the military. By implying ideological complicity with the war aims of the state, he was classifying it with the content of the more strident symposium on world history and saying that its participants were willingly involved in the formation of an ideology of "total war." We know that Takeuchi Yoshimi, after the war, discounted the ideological utility of the symposium, described its content as nearly "empty" of substance, and condemned it for linking its critique of modern culture (which he applauded) with the war in Asia (which he deplored). Yet both symposia were apparently targeted for surveillance and even censure by the military, which they frequently failed to evade. Whatever its uncertain status at the time and even later in the meditations of Japanese intellectuals, the symposium on modernity intimated a complicity with fascism that ultimately marked the historical conjuncture of the 1930s in Japan and elsewhere.

If the symposium on modernity was less devoted to directly supplying a cultural scenario for "total intellectual warfare" (as the Conference on the Meaning of World History was promising) and remained silent on the role of the Japanese state in bringing about war—the subject with a capital S (as Louis Althusser identified the modern state)—it nevertheless managed to provide powerful if inadvertent ideological support for the idea of *kokutai* as it was being articulated by the military and the Ministry of Education in the late 1930s. The "amuletic" signifier *kokutai* was understood to mean a conception of an essentialized and exceptionalistic culture capable of resisting historical change.[17] Above all else, the event of war was seen as merely the moment to assess the broader cultural consequences of Japan's modern experience which many believed had brought the nation to this fateful point in its history since the Meiji Restoration. But we have seen that writers like Nishitani and Kamei dated the origins of Japan's modernity to the 1920s, after World War I, and the shocking experience of massive industrialization and the material transformation of Japanese life induced by broad-scale cultural importation. As Kawakami Tetsutarō reminded the symposium, the war served to reaffirm for Japanese a long-standing conflict between the "blood of the Japanese" and "Western intelligence," between the dislocations accompanying the installation of a modern order and the rapid destruction of experience and memory, between a world the folk had made over the long duration of history and the implantation of one that was made for them in the brief history of the present. The event of the war would not have been possible had there not been this prior history of modernity in which the very capacity to experience the shock of transformation had already been put into question and was being discussed by thoughtful people. Hence, the convening of the symposium on modernity, perhaps unprecedented among modernizing societies (even though Germans have, from time to time, discussed their unique route to modernization, the *sonderweg*) became an event that *em*bodied the idea of modernity and the search for its meaning, which an entire generation of writers, thinkers, scholars, and artists had already conceptualized, discussed, and worried about.

What is so important about the symposium is that it strove to distance itself from the event of war in order to better understand the very eventfulness that had transformed Japanese society so completely in the interwar period. In so doing, the symposium risked becoming yet another event in the modernizing process—the very history of modernity—whose meaning, its "historical reason," it was now trying to grasp and evaluate. While the symposium sought exemption from the eventfulness constituting modernity, and which undoubtedly led to war, it now yearned to understand the proliferation of events as the condition for overcoming modernity's excesses; its status as an event only guaranteed that it would remain merely another episode in the process of modernity, inside it rather than occupying a critical space outside of it. For this reason the symposium was part of the very modernist gesture that had already framed a critique of modernity and thus supplied an ideology for its persistence capable of resisting a final overcoming. Modernity was already an overcoming, as I suggested earlier, and any attempt to imagine an overcoming of an overcoming could lead only to a reaffirmation of the very processes of modernity that induced people to think about eventfulness and change. This unintended irony was never recognized by those Japanese who eagerly dreamed of overcoming modernity. In this regard, it was precisely the modernist dismissal of an antecedent history that supplied the capitalist sociopolitical order in Japan, and wherever else capitalist modernization had taken hold, with the image (representation) of an eternality that could never be overcome. For to be overcome would have required acknowledging the passage of historical time from one stage to another, as yet unenvisaged, moment. But accepting this conception of changing temporality would surely have entailed recognizing that capitalism itself must one day be overcome and replaced by a new social and economic order.

As a result, the substance of the symposium's discussions recuperated all of the major ideologemes produced by the prior discourses on modernity during the previous two decades and reaffirmed the autonomy of "spirit"—culture—which was another meaning for Nishitani's (Nishida's) conception of a nonmaterial "subjective no-thing" (*shutaiteki mu*), permanent and always present in the national life of the folk. The "affirmative" role played by culture, its offer of an independent space for critique (another principal modernist gesture), was seen by modernists as the best defense against capitalist commodification, alienation, social abstraction, and the mechanization of daily life. Mindful of the vast contradictions introduced by modernization, signified by the struggle between preserving the memory *of*, rather than from, the interwar discourse on modernity looked to the cultural endowment for the inexhaustible source of authentic difference as a defense against the homogenizing world of capitalist abstraction. In this search, writers and thinkers focused on resuscitating an auratic authority in "nuances" and "shadings," as Kamei Katsuichirō explained to the symposium and Tanizaki Junichirō expressed a decade earlier in his melancholic lamentation for vanished cultural masteries entitled *In'ei raisan* (Praising shadows).

What the event of the symposium disclosed was that the assessment of modernity preceding it often slipped into an adversarial assault against the West, especially the United States—pejoratively known as "Americanism" (in the late 1920s and the time of the conference)—that led to waging intellectual war with history in order to resist being assimilated by it. Specifically, this struggle against history meant fending off the progressive segmentation of time and the swift succession of events that constantly threatened to undermine any chance for stabilizing daily life. But the struggle also sought to stem the confusion caused by the splitting that resulted from mapping the historical experience of the West onto Japan. (One of the crueler ironies of this historical episode is that the West—the United States—virtually demanded the Japanese to abandon their own modern history—the experience of capitalist modernity—when it made the return of its colonial possessions in China a condition for preserving the peace in the Pacific. In short, Japan was being asked to cease behaving like the colonial and imperial West, which had been its model for modernity!) Yet the symposium, even though clearly an event, was supposed to announce an end to the eventfulness that was so much a part of the narrative of capitalist modernization. Despite its intense concern for the status of history, it managed only to mount a displaced critique of the imperial claims of its grand narrative, setting its sights only on the level of representation and not on the political economic system that authorized it or the contradictions it produced. Regardless of the symposium's own modernist dissatisfaction with capitalism and its disavowal of "Americanism" as the sign of mass production and cultural dilution, it never got around to directly constructing a critique of capitalism as a political and economic system. The symposium targeted history simply as representation of Western experience that had no referential role in explaining Japan's modernization. In making this move, it echoed earlier complaints against the hegemony of historical consciousness by either disavowing it altogether or trying to envision a new and more authentic mode of historical existence outside of the progressive story line that announced only the regime of sameness and homogeneity under the "universalistic" claims of reason. As an event, then, the symposium joined the vast assembly of eventfulness filling the space of interwar Japan and prompting its most sensitive observers to call for a pause in the unending and dizzying chain of change to grasp "whatever reason of history" was embedded in the succession of events. Rather than seizing hold of the opportunity for reflection provided by a pause in history, the symposium simply recuperated the genealogy of Japan's modern experience and rehearsed all of its aporias and contradictions, displaying one more time what Takeuchi called Japan's "Gordian Knot," as if the act of enunciating them again would finally expunge them from the national memory or, at the very least, offer the promise of expiation for having lived through them.

But the symposium also opened up to the very context of industrial modernization that subsequent discussions on culture and community—what I have called the discourse on the social—had tried desperately to conceal by enforcing the image of timeless and eternal structures and subjectivities. While the thinkers who mounted this discourse on the social aimed to imagine a timeless "experience" or "existence" produced by an act of "involuntary memory," fearing that experience itself could not survive, other thinkers whom the symposium dismissed or ignored saw in the moment of modernity an unevenness that only the future could bring to completion, not by an act of overcoming but through the process of being overcome even more thoroughly by the modern, by living it to completion. But this very unevenness, perceived and unperceived, as we shall see, imprinted its historical watermark in the appeal both to an image of a timeless and eternal moment or place in the past and to the promise of one that was yet to come.

AMERICANISM

It is one of the paradoxes that those scholars who have written so forcefully on the symposium, like Takeuchi Yoshimi and Hiromatsu Wataru, have generally dismissed the content of the discussions as trite and empty and have chosen to concentrate on the major intellectual affiliations represented by the participants. Instead of confronting the content of discussions, these and other writers have frequently appealed to its immediate intellectual context and thereby reduced the symposium to previously prepared positions that had already been articulated in prior discourses. Lost in a thick description of background context characterizing contemporary ideological formations, the event disappears as nothing more momentous than a passing blip on the screen of the "current situation."

But the symposium stood as a sign of the very overdetermination of cultural critique and discourse that these three formations (Kyoto philosophy, the Japan Romantic School, and the Literary Society) represented as merely the most recent manifestation of what had been a ubiquitous and continuous activity since the end of World War I. Far from being the empty vessel marking the place of already fixed positions of Kyoto philosophy, the Japan Romantic School, and the Literary Society, the symposium was a profoundly meaningful, meaning driven, if not ambivalent, condensation of all those fears, anxieties, and doubts thoughtful Japanese had expressed over the spectacle of a process of capitalist modernization that was threatening to disrupt and transform their life materially beyond all recognition and eliminate the capacity for recalling an enduring experience. If the symposium tried to call a moratorium on eventfulness, as I have suggested, and halt ceaseless historical change, it also reflected, especially in the ideal of overcoming so current throughout the 1930s, an overwhelming desire to bring an end to a reliance on Western industrial life, with its laws of endless specialization and division, as the preparatory move to envisaging a time for restoring cultural wholeness. Ridding Japanese society of fragmentation and alienation, not to forget the loss of fixed meaning resulting from unrelieved reification (capitalist social abstraction), would, it was believed, secure an identity sufficiently different from the modern West capable of rescuing the race from the homogenization promised by cultural colonization. In the words of the critic Tsumura Hideo, one of the most vocal participants in the symposium, this process of dissociation would lead to new cultures constructed on the site of "new life spheres in both Europe and Asia" (118–119). A modernity that insisted on imitating the West risked causing a "contagion," a "historical sickness," and produced only a surplus of history, an "excess of historical consciousness" according to the literary critic Kobayashi Hideo, which inevitably stifled intellectual creativity and cultural originality.

Echoing a Nietzschean postmortem on bourgeois culture in nineteenth-century Europe, Japan would thus be forced to enlist its own modern culture from the "vast storehouse of theatrical masks and costumes" that "Europe's past has become for it."[18] It is instructive to note that the symposium managed to recuperate the same contradiction between repudiating modernity yet frequently approving of European culture that had stalked discourses dating from the late Meiji period. But this move was made possible by arguing that American civilization—Americanism as it was called in both Taishō Japan and Weimar Germany—constituted a second term that signified a negative reflection that aimed to replace quality with quantity, value with desire and interest. As Japanese conceptualized Americanism from the late 1920s on, it was increasingly seen as a distorted inflection of European civilization, which it now threatened to overtake everywhere that mass production and consumption had managed to establish a cultural beachhead. What the symposium called for was the discovery of a method that might successfully eternalize the forces within culture—what the poet Miyoshi Tatsuji explained as "rediscovering the Japanese spirit" (137) and finally bring to an end the destructive surplus of historical consciousness that swept away all fixities and durations before it to prevent the "continuity of anything." If such a program were not enacted, art and imagination would perish. This concern for the specter of historical surplus and the need to find its corrective by returning to the ground of cultural authenticity was, in fact, the way discourse prior to the symposium had already recoded the historical prob-

lem of the interwar years and the relentless production of everydayness
made possible by the transformation of the Japanese political economy
from the time of World War I.

The perception of everydayness produced in the 1920s and 1930s (conceived first and perhaps most enduringly as a figure of discourse) had
increasingly been linked to the installation of mass culture (especially consumption) in Japan and elsewhere after World War I, with the momentary
disaccumulation of capital that came with peace and the desire to capture
new markets by producing consumer goods. This interlude was gradually
called Americanism or Americanization and usually signified progressive
mass consumption driven by desire rather than value. It is important to
note that the question of value was already being intensely engaged by
neo-Kantian philosophers who were celebrating the primacy of what they
called "culturalism" (*bunkashugi*), which was glossed from the German
geisteswissenschaft and represented the equivalent realm of human value
to the claims of objective truth promised by natural science. I shall have
more to say about how contemporaries in the 1920s figured this new
cultural configuration as Americanism, not because it was necessarily
being lived evenly by the masses who were flocking to the cities to be both
producers and consumers of new commodities, but because it constituted
the overdetermined image and promise of a genuinely different kind of
culture available and accessible to the new social constituencies that accompanied capitalist modernization in Japan.

By the time the symposium met and took stock of the preceding two
decades, the everydayness of the masses and their culture of consumption
were bonded to the idea of Americanism, which represented, for the participants, the condensed sign under which Japanese culture was now collapsing into valueless mediocrity, shallowness, and triviality. All the ills
that had poisoned Japan were found in Americanism, which, for most,
was the model of modernity that had to be overcome. Americanism referred to the importation and adoption of commodity culture that came
with consumption immediately after the war: radios, automobiles, telephones; Western clothing, housing, and foods; new and more accessible
forms of pleasure and entertainment, cafes, bars, department stores, movies, etc. Seen as a distinct and lively material culture appealing to the
desire of the masses for endless consumption of commodities, the trope
of Americanism soon took on the association of a negative image that
could, as we shall see, easily mobilize the effort to imagine its positive
other that represented value, quality—all that was genuinely good, beautiful, and true (values that had already been embraced like a shield of armor
by Japanese middle-class intellectuals in the 1920s). The threat of merging
producers with consumers reinforced a division of culture into high and
low, the former devoted to enduring value and the latter mired in the

desire for commodities. This division matched a more consequential one that increasingly associated democratization with mass political participation, what in Europe was already being proclaimed by writers as diverse as Ortega y Gasset and Karl Jaspers as the danger of mass politics that increasingly appeared to challenge established political arrangements that promised to preserve the control of an elite, whether it was an older aristocratic class, or the upper bourgeoisie, or the progressively fashionable "scientific" managers and planners—faceless bureaucrats—pledged to linking the interest of the state to rationality.

For the symposium on modernity, Americanism was simply a more recent manifestation and reminder of Meiji *bunmei kaika*—the period of "civilization and enlightenment" of the 1870s and 1880s when Japan embarked upon importing the material and technological trappings of modern life. Since that time, the image of Meiji had become a trope for superficiality that continually prompted critics to reduce its achievements to mere technology. "The crime inflicted on our country by Western civilization," Nakamura Mitsuo wrote in a supplementary article before the symposium (" 'Kindai' e no giwaku"), "is the problem that needs to be most discussed." "Western worship" resulted not simply in changing "our lives" unalterably, according to the importation of a foreign civilization, but also in sustaining changes in spiritual life (152–153). For that reason alone, he argued, it could not be easily dismissed or rejected, as if it were last year's fashion. Not simply the acquisition of things but customs that have been fully integrated into daily life disclosed the nature of the changes that had been introduced. Nakamura pointed out that an example of how Western custom had become second nature in Japan was the practice of "sea bathing" that had become "widespread in recent years" (153). The same could be said of the use of telephones, cars, and radio. In fact, people rarely thought that imported things were from the West, owing to a process of appropriation that had successfully assimilated the new and novel into Japanese life. In politics, economy, and even the realm of culture, he added, it could be easily said that the life of contemporary Japanese had not yet eliminated "traces" from the pre-Meiji era, but the revolution of life-style that has taken place since the opening of the country (1854) had occurred in the relatively short span of eighty years and was a characteristic of "our so-called modernity." Yet in that passage of time Japan had experienced an unprecedentedly "confusing and violent" transformation as in no other period in the nation's history or anywhere else in the world.

Nakamura was right on both counts, and it is easy to forget today that Japan's modernization was a singularly unique long march accomplished in a relatively short span of time that was both violently jarring to settled customs and probably without historical parallel. Worried that the rapidity of the process had projected another meaning of the modern that had yet to be theorized and analyzed, Nakamura was anxious too that Japanese, who had absorbed modernity, often failed to understand fully or even adequately the very elements that constituted the "spirit of European man." "Why is it so difficult," he asked, "to make these elements into a common sense?" (156). The form the importation of Western culture took was determined by necessity, provoked by the imminent threat of colonization. Hence necessity, not always the best reason to adopt foreign social and cultural forms, dictated both the speed at which Japanese transformed their society and the adoptions that would best guarantee Japan's continued independence—military technologies and the infrastructure of the modern state. Nakamura's observations revealed both that unevenness existed between the West and Japan that was not understood by the West and that the speed of modernization had in fact affected the substance of spiritual life.

One of the interesting ironies of Japan's modernization hinted at by Nakamura was that the speed of the process resulted in constructing a society based on speed and sensation. "Western civilization for contemporaries [of the early Meiji period] meant realizing a society committed to using machines" (157), which refracted the nineteenth-century European preference for science, technology, and utility. Westerners viewed this development in Japan as superficial, even though it betrayed a misrecognition of the degree to which Meiji society not simply had understood the "external forms" but was devoted to absorbing the "spirit of the West" as well. But because Japanese imported Western culture without having the leisure of controlling reception, the spirit was formed in a period of "unwholesome digestion." Anxious that a "deformed spirit had been fomented within the unconscious according to the oppression of foreign culture," Nakamura was convinced that Japan, under the circumstances, would never possess deep enough roots to heal itself, fearing that in the end the nation would forfeit the practice of diligently considering things in and of themselves to simply and expediently adopt what was at hand in response to the "superficial movement of the times" (163). The cultural disorder that had marked Japan since the Meiji era lay in the production of an unequal power relationship between Japan and the West and insufficient Western understanding shaped by this unevenness that now urgently required "redressing" (164).

Others, like the former Marxist turned enthusiastic convert to the Japan Romantic School Hayashi Fusao, supported Nakamura's conviction that Western civilization had been forcibly imposed upon Japan out of the necessity of maintaining autonomy in a hostile social Darwinist world where colonial supremacy served as the emblem of successful survival. But he refused to recognize that its implantation resulted in anything more than a "submission to Europe." In his opening remarks to a session on "The Substance of Meiji Civilization and Enlightenment," Hayashi explained to the symposium that only Japan had resisted the Western threat by borrowing crucial elements from its scientific and technological arsenal. But "civilization and enlightenment," he added, "adopted only useful things the culture had to offer, not its foundational principles" (239). Even as Meiji civilization was being installed, a number of voices surfaced to protest the utility of such sweeping importation of cultural artifacts and call for a return to foundations as a corrective. Prefiguring a view he was to articulate after World War II, Hayashi proclaimed that the East Asian war would, with great difficulty, bring an end to the domination of "civilization" and "enlightenment." Yet the real problem that faced the nation was the enemy within, as well as without, lined up to subvert the country domestically just as surely as imperial powers lay ready to strike at Japan. Even though he was convinced that thinkers in the Meiji era were neither as "susceptible" nor "faithful" to Western thought as those living in the present (241), earlier pioneers of the Japanese spirit such as Saigō Takamori, Okakura Tenshin, and Uchimura Kanzō had already encountered forceful "enlighteners" in their own struggle to prevent Japan from succumbing totally to the seductions of Westernization. If utility drove Meiji Japan obsessively to embrace civilization and enlightenment, the problem was why so many Japanese were attracted to their allure. It was not merely the impulse to defend the nation that enlisted such enthusiastic converts but rather something else that must have magnetized Meiji Japanese to their power.

Nishitani Keiji wondered why influential and profound systems of thought such as Buddhism and Confucianism were so readily abandoned for the superficialities of Spencer's theory of social evolution, reminding his generation of what in the present were still audible echoes of late Meiji Japanese, like Tokutomi Sohō's celebration of social Darwinism as the principle capable of explaining why some societies progress and others remain stationary, or even Lafcadio Hearn's effusive praise (in Kokoro) of Spencer as a genius. The answer was given by Suzuki Shigetaka, who proposed that while the implantation of civilization was necessary in the Meiji period, Japan's experience represented simply a local inflection of what he saw as a dominant world view that could be found everywhere in nineteenth-century Europe, Russia, and the United States. If adoption of civilization inspired critique and even the desire to return to foundations, Japan was still part of a larger world system and thereby connected to a critique of civilization already begun in Europe. In other words, the critique of Meiji enlightenment should be understood not as a local response but rather as part of a larger assault on European bourgeois civilization. Acknowledging the baleful influences in Japanese life introduced by Meiji civilization, Nishitani nevertheless saw it as a moment, experienced by other nations as well, that changed the course of Japanese society from feudalism and its rigid status system (*mibun no sabetsu*), bent on classifying samurai and commoners (peasants) hierarchically, to a liberal order with its equalization of classes. It is interesting to note the irony, not recognized by Nishitani, of using European historical and chronological categories to show how the Meiji Restoration represented a transition from feudalism to a liberal bourgeois society, and thus the degree to which such categories had become commonsense or second nature to Japanese, who never questioned the aporia of their representational status, even though the symposium and others had long problematized the question of representation. This transformation constituted a fundamental condition for establishing a unified Japan (when before there was only the loosest confederation of domains) in the form of a national state centered on the imperial court. But what Nishitani saw as a necessary condition of modernization, Hayashi pictured as "decline" (*daraku*); while Nishitani proposed that enlightenment was linked to the establishment of popular rights (*jiyū minken*), Hayashi rejected the equation altogether and reminded the symposium that unification was the product of "bureaucratic policy," "national policy." "As for the popular rights movement," he proposed, correcting Nishitani, "it was opposed to the enlightenment of government dominated by a clan clique" (242).

This dramatic interchange offered a rare glimpse of genuine conflict, which must have been for the most part edited out of the original transcripts when they were being prepared for publication. We can only guess at which moments signaled disagreement and conflict; that the editors wanted to present a smooth and untroubled narrative of assent and agreement is not surprising and needs no explanation. The following interchange demonstrates both the nature of disagreement over the meaning of Meiji, which I think was polarized in this instance, and how the symposium assimilated discord to achieve the effect of an untroubled narrative that aimed to show that despite Japan's incorporation of Western civilization, some basic spirit remained solidly in tact and unaffected to assure an identity of difference:

> *Nishitani:* Well, civilization and enlightenment and the popular rights movement were connected to the enlightenmentism of the Western eighteenth century. Can't we say that this philosophy entered Japan?
> *Hayashi:* Not so. The subjectivity of scientists who try, unreasonably, to make connections produces all kinds of unfortunate conclusions.
> *Nishitani:* . . . If it is said that individualism today is a bad thing, can't we also say that at the point it abolished the closed class discrimination of the feudal period it performed an unusually great, meritorious service?

Hayashi: Shimazaki Tōson went to France and was surprised [to see] that the class system was majestically still present. I went to Peking and surprisingly the class system still prevails in all its grandeur. But in Japan it has not survived. The liberal movement never destroyed the class system in Japan. It was the Meiji Renovation (*ishin*). What was the Meiji Renovation? It was a Restoration (*fukko*). The model loyal activists (*shishi*) had in mind was not France or the United States. The original form the *shishi* held in their head was Japan's antiquity. It was a classless time, when people directly served the emperor. Will awareness of the Western-style system of individualism exist in the history of Japan? (242–243)

Meiji was expediency, utility, technology, and materiality, even though it had been driven by a spirit unique to Japan alone; it was merely civilization—external and superficial—not yet culture, which in the early twentieth century was seen increasingly by middle-class intellectuals and writers as "spirit." This emphasis on spirit privileged both subject and the goal of self-formation (*kyōyō*) through the practice of a humanistic discipline and the cultivation of absolute value—precisely the kind of program Nishitani would propose for the achievement of "subjective nothingness" (18–37). Like other bourgeois intellectuals in the Taishō period, philosopher Abe Jirō, in his celebrated and widely circulated text *Santarō no nikki*, presented a *bildungs* hero of his own life—Santarō—and his endless meditations and soliloquies on the status of his self. Such texts invariably distinguished the search for self-refinement and completion as a spiritual quest from the more mundane, material utilitarian, and ultimately superficial preoccupation of the Meiji enlightenment. The distinction made was usually between a civilization of the surface and a culture of depth (already articulated by the writer Natsume Sōseki in his critique of enlightenment before World War I)—what Hayashi, in his essay "Kinnō no kokoro"—perhaps the most determinate critique of Meiji enlightenment at the symposium—described as the "loss of the gods" caused by a literature (naturalism and realism) that forced the young to "forget the emperor" and "forget the country" (104).

By the time of the symposium America had become the negative model of a superficial and material civilization in the continuing struggle inaugurated in the Meiji period for the liberation of the spirit, an even more powerful successor to Meiji civilization that unleashed the full, terrifying potential for disorder and mediocrity inherent in individualism and democratization. Above all else, Americanism destroyed memory and encouraged social forgetfulness. For Japanese and so much of the industrial world, Americanization signified the emergence of the masses in both culture and politics and invariably produced a reflexive revulsion and fear of the new social constituency of the masses—political and cultural democratization. What paralyzed the older ruling classes, as well as the more recently arrived bourgeoisie in the developing industrial states, was the prospect of greater accessibility for wider consumption of new mass-produced products and new forms of popular entertainment that threatened the sovereignty of spirit—a putative traditional culture now transmuted into the image of high culture. It was, in any case, the continued persistence of depth and durability against the devastating challenge of newness, superficiality, and the shock of rapid change—the principle of capitalist laws of development—that became the work of cultural discourse before the war and constituted the polar models the symposium was determined to reconcile by overcoming the latter and liberating the former. But the task was clearly impossible since the symposium, quite early, had trouble deciding which modernity needed to be overcome: nineteenth-century Europe or the Renaissance. America and Americanization seemed to offer an illusory way out of the dilemma by supplying an image of negativity, a distorted reflection of European culture that was not only quite bereft of either value or enduring standards but now posed a threat to all that was true, beautiful, and good.

Even though the distinction between civilization and culture was actualized in producing the categories of high and low culture, nothing better illustrated the challenge to the survival of high or, frequently, received culture than the figure of Americanism as it came to be understood in the late 1920s. At the opening of the symposium, Kawakami Tetsutarō posed an initial question. If in the capitalist modernizing process, Europe and America were originally related to each other and subsequently diverged, then what could be said of Japan since it was related to both by sharing the common ground of modernity? (174) Since he, and others, believed that contemporary Japanese history was, in effect, world history, all developmental routes inevitably led to modernity. Yet this discussion on the genealogy of the modern disclosed how Japanese could easily identify their own origins in the collapse of European medieval unity (as put forth by Yoshimitsu Yoshihiko, 180–182), the Renaissance (Suzuki, 175–178), and the eighteenth-century Enlightenment and French Revolution, the emergence of industrial capitalism (179), and the development of science (Shimomura, 186–188). By the same measure, the Americanism installed in Japan after World War I was seen as continuation of this narrative of modernity as the latest stage of a world history Japanese and others were living in the interwar period. While Japan had imported forms of modernity after the Meiji Restoration, Kawakami observed, and in fact taken on the entire culture of nineteenth-century Europe that had been produced historically, culture in Japan followed no discernable historical or developmental trajectory and seemed to be "not concerned with persons" (254). By appearing here and there, without any apparent historically induced direction, it risked looking like a "perversion."

Kawakami's reason for calling attention to the absence of a culture that had developed historically in Japan was to introduce the conviction that even American culture, however much it seemed to have diverted from classic European models, represented a certain development derived from European culture. Despite the baneful associations linked to American-ism, it was still a product of Europe, and the symposium had to consider this relationship.[19] "The Japanese modern boy and modern girl (*mobo, moga*) imported the thing called American culture and . . . writing has curiously described their life as one without roots" (254–255). It was Japanese culture at a laughable level, he added. But it wasn't laughable because there existed this "frivolous human species called the *mobo* and *moga*." What are we to make of the appearance of so much of this life-style within a culture that regards it as suitable for Japan? Kawakami was asking the symposium to consider what had hitherto been considered as frivolous and dismissable in a culture that so readily was willing to em-brace Americanism to a point where it had become a hegemonic style. The real question was how an equally rootless and apparently ahistorical culture could be so easily implanted in Japan, and how it differed from Japan's own modern experience of cultural rootlessness. Culturally laugh-able, to be sure, especially when compared to the accomplishments of European high culture, but the figures of the modern girl and boy, draped in bizarre dress, wearing outlandish makeup, and behaving in a way that called attention to themselves, were discounted as an odd and "frivolous race" (*keihaku na jinrui*). But Kawakami was convinced that their ubiq-uity demanded serious consideration by a symposium devoted to under-standing the modern. What he imagined as widespread was probably an exaggerated figure that had, since the late 1920s, constituted the unstated fear threatening social order and the processes of cultural reproduction that had prompted the formation of a discourse on the social. Responding to the essay by Tsumura Hideo ("Nani o yaburu bekika"), Nishitani fur-ther observed that this Americanism not only was present in Japan but had permeated Europe as well, and the reason for this now needed to be explained by interrogating the "character possessed by Americanism" (255). A rootless American culture superimposed upon a rootless nine-teenth-century European culture that Japan had imported simply overde-termined a rootlessness that could only oblige Japanese to dig even deeper below the surface to find what remained unaffected by capitalist change and thus fixed and anchored in their own historical development. Once the modern present was contrasted with a historical experience and devel-opment that did not lead to modernity, as Europe's past had, it was then possible to recognize that there existed both cultural and economic unevenness within Japanese society. But before unevenness became the basis on which to theorize cultural difference, a theme I will take up later, the symposium recognized that the overdetermination of surface could be avoided only by problematizing the category of historical consciousness—putting into question the category of history itself (Kobayashi)—and by rethinking the status of representation (both expressive and political) and "rediscovering the classics" (Kamei, Miyoshi Tatsuji, Hayashi, and Kobayashi).

Clearly, the issue confronting thoughtful critics was the spectacle of modern everyday life as it was being lived by the masses in the new metropolitan centers and their surroundings and the supremacy of industrial production. By the 1930s cities like Tokyo, especially, usually horrified Japanese who returned home after long study spells in Europe, when the shock of recognition prompted revulsion (Watsuji Tetsurō) and shame (Kuki Shūzō). The initial response to the spectacle of Americanism and the reason for its capacity to sweep over the more settled culture of Europe and the recently acquired forms of modern civilization in Japan was made by Tsumura Hideo, both in an article prepared for the symposium and in his opening remarks to the assembly. Tsumura shared with most the conviction that the problem Japan and Europe faced was America and its principal export, "Americanism." The war in Europe and now East Asia offered the historical opportunity to end the harmful and hegemonic influence of Americanism and to inaugurate a "new European culture" and create a "new East Asia cultural sphere" (118, 121).

Tsumura, a film critic with a rather broad cultural reach, was persuaded that Japan stood on the site of a vast and fateful cultural conjuncture. The conflict that was being waged in Europe and East Asia was a cultural war. (Kyoto philosophers like Kōyama Ikuo and Kōsaka Masaaki were already articulating this argument.) The nation had not entirely lost its traditional culture—spirit—even though it had absorbed both the old culture of eighteenth- and nineteenth-century Europe—modernity—and American material civilization (123). Owing to the new conjuncture, culture was used "cheaply" and in a "variety of wondrous ways." During the Taishō period, for example, virtually everything was prefixed by the word culture. As if to show that no meaning was complete and finally fixed unless it signified the cultural, there was a great rush in the 1920s to participate in what was then called a "cultural splash" (*bunka donburi*). Hence, there were culture homes, culture drawers, culture kitchen ranges, and more, all testifying to how Japan had received the "bad influences" of American material civilization. The term culture had been entirely absorbed by material artifacts, leaving nothing for the realm of spirit (123). "I see this as the influence of Americanism," Tsumura proclaimed: something that expanded the meaning of culture and caused its necessary dilution. For Tsumura, because he was a movie critic immersed in film, the problem of culture was "no longer limited to considerations of elevated questions concerning only learning, art and thought," even though culture critics in Japan consistently refused to take seriously the claims of the new material culture and how it had changed Japanese life. The very elasticity of the term revealed the lasting impact of Americanism in Japan during the interwar period. Current usage, he noted, included "culture underwear" at the same time as the word was used to denote a cultural organization or society. Similarly, culture also embraced the customs of women students who dashed around the city to obtain the signs of being identified with this or that physical athletic group. While photographs of Deanna Durbin and Tyrone Power were found everywhere, as were "pretentiously" decorated beauty salons and contemporary Tokyo coffee shops, phenomena nobody would consider to be wondrous, they must nevertheless be taken seriously because they participated in Japanese culture. Sometimes, he observed, people would take seriously the enthusiasm of the masses for women's sword matches in Asakusa, the lunatic attractions of Americanisms, and watching cheap movies like a "A Wife's Pedigree"; at other times even the drunkenness of large groups of boys and girls was taken seriously as cultural phenomena. Blues music overwhelmed the recording world, and large numbers of people welcomed and mastered current songs like "Sun on the Lake." American material culture in the 1920s and early 1930s, according to Tsumura, was absorbed in staggeringly large quantities, as were its informing values, which constituted an even more serious danger to settled life. After the 1920s Japan imported new life forms that invariably were accompanied by new commodities produced by American civilization, whose "life-customs" acted as a contagion, violating everything they came into contact with. By the 1930s students were no longer interested in the masters of European high culture like Tolstoy, Strindberg, and Dostoyevsky, whereas these artists had been seen a decade earlier as the sign of the modern spirit. Instead the youth of the 1930s preferred the "charms" of European and American movies, and large numbers constantly showed up in Asakusa where they learned their Tolstoy and Dostoyevsky from the movie versions of *Crime and Punishment* and *Resurrection*. Tsumura disparaged contemporary cultural critics (*bunjin*) who willingly closed their eyes to shut out "vulgar customs" in order to discuss the purity of Japanese culture. These critics must be forced to confront contemporary reality and be made to seriously consider and examine an Americanism they had overlooked in order to understand how much harm this culture had inflicted on the construction of an East Asian cultural realm in the future (124).

The principal reason for the swift spread of Americanism, Tsumura explained, was the "impoverishment of life and moral disorder" Europe experienced after World War I (255). The ruined landscape of postwar Europe was the ideal environment for receiving the optimism, speed, and eroticism promoted by American films. French cinema, which had been a world leader before the war, was overtaken by American film, whose technology and capital easily penetrated France and literally threw its movie industry into a disarray that took ten years to rectify (120).

If film was the agent of Americanization sweeping Asia after the war, as many believed, it was the power of capital that fueled its global expansion. During the symposium Tsumura pointed out how Hollywood was capable of putting up large outlays of capital, amounting to as much as two million dollars for the production of a single film. Clearly, America had come out of the war as a creditor nation, and the world's financial system twenty years after was still being driven by the dollar and the pound. What seemed to interest Tsumura most was the link between an all-powerful dollar facilitated by American war loans—in an environment of weaker national currencies—and the massive growth of the American film industry (128), which plainly was America's principal export. It was not only the power of the dollar and superiority of American productive techniques that accounted for both the spectacular spread of the Hollywood film and the global conquest by Americanization. Equally as important was the fact that America itself was a country that possessed no traditional culture, as such, and thus had no access to a solid residue of durable values capable of being mobilized to resist the desire for commodity consumption; nothing could stand in the way of creating and producing consumer products and expanding the need for them (255). Tsumura, especially, saw in this cultural lack a fundamental explanation for the swift success of the American film and its portrayal of the very social conditions that had produced it. He was particularly concerned to show that its global conquest also brought before vast audiences the constant image of a society devoid of depth, driven only by the most superficial activities of daily life such as endless consumption of commodities and entertainment. "Because the American film accurately reflects this fact [of a society lacking a traditional culture of depth]," he announced to the symposium, "it was able to give birth to a worldly and universalistic appreciation. Since its customs, habits, and morality lack complexity, unlike Europe's, the result has been films that can easily be understood by our commoners. For a long time, the American film, even in East Asia, brandished violence (*moi*) but was easily understood by primitive peoples of Malaya and the Netherlands East Indies by showing Westerns and pure farce [slapstick]. The original spirit of the American film privileged (*taisetsu nisuru*) movement that revered speed (*supīdo*) and it was precisely for this reason that it didn't rely too much on words" (256). Even with the introduction of the talkies, Tsumura observed, American films failed to deviate from this emphasis on action and rapid movement that still made understanding easily accessible. In fact, talkies facilitated the spread of the English language globally over other languages, and this reinforced the popularity of American film. Hence the incredibly accessible nature of the American film in the interwar period, its almost universal capacity to win reception and induce broad understanding, derived principally from the absence of an informing traditional culture. Yet it surely also conveyed the spectacle of a world held together by easily understood activities and the circulation of objects that even the natives of island Southeast Asia, not to forget the backlands of Japan like Kyushu and Shikoku, could recognize and desire in their own daily lives. Watching the American film reflected a shallow culture of things and conduct that signified a "demon pleasure" (*maraku*) capable of deceiving not only the "ignorant masses" but also intellectuals who had declared their exemption from its baneful influences. But intellectuals only overlooked assessing its harmful consequences, whereas the masses enthusiastically submitted to it and immersed themselves in it without reluctance. As Kawakami Tetsutarō put it, the culture offered by the American film tapped the deepest dreams of people of certain classes. A man who earned thirty yen a month could feel like he was riding on a jewel-bedecked palanquin for an evening (258).

Tsumura and others were thus convinced that the American film was the principal agent for introducing and putting into place a life-style that corresponded to American material civilization. He, especially, was persuaded that national policy had erred by permitting the "demon pleasures of Americanism" entry into national life. Not even the colonial territories of the Dutch and the British in East Asia had escaped the force of its dominating conception of daily life. "Today," he complained, "we see the circumstances that . . . the true culture of the motherland, over and beyond being a colonized territory . . . has been given over to the conquest of American film" (126). By constantly advertising American customs, film had engulfed all in an endless cycle of desire for the daily life it presented. The American film was villainous because it presented a face without altruism (in contrast to even Soviet cinema)—pure self-interest and the image of individual satisfaction and the promise of forgetting the immediate past—offering to a fatigued Europe after the war an effective narcotic in the diverse appeals to eroticism, jazz, and optimism. The novelty of "new world" social customs became, everywhere, the standard determining the conduct of global societies (256).

Tsumura went even further in his condemnation of Americanism and its evils. American social organization had dramatized the mixed life of diverse races. But the principle of diversity as a lived reality went hand in hand with the development of a criminal society that was beginning to have consequences for the world. If it was natural that "swinging new customs" like the development of criminality appealed to European curiosity, the appearance of an entirely new social imaginary called America was not simply a surprising spectacle for Europeans (and Japanese) but a problem that now necessitated the task of overcoming. Suzuki Shigetaka, in this connection, acknowledged the importance of the American experience in constructing a new social order comprised of a diversity of races. While he refrained from classifying the United States as an outlaw society because of its racial mix, he wondered if there were not, in actuality, two white races, one composed of the original European-centered world and the other—American—located within the perimeter of colonial lands. Seen from the perspective of world history, the appearance of a white America introduced a new meaning. Just as intellectuals had scorned the culture of the *moga* and *mobo*, without evaluating its importance for modern Japan, they had rushed to dismiss America as still another manifestation of the conquest of a superficial material culture. Suzuki counseled his fellow participants that easy and unreflective dismissal had made America a problem, especially the Americanism that has been imaged in books and common sense, the Americanism that had exerted such powerful influence on Japanese life through the motion pictures: an Americanism driven by the vast power of capitalism and its forces of production. "In contemporary life," he exclaimed, "it is an unfortunate reality that we appropriately speak of an insubstantial civilization against one of substance." Overcoming this habit of mind was difficult and could not be done by merely denying the progressive spirit for one more in keeping with "substance," by not accounting for both the progressive side of American culture and the "prohibitions" demanded by the spirit of Puritanism (259).

It was Hayashi Fusao who reintroduced the image that identified Americanism and the specter of the masses. The problem of mass politics and culture had been a primary preoccupation of bourgeois writers and modernist criticism in Japan and elsewhere during the interwar period. What was most fearsome about Americanism was its capacity to bond mass politics to mass culture. Hayashi shrieked that "the American film seizes the heart of the people (*minshū*) through democracy, American democracy takes hold of the heart of the people in countries that more or less have had bad politics" (referring to both the United States and the Soviet Union) (258). Democracy, he reasoned, seemed to fill a political vacuum that had not been properly occupied and, worse, invariably appeared as the sign of political failure. The movie was an "amusing thing for foolish people of the world," for every Tom, Dick, and Harry even in Japan. Fools were everywhere. Democracy had taken root, and the film both signified the link between democracy—mass participation in politics—and everyday life and portrayed it routinely as a lived reality (258).

Against this wide, sweeping denunciation of the film, Tsumura Hideo, a film critic, rejected the claim of a necessary relationship between mass politics and culture (Americanism) and the agency of the film. "You've repeated the remarks of a coarse fan who reduces the film to lewdness," he retorted. If the film was considered from the perspective of efficaciousness, it was a more elevated device than the way it had been thought in the present. The masses were not the only ones who were exposed to the superficialities of Japanese film and the easily available shoddy products peddled by American movies and capitalism. Film culture was also broad and elevated, and, as he suggested elsewhere, it was the quintessential modern form because it came with the end of modernity and was thus opposed to its spirit (131, 258). For this reason film, because of its capacity to dispense news documentaries, would be useful in the construction of a new order in Europe and East Asia. Even though the bulk of American film was "froth," it still possessed great utility. While the American discovered radio, he said, it is being used more effectively by the Germans (and, he could have added, by most fascist regimes).[20] This was also true of the film, clearly referring to the documentaries of Leni Riefenstahl. Echoing sentiments that called attention to the current aestheticization of politics in the fascist use of film, Tsumura proposed that Germany had used film effectively by making documentaries that would, presumably, actualize the reality of the new order for the most ordinary viewer. American film-making was capable of portraying only the modern spirit, which increasingly, as we shall see, meant presenting a content that seemed to be dominated by jazz and "crazy dance styles" and represented nothing more than speed; it never exceeded repeating itself. By contrast, German documentary films like "Festivals of the Folk," "History of Victory," and "Triumph of the Will" pointed to "a true overcoming of the modern spirit." In fact, the film of the future—Italian and German—would be documentary rather than literary, like the film of the past; the world of French and American cinema was dominated by creative screen writers (131). Doubtful of whether or not American film technology would continue to progress, even though it was rooted in "productive circumstances" and a "film science," Tsumura was convinced that its development as a visual culture capable of representing the decline of American national character, morality, and customs was probably slight (132). What he was referring to was the evolution of film culture into a medium of documentation sensitive to the contemporary situation and capable of portraying the reality of fact rather than fiction. (Ironically, this was the task the Marxist philosopher Tosaka Jun had earlier assigned to journalism.) Yet this enthusiastic celebration of the German documentary betrayed a blindness that prevented him from seeing how these new productions were implicated in constructing fantasy rather than reconstructing the reality of a new order.

This discussion about Americanism dramatized the problematic nature of modernism. For most, the Americanism that seemed to dominate the contemporary world was a depravation of the modern spirit. Modern spirit was, in turn, principally identified with the nineteenth century and revealed an opposition to material civilization, possessive individualism, hedonism caused by money, and ceaseless consumption unleashed by finance capitalism. At the heart of this vision of modernity was the spectacle of endless change, endless motion, the constant revolutionizing demanded by the capitalist forces of production that constituted the great nemesis of all cultural criticism since Nietzsche. Tsumura differentiated the modern from the contemporary (an obvious Heideggerian gesture), which marked the site of decline. In response, Suzuki Shigetaka wondered if Americanism actually represented modernism or whether it simply occupied a different place in the perspective of world history (259). But regardless of its location, it was important not to condemn the development of science and the growth of material civilization out of hand. Even if the United States was hegemonic, Japan was very much a part of this global process. The real dilemma was the recognition that while the human spirit creates machines for its own use, it is eventually "devoured" by its own creation. The problem appeared to be not so much the impulse that clearly denies the nature of contemporary life as it was the imperative to discover how humans, who are inevitably condemned to living in a material and technological world, learn how to control their creations. While such an approach necessitated an elevated ideal, the problem, as Suzuki envisaged it, was that democracy, technology, and capitalism stemmed from a commonly shared foundation. Because of this interlocking relationship among democracy, especially its propensity for mass culture, capitalism, and technology, it might be necessary to imagine a vastly different conception of human order and need. In this connection, Tsumura proposed the establishment of a new economic system based not on exchange but on usefulness (127–128), while Hayashi's nostalgia for imperial loyalism reminiscent of samurai activists who had sacrificed themselves to the Restoration promised a new start based only on willful action and nothing else.

It is difficult to know whether Tsumura's recommendation represented an echo of Marxism or simply an instance of the current desire to return to some form of communitarianism. Even though Japan needed to overcome modern technological civilization, overcoming rarely meant total elimination. Capitalism and technology had altered the style of living by making things easy, convenient, and efficient. Cheaply made goods were available in abundance and had literally colonized everyday life in Japan, as Nakamura Mitsuo had observed. The consequences of this process of rationalization clearly homogenized everyday life, just as democracy equalized social relationships (127–128). The bonding among democracy, capitalism, and technological civilization was inscribed in this process of homogenizing and equalizing, driven by the unlimited acceleration (*supīdoka*) of everyday life, which many believed was its most dangerous dimension. For the symposium, speed was the sign of the vast discontinuities in life Japanese had experienced since the Meiji period and revealed itself in an excess of historical consciousness that emplotted the world as ceaseless development and change. But speed was also linked to the constant homogenizing and averaging that troubled people like Suzuki, Tsumura, and Hayashi. If the ideal of America was to elevate the material standard of living of the masses (reflecting capitalism's great but unfulfilled promise to even the ground of development), it still risked producing the average and the same everywhere. Tsumura was confident that if technology were used adroitly, there might still be hope for an overcoming of the modern, but, as Kawakami Tetsutarō had insisted, "it is not technological civilization that has become the object of overcoming . . . [because] for spirit the machine is not within view" (261). While Kawakami praised Kobayashi Hideo—hitherto silent in the discussion on Americanism—for having observed that even though spirit (culture) dislikes the machine, it doesn't struggle with it as an adversary, the discussion slipped into a celebration of the primacy of spirit or culture—but with disagreement:

> *Shimomura:* I think that's inexcusable. . . . We have to problematize the spirit that makes the machine.
> *Kobayashi:* Even though the spirit creates the machine, spirit is still spirit.
> *Shimomura:* We must problematize this spirit that makes machines!
> *Kobayashi:* It is not a technological spirit! Spirit must create the machine, but the spirit that does so is spirit! It is the same as the spirit that creates art!
> *Shimomura:* ". . . Spirit (*seishin*) and spirit/soul (*tamashii*) have accomplished a modern revolution. Until today the spirit—*tamashii*—was something that corresponded to the flesh, but in the modern period the character of the body has changed. It is not a fleshly body. The organism that makes the machine like an organ of the self is the modern body. The ancient spirit is not able to manage this new body. I believe that we must look for a new spirit. The tragedy of modernity is found in an ancient spirit that cannot follow in the wake of the body, the machine. Regardless of the

problem of whether to retire to the rear or advance to the front, it is no longer possible to turn back. I think that the spirit that creates the machine is never material." (261)

Even modern technology, according to the Catholic theologian Yoshimitsu Yoshihiko, passes through "magical meaning" that anchors the pursuit of unlimited materiality and speed. The mystical is the backside of the whole process (263). Hence the necessity of the overcoming is manifest in the rediscovery of spirit itself and its true vocation to extract from sheer materiality the aura of a creative impulse that is not bound to what it has created. In this time, he added, spirit no longer controls either the course of civilization or the itinerary of the machine. Spirit has been emptied out of both, and this marks the place to begin the difficult task of overcoming the modern. To envisage an overcoming in this way meant acknowledging it was a "problem of repetition" that involved returning to origins in order to start anew to discover the spirit and soul that had been lost.

But, as we shall see, what had been "lost" and forgotten had never really existed; the memory of a past time was the invention of the present. It was precisely this sense of a "repetition" that promised to lead the present to the self-discovery of the spirit. Because spirit was not material, it was in a position to escape the snares of representation and the desire of historical consciousness to capture it in a progressive narrative. In this way, spirit, according to Kobayashi, was still spirit and remained outside modern rational modes of explanation.

THE PROBLEM OF REPRESENTATION AND THE STATUS OF HISTORY

For the symposium, the problem of representation was linked to the specialization of knowledge that had characterized the commitment to instrumental rationality and a division of labor that marked off the modern from all preceding epochs and was, perhaps, its distinguishing sign. What a divided knowledge managed to produce was an endless series of partial representations that were constantly changing. These could offer no chance of aggregating or linking up with each other to produce a totality of what could be known. Instead, the division of knowledge into fields resulted in armed encampments where each claimed privilege for its own, partial view of the world. In brief, the full impact of alienation and the instability of representation was experienced first and perhaps most intensely in the commitment to a new mode of knowing. The acquisition of modern knowledge convinced Japanese that what they possessed before the advent of modernity was a whole and coherent body of knowing that now was being replaced by a multiplicity of divisions that had no chance of ever being brought together. Hence, the adoption of modern knowledge resulted in producing loss of a prior object.

After the Meiji period, thinkers attributed the characteristic failure of "civilization" (*bunmei*) to the loss of wholeness, the extreme differentiation of work, and the proliferation of specialists everywhere (233). The ensuing specialization of knowledge and the installation of a new division of labor distorted and thus separated a world once thought to have been whole but which now lay in fragments. For Kamei Katsuichirō, this new, instrumental knowledge had destroyed the unity of the Japanese spirit. In his opinion, there had been a few heroic pioneers in the Meiji period, like the Christian activist Uchimura Kanzō, who reacted early to this rationalizing trend and tried, with the example of their lives, to resist the inevitable. Even though Uchimura had been originally trained as a specialist in marine biology, he refused to become a specialist. It was for this reason that he pursued God, the "universal thing" lodged in all things and work. In a later discussion, Yoshimitsu would refer to this immanentism as an expression of "pantheism," but it was not the same thing. Uchimura read and interpreted theology widely and was convinced that it embraced politics, economics, philosophy, history, and natural science. Even after enrolling in a theological school in the United States, he refused to become a specialist, that is, a minister, and insisted that he wanted only to be a layman, an amateur (234). Hence, the meaning of his idea of "nonchurch" Christianity (*mukyōkai*). According to Kamei's account, Uchimura chose to pursue a purity toward God that would be no different from being inside Him. While this was only one example of how an individual struggled with European civilization and the demands of instrumental knowledge, the pace of importing new knowledge and skills quickened after the 1880s and spread rapidly in the subsequent Taishō period.

What troubled the symposium most was the recognition that the knowledge imported was principally informed by its apparent utility and promise of speed and rationalizing capable of producing untellable numbers of specialists. By the same measure, the universities had singularly failed to produce "philosophers of real life" and forfeited the responsibility to find an image of the whole person. Instead, they settled for developing "scholarly schools belonging to different doctrines." Shimomura Toratarō and the scientist Kikuchi Masashi tried defending the necessity of specialization in the sciences and rejected suggestions that called for other arrangements. The discussion between Kamei and Shimomura revealed one of the persisting tensions of the conference between the claims of science and the authority of spirit, between the present and the belief that there was no possibility of turning back the clock and the con-

viction that what had been lost had to be resuscitated. While Kamei acknowledged that any turning back might constitute a "decline," he was
also convinced that specialization actually undermined service and appealed to the example of Uchimura, who served God while working as
an expert on sea life. "He tried to restore the character of wholeness (*zen-
jinsei*) to himself by believing in God." But, unfortunately, specialization
was a condition for doing science and the price paid for the forfeiture of
wholeness (235).

According to another participant, Moroi Saburō, the question raised
by specialization concerned understanding whether the conditions of modernity must inevitably be based on the division of knowledge (236).
While he was made aware of this question when studying in Europe, he
acknowledged how unbearable it was for him to see Europeans actually
represent their differences from each other and from non-Europeans.
What the episode suggested to Moroi, who undoubtedly must have repressed an experience in racism, was how Europeans had convinced themselves that Japanese were musically weak. In it, he seems to have recognized that Europeans were committed to differentiating themselves from
all others, including other whites, as if it were a moral imperative, even
though it was well known that "90 percent are basically the same" (236).
Instead of proceeding from some conception of the whole and its unity,
they resorted to differentiation produced by specialization and the division of labor. The great injury inflicted by *bunmei kaika* was the loss of
self-awareness—a kind of alienation that prevented people from seeing
and thus representing the whole as a unity (238).

This seeming distrust of the baneful influence of specialization and its
destruction of total understanding was related to the question of representation and the stability of meaning. No problem seemed more important
in the interwar period than those considerations that prompted thinkers,
writers, and artists to worry about the capacity of art and literature to
accurately represent the real in a society in which reality was subjected to
endless differentiation. But it should be stated that the problematic status
of representation was linked to an equally compelling perception that recognized in modern society the specter of social indeterminacy produced
by ceaseless social and technological change, new patterns of consumption, the rising expectations of new classes, and the constant revolutionizing of relations of social production in the 1920s. Often, the effort to
determine or fix principles capable of guaranteeing lasting social cohesion
fused with attempts to regain the ground of authentic experience or practices (announced by all of those calls for what Miki Kiyoshi identified as
"foundational experience," *kisoteki keiken*), which could lay claim to an
identity with origins or some autonomous (spiritual) act of creation outside of any historical scheme or process. This, it seemed, offered immunity

from the dizzying changes demanded by capitalist modernization. During the interwar period, the principal problem Japanese writers and thinkers faced was how to save art and culture from the instability of representation, which increasingly was being yoked to a program charged with reflecting only constant changes in the life-world. By the same measure, this relationship between social reality and its mirroring effect threatened to undermine the fixity of enduring agency and value. If art and culture represented merely a reflection of real life that was now being lived and experienced daily, then its only vocation was to show how life itself was in constant flux. Under this constraint, art and culture could only reflect the passing, "the transitory and fleeting," the fragmentary that had no chance of being grasped before the shards of experience disappeared. The task, as envisaged by so many modernists, many of whom were active participants in the symposium, was to show how art was able to escape the uncertainties of social change and reflect or signify a life endowed with enduring and lasting meaning. This is what the critic Kobayashi Hideo referred to as the "commonness of everyday life": that which manages to escape historical change and outlasts its ups and downs. It was also this sense of a common experience that historical representation inevitably missed.

What the symposium sought to do was remind contemporaries of the necessity of reviving a memory and experience that had not yet been assimilated to or destroyed by the shock and sensation of modern life. Participants like Kobayashi saw the social experience of modernity as a form of forgetting that repressed a true history consisting of the continuity of "commonness" in a cultural unconscious. Like so many of the thinkers of the interwar period, those who participated in the symposium pointed to the necessity of a revolution that would unleash the dead forms of tradition. Where they erred, I think, is in believing that such forms could be enlisted from outside modernity, as if they were as yet unrealized socio-temporal forms. Only a few thinkers like Gonda Yasunosuke and Tosaka Jun were able to see that this act of remembrance had to come from within the temporal forms of modernity itself. If thinkers like Kobayashi counseled amnesia concerning the present—which always meant the status of the everyday—then the task was to forget about the modern for the past. Despite his effort to distance his approach from historically progressive schemes, his own conception of continuous commonness merely recuperated an older historicism that mapped the new onto history as a whole and established an abstract continuity with the past. In this way, historicism, and Kobayashi, presented within modernity the past in terms of its "value as heritage" or, as Yanagita claimed, describing his "discovery" of Okinawa as a cultural "treasure ship." But it should be pointed out that the symposium largely agreed on the necessity of forgetting and even discounting the constitutive work of the present, what Marx called the "current situation" and Tosaka Jun identified as the "now" (ima).

Rather than returning to remembrance to derive a new form of historical experience immanently from the experience of the crisis of the older order, the symposium, following the example of an earlier discourse on the social, sought to recover memory as an unsullied form in artwork and practices that had escaped the mediations of capitalism and modernity. This meant identifying the status of agency in an artwork, in aesthetic, cultural experience or in a religious practice because it was presumed to be outside of modernity and temporality and thus could hold out the promise of a "prior grounding in a 'pure' practice of representation, one that enjoys a grant of autonomy from the object."[21] For the interwar period this search involved finding a practice that had successfully evaded the constraints of an objective world that was never the same, for one that never changed in its decisive aspects. Specifically, the gesture inscribed in all of those efforts was to produce a "pure literature" free from the mediations of society or history, or to resuscitate an experience unaffected by reification—social abstraction—or, as Nishitani Keiji proposed, to re-situate a different philosophical conception of subjectivity, a "subjective nothing" rather than a "subjective self." Such a move appeared to enable the "aesthetic" (which included religious and cultural production) "to transcend the fall of representation as the basis for the formation of subject/agents."[22] For Japanese modernists, this entailed a distrust of anything that was submitted to representation because it was already mediated by capitalist abstraction to constitute a kind of secondary revision that removed the object from immediate experience. The task aimed at locating an artwork or practice that signified the immediacy of experience and not its intervening (social) mediations. Writers and thinkers of differing persuasions, as we shall see, sought to secure accessibility to the authority of an immediate experience that was indistinguishable from the artwork or practice that represented it, rather than relying on "modern, interpretative modes" that invariably fabricate and distort (228). Avoiding these secondary revisions was important, as Kobayashi suggested, because they screen out the authentic by virtue of their dependence on the mediations of "thought" and "literature." "If I may speak bombastically," he declared, "I think ... that that Western things are usually interpretative is an interesting opinion; they have produced interesting criticism, interpretations and essays. And, we move from one place to another because of such interesting things. I myself have thought so. When one is trying their hand at this kind of writing, and somehow adhering to a logic, it is all trifling when it comes to feeling with the gut. By considering either literature or thought without the head, you'll gradually come to feel it in the body. Things like content and circumstances that are written about are worthless. Literature is only gradually caught sight of like an artistic object you sometimes feel in form" (246). Kobayashi was pointing to the interference caused by thinking and the deliberate effort to create literature by fictionalizing circumstances for content, an operation that was indistinguishable from "interpretation." One does not think literature but feels it in the "gut," the body; it signifies its presence not in content but in enduring form. Kobayashi believed it was social abstraction, manifest in specialization and differentiation of knowledge, that led to the substitution of experience, seeing, and feeling by analysis and interpretation.

This distrust of mere interpretation in a capitalist social formation invariably required making some effort to get outside of it in order to think or, better yet, feel the concrete. The problem in Japan was further complicated by the recognition that it was questionable whether Japanese sentiment (*kokoro*) and spirit (Tsumura Hideo used the German *geist* to ironically make the point) could adequately be represented by Western skills, modes of apprehension, concepts, and instruments. Moreover, there was the overdetermined perception throughout the 1920s and 1930s of the historical role played by uneven development, the dissonance in modes of being, between Japan and the West, colonizer and colony, and within society: the discovery that people were occupying spaces marked by differing modes of production and temporalities that were co-existing with capitalism in the Now. To find a way out of the mediations of capitalism it was necessary for the artwork—culture itself—to become a stand-in for the lost historical agency, what had been effaced by both a moving history and the reliance on Western codes of representation and historical narratives of progress. In this endeavor, Japanese sought to replace the presumed universal ground of capitalism and social abstraction as the source of all activity with the "seemingly concrete but historically indeterminate agency of the artwork," or, as Nishitani put it, a "subjective nothing" (which resembled a religious experience) or the folk or the Japanese spirit itself. By making this move to find a grounding for a living and enduring practice rather than a mere representation of the fleeting and the fragmentary, Japanese sought to resituate in their present the claims of pure presence associated with the permanent artwork (Kobayashi's form), an aesthetic, cultural artifact, belief, or an authentic experience untied to the conditions of historical production and unaffected by historical change. Under capitalism, the spectacle of modern life in Japan in the interwar period put into question the relationship between representation, increasingly seen as an abstraction of reality, and the represented, the concrete experience which, miraculously, had managed to escape the devastations of representation, now renamed as "Americanism."

In his supplemental article "Gendai seishin ni kansuru oboegaki," Kamei Katsuichirō alerted his fellow conferees to what he called the "crisis of words" and the grief he felt in seeing the "decline of wonder when the specialized words of thought and situational terminology become people's words or the signs that adorn their words." Whatever the case, this trend pointed to a confusion in the usage of contemporary language symptomizing the alarming decline of "spirit" (6). Originally, words were formed to speak "positively" of the "flood of emotions" that were difficult to express—emotions that constituted a "piercing" that inclined the "whole soul." It was the same with love and grief, where words were employed to express a thought or feeling that was inexpressible. Words interlocked with beautiful facial expressions and deep shades, but they made a wager with life. "I feel a violent nostalgia for a language that brings out the many shapes and reflections of original values, that is like the motions of a dancing girl." What he regretted most was the decline of sensitivity toward words (7). Instead of people consciously taking care to use words correctly, recognizing at all times the hard labor involved, there is only a "tampering" that produces a "daydream language." Contemporaries, he advised, had lost the sense of surplus meaning embedded in a single word, the multiple meanings a word might evoke if used properly and carefully.

The appeal to a more authentic practice of word usage signified the possession of the meaning of history. Yet the gesture also implied that meaning was infinite and never exceeded itself, that it could always be found, despite the accidents of history and the dross of contemporary life. While stopping short of calling for a restoration of an archaic language suitably fitted to express a range of emotions and feelings, like nativists before him, Kamei acknowledged disappointment with people who no longer pursued the echoes of origins and traces of mystery still locked in language. When the ancients tried to copy the classics, belief blossomed because they had "thoroughly grasped the superb spirit buried in a word." Copying was not carried out because of the absence of a print technology. A sense of belief in the surplus meaning found in words would determine how to experience the unlimited thought lodged in one word of the classics, how, in fact, to narrate its hidden beauty. Contemporaries, he complained, value things only according to the form of what is being used.

Kamei's critique of representation was instantiated by the collapse of language usage; it derived from a deep dissatisfaction with the consequences of modernization itself. Everywhere he looked, he saw language developing into hardened clichés, jargon, empty conventions, without referents, causing a heavy reliance on slogans (especially among the left). In response to this crisis in representation, he explained that the development of language into slogans was simply an extension of the Meiji enlightenment and its singular commitment to utility and machine civilization. Since that time, the masses, who had raced to embrace the most shoddy goods introduced by the "enlightenment," had rapidly succumbed to the forms of language that were easiest to understand. Unschooled and thoughtless, they degraded the original beauty and sternness found in words, whose meanings collapsed into nonsense and unintelligibility. This dissolution of proper language usage, accompanying the production of degraded products, was caused by democratization, which, like its left wing off-shoot, communism, uses language instrumentally, as pure utility. During the 1920s and 1930s, he observed, communists and liberals alike appeared precisely at the moment when language was being emptied of its meanings and replaced by formulaic phrases. Only slogans were understood, he intoned, and Japanese society was faced with an immense crisis whereby the "spirit" was being swamped by the processes of equalizing, averaging, and vulgarizing (9). But the persistence of slogans also meant the disappearance of referents and the culture of reference that once, it was believed, gave shape and meaning to words. It also signaled the reduction of language to the function of interpellation. In Kamei's critique of representation we can see both a grasp of the process by which language usage reflected the commodity-form and the fear of mass culture.

At the heart of this process of language debasement was the shock of speed and the commodification of language such that words lost meaning as quickly as yesterday's fashion. Like the commodity form, newness became a stimulus of demand that always antiquated the most recent past. In the interwar period, speed and shock were seen as formal principles of perception in film, photography, and contemporary journalism. But Kamei saw these new media only as conveyers of information and as obstacles to communicating social experience. If speed destroyed antiquity as a stable historical referent for the present, it also closed the distance between the modern and the new. The world Kamei surveyed was one where the modern and the new were rapidly becoming synonymous and temporality was appearing as the ever—always—the same within the new. Kamei exemplified this process of how language in the present reflected the impact of speed and its transformation into slogan and cliché (the commodity form) by turning to the past. When the Edo period poet Bashō took a trip by foot (in one of his journeys), it took him a long time to get there and allowed him to record the journey in a poetic diary. By train it's a matter of a few days. But the time he spent on the road was necessary to allow him to "see" and grasp the meaning of the scenes he was encountering rather than numbly recognize a blurred landscape from the window of a railway car. By contrast, moderns construct meaning by viewing people, villages, and scenery as they pass by the window of a moving train. As a result, modern seeing never allows people to get into nature, grasp its movements, and learn to love it. For Bashō, "seeing" was the same as the word for "following in resignation" (13, 14). The danger is speed, as Natsume Sōseki had observed years earlier, and the taking of short-cuts. Taking three days to get to a destination violates the original meaning associated with the word for travel.

Speed produced condensations, slogans, clichés, and what Kamei detested most, frankness, a plain directness undoubtedly produced by democratization and its insistence on equality. Healthy language depends on silence, on pause, not the noise of modernity where both sound and meaning are drowned in a ceaseless din. Everyone has become too talkative, and nothing gets communicated except information because clichés and slogans have replaced words. Modern enlightenment "violently tramples on the beauty of representation, which secretly performs the subtle things in concealment that only a delicate sensation can handle flexibly, as they come" (10). Contemporary civilization has completely undermined the power to represent things as they are. Speaking frankly and "crudely" prevents speakers from exploring a broader range of meaning and association. The intense compulsion to talk excessively and say all, without leaving something out, was prompted by rationalism and its "desire to explain" everything, which he attributed to an "impatient utilitarianism" and poisonous "sensationalism." (Kamei's criticism recalled Tanizaki Junichirō's earlier observation that the incandescent light bulb illuminates everything and thus prevents the existence of shadows and nuances, things half concealed in darkness, that was so important for an earlier aesthetic.) In Kamei's view, the new media of radio and print journalism exemplified this worrisome desire to explain everything and leave nothing to chance or imagination. If the conduct of war, he wrote, is covered by radio or the newspapers, it is easy to see that the reports dwell only on surface events and occurrences and often neglect the "fine feelings" and "shadows and nuances" embedded in a noble action. Praise might prevail, but the form strives only for minute detail reducing the report to its narrowest dimensions and constantly repeating the same.

Kamei's perceptions evoked the possibility of mechanical forms of reproduction actually destroying the auratic qualities of an experience by resorting to detailed representations that overlooked shadows and nuances. "When those who return are heroic spirits," he asked, "who talks too much? Writers and reporters who hasten to the war heroes' home place . . . ? Will they try to narrate thoughts and emotions difficult to tell because they are noble and aristocratic?" Kamei was not so sure and lamented what appeared as a polluting of nobility and beauty because of hurried frankness and directness. (11). Worried that Japanese would end up "submerged in a pool of forgetfulness," speed and the desire for detail destroys and omits what is truly important and what cannot be captured by mere description. What remains singularly vital in representing things is silence and solitude, while the obsessive trend toward greater "frankness" produces only greater emphasis on self-apology, adding more and more commentary on the discourse of the self. In fact, frankness and self-apology were necessary conditions of a discourse on the self. Losing emotions in contemporary speech inevitably risked disregarding how to adequately narrate an event or scene and the inevitable fall into "political ideology."

If words, for Kamei, had lost their power to express the ineffable, photography and film were no more effective. Both film and photography aimed at taking shots of things without making the necessary distinctions concerning importance. Like reportage and the failure of detail to capture the full story, the photographer was no more capable of distinguishing those aspects of a thing, person, or event that are notable, beautiful, strange. When photographers focused on the old statues of Buddha in Yamato and tried with film to make conspicuous the figure itself, they invariably eliminated the statue's luminosity (*hikari*), its aura, which is marked by its location inside a dark and secluded main temple. Ancient art found in Nara temples conveyed an implacable aura produced by the statue's location inside a temple that subjected it to the constant play of shadows.

Owing to its capacity for reproduction and distribution, it was normal to expect photography to raise the aesthetic consciousness of the people. But in actuality, it only managed to deceive the viewer, who was never in a position to grasp the inexpressible aura of the artwork. And in this way photography differed little from the contemporary debasement of words. The trusting spectator of such a photograph, believing that the object had been authentically (*seikaku*) reproduced, lost sight because of the surprising inauthenticity of the representation, which was only a poor copy of an original that forever remained out of focus. The viewer thereby always fell short of grasping the feelings shadowed in the mysteries associated with the original object, as the photograph concealed its inauthencity by appealing to authentic forms and claiming to reproduce them. Yet, the photograph had managed only to induce an optical illusion where the viewer was made to believe that he/she was seeing the authentic thing. If photography made available the art object to a greater number of viewers, it also jeopardized receptivity by threatening to plunge it into a "paralytic condition" (12). What Kamei was pointing to was the disappearance of experience itself, the possibility of communicating it, and the inadequacy of new forms of representation like photography and print journalism to serve as substitutes for the lost aura. But he also appears to have been inadvertently acknowledging the impossibility of laying hold of the subject who was in a position to experience the auratic because it was always slipping, shifting, never remaining in a fixed place.

While Kamei's critique of representation concentrated on the new technologies of mechanical reproduction that eliminated aura and undermined true receptivity, the symposium seemed to be more concerned with determining whether Western forms of art had been "honestly imprinted on the Japanese." This emphasis, which did not preclude considerations of mechanical reproducibility, referred to the role played by Western art forms in the creation of a new, synthetic culture combining East and West (212). On this issue, the musician Moroi Saburō proposed that while Japanese had not yet developed a new musical tradition in the Western idiom, Western influence had been implanted in "the creation of new musical forms." But to resolve this question, it was necessary first to determine whether it was possible for Japanese to represent their own feelings and sentiments with Western techniques, modes of composition, and instruments. The literary critic Nakamura Mitsuo was persuaded that Japanese had not yet absorbed the emotionality needed to grasp Western music and the structure of feeling that had actually been implicated in the production of musical forms. Moreover, there was a large difference between musical forms employed by the Japanese and those of the West.

According to the composer Moroi, the mood or feeling (*kimochi*) of Western music derived from song (*uta*), whereas in the Orient the narrative had been essential. (It is interesting to note that Orikuchi Shinobu, who was not at the symposium, had observed a decade earlier that the origins of art in Japan derived not from lyric poetry and love songs but from narratives chanted by (female) mediums during auspicious religious rituals imploring the gods for yearly abundance and the continuing good fortune of the community.) "I like composing music that narrates," Moroi explained. "Japanese audiences don't like listening to these [Western] songs, principally because they can't penetrate the sentiments of the composer. When older folk in the countryside hear songs on the radio that rely on Western vocal techniques, if they are over forty years old, they have trouble staying tuned in to them for more than twenty minutes. They usually get up and say: 'Its too weak,' and they believe the young are weak for listening to this music. Eventually, they turn the radio off and say its safer not to listen. The lamentation of these Japanese wouldn't be understood by Western musicians" (212). In this connection, the film critic Tsumura Hideo called attention to the practice of contemporary singers using Western vocal techniques to sing Japanese folk songs as a means of overcoming the incomprehensibility of Western musical forms. But he was also convinced that the method produced strange effects that simply would not be welcomed by Japanese audiences. It was a "joke," he declared, but because it was being used repeatedly in current Japanese films it was a problem that still needed to be confronted. As an example, Tsumura referred to a recent "boring movie" called "Yamato," where the singer, employing the Western method to vocalize Japanese songs, sounded as if the song was being blurted out. The effect destroyed the whole mood of the film. Despite the best of intentions to revise vocal techniques so that they relied on Western song styling, the episode dramatized the impossibility of this approach because it had no connection to the "Japanese thing." While it is hard to know what Tsumura meant by the "Japanese thing," since it was one of those loose signifiers everybody was using in the 1930s, he explained that the music that best represents the Japanese spirit is "autumnal" and thus must bring out a sense of the "South" (214). The difference between the Western vocal tradition and its Asian counterpart is that the latter, according to the poet Miyoshi Tatsuji, "crushes the voice," as manifested first in the recitation of Buddhist sutras but amplified in No performances deriving from the fifteenth century.

The move to identify an authentic musical mode in Japan and situate it in the present favored the tactic of rejecting newer forms of composition like primitivism, symbolism, impressionism, and expressionism for a neoclassicism that pitted rigorous objectivism against the subjectivism that had characterized previous modes of modern music. Its objectivism was based not on a set of contradictions between actuality and passion but rather on the beauty of order as it was constructed according to the requirements of sound. Privileging form and promoting the application of formal principles served as an effective check against the formlessness and excessive subjectivism of romanticism. But, he added, form, here, was not structure but surface, a purity of expression, something that was not necessarily linked to representing. For Moroi, this neo-classicism constituted a form of "restoration" and an "overcoming of the modern," not necessarily a wholesale rejection, which was no longer possible, but rather a procedure that permitted a "seeing through with our eyes to the essence of Western culture" (54). While grasping the essence of Western culture would reveal what needed to be thrown out and excluded, it would also, at the same time, underscore the importance of "know[ing] the classics of Japan" (55).

If Moroi's pursuit of antiquity fell short of recommending a recovery of the totality of its forms, as if driven by an insatiable nostalgia, it managed to call for an approach that would consider the origin of things and acknowledge the constant pulsations of the past in the present. In this way, neo-classicism had been able to announce its own "overcoming of modernity" that might now supply a model for the kind of overcoming the symposium was seeking. Although it was urgently important to rid Japan of senselessly borrowed elements and the informing impulse of "blind imitation" that ceaselessly drove it, it was also evident that a complete rejection was never possible. Moroi's recommendation of a restoration more spiritual than formal pointed to a strategy that merely "contemporizes court dance music" or "introduces Western musical instruments in performing rituals of ancient tales" (*naniwabushi*). The first, guiding principle of this program, he explained, required being touched (*furiru*) by the spirit that has continually informed Japanese music and given it life. When "we [Japanese] encounter transitional times of national self-reflection like the present and seek to overcome a Japanized modernity, the effort must be correct because the classics hold an important meaning for us" (53, 55). The appeal to the classics authorized a program that recognized the importance of "constructing our own culture," which, at the same time, was driven by an active "recovery of spirit." Specifically, this move required a return to a native structure of feeling and sensation, much like Tokugawa period nativists had promoted in their own struggle with an alien civilization. As contemporary artists entrusted with this task, it was necessary to obey the "order of spirit" (57). Moroi insisted that Western music could not adequately represent Japanese sensibilities because it had lost contact with the original spiritual order and was shut off from following the proper path of sensation. Spirit was "master of both form and sensation" and hence identical to the pursuit of the classics and an "adherence to origins" (57)

As a response, the critic Kawakami Tetsutarō accused Moroi of "overbuying" neo-classicism since it was merely one among many modern, Western artistic forms. Kobayashi Hideo asked whether modern music "yearns for an ancient place or has failed to reach it yet?" (206). "While I haven't listened to your [Moroi's] music," he confessed, "where do you get the hint of spirituality . . . is it from traditional Japanese music? Do you dislike Japanese music? Hasn't it been discovered yet?" Moroi's defense claimed that he had never rejected the meaning of traditional Japanese music, which possessed its own beauty that required willing listeners. The problem came when one tried to introduce its formal elements into composition. There were people who relied on studying the great ancient songs of the *Manyōshū*, while others submerged themselves deeply in the conventions of modern music. But, he added, "its not as if one could get a hint of traditional music in such situations; I'm not saying that its a bad thing to try to get a 'hint' out of using [instruments like] the *koto* and *samisen*" (210). Yet the problem remained intractable for a Japanese composer who, wedded to Western musical modes and instruments, might try to create a new Oriental music from this location.

It was still questionable, according to Tsumura, whether the structure of Western music supplied adequate means to represent a Japanese "geist." Song and poetry were not served well by Western musical and vocal techniques. For Tsumura, the experience of contemporary Japanese musical composition was following the fate of the Japanese film. Although it was a commendable gesture of people like Moroi who tried to represent the spirit of Japan by employing Western musical techniques, it was still doubtful whether it was possible to use Japanese instruments in the attempt to create symphonic music capable of appealing to contemporaries. When effort was made to express the "heart" of Japan with Western musical techniques, there could only be pain and contradictions. Japanese first learned film making from the Soviets and the Americans. Owing to this inaugural reliance on foreign examples and the imitation that comes from using such techniques for representation, innumerable films were produced that simply failed to express the Japanese soul. But it was also true that film-makers had not worked with the "true customs of Japan" (211–212).

In fact, the very techniques and skills employed to make films collided with efforts to represent the Japanese spirit, frequently producing strange effects like seeing the use of Western music in a Japanese historical film. But it was impossible for film and music to communicate such ineffable spiritual durables like the No, Japanese dance (*gagaku*), and aesthetic attitudes like *sabi, wabi, yūgen*, each in their own way pointing to the unrepresentable, the Japanese sublime (211–212). Not surprisingly, Tsumura discounted Moroi's own efforts at finding a suitable means of representing what was essentially Japanese with Western techniques (211).

Although the use of Western technology and artistic methods could not adequately represent Japanese sensibilities—the putative spirit of the race—it also prompted a consideration of how Japan's modernity would actually be represented. Specifically, this turn in the symposium came when Kawakami Tetsutarō raised the question concerning the form of civilization that had entered Japan and whether Japan had historically conformed to it. In response to this initiative, Kobayashi Hideo, who had already emphasized the importance of returning to the classics as an antidote to a poisonous modernist literature, proposed that the history of Japanese literature since the Meiji period had been based on a misunderstanding of Western literature, which itself had misrecognized its own world. Kobayashi was convinced that the problem of assessing the role played by modern Western thought in Japan and determining the nature of a modern literature required understanding the "political crisis" that had apparently provoked these considerations. "The arrival of a political crisis," he noted, "now gradually pricks both healthy reflection and research" (217). He no doubt was referring to the political crisis of the 1930s, which had already led to domestic spiritual mobilization and Japan's progressive drift into a war against Anglo-American imperialism now powered by the promise to rid Asia of the burden of the white man's oppression. But he also could have been referring back to the earlier Meiji period, which had been produced by another "political crisis." During the symposium, Kobayashi declared it was more difficult to discover genuine "Japanized principles" than it was to determine the form of modern thought and literature since their inception in the Meiji period. Similarly, it was more problematic to lay hold of a common experience than it was to identify the ever-changing new. But as a distinguished literary and cultural critic even before the symposium met, he had already framed his interests by the modernist problematic to find, without becoming a revolutionary, a stable grounding for an authentic experience capable of resisting the revolutionary force of capitalism. It was this impulse that drove him early to dismiss history altogether as an abstraction and to embrace the formalism of the *shishōsetsu*, its embeddedness in the concrete experience of everyday life, to celebrate Dostoyevsky, Baudelaire, and Mozart, and ultimately to appropriate Henri Bergson's theories of time and cognition to help him configure his own approach to poetics and aesthetics.

Before the war, Kobayashi had thus already committed himself to a defense of poetics against history, a spirited celebration of the claims of art and poetic genius that manifested "self-consciousness" and "spirit" against the "various designs" of literary theory, especially rationalism and scientificity. His dismissal of the representational claims of history and historical consciousness was a remarkable prefiguration of Claude Lévi-Strauss's later denunciation of history as "fraudulent outline." In Kobayashi's thinking, the assault against abstraction settled on Marxism and was propelled by the conviction that theory abstracted and schematized, thus inhibiting the realization of concreteness. While this approach constituted an obvious response to the consequences of capitalist social abstraction (the regime of reification and the disappearance of the referent), it was one shared also by Marxists, who had put into question the status of referentiality in representation, only to find themselves now being condemned for sustaining the very system they hoped to destroy.[23] Hence, the target of Kobayashi's critical practice in the 1930s was clearly the specter of abstraction that had set "rational limits" on the imaginary and history and thus constrained the powers of creativity in order to project a narrative of rational (and capitalist) progress, a "fraudulent outline" that inevitably excluded what was most essential in human experience. What he favored most in these years were examples of expression that rendered concrete an individual's experience of "self-consciousness." This was best realized in the hybrid literary form called the "I-novel," which symbolized a watermark of Japan's uneven development in the interwar period. Even so, Kobayashi wanted to show that this form derived from the "social traditions of Japan" and the "traditional aesthetic sense."[24]

Kobayashi acknowledged that through a reading of Dostoyevsky, he first learned how modern Japanese critics had distorted his image. For this reason alone, he felt compelled to "return" the great writer to his original "shape." (Years later, Kobayashi would make the same declaration in the opening pages of his magnum opus on the nativist thinker Motoori Norinaga, whose figure, he believed, had been distorted and bent by historians and historicizing.) Reading Dostoyevsky apparently revealed to him the itinerary of discovery by a modern who had found the people of Russia and its spirit (*kami*) after a time of massive social upheaval. The significance of Dostoyevsky's project lay in his refusal to represent nineteenth-century Russia and the society of a modernizing Russia as his themes. Rather he was a writer who actively struggled with these subjects and won. According to Kobayashi, his books resemble a record of a war veteran who has come through combat alive and intact to tell another, truer story. Dostoyevsky demonstrated how the writer must constantly struggle with questions concerning literary and artistic vocation and determine whether literature is pledged to the task of representing society and the age or should follow an altogether different path in order to defeat both the age and society in which he lives and writes (218). Writing in the midst of a raging cultural tempest caused by Western individualism and rationalism, Dostoyevsky's great achievement was to escape the constraints of both and literally "overcome" them. Above all else, he was a Western man who warred with the West and triumphed.

At the heart of Kobayashi's refiguration of Dostoyevsky as a model of an "overcoming" and his own critique of representation was the desire to resolve the conflict between poetics (art) and history. During the conference on "Overcoming the Modern," he was able to reassure his audience that it was unimportant to worry about history or the historical conditions attending the production of a great work of art, such as Buddhist sculpture of the Kamakura period or indeed any epoch. Artworks, he announced, outlive their history to constitute a material reminder of the aura of an enduring spiritual inheritance. The sign of its inheritance was the capacity to withstand ceaseless historical change. The problem facing modern society was the fragility of representation, reflected in the claims associated with historical narrative which are always reducible to acts of interpretation. But even before the conference, in an article called "Rekishi to bungaku" a year earlier, he sought to elaborate upon the views on history he had first introduced in his work on Dostoyevsky by demonstrating that what was commonly regarded as historical consciousness failed to "touch" the heart of history. The root of the diseased conception of humanity was a modern historical consciousness that concentrated on only interpreting (representing) history as something other than what it actually was. While he aimed at Marxism in this essay, he included other "rationalistic" theories of history and historical practice committed to narrating the plot of progressive development, as well. "In every period," he wrote, "there are words that are idolized . . . and manage [to control] the intellectual world at the time. In antiquity, there was Buddhism, as well as the gods (*kami*). In the Tokugawa period, there was the word denoting 'heaven'; in eighteenth-century France, it was 'reason.' But in our age, I believe it is probably 'history.' " Recalling his own youth, Kobayashi complained that history had been badly taught; students were forced to memorize large bodies of uninteresting and trivial facts with no apparent purpose (295). But whenever there appears a failure to arouse a "healthy interest in history," which meant "sentiment toward history" (probably historical consciousness), there will be no chance to "inhale such things as the idea of *kokutai*" (296). This idea of "breathing in the national polity" can never be realized by listening to this or that person (like students listening to history lessons from a teacher) but constitutes a different form of understanding that "dwells within the recesses of love for the history of one's country." Where Kobayashi broke with Marxian and other rationalistic historical schemes was over the question of what counted as a proper historical consciousness. In the enthusiastic "welcoming" of Marxism in Japan and its privileging of an awareness of the stages of historical development (and progress) all societies must understand and follow, "honest history got lost" (296). Fraudulent outline—"tinted glasses"—prevented people from seeing anything, much less grasping the "secrets of history," and only those who possessed true awareness refused to close their eyes to the paradox.

What Kobayashi meant by "honest history," an actual history suppressed by historical schemas, was to be found in earlier writers like the twelfth-century "hermit" Yoshida Kenkō and the eighteenth-century nativist Motoori Norinaga, who were committed to speaking about only those things they were able to grasp immediately, without resorting to "devices" (*karakuki*). This "program" to rescue actual history from the iron cage of historical reason required juxtaposing the personal and direct, immediate experience of everyday life to the grand designs of an impersonal, event-driven philosophy of history filled with great men, kings, and generals—in fact to narrative itself. With this move, Kobayashi came close to constructing a critique of history mounted earlier by the native ethnologist Yanagita Kunio, who saw in history not endless linearity and seriality but timelessness and repetition. For Yanagita, as we shall see, the subject of history was custom and the folk who repetitively lived it.[25] In defining his own understanding of history, Kobayashi preferred to describe the method as "feeling with my gut." Even though it came perilously close to that sense of feeling into—*einfühlen*—hermeneutics had established as a condition of "interpretation," no world historical scheme was ever competent to incorporate as an operational procedure, much less account for those things one ordinarily feels. His program insisted on positioning the "necessity" of everyday life (which he contrasted with "historical necessity") against the vast causal networks contemporary historians and philosophers employed to understand the movement of history. Everyday life was filled with accidents, contingencies, and chance that were capable of escaping philosophies of history and all forms of emplotment and "producing a simple historical emotion" everyone was in a position to understand by virtue of their own concrete lived experience of daily life. The grief of a mother for a lost child was an event that was no less historical that never entered grand historical schemes of narrative, yet it was an emotion that all could understand at any moment. Kobayashi saw literature, which always follows nature, devoted to the vocation of transmitting this understanding of history.

Once history was seen simply as fate, the play of accident and chance, the profundity of emotion and grief expressed by a mother for the death of her child (his favorite example), then it was not really so different from nature or indeed literature. The only difference he could discern was that while nature's existence was unrelated to humans, history was impossible to make without them. In time, Kobayashi would move to assimilate history to nature altogether—to nonbeing—by reducing it to what he called a "second nature" or "tradition." History, he wrote, at about the same time in an essay on the Buddhist concept *mujō*, flees from thought that constantly strives to discover new interpretations and "comes to be reflected only [in those immutable] forms that are difficult to move the more one looks at them" (315). Interpretation, reducible to representation, simply obeyed the law of ceaseless change. Turning to Mori Ōgai's late decision to write historical biographies, he proposed that "beauty is only that which rejects interpretation and does not move" (315). Grasping the "true spirit of history" meant perceiving the fixed, unmoving forms, as he advised his fellows participants in the symposium, and required the operation of some kind of mnemonic power of recall (*omoide*), not simply remembering as one does a chronology of events recorded (*kiroku*) by historians (295, 315). Only a poetic genius like the fourteenth-century historian Kitabatake Chikafusa or the Tokugawa nativist Motoori Norinaga possessed the power of direct "intuition" and "insight" to penetrate reality. Only the poets of the *Manyō* who were "firmly embraced by the heart of history, as they were enclosed in the heart of nature," could see through the distorted explanations that "covered" human beings. But if one failed to possess such genius, it was still possible to "polish mightily the mirror of the self" in order to see the "true shape" of things (312–313). For Kobayashi, Kitabatake's imperial genealogical history was an example of history as a mirroring of the self, since its author "repeated the necessity of polishing the mirror of his own *kokoro* to understand his nature." Accordingly, he produced a historical view that was based on fixity and a sense of the "unmoved" that was empowered to reveal the "mystery" and "secrets" called the history of Japan, which has never "known how to participate in a theory of change" (313, 295).

History was not rote memorization and recording "trivial facts" on paper but rather the act of recalling an auratic experience, what Kobayashi increasingly called "commonness," the "normal," the "continuous," all covered by the word *tsunenaru* (316). In his essay "Mujō to iu koto" (1945), he confessed that the act of "recalling" relieved him from simply being one kind of animal among others, which was his way of describing historians who busily record only what they have memorized. The reason why historians obsessively record the most trivial intelligence stems from their inability to "empty their minds" to "recall." But, again, the operation of "recalling skillfully" was beyond the reach of most people, since contemporary society amply shows it had lost sight of the "common" and the "continuous." Kobayashi recognized that the vast social transformation resulting in Japan's modernity required an immense effort at social forgetting. In this process the capacity to "recall" the enduring and the continuous had been all too quickly forfeited to thoughtless amnesia. Instead of forgetting the past, people should forget the present. The immense task confronting contemporary Japanese society was how to rescue the experience of those poetic geniuses of the past who exemplified their own struggle to remember the common and the continuous. Their effort disclosed how the present might raise up from the depths of a collective being the vast structure of recollection. Kobayashi was convinced that he could perceive in those expressions of how life should be lived not simply the lived social life whose essence had never really changed, but glimpses of what had endured. Not the "places of memory," the multiple mnemonic paradise dreamed up by recent French historiography, but rather the place where a certain kind of life had been lived and the vocalization of its subsequent memory in literature. This is what Kobayashi elsewhere called the "literature of the lost home," where the site was linked to the act of expression itself, of creativity, serving as the referent for what people understood, felt, and knew, which always meant the self-conscious effort to imagine how life should be lived.

At the symposium, Kobayashi, in a self-consciously, ironic gesture, described the modern West as tragic, occupied by "elegant tragedians," while modern Japan, bent on slavishly imitating it, appeared only as comic. But, "the elegant comedians have not yet come on to the stage" (219). What he apparently was referring to was the Japanese determination, demonstrated first by naturalist writers in the first decades of the century and then by their left-wing successors, to yoke the act of literary production to social life. Even when social and historical conditions are investigated to determine how they have produced the formation of a certain kind of literature, the results never get any further than identifying the dross and wreckage the great writer has victoriously weeded and thrown out. The examination fails to grasp the spirit that has won over both history and society. Overcoming the modern, as Dostoyevsky had shown, is discovering the living effect when writers transcend their time and place. True literature, like enduring art, leaves its history and society behind, even as it marks the place of its own history.

For Kobayashi, the example of Dostoyevsky necessitated conceding to the prospect of a complete change in how history should be viewed and grasped. If modernism inspired a vision of history that privileged incessant change, ceaseless movement, and succession, was it not possible, he wondered, to envisage a history that was unchanging, static, timeless rather than timeful? Drawing upon the science of mechanics as he understood it, Kobayashi proposed that since changes in strength were called "dynamics," there should be a comparable theory called "statics" that constituted its opposite, inertial immovability. It was the singular weakness of moderns to forget about the existence of a "statics" of historical energy and to overlook the real possibility that things remain fixed, stationary, unchanged. Literature and art always appear in the form of either harmony or order, but never in one devoted to transforming power. They appear in a form that seeks to equilibrate power, not alter its properties. "Isn't it a happy circumstance," he stated, "when order and harmony are achieved by certain writers who, at odds with their times, manage to strike a balance?" (220). The occurrence of this optimal condition signifies how certain artists who have been dominated by their age are persuaded to respond to the challenge of its requirements. Great writers never bend to the demands of their age, nor do they take flight and try to separate themselves from it. They conquer it. The situation is always the same for them, as they are in a tense, staticlike relationship to their circumstances. Here, he wanted to link the great writer to the classics in both East and West. When the classics are seen from a perspective that considers history as change or progress, they will appear different from later, great writers. But the struggle between the relation of classic art and mere history has always been the same, and the artist has always confronted the prospect of overcoming history and society without taking flight from it. Humans have always been waging war, and those who have managed to "penetrate" this "thing" (the struggle between art and history), to grasp its lesson and master it, are, after all, eternal, immortal. Through this optic, Kobayashi wanted to reconfigure the relationship between history and classics in Japan, which, until the present, he remarked, had been seen as identical but were now separated.

During the discussion, Kawakami asked if "statics" should be called something like the "universal human science" rather than history, to which Kobayashi replied, "or an aesthetics." The problem was whether Kobayashi's vision of history as statics was simply another level of the historical process or an entirely different kind of consciousness separate from it. Even the greatest writers, Nishitani Keiji added, transcend history, which they simultaneously remain deeply rooted in, and this was the true meaning of the historical. People lived in the flux of change but were able to get out of its vortex. Nishitani was referring to his own conception of the subjective nothing embedded in religious sentiment that he believed was capable of supplying people the means with which to live in history at any time yet remain removed from it. This conception of subjectivity, what he called "true subjectivity," was juxtaposed to one founded on the sovereignty of the self. Nothingness (mu) did not literally mean no thing but rather conveyed the presence of a subject that did not possess something objectively, as against "an ordinary self" that is considered substantive because it possesses all things and is possessed by them. For Nishitani, perhaps Nishida Kitarō's most faithful student (Kōyama Ikuo and Kōsaka Masaaki by this time had fled to Hegel and to outright fascism), the ordinary self was mired in a world of things—history and society—which the subjective nothing has avoided because it is not constrained by possessions. As it rejects the "possessing, grabbing self," it has only "nothing" before its eyes.[26] Life can never be solely limited to acts of "possessing" and grasping things as "possessions." There is only movement, Nishitani explained, which essentially seizes the actuality of "living directly from the perspective of interior intentionality within the self itself" (24). The importance of this conception of subjectivity is that it afforded humans the possibility of transcending the mundane world of society, politics, and history and conformed closely to Kobayashi's ideal of the "eternal," the "common," and the "enduring," which also called forth associations of Yanagita Kunio's own formulation of the "eternal and abiding folk" (jōmin), whose unchanging life was known through enduring customs and practices.

While Kobayashi called Nishitani's version of history dialectical, and one that was still safely within the framework of change and movement, I think he misrecognized its powerful religious grounding and the apparent prospect of consolation it offered in its promise of transcendence. Unsurprisingly, it came close to resembling his own celebration of the static and the vision of the great artist who was able to overcome the times without fleeing them, the passive as against the active, or rethinking the passive now as active. But this solution risked encouraging the same kind of political consequences of indifference. Kobayashi was also suggesting that Nishitani's grasp of history and the historical were still founded on the presumption of change, even though his own conception appealed to a science of mechanics that still required a "statics" to complement its "dynamics." If history was historyless, without change, then what actually changed was not necessary to the true vocation of history. Kobayashi's model of mechanics produced a double-tiered history, in which change takes place at one level as certain things endure changelessly at another; only the latter qualified as actual, concrete existence, while the former remained locked in abstraction. "Bashō esteemed the word that meant 'immovable current,' " Hayashi Fusao offered as a resolution, but he reminded his audience that in the "progressivist education we've been raised in, we were taught only that things progress, change, that is, they move on and we're thus blinded from an unchanging existence. The theory of progress is the modern superstition" (221).

Still puzzled that Kobayashi named his version of the historical as immutability, Kawakami wondered if history was not simply a form of chronological seriality that identifies those who have born earlier from those who come later. Kobayashi's response was affirmative but reminded Kawakami that he had omitted "theory" (rikutsu). Reading for some time the history of Japan, he acknowledged that he had encountered only historical interpretations, views of history, representations, not history. But whatever else they are, they're all trifling and in fact worthless. He explained that he had gradually come to understand that history is not perturbed or disturbed by such things as contemporary interpretations of our contemporaries. It is necessary to first recognize that there is a beauty in history. "However we presently interpret history, evaluate it, criticize it, we are not able to reach its beauty. That history is beautiful stops [conventional] history and this means that humans who are dead ... exist in a form beyond our interpretations. The form that demonstrates this is understanding history" (222). To make this point, Kobayashi turned to one of his favorite periods in Japan's history, the Kamakura age of the twelfth and thirteenth centuries. Convinced that it was not possible to understand it in its entirety, he was also persuaded that whatever interpretation made of it, whatever the effects of the preceding Heian period on it, whatever causal explanations the historian chooses, whatever dialectical interpretation employed, the form called the Kamakura period will remain "unperturbed" by whatever good account. The time of Kamakura would always reside outside of an interpretative net, managing to escape full scrutiny, representation. Historical ages, like Mt. Fuji for painters, constitute forms that remains unchanged, unmoved, fixed, and never exhausted either by the artist's gaze or the historian's perspective. Yet, like some vast, formless pool of "magma," recalling Cornelius Castoriadis, it is capable of producing endless forms because of the power of imagination and creativity. For Kobayashi, Kamakura represented an imaginary whose contours could never fully be known. Because there still continues to exist an "unusually, great mystery," like surplus, that is not seen in historical facts, the art treasures of the Kamakura period that still remain available for contemporary viewing have an independent beauty that exceeds contemporary criticism and interpretation. "The art and emotions of the Kamakura period, its customs, thought, must be felt by me" (223). Although admittedly visionary, Kobayashi was convinced that his version of history was vastly different from a contemporary historicism that had sought to represent the "Japanese thing" in a trajectory of progressive movement and required all life to be submitted to its proper historical explanation. He compared his vision of history to Plato's conception of ideas which, he proposed, was not visionary.

According to Nishitani, those touched by the eternal in history were able to overcome a variety of circumstances and conditions peculiar to their times to encounter the eternal directly. Through the endeavor and spirit of the individual, beautiful form is imagined, created, and made. Even though this eternality appears in form and aspect, the spirit and endeavor that made them "are ours and must be maintained." Nishitani proposed that Japanese, now faced with the time of the present and needing to find a way out of it, confronted the same spirit that had created the eternal throughout history. The spirit he was referring to was the same as the one that had moved the ancients. It was a spirit that would liberate people from the constraints of temporality and the limitations imposed by place. Counseling action, doing and making rather than merely observing form and aspect, he advised following the traces pursued first by the ancients. Like earlier nativists, Nishitani now called for the effort to make the spirit of the ancients one with contemporaries. Because of its immense capacity to serve any present, it was earlier called the "immutable thing." An unchanging spirit informed Plato's thought, but it was the spirit of the person who was philosophizing and purifying the soul that explained the vast diversity of his thinking. Since the present age now confronts a variety of problems, it is important to recall the example of Plato and the informing spirit that has remained unmoved, even though it is capable of producing a diversity of ideas and solutions. "If Plato were born today," Nishitani speculated, "we can say that he probably could have constructed a different kind of philosophical vision, but it would still have been driven by the same spirit" (224). Had he lived in the present he would have struggled with it. What Nishitani's argument disclosed was a belief in the existence of eternal forms that never change, regardless of history, and how the work of an unchanging spirit is manifest in the representation of a variety of forms and aspects. He was confident that this spirit continued down to his present. It is understandable for historians to fasten their attention to movement and change and juxtapose them to the immutable that is incorporated into it. But this is not available to philosophers or writers, who are obliged to find a way that lives within them while struggling with contemporary existence. This task requires them to accomplish their projects at a level that is constantly changing within a temporality and space that is unchanging and unmoving. This seeming paradox is what Nishitani meant when he asked whether change and mutability appeared at the same moment since history could not be separated from the self because the self was always a part of it. Yet this question was satisfied by the historian Suzuki Shigetaka, who proposed that contemporary historical consciousness leaned too heavily on the side of change in accounting for shallow and superficial things but should make the effort to recover the immutable, the lasting, and unchanging. A few years earlier, the philosopher Watsuji Tetsurō named this process "doubling" (nijū seikatsu). Historians eschew progress for development but rarely pursue the question of whether or not such schemes should be overcome (230–231). For them, the goal should be no different from that pursued by writers and artists, which was to account for change and succession within a framework of fixity and immutability, within the eternal and enduring.[27]

In Kobayashi's opinion, moderns have always believed that they and their accomplishments are superior to the ancients. It would be an unfailingly modest feeling to acknowledge the impossibility of going beyond what the ancients had accomplished. But he was fearful of detecting an unwillingness to do so among his contemporaries, who stubbornly clung to the meaningless presumption that living in their present was better than living in a past time. Because men live in a present, they believe they are required to open up a different place for themselves. The conceit of superiority and originality must be contrasted to the work of truly great artists from past times, who have never suffered from excessive self-adulation. The mark of a great writer like the poet Masaoka Shiki, for example, is the absence of this conceit that puts his moment over the past but manages to disclose at the same time the presence of genuine modesty and humility when confronting the poems of the Manyōshū. Shiki, according to Kobayashi, always used these ancient poems as his standard before embarking upon his own poetic project. His work brilliantly demonstrated the "classic within the classic" (226). Yoshimitsu Yoshihiko reiterated for the symposium the necessity to get beyond modern interpretative modes such as theories of "biological progress." "In the spiritual world," he asserted, "the philosophy of 'progress' is clearly a lie" (228). The reason for this is the 'reality' of spirit, which is beyond proof. Owing to the reality of spirit's existence, its "self-affirmation as reality" intersects with history at the level of faith and belief. History is not meaningless. By reason of the traces spirit deposits and leaves behind on its itinerary, we will suffer the same pain it experienced when it made these conditions. For Yoshimitsu, this was simply another way of recommending to moderns that they should recognize the necessity of following in the tracks of the ancients and the impossibility of trying to separate contemporary life from the effort to locate the archaic (229). "Being touched honestly by the ancient path," Nishitani explained, "begins with walking on the road of the self by oneself" (229). Similarly, if humans are able to exclude all of the diverse encumbrances of social life and truly seek and reach the honest forms of actuality (*genjitsu*), they will grasp the beautiful (230). It is important to note that in making this statement that equated the beautiful with "actuality," Kobayashi was appealing to an already well established discursive convention of the times that had pitted the "actual," conveying the association of the "concrete," against the nominally real, the everyday life of the present (*genzai*), which was seen as abstract, formless, mutable. The evil that must be thrown out is the view that tries to reach the real through the "schematization and mapping of an expanding history or sense of reality that jams the head of modern man to the utmost" (230). Where there is sometimes a sense of wonder and at other times respect, there is neither temporality nor development. Artistic creativity is found where history now occupies the domain of the classic; inspired by encountering the traces of the ancients as a standard to follow, it is without temporality or any hint of development. Even among ordinary folk, the experience of appreciating the classics teaches this truth. Echoing his contemporary, the native ethnologist Orikuchi Shinobu who had already named folkloric studies (*minzokugaku*) as the "classics of life," timeless and always, already there, Kobayashi was convinced that this recognition was the "experience of our everyday life." Here, he came closest to both contemporary folklorists and cultural theorists (not to mention Marxists like Tosaka Jun) who had already formulated a poetics of daily life in contrast to the everyday life that was being lived and experienced under capitalism, one that was still, imbued with form, timeless, immutable, and nondevelopmental, as against a bristling and noisy life of movement and the ceaseless succession of time, activity, and formlessness—a life, as Kamei Katsuichirō put it, that was viewed from the window of a fast-moving train.

If representation and the schematic emplotment of historical progress failed to express adequately the Japanese spirit or identify the eternal and immutable within temporal development, then it appeared necessary to find a ground that would secure for society an anchor in an ever-changing present, an "actuality" that would guarantee that what was seen as an ineffable and irreducible endowment would not be assimilated to capitalist abstraction. This was, of course, the immense purpose assigned to a program of "overcoming the modern." Increasingly, the program pointed to digging deep into the native soil of cultural difference to find a collective experience capable of distantiating the modern without abandoning it altogether. Clearly, the symposium's agenda and the subsequent discussions were driven by a recognizable modernist concern for the nature of the artwork, culture, concreteness against abstraction, representation as a distorted other of pure practice, mystery, creativity, beauty, and origins, these latter necessitating the identity of memorative communication in the struggle with a degraded, performative present. Yet it is difficult not to recognize in this vast, holy grail-like quest that all of the weighty concerns were being discussed in an environment that scarcely acknowledged the existence of a war that was being waged outside of Japan (even though the conference was called to discuss the meaning of the war in relation to Japan's modernity), and that a history of imperial expansion, not necessarily Japan's modernity, had brought the country to this moment. Only the film critic Tsumura Hideo, in his supplementary essay, referred to the current situation when he proclaimed that war would necessarily result in global reordering and the establishment of new cultural and political spheres in Europe and East Asia. For him, the war was clearly provoked by Anglo-American capitalism, and victory would promise to bring a new economic system based on "things" rather than "money" and thus destroy the "poisonous materialist civilization" founded on the international domination of Jewish financial capitalist power. The war would make possible the achievement of an even greater and "healthy life of the races" and ultimately eliminate the corrosive "Americanism" that had held Japan in its thrall since the 1920s, a "demon power" whose values should be eliminated (129).

While the symposium was constrained from saying anything critical about the causes of the war and its subsequent conduct, it is still surprising to recognize, save Tsumura's paranoid and racist outburst, that no mention was made of the event raging on in the Pacific. To be sure, the idea of overcoming could be read allegorically or simply as a displacement for a war most believed was being fought against the imperialism of materialist civilization and the "demon power" of Americanism. In many ways, the symposium was a continuation, by other means, of the struggle against an everyday life introduced by capitalist modernization that had been fiercely contested since the 1920s by all kinds of social and cultural theorists, writers, and thinkers, who saw in its growing hegemony both a dilution and diminution of an essential cultural endowment. But that phase of the struggle had been fought primarily by middle-class intellectuals, who had, it seems, already forfeited any role as agents in the political process in order to serve the higher vocation of cultural custodianship against what they feared was the proletarianization of culture. By the time the symposium met, the target had shifted to the globe, to the great imperial democracies of the United States and Great Britain. Perhaps these provided the sign of modernity itself for Japanese, and the world histori- cal mission aimed at eliminating the centers of industrial capital that pro- duced the poisonous leveling and homogenizing that had seized hold of Japanese society since the end of World War I. It was for this reason that the symposium, like the modernism of the preceding two decades, put into question both the reliability of all those modes of representation that presumed to speak for the ineffable but merely managed to miss it in the rush to signify the timely, and the history that supplied a narrative of progress in which the spirit no longer played a recognizable role.

To solve the problem of representation, the symposium ultimately sought to identify a general ground that promised to resist the challenge posed by material civilization inscribed in the routines of modern, every- day life. Thus might they remove the fear that Japanese would disappear into that large, boundless realm of sameness called modernity. What parti- cipants offered as an "overcoming" was a rediscovery of the classics, the return of the gods and, with Nishitani, a new kind of subjectivity that owed as much to modern philosophy as it did to Buddhist metaphysics. Whether the symposium was appealing to rootedness or transcendence, it came down to the same thing. The recovery of the archaic traces was really no different from the return to some form of religiosity that prom- ised immunity from the present in transcendence or even Hayashi Fusao's quixotic reclamation of the "spirit of imperial loyalism" that had moti- vated Restoration heroes like Saigo Takamori. The symposium seemed to agree that a return to the classics would lead to a reencounter with the Japanese spirit (264). Kobayashi acknowledged that he now felt a great shame for an early, youthful infatuation with French novels (even though his conception of time, history, and memory owed much to Bergson and Proust) and American films but recently had begun to understand classic Japanese texts like the "Histories" (*kiki*, denoting the *Kojiki* and *Nihon- shoki*) and the *Manyōshū*. The poet Miyoshi Tatsuji, who also wrote a supplementary essay on the classics and the Japanese spirit, believed that even though the Ministry of Education had taken up the classics as a subject for instruction, the troubling problem had always been the ab- sence of any genuinely consistent and continuous program to teach them. Miyoshi rejected, *tout court*, any effort to reintroduce the classics to "cor- respond to the state of things" as they existed and called this an unwanted "accommodationism" (265, 266). Understanding the classics, according to Kawakami, meant gradually portraying the image of humanity firmly, as if it was finally engraved in the mind's eye. But returning to the classics to grasp the original spirit of Japan also risked slipping into an uncritical celebration of wonder and mystery, an unrational knowledge, if not slid- ing into the irrational itself, which some in the symposium were quite willing to express (191). It was, in any case, Kamei who historicized this reclaiming of the classics despite Miyoshi's warning against accommodationism that made their recall a momentary experience. "Since the China Incident" (a euphemism for the war in China), he reported, "there has been a cry for a Restoration of the Japanese spirit," and this has meant "reading the classics more widely. But will this bring [us] direct relief from the modern?" (201).

By putting the question in this way, Kamei could explain his doubts about the usefulness of the project of introducing the classics compared with the utility of restoring a sense of faith and belief. Returning to the classics for spiritual meaning and nourishment was apparently the same as expressing a yearning for magic and mystery in science (191, also the discussions of Shimomura and Yoshimitsu, 192–193, 194). For Kamei, the disappearance of faith and belief marked the modern loss of the gods, which had originated with the incorporation of the Greek (Western) myth of Prometheus's theft of fire from the gods. Since this archetypal episode, gods and men have been locked in a continual struggle, with humans using science and technology as their weapons (199–201). Nothing seemed further from the mythic narratives of the Japanese than this Western story of an inaugural breech between humans and their gods and the ensuing struggle. In Japan, the gods struggled only with other gods. In this discussion, Hayashi was not alone in equating the Promethean myth with a separation of culture from nature; the gods represented nature while humans broke away from their dependence, armed themselves with fire power, and went on to create culture. The Japanese myths identified the gods with nature, which was given to humans as a gift they were obliged to repay by cultivating the land and reproducing the conditions of existence for each generation. What was primary in this relationship between the Japanese and their gods was the recognition of reciprocity (repaying the blessings of the gods), not struggle and competition, founded on the human willingness to submit to the divine dictates of the gods.

Kamei saw the problem of modern disbelief, stemming from decades of confusion, as the principal cause of widespread misery among humans who "have been exiled from the gods" (200). Reviewing the life led by Japanese in the 1920s and 1930s, he concluded that these decades were characterized by an experience of disbelief. Why he distrusted the return to the classics as a solution to the contemporary problem of the modern reflected his own conviction that this kind of activity tended to dissolve into mere interpretation and representation, rather than supplying a course of action. Belief and faith, on the other hand, were never matters of interpretation but rather significations of acceptance and even resignation. Kamei, like so many of contemporaries, saw modern life as a vast prison (in some instances it was also seen as a madhouse) where the inmates, the Japanese, could no longer communicate either with each other or with the world of nature and their gods. Since, as he believed, contemporary Japanese had lost contact with their deities, he was equally sure that an overcoming could be accomplished by returning to a belief in the *kami*. To this declaration of faith, Nakamura Mitsuo added that it was not simply enough just to believe, but also important that one live their faith and see the gods in their self, "experiencing and seeing [them] in one's hand" (203).

Where Kamei and others looked to a return of faith in the old religious practices of the Japanese, in the gods, Nishitani Keiji saw religion (like Yoshimitsu) as the "absolute ground" (*zettaina mono o tatte*) and thus the place that marked where humans "mourn for the powerlessness of the self" (192). It was the nonself derived from Buddhism—the no-thing opposed to the I—that constituted the true subjectivity Japanese should embrace in this critical time. For Nishitani, the subject was able to receive genuine release from the world of things through transcendence offered by the absolute. Indeed, the absolute constituted a clear rejection of the world of culture itself. It was, he wrote, "a religious freedom, a complete freedom from the world" (25). Freedom of this kind was found in "Oriental religions" and constituted an "Oriental freedom" that was capable of resolving the troubling problems of science and culture because the act of transcending the self-righteous self, the obsessive awareness associated with modern subjectivity, will establish an inseparable bond between the natural world and the body, the heart and its cultural realm. The religiosity of the subjective nothing, Nishitani cautioned, is never easy to attain but nevertheless "permeates actual existence and thus conforms to a national ethical intention which is the unique condition of Japan." If it was not exactly a return to the gods, it was still a reunion of the self with the ground of nonbeing, nature.

Regardless of Nishitani's slip into exceptionalism, he was expressing a sentiment shared by most of the participants that already had been revealed in the discussions on the specialization of knowledge. The various appeals to the classics, the gods, and religious subjectivity establishing real difference promised, it was believed, the prospect of leading to a new kind of human (actually Japanese) that was whole, complete, undivided, who would, in turn, make up for the lack and incompleteness attributed to, if not lived and suffered by, Japanese and Asians by a putative universalism whose claimants proclaimed both completion and coherence. It was this Western misrecognition that fueled the symposium's desire for an overcoming that might achieve an image of modernity that was itself a substanceless fantasy (yet gave credence to some of its critique) of a modernity made in the West. At the same time, we must always balance the intellectual passion of this critical practice with the symposium's refusal to engage the status of Japan's war in and against Asia and the particular form of modernity its armies were forcibly imposing on subject peoples who had just recently been liberated from White Man's imperialism. One of the immense paradoxes of the symposium was how this blindness to its present—the war and Japan's conduct in Asia—seemingly served as the enabling condition to revisit the past of their present, which was supposed to illuminate the path to overcoming it. But instead of leading to a restored past in the present, it disclosed the figure of a future yet to come that would exceed both past and present in its will to modernity.

It is, nevertheless, important to point out that the very critique mounted by Japanese against modernity prefigured precisely all of those doubts and obsessions concerning subjectivity, cultural difference, and even racism that have become the signatures of a Western and putatively global discourse that marks our own historical conjuncture today, almost sixty years after the symposium first raised them in a different context.[28]

But even if the symposium found itself locked in a fantasy inspired by Western misrecognition and the dilemma of overcoming an overcoming, it is still important to recognize that it looked back upon more than two decades of meteoric eventfulness to discover what another modernist, James Joyce, writing in the first decade of the twentieth century, had already grasped as the effort to escape a nightmare that was history. Instead of restoring what had been forgotten or lost, what the poet Hagiwara Sakutarō described as "forfeiture," rescuing the old as a temporality within modernity, or even inventing the loss of a "found" object to orchestrate nostalgia, the symposium merely overdetermined the memory of the past of capitalist modernization and the vast material and spiritual transformation lived and experienced by Japanese and what lay in store for them in the unenvisaged future. It had narrativized precisely the eventfulness it wished to overcome and managed to reaffirm the historicity it promised to eliminate. The only destination reached by the symposium on overcoming modernity was the place where Japan itself had been overcome by modernity.

CHAPTER 3

Perceiving the Present

THE PROMISE OF "MODERN LIFE"

At the same moment that popular discourse exploded in new media like film, mass-circulating magazines, opinion journals, radio, and newspapers to figure and fantasize the new everydayness that was being installed in Japan's larger cities in the 1920s, thinkers, social researchers, and critics were busily involved in envisioning the experience of modernity and its constituent elements—speed, shock, sensation, and spectacle—through an optics that produced differing effects according to the angle of the lens through which experience was being refracted. These refractions distilled certain intensities in the experience of modern life and privileged others to present a vision of everyday life that was both enabling for the present and promising for a future as of yet unenvisaged. What is important about this activity is the way it centered the category of everyday life—its performativity in the present—as the informing principle of modern life. It made it both a condition of social research and critique and the occasion for looking to a new social and political imaginary in the future. Far from imagining everyday life as a source of negativity and mediocrity, as Martin Heidegger was already formulating in *Sein und Zeit* (1926), thinkers as diverse as Kon Wajirō and Tosaka Jun saw in the performance of the everyday an escape from a binding past that still managed to lay claim on the present and the full promise of modern life—including the hope for a better future.

We must, in any case, try to account for this overwhelming, almost overdetermined, interest in and enthusiasm for everydayness in the 1920s and 1930s when, according to Kon, Europeans had not yet focused on this dimension of modern life. While this assessment was not entirely true and might easily be taken as an expression of self-aggrandizement employed to make Kon's own program (called "modernology") of studying everyday life appear unique and original, it is, nonetheless, one of the interesting problems of Japan's modern history that so many thinkers were intensely concerned with the status of everydayness—a concern that often matched and even frequently exceeded European considerations. In Europe, concern for everyday life after World War I was dominated by the work of two thinkers, Georg Lukacs and Heidegger, in the shadow of

Max Weber's meditations on the identity of modern society. Lukacs had powerfully formulated the way in which the commodity form mediated social relationships and the consequences of its effects for producing a "reification of social life." Heidegger had reduced *alltagslichkeit* to the mediocre world of the They (*das Man*)—the domain of complete negativity—and insisted on returning to the temporality of Being's "authentic historicality." Heidegger's conception of inauthenticity was thoroughly dehistoricized, as Lukacs's understanding of reification was deeply embedded in a particular history of the capitalist present that marked, historically, its production. Even so, they were talking about the same kind of social formation. Among thinkers of the beleaguered Frankfurt School, there were attempts by Walter Benjamin and Siegfried Kracauer, especially, to imagine the role played by everyday life in mass society and advanced capitalism. But this intervention, which undoubtedly aimed at countering the negativity associated with everyday life, often shared Heidegger's dim estimate of the masses and its consequences for both culture and politics. Kracauer's brilliant essays on everyday life and his critique of the German white-collar class (*Die Angeststellten*, 1930) went a long way to simply confirming the effects of commodification on the masses and its political and cultural consequences for producing spiritual "homelessness," while only Benjamin seemed willing to envisage a new historical materialist program that could acknowledge the existence of alienation in the everyday brought on by commodification and routine yet at the same time see in it the "mystery" of genuine possibility. If Marxism in general remained slow to respond to the category of experience in modern life, owing to the confidence invested in analyzing systems and structures, even Frankfurt Marxism shied away from everydayness in favor of an overwhelming concern that expressed a fear and distrust of the masses and the new culture industry. In short, their work reflected more conservative misgivings that had already been articulated by thinkers and writers during the decades of the twenties and thirties. During Italy's fascist regime, Antonio Gramsci worked out a conception of common sense and ordinary culture that closely resembled the everyday world and its difference from modernity. And in the Soviet Union, at the moment Trotsky was complaining how the daily life of workers had become commodified, constructivists like Boris Arvatov were trying to conceptualize a socialist everydayness that would make the consumer into a subject free from the commodity fetish by transforming objects into use-value.[1]

Japan perhaps came closer to the Soviet experience of seeing the everyday as the site for utopian aspiration. But this is not to say that there weren't Japanese who, following Heidegger's lead, sought to forget about the performative present altogether in favor of recalling an indeterminate past. Thinkers like Yanagita Kunio, Watsuji Tetsurō, and Kuki Shūzō, as I hope to show, tried mightily to offer what they believed to be a more enduring and less dangerous alternative to the new everydayness being lived and fantasized in the cities; they sought a theory of cultural reproduction that would check the production of the new culture based on things and consumption rather than custom and value. With their call to memory of a past age or in their move to poeticize a mode of existence, they appealed to cultural forms and practices that claimed for themselves an as yet unrealized sociotemporality outside of a temporal and temporalizing present. To offset a present that alone gave direction to history, they recalled a historical reason that already prefigured the whole history of the race from past to present and forged, therefore, an abstract and fictive continuity between then and now. The strength of this philosophically bankrupt archaism, as it was called by Tosaka Jun (and recently articulated in a critique by the contemporary Italian philosopher Gianni Vattimo that often resembles Tosaka's earlier view), is manifest in its capacity to persist down to the present, well after the historical crisis that produced it, and is still expressed in all of those attempts to show that no fundamental difference separates the Japanese of today from their Stone Age predecessors.

Yet, the Japanese, when contrasted to Europeans, seemed more enthusiastic about the promise offered by the new everydayness and thus willing to explore the possibility of newness for a life vastly different from the one most recently lived in the immediate past. New social constituencies and subject positions like the people (*minshū*), the masses (*taishū*), the modern boy (*mobo*), modern girl (*mogarū*), cafe waitress, bar maid, and so on, validated by recently introduced commodities people were encouraged to buy and use, called attention to a new kind of social life in Japan for the first time in its history, sometimes called *modan raifu* or simply *seikatsu*. What distinguished this conception of modern life, as we have already seen, was its materiality and its embeddedness in a culture of objects and their circulation. Its very materiality—its embeddedness in objects and their circulation—constituted the sign of a historicity of the present, its historical moment, the temporality of modernity. The question that thinkers tried to answer related to the givenness of the historical present and how it showed itself as present. But what the now of the present offered was little more than a minimal unity empowered to organize the experience of the everyday. That is to say, to speak of the present, as against merely the modern—the regime of the new—denoted the unification of a multiplicity of givens in a minimal unity of meaning. Moreover, it was a unity in time, marked by a kind of synthesis of apprehension, reproduction, and recognition, what Kantians called the "synthetic unity of experience." And this minimal unity of the present, however precarious, was increasingly seen by thinkers as the actual and unavoidable experience of everydayness which everywhere in the industrializing world—colonized and noncolonized—was identified with the distinctively modern, even though it sheltered a difference from the merely new.

When Tosaka proposed that everyday life provided the principles to organize both time and space, or Gonda Yasunosuke declared that people's pleasure derived from the experience of everydayness, or Kon Wajirō insisted on seeing daily life and its transactions in home and on the streets as the source of subjectivity, we are confronted with not the simple expression of enthusiasm for the newness of "modern life" but with the conviction of what this new life had come to mean for Japanese living in a present they saw constantly opening up to a completed future. A partial explanation of this inordinate emphasis on everyday life, I believe, lies in the discovery of a personal and private world of experience available to large numbers of people for the first time in history now being installed in the 1920s and immediately juxtaposed to the public world of state and social system.

For many thinkers, the new culture of the people promised rationality and efficiency, not to mention accessibility and availability, what Hirabayashi Hatsunosuke celebrated as the scientific method in everyday life. Before, rationalization had been restricted to the state and public realm. In fact most thinkers could agree that rationalization in the register of everyday life called for a remodeling, what contemporaries called a "reconstruction" (*kaizō*), of custom especially, and of those conditions of social life associated with shelter, clothing, and food. Without the rationalization of the "means of life" (Kon's words) and "life attitudes" linked to institutions implicated in everyday life, there could be no chance for the development of a democratic subject.[2] Modern custom announced rationality and the coming regime of rational expectations when people would be in a position to know what choices to make for themselves. (By end of the decade, Aono Suekichi was reporting how the Japanese white-collar class had exceeded its capacity to satisfy such rising expectations and was collapsing into psychological malaise.) The appearance of modern life was seen as rational, efficient, and even scientific, requiring at all times the steady flow and circulation of information and knowledge. It was for this reason that thinkers like Tosaka naively invested so much confidence in new modes of communication like journalism, newspapers, magazines, and reportage. The opening of the decade of the 1920s was greeted with optimistic calls for the establishment of "cultural living" (*bunka seikatsu*) by enthusiasts like Morimoto Atsuyoshi, who quickly identified the modern with the prospect of "rational, efficient living." For Japanese this meant the possibility of rationalizing those segments of life that had remained outside of the modernizing process.[3] Everydayness was increasingly understood as that surplus left over from the public realm, the residue left behind by an official public domain of state and society that had no everyday, no place for its experience, no room in the officially sanctioned separation of public and private realms and its metonymical mode of relating. But if it was a product of a leftover that exceeded the boundaries of more formal categories like public and private (already marked off in the Meiji Civil Code), it was considered by many as a space in its own right, a spatial category—what Tosaka called "everyday space" (*nichijō kūkan*)—that housed the new experience of living in the Now on the streets recorded by people like Kon Wajirō and Gonda Yasunosuke. The identity of this new space characterized by the experience of everyday life posed a challenge to both received social relationships and the tidy (and officially ideologized) organization of society into public and private (state and civil society) that delegated duties and determined conduct and behavior. For some, transforming the experience of everydayness to conform more closely to the requirements of rationality constituted the principal condition for remodeling society itself and altering the received political and social relationships in the name of science.

If the discourse on modernity was constituted in new media and necessarily overdetermined certain objects and images, social thinkers drew upon this vast inventory to imagine and figure a new reality they hoped would be lived and experienced more intensely, permeating all sectors of Japanese society. Although the new "modern life" was identified principally with the large cities, few denied that it would become ubiquitous in the near future. This recognition of the power of everyday life to expand and reach every corner of the country explains why so many thinkers were committed to seeing it as the basis of a new social body; it also explains why so many turned away from the present to find lasting alternatives in the construction of fixed conceptions of community and culture. Yet the first impulse in the 1920s and early 1930s was to take stock of the experience and determine what it meant for society and its future. As a result, the "experience" inscribed in the discourse on everyday life was inflected in such a way as to supply the raw material for producing a secondary revision capable of imaging the social totality. Thinkers and writers, usually progressives and Marxian, saw in the new configuration the occasion to evaluate its key imaginary dimensions such as custom, the people, and the masses; they saw it as the starting point for envisioning a new kind of human order that might yield the prospect of a better life. The idea of a better life retained the faith in rationality and science but in time developed a political purpose that took precedence and began to visualize new forms of political society. More often than not, this impulse exaggerated the crucial role to be played by science in the construction of a new social and political order for the masses. But what seemed to link a diversity of thinkers, writers, and social researchers in a common effort was the belief that what lay before them was still unfinished and incomplete, despite the worrisome effects of capitalism such as alienation, consumption, and commodification. In this regard they were convinced that they were responding to the demands of a historical conjuncture marked by the advent of new social imaginaries like the people and the masses, their lives, needs, and desires, and that in meeting the requirements of this conjuncture—submitting to its historical necessity—they were imagining how modernity might be completed. Above all else, they recognized the importance of new customs, new social relationships, new forms of work and leisure, and new patterns of consumption as the basis of both a proper social science founded on observation and critique, and a program of social construction.

What this program entailed was a confrontation with the phenomenological present and a recognition that the everydayness of *modan raifu* was, at its center, colonized by the commodity form and its effects. Both its capacity to conceal (and thus induce social forgetting), its enabling conditions of production, and its aptitude for interpellating consumers revealed its role in making the everyday the space of differing historical temporalizations. At the same time the everyday became the only place for producing anew the redemptive power associated with tradition in the time of modernity. If the commodity form produced the ever new in the ever same, thus "atrophying experience," it would yield the necessary difference to transform the empty, homogenous time of the Now. It should be recalled that progressive thinkers like Tosaka and even Kon opposed the Now to the present, rather than past to present. The distinction derived from a prior phenomenological classification that differentiated the "present" from the now of immediate experience, what Benjamin once described as the "now of recognizability." In this formulation, the present was seen as belonging to the order of history, whereas the now was the lived moment. Deciphering "social hieroglyphics" for the social and historical character of the labor that produced them as objects that became commodities, while putting into question the very history they were made to have consumers forget, Japanese thinkers envisaged an everyday world filled with alienation brought on by routine yet still filled with possibility, the different in the same: the place of transformation. Social thinkers were thus left with the choice of finding a way to break through the commodity form that dominated modern life either to restore its forgotten history (Gonda), or to show how consumption was actually constitutive of a new subject capable of making choices for the first time (Kon), or to transform the daily objects in order to release a new aesthetic consciousness (Murayama), or to conceptualize it into a space that structured its temporality into accumulative layers that could only be disturbed by exploring the possibilities they offered at any given moment (Tosaka). This revolution came from *within* modernity, neither from the kind of repetition of custom or cultural stratigraphy envisaged by Yanagita Kunio and Watsuji Tetsurō, nor from an unrealized social and cultural form that the present had forgotten, as "recalled" by Kuki Shūzō and Kobayashi Hideo. Whether it was the Marxist critic Hirabayashi Hatsunosuke calling for the establishment of a new mass culture or a "culture of feminism," Tosaka Jun rethinking the relationship among custom, morality, and everyday life and finally defining everydayness as a spatial category that contained historical temporality comparable to the laws governing physical space, or Kon Wajirō, standing on Ginza street corners to put into practice a new discipline devoted to studying the modern (*kōgengaku*), this secondary revision upheld the claims of modernity as the product of a determinate history directed only by the present and a different temporality that would, according to stages of development, ultimately yield hitherto unimagined new forms of human existence and experience for Japan's masses. In this regard, the heady optimism manifest in the powers of the modern evoked—if not aped—the atmosphere of the carnivalesque. In this it recalled both M. M. Bakhtin's conception of how everyday life is capable of exploding into utopian aspiration, that is, the experience of Soviet Russia in the 1920s which produced this Bakhtinian inflection, and the enthusiasm for artistic and cultural experimentation that momentarily offered a glimpse of an unfulfilled future. In fact, Japanese in the 1920s were driven to see in the hard commodification of life the promise and design of an even more human order reached not by overcoming modernity (which in the late 1930s was nothing more than an escape route to a national fantasy) but being overcome by it, by bringing it to completion.

THROUGH THE "PRISM OF THE MACHINE"

Nowhere was this more true than in the writings of Murayama Tomoyoshi (1901–1977), an artist, sometime admirer of Italian futurism, filmmaker, and dramatist who appealed to "constructivism" as a program that promised to bring about a reconstruction leading to a completion of Japan's modernity. Murayama was involved in a number of projects during the 1920s after he returned from Europe and was one of the founders of MAVO, a gallery and society directed to presenting an avant garde artistic program through staging exhibitions that were deeply implicated in constructivism.[4] Anxious to account for both the intense industrialism that had taken hold of Japanese society after World War I and the hegemony of "bourgeois art," Murayama proposed that "constructivism" had surfaced in the Soviet Union with the "destruction of capitalist society" and the establishment of an "order where socialist art, proletarian art would become the unrivaled sphere of activity."[5] Murayama was apparently attracted by the recognition that bourgeois artists, who had played no role in the revolution, showed no "pity" for the passing of an older culture. Instead, they saw the moment only as one where art had ended. Artists who no longer hoped to return to the art of the old period took a "great leap" toward industrialism. "Painting as communists, a plaything ended with the New Economic Policy" (GKKG 59). "It was," he announced, "a Copernican Revolution from the standpoint of form and art and constituted the spark plug for the unprecedented planning to inaugurate an art of new productive organization." Constructivism showed how and why art, rooted in an industrial system, should have a social character, the very objects that were colonizing everyday life, like "post cards, stamps, umbrellas, ties, chairs, futon, handkerchiefs, towels"—all functional things—can be enjoyed as art. In fact, these objects that inhabited the space of everyday life and were used daily necessarily possessed both use-value and artistic value, signifying the necessarily identity between life and art, rather than its separation when such objects are removed from the aesthetic domain. Murayama derisively called attention to "priests of art" who maintained skills devoted to constructing things without art and viewed them as obstructionists. Art for art's sake, which had dominated the conventions of bourgeois art, had to be destroyed completely, something the Russian Revolution made possible. "Productivism," he wrote, "proclaims a complete war with pure art. It buries individualism in art and calls for the collective" (59). More importantly, it announces that an art lacking practicality does not qualify as art. Constructivism was formed in a productivist environment and immediately met the requirements of a new political and cultural order.

Murayama plainly recognized the new hegemony of industrial society—what he called productivism—and its profound implications for art and culture. While refraining from calling outright for a revolution in Japan, he saw industrial society as the wave of the future and the end of capitalist social relations. Communism, he insisted, maintains, above all else, the "social character" of art. In the present, marked by an individualism dissolving into anarchism, new modes of artistic production are appearing that clearly are purposeless. The reason for this unhappy state stems from the defect of "separating" new modes of art "from reality" that disposes them to "subjectively construct forms"(60). Convinced that artistic subjectivism signified an "illusion" produced by a tendency to absolutely elevate aesthetic formalism and abstraction over any other consideration, Murayama observed how easily artists fall into a "boasting" self-praise that places the self at the center of existence, which is clearly contrary to society. It is important to recognize in this passage an early concern for abstraction and formalism and the primacy of the individual self, which later critiques would make as the centerpiece of critical practice aimed at Marxism and its own failure to produced a science of the concrete. In the early 1930s, as we shall see, writers like Kobayashi Hideo denounced Marxism precisely for its reliance on abstract categories and formulaic and schematic thinking removed from everyday life. With thinkers like Murayama, the machine constituted the concrete subject of everydayness because it was authorized by a social reality dominated by productivism. For many thinkers, later, modernity itself, the substitution of the machine for (human) spirit, was the abstraction, removed from the vital forces and experiences of the Japanese folk.

In Murayama's account, constructivism as a strategy employed to implement productivist requirements was identical with life. What a productivist society demands is an environment for "creating functional forms socially, produced from pure, objective methods, that would correspond to the social whole (sōtai)," free from the "selfish, accidental mood of the individual" and its "subjective (shukanteki) taste." It is important to note, in this regard, that Murayama's designation of "subjective" as shukanteki suggests an identification with passivity, nonaction, the observing subject, instead of the acting subject (shutai). Aiming to remove all signs of the subjective individual in the production of art, who would automatically be driven to make things according to personal taste, Murayama was convinced that this distraction could be avoided by privileging the primacy of the social collective. But this idea did not necessarily mean shifting the site of subjectivity to the people, the minshū. Rather, the location of subjectivity seemed to hover somewhere between the social collectivity, represented by the indeterminate masses, and the machine. For the constructivist program, what counted was the decision to "utilize diverse materials for art, manufactured technically, drawn from the natural world" (60). Yet such a move was never intended to imitate nature or cope with the natural world. Nature was seen as merely a large reservoir that supplied raw materials for human production; it could not be considered either as a model for society or as a domain that needed to be distanced. Out of the diverse materials made available by nature, it was simultaneously necessary to shape the objects of actual life for human use. While emphasizing the necessity of submitting to the laws stipulated by the peculiar properties of raw materials, the creation of art in determinate forms passes through the mediation of social utility. The task of constructivism in the new society, as Murayama saw it, recalling the meditations of Boris Arvatov, was to make socially useful objects that were also beautiful, whose value, nevertheless, was determined by their utility rather than their capacity to pose as commodities for exchange. Constructivism represented "one kind of social organization" devoted entirely to the "art of cooperation." "It is the things people eat and drink" (60).

But the principal characteristic of the new social order Murayama was conceptualizing, and thus its subject, was its passion and love for the machine. "Constructivists like Hans Arp and El Lissitzky saw this age and society through the prism of industry. Far from trying to impart an illusion on canvas with the help of colors, they used and worked with glass, steel, and wood; their near sight saw only the [figure of the] machine in these materials" (62). For communists, especially, the "machine was the god of rescue bringing forth the ideal society of surplus production" (61). Nothing symbolized more the departure from the past than the appearance of the machine, which had no need to "drag out traditions summoned by amateurish [and dilettantish] tastes that were [supposedly] delicate and refined." Murayama pointed instead to the necessity of "loving the beauty of the bluntly courageous machine" (61). (Here he closely resembled the delirious futuristic celebrations of Marinetti.) The presence of the machine pointed to an organization devoted to realizing a program of practical utility connected to the requirements of industrialism itself. But it is important to suggest, in this connection, that he earlier (1920) had made a point of distinguishing his brand of constructivism from the Soviet inflection. Called "conscious constructivism" (*Bewusste Konstruktionismus lishikikoseishugi*), his brand was powered by the "pursuit of a higher unity" that sought to resolve the "rivalry" between subjective conceptions of beauty and its opposite—ugliness. Convinced that a supreme effort of the self had to be made, Murayama, in a later reflection, acknowledged that while his study of Marxism and the workings of the dialectic had "cooled within himself," even "conscious constructivism" would fail to realize its program of tearing down existing structures as long as it remained locked in the prison of idealism. What was needed, above all else, was a thoroughgoing materialism which even Marxism, in the early 1920s, was apparently turning away from for what appeared to many as an idealistic (Lukacsian and Hegelian) theory of cultural form.

In any event, the promise of constructivism lay in its capacity to unify mathematics and art, artistic labor and the factory. Eschewing the importance of the "plan," which simply was a romantic hangover that, by looking to the past, it inspired only the most personal fantasies, constructivism derived its inspiration from the present through its encounter with industry, technology, and science (63). It borrows tools and materials used in the industrial process, such as cylinders, steel, glass, concrete, spheres, and triangles, and derides the beautiful to seek life stimulated by strength, clarity, and brains: thus the "mechanization of art and thereby life itself." In such a society, marked by the "constant cooperation" of the masses and equality everywhere, the artisanal products of individuals would appear as "medieval," "bourgeois," "unnecessarily extravagant," and totally inappropriate for the present. Murayama looked for the identity of mass society and the productive system in the processes of quantification. Nothing was outside quantity production in this area, he insisted, pointing to how large numbers of people were drawn into concentrated spaces, invariably reproducing the example of the factor that had managed to assemble numerous workers under a single roof. Quoting with approval from Romain Rolland's *Theory of Mass Art* that "a painting without walls to hang on is painting while one hanging on walls is not painting," Murayama wanted to emphasize the necessity of putting art at the disposal of the masses rather than cloistering it in confined museums serving only the few. Quantified production meant increased numbers of people embracing the mechanization of art, an art that was found everywhere in objects people used in everyday life. Here, he was calling attention not merely to the more familiar observation concerning the mechanical reproduction of art but rather to a mechanization of life that put useful things that were also beautiful at the disposal of the masses. Yet, Murayama was clearly referring also to the representation of this "mechanizing" process in printing, photography, and film—all signs of mass society, mechanical reproduction, and the reproduction of quantity. Printing especially imparted the image of a "new life," not just in its infinite capacity to reproduce sentences on a page and pictures of paintings, but also in bringing about a different understanding of the value of originality. No longer restricted by the hand of the artist, the hallmark of both creativity and originality in the past, originality could now refer to mechanized productions of art in film, photography, and printing (68).

Architecture, especially the construction of buildings of scale, captured the constructivist imagination since it involved a workable synthesis of industry, art, and production. According to Murayama, the architecture of the cities was not rococo, renaissance, secessionist; it had to be rational, economic, and industrial. In production sites, factories, schools, hospitals, *misemono shōya*, tunnels, warehouses, theaters, and restaurants, all had to be constructed and the forms should obey the properties of the materials designers and builders decided to use. The motto for architecture was "necessity alongside convenience." Murayama's inventory of architectural sites inevitably acknowledged the concentration of large numbers of people in constricted urban spaces that required the services of new structures for work, business, and play. But, once more, he was quick to add that the special characteristic of constructivist architecture was its dependence on industrial production, its "industrialization," as its ideal "progressed" from the building of industrial houses to the idea of large city constructions (70).

In this celebration, the industrial factory, the site that brought art, production, and quantity together into a harmonious synthesis, dominated the new cityscape. It was the factory that served vast numbers of people who had congregated in the urban space to become the masses who, in the constructivist vision, would forever remain in the shadows as objects in the great machine called society—at least until Charlie Chaplain showed them how to become cogs and agents.

"THE MAN OF THE CROWD": THE ACTUALITY OF MASS CULTURE

It was precisely this optic refracting the figure of the people in the prisms of the machine that caught the attention of Marxian critics like Hirabayashi Hatsunosuke (1892–1931). Like many of his contemporaries, he sought to determine the meaning of the category of the "people" for an emerging culture in the 1920s and ultimately defined the "actuality" of this new social constituency as the subject of a society still dominated by a vision that denied this privileged status. Hirabayashi argued that an emerging culture, whose signs were appearing everywhere, had to be acknowledged as a reality, and with it the role played by the people. In this struggle, he posed the proposition that the "problem of a people's art today is not one that concerns pure art so much as it does the people."[6] While he resembled Murayama in his dismissal of the claims of pure art, convinced that a virtual technological revolution of art was under way, he departed from the constructivist in upholding the primacy of the people—the masses—who had flocked to cities to live, work, and play. So transforming were these new technologies that he believed they produced political consequences of immense importance. Print technology and paper manufacturing would lead directly to the development of democracy and the recent and widespread prospering of new literary forms like the novel.[7] New technologies like film, photography, and radio, spurring mass consumption, not only greatly altered the terms of artistic production but, more importantly, made art available to larger numbers of people. If Murayama seemed hostage to culture, and the masses to the machine, Hirabayashi saw the hegemony of the people reflected in the production of an entirely new kind of culture.

At first, Hirabayashi's purpose was to validate what he referred to as the "actuality of the people." In the 1920s, and before the Kantō earthquake of 1923, there was, perhaps, an intensive concentration on this new imaginary called the people (*minshū*), which, for many, was employed as an abstract political subject recognized by social democrats and reformers. They were viewed as a natural constituency that could be mobilized rather than as the subject of capitalist modernity. "Among us," Hirabayashi wrote, seeking to demonstrate the reality of the *minshū*, "there are men who portray the wretchedness of workers' lives with extremely melancholic brushes. There are men who have been lecturing on the capitalist system from the standpoint of novelistic fiction. But the people do not offer too much good will to them."[8] The people have no need of instruction; rather, they need to be understood. "More than a teacher, I hope for a friend [in the people]." Characterized by unlimited trust inscribed in their strength, the people represented a bottomless reservoir of wisdom and experience. It is interesting that Hirabayashi's faith in the imagined figure of the people prefigured later attempts by folklorists and postwar intellectuals like Yoshimoto Takaaki and Shimizu Ikutarō, who invested the folk with an enduring knowledge superior to Western and Enlightenment intelligence.

The problem of a people's culture stems from the existence of prevailing social institutions; if people fail to understand, it is less their fault than the responsibility of a social environment that has blinded them to their own interests. As a result, contemporary society is divided between the reality of the people, whose existence is a fact, and a leadership and bourgeois class that has failed to acknowledge either the actuality of the people or their needs. In Hirabayashi's text, *minshū* was identified with the worker, in the context of an argument that emphasized the paucity of available legal holidays that would give adequate leisure time for cultural activities and its poor and unproductive utilization. But the principal reason determining the scarcity of leisure time for culture was the capitalist system's opposition to granting workers time off. Hirabayashi was convinced that if workers were given more time off, they would spend it reading books from the domain of high culture. If workers lack a "sideline," as he put it, and spend their holidays sleeping late, drinking, and playing with women, they will have no life. It is important to note, despite Hirabayashi's almost puritanical program for workers, that he was still proposing a necessary relationship between work and leisure, a link between labor and everyday life. We must also read this recommendation as a desire to make the people into subjects capable of occupying the position of knowers entitled to speak about their own lives rather than the voiceless, negative other of modernity. In this regard, Hirabayashi's effort to vocalize the worker resembled Yanagita Kunuo's contemporaneous desire to listen to the folk, yet another other of modernity. Leisure was more important than art, as such, and along with bread and sleep, it was linked to the worker's capacity both to reproduce the social conditions of his labor and to realize "freedom." If, as he believed, reading was a low priority among workers, the reason for this devaluation lay with society at large. Censoring people for not having understood art revealed only the vast disjunctions in contemporary social structure and the prohibitions that have been put into place to prevent workers from realizing the promise of culture offered by leisure time. In Hirabayashi's vision, the right to leisure meant the right to culture. While the people lack sufficient leisure time to read books, they also lack the funds with which to buy them. When Hirabayashi made this point in 1921, the great publishing and distribution revolution in Japanese society had not yet started. Yet, in a few years the production and distribution of cheap books for a mass audience had firmly taken root, and publishing houses like Iwanami and Kodansha were becoming overnight household names. But it was still a persisting truth that the sacrifices required of a working-class family merely to attend a performance of the kabuki was too much to pay in weekly wages and allotted days off. As a result, the awful gulf between "the people and art widened."

"How best to bring them closer?" Hirabayashi asked. The solution to this problem had less to do with improving the management of theaters, widening educational opportunities or even making books more available by lowering their price than it did with the living conditions experienced daily by the people. The answer was provided by "reconstruction" (*kaizō*). Deeply involved in the contemporary craze for "social reconstruction and its program aimed at remodeling the institutional infrastructure," which held Japanese society in the early in its thrall, Hirabayashi concluded that the times were not yet ripe for carrying out any transformation that had a chance to last. But the widening gap between culture and the people plainly showed all that any resolution must come from society rather than the people. It was impossible to accomplish a social reconstruction on a piecemeal basis; it had to be generalized. Any attempt at reconstructing people's culture through a route that bypassed the social system altogether was like bypassing the Pacific Ocean to purify the waters of Tokyo Bay.[9] Art and culture would never be freed from the monopolization of class privilege unless a general reconstruction of society was undertaken. The path to a general reconstruction lay not in destroying completely the old art that had been once valued. Rather, what is to be valued is to be resuscitated from the ruins and resituated in a new social environment alongside the new. Cultural shards from a now discounted past must be reworked into modernity, placed in a different temporality from what had produced it and made it subject to the pulsations of the new. "We have no authority," he declared, "to criticize the emancipatory movement of the people under the pretense of an eternalized art." Without constantly "negotiating the relationship between the people and culture," the eternal in art will never be found. The people's life approximates art. "Do the great voices of the great poets of the past addressed to the people reach their ears today?"[10]

A history of the culture of one segment of the human species is only true when, as in antiquity, science, art, and religion are bequeathed to the masses; when such a bestowal only scratches the surface and changes nothing, it fails as a true history of the human species. Worse, it is not a true culture because it benefits only the few and reinforces their efforts to prevent further change. For Hirabayashi, it is not surprising that culture and history change only when social conditions change. What he was interested in promoting was the elimination of an aesthetics and culturalism "devoted to the completion of art constructed on the basis of oppression and exploitation." While this meant replacing the producers and custodians who have consistently used art and culture to maintain their hegemony, it did not mean ridding society of older forms of art, philosophy, and science. In Hirabayashi's view, what counted were the producers—the people—whose active involvement in the making of culture would seal the separation between custodians and producers. "Our aim," he wrote, should be "to rescue culture that has become the victim of utility."[11] The problem was not so much in understanding of art as art, science as science, as it was recognizing and respecting the independence of both, and thus their resistance to being fixed, linked to a single class and their openness to history. Only the present directed the movement of history.

As an early enthusiast of *proletkult*, Hirabayashi saw the present as a different temporal moment designated to begin the struggle with a received, hegemonic culture, "fighting it," as he put it, in order to exclude those things that had reinforced the separation between culture and the people. Everywhere there were signs of an emerging culture rooted in everydayness and the commodity form and the progressive modernization of life. "Sheik boys" and "flappers" strolling aimlessly in the Ginza, he observed, were not all there was to the changes taking place. Behind these surface changes, there was the regime of economic and political rationality, which, as the "mother of modernity," was reflected in the growth of the urban arts. Modernism, as he understood it, referred to the ceaseless production of the ever new, the fresh, and the innovative, driven by new forces of production. But rather than focus on the modes of production, he turned his attention to the transformation taking place in the forces of production—in technology and science—and the increasing mechanization of everyday life. Echoing his contemporary Murayama Tomoyoshi and his own romance with the machine, Hirabayashi never went so far as to make the machine the acting agent of society, even though he risked eliciting critical denunciations from fellow Marxists like Ōya Sōichi, who complained he had forgotten the "reality of the people for the machine." Nevertheless, Hirabayashi envisaged a narrative for the modernization of Japanese society and the emergence of everyday life that was linked to the development of technology and subsequent technicization of culture. In his narrative, mechanization moved through three stages: (1) The appearance of the machine came with the imitation of Western clothing, food, housing (calling attention to the "culture houses" of the 1920s), new activities such as eating out, using the car, and the trend toward the "quantitative" production of goods and commodities for consumption. At the heart of this stage was electric power. (2) Acceleration of the pace of life and the growing importance of "speed." Here, he observed that the tempo of life has changed as a result of increased mechanization and the condensation of space in time through the development of new forms of transportation and communications. And (3) the influence of technology on the human spirit. The machine, he proposed, promised the realization of a bright future, one lived by the proletariat, and revealed glimpses of how an ultramodern society might configure a new culture and social order that was progressive, rational, and scientific. Faith in science to produce a genuine people's culture seized not only Hirabayashi's imagination but also the attention of many contemporaries like Tosaka Jun, Tsuchida Kyōson, and Nakai Masakazu. What this faith seemed to disclose was the people's capacity to fulfill its historical mission to produce a scientifically based culture that would emancipate them from oppression by joining leisure to work, unalienated existence to daily life, and concreteness to experience.

Hirabayashi's own enthusiasm for the processes of technological change and how it intersected with cultural production fell short of full determinism since agency still resided with the masses. Yet, there is no denying that he drew a close, almost homological, relationship between the forces of production and the appearance of the people, who represented for him the force of the social relations of production. In his view, technological mediation, which grew out of productive social relations, mediated received forms of art and culture and made possible broader communication and innovation. "Film art," he asserted, "is not determined by social organization alone but is born according to the invention of moving photographic machines. But the film, it is good to say, imparts great impact on . . . established art. The invention of the microscope gave birth to bacteriology, and bacteriology was similarly related to producing a great revolution in biology and medicine." Similarly, the changes that take place in literature and art are not simply occurrences in the superstructure but movements stemming from the base of society. For Hirabayashi, this formulation reflected no simple economism but rather a more complex understanding of base as a broader socio-ideological realm that registered first the great shifts society and polity would later refract. The machine made by the hands of the technician reaches directly to the domain of culture and changes its "modes and shapes." Any investigation of literature and art cannot fail to avoid considering the role of technological change. In a word, "machines alter art." Yet, at the same time, he was aware that those who recognize that art had become mechanized and determined by social class might cause "certain people to shiver."[12] He was certain that such people would have been the first to oppose the heliocentric theory or the development of evolutionary biology at an earlier time. Technology would bring art and culture closer to the masses, which until recently had been removed from life and enjoyed only by the few. With its capacity for altering received cultural forms and generating newer ones and its potential for mechanical reproduction and effective circulation, technology promised to take art and culture from the monopoly of the bourgeoisie and resituate it within the masses.

The point to Hirabayashi's meditation on the relationship between technology and culture was to demonstrate how closely they were linked in contemporary life and how completely everyday life in the 1920s—the target of cultural production and the site of its consumption—had become dominated by film, photography, print journalism, and radio. These technologies were finally indistinguishable from the experience of daily routine; technology and mass culture were indissoluble. It was far from his intention to diminish the actual agency of the people in the production of culture. But it was precisely this observation and his promise to support it with "actual facts" (jijitsu) that ignited an attack launched by Ōya Sōichi, who appealed to the authority of the same "reality" which he identified with the people. What appeared to be at stake in this controversy between two Marxian critics was the status of the real at this historical moment. With Hirabayashi, there was no backing off from his earlier enthusiasm for proletkult but only the supplementary recognition that everyday life was saturated with the effects of technology as commodity and means of communication; these now had to be taken into account in any further consideration of contemporary and future cultural formation. The very technology and commodity form that anchored everyday life was seen by Ōya, on the other hand, as simply modan sō (modern customs) that signified only the presence of a superficial, Americanized, and diluted cultural formation, doomed to self-destruct before the construction of a genuinely new, people's culture he scarcely envisioned.

For Hirabayashi, the paradigmatic example of the fusion of new technology and mass culture was found in the implementation of radio drama. It was different from stage plays, he explained, because it was "formed" through the mediation of "sound waves" (GKKG, 73). Radio was comparable to print technology—journalism and novels—insofar as both brought about a great transformation in making culture accessible to larger numbers of people at the same time. Moreover, these new, technologically enhanced media demanded a shift from the eye and seeing to the ear. Like print, the sound waves that came through a radio box could be received easily, even while the listener was doing something else (76). The audience did not need to go to a music hall, a theater, or any public space to listen to a drama and could appreciate and enjoy news, lectures, and music while lying down. Hirabayashi recognized that sound required new devices and procedures that could make up for and even supplement the written word that the reader could see in print. In his view, the utilization of sound waves opened up a new realm in cultural production and consumption, not just as a significant supplement to print, but as an entirely new practice made possible by the perceptual category of sound. In this sense, radio matched film perfectly, as both media were actually driven by the new categories of perception represented by speed and sound. The impact of sound on culture expanded the horizons of art and literature and disclosed a veritable cultural revolution (77).

By the same measure, film was even more progressive, even though contemporary critics had originally condemned its appearance as nonart. For this reason it steadily announced its own independence from the theater. "In Japan," Hirabayashi wrote, "borrowing the words of Mori Iwao, film managed to exclude all the theatrical conventions and had therefore to create a new cinema from scratch" (78). Film in Japan was, from its inception, separate from the stage, and this independence attested to the fact that it had originally been a people's art form. What changed it, and even radicalized or "mechanized" it most, was the introduction of sound (81). Hirabayashi claimed that this technicization of the film and growing differentiation of its production process signified "progress and specialization." The history of social progress, he asserted, has always been acknowledged to be a history of the social division of labor. The progressive history of art (culture) reflects the history of the specialization of artistic activity. In less than a century, the Industrial Revolution and its promotion of machine production has changed the modes of human life. If cinema required new scripts, radio different kinds of drama, music different compositions capable of expressing "mechanical sounds," we have reached a state where it is difficult to determine whether humans manage machines or vice versa. Even though wars in the past and present have seen humans acting as subjects (*shutai*), there is still a vast difference between a struggle based on individual combat, when men shouted their own names before battle, and modern conflicts that employ tanks, poison gas, and steel engines. Ancient art was independent of machines, while modern artists have become enslaved to them. Although humans make machines, they are ultimately led by them. How, he asked, is this paradoxical relationship realized in culture (84–85)?

Hirabayashi argued from history. The means employed to communicate thought was not necessarily limited to the use of writing. Different kinds of sculpture were capable of communicating ideas without using either sentence or words. But because writing has been made to appear as the sole means of transmitting thought, it is no small event that discovers modes of expressibility and understanding other than writing. Communication today depends upon the use of signs—semiology— driven by the power of electricity on radio wave transmission (86). Even science has come to be expressed in signs that have little or no reference to words and sentences. What seems to have occurred to him is the observation that writing had to be deprivileged and resituated to take its place as only one among other modes of notation in a larger system of signs. Only literature, emphasizing particularity and originality, defended the importance of writing as an "impregnable fortress" and as an eternal and unchanging means of expression. It should be noted, again, that Hirabayashi was putting forth this idea precisely at the moment when folklorists like Yanagita Kunio and Orikuchi Shinobu were trying to show how the folk had remained voiceless and excluded from written records but had nevertheless expressed themselves and their lives in custom and religious practices. But, he remarked, the fortress had been shaken to its foundation with the emergence of radio and cinema, by the appearance of everydayness whose experience conformed to the masses who had come to the cities to work and play, and in the media. Hirabayashi speculated that if the discovery of radio had predated moveable type, printing presses, and paper manufacturing, the dissemination and popularization of novelistic literature would not have occurred. To widely disseminate portions of a novel using old block prints would not be economical or politically feasible. But the invention of moving pictures and radio might have made room for the sudden appearance of literary forms like the novel because of the possibility of rapid diffusion and circulation. In brief, the technology that colonized everyday life meant producing cultural forms that would rapidly enter into the domain of popular consciousness at a pace that earlier, print technology could not have matched.

What seems important about Hirabayashi's meditations on new forms of expressibility made available by technology was the recognition that writing did not represent a completed narrative progress of humans from their "common ancestors" and monkeys. Writing was probably nothing more than an invention of a certain moment in history. Even Orikuchi Shinobu was proposing, at the same time, the existence of a literature before literature, that is, before the adoption of writing in Japan. With Hirabayashi, literature exemplified merely a "technological metamorphosis" at this moment in history. "If, as I've argued, the printing press were invented after the moving pictures, it would have been necessary to translate the film and make it into a novel, rather than adapting the scripts of today's novels and plays to the cinema" (86–87). In a world increasingly internationalized, literature is burdened with real limitations. Since it is organized on the basis of words and sentences, it is important to recognize that words and sentences do not have the same meaning for two people from countries who know only their own language but also wish to exchange ideas. But moving pictures revive and revivify visually concrete things and actions that can break open these barriers to understanding and mutual exchange far more easily than literature. Hence, the urgency of importing foreign films as against expecting people to read foreign literatures in the original languages. Yet, Hirabayashi's celebration of the moving picture over literature, viewing over reading, easily overlooked the immense number of translations that were being published in the 1920s in cheap, paperback editions. Even so, he was still troubled by the act of reading and what it implied. Literary works, he argued, had to follow and portray an order of things, driven by a logic of narrative, and were thus constrained from presenting multiple images simultaneously in time and space. The capacity to present the simultaneity of space and time, the spatializing of time and the temporalizing of space, conformed to a perception of contemporary reality that was expressible in film and to a certain extent on radio. Literature's greatest defect was its unsuitability as group art since it focused on the singular, the linear, and the individual. But because humans have recently become more "socialized" (*shakaika*), literature, which has always been a solitary and isolated act of a closeted individual, cannot meet the demands of the masses who throng in public spaces. While it is not clear why individuals could no longer enjoy a text as a solitary activity in a mass society, Hirabayashi was apparently pointing to the gathering of sheer multitudes in public spaces, like movie houses, to enjoy a performance of a story that previously was a pleasure restricted to the few. As a result, literature was no longer "unified with the progress of everyday life" (88). Convinced that culture was at the threshold of a technological revolution, he felt that its effects could no longer be ignored or dismissed.

But this conviction in an immanent cultural revolution announced by technological advances prompted Ōya Sōichi to denounce Hirabayashi for adhering too closely to the conventions of art, as such, to the neglect of politics: the privileging of critique or the "specialist" against the claims of the "amateur" (*shiroto*), whom he identified with the "people." The problem, as he saw it, stemmed from an unresolvable relationship between the claims of political (or social) values and aesthetic values informing the production of art and culture. For hard-line Marxists in the 1920s (Kurahara Korehito, Katsumata Seiichi), no apparent conflict existed because "art and politics are laid on top of each other, like two straight lines."[13] To think there could be cultural values outside of the political was a grave misrecognition, since the former was completely implicated in the latter. But regardless of this declared imbrication of the political and the cultural, the relationship was not so easily soluble for Marxists who were committed to constructing a theory of action capable of accounting for the struggle and final victory of the proletariat as well as a cultural program that could resist being assimilated entirely to an ideological and political strategy. For Hirabayashi, who problematized the relationship between culture (art and technology) and politics (the progress of the people), the matter could not simply end in a conflict over the priority of politics and culture. Instead, it involved a broader set of relationships between ideology and science, history and cultural essentialism, people and leadership, class and the masses. Arguing that Marxism possessed no fixed theory of culture, as such, or even of art, the present provided the occasion to "rethink" (saigimi) this possibility of seeing art as a means and movement that could be put into serving the victory of the proletariat. But culture, and especially art, could not always be submitted to the judgment of political values. No one has yet objected to the fact that the works of writers like Edgar Allen Poe and Baudelaire, he observed, are not in the service of the proletariat victory. "Besides acting as a spur that pushes the good fortune of humanity in general," he continued, "not one of these [writers] was considered a Marxist."[14] Accordingly, Hirabayashi was proposing what clearly was a Lukacsian argument that held that even if writers were not necessarily Marxist, their works could be put into the service of the proletariat and contribute to the purpose of the people. Great writers, as Lukacs observed of Balzac, could reveal a good deal about their times, especially class relations, even though their ideology might differ from the progressive forces of history. This argument resembled Hirabayashi's belief that technology and the forces of production could play a commanding role in advancing the cultures and arts of the people, even though they were not necessarily proletarian devices.

Immensely misrecognized by Ōya, who complained that Hirabayashi's emphasis on cultural/artistic values was bonded to the privileged "technology" of writers that had excluded the agency of the "amateurs" in their considerations, a cultural theory that appealed to new technology risked becoming a reactionary position that ignored the flow of history. Ōya's argument rested on the conviction that his moment was the time of the masses, the time of reality, as he called it. Behind this view lay hidden a metahistorical explanation that mandated that at certain moments of transition, "reality led technology in the arts," while in moments of pause, "technology led reality." Writers in a time of transition, which for Ōya marked the age of the masses, were always concerned with "what should be portrayed rather than how it should portrayed." Conversely,

when writers produced in an age of "comparative smoothness" their attention turned to "how they should portray rather than what."[15] For Hirabayashi, this distinction was simply an alibi that revealed a "famine of
material" and intellectual bankruptcy.[16] If Ōya condemned Hirabayashi
for separating art from "our social life," it undoubtedly derived from his
own inability to grasp an argument that had proceeded from a vision of
everyday life embedded in technological innovations that already were
changing how people would see, hear, and even behave.

In one of his last essays (Hirabayashi died young, in 1931, while abroad
in Europe), the essay "Nihon kindaiteki tanteishōsetsu—toku ni Edogawa
Rampo ni tsuite," published in the magazine *Shinseishin* (1925), he proposed that the reworking of older, generic forms into newer ones like the
detective story, which he believed was the popular favorite of the people,
was more important than the role of technology in mass culture. Concentrating on some of the writings of the mystery writer Edogawa Rampo,
Hirabayashi explored the meaning of this new, hybrid form that appeared
in Japan only recently, owing to lag in the development of the novel itself,
and had been realized in the West.[17] His enthusiasm for science and technology spilled over in his praise for the detective story, which, for many
contemporaries, including proletarian writers, constituted a worrisome
sign of decadence in mass culture. Hirabayashi was the first in Japan to
take the form seriously as the mark of a new cultural formation. It was,
he believed, the implanting of a "scientific civilization in Japan that gave
birth to the detective novel." While many have argued that the detective
story developed slowly and incompletely because the design of the Japanese house was not "suitable to frankly secret crimes," others proposed
that human relationships were different from those in the West, while still
another group attributed the reason to the bureaucratic domination of
everyday life and the people.[18] But the principal reason for its slow development was that Japanese modern life and science were in their infancy,
germinating in new soil to blossom forth at the right moment. The development of capitalism, especially from the time of World War I, accompanied by greater scienticization of civilization, brought forth greater con-
centrations of wealth, the emergence of a new class of businessmen,
elegant styles of living, the development of credit transactions, and the
exponential increase in dishonest and corrupt officials and financial elite.
Hence, the appearance of the detective novel constituted a historical watermark of "social conditions" marked by the development of science
and the analytic spirit, which became the basis of detection. According to
Hirabayashi, the popularity of Rampo among a mass readership was also
related to the recognition that "he [Rampo] was the one writer among
the Japanese detective novelists who clearly recollected (*kioku*) the contemporary 'I.' "[19] What he plainly meant with this observation was that

Edogawa Rampo's novels and stories constituted a vast reservoir for contemporary memory and recollection. His stories were invariably about people who came to the city from the countryside, found themselves alone, literally living on the streets, and fell into a episode that demanded some form of recollection of past relationships, elsewhere. In Hirabayashi's opinion, Rampo's stories and novels represented something more important than merely momentary but forgettable entertainment. Stories like "D-zaka no satsuji jiken," "Shinri shiken," and "Kurotegumi," published in pulp magazines, appealed to a mass audience precisely because they were embedded in social relations, experiences, and an environment that could be easily identified with the life of a readership living in the cities. Like newspaper stories, which often supplied the writer with an incident, detective stories were centered on an event that concealed more than it revealed but whose surface account pointed to the existence of a fuller narrative that required disclosure. This was, of course, the job of the detective, to dig beneath the surface event in order to restore the full, explanatory narrative. His methods were scientific and inductive, and his "laboratory" the vast city that supplied the place where he carried out his "experiments" in verifying facts necessary to constructing the true narrative of the event. Rampo's hero, Akechi, is actually an amateur; his locale, the streets, bars, coffee shops—the new world of everyday life of the cities, appearing to the reader as recognizable, concrete, and familiar. People are often separated from friends and relatives, living alone in a boarding house full of strangers; their lives are structured by the neighborhood, its coffee shops, bars, restaurants, and the commodities and entertainments of mass consumption. Indeed, the "readers of detective stories, like the lovers of moving pictures, are a kind of expanded group of critics. This criticism of fans was often impartially fair compared to the criticism of specialized critics."[20]

Rampo's detective stories were rooted in reporting social relationships that were not locked into personal considerations and friendships but rather explored the broad range of social situations newcomers to the city would encounter. Even more important, his stories underscored the primary role played by memory and recall among the new city dwellers, as referents to a history and experience lost in dislocation. This world of memory and history was what Yanagita was already trying to evoke in his concentration on custom and practices associated with the countryside newcomers inevitably left behind when they migrated to the cities searching for work and a new life. Social relationships were thinned out, and people were forced to see things differently even as they shared a common experience of everydayness that structured their lives. In Hirabayashi's thinking, the formation of this world had less to do with the "reality" of a mass age, unlike Ōya's, than with a struggle (a "groping," as he put it) to grasp the cultural configurations made by the people from a "perspective that treaded on the meaning and limits of what had already been conceived."[21] What this entailed was assessing the relationship between new technologies and the experience of everyday life lived by the masses.

PHILOSOPHIZING EVERYDAY LIFE

If Hirabayashi saw in contemporary society the effects of science and technology mediating mass culture, Tosaka Jun (1900–1945), who accepted this observation, went further to actually reflect on its meaning. More than any other thinker of the age, he viewed his present as a philosophical problem that needed to be interrogated, when others merely assumed its phenomenality as a given. Yet it was, in fact, this phenomenological present, filled with unrealized meaning giving direction to history, that required philosophical analysis. One of the interesting accomplishments of Tosaka was to investigate the phenomenon of the present as it was occurring before him, rather than, as in good Hegelian fashion, accepting the inevitability of time usually represented by the Owl of Minerva's flight and the recognition that philosophical reflection always comes too late. By proposing that "thought had become quotidianized," Tosaka not only prefigured and thus anticipated Henri Lefebvre's effort to show that everydayness should be seen as a subject for philosophy by almost twenty years, he tried also to demonstrate why everydayness was a philosophic category that needed immediate attention. This observation was no doubt inspired by his reading of Heidegger, but its most immediate impulse stemmed from his recognition both that literary modernism was grounded in the self and individual experience and that the accelerated tempo of everyday life was being colonized by new customs that were colliding with older conventions. With his contemporary Tsuchida Kyōson, a progressive advocate of *proletkult* and worker's education, Tosaka systematically identified everyday life with newly established customs that thereby demanded interrogation for meaning. In his later and great text on the Japan ideology (*Nihon ideorogiron*, 1935), he forcefully juxtaposed this image of modern life filled with new customs to the fictive abstractions of national culture in order to reveal the utter bankruptcy of all those pronouncements claiming the eternality of Japanese culture.

Tsuchida, like many contemporaries, was riveted to the search for a sociology of the newly emerging social constituencies of the 1920s, such as the "people" and the "masses." As a Marxist severely critical of the conduct of Marxism in his day, he embraced in his essay "Taishū no shakaigaku" (1932) many of the persisting themes of the times, focusing on the category of "society" and its meaning, "essence," "laws," etc. Where he came closest to Tosaka was in his proposal to "sociologize philosophy." Both men believed that any proper analysis of the social must confront and engage the content of "actual social life," which ceaselessly changed and shifted ground to produce the historical surplus identified with everyday life. Instead of following a phenomenological perspective that sanctioned the acceptance of things as they are, both turned to everyday life as it was being lived and experienced to find concepts adequate to describing its fluidity. Yet, newness was only half of the problem. "Analyzing a problem," Tsuchida wrote, "its realities, we must reflect upon such questions as reasons why new phenomena and forms come to develop from the lifestyles of the past."[22] To determine their meaning, even Marxism has to be rendered adequate to catch hold of the changing scene. In his theory of the masses, Tsuchida attacked "critics of civilization" who willfully ignored everyday life, just as Tosaka condemned a philosophical practice that ignored the role of "clothes."[23] While Tsuchida concentrated on the agency of the masses, and the necessity of educating them for this role, Tosaka looked beyond to the appearance of custom itself as an agent of what he called "actuality," which, when investigated, would disclose its hidden or suppressed history as a condition not only for putting into question established and fixed moralities, but for reworking them in the present into new conventions capable of satisfying new needs. More significantly, Tosaka sought to locate the ground of custom (*fūzoku*) in the masses. "From the very beginning," he wrote, "this thing—custom—is certainly a mass phenomenon. Therefore, any concern for it must be related to the masses since it is something easily understood in the space of mass interaction. Whether it is a picture portraying custom, notions of customary beauty, or ambiguous words, it will circulate without trouble as a mass product throughout society" (3). As a phenomenon produced by the masses, and not, as Yanagita was proposing at the same time, the "ordinary and abiding folk" (*jōmin*), what Tosaka called the "popular" was identified with large numbers of people mutually interacting with each other. Where Yanagita saw custom as an alternative to the commodity-thing, as a kind of defense against its saturation of everyday life, Tosaka, as we shall see, envisaged it as the expression of the commodity form.

Yet, it seems that the observation that linked custom to the popular and mass life was only possible from a perspective that distinguished between what had appeared and was as yet unaccounted for and the identity of traces of earlier forms of social custom received from the past. In the absence of any serious concern for the status of custom and how it evolves into morality by concealing its history and link to forms of sociation, Tosaka noted a certain unevenness between the presence of custom in the present and its vanished past, between what now claimed eternality and its historical conditions of production. "It is a mystery why Carlyle, in

Sartor Resartus, didn't write a philosophy of clothing. Whatever the case, philosophic study hasn't discussed this question, even though it—philosophy—is less in daily view than clothing" (1) It might be that considerations of clothing have never reached the imagination of the English and that it might be necessary to turn to Germans for a philosophy of clothing. Carlyle contrived to begin such a discussion on the philosophy of clothing through his fictional German philosopher, Professor Teufelsdrockh ("Devil's shit"), whose book on this very subject had just been published. His philosopher is a follower of Adam Smith's theory of the "concealed body" who is not interested in the mundane world and is ill-disposed to all forms of human ornamentation like clothing, even though he has written a philosophy of clothing. He is, in short, a "transcendentalist" who believes in "pure reason" abstractly in the idiom of German idealism. But the fact that he emphasized a concern for the social and historical reality possessed by clothing has a personal meaning for Japanese today. Tosaka worried that despite the indispensable importance of its reality for social and political meaning clothing possessed in objective history, there has not been much attention in philosophy, literature, and art since Carlyle. Not even the German love for philosophy has managed to develop a philosophy of clothing. Kant once noted a philosophy of the barbershop he found advertised in an English newspaper, and Hegel criticized the philosophy of the shoe shop. And that was it for philosophy until the present. The problem, as Tosaka formulated it, was that even though clothing possessed a material reality, theoretical concern for it has been exceedingly "thin." During the French Revolution, the appearance of the *sans culottes* dramatized for many a new intellectual meaning, since clothing and dressing had always symbolized the economic life of the people, class membership, and ideology (3). Because of this powerful symbolization, he added, clothing possessed a social reality that contemporaries could no longer ignore or dismiss as mere banality. For Carlyle, he reminded his readers, clothing symbolized the human species; for himself it reflected custom. The task facing contemporary society was, therefore, to supply a theoretical understanding of custom Carlyle had overlooked and show how it had been produced by a determinate history it concealed as a condition of its claim to eternality.

Tosaka's interest in custom must be situated in a context that includes those folklorists and cultural theorists who were already settling on custom as the irreducible but still living trace of an "eternal and abiding folk" and upholding its claim as a link to origins and as an agent in history. He saw custom at the heart of any social order but also recognized that it was susceptible to change. "Humans who have no customary life have no society." Despite its close identification with the popular, social analysis has clearly failed to grasp its formal nature and its movements. "Since a consideration concerned with every kind of phenomena of social life must take hold of the character of the popular (*taishūteki*), the means of actuality must be regarded as one of the most important points for theory. In social theory, the understanding of the popular should never be omitted" (4). By calling attention to the relationship between custom and the popular (or masses) in social theory, Tosaka foregrounded both the historical and social conditions implicated in the production of the customary. Custom, he argued, was intimately related to social convention, and conventions were ultimately determined by diverse forms of relationships in the working lives of individuals that derived from the production structure of society. Moreover, custom functioned to develop and maintain the political and legal systems as the order of society. Finally, it was the site where social consciousness and ethical rule were ideally guaranteed. When conventions are broken down into personal effects and speech habits, they most likely become customs. For this reason, he reasoned, custom is the product of the basic structure of society. But it was not, as Durkheim would have it, the source of social solidarity, the binding that made society possible; rather, it was an effect produced by social structure. Hence, the substance of society "acquires skin and flesh, beauty or unsightliness, that extends to what we call custom. Ultimately, it ends in clothing" (4). As a social effect (*ketsuron*), it is thus the most straightforward surface phenomenon in society, its physiognomy, the "clinical sign of social life," and a "symptom of the times by which to diagnose the social." Tosaka added that the word for "decadence" was another term for diagnosis.

If custom is educed from the social base, it is nothing more than an abstraction. Yet, it also possessed concreteness because it is an embodiment of something else. This double character, calling attention to weak and strong functions, showed that custom had to be seen as a theoretical category of social reality and analysis. Ordinary social science, posited on the primacy of the superstructure, phenomenality alone, had failed to discover the living location of particular social phenomena like custom that the materialist view had been able to uncover. The reason for this, Tosaka believed, stemmed from a method that was capable of distinguishing custom's abstract and concrete dimensions. What this meant was that even though custom might appear as one thing, it could not be fully grasped unless it was related to a specific social and productive base. At the same time, Tosaka acknowledged that custom, accompanying a specific social formation, reflected the human consciousness developed and educated within the system. Under this circumstance, it corresponded to a segment of the ideological superstructure by embracing both the materiality and the ideality of an appearance that functioned to conceal its origins in a determinate system of productive relationships. It was both concrete and abstract. Custom, for Tosaka, obeyed the logic of the commodity form. Careful to suggest that custom was not an economic, political, or cultural phenomenon, as such, but acted as a generalized and common phenomenon, it behaved like the commodity form, by penetrating all levels of the social formation. Understanding custom on the model of the commodity form demanded an analytic approach that would establish the "order of the structure of things in the social system as the primary standard of analysis," in order to avoid the blindness of a social science that "grasps the phenomena, those generally common signs of a living society," as its basic elements (TJZ, 4:274).

By contrast, bourgeois social science substituted symptom and sign for substance, ideality and abstraction for materiality, autonomy for connectedness. In Tosaka's view, the most extreme example of this failing was not always the work of cultural theorists like Watsuji Tetsurō, whose *Fūdo* he targeted for critique, but also of contemporary social researchers like Kon Wajiro, whose "modernology" was an example of an approach that clung only to surface and phenomenality without interrogating what it concealed. The worst example of this practice of "grasping" phenomenon only at the surface level, without accounting for the immense complexity of "custom," were newspapers, which reported events at a "most unsteady level." For this reason, newspapers dwelled only on the popularity or baseness of custom but never considered whether it qualified as a major social problem. Tosaka complained that society (*seken*) was always sensitive to fashion and that it was a "terrible meddler." What he meant by this condemnation was that society, in general, was always an opponent to the new and would purposely trivialize such things as "modern customs." The "custom of modernism," he added, was not only "reflected in society's eye as a scorned object; it was also its ordinary common sense." Here, custom is not seen as a social problem but only as a "trifling" given that is a "condition of the idea of popular custom." At this point, Tosaka's conception of custom, whose behavior he assimilated to the commodity form, converged with his elevation of the category of everydayness (*nichijōsei*). Like custom, everydayness had simply been taken for granted as unworthy of further reflection. In this way, women who work as prostitutes are seen not as a social problem but only as objects of teasing and pleasure. The commonsense understanding of everyday life saw it as simply "customary" and "vulgar," dull routine, prompting philosophers to juxtapose it to the "transcustomary" (*chōtsūzokumono*), which they privileged as a proper object for philosophic speculation (4:136, 132–135). Just as Yanagita dismissed historiographical practice because it privileged heroes, battles, and politicians, philosophy, in Tosaka's view, discounted the everyday because of its triviality, insignificance, for a world that exceeded the common and customary. He appeared concerned with the way philosophy had turned away from the reality of contemporary custom, the world of everyday life that was being figured in mass media and lived on the streets, removing its "experience" from serious consideration. Through the mechanism of what he identified as philosophy's new vocation, reality was transmuted into a "transcustomary thing," displaced to a world of abstraction rather than to a position of centrality. Custom, he observed, had to be resituated within the process of capitalist development, and this required "revising the idea of custom as something that should not only be grasped as popular or base" but "refashioned into a category that had theoretical meaning" (4:276).

For Tosaka, the task of such a new categorization would first be to determine why custom "corresponds to morality." The identity of custom and morality signaled a return to the prevailing practices of everyday life, to the customary rather than the transcustomary. With this move, he had opened the way to interrogate custom for both the meaning of its contemporary practice and its concealed historical and social conditions of production. The reality of custom is something made by society for all its members; it carries with it social oppression and coercion. According to Tosaka, this coercive dimension of custom "provokes an easy and comfortable feeling by acknowledging moral and ethical authority" (4:276). Convinced that the most representative norms corresponding to custom were those that concerned sexual relationships in society, he also saw that sexual mores constituted the content of surface, commonsense morality that needed to be examined. While he was ready to recognize that "one kind of antisocial image, called corrupting customs, pointed to the destruction caused by sexual practices," inviting the intervention of political moralists and the police who saw it as a great problem for society's public morals, he was concerned with how all custom became "completely moralized."

"Recently, the discussion of love-making, as one of the problems of morality, has appropriately become widespread." Referring to the current craze described as "erotic, grotesque nonsense," Tosaka sought to connect the concern for custom and morality with his interest in the materiality of clothing. Sexuality, he observed, close to the pulsations of contemporary everyday life, has an intimate relationship to clothing. Nothing better than clothing, today, represents sexual differentiation in society and discloses both moral and sexual meaning. Recuperating an argument he made in greater detail in his *Nihon ideorogiron*, where he identified morality with common sense, Tosaka recognized that it was precisely the capacity of morality and custom to pass as common sense, something that went without saying because it could come without saying. Custom, in this commonsensical idiom, was able to escape examination and win for itself the immunity of acceptance because it was rooted in the claim of consensus. In this regard, he observed, custom was rarely submitted to theoretical and scientific investigation, which, for the bourgeoisie, always reflected a transclass and transparent perspective, above immediate interests. The problem is not whether or not something is good or bad, but rather the necessary and more difficult task of determining scientifically how defects might be relieved. It is not enough to condemn, for example, out of some reservoir of common sense, the sale of women into prostitution while failing to consider how the practice might be eliminated. Morality is antiscientific, antitheoretical, and anticritical. Too much contemporary social science dwells on detailed descriptions of phenomena, but too little has been executed with the purpose of overturning customs and moral norms that serve only to condemn, coerce, and blind society to resolving its gravest problems. "We must overturn the idea of morality itself," he demanded, "rather than overthrowing this or that fixed moral norm or sentiment." If the idea of custom is merely linked to moral norms in its phenomenological sense, thereby enforcing the appearance of a natural coupling, he feared that the result would end in a "nonsensical, embarrassed category," theoretically useless. Instead the relationship itself, its social and historical location, must be scientifically probed. Tosaka looked to literature and its own experience in treating morality to find an "effective category" with which to apprehend the phenomenon of contemporary morality (4:277).

As a theoretical concept, custom simultaneously emphasized the reason why it belonged to morality and projected an intellectual content. The customs of the country are ordinarily called national characteristics and are thus said to reflect the national thought and sentiment of the people. To this extent, thought is represented in custom, and custom is expressed in thought. But representation (hyōgen) denotes interpretation or hermeneutics and never counts as a scientific explanation. Even though custom has been ordinarily seen as a representation of thought and thinking, thought, itself, never reaches the point where it is able to determine what custom actually is. Thought is an idea, while custom is something that can be seen. There are no "wizard words," he announced, to show that ideational thinking becomes the landscape for custom; custom only gives expression to thought, indicating and giving expression to its presence only, despite its reliance on words. Yet, the materiality of custom, its thingness through which the idea is expressed, points to the recognition that custom is capable of disclosing meaning. Hence, custom ends up by calling attention to meaning by way of the intellectual content associated with morality. Its meaning is ultimately derived from morality itself, which always conveys a reason. For that reason alone, the moral problem was always a problem for thought. Tosaka believed that this conclusion was not only "helpful" in arousing interest in the special characteristics of social reality that contemporary custom possessed and thus calling attention to its "popular" or "masslike" dimension; it also permitted establishing a broad-based consideration of theoretical, literary, and cognitive content identified with the category of custom. Confident that this discovery enables connecting a "glimpse of trivial themes" directly to the central problematic of social theory, he was equally sure that it would also help in finding the theoretical meaning occupied by the category of the customary as the reflection of real existence for the arts and culture in the structure of knowledge. With this move, Tosaka believed philosophy would be reunited with its true and original vocation by returning to an investigation of the relationship between phenomena and their material conditions of production, which, in his time, pointed to the fundamental problem of the popular and masses in art and culture. What he sought was a method that would locate the social position of morality, the process by which the customary became moral norm and morality became common sense. This led him to the problem of a ground and its identification in production relationships, the subsequent ideologization of morality and its class content.

Everyday life put into question the status of the customary by producing new practices that clearly were colliding with received conventions. But custom, he remarked, was simply the shell that both concealed and revealed the kernel of morality, since custom was used to substantialize morality (4:278). Hence, custom was the embodiment of morality, even though it marked what was abstract. This "skin," as he called it, this sign, supplied morality with a grant of immunity from scientific interrogation and authorized its acceptance as natural. This appeal to naturalness, actually concealing concrete class interests, was custom's most powerful function and the reason it now had to be examined for its connection to morality and the thought it expressed. It is interesting to note that Tosaka was persuaded that this appeal to naturalness conveyed by custom—its claim of consensuality (common sense)—dissuaded social scientists from probing its meaning. This analysis of custom was prompted by a contemporary craze that either embraced the new uncritically, discounting "modern custom" for some as yet unenvisaged model, or appealed to an indeterminate, unchanging, and static customary life capable of revealing the essentiality of the folk. Whatever the case, the very effacement of custom as a problem for reflection and inquiry, rather than description and recovery, the very reason for its banishment from philosophy, explains why everyday life itself had escaped the attention of thoughtful analyses. For, as Tosaka observed, everydayness resembled the customary in a number of ways, but none more closely than in the contemporary dismissal of both as trivial, banal, vulgar, and unworthy of serious investigation.

Tosaka reasoned that the contemporary desire to see the everyday as an occasion to envisage its other, the realm of the transmundane, constituted a "marked characteristic of the worldly," inasmuch as it signified a retreat from what was near at hand for some transcendental perspective removed from an immediate world of things (4:136). People look upward and start talking about what is beyond reality at the moment they begin to realize they are surrounded by unsatisfactory conditions that cause them to take flight to the spiritual sphere and to appeal, like Buddhists, to "what is a contrary worldliness." The "one modern philosophic term that has been understood most vulgarly has been the word for everyday life (*nichijōsei*)." Its absence in serious reflection represented only the rejection of the contemporary world of lived reality for a fanciful realm of the spirit. To see everydayness as vulgar is to judge it as exceedingly unworthy and to mark its presence as a decline from some loftier, original life. There is no objection on this point among so-called residents of the everyday or the deeply religious who live what they believe to be the original life. Insofar as everyday life is a theological term, it is able to determine things unconditionally. Nevertheless, "the religious system of classifying can be useful in sorting out, according to class membership, those who live an original life from the proletarian masses (who have been impoverished since antiquity) who presently inhabit the everyday life. This is nothing more than acknowledging that those who do not believe in everyday life are namely religious people in the widest sense of the meaning" (4:136) Accordingly, this view sees everyday life as nothing more than either restraint or blind obedience and thus presents it as a superficial phenomenon. As a result, it concentrates on those places of everyday life that make everydayness appear as yet incomplete. Everydayness should not consider the mundane but rather the "divine" directly (4:137). Since "speaking" is philosophy rather than theology, "we must use the idea of this everydayness philosophically, not theologically" (4:136). Recalling his earlier meditations on custom and the proposal to imagine it as a category submitted to interrogation, Tosaka discounted any attempt to displace everydayness to the transcendent world of theology and the extra-mundane as culturally obtuse and politically dangerous. Theologians, whom he described as "philosophers of the other world school," detect the special characteristic of everydayness in its relationship to people. That the average person of society speaks and thinks convincingly suggests that everydayness is lodged within the humanity of a single individual. It is often explained, he observed, that the reason these activities are called everydayness is that they are bonded to convention that the necessity of history follows. But this was a clearly mistaken view because it failed to rise above the commonplaces of belief and literature and fell back on accepting convention and historical necessity as formulated in a literary idiom. (Tosaka actually called this "literaturism"—*bungaku-shugi*—which referred to established modes of literary production that privileged formalism and something called "pure literature.") "The problem," he concluded, "was a philosophical analysis of everydayness."

It should be pointed out here that Tosaka's refiguration of everyday life and his program for philosophizing derived from Heidegger's prior critique of everydayness (*alltaglichkeit*) articulated first in *Sein und Zeit* (1926). This reliance is more evident in Tosaka's texts on space and the space of everydayness. In the "Nichijōsei ni tsuite," the sign of this Heideggerian presence is manifested in the discussion that identifies otherworldliness with an originary life that has, in the present, declined to mere averageness and mediocrity, to the world of the They. Far from wanting to eliminate everydayness as a category for reflection, Heidegger's aim was to rethink it philosophically, as Tosaka was now proposing, in order to relocate in its primordiality Being's originary and authentic existence. But the everydayness of his present, what he referred to as the "average," the "publicness" of Being's immediate existence, constituted a descent from "authentic resoluteness" Being had originally known, authentic historicality which the present had obscured. For Heidegger, the present is open to the possibility of detaching Being from all the conventionalities associated with the "They" and returning to an originary primordiality to deprive the "today," the "now," of its character as "present.[24] In Tosaka's thinking, this appeal to the primordial, which he called the otherworldly and compared to Buddhism, was still religious and therefore constituted an effort to think it as the activity of theology rather than philosophy. The degraded everydayness Heidegger had identified with the modernity of his present, which now offered the "moment of vision anticipating repetition," was precisely the daily life Tosaka was now submitting as a candidate for serious reflection. Despite Heidegger's claim to writing a philosophy, Tosaka renamed it, and all of its variations, as theology. Very early in his seminal essays on space (notably "Kūkan gainen no bunseki," 1928), he distinguished his view of everydayness from the Heideggerian understanding of "commonness" or "ordinariness (*futsūsei*) by arguing that even if the former seemed to point to the latter, defined as ordinary conduct in society, they were different. Commonness is a reality that provides only for general conduct, while a consideration of everydayness is the task that has been assigned to asking where this place must be located where reality is generally carried out By referring to a location, Tosaka was reducing everydayness to space, an everydayness "formed in that place" where the "idea," which he linked to the "commonsensical," is not given but must be pursued and discovered (1:491). Similarly, he advised separating space from the spatial (*kūkansei*) which, according to Heidegger, remained identical to constrain the subject (*shukan*), and thus its existence to the confinement of the spatial (*kūkantekina no de aru*) (1:516). I shall return to this linking of everydayness and space below.

For Tosaka, everydayness was a repetition (*hanpuku*), the repeating of a cycle where "we daily practice love, reflection, and planning under determinate conditions of a fixed society" (4:136). But he warned, as if admonishing contemporary fellow Marxists, that it was not possible to carry out everyday life by merely following things as they are, historical necessity and received convention. The reason for this rejection of the force of mechanical necessity lay in his conviction that everyday life survived only by destroying received conventions and constructing new necessities. If this were not the case, he asked rhetorically, why do we bother eating? While there are always people who believe that an originary existence outside of a degraded daily life is a necessity (Heidegger), the one completed, the other still incomplete and fated to remain so, the characteristic of everyday life was, at bottom, life and living itself, as it repeated the cycle of loving, planning, and reflecting. In this sense, everydayness was never complete, as theologians imagined an other world to be, but always in process of being completed, which came only in the last instance, as it were. The problem, he confessed, was knowing less how to represent everydayness as the space of the "people" and how to avoid a "pedantic" approach for one capable of grasping the everyday in its intensity through literature (4:137). Too often, Tosaka observed, the characteristics of everyday life are, in reality, nothing other than characteristics of life itself. But, he warned, it is also important to recognize that these characteristics inhere in the nature of places that can never be said to be commonplace, realized faithfully and nobly, even if the design of material relationships at first appears complex and confused (4:137). When speaking of the very common, its existence seems always to be where it is never talked about. What he was referring to was the "irresponsibility" of those appeals to the aimlessly lofty and deep, the vocation of theologians who have forgotten the commonplace and the ordinary, the worldly and the material. Hence, the characteristic of actual everyday life, its materiality and concreteness, was not only its flesh and sinew but all that embodied conditions substantively. Calling to mind Kobayashi Hideo's own view of history as the record of commonness, or even Yanagita Kunio's rejection of received historical narratives because of their incessant preoccupation with heroes, generals, great political figures, wars, and battles to the neglect of the voiceless common folk, Tosaka identified everydayness with the materiality of the commonplace, the things colonizing the life of ordinary people, customs that were always changing—all this as over against the extra-mundane claims of the lofty and profound.

This understanding of everyday life was made explicit when Tosaka discussed the status of reality, the real (*genjitsu*) a term used widely in philosophic discourse in the 1930s. Although the term referred to the real, as such, it was able to convey the capacity of grasping concreteness abstractly. At the same time, it was capable of making whatever "reality" into an "unreality," or even a "false reality." For Tosaka, *genjitsu* acted as a code for idealist philosophers who envisaged a reality at a higher plane of existence than at the level of mere, actual occurrences of society. Since it proved to be a conception of reality that resonated with echoes of the abstract rather than the concrete, it was quickly embraced by the "apostles" of "will," "subjectivity" (*shutai*), or the "personal" (*shinpen*), who have wrongly imitated actual reality. This mistaken idea and the effort to imitate the real is basically and categorically different from the actuality of everydayness that disclose a "true reality, that is, it provides the characteristics of the everyday life of humanity. The principles of everydayness are formed in no other place than there" (4:137). What he meant by locating everydayness "there" or in "that place" (the Heideggerian *Da*, thereness, as he was to propose in his essays on space) was the realm that had been concealed by a false or imitated reality, whether it was the idealized transcendent or the regime of the modern and the ever new. Everydayness was not simply the real, as he envisaged it, embedded in materiality, it was also the original of a copy that philosophers, thinkers and writers had misrecognized as the real thing.

Its hard to know who Tosaka was targeting, since there were so many contemporaries who had invested in the word *genjitsu* this sense of an abstract, lofty, and nonmaterial meaning that was prior to and superior to the lived reality of everyday life. Kuki Shūzō, as we shall see later, was surely the most obvious candidate since his *Iki no kōzō* (1929) began with a consideration of "reality." But there was also Watsuji Tetsurō, whose particular brand of idealism Tosaka had criticized on a number of occasions. Nevertheless, it is important to say that this identity between *genjitsu*—reality—and an idealized imaginary enlisted from history or discerned in traces became the subject of Tosaka's searing critique of what he called the Japanese ideology in 1935. Acknowledging his own disbelief in the word *genjitsu*, he could only conclude that for those who employed this meaning it was an easy and convenient pretext for deceiving others and themselves.

In its place, Tosaka preferred to use the word "actuality" (*jissaisei*) to express the rules of everyday life (4:137). This term had been in the service of metaphysics and used even by the Italian philosopher of fascism Giovanni Gentile, a Hegelian idealist. Metaphysically, the term usually conveyed the meaning of movement, marked by action; insofar as this world of actuality is not more than a material domain, it is in the end an impossibility. Other examples propose that real actuality is never found, as its basis is in pure consciousness. When the idea is used in this manner by philosophers, he explained, the category of actuality is clearly unconnected and opposed to everyday life. Avoiding these idealistic dangers, Tosaka wanted to show how the word for actuality was really linked to facticity and temporality. The Manchurian Incident, he wrote, was not a philosophic problem, as such, insofar as it was related to metaphysical principles. But it was an "actual event in the problematic of events" of the day that was not possible to view or see again. It was an event that would not occur again. If the problem of everyday life omits such an event or actuality, it forfeits any connection to content and thus necessitates a consideration of the commonest event philosophically and from a literary perspective. Yet if actuality, which has been imprisoned by a hermeneutic metaphysics, is conceived as an event embedded in everydayness, it will be possible to make well-informed judgments.

Everydayness, in other words, must be relieved of the burden of metaphysics, which blinds or screens the actual from consideration, removing it from history, the current situation, the now (*ima*). This is how he put it in his essay on historical time and the principles of everydayness, which demonstrated how the everyday was made into a mechanical experience bonded to convention and necessity (3:95–104). Eventfulness enters everydayness and thus gives it new meaning, as against the structures of routine and repetition, which constitute its content, yet everydayness, at the same time, mediates events and circumstances in such a way as to make its meaning accessible to the moment. Everydayness was the site of contemporary events, the performing present, the "now" of the "current situation," which alone was giving direction to history and thus supplying it with meaning. But it was being concealed, occulted by a metaphysical conception of reality—*genjitsu*—that would ultimately locate the "real" in an archaism and utopia of primitivism that more conventional (vulgar) Marxists could keep no watch over. Yet, by the same token, Marxist historians and others were rushing to analyze the late Tokugawa period instead of their present and concluding that, by implication and the logic of contiguity, the present had already been prefigured and thus completed in this specific past. Tosaka's penetrating critique of both hermeneutics and historicism, which would have had to include the Marxian historical narratives as well (even though he never explicitly criticized contemporary Marxists in print, as far as I can determine), revealed the fiction of mapping the present onto a completed past to provide a spurious continuity. In this sense, there was probably little or no real difference between cultural exceptionalists who wanted to show the enduring and eternal character of Japan's culture that bonded past to present, on the one hand, and Marxian narratives on the nature of Japanese capitalism of the 1930s, on the other, that aimed at showing that the present was simply a continuation of a past that had neither realized the necessary conditions for either a bourgeois revolution nor prevented its absolutism.

In its own way, this past was still complete in its incompletion It is important to suggest that this move to link the Manchurian Incident to philosophy's true vocation of critical practice called attention to both Japan's imperial adventures and the process by which "actuality," as it was named by *genjitsu*, worked to turn both philosophers and historians away from the momentous events of the time that were demanding analysis rather than engage the historicity and meaning of the "now." What Tosaka seemed to be proposing was that historicism and hermeneutics, cycled into a common sense inscribed in newspaper reporting, sought to detraumatize events in the contemporary historical world that were acting in an overdetermined way as causal forces by removing them from the plot structure in which they had acquired a dominant place and either inserting them in the past or displacing them simply to considerations of generic conventions. The effect was the same since the events were now situated in a subordinate place or simply neutralized in a conception of another world more abstract than concrete, more "real" than actual.

Because a "willful hermeneutics that has been mysteriously metaphysicized rushes into actuality after the reporting of matters of fact," he was convinced that the writing about everyday-like events and occurrences could only be judged and talked about as "creampuffs." What he meant was that the news was simply being sugar coated and disguised as sweetness. In short, a particular view of metaphysics invaded accounts of everyday life to make them appear benign, harmless, unimportant. Even though talk about daily rice and tea is presented in terms of the essence of conventions, "isn't it a more important contemporary problem of everyday life to know whether boiled tea and rice are going to be really sufficient for the masses today?" (4:138). It is hard to exaggerate the significance of this prescient observation of how metaphysics and hermeneutics, indeed how a recondite philosophy seemingly removed from the rhythms of everyday life and indifferent to them, enter unnoticed into the common sense that contemporary journalism is supposed to express. Almost unnoticed, philosophy then mediates the coverage of daily events and occurrences either to make them appear other than they are or to displace and thus neutralize the more urgent consequences of such considerations.

For Tosaka, nothing seemed more important for grasping the "principles" of everyday life than the nature of the current situation. The question of everydayness puts before contemporaries the reality of everyday life implicated in the problem of the current situation (4:139). Moreover, this concern for the current situation should not be limited to materialists alone but should interest philosophy in general. But he also recognized that a concern for contemporary affairs had become the criterion for determining whether or not a philosophy was materialistic. When there is a manifest concern for contemporary affairs, then there is also the criterion that shows whether or not the treatment of the current situation is scientific. Acknowledging that it was important to represent the scientific treatment of content from a literary perspective, he also claimed that this approach should never encourage the tendency toward the "mechanical" as illustrated by contemporary "literalistic speculation" (*bungakushugitekina shikō*). Too often, people move from scholarship to journalism, like the Italian social thinker Vilfredo Pareto in his last years, in the "style of a critique of contemporary events," and are berated as bad scholars by others who believe that learning should be kept pure from the current situation. (This is not to say that Tosaka approved of what Pareto was writing, which he didn't.) Tosaka observed that a pure philosophy that leaned toward abstracting everydayness might constitute a hobby for "deep philosophers" and "literary men," much like salarymen chanting No on their lunch breaks. But as a hobby it was not really so different, since the turn to everyday life by deep philosophers might become an "avocation" itself. Whatever the case, he was convinced that readers would soon discover how the otherworldly has no fidelity in life. Worried that in his day the philosophical meaning of journalism was scarcely understood, an even greater deficiency was the failure to recognize this as a problem. By the same measure, he was convinced that, due to its nature as the site of the current situation and its eventfulness, it was impossible not to problematize everyday life philosophically. To envisage the current situation—the now—philosophically opened the way to evaluating and even judging those "journalistic phenomena" that concentrate on daily eventfulness (*jijisei*) and to explaining why, therefore, they are necessarily a problem of actuality for both literature and philosophy. Hence, the problem of everydayness was intensely bonded to the question of the "situation" (*jikyoku*), implying, of course, the recognition of a specific temporality. While Tosaka complained about "theologians" and "Buddhists" yearning for an otherworldly authentic life, he was particularly dissatisfied with those (perhaps like Kon and Gonda Yasunosuke) who marked time by holding only discussions on whether or not everydayness was an "easy going" life style of society's masses. "Inasmuch as these people are not Buddhist priests, I can't help saying that something is extremely wrong" (4:139). "Theologians," "metaphysicians," and "literary consciousness" (devotees of "pure literature") "have employed interpretative categories toward the actual problem of current reality by absent mindedly looking back in a stupor" to miss both the vast spectacle taking place before their eyes and the necessary relationship between newspapers and history, journalists and historians.[25]

But Tosaka also warned against a "historical philosophy" that aped metaphysics to exclude an analysis of contemporary events from historical consideration altogether. This was another of the "modern attitudes of metaphysics" (4:140). The history of the real, he argued, was never grasped according to "historical sensation" (referring to the empathic approach) or the historical philosophy that accompanied it; it was seized first through the articulation of a necessary social consciousness (a journalistic sense of contemporary events) and its analysis. The mundane and vulgar realm imagined by the otherworldly school that so disliked everydayness now takes reprisals on everyday life by making the self the axis of its concerns, even when it is considering the problem of history. What he seemed to be expressing was a hope for a "return" of the fundamental opposition between "historical philosophy" (*rekishi tetsugaku*) and historical materialism, the former recently articulated by his friend Miki Kiyoshi in his transit from Marxism, the latter misrecognized by an economistic Marxism informing the contemporaneous historical debate over capitalism which he was in process of trying to rethink. In *"Rekishi to benshōhō"* (1934), he promoted a Kantian conception of dialectics that authorized a reason that should bring about a union with sensibility, a speculative mode that should play a role that first takes existence into the self at the moment autonomous action is contemplated. This dialectic that established a link between existence and speculation was juxtaposed to a Hegelian version that promised to "advance outside of speculation [theory] but terminated in the world of theory. It never got beyond the developmental form of the idea, the concept" (3:76). As we shall see, the favoring of a Kantian dialectic over a Hegelian revision produced an entirely different conception of history rooted in material existence and the possibility of contingence, in opposition to one that obeyed the logic of a developmental narrative that remained locked in the concept and bonded to a totality. The purpose of problematizing everydayness, Tosaka was convinced, was to recall the function of criticism itself as a response to the current situation. By criticism, he meant the turn toward active reflection on the current situation (*jikyoku*) demanded by the occurrence of contemporary events, which constituted the best defense against a "metaphysics of interpretation" that managed to produce only the "principle of criticism" rather than its actual practice. And it was for this reason that he insisted on the "scientific necessity" to "scorn" the claims of a "trans-everyday world" (3:140).

But Tosaka's call for a "return" involved a more fundamental desire to recall philosophy to its true vocation as the commonsensical arbiter of everyday life. Tosaka had, on numerous occasions, investigated the status of common sense and its original relationship to (Greek) philosophy.[26] The present offered an urgent reason to reconsider the role of common sense and how it related to philosophy. "When speaking from a certain commonsensical perspective in Japan at this present time," he wrote, "nobody has yet actually considered that philosophical learning and research, for some time now, has belonged to a special world separated from any everyday life, where it once resided. Philosophy permeates common sense nearly completely, and it is good to say that it is used correctly there where it should be used." "Insofar as this is seen, it is best to say that philosophy, at least, is becoming properly everyday-like [quotidianized]" (4:162: "Tetsugaku to bunshō"). Tosaka argued that philosophy, in its full and final meaning, would become everydayness and thus be elevated to the everyday as it mode of articulation. But he was also concerned to explain why the present had provoked the question of philosophy's original relationship to the everyday and commonsensical, and why it had departed from this venerable genealogy to become a specialized language figuring other worlds. The present seemed appointed to inaugurate an excavation of this relationship of philosophy to worlds other than the everyday.

Originally, he explained, philosophy distinguished itself as a literary science by its contemplation of the everyday (4:164). If literature was close to the everyday and the commonsensical, philosophy also conveyed the same original meaning. By recognizing that philosophy shared an identity with the everyday, he was also aware of the fact that the Greeks envisaged the possibility of philosophy becoming unnecessarily difficult, a mode of reflection that easily slipped into academic pedantry. Tosaka proposed that while philosophy was once said to be everyday-like, today it has become necessarily very difficult. And the reason for this is that its essence is an "anti-everyday-like, anti-commonsensical philosophy." What he was driving at in this meditation on "Philosophy and Writing" was the apparent separation of philosophy from the world of existence and its acquisition of a complex, technical vocabulary used to figure other (metaphysical) worlds. The path of return lay in reinvesting or, as he put it, "tempering" philosophical language with "everyday words" or words from the world of common sense. Unlike other sciences, he explained, philosophy "is an effect that comes from an everydayness" and should avoid scholarly specialization (4:166). What marks philosophy especially is only its "everydayness," which, he believed, it had forfeited in the interest of becoming specialized and academicized; the result was "scientific stagnation." With its increasing dependence on "technical words," philosophy risked losing its connection to its referent. Even though it has been saturated by a technical language, it still must seek to preserve to maintain a "direct relationship" between technical words and "everyday words." The link was provided by the recognition that philosophy was never able to completely create a technical vocabulary so that its technical words would still reflect and retain a connection to its base in everyday speech (4:167). After philosophical terms have been refined from everyday speech, the problem that emerges is the relationship between philosophic vocabulary and national language (kokugo). But it is not simply that national language signifies the "breakup" of local dialects for the creation of a standardized language. Even more important is the "breakup of several kinds of class language" (4:168). Words and sentences as living expressions possess a classed segmentation, as if they were restricted codes. What becomes a problem for philosophy is, of course, the classed opposition between scholarly terminology and popular speech. The opposition between technical and everyday language invariably enacts a confrontation between classes.

It is interesting to note that Tosaka saw the crisis of meaning deriving from philosophy's separation from its referent in the everyday world. But while he privileged the primacy of everyday speech, he was also fully aware of the segmenting process that takes place in actual language usage according to class position. This argument had been forcefully made a decade earlier by the Soviet critics M. M. Bakhtin and V. Voloshinov in their classically prescient attempt to think through a philosophy of language for Marxism. What they observed was that everyday speech was the basis of communication and therefore the "arena" of the class struggle, which was always driven by the contest over whose meaning and voice would prevail.[27] For Tosaka, the loss of the referent, which meant the disappearance of everyday life, conformed to the contemporary modernist concern for both the stability of reference and the necessity of concreteness in a social order where both seemed to be disappearing into social abstraction. Yet, the problem was even more complex since everyday speech itself was segmented along class lines. The language "deeply systematized by the philosophies of Kant and Hegel," he asserted, "was the everyday language—the language of townsfolk—which they completely refined" (4:169). In Japan, the problem of language usage was complicated by the importation of European terms and translation into putative equivalents. In fact, philosophical language was itself an importation and not an effect of the usual agglutinating process that produces it from popular speech. For Tosaka, this fact accounted for the markedly distinctive separation of philosophy from everyday life in Japan, more than elsewhere. Philosophy in Japan, he wrote, was not only a "classed tolerance that digested popular language used by the masses; many of the philosophic narratives were left behind as a variety of ornate, bureaucratic writing." As a result, the popular language of everydayness remained apart from the formation of a philosophic idiom from the start, preserved by the masses yet used only in translating activity. Literature, by comparison, progressed rapidly, while the existence of philosophic terminology and writing stalled because it constituted a problem unrelated to everydayness and the popular. Although his own advice to return to everyday speech, the language of the masses that had remained separated from a specialized philosophical vocabulary, conformed to the general modernist program of finding a stable referent, it still risked carrying the unstated presumption that commonsensical speech had been, in a way he never explained, able to resist the reifying process and its regime of social abstraction. It was important, he believed, for philosophy to return to its roots in common sense. Specialization constituted a form of reification, inasmuch as the division of knowledge characterizing philosophical reflection diverted it from addressing the everyday. "This specialty," he insisted, "must be returned to the world of common sense again. Moreover, it is necessary to dissolve it philosophically and honestly into the commonsense world. That is the problem of philosophy. The problem of philosophy, in a certain meaning, is the problem of contemporary eventfulness, the problem of criticism. A philosophy that does not understand the 'problem of actuality' is not philosophy" (4:173).

If Tosaka sought to return philosophy to its original involvement in the world of common sense, he also wanted to relieve history from the curse of historicism—its dependence on metaphysical categories and narrative development under the sign of hermeneutics—in order to turn it back to the materiality of daily existence (3:69–77). The final (*saigo*) principles of history are the principles of everydayness or, alternatively, the "sense of the actual" (3:72–73). In his understanding, selecting as an example from past occurrences and citing it as real is not yet a historical actuality. "Reality," he pronounced, "is a connected totality of the final *Konkreta*" (3:73). What he plainly meant is that the principles of history cannot correspond to an order that is outside history. The principles of history are "materiality" and "massness" (*shitsuryōsei*), which are not "imparted" through form but are themselves the final principle of the self. To explain history from the perspective of an "originary history" (*urgeschicte*)—or "eternity"—is to deny the "principles of history" and the historical itself. According to this explanation, Tosaka warned, "historical existence" does not "increase the character of its existence," progressively and exponentially, but instead "weakens" it and is "distantiated from existence." This approach proceeded from "metaphysical categories" that tried to reduce existence to history, which itself was nothing more than the "idea of an originary history," "eliminating" history, as such (3:74). The problem for idealism has always been its misrecognized identification between the metaphysical meaning of practice and practice itself. Tosaka wanted to liberate "practice" from its constrained idealistic identification. Practice as a philosophic category, as existence, was yoked to the ethicality of the individual and the level of social morality, and thus resituated as historical, social, and productive activity.

To this end, he demolished the principle of historical temporality based on the hermeneutic category that always looked back "absentmindedly" as if mesmerized by the lure of the past for the immediacy of space. By space he meant "everyday space," where actual existence was carried out and which structured its own sense of time in the present, the now. Tosaka's tactic required dismantling received categories of historical temporality, especially those that seemingly authorized developmental schemes founded on an originary history to show how the present of everydayness supplied the principles of historical time. Once he made this argument, he turned to demonstrating how everydayness signified genuine materiality—precisely the principles of materiality and massness he previously located in history. The priority given to space would organize historical time differently from an approach motored by the presumption of an "originary history" or "eternality." He managed to envisage a new and radically different purpose and task for historical materialism, an ambition he apparently shared with Walter Benjamin and perhaps Antonio Gramsci, who, at the same time, were trying to imagine a conception of history that would open the way for practice in history that historicism, in all of its forms, had simply foreclosed. With Tosaka, the refiguring of historical materialism revealed the shadow of both Kant and Heidegger (as it did in Benjamin) rather than Hegel and Lukacs and allowed him to emplot a history from the present, rather than a fixed past, from material existence in the now, the "current situation" that would subsequently recall a certain past, rather than from a past that would undoubtedly forget the present. As a loyal Marxist, he never addressed the contemporary controversy among Marxist historians raging over the nature of Japanese capitalism, even though his rethinking of historical materialism diverged sharply from the more familiar developmental and economistically emplotted narratives historians were constructing to show how Japan had either fulfilled or come up short of satisfying the conditions for revolution in the mid-nineteenth century. What his silence denoted is hard to say, but what his own version of historical materialism based on the immediacy of the present and the primacy of critique earned for him was lasting dismissal by both Marxists and historians, much like Benjamin's own program for a revised, nonhermeneutic, and noneconomistic historical materialism.

Tosaka's program hinged on a critique of received categories of historical temporality that all historicisms presumed as a given: the temporality that mediated both the trajectory of the succession of events and the causal relationships supplying it coherence. In his one of his most profound and original essays, "Nichijōsei no genri to rekishiteki jikan" (The principles of everydayness and historical time, 1934), he showed his certainty that everydayness was related to the "abstract structure of history," even though it was absent in most considerations seeking to elucidate the "mystery of history" (3:101). Any discussion concerning the structure of history must inevitably return to the theory of time, historical time (*jikan*), and must therefore try to determine its nature. By reasoning that history must always draw its principles, its general structure that is historically temporalized, from conscious phenomena outside of history, he proposed that the principles informing history are thus not found in history itself, as they are adaptations from another domain or extractions from nonhistorical principles (3:96). Historical time either is nothing or inheres only in a nonhistorical temporality. What Tosaka was advancing was the idea that historical time could not qualify as a phenomenological thing or object, as such, but rather corresponded only to consciousness. But in natural science, time is quantified, calculated, enumerated. Quantification, in this regard, refers to a process of enumeration and spatialization that thereby introduces the operation of "cutting time up," mincing (*kizami*) or marking it. At the same time, people are familiarized with this idea so that they expect to understand time as a set of discrete segments. It is because of this cutting up of time that ordinary people consider time as time. The operation of marking time (mincing it) breaks into the continuity of pure time and opens up a gap that always involves seeing it—temporality—as the gap of time rather than merely the gap in time. Even the claims for the flow of consciousness as pure continuity require this operation of marking, mincing; without it, one will never know time. Tosaka acknowledged that marked time (*jikan*) was often confused with pure temporality (*toki*), which constituted "a reflection of eternity," its "shadow," perhaps, the lining or backside of marked time, but the temptation to treat it in this manner risked forgetting the necessary operation of cutting or marking. Because time is time, there must be minced segments. In natural science, this cutting up acquires a meaning by and of itself, an autonomy that is substituted for time itself. Temporality, he observed, is defined through the process of dividing it into segments like the hour and day, by time limits (*jigen*). This exaggerated emphasis on the process of cutting up time into discrete segments refers simply to its quantification. It is from this perspective, in any event, that natural phenomena like the revolutions of the globe are made as the basis of calculation. Tosaka recognized that this understanding of time "overstated" the function of marking and overlooked its actual content or substance; the operation of cutting worked externally and contingently and was unrelated to the content of time.

Overstating the function to relieve time of its divisions transmutes segmented time into pure temporality, eternalizes time into eternity, "stopping it" and "making the present eternal" (3:97). The reverse operation that overstates the role played by marking ultimately spatializes temporality and robs it of its timefulness. In both cases, historical time is denied any possibility for appearance; in the former, there is simply no historical temporality as a first principle in the idea of time; in the latter, what makes marked time pure temporality is what eternalizes history and makes it circular. History becomes Nietzsche's "eternal recurrence." The cosmic diagrams portrayed by Dante sought to represent the movement of a Christian historical philosophy that paralleled natural scientific time and its conception of an eternal cycle based on the movement of the heavenly bodies. But in this process, Tosaka recognized the effect of actually disregarding historical time and inducing forgetfulness of the normal cutting of time. The usual idea of historical time and temporality is where the process of marking is neither excessive nor too little. It was at this point that Tosaka turned to the problem of how historical temporality was divided. Accepting the received conventions of historical chronology, he acknowledged the role of the period (*zeit*) as a basic unit and marker in the historical process. The period or age, he wrote, refers to an epoch (*epoché*) and thereby signifies the introduction of a point of pause or cessation to differ sharply from the natural scientific cycle. Instead, it closely resembles the logic of grammatical markers that punctuate pauses and stops (3:98). The actual marking or cutting up of time derives from the content of time itself (in contrast to scientific quantification) and, unlike scientific time, is neither contingent on nor external toward its content. Hence, historical time is segmented into periods (*perioden*) according to its content which is, more or less, unlimitedly diverse. While historical temporality always ends in a specific content that is not necessarily formalized, what is important is the idea of character (*seikaku*), which, like a grammatical trope, organizes the pause or cessation demanded by the *epoché*. Out of the diverse conditions constituting content, it is the identification of character (or characteristic) that governs the selection, grasps content as content, and organizes it. Historical temporality, denominating the unity of diverse characteristics, segments and partitions them into fixed periods. These characteristics must be differentiated from the individual (*kotai*) or *a-tom*, which are indivisible (at least in 1934 it was thought so) but are produced through a process of "partitioning" (*bunkatsu*), which, he believed, constituted the basis of cutting up time. The duration (what Tosaka called "quantity") of a period depends upon the nature of its characteristic, whether or not it is susceptible to change. It is for this reason, he added, that historical periodization is the opposite of the cycles of natural science, since this difference—marking divisions according to periods—derives principally from the content of historical temporality, whereby character acts as the means that grasps it.

Tosaka compared historical characteristic to the monad, which was supposed to possess the capacity to either swell and enlarge itself or contract while it keeps its windows open and breathes the air freely. According to this model, history becomes heterogeneous, which supplies it with its only meaning of continuity. If the characteristic constitutes the idea or means by which to "seize hold" of content, people are no longer in a position to either conceive or create it since it is something that is produced. (Here, Tosaka was obviously hinting at Marx's famous declaration that men do not always make history but find themselves in circumstances that have been made for them.) "Character is like the maturation of the fig which falls by itself when time ripens from the tree of history. When these fall, people must unerringly receive them in hand. It is only good if people discover a definite or fixed characteristic within history. But how they receive this ripened fruit skillfully for their present depends completely on the character of people themselves. How their character is linked to the characteristic of history is determined by the period. The problem is like returning to their historical sense" (3:99). Still, Tosaka worried about what actually caused the maturation of the tree of history to finally shed its fruit, what actually determined the nature of a characteristic that constitutes a period in historical time. The answer was provided by politics, which, according to his logic, is driven by social relations and the material forces of production, as it is played out it in the "rising of classes" (ran). (He used the character for "basket," whose sound is homonymous with rebellion, ran, apparently to evade the gaze of censors.) Tosaka described discrete periods as "living bodies" that obeyed something like a life cycle that brought them to an end, to be regenerated in another "living body." While he eschewed a specifically organicist conception of periodization, he saw the various epochs interacting with each other in dialectical succession to constitute the totality of historical time. Yet he was persuaded that the diversity of periods, each bearing the mark of its own characteristic that partitioned it off from others, constituted a continuity of diversity or heteronyms, a kind of ruptural unity, as Althusser would call it later, where each period, however diverse, functioning as a historical individual, refers to a part at the same time that it calls attention to the whole (3:100). Visualized as the relationship between part and whole as a layering on the same level, the period, nevertheless, is determined by the idea of the characteristic that selects without flattening its solidity or three-dimensionality. What Tosaka hoped to show was that even though there was a tight relationship between part and whole, the part was not flattened out to accommodate the whole, but rather retained its individuality, its "three-dimensionality." In this regard, historical temporality possesses the same value as the characteristic.

The really important question for Tosaka is why historical temporality had become such an urgent problem in his present. The motive behind this concern was the "reality people were living in this historical time. This is the time of our lives which must now be recalled again" (3:100). While we live in the present, he continued, we must see how the present is situated in "our historical time." At the heart of this question was his own desire to show that the present possessed its own historical temporality because it was a period, a slice of time cut off from others, that announced its own distinctive characteristic. Aware that certain men, as he put it, stretch out the present to include eternity itself, fuse the past to the present, the future in the present, the present in the present, and so forth, the present ends up equaling the past; the not yet becomes time that equals temporality that equals eternity. With this move the now becomes eternity and the present disappears. Still others consider the present (*genzai*) as a geometric point that cannot be lengthened. Hence the unit of time that is thought to be the present is immediately the past. These two extremes, which are similarly mistaken, never manage to get beyond the wrong side of the idea of the present because they fail to consider the present as a period where the cutting of both sides has taken place. The eclectic explanation imagines the present either as a "differential calculus" or as something that brings out the "fringe" (3:101). Whatever the case, all of these positions deny the present of its periodicity, its temporality inspired by the idea of phenomenological time that permits consciousness to live in its conception of time but never the body. According to Tosaka, living is always done in the present, "in a period named the present, properly in modern times (*gendai*)." But that life is lived always in the present age does not seem to teach anything new, and it is for this reason that it is important to see the present, unlike phenomenologists, as a period that has surfaced according to the marking (cutting) of historical time. In this respect the present possesses limits that are seemingly infinite but not entirely so.

Although Tosaka recognized that the duration of this present, like any other present, would depend upon its own characteristic, he was equally sure that its uniqueness was testimony to its characteristic rather than constancy of its longevity. He was also convinced that the uniqueness of a period reflected the accent of the whole of historical time which is located in it. Because the characteristic of historical time brings out in almost condensed form its most intense points, its focus, the solidity of historical time is concentrated in this place (3:101). What this move encouraged him to propose is the discovery of the "kernel of the crystal": finding in the present the condensed meaning of historical time as totality. By the same measure, this discovery would authorize advising both historical action and the production of historical narrative to make the present the "starting point of its coordinates." The present, for him, was the site of both necessity and flexibility, which meant crystallizing the "kernel" in the "today" or the "now," that is, making it visible. This now, he observed, brought out the same nature as the present, the contemporary, the real, since both the present and the today shared the same principles of meaning. But the present would belong to the order of the history, whereas the now remained outside of it, constituting the space where a potential history of the present could be produced. It is the place that "surfaces through the cutting up of historical time"; the present acquires its identity through the act of cutting up time into small but limited durations (3:101). Tosaka, disclosing an indebtedness to Heidegger, sought to collapse the present age into the now to show that the now was where life was carried out and where the present was given its distinctive temporality. A today that epitomized the present age and shared with it the principle of meaning was the "principle of everyday" (*nichinichi*). Hence, historical time was governed by the "principle of everydayness." In his thinking, the present was inevitably "minaturized" in the today (*konnichi*), even more in the now (*ima*). By the same measure, the now served as a metonym that was capable of disclosing the nature of the present and contemporary reality (*gendaisei*) which it shared.

Tosaka reduced the vast, seemingly endless flow of historical time to the most basic unit of existence, the day-to-day interactions that structured experience. "This is the time of our lives." Everyday life was driven by the principle of repetition, each day repeating itself, repeating the same things that had happened the day before. "In the long run," he explained, "while the principle that brings out dailyness and this or that day repeats the same thing everyday, where every day is still a separate day despite the common daily occurrences [that make them look alike], the principle of an inescapable everyday life absolutely shelters the kernel of the crystal of historical time, the mystery of history" (3:101). In the repetitive and routine unfolding of one day after another, each resembling what came before and what was to come tomorrow, lay concealed the "kernel" of historicity (the "crystal"), the mystery of time's difference. Yet it is important to notice that that everydayness actually "sheltered" the "kernel of the crystal of historical time," concealed it. Everyday life, unlike history, was a concealment, blurred in repetition and routine; its investigation was necessary if the historically concealed, that is, the crystal of historical time, "history's mystery," were ever to be revealed, made visible. In a sense, Tosaka's conception of everydayness resembled his view of custom and the commodity, both of which managed to conceal their principles of historical production to appear natural, unhistorical, without time and character. Embedded deeply in a nonhistorical everyday life was the kernel of history that needed to be drawn out. By proposing that the characteristic (*seikaku*) differentiating historical time has the same value as everyday life's claim to historical temporality, Tosaka was able to identify the relationship between the now and what would become the historical present. The relationship approximated one between part and whole. Everydayness offered a glimpse of what would be known as the historical character of an age. When it is remarked that the present always reveals the necessity and flexibility of today, this means only that it is responding to the necessity of practical life. Although there are large numbers of *discriminating* rich people endowed with the means to lead excessive lives, the present for them will probably offer unlimited opportunities for deferral and diversion. The reason for this is that they can do without the today if they choose, defer what to do today to an indefinite future; if today is bad, tomorrow, the day after, will be good. But no such alternative is available to the worker, who, by contrast, must work today without fail since tomorrow may be worse if he does not. For them, the present is always today, and insofar as history is practical, the present is packed into the today. And in this way the principle of "today," the principle of "everydayness," directs historical temporality as a unity.

If everydayness corresponded to a contemporaneity that qualified actuality, it also signified the domain of praxis (*jissensei*). Despite his enthusiasm for practice in everyday interaction, Tosaka cautioned that these principles of reality were not the same as envisaging possibility (*kanōsei*) for the future, which belonged to utopian speculation generated by idealistic philosophy. Tosaka was unambiguously emphatic in insisting on making a sharp distinction between the relationship between "actuality" and the possibility of a utopian future, which he classified as "ideal," the "imaginary," "expectations" that had more to do with the reverse of everydayness than with the realities of day-to-day experience. What prompted him to make this distinction was quite conceivably his already declared opposition to a dialectical progression moving toward the accomplishment of a distant goal that remained entirely confined to theory and consciousness. But he also objected to placing contemporaneity and possibilities for the future on the same plane, side by side, as a formal coupling that seemed to share the same identity even though they were vastly different. People experienced everydayness day to day, yet the presumption of achieving some sort of utopian possibility did not have the same substantive reality as daily experience. In fact, it had no reality whatsoever even though it was ranked with daily existence. Its presence invalidated a theory based on everyday actuality and made its practice entirely impossible (3:101, 103).

The criticism against placing contemporaneity and possibility on the same plane stemmed from a conviction that work in the now, and not the Heideggerian recognition of one's death, the demands of a futural destiny, structured one's life, one's destiny, as it were. It was work time, limited by the time of one's death, that necessitated the urgency of doing today, in the now, what one might want to defer to tomorrow but cannot afford to do so. Because "death's time comes," it is necessary "to put work into order within a fixed period of time" (3:102). The contemporary, the characteristic named as the now, independently constructs an "order of values" suitable to its angle of vision. This meant that a person—the I—is not permitted to measure the value system produced by the actuality of today with tomorrow's, according to a set of possibilities fixed by a future that has not yet come about. Today must put into order the business of today, just as tomorrow must settle the business of tomorrow. From the standpoint of unifying one's limited temporal life, this is an absolutely inescapable fact because, he explained, one must construct an organization that determines what is to be done before and later when planning work. This structure, the present, which Tosaka named as the "today," imparts a rule of perspective that reflects this arrangement of business, where today constitutes both a historical totalization and its spatial configuration. While the principles brought out by common day-to-day existence are those associated with everydayness, it is important to envisage the individual who is an "I" in society as a member of a class, just as it is essential to see the single day that has been identified as the today as a day in world history, in order to avoid giving the impression that the individual is imprisoned as a solitary inmate in a routinized everyday removed from the broader world. This allowed Tosaka to propose that historical time had to conform to an order that permitted no exchanging of today for tomorrow, today for yesterday. Unless this mixing of series is avoided, the present will become (mis)identified with possibility, and "actuality" will be disregarded. His complaint was, again, directed against a formal theory that mediated things by lining them up on the same plane because it was driven by the law of contradiction that could not tolerate nonidentity. If things were distributed to other levels, rather than being limited to the same plane, it would be possible for differences to appear rather than forcing identities. The argument was based on the presumption that while a thing with one identity, say A, exists on one plane, it might be possible for it to become something else on still another level, such as "beta." Allowing for the existence of at least two levels invalidates the law of contradiction and introduces multidimensionality and thus the possibility for difference. A thing might be one thing in one section but something entirely different in another because it possesses concrete diversity. The significance of this theory was that it made allowance for the existence of dimensions (which Tosaka incorporated into the dialectic), which called attention to the structure of space more than temporality, a kind of sedimentation of levels where location would determine the identity of an object that would change as it was resituated on other levels. But the relocation of a thing is a characteristic that shows how it develops historically in several manifestations—something equivalent to a conception of historical change. Tosaka believed that dimensionality, the movement of a thing from one level to another where its identity changed, corresponded to historical time. But this need not have implied either progressive linearity or endless repetition, even though we can discern a repetitive dimension in the move from one level to an-other that marked the same with difference. Rather, Tosaka's theory of history came close to a view, articulated in our time by Deleuze and Guat-tari, that decodes and recodes received practices, deterritorializing and re-territorializing them in any given present.

Clearly, this conception of historical time was spatial. Days accumulate on top of each other in succession, but today and tomorrow are not inter-changeable. The perspective of the present, the now of today, is always the time of work, not tomorrow, which may never come. In this way, Tosaka insisted, the today, the "now, has dimensionality and solidity to it," and practice must conform to its immediate situation, its historical moment. The task for theory was to follow the principles of everydayness, to "unify completely with the dimensionality of the now of historical time" (3:103). In other words, the temporal perspective, the differentia-tion between fore and after, indeed the difference between foreground and background, would mean a difference in theoretical values, the difference between a reality that was at hand and one that had not yet been realized. Temporality was thus cast within the space of everyday life, determined by its "thereness" (soko), just as Tosaka's contemporary, the linguist Tokieda Motoki, was in process of envisioning what he called the "scene" (bamen) of speaking that would supply the material referent to language usage.

A few years later, in 1936, Tosaka turned to explaining how everyday-ness was primarily spatial and material. In all things, he wrote, "we trans-mit our daily lives through the management of . . . space" (3:239). In fact, three modes of space—intuitive space (psychological space or the space of representation), geometric space (mathematical space), and physical space (actual space)—are all connected to everyday space (3:260). Everyday space was thus a direct abstraction of space itself, a nondifferentiated ex-pression of space produced by people putting it to practical use. Histori-cally, everyday space was expressed by the "where" (doko, izuko), "topos" or "locus" (basho), and "situs" (chi-i), that is, whereness, loca-tion, and the situation within space (3:261). As for the characteristic of existence, it was expressed by the "there" (Da), testifying to its "unique objectivity" that was the only way to describe space. This Da-ness signified a materiality determined by the attributes of extension, continuity, succes-sion, and length. In this space, humans manage their practical activity ac-cording to matter within a presentness (ima, konnichi)—the now, today—and its repetition (3:264). For Tosaka, everydayness always returns to ma-terial despite the abstracted philosophical modes that seek to differentiate its substance. If this was the case, then it was important to examine the history of philosophy in order to reveal how it had effectively repressed and even effaced the role played by space as a central problem for reflec-tion. Illuminating this real, hidden history not only would demonstrate the commanding role once occupied by space and materiality in philosophic speculation but it would invert the structure of historical narrative itself to reveal how history must revolve around the space of everydayness rather than be driven by the itinerary of the idea (and Being) and its fulfillment in time. Under this charge, historical narrative would, by necessity, no longer follow a linear trajectory but acquire both a different form and content that structured its temporality into accumulative layers that could only be disturbed by critically exploring the possibilities they offer or make accessible at any given moment. Only critical practice was able to upset the hold of sedimented conventions and envision new custom. While Tosaka's theory of everyday space resembled the structure of sedimented cultural layers Watsuji Tetsuro identified as "stadialization", where the earliest strata of cultural layering continue to reflect through later accumulations to attest to permanence and self-presence, it rejected this palimpsistic effect out of hand and sought to undo its effects by assigning to critical practice the task of constant vigilance over daily affairs.

We must recognize in Tosaka's thinking a Husserlian gesture that sought to demonstrate how perception derived from everyday experience and thus lay at the heart of all subsequent reflection. The importance of this observation is that it explained how perception based on what was experienced was inverted into abstraction and the claims of universal transcendence associated with mathematics and later science. Like Husserl, who proposed in his *Crisis of European Science* that geometry had grown out of the use of everyday modes of measurement which ultimately were repressed to make it appear transcendental, Tosaka argued that all conceptions of space, however abstract, scientific, and putatively transcendent, originated in the space of everydayness, even though this history was buried or concealed in the subsequent history of science. Practices derived from everyday life and experience, and these latter were shed as they metamorphosed into science. But it is important to note also that his argument identified not only the loss of everyday space in the original production of science but also the equally crucial relationship between spatiality and materiality. In a sense, his discourse on space aimed at resuscitating the "memory" of this lost and now forgotten linkage and resituating it in the present as its sign and the site of its privilege. The present signaled the reappearance of an everyday life embedded in material things that structured lives and experiences and mediated existence in the now, as it had in the beginning of human history.

Tosaka's appeal to everyday space as that which was repressed in order to uphold the claims of scientific transcendence was an effort to get back to the materiality of existence and the historical moment when everydayness had first emerged in philosophical reflection. By the same token, the act of recall was necessary to rescue the authority of everydayness as it was being lived in the present, the now. Clearly, he was targeting the practice of prevailing philosophic idealisms and especially Heidegger's dismissal of the everydayness of the present—the regime of mediocrity and the average—and call for a return to Being's primordial conditions and authentic existence. If Heidegger sought to eliminate everydayness, as such, he was convinced that the present represented a descent as it was now being lived by "them." As a response, he also wished to return to a place where Dasein had been originally united with its true vocation and destiny. For Tosaka, this view of Being still retained more than a hint of idealism and subjective intention—a criticism made also by Nishida Kitarō—and seemed to recuperate the sovereign self and its separation from materiality. In fact, he believed that the priority of space and its problematization, not Being's original intention, was the historical basis of philosophic speculation (3:240). Presocratic philosophy, especially what was called "natural philosophy," revolved completely around the problem of space. To demonstrate the existence of this prior foundation, he excavated a different narrative which both the history of philosophy and the history of science had forgotten. First, Parmenides liked to look at the category of existence (*sonzai*) as an object of theory. What this meant, in Tosaka's understanding, was that commonsensical material was prior to the awareness that it belonged to a philosophic, universal awareness (3:264). But existence for Parmenides meant "spatial existence." Second, Pythagoras understood that the principle of existence was numbers, which were connected to diverse mysterious characteristics. Hence, one-1-was a point, two-2-a line, three-3-a plane, and so forth. Even though Pythagoras was not always considered a participant in natural philosophy, he never abandoned the basic attitude of archaic Greece, which considered existence as related to space. Third, a view that saw existence as spatial undoubtedly took notice that space was also a void, that it had no existence itself or being but rather appeared as no-thing. Although existence was in space, it was not spatial itself; existence and space were thus separated, opposed, one "squeezing out" the other. But it was necessary to concretize existence if it was to achieve unity, and this was the purpose of Democritus's theory of the atom, which, it was once believed, constituted the most basic, indivisible unit of matter. Socratic thought and its aftermath argued that existence escaped from the constraints of spatial attributes to become formless, spiritual. As a result, space came to be regarded as only one among many distinct features of existence and thus lost its centrality commanding Greek philosophical speculation. It was reduced to questions of consciousness or values, or spirit or culture. Tosaka wondered why it had been so belittled, so trivialized in his day.

The narrative proposed that philosophy, since Plato, had omitted the claims of natural existence for the privileging of attributes that "tried to impart a spiritual, anti-material conditions" as its original vocation. Idealistic ontology supplanted the previously held view of material existence; this inspired the "cold reception" toward the problem of space. Socrates had such distrust for the basic problems of natural philosophy that he had no hesitation in classifying it under sophism. But Plato showed the greatest "distrust" in the *Timaeus* with the so-called Platonic idea, which Aristotle later repeated. Diminishing the space problem attended the introduction of idealism, just as the respect for it was originally accompanied by the formation of materialism (3:243; also 224–225). Hence the problem of space rose and fell with materialism. Paradoxically, the "basic revolution" announced by the idea of materiality unexpectedly prepared the ground for its effacement in the wake of the idealist revolution. The atom, as the "final" unit of matter testifying to an existence that could be divided, could not help but be maintained in a fixed shape, form, and aspect. Matter was not seen only as existence but as materiality that acquired fixed form, which authorized its claim to the name of existence. In time, this "existence" evolved into the mathematical forms of today. Tosaka reasoned that an existence of existence, the essence and substance of existence, was located not in matter but in its representational form. Matter and existence were thus separated, revolving round an opposition between existence as form (representation, the figure, the idea) and formless matter (3:225).

The importance of this historical narrative is that it sought to locate the hidden origins of philosophy in a materialism and spatiality that subsequently were overthrown for the idea, form, and primacy of temporality. (Again Tosaka came close to the arguments Watsuji Tetsuro was already making in his own effort to differentiate East from West by showing how the former privileged spatial relations while the latter prioritized time.) Yet his account must also be read against contemporary historical practice that still, despite even the Marxian inflection, privileged idea and its fulfillment in time. It should be recalled that Tosaka insisted that all considerations of space derived from the everyday. "Before people structured space psychologically, physically, and geometrically," he wrote, "it was necessary to have a general idea of space." Because this meant a spatial idea formed before the appearance of "specialized" knowledge, it could only refer to the "nonspecialized" idea of everyday space" (3:226). This understanding of everyday space represented the most direct spatial idea people put to practical use in their daily lives. The subsequent move to differentiate space called attention to either the absence of an idea of everydayness altogether or the recognition that philosophers actively forgot that such an idea has actually existed (3:262).

At the heart of everydayness was its "thereness," its *da* character, as he put it, which was capable of uniting the diverse forms of space and demonstrating a genuine "objectivity" in contrast to Heidegger's "anthropological" concept of existence embedded in Dasein—Being there—and its associations of subjectivity (*shukanteki*) (3:263). The surety of spatial objectivity meant the domination of materiality—matter which, unlike the world inhabited by the Heideggerian Dasein, was not the name for any separate existence but rather expressed existence in general itself. "In our everyday lives," Tosaka proposed, "we live and depend upon material substances and call this 'actuality' (*jissai*)." Everyday space is none other than this scene (*bamen*) of practical and material circumstances people find themselves in, a thereness that returns humans to the source of space itself, and to their original understanding of the world they inhabit. Yet, it was a world grounded in materiality, in what could be experienced and its spatial location, that linked Tosaka's narrative of origins to the present of "modern life."

HISTORICAL FORMATIONS AND PEOPLE'S PLEASURE

Even as Tosaka was excoriating both social researchers like Kon Wajirō for being locked in the phenomenological object of modern life and "theologians" whose eyes looked upward and yearned for an otherworld free from the vulgarity of the present, Gonda Yasunosuke (1887–1951) was already committed to dissembling the idea of national character (*kokuminsei*) as it was being currently articulated. In his view, the idea of national character froze the determinants of national life (summoned by Tosaka's powerful critique of "archaism") and a promiscuously mapped present onto a completed past as if nothing substantial had changed between these two moments. "I carry doubts toward considerations of 'national culture,' " he wrote, because "it imparts fixed, unchanging conditions from the beginning of national life down to the present" (GYC, 4:32). Recalling Tosaka's blistering dismissal of the metaphysical and theological versions of society that appealed to the transcendent, Gonda argued that the idea of national character functions like an unyielding geometer that resembles the commandment of the gods themselves who have delivered a "destiny that must reveal a fixed nature." Insofar as national life is transmitted into an indefinite future by virtue of this fixed nature, it is a circumstance that cannot possibly be considered. Nothing really could change between past, present, and future, and there is absolutely no way that things can be decisively altered. Moreover, the fixity of national character exempts national life and culture from all subsequent criticism. While Gonda was no doubt reflecting on the spate of studies on national culture inaugurated since the late Meiji period, transmitted through countless spiritual and cultural histories in the 1920s, a range that includes writers as diverse as Haga Ya-ichi and purveyors of national literature and philosophers like Watsuji Tetsurō, he was also prefiguring the production of other texts devoted to reducing culture to fixed, unchanging, and natural essences.

A tireless social researcher who studied popular forms of pleasure and entertainment in the 1920s and 1930s, Gonda's intellectual alignments moved rapidly from Marxian-inspired critical practices in the 1920s to fascistlike theories of mass national culture in the late 1930s. Yet throughout he clung consistently to a view that saw the formation of national culture in the construction of people's pleasure. And the history of pleasure would reveal not the fixity celebrated by essentialists and archaists but rather the changes signaled and demanded by modern life. What he sought to put into question was the enunciation of transcendental principles promoting "the most beautiful life" and "the most good" that elevated "national character" to the lofty heights of otherworldliness (4:32). While clearly referring to Nishida Kitarō and other "transcendentalists," Gonda was actually targeting the role played by a dominant "culturalism" (*bunkashugi*), as it was then called, and its commanding voice in the cultural discussions of the 1920s. But culturalism was simply a recoding of the claims of fixed "national character." In each period of the nation's history, he argued, the principles of national character unfailingly appear to inform national life. The history of the nation is nothing more than the record of the "activity of this 'national character.' " When the nation's people are viewed from this perspective, the apparent source of their inspiration and contemporary conduct is drawn from this idea of national character, the force that "makes national life" (4:33). While this critique was also made, later, by Tosaka Jun, in his identification of a fictive, ahistorical archaism with the Japanese ideology, Gonda was virtually alone in the 1920s in discerning the effects of a Neo-Kantian culturalism that repressed historicity for timeless values and eternal images of national character. It was in fact this culturalism that later spilled over into the vulgar and intellectually indefensible archaisms fascists upheld as the sign of Japan's true uniqueness and racial superiority. He claimed that this view of life, called "transcendental culturalism" (*chōetsuteki bunkashugi*), possessed an inherent danger that "should be subject to criticism," if not outright denunciation. Among the peoples of the present, there are such vast differences that none of them can be thought to possess an identical nature, as he was convinced that Japanese, Russians, North Americans, French, Germans, English, Chinese are marked by differences in thinking and feeling among and within societies. Whatever differences separate one national group from another derive not from some ineffable and irreducible essence but are simply the "last effects" of a long and complex historical development, the most recent manifestation of a vast signifying chain rather than a first cause that attended the formation of the race at its beginning. What Gonda insisted on was the primacy of national life itself as the source of whatever characteristics are associated with a specific group.

Ideologues of national character are thus concerned with locating an "absolutely unchanging" essence that produces national life and supplies it with exemption from further change. While he could recognize a shared common ground with national ideologues that held to uniqueness of different national characteristics, he distanced himself over questions of interpreting growth and development. Where he differed from most contemporaries worrying about this problem was in his rejection of a belief that actually "recognized" the possibility of locating an unchanged and unchanging national essence. Here, he declared his own desire to "abandon" the presumed revelation of national character people believed could be detected in popular pleasures for a view that promised to apprehend "the national dispositions that appear in the pleasure life of the people" (4:33). Rather than accepting the assertion that pleasure always reflected this unchanging national character, Gonda embarked upon investigating it for its varying conditions of productions and those crucial moments of change. There is no reason whatsoever to believe that the ways of feeling and thinking about everyday things among the outcasts (*burakumin*) who lived in the mountains during the Nara period, or those who inhabited villas in the Kamakura era, are the same as those people who today live in Tokyo and Osaka. Both the force of time and social location—class—produced crucial differences between these various groups. "The peoples of the mountains of Asuka should exhibit that nature, just as surely as the inhabitants of single flat bungalows (*hiraya*) must demonstrate their own nature." If differences in time, place, and class accounted for recognizable differences between groups, even though they shared a common racial ancestry, it was also true that the conditions that marked their existence would be carried through to the future. "The character of outcasts," he remarked, "has from the beginning been endowed (with distinctive characteristics) and accompanies the community well into the future" (4:34). Because of this history, Gonda wanted to propose that these communities constituted microcosmic representatives of countries and thus reflected the same kind of differences observed among larger national groups. "A reality today," he wrote, "is recognizing the peculiar differences in national natures among the people of the nation." Hence, national character does not invent national life; national life produces national characteristics in time. Insisting upon the recognition of differences occurring in both differing temporalities—history—and spatial environments—social location—Gonda's argument aimed at showing how

national life was always plural and the product of distinct historical formations that had come into existence in certain moments of a nation's
history. What affirms national life was "social environment," as well as
climate and topography. But in the present period, the strongest elements
in the making of the social environment are "social and economic circumstances." In a number of texts produced throughout the 1920s, Gonda
embraced a "materialist view of history" toward the present and thereby
understood the formation of national characteristics within the framework of this critical practice. Years later, he would change his mind about
the veracity of materialist history, but he would always retain his faith in
popular pleasures.

More than any other dimension of contemporary social life, the pleasures of the people expressed both national life and the peculiar characteristics informing it. Modern society supplied a vast social laboratory of
lived experiences that differed among its several, constituent groups and
diverse geographical regions. How people enjoyed themselves, the pleasures that attracted them, was identical with the production of culture
itself. Gonda was also persuaded that such practices would disclose the
unobserved natures that qualified and quantified social differences. National life constantly changes its conditions according to more fundamental transformations in social and economic circumstances. But these
changing conditions will also be registered at the level of people's entertainment. While both cultural production and pleasure appeared as superstructural transcriptions of larger shifts in the economic and social structure of national life, they were by no means less important or less reliable
indicators of history. "What is the basic keynote of popular pleasure
among the Japanese today?" he asked rhetorically, and answered: "I want
to say again that it is in the ideograph denoting o ["honorable," "august"]. Japanese who ask about the meaning of the ideograph o are told
that its presence refers to the pleasures of their life." By merely adding
the prefix o before words used in everyday life, it is possible to denote the
presence of pleasure. Instead of eating sushi and rice and sipping soup
and noodles in order to stave off hunger, it is possible to place the desire
for satiety completely outside of consciousness by putting the suffix o
before words for eating, noodles, and sushi. "It is the keynote of Japanese
popular pleasures to eat o-sushi, grill o-mochi, accept o-shufun [noodles
in broth]" (4:35). Consuming o-kashi and drinking o-saké, Gonda added,
was not the same as simply filling the stomach with sweets or getting
drunk on rice wine. People ate o-kashi or drank o-saké merely for the
pleasures of filling themselves with wine and candy. By the simple addition
of a honorific prefix, the ordinary, mundane, functional, and necessary
became the extraordinary, the luxurious, pleasurable, without instrumen-

tal utility; the prefix o empowers a radical transubstantiation of everyday life where the most familiar objects at hand are defamiliarized, made strange, as it were, thus casting an entirely different light on what was seen as habit, routine, and necessity. In the simple act of consuming and drinking, Gonda observed, no other meaning was necessary. Only the tactility presented by the candy and wine—the ambiance of its materiality—was meaningful. While one learned floral arrangements to become skilled in the art, practiced the biwa, memorized the samisen to become a master, none of this applied to the pleasures of the people. The questions of skills and mastery had to be situated outside of the idea of people's pleasure, so that one learns o-hana, presides over o-cha, augustly practices the o-biwa. The same was true of New Years. The change of the calendar (called o-shōgatsu-the august, punctual month) observed by all Japanese referred to the new year and everything associated with ritual, ceremony, and commemoration. Yet the prefix is inappropriate when used to only signify a first month or first day announcing some kind of activity, like artisans who always represented rest days like the first and fifteenth of the month by affixing the prefix o to them (4:36). The first of the new year was unique and different, and the term o-shōgatsu could be used only at this fixed time. What is conveyed by the prefix is not simply the acquisition of formal skills but rather the range of pleasurable associations unleashed by an activity or an observance.

Hence, Gonda wanted to strip popular pleasures of any hint of utility or instrumentality. When Japanese, for example, observed "flower viewing" (o-hanami), they did so not simply because they wished to see the first blossoms. The term did not literally mean "watching or looking at flowers," as such, but rather "august flower viewing": a total activity in itself. "Spreading out a straw mat and blanket under the blossoms," he wrote, "it is o-hanami when opening the o-bentō [lunch box] and drinking the o-saké. The beginning of spring in the country decorated by flowers enters the stomach. The flowers are, perhaps, outside of and incidental to the occasion and its assorted and associated activities." Accordingly, it is outside the area of consciousness itself, submerged in an unconscious; and it is the time of o-hanami when the "self gets drunk from a bottle of sake . . . dances madly under the blossoms until one becomes identified with the flowers. A similar experience occurs when one goes to the honored stage—o-shibai—rather than a play (geki)" (4:37). In short, Gonda was acutely aware of how the addition of the prefix o constituted a honorific and exalted title or name (keigo), implying a more refined and elegant manner of speaking. But rather than seeing it as merely a sign of politeness, he wanted to show how it had been appropriated by commoners to produce a distinct popular culture, how it worked to transubstantiate an event into an occasion experienced by the people who expressed their "nature" through it. He saw this transmutation as a "self-driven purposeful goal" that had remained "hidden" even though it had been at the heart of the "people's pleasure life" down to the present. Yet it also signaled how the "other's purposive idea" was "inverted" (*tenkai*) into the "personalist aims" of the people. The importance of this observation was that it recognized the relationship between official or high culture and its appropriations to produce popular culture. The sufficiency of reaching a goal, he reflected, is a certain thing whereby the submerged purposeful activity becomes the cipher that informs the living pleasures of the people. Moreover, "it strongly desires to transform the various purposes of the other's goals into self [the people's] driven goals" (4:38).

Gonda rearticulated the living characteristic of pleasure in a lecture he delivered in 1923 that discussed the relationship between "philosophy that escapes life" and one that is embedded in it. Turning to his favorite object of research, the Asakusa district of Tokyo, long noted as a pleasure quarter, he declared that the shift from a philosophy that fled life to one that was capable of affirming it was found buried in the miscellaneous struggles and pleasures in this time and place, pleasures that reach all the way to even the coffee house. What he seemed to be calling attention to was philosophy's traditional vocation to eschew and dismiss the mundane things of the world, like those "hermits who live quietly and inhale dew drops deep within the mountains" (1:108), but who forget the so-called vulgar affairs of human life. In his present, philosophy was no longer a thing of study or seminar rooms because it had become a "thing of the streets." The reason for this migration of philosophy from the sheltered seminar to the open streets is that society itself has changed so rapidly and definitively, owing to accelerated capitalist development. Philosophy must follow in its wake or risk disappearance. Here, Gonda seemed to be registering a proper Hegelian observation that philosophy was always too late. Philosophy, he insisted, must be formed from within the life of humans who are living their lives and experiencing the new. Prefiguring later efforts like Gramsci's to reunite mental and manual labor, Gonda proposed that "men who live in this society and move within its truths are all philosophers" (1:109). The present is a period appointed for philosophy to exist in the everyday, in the materiality of its things that have come to dominate contemporary existence. In fact, philosophy has to leave the study and the classroom in order to be able to "vehemently" express "the everyday life of people in Asakusa," where both play and work merged. Life, the living, always produces the idea, not the other way around; a new mode of existence is always produced from this process in which "everyday reality creates thought" (1:116).

Modern life, as Gonda understood it, was identical with the ever new and same, what was fashion and fashionable (*ryūkō*) in the present. In a number of texts produced just before and immediately after the earthquake of 1923, Gonda explored the relationship of the people, pleasure, and the popular. Part of this intense interest undoubtedly grew out of what Yoshimi Shunya has referred to as a "problematizing" of people's art and the theory of people's culture after World War I. We saw earlier how progressive writers like Murayama Tomoyoshi and Hirabayashi Hatsunosuke turned toward figuring the people and the popular as the subject of cultural production, if not as the actual object of cultural analysis. The genealogy of this theorizing of popular culture dates back to Honma Hisao's *Minshū geijitsu no igi oyobi kachi* (1916), aimed at Ōsugi Sakae and Yasunari Sadao, a text that sought to envisage the task of "people's art as a mechanism or form of movement that cultivated general commoners or the working class."[28] Since the people, themselves, according to Honma, lacked the ability to create a culture they actually conceived, the only way they could be assisted in this vast undertaking was through a process of "refinement" (*kyōyō*)—the old staple of the Taishō bourgeoisie already being promoted as an individualistic ideal by thinkers like Abe Jirō and as a Japanese gloss of the German *allgemein Bildung* by writers like Mushakoji Saneatsu. What this program entailed was the act of "imparting a kind of refrigerant, above all else, on the mind and body, which are inflamed, exhausted, and fatigued"[29]—in other words, chilling or freezing and thus harnessing the passions that already were exploding in new cultural expressions. The issues raised by the problematizing of popular culture were twofold: First, what people does *minshū* in popular art refer to? Are the people simply the "working class" or the urban proletariat? Does it involve a general humanity that might include the bourgeoisie, etc.? Second, is the people's art for the people or one by the people? Between art and the people, Ōsugi argued, there was the problem of the preposition.[30] While this debate ran through the opinion magazines throughout the 1920s, with proponents coming down on both sides of the "proposition"—"for" and "by"—Gonda differed from both those who promoted the ideal of *Bildung* for the popular classes and those who ended by investing the state with the role of purveying and producing people's culture. If thinkers like the anarchist Ōsugi and the Marxists Hirabayashi and Kurahara Korehito were seeking to figure the people as the object of their cultural production, their arguments more often than not never exceeded recuperating received and established conceptions of how art/culture were supposed to function. When Gonda turned to the question of popular pleasure as the key to understanding culture itself, he also resolved the status of the popular and the role played by the people in cultural production. Too often, he observed, the most radical proposals fell back on the leadership of the intellectuals, even while acknowledging the possibility of cultural creation among the urban masses because, according to one commentator of the contemporary scene (Ōbayashi Muretsugu), the received pleasures of the people were "old, low grade" and did not fit into the "molding" of pleasurable desires of the new age.[31] As early as 1920, Gonda wrote an essay as an entry into the ongoing discussion concerning the role of the people in the production of culture called "Minshū bunka ka—Minshū no tame no bunka ka" that tried to clarify the principal subject and status of the people's agency in the formation of popular culture. Again, he called into question the claims of an older philosophy and the necessity of now constructing a new one close to the interests of everyday life. But thought was always too late to seize hold of the changes people were living and experiencing, and it had failed to keep pace with the demands for "reconstruction" that the new age and modern life were announcing. In this respect, philosophy was neither reformist nor enlightened. Its failure derived from the inability of intellectuals—producers of thought—to move beyond the vision of a past cultural history they have embraced and now cannot let go. But as producers of thought, they also believed they occupied positions of privilege in the production of culture. History had shown the pulsations of progress and change easily confirmed by looking at "the actuality of contemporary reality moving before our eyes today" (4:18). Present-day thinkers must be jarred into recognizing the changes in reality going on before them. Reality, by the same measure, does not pay attention to the "intellectual frolicking of thinkers; it changes gradually." Historians might explain its occurrence a hundred years after the fact, but thought is apparently completely powerless to capture its presence and give shape to it.

In the current discussions, Gonda observed that intellectuals seemed to have no confidence in their own positions and interpretations concerning the people's movement. What surfaced regularly as explanation was simply the idea of culture itself, and what gets forgotten are the people. Noting a disparity between the idea of culture and the "reality" of the people, he argued that intellectuals appealed to the former in order to understand the latter and thus risked submerging the latter in the former in all subsequent discussion. This tactic was named culturalism (bunkashugi) and privileged the eternality of the form of culture over the productions of history (4:21). Culturalism in the early 1920s was, in fact, possible because of the anxiety produced by the presence of the popular in the production of culture. The problem culturalism sought to elide was the status of a popular culture and a culture for the people; that is to say, the proponents of culturalism aimed to incorporate the merely popular into the larger, eternal claims of beauty, the good, and the true. Yet any culture of the people, whatever its historic promise, authorized the position of the intellectual to create what the people clearly were incapable of doing for themselves, which was to assert values that were associated with the bourgeoisie. In this discussion on culture, Gonda saw how class was able to co-opt precisely those elements in society that constituted a challenge to its ideology and political position (4:26). Concentrating on culture, it was hoped that the people and a people's movement might be discerned within its precincts. The culturalist argument held that if culture is the highest standard for all, then the people found and possessed meaning by completing it. They would find their sole reason for existence "only because of the formation of culture" (4:22). Hence, the people were necessary for the completion of culture, and the popular movements acquired purpose only when seen for their possible utility in realizing the greater totality of culture. While this wing of culturalists did not necessarily reject the claims of a genuine "people's movement," as such, and even sympathized with it, its focus fastened onto the whole rather than the parts comprising it. Gonda noted that the "most important thing for these thinkers is the transcendental ideal represented by culture. They think that the most sublimely beautiful thing called culture informs what is produced in the world of human species down to the end of history itself. . . . The human species exists in order for it to realize the highest principles of the universe and humanity" (4:24).

Gonda saw that culture during his time was being identified with values—the good, true and beautiful—values which exceeded history and surpassed mere human desire, and which ultimately resulted from contributions made by politics, religion, morality, art, philosophy, and science. Culture was the sum of the values produced by this (collective) human effort. "The history of the past of the human species," he wrote, "was the record of the development of culture; the present of the human species is the reality of the hard struggle (funtō) in realizing this 'culture.' " Its fulfillment, he added, must be in the ideal place where this cultural expression is completed (4:24). Once aristocratic culture evolved and reached its fulfillment, it turned its "seat" over to the bourgeoisie, which has since advanced the cause of value one step further. But bourgeois culture had stalled in its tracks, holding on desperately to what it already had accomplished and possessed, consolidating its "position" and thereby inhibiting the further development of culture. This explained why culturalists were able to express sympathy for popular movements but were, at the same time, incapable of doing more (4:25). If one wing of culturalists was "despots of culture," the other was its "addicts" (wakudeki), owing to their all-consuming commitment to transcendent values rather than to the world in which they actually were living. The content of their culturalism never exceeded the class that produced intellectuals who promoted the idea of a transcendental culture, despite the claims of universalizing values. It is important to recognize in this critique Gonda's differentiation of values from desire and history and how the former was already being summoned against the claims of the latter, especially as it was figured in the commodity form colonizing and being experienced in "modern life." That is, we must see in this attack on culturalism his acknowledgment of a polarization between the claims of pure, absolute value and the operation of desire and consumption as the sign of a lived history.

If culturalists were divided between those who simply elevated the totality of culture above all considerations and those who believed in the necessity of its completion ("cultural despots" and "addicts"), Gonda detected a third group that simply discounted any identity with the people and despaired of the possibility of the popular classes ever creating their own culture. What they seemed to promote was the conviction that people share in and then enjoy a culture already produced by the upper classes that would be "adjusted" to meet the requirements of popular consumption (4:6). This strategy was called the "popularization" and even the "democratization" of culture, even while it led to another misrecognition concerning the capacity of the people to do more than serve as passive receivers of watered-down high culture. (The first misrecognition was the culturalist conceit that held to pitying the laboring classes because they were without power or ability.) Because the people were "pitiable," established culture had to be "adulterated," mixed, made easy, as Gonda put it, with "salt water" to make it swallowable. It was hoped that the people might "taste" the stimulation of aristocratic or bourgeois cultures, however diluted. This was called the principle of "kind treatment" of bourgeois culture, and Gonda condemned it as a social policy at a cheap price. Social policy had already led to advocating educating the people, so that they might be in a position to create their own culture, even though the models that were inculcated belonged to the middle classes. Rejecting this program for the deception it was, Gonda dismissed all schemes that employed the category of culture to discuss the place of the people in modern society. Inevitably, such schemes worked to displace the popular as subject/agent for some arrangement that would affirm the role of both the intelligentsia in producing culture and the bourgeoisie in their shaky claim to cultural hegemony as the natural successors of an older aristocracy. It is also important to notice how the lower classes were made to identify with upper-class culture as a means of hegemonizing them and securing social solidarity. In this respect Gonda's observations resembled Antonio Gramsci's recognition of the partial hold the ruling class maintains and the necessity of working out hegemonic relations that invariably involved the deployment of culture. Whether intellectuals constructed a culture for the people or managed it, the real problem was that such a culture must emerge from the people themselves, through their own agency, from within those objects and practices that dominated their lives and experience. If intellectuals failed to grasp this understanding, there was still no reason to feel any "anxiety" for their loss. For Gonda, the idea of a "people's culturalism," as all these positions implied, was oxymoronic, an unwanted impediment to understanding the place of the popular in contemporary, modern society. To "truly" complete a "popular culturalism," he concluded, it is imperative to be extricated from the ghostly "apparition" of "normal culturalism," the "past time of intellectuals," in order to make its demise the most urgent business of the day (4:31).

What Gonda recommended was a conception of culture derived from the historical experience of pleasure and laughter. This meant abandoning the category of culture altogether, since its utility seriously excluded the role of the people and the popular. On this point he was clear: culture was the product of the "self-intoxication" of the "abstracted, idealistic intellectual class" who were not in a position to exhibit anything about ordinary people (1:309). He saw the appearance of the popular as a kind of "uncanny" that modern society presented regularly in a diversity of manifestations to remind the present of the past (history) and the people (4:58). Historically, all groups have produced their own forms of pleasure and entertainment, forms that were deeply rooted in the particular lived experiences of social groups. In this sense, the production of pleasure stemmed from play itself, which in Gonda's thinking constituted the principal content of any cultural configuration. While one interpreter called his "Minshū gorakuron" (1931) a "strangely academic" text, it was here that Gonda quoted approvingly a German scholar (Bucher) that "play is older than work and art precedes economic production" (1:406, 203). Nothing seemed more evident than the coupling that pleasure was both historical and a product of people's "everyday life" (1:23). With the inauguration of capitalism and the rapid modernization after the Russo-Japanese War, and especially after the "European War" (1914–1918), Japanese society experienced the expansion of vast social and economic transformations and the sharpening division between rich and poor, producing the "people" without money or leisure time (1:24). It was because the people had no money that they had no leisure time; as a result they were not able to take hold of pleasure, which had been a principal condition of the older artisanal cultures of the Tokugawa and early Meiji periods. "The people were separated from pleasure, and pleasure took flight from the people" (1:25). Their lives fell into futility and emptiness but not hopelessness. In time, he continued, "these new people" became dissatisfied with their condition and began to work for the creation of pleasure that reflected the things of their daily life. These people, he claimed, gave birth to pleasures by themselves from their actual conditions of social existence that supplied new forms of entertainment. The principal form of entertainment embraced by the people in modern life was the moving picture.

Of course, the "new people" he was speaking about were the social classes produced by capitalism, who, through the mechanisms of exchange, circulation, and consumption, gave lasting expression to the apparition of the "popular." For Gonda, the people provided a new set of pleasures, but it was the movies that especially corresponded closest to capitalism. (The other two favored pleasures were theater and "gatherings.") What he wanted to emphasize was the relationship between these classes in a new social formation and their capacity for producing their own pleasures, that is to say, culture. People's pleasure was a reality, he asserted often, a "natural product," rather than an "artifice" derived from idealism and excessive conceptualization (1:289, 290). It is found where people live and work, embedded in their lives, not in the idealized fantasies imagined by idealists (1:310). Because it is "joined to the real lives of people, it becomes their problem, not that of the intellectuals" (1:311). Here, Gonda argued that the "original text" of play could not be found in Maruzen's book store, where it was impossible to even discover the word "people's pleasure" (*minshū goraku*) in the store's catalogue but in only Asakusa, the playground of the new classes, especially the working class, and Gonda's primary site of research (1:292).

The development of capitalism brought a quantification in production, in the period after World War I, and a greater demand for luxury items (1:314). It also introduced the phenomenon of capital concentration and the formation of new social classes in the sites of capital. Gonda observed that the growth of capitalism produced two principal classes in social life: the propertied class (bourgeoisie) and the proletariat (*musanshakaikyū*). The latter replaced the older artisanal and commercial workers of the Edo and early Meiji periods to become the central component of a new constellation in the "new age" called the "people." As a social group, it proliferated rapidly and steadily so that the "center of gravity of the people today" is with the proletariat. By the same measure, the nature of popular life also changed swiftly to reflect the new social arrangements and the paucity of resources that produced a marked "lack of money" and "meager leisure" (1:315). Caught in an economy where they were forced to procure ready-made goods, workers were made hostage to both the lack of funds and the instability of the job market. Scarcity of leisure time and lack of money meant that workers had available few opportunities for experiencing pleasures and entertainment. In Gonda's thinking, this was a serious deficiency, since pleasure was not to be considered a "luxury," but rather "one of the most important dimensions of the real life of [the people], like eating when hungry, drinking when thirsty"

(1:319). People without pleasure, he insisted, are dull and dry. More, they are dead. What he envisaged was a role for pleasure in the general representation (and reproduction) of the worker's labor power. Hence, pleasure would serve as a means for "directly assisting scarcity and the extreme fatigue by satisfying a desire for entertainment capable of supplying strong stimulation" (1:320). It is interesting to compare Gonda's defense of pleasure as a powerful element in the reproduction of the worker's labor power to others elsewhere, like Siegfried Kracauer, who were beginning to see in modern forms of entertainment "distractions" and the ominous domination of the commodity form and the culture industry.[32] By the end of the decade of the 1920s, Gonda's contemporary, the social critic Aono Suekichi, was recording the devastating social-psychological disappointment of Japan's white-collar workers, who were having trouble satisfying their desire for pleasure and consumption in a time of unemployment and scarcity.

We know from the theorizing in Gonda's "Minshū gorakuron" that pleasure implied a conception of utility that might avoid simple mechanical reproduction yet find a place for it beside production (2:211). Pleasure had to stand together with production, he reasoned, since a pleasure serving creativity was equivalent to "production for creativity." Regardless of his insistence that pleasure was never simply a "servant of production," it is hard to avoid concluding that it still functioned in the process of reproduction—after all, it was like the necessities of food and drink. Pleasure, Gonda was fond of saying, was "one expression of life." It is important to mention in this connection that Gonda juxtaposed "pleasure as reality" to pleasure as "serial policy," which meant the thesis on reproduction (2:207).

If play and pleasure, which constituted for him a "social reality," could not be "separated from the actual everyday life of the people," then their location was of primary importance. Gonda was convinced that the focus of pleasure was the Asakusa district of Tokyo, which he would identify with comparable quarters found in other cities, like Osaka, Kobe, and Okayama. These were the great metropolitan cities and their regional satellites, where growing armies of workers became the fulcrum of the people whose need for pleasures was as great as for food and drink (1:302–303). "It is not an abstract ideal production scholars fabricate in their studies (referring to the presence of popular pleasures); rather it is the product of concrete things (*mono*) social life brings forth from the streets" (1:16). Because pleasure could not be separated from the space of daily affairs in the cities, leisure and work would form a complex relationship in which the time of one activity would constantly criss-cross and overlap with the other.[33] Gonda recognized that the bases of people's pleasure had changed from the early modern period to the present, from principally an artisanal and commercial economy to industrialism driven by capital and the worker. This acknowledgment affirmed both the role played by history in the development of pleasure and the production of difference manifest best in the co-existence of differing forms of entertainment signifying different temporalities (1:313–342). "We can detect the fact that the birthplace of people's pleasure as a new idea resulting from the necessity of contemporary social and economic life was first in city life. Investigation has resulted in anticipating its organization rearing inside the life forms and living consciousness of the proletariat living in the cities. In reality, people's pleasure is a transformation of reality created, sown, and fermented in the great cities that are identical with contemporary social life. . . . The ebb and flow and changes in people's pleasure is something that should express this in the most modular form of urban, people's pleasure." Grasping the changes in the development of people's pleasure in the cities and among diverse cityscapes will supply an understanding of the actual ebb and flow of entertainment (2:291–292). Whereas the older artisanal forms of pleasure were not necessarily restricted to the great cities and required more leisure time and money to pay for the obligatory instruction in the performative arts, the cities under capitalism introduced an "entertainment industry" (kōgyō) devoted to "material pleasures," divided into the "movie industry," the "theater industry," and the "variety hall industry" (yose), what he called, in obvious allusion to the Three Imperial Regalia, the "three pleasures of the cities" (toshi sandai goraku). These city entertainments, compressed into quarters like Asakusa, were both spaces of play and the raw material for the creation of an "original text" of people's pleasure that did not yet fully exist but was in process of taking shape. The space of play overlapped with the textual space that investigation would construct.

As we already know, Gonda viewed city dwellers as the urban poor, lacking money and leisure time, whose lives were fragmented, separated, and alienated from both the process of production and the consumption of commodities.[34] The "content" of culture signified the "ephemeral" "ready-made goods," the intuitive rush to instantly taste pleasures before having them explained, "the deeply emotional," especially in response to "strongly stimulating" entertainments, the graphic, imagistic, and the cheap (1:320). Gonda's research agenda followed these consumers, just as Kon Wajirō tracked the walkers on the streets and in the parks, into department stores and the pleasure quarters, where he carefully tabulated the quantity of people who attended variety halls, movies, and theater. He also compared locations of pleasures in other cities like Osaka, Kobe, and Okayama, using Asakusa and its denizens as a baseline. Concentrating on securing qualitative materials, as well, he executed in-depth interviews with performers, usually "street performers," his favorite subject. Despite his own desire to map the quantitative/statistical incidence of consumers and audiences, his surveys invariably called attention to the importance of work, class, and social location. Much of his research was focused on cultural "spheres" or "zones," like the Asakusa, found in the larger cities. Even children fell under his research gaze as important objects of investigation, and Gonda showed early how they gravitated increasingly to movies. As early as 1917 he demonstrated the number of times children in certain age cohorts would attend movies. They favored action films and comedians like Charlie Chaplin and his numerous Japanese imitators. In fact, Gonda recorded that children literally lived in cinema houses, where they "drank lemonade," consumed large quantities of "caramels," "sembei," and "bread," all sold there. These children came for enjoyment, where they were able to raise their voices, "forget themselves" for a moment, and escape the routines of everyday life (1:84–87). But Gonda also perceived that many children who attended movie houses strayed from watching the screen to playing and talking with friends. "There are no teachers nor textbooks in the heads of these children," he remarked, "only Chaplin and Matsunosuke led and guided them" (1:98).[35]

In addition to identifying entertainments enjoyed by differing classes of people, Gonda was also interested in the larger comparative perspectives his surveys reflected. His research itinerary took him to a variety of cities, resembling Yanagita Kunio's almost endless moments on the road searching for remaining traces of an authentic life. While Asakusa enlisted its audiences from intellectuals and workers, Osaka's pleasure zone—Tennōji—by comparison recruited its clients from classes closer to the petit bourgeoisie. In this decisive way, it differed from Tokyo/Asakusa, which attracted throngs of proletarians (1:253, 273). By making this class distinction, Gonda could propose that workers and intellectuals were able to act independently in making their choices, while the petit bourgeoisie, deriving from Osaka's older commercial and artisanal classes, were still locked in a system of "patriarchal conduct" (1:253). Furthermore, Okayama's pleasure quarters were even more intellectualized (places of the "intelligentsia of the intelligentsia"), and the installation there of a pleasure sphere like Asakusa was clearly impossible (1:258). What this meant for him was that Okayama's pleasures followed a more rigid division of labor spread throughout the city. The difference may have stemmed from size, since the city was clearly smaller than Tokyo or Osaka. But it also had to do with history and development. Okayama's pleasure quarter, called Hōkan-chō, emerged in the early Meiji period when the domain's *shizoku* population was forced to cash in their hereditary stipends and thereafter make their own living. With cash settlements, many drifted to what came to be called the Hōkan-chō and became small shopkeepers with varying degrees of success. Kobe, on the other hand, seemed to resemble Tokyo/Asakusa most and disclosed similar patterns of establishing cultural spheres that marked class differentiation. Unlike Okayama in the 1920s, Kobe was heavily proletarianized (1:265), and while its petit bourgeoisie paralleled Osaka's, its intelligentsia differed from the one located in Okayama. Kobe was the site where the "new proletariat" and "new salarymen" converged to share a common antagonism toward received and traditional forms of entertainment that actually "denied" them their own "authority" (1:266). In this regard, Gonda noticed that the newly emerged salarymen showed a striking fondness for the "exotic" that also prompted genuine enthusiasm for "destroying older forms" of pleasure.[36] While these two classes had developed markedly "differentiated" tastes and methods when compared with the "bartender" tastes of intellectuals and the traditional tastes of the smaller bourgeoisie, the disparity was not as great as imagined. Nonetheless, there was "exotic Kobe," the "union of materialist Kobe, its materialistic utilitarianism, and exotic taste" (1:267). And this sense of unevenness was best represented in "producing beef sukiyaki," a fusion of Western and Japanese cuisine, even though it fell short of replicating the *gemeutlich* (*kimochi*) of Asakusa, which Gonda renamed as the "crossroads of posters" (1:268). In Asakusa, the mixture of cultural styles was everywhere and constituted the unique sign of its pleasure world. When one's eyes are awakened to Asakusa, one does not see "moving pictures in it, one does not see theaters, or arcades, or small drinking shops, or even Kannonsama, or flower shops and tall buildings. All of these are gathered in this zone and thus lose their individuality to make what is called 'Asakusa.' " (1:269). What is seen in Asakusa is simply "great differences." People who seek only to portray Asakusa as the site of movie houses are mistaken. They are there, to be sure, but so are all of these other shops and activities, producing a configuration in one place that signified "a world," "a certain kind of atmosphere" (1:270). But, he insisted, it is in reality a separate world, marked off from the rest of the city by virtue of what it offers, yet vastly different from the earlier, cordoned pleasure quarters of Edo (Yoshiwara), which supplied sanctuary in an idealized world—the "floating world"—for merchants and samurai. Asakusa was a place the people of the present have produced, "the central place of pleasure the people have constructed from the expansion of actual, everyday life" (1:272). The differences between Tokyo's Asakusa and Edo's Yoshiwara, he recorded, was a difference between the contemporary proletariat and the Tokugawa *chōnin*. "One lived in Asakusa, day to day; life there was simply goods and commodities, without personal purpose, motivation" (1:279).

Asakusa represented a world of differentiated pleasures that constituted a totality. Both the perception of difference and the imperative to compare led Gonda to imagine a culture of pleasures constituted of coexisting, heterogeneous class elements with new and older forms of entertainment. A contemporary writer and critic, Soeda Azenbō actually put it better than Gonda when he wrote in "Asakusa teiryūki" (1930) that "the Asakusa of fools is at the same time the Asakusa of wisdom. Asakusa is not a world of theory but one of action. It is the zone of the concrete."[37] In Gonda's research agenda, nothing seemed more important than examining the "living society" as against merely applying religious and philosophical principles, and nothing seemed more appropriate methodologically than the technique of "interviewing" "living reality," which, for him, expressed a "universal law down to the smallest blade grass in the fields" (2:15). Devoted to a rigorous empiricism based on punctual and precise observations supplemented by intensive interviewing, his method required that he first select a set of entertainment forms before embarking on the actual social search. The technique underscored the importance of co-existing forms of pleasure from past and present, the mingling of the new and the old, the old in the new, Japanese and Western, to become the basis of a conception of culture marked by differing temporalities, where culture appeared as a configuration housing a number of nonsynchronisms very similar to Yanagita Kunio's perception of the co-mingling of past and present customs.

At one level, this nonsynchronist cultural imaginary pointed to precisely the uneven development capitalism was invariably producing through its ceaseless deterritorializing and reterritorializing of labor and capital. It also represented, in still another register, a hybridity that both Gonda and Yanagita would evaluate as a new cultural constellation figuring Japan's modern experience. The coexistence of different forms within the same cultural realm and the constant co-mingling of elements that testified to different temporalities and histories, if not social spaces, would only mean that the unevenness that marked contemporary Japan would eventually be overcome in the achievement of uniform evenness in both political economy and culture. Comparison and the perception of differences—unevenness—became the sign of vitality and a possible defense against the threat of a promised homogenization and averaging, even though it also risked the entrapment of political strategies like fascism that promised the retention of older cultural and social forms in the midst of a capitalist society. What this view entailed was misrecognizing the capitalist process of deterritorialization that literally destroyed the received culture of reference to create the spectacle of ocular unevenness as the first step in an eventual refiguration, not as the last step in settling accounts with the received culture. With Gonda, and many others, it was possible to understand how capitalism had led to the present, but what he feared most, and what his own vision of a mixed culture circulating elements from past and present, Japan and the West, revealed, was the continuing march of capitalism that eventually would eliminate unevenness—the culture of difference—for one of evenness, leveling, and the homogenizing of the cultural ground. It was this fear of "modern life," as he and others were calling it in the 1930s, together with the historical conjuncture in which political choice and decision converged with the representation of cultural form that led Gonda, and others, to embrace fascism. Gonda's agenda aimed at halting the very process of deterritorialization that had led to the present conjuncture by transmuting the national consumer into the national community.

Before he reached this place in his intellectual journey, Gonda's research led him to the streets of Asakusa where he spent a good deal of time observing and interviewing both the participants in and producers of people's pleasures. This research, recorded in "Goraku gyōsha no mure" (1923), was a vast, panoramic catalogue that sought to identify the principal places of production and their principal agents, such as the women in bars and "guest" trade (prostitution), performers, streetwalkers (unlicensed prostitutes), restaurant waitresses, *machiai* waitresses, cafe waitresses, noodle shop waitresses at boarding houses and inns; the society of artists—performers, storytellers (*rakugoka*), comedians, professional storytellers (*kōshakushi*), "masters of polite accomplishments" (*yūgei*), dancers, *biwa* players, singers, floral arrangers, tea masters, *shakuhachi* players, songs played to the accompaniment of the *samisen*, street performers of all kind, etc." (2:4–178). In this vast inventory mapping entertainment on the streets, whose content is filled in with numerous interviews he conducted with the various agents/subjects of popular pleasures, what distinguished and characterized this world most was the spectacle of difference produced by the coexistence and circulation of heterogeneous elements representing different historical moments from past to present. Gonda's statistical surveys, matching the later surveys of researchers like Kagawa Toyohiko and Andō Masayoshi charting the migration of young women from the countryside into the fleshpots of the larger cities, were undergirded by qualitative data (as were Kagawa and Andō's portraits, driven by powerful moral outrage) culled from countless interviews. Here, moreover, his method converged with the program of Kon Wajirō, who was, perhaps, given more to recording observations made on the streets and other city sites than to interviewing subjects. With Gonda, however, we have the breakdowns of brothels by districts and the numbers of women employed in them in a given year, say, 1921. Like Kagawa and Andō ten years later, he also calculated the number of clients serviced in the various houses and their gross revenues (2:28–38). In this regard, he identified diverse regions women were recruited from, distant prefectures like Niigata, Akita, and Yamagata, and closer districts contiguous to Tokyo, described their living circumstances, working conditions, costs, payments, and general everyday lives (2:31). This detailed information concerning virtually every aspect of the lives of licensed and unlicensed prostitutes came out of a direct engagement with the subjects in their milieu.

But if prostitutes captured Gonda's statistical imagination, it was the street performers he was most concerned with portraying qualitatively. It is important to notice, in this connection, that his inventory of popular pleasures included an array of traditional forms that were still being practiced in Asakusa in the early 1920s. Among these, the street performers (*daidō geinin*) there were people of the *nagashi*—strollers—and their various skills included monkey trainers, street *shakuhachi* players, *enga* singers, and a variety of performers possessing ancient storytelling skills, like sword players, shell game artists (*kaganouke*), street storytellers, and hand puppet performers. Worried that these street performers were beginning to dwindle in numbers, Gonda recorded that they were being seen less in the larger cities, even though they still retained their hold on entertainment districts in medium-sized and smaller towns (2:117). It was extremely "grievous," he seemed to lament, but a condition that nevertheless "couldn't be helped." If today one goes strolling to small towns and villages in the countryside, they will see that the older forms of street performing still persist. The relative social importance of street performers constituted a sign that attested to the actual completion and noncompletion of contemporary everyday life and thus signified the variation of local characteristics and unevenness marking the process of capitalist modernization between city and countryside. Whereas Gonda would, in the early 1920s, see the unevenness between city and countryside in the relative position occupied by street performers in the respective sites, Yanagita Kunio would, by the end of the decade, use the division as a warning signal that showed how the large cities were draining human and material resources out of the countryside and how the latter was being sacrificed to the former. But this should not be taken to mean that he saw the plight of street performers as merely a statistical datum that required no further commentary.

For Gonda, the "great meaning" of conducting research on the position of these street performers in contemporary life lay in discovering the degree to which older forms of people's pleasures were actually disappearing (2:117). In this regard, his concerns for cultural conservation dovetailed with the projects of contemporary native ethnologists who were already busily involved in collecting customs and practices before they vanished under the imperatives of capitalist modernity. What Gonda wanted to do with his interviews of street performers was preserve the last remnants of dying arts, to retain, much like Yanagita and Shibusawa Keizō working with folk custom and practices, the traces of Asakusa, even as he recognized that progress would inexorably continue to throw up newer forms of popular pleasures like the movies and variety halls that already were beginning to capture the patronage of large numbers of people. But at the same time, he was undoubtedly pained to recognize that the older forms of entertainment were losing their power to attract large numbers of audiences, who, for one reason or another, simply lacked the patience and knowledge necessary to appreciate them. Street performers, players, and artists, and their would be successors, he confessed, were doomed to disappear soon.[38] In this acknowledgment, Gonda first revealed an ambivalence over the putative benefits of material progress driven by the forces of history and the manifest prospect that any desire to preserve the older forms from subsequent historical change was clearly impossible. "Why are these wandering performers (*hōrō engeisha*) dying out today? When speaking about the transformations of the 'heart' of contemporary people," he charged, "it has taken place especially in the great cities. I have come to believe that it might be the case that the streets have changed, a result of the increasing complexity of communications machinery. The decline of street performers is [found] there . . . The streets are for walking and have no other purpose" (2:119). Yet he knew that this was precisely the inescapable point of the kind of material progress inaugurated by capitalism that projected everydayness into life on the streets, where others like Kon Wajirō were already carrying out research in contemporary custom. Even for Gonda, the streets were the location of "modern life."

The development of modern cities, he noted, made possible the great thoroughfares that led to the erection of halls and stages for performers but also eliminated the street actors and players. Streetcars were now accessible in literally all directions, "dashing along at high speeds of more than 50 miles per hour"; the streets were congested to such a dizzying degree with pleasure cars, taxis, and buses that the "comfortable life" recalled by street *shakuhachi* players and the world of players was decaying and no longer "permissible." What had once been praised in the Edo period for its art was now performed as a marginal existence and "ephemeral life" (2:26–127, 138). Virtually at the same moment he was eulogizing the disappearance of street performers of traditional arts, he was also pointing to the installation of "modern life," which the "apparition called the modern city" had produced in "life on the streets."[39] These remarks appeared in a text published in 1931, several years after the Tokyo Earthquake and the destruction of many of the older sites of pleasure he had studied. While it is hard to know why Gonda, an avowed proponent of a "materialist history," should now grieve the passing of arts and performers that belonged to an earlier, feudal age and mode of production, it might be explained that he saw in these practices and activities an immediate and direct means of communication between street performers and audiences in a public social space through an actual reading of the lives and experiences of the performers. But what seems clear is his mourning for the passing of an artisanal tradition and the social relationships associated with it. The newer forms of entertainment, especially those that took place in large movie houses or variety halls, diminished the possibility of such direct contact between performer and audience. His own desire for direct access to reaching this more remote society represented in his interviews with performers pointed to an inaugural conception of mediation unaffected by a system of exchange values and thus the traces of a world unmediated by either distance (exchange) or technology.

As early as 1923, Gonda had seen that capitalist society was in the grip of a system of exchange value and what he called the circulation of "things" (*mono*)—consumption and commodification. This early observation was made in a broader context that considered as commonplace "consumers demanding fashionable goods" (4:60). Here, he proposed that modern society was not a time that actually acknowledged the "meaning of life" in the fulfillment of natural desires. Instead, modern society fixed life's meaning in criteria that concerned only the capacity of people to buy; what was truly important was whether a person was or was not able to purchase things. The things, themselves, possessed no meaning apart from the price fixed to them by the system of exchange value; the "significance of life" was entirely determined by the possibility of consumption. "Even enduring discomfort by wearing a summer cloak while scratching the sweating skin," he wrote, "is a condition that acknowledges only the significance of life in buying the cloak." It is less a question of liking or disliking an object, through the mechanisms of what he called "fulfilling natural desires," than of simply buying things. People yearn for and even miss grasping meaning when they seek only to "possess a thing." Hence, pleasure, based on "natural desires" (increasingly a code for use-value), loses its original meaning in contemporary society and is replaced by the "desire for possession" that recognizes the locus of meaning in the sole act of buying a commodity (4:61). No distinction is possible between "inconvenient commodities" and "inexpedient things," since use is no longer operating in the transaction. Immersed in the act of buying, consumers no longer know where to stop in their pursuit of purchasing popular commodities. In this world, fashion, the ever new in the same, rules, and all meaning now derives from the simple act of "entering the thing into anybody's hand." "Man does not determine 'things,' as such, but 'things' manage man; man does not dispose things but things dispose man. Man, therefore, becomes a worn-out horse (*doba*) of fashion; spurred on only by the popular and the fashionable (*ryūkō*) that causes the suicide of the man inside the customer" (4:63). It is evident that Gonda understood early how the demand for things simply strengthened the regime of desire which is never fully satisfied, until the last lonely instant. The commodification of life led to the disappearance of humans, who were rapidly being replaced by consumers seeking the ever new in the same. In modern society, he asserted, managers "create fashion"; things are not produced and circulated because of need and use but because the new is always in demand. Popular commodities must be situated within this framework in which demand is created for things people do not necessarily need. But this structure, in turn, was driven by the production of great quantities of goods that override choice according to the likes and dislikes of consumers. And this meant "making in great quantities the demand for goods of a similar nature and similar form," in short, homogenization (4:65). Concentrating on "big capital," it was necessary to carry out mass production of similar goods whose only consideration of value depended on whether or not they could produce a profit. In this way, "things" actually select people, interpellate them, recalling Benjamin's later description of the commodity form (4:66). Individuals are oppressed, crushed, leveled by this "apparition" of change, the domination of the popular, the fashionable, and the ever new in the same (4:67).

Eight years later, on the eve of a sustained silence that was to last five years, Gonda returned to this theme of production for commodification. The central purpose of contemporary society, he wrote in "Minshū gorakuron" ("Shakai seikatsu to minshū goraku"), is production. "The trend that elevates 'things' . . . and ignores 'life' is the philosophy of the new privileged classes. . . . This intellectual trend . . . sacrifices this 'life' and praises the move to elevate it to the political mansion of 'things' " (2:209). But this trend was most consequential in producing a new class that lived to oppress less privileged people and whose vocation was "dispossession by force." If the first Renaissance released human life from religious superstition and domination, the second must save human life from the additions of the present day (2:210). There can be no adequate human life for production, no everydayness for "things." What Gonda seemed to be calling for was the rejection of a view that saw production serving creation and pleasure that reproduced for production. Under the constraints of this regime, only the received system of relationships would be sustained through a process of simple reproduction in which pleasure could only have a mediatized and predictable role. For a moment, Gonda's theory of pleasure resembled Bakhtin's meditations on laughter and the carnivalesque, inasmuch they both saw pleasure exceeding the demands of replicating the social order. It was the force of this perception he saw in the residues of earlier forms of entertainment and pleasures situated on the streets and in the direct relationship between the performer (producer) and audience (consumer), now daily disappearing from the large cities.

Gonda favored these older arts because they were performed in the streets, where people could gather and meet each other without fear of being driven out by cars or buses.[40] Similarly, he was quick to propose, after the earthquake, that it was necessary to "abandon attachment" to the places fire had destroyed and to the circumstances that once existed before the sites had been destroyed, a view he shared with Kon Wajirō (4:146). After surveying the restoration of Tokyo in 1924, from quarter to quarter, and praising the efforts to resuscitate life as it had existed before the catastrophe, he concluded that the dream of yearning for a return of conditions as they had existed before places had been destroyed by fire would eventually fade if those burnt out sites were not restored to their original shape. He was convinced that a "starting point" that aimed at restoring the old was mistaken. The reason, again, was history. Lacking access to the social life experienced before and at the time of the quake and the economic development accompanying it; any effort to "leap" into the restoration of the imperial capital and reconstruct a "new Tokyo" along such familiar lines must be mistaken. What is important instead is planning for a new social life. "We must," he advised, "discover the true process that should transport us to the future by considering the social and economic relationships that are emerging at the present time" (4:146). The parts of Tokyo that were destroyed represented the confluence of social and economic conditions that now belong to history and have been overtaken by a new combination of forces.

> The street cars are revived in fresh verdure, the early summer sun dances on the pavement. . . . Ginza street has the exotic scent of towns like Singapore and Barcelona, women in short bobbed hair and bell bottom trousers, remainder sales of old fashions, flashy coats that signaled elegance (*shibui*) [coloring from women's scarves], smooth, expressionless faces like the surface of ivory comes into sight among the thin neckties that differ from the string cords of *haori* ; even though the fat, short legs of women are an inheritance of a long tradition that should not be grieved, we are still caught in the physique of a small people who wear simple clothing that also have a taste for the abnormal and strange (*hentaiteki shikōsei*) and adore American actresses with whom they have become intimate at the movies, dressed up in flashily designed kimono like the apparel of cafe waitresses with darkened lipstick, rouge resembling monkeys, they continue moving the coquettish fans composed in ideographs that lengthens and narrows the eyebrows. When movie houses are swept up and the surging crowd is pushed out, the cafe lanterns are red, at the time the jazz music in the dance halls begin to blare. The men and women emerge cheerfully and dance excitedly. Moving, living. (2:240–241)

In this long passage, Gonda employed the technique of photomontage to catch the speed, spectacle, and blazing colors of modern life on the streets. There is little or no syntax or order here, only the juxtaposition of simultaneous images appearing like flashbulbs, movement, energy. The explosion of images, color, and people and things in movement constituted a constellation of things coming together to signify "modern life" (*seikatsu*)—the everydayness of the Now Tosaka Jun targeted for theoretical reflection. Even in this montage, Gonda discerned "a taste for the abnormal and strange" that had appeared meteorically among groups called the "modern boy" and the "modern girl," whose presentation of self was patterned from American movies announcing the advent of the age of the flapper. Gonda advised that it would be regrettable to overlook this "taste for the abnormal" which, at the same time, furnishes both a "certain charm" and a "certain revulsion." While this aptitude was a product of the cities, it also represented a widespread change that would eventually penetrate every sector of Japanese life. Hence, it was unreasonable to expect that the "smells of old Edo" would still persist. The "modern everydayness" was still restricted to those areas where the life of the new age was stirring, special places where the new was being lived. These locations were the Ginza, the cross streets of Marubiru, Hibiya, Shinjuku, Kagurazaka. While the people who actually lived in Ginza, Shinjuku and Kagurazaka were a special case, workers in these districts lived elsewhere in the city and came to these locations daily for work. The cafe, bar, restaurant, movie house, dance hall all became the seat of "modern life" and extensions of the streets, as one form of *strasse*, as he put it. Gonda claimed that this form of life did not flourish in the household and thereby offered a release from its spatial and emotional constraints. As for the modern boy and girl, who were the protagonists of modern life in the streets, the act of returning to the household resembled "a tiger whose fangs have been extracted, a cat whose whiskers have been cut" (2:242). Gonda wanted to associate the *gaitō*—the street—with the boulevard and *strasse* as an equivalent to European thoroughfares which had been the centers of modern life. Modern life, he believed, created the streets that produced patterns of living that were neither ordinary nor regular, composed of the time of an unconnected, diverse humanity and the time of leisure separated from production when consumption ruled.

Accordingly, modern life was formed on two basic principles: the "image of abandoning productive life" and the "emancipation of life in modernity" (2:244). Modern life prompted people to abandon work and family, as Aono Suekichi documented the process, to forswear the great crucible of productive life centered on the household to seek escape from the burdens of labor, relief from the hardships of home and its entailing obligations. The streets clearly offered an escape route. Modern life encouraged emancipation in all forms by prompting a frontal attack on feudal residues as a necessary condition for constructing a new life based on equality and freedom. The temptation of abandoning the burdens of a productive life, Gonda reasoned, energized diverse groups to construct new lives on the streets. What seemed to worry him was the very elasticity of modern life and its introduction of "necessary evils," referring to the "taste for the abnormal and strange," which by the early 1930s plainly pointed to the spectacle of eroticism and the strange (*eroguronansensu*) new forms of entertainment, social relationships, and sexuality that had spilled over from the streets and were being daily dramatized in newspapers and in the fictions of writers like Edogawa Rampo. The emergence of these newer pleasures made the older precincts of entertainment no longer necessary. The streets signified surplus that led to inexhaustible possibilities of play and consumption that might require greater vigilance in the future. The desire for the abnormal developed particularly "without regret in places like the Ginza, Hibiya, in movie houses, especially those specialized in featuring Western films, in restaurants, dance halls, in the streets" and became what people enjoyed most. "Modern life's penchant for the abnormal danced on the pavements reflected in the early summer sun, around the benches shaded by verdant freshness, on the sides of cold marble tables" (2:247).

For Gonda, the preference for abnormal tastes prefigured the end of people's pleasures. The recurring image of abandoning the productive life for endless play and what was described as "life emancipation" undermined the "equilibrium" provided by labor, the necessary relationship between the time of work and leisure time (2:245). He feared that the separation of cultural production from the everyday life of the people would lead directly to the forfeiture of independence such a culture represented, replaced by the regime of consumption and commodification— the domination of the thing and the evacuation of all meaning. The most serious consequence of this process of endless and meaningless commodification would be the homogenizing of both consumption and things—the ever new in the same—and the leveling of popular entertainment. Gonda referred to this process in a number of ways: the "unification of taste among the people" and "proletarianization" plainly called attention to the homogenization of culture (4:171). All of this stemmed from the progressive elimination of the mixed and uneven cultural configuration that had characterized people's—working class—pleasures in the period before the earthquake. He called this new circumstance "taste without tradition" and wondered about the effects of a contemporary culture now separated from "convention" to embrace the "taste of nonsense," where everything invariably gets exchanged into the "trifling" and the "silly" (4:169). Attributing the progressive leveling of life and the loss of social distinctions between classes, occupations, gender and age to economic, political, and social freedoms introduced by modern society, he increasingly held up the example of how medieval society maintained sharp distinctions between these social categories as a historical model that demonstrated the necessary correspondence between pleasure and proper social constituencies. In that distant time, the diverse social groups possessed their own, unique forms of pleasure to reflect a feudal class system even in the domain of entertainment. The crossing of boundaries was prohibited and offenders "were frowned upon as people who disturbed social order and peace" (4:170). Yet, Gonda was clearly romanticizing the feudal past and exaggerating its own rage for order, refusing to recognize how steadily those barriers separating zones of class entertainment were daily violated by both peasants and samurai, and how this very mixing of elements gave late Tokugawa culture its vitality. At the same time he was upholding the order of pleasures of medieval society as a mirror for his present, while Kon Wajirō, as we shall see, was celebrating its disappearance precisely because it restricted taste and consumption to the privileged classes.

People were now free to participate in any kind of pleasurable activity as long as they could pay for it. Gonda referred to this removal of social constraints as an "opportunity for evening out pleasure" and the occasion for producing the phenomenon of a "unified taste" shared by the people as a whole. This trend, in turn, led to the unleashing of a process of "democratization of the older class and traditional pleasures" that survived the demise of the feudal order and the "smashing of a unique tradition of pleasure," prompted by the "birth of new pleasures that conformed to the idea of a reborn pleasure community (*goraku kyōdo*)" (4:170). Various dance styles, golf, Western music, and No drama that inundated aristocratic taste were rapidly generalized, diffused throughout society, made accessible to all "without restraint," who were now free to gather in one place to enjoy them. If this represented proletarianization at one level, at another it inspired a "mood of opposition" to both tradition and custom. Finally, the new culture of play encouraged resistance to "authority" and "power," especially in its most extreme forms of expression represented by the "taste of nonsense" that was supplemented by the movies and theater. What Gonda was referring to was the obvious flouting of conventions and moral codes new forms of entertainment risked as a condition of their own practices. In this respect, the most representative medium was the contemporary, popular "revue taste" found in theaters and variety halls, which always seemed to emphasize "fascinating excitement" that produced a jumble of sexual rapture and quite lukewarm sensation to constitute a "unification of illogicality" (4:171). But opposition to authority and revue taste favoring nonsense were different moves derived from the same source. Gonda was convinced that the source was the impulse of denial toward convention encouraged by materialist society under capitalism, "an unlimited hell."[41] He saw this development as a betrayal of the people who now were consigned to a "prison" of endless trivial entertainment that managed only to titillate. Homogenization and a lowering of taste to the most common denominators combined to destroy the older people's pleasures in which they could find themselves (2:20–21). Even more worrisome, the process was beginning to penetrate the countryside, the remaining site of all the traditional forms of class and regional pleasures, which were being thrown into a large melting pot called "national life" (3:23). If an earlier people's pleasure had been produced from the everyday experiences of workers, the new, national masses (*kokumin taishū*) must now endeavor to construct new forms of pleasure that conform to "large-scale organizations," "the technology of machinery," in order to be aligned with the "new movement of industrial arts that must introduce beauty—through the machine—into the life of the national masses."[42] What had been once produced by the people had now become the task of large-scale organizations, capital, and the state.

By the early 1930s, Gonda was beginning to envisage another kind of national community that would conform to the very evenness of capitalist modernization he had earlier criticized. He believed that this call for a national community producing new pleasures would resolve the problem of a society of national consumers caught in the ceaseless allures of homogeneity and a preference for abnormal tastes. Here, he appealed to the formation of a new culture that would enlist the "joy of the masses" as its standard. While this identification of the joyous masses recalled an earlier constructivist program and now came close to the productivist nightmare of German national socialism that linked joy to work, it also converged with the communitarian and cultural projects promoted by contemporaries like Yanagita Kunio, Takada Yasuma, and Watsuji Tetsurō. The newly awakened pleasure will be erected on the life of the nation's masses, "by sprouting a harmonious solvent" capable of fusing the mingling of new and diverse pleasures. A new formation of national pleasure would reproduce the mixed and uneven culture that once marked the place of people's culture. Perceiving the steady diminution of pleasure and the decline of traditional entertainment, fueled by a relentless process of "equalization" and homogenization as the necessary condition for establishing the forms of "newly emerging pleasures," Gonda was undoubtedly driven to this extreme by the recognition that older entertainments had once constituted an important element in an uneven mix that corresponded to the historical location of the "people," the workers. The earlier culture of pleasure was one marked by restraints and conventions that meaningless commodification undermined. Widespread homogenization, the lowering of tastes, and the drift to "nonsense" inspired by American movies and revues encouraged opposition to authority and the establishment of a culture of pleasure without restraints, open to all, available to everyone to enjoy themselves as they pleased. This move to reinstating a culture of restraints disclosed obvious social fears in the 1930s and a kinship with political agendas aimed at aligning the masses to communitarian expectations within the midst of a capitalist society. Gonda, like so many, contributed to the growing vocalization of fascistic solutions to the crisis of capitalist civil society, the "gathering of fascism" Alice Kaplan has identified in the France of the Third Republic, where the divisions that characterized modernity would be rewritten and effaced for the image of a gemeinschaft where the people and the masses would be reborn as the folk. But it is also true that Gonda lamented what he saw as the loss of historical formations before the cruel and relentless regime of the ever new in the ever same. In his program, the turn to a new culture serving the national community (not consumers) was a call for restraints and conventions managed by the state and large-scale organizations, and not by the people who lived, worked, and enjoyed themselves on the streets. Commodification, leading to a "preference for abnormal tastes," introduced a crisis of consent in Japanese society. What he seemed to fear most was the bonding of watered down tastes with a generalization of pleasures, sameness—the bland horror of the everyday—which he attributed to proletarianization.[43] To prevent the withdrawal of consent provoked by the "liberation of everyday life" and the "abdication of a productive living," Gonda sought to envision an arrangement that might resecure consent by refining the terms of the culture of pleasure. Culture was a negotiation between various groups and different sites, whose differences would be inscribed in its formation. The concept of a renewed national community thus aimed at securing a hegemonic arrangement that might help realize the partial completion of a unity (or some suggestion of it) he feared was slipping away under the driving force of commodification, "equalization," and the loss of standards. It was, he acknowledged, precisely the absence of a such a unitary conception that ultimately prompted the state to appropriate all of those theories capable of promising unity or restoring the historical unity of the Japanese people.

In 1937, the year of the Japanese invasion of North China (euphemistically described by contemporaries as the "China Incident"), Gonda's conception of people's pleasure had rotated 180 degrees from where it had been ten years earlier.

The contemporary period in which the bell at daybreak rings out loudly the dawn of a new East Asia announces the founding day of a new order that drums out the indomitable will and violent passions for the establishment of

a new system in the domain of national life. This holistic ideal and the sentiment for national cooperation acknowledged a completely different meaning
and function toward the pleasure life and the pleasure of the nation's people
who have been entrusted to individualistic selfishness hitherto too freely neglected. It is nothing but the pursuit of a completely new direction and policy.
The "national people's pleasure" has become the new demand of the age."[44]

Despite the ringing of bells reverberating throughout the land proclaiming a new order, Gonda had clearly turned to endorsing state and
large-scale organizations of incorporation—corporate structures—as the
basis of founding a new national community and its pleasures. It was
almost as if the task of defining pleasure was reduced to national life
itself, where the community was organized along the lines of national
enjoyment—"enjoying the nation," as Slavoj Žižek described nationalism
not too many years ago. The solution to unevenness was national unity,
which demanded national enjoyment, rather than the mixed and historically marked pleasure experienced by workers and other social groups
earlier. Gonda easily acknowledged that since World War I, the pleasure
of the masses had been rooted in the moving pictures established on the
"wave" of social democracy, economic liberalism, and individualism.
People's pleasures had evolved there and developed within these determinate limits. But the China Incident seemed to change all of this. The
"situation," as he put it, has ended "people's pleasure," as such, and
given birth to the idea of "national pleasure" (3:13)! The outbreak of
the war signaled diminution of pleasure, a "vacuum," in which people
watched only newsreels. The "excitement" at the time of the "Fall of
Nanjing" turned into "tranquilized deep emotion" that revived again the
desire for a new pleasure within daily life. Gonda saw in this new cultural
formation an awareness of how the force of habit had taken in pleasure
unconsciously, how "pleasure was not play for wasting leisure" but rather
a "provision of life for continuing at any time the tranquil heart while
being serious." The "economy of consumption" derived from the war
"sliced through and diminished the excess fat to provide a starting point
for a true life request of the people, a real self."[45] Yet, he was also aware
that this new awareness necessitated rethinking the relationship between
"mass character" and "leadership," "freedom and law" and pleasure and
education. But we can see that the move already revealed how far he
had departed from an earlier enthusiasm that linked the formation of
pleasure to history. He had committed himself to the authority of large-
scale structural management to administer pleasure—what could only result in recuperating the very homogenization he had feared and now
sought to avoid.

STREETS, SHELTER, SUBJECTIVITY

In an essay written in 1929, titled "Gendai no fūzoku," and published in a multivolume series on custom and life history edited by the historian Nakamura Kōya, Kon Wajirō (1888–1973) included a number of drawings he made at locations where he was conducting research. Among these locations was Inogashira Park in central Tokyo. The drawing was a topographic map filled with numbers, next to symbols denoting women, men, children, ages, and so on. The map is entitled "Inogashira-koen no picnic no mure" (Picnic groups at Inogashira Park) and is dated April 18, 1926, 3:10 in the afternoon. Signaling the first outbreak of spring in Tokyo, the custom was for diverse groups to spend a few hours outdoors in this and other city parks to picnic, sit, or even sleep. The illustration is accompanied by a short description and explanatory legend. Kon explains that the illustrations stem from an investigation carried out at the time of "flower viewing" (*hanami*), already discussed by Gonda as a form of popular pleasure, at a park known for its seasonal flowers and on a bright Sunday afternoon.[46]

There was nothing frivolous about this mapping, even though it might at first appear strange to assemble a topography of a park marked by different groups of people involved in diverse activities. What is interesting is the detail of the legend Kon provided that identifies precisely people and groups, their positioning in the park and their differing activities.

(1) Three young girls, one middle-aged woman, two boys gathering herbs; (2) a young boy, middle-aged woman and a girl sitting on a bench eating boiled eggs; (3) group eating mandarin oranges; (4) middle-aged woman eating mandarin orange; a middle-aged man smoking; another middle-aged man eating candy (*kashi*); (5) everybody eating Nanjing tofu; young woman holding a child and feeding it milk; (6) child watching three soldiers; (7) two boys dressed in sailor outfits (*hanten*) fooling around after getting off their bikes; (8) group of eight men drinking sake; six of them lying on the ground on their sides; (9) two men, silent, sitting together on a bench; a woman inhaling on a cigarette; (10) eight boy scouts cooking, eating; remnants; (11) girl in Western clothes, drinking citron while standing; (12) two young men lying on their sides; (13) young woman and middle-aged woman; the younger woman is holding a baby; (14) woman searching for a toilet, confused, holding paper; (15) accompanying a dog;(16) old man and baby buggy; pointing to a peddler; (17) two men eating donuts; (18) reading a bible; (19) watching quietly, while conversing; (20) scrutinizing scenes in the direction of the pond.

Kon offered the explanation that "these are the lives of moderns, pieces of customs. Like butterflies, they are shapes flying about" (32). No other narrative is supplied since the configuration and its content tell their own story, about modern life and how people choose to spend some leisure time. Yet Kon's description is as rich and precise in detail as Seurat's earlier pointillist masterpiece "La Grande Jatte," which portrays an array of people sitting, lying down, and generally enjoying a warm afternoon in a Parisian park. The importance of both portraits, or at least what they share, is a valorization of detail concerning how people are dressed, their bodily placement, and what they are doing. Kon, who was trained as an architect and was a gifted draftsman capable of producing talented drawings, must surely have known about the Seurat painting.

This inventory of people filling in the precincts of Inogashira Park derived from a prior explanation of a new understanding of contemporary custom and the "science" of its study, which he called *kōgengaku* (he translated this as "modernologio," which was undoubtedly the word in Esperanto) (5), revealed both a method for research and the principal concerns informing his broader program. Yet behind this program, which Tosaka Jun already dismissed as simply phenomenological and too descriptive, was a desire to make sense of the modern life established in the large cities, especially Tokyo after the earthquake of 1923, and the role played by the formation of modern custom in negotiating this experience. "Our research object," he announced, "avoids the abnormal. It is, in general, the everyday of society and people (*minshū*) [who inhabit it]" (5). While Kon wanted to use the "pretext" of an introduction to the understanding of modern custom to determine the contours of the field (Bourdieu's idea of the *champ* would be more appropriate), and the attributes and method that best suited an examination of modern society, he recognized that "our *kōgengaku*" has also become a "study of consumption in life" (15). He saw, quite early, that the buying of "commodities" formed an integral part of understanding modern life rather than representing a simple whim of curiosity. Research showed that there was marked imitation in the patterns of buying, and the observable occurrence of a "a wave of custom transmitted by imitating the upper classes," forging a form of mimicry perceived by the French sociologist Gabriel Tarde (whose work Kon was acquainted with) in his classic book on imitation, which sought to explain how the lower classes imitated upper class custom and style. In this regard, "imitation," or, as it has been more recently and fashionably renamed in postcolonial theory, "mimicry," was seen as a cement sealing social solidarity in industrial society and the apparent guarantee for averting class antagonisms and open conflict. For Kon, it was less a prod toward securing social solidarity than a channel for circulating differing customs and commodities on a mass scale. Acknowledging the purpose of his work to explain these phenomena quantitatively whenever possible, his concerns seemed more riveted to the multiplicity and proliferation of commodities and custom, its sheer volume as a sign of modern life. The constant flow of goods and people and their seemingly endless and inexhaustible capacity for interaction signaled the regime of the truly modern; objects and people in constant interaction constituted the great narrative of modern life. Embedded in this process of quantitative commodification was a conception of subjectivity and the possibility for producing an endless tableau of subject positions people were able to slip in and occupy or evacuate for still another in their daily encounters on the streets and public spaces of the great cities. *Kōgengaku*, he proclaimed, deals with commodities as "use objects," and while they are the same, each, when confronted, still manages to be seen from a different angle of vision or perspective (14–15). Despite the appearance of the ever same associated with the commodities, their "lives" took on the aspect and attribute of differences, much like the people whose lives were in constant interaction with things. Hence "modern studies" is founded on the principle of studying everywhere the "situations" in which commodities are used. Kon, here, called attention to how commodities might appear differently to different people in different locations, how their use, despite their apparent sameness, will vary according to person and place.

Places targeted for investigation should begin with the household, since the family constitutes the principal component of social structure. The life of the family is administered within the confines of the household. But there are other important sites as well, where investigators can find the conduct displayed by people buying commodities: schools, the military, the theater, and the streets. All of these sites represented spaces where the interaction between things and people took place and where the act of purchasing would disclose how the object might be used. Kon's emphasis, in contrast to Gonda's observations, disclosed the primacy of use, utility identified with the commodity, rather than the empathy elicited by the thing as it appealed to individual desire and interpellated the buyer. Aono Suekichi, as we shall see later, went even further than Gonda in showing how unfulfilled consumerist expectations—the pain of being interpellated and not being able to respond—drove the white-collar class (*sararīman*) to despair, panic, and unhappiness. From the perspective of seeing use-value in the commodity, Kon was convinced, perhaps naively, that his investigations would ultimately bring out the "social meaning contained within these commodities" (15). What he seemed to mean by "social meaning" is hard to know in a context where goods produced for mass consumption necessitated the repetition of the ever new in the ever same. There is more than a hint in his writings to suggest that his interest in modern custom, which he saw as the vocation of his conception of urban ethnography, opened the way to considering the importance of commodities and the social meanings people attached to them in and by the act of consumption. The commodity as custom under the sign of rationality was how Kon differentiated the modern present from both the nineteenth and eighteenth centuries.[47] In the act of buying, people were not seen as exercising some sort of "resistance" by choosing one commodity over another and using them in different ways that did not necessarily conform to their intended use. Attributing to commodities a social meaning and life, he was convinced that the act of buying itself empowered the buyer with an agency, inasmuch as the actor buyer was performing as a subject who was now acting on the object. Buying and consuming was an act of conferring social meaning on the thing, according to Kon, and this recognition disclosed a conception of subjectivity—people occupying a position of knowing what they wanted and why, and thus capable of acting on this knowledge. This grasp of the modern subject and its formation in the process of commodification and consumption was intimately related to his research projects, which concentrated on observing people in different locations and situations, usually in open, public spaces—the streets, parks, sometimes large department stores (one of his favorite locations)—where he recorded the vast diversity of subject positions people were capable of assuming, as signaled by their clothing, body language, and conduct. While Kon envisaged the creation of subject positions as a "construction" closely linked to the styles associated with certain places like the Ginza, he never showed any sensitivity to the power of the commodity to masquerade as modern custom in its unrelenting effort to induce people to consume. In this regard, it is as difficult to know which was actually subject and object as it is to determine the real source of social meaning. But in his effort to mark off the place of the observer from the observed, as we shall see, he tried to differentiate subject from object and fix the content of both and the order of the relationship.

Initially, Kon believed that an accumulation of research would lead to a draft for a guidebook on modern man (16). Cautioning his readers that he was not solely concerned with gathering information for utilitarian purposes (even though his research projects were often funded by city agencies), he believed that the gathering and selecting of social facts useful to explaining the conditions of modern life would yield a beneficial knowledge of contemporary custom and result in the subsequent transmission of the style of living characterizing contemporaries to later ages. Here, he rearticulated the desire of contemporary native ethnologists, who were already seeking to record the customs and traces of folk life to preserve what clearly was vanishing from the scene, with the goal of transmitting its memory to future generations who would no longer have the opportunity to either experience such a life or even observe its remains. Kon was convinced that the customs of contemporary life would undoubtedly pass into memory and history, overtaken by as yet unenvisaged forms of life that would thus necessitate supplying an account of the "living styles of contemporary man." It is interesting to note that the early postwar films of Ozu Yasujirō actually accepted this task of trying to reconstitute precisely the space of modern life Kon was describing as contemporary in the 1920s and 1930s but which was rapidly disappearing in the postwar world of the 1950s and 1960s.

What now seems so extraordinary about Kon Wajirō's program is the decision to transform the contemporary social formation into a totality he called the contemporary (*gendai*) that immediately required the figuring of a method of investigation appropriate to its conditions. In fact, contemporaneity, like Tosaka's now, constituted a form of historical totalization that insisted upon a different relationship between the present and the past. The past, in Kon's thinking, appears only to show how different the present—the contemporary—is; and while there is a narrative of the development of social custom since the eighteenth century, taken from Tarde's analysis, Kon is not at all interested in establishing a continuity with it through a category of tradition. The present is a moment of genuine difference, offering new forms of historical consciousness; the present of *gendai* is defined historically by a negation of a past which represented a historical mistake. While this view of the development of custom, as we shall see, consisted of sequential stages, one following the other in chronological time, these stages did not necessarily follow each other in a causal order, even though the present signaled the regime of rationality. What Kon aimed to show was how the historical antecedents of modern custom—the feudal and early modern pasts—were ultimately turned into a "now-time" that came very close to Tosaka's conception of the "now" that totalized historical time and designated its locus as the "thereness," the space of everydayness. If, as I have suggested, Tosaka remained silent on conventional forms of historicist temporalization, as it was being vigorously practiced by contemporary Marxist historians embroiled in the great discourse over Japanese capitalism, and promoted instead a conception of history devoid of developmental and linear dispositions, we can assume that he was dismissing narrative for a different form of historical consciousness that moved from one level to another, from decoding to recoding, in order to find difference. By the same measure, we can see a comparable shifting of the focus of historiography away from narrative forms of historical totalization to the kind of montages people like Gonda were already employing to describe the spectacle of modern life. Yet this move, like Tosaka's penetrating critique of historical temporality, can be said to have put into question a conception of modernity based upon the presumption of a temporal continuity with the past.[48] Within both the historicist Marxism driving the debate on Japanese capitalism and later modernization theory, this restitution of tradition through the newer expression of historical continuity would provide the same temporal framework and thus similar conceptions of modernity that represented different sides of the same, bad coin. But in the cases of Tosaka, Gonda, and Kon modernity was envisaged as a distinct form of historical temporality produced by a range of social practices, forms, and a qualitatively different kind of experience that resulted in "a decisive mutation of historical experience capable of deriving meaning" from either a relationship to the past or tradition or to a different level of everydayness.[49] In Gonda and Kon, we find the explicit turn to historicizing temporality by appealing to concrete cultural forms, while Tosaka shows through the critique of specific custom and the resituating of the space of everydayness how history is repressed and how the present—the now—demands a critical practice based upon understanding the current situation.

Kon's definition of the contemporary coincided with the moment after the Kantō earthquake when the massive importation of American material culture that came in its wake formed an overlay of received customs and practices, old and new, that had survived the natural disaster. The sign of this culture, which had already transformed the life of American cities in the 1920s, was the commodity; its modus vivendi was desire transformed into value to produce the effect of mass consumption. With Kon, the commodity became a poetic object. Yet behind the "commodity . . . bathed in a profane glow," as Benjamin described its attraction to unknowing buyers, was the larger figure of the commodity form, which, as Gonda perceived, was already becoming the model for social relationships in Japanese society. Hence, *gendai* was bounded by the years following the earthquake—from 1924 on—and the subsequent installation of modern life in a Tokyo that had to pick itself up and reconstitute its space. Despite the power to figure a discourse that might not have been as ubiquitous in lived reality as it was in the imagination, there was agreement among a number of contemporary observers that the pace of Americanization was quickening after the earthquake and may very well have been propelled by the necessity of reconstruction. Even so, Gonda had already supplied testimony to the hegemony of newly imported Americanized forms of mass entertainment, movies, radio, that had been firmly implanted in Japanese society by the latter half of the 1920s. So compelling was the evidence for change that it persuaded Kon to propose that new economic and political conditions demanded that those sites that had burned down after the quake should not be resuscitated in their original form. If Hirabayashi Hatsunosuke celebrated science and rationality, Ōya, as suggested above, dismissed it as "incomplete," "superficial," possessing neither "ideals" or morality. We know that Tosaka Jun imagined both a modern temporality and space of everydayness that would require new customs and morality.

Kon saw the contemporary as a "moving present (*ugoki tsutsuaru*) developing before our eyes" (1).[50] "If you take one step outside the door," he exulted, "you see the spectacle that I will make as my object." But his fashioning of a new object of investigation and its corresponding method was also encouraged by the rebuilding of Tokyo as well. Everywhere he seemed to turn, toward households of the middle class, to diverse meeting places, the fields and gardens, there is "contemporary custom." Activities like sitting and reading a newspaper or turning the pages of a magazine do not always necessitate an explanation. But, he added, these are things that immediately call attention to the contemporary, which is actually moving all the time and demands to be grasped (2). Grasping and then narrating it, he acknowledged, is a difficult task. Kon confessed that his interests in the contemporary began after the earthquake; the destruction caused by the catastrophe immediately aroused his concern for the uncertain status of customs, at which time he embarked on a number of collaborative projects with his friend Yoshida Kenkichi, such as "1925nen shoka Tōkyō Ginza fūzoku kiroku," "Honjo Fukugawa himmin kutsufukin fūzoku saisha," and "Tōkyō togai fūzoku zatsushū," published in *Fujin kōron* in 1925. Although these studies established the mode of investigating the cityscape by concentrating on the details of customs as they appeared to the observer in the streets of Ginza, recording the ratio of people looking at show windows, changes according to the time of day, age, gender, occupation of people strolling along its streets, they do not explain the impulse informing the new "science" of *kōgengaku*.[51] The technique was, of necessity, metonymical; the details of Ginza life observed ("Ginzabura") called attention to a larger image of the "living styles of contemporary cultured people."[52] His motive was first propelled, according to his own testimony, by a concealed intention to analyze phenomena like custom and popular fashions in concrete settings. "After studying industrial design in the late Meiji," he confessed, "I fell into despair" since it apparently failed to satisfy him. Folk life and custom already constituted the subject of the new "native ethnology" implemented by Yanagita Kunio and his followers, but this direction held less attraction to Kon who felt he had already said what he wanted about traditional farm architecture and the life it housed in a book published on Japanese rural folk houses. He was apparently more interested in observing and recording customs that were always in process of being made rather than preserving and even conserving those practices from the past that still lingered on in traces in the present. It was in this context that he returned to the city and inaugurated *kōgengaku* as an "actual investigation of everyday life" as it was being lived in the cities by civilized men whose selves were embedded within contemporary customs.[53] This shift "occurred around 1923, immediately after the earthquake. I collaborated with an artist as others soon fled this capital of death. We stood for hours on the soil of Tokyo and viewed the reality of the city at that time. Both of us felt that there were many matters that needed to be looked at. I began painting somehow, while serving as an office manager. Still, I was able to do some light investigating by wandering daily on the burnt fields. It was distinctly from that time that I rejoiced over the fact that I was recording a variety of things that caught the attention of my eye"[54] Kon investigated this "ruined earth" (16) and was urged on to record what he was observing by sketching the jerry-built shacks that had been constructed on the sites destroyed by fire. The method of recording and sketching was one he had already put into practice when doing his earlier researches on country homes.[55] It is interesting to note, in this connection, Kon's conception of ethnographic reporting, which easily incorporated sketching as a substitute for photography that his great contemporary Yanagita Kunio, we shall see, refused altogether because it risked putting the observer outside of the scene rather than in it.[56] While this move dramatized the problem of how subject related to object, which I will turn to later, Yanagita sought to efface this difference by merely eliding the observer with the observed and thus appealing to the power of empathy to overcome the two moments. Yanagita collapsed knowledge of the native into native knowledge to erase the distinction between himself and those whom he studied since they were both within the same scene. With Kon, there was no claim to a privileged native knowledge, even though his observer was very much in the scene of the observed and shared their customs as they navigated their way through the streets of the city. There was still the recognition of a distance between the researcher who stood on street corners and recorded the movements of passers-by who constituted the situational crowds that passed through Ginza throughout the day. Before the earthquake, he saw a kinship and "similar frame of mind" in the production of records within mountain sites and inconvenient rural areas. Even Tokyo at that time, though complex, was considered an easy place to record the circumstances of city life. After the earthquake, the situation changed and the dialectic of appearing and disappearing custom became an intricate weave that required different kinds of methods of investigation (KWS, 1:16).

We must pay close attention to Kon's awareness of self-reflexivity, which marks his science of modern studies. His desire to situate himself in the actual site of investigation was obviously an appeal to the authority of witnessing the comings and goings of a specific scene as it passed before his eyes. Unlike Yanagita, with whom he has been frequently compared, Kon based his authority on the experience of observation rather than hermeneutic privilege. Whereas Yanagita sought to collapse his perspective into the experience of another rather than present a knowledge of it, Kon proceeded from the presumption that modern experience was separate from a knowledge of it and thus required a method of investigation that would, in fact, take this division into account. This meant that he was interested in trying to extract a knowledge of the experience of living in a modern scene. In the essay "Kōgengaku to wa nanika," he proposed that investigating and analyzing contemporary custom as it appeared on the surface of group life, the relationship between subject and its object, between researcher and the researched was like that between the civilized person and the uncivilized, the doctor and the patient, and the judge and the criminal. "If we [the investigator] are separated from the customary lives of the average person and are not aware that we are living in an objective position, we will feel extremely isolated." In other words, Kon wanted to fix the place of the observer outside of the site of investigation for analytic reasons, even while recognizing that this was something of a fiction. The doctor had to remain impartial—objective—in order to cure the patient, yet he was also part of the human situation. While constructing our own life as individuals at the same time, we are prepared to acknowledge that we stand in a position that observes the life of society. The relationship between "we" and "contemporary people" resembles the relationship between "oil" and "water." Even more dramatic, Kon explained that researchers of the modern were no different from botanists and zoologists and stood in the same position and enjoyed a similar perspective of observation, even though the object (taishō) was different. "When illuminating the attitude of archaeology," he advised, "the mental state is toward remains and relics." But for modern studies one looks only at the commodities in show windows on the streets lined up as exhibition objects in a historical museum (1:17). Even though it is easy to admire those things that pass before the eye, he warned, it is important to execute a recording and analysis of them because it is often forgotten that the stage occupied by the "wandering shape of the modern girl" is also the "life we, ourselves, are living, engaging in the work of research standing before these, within these rooms, [sharing] in the existence of the modern girl" (1:18).

It is, of course, important to note that Kon's formulation of a new method of studying Tokyo and collecting ethnographic data corresponded to the resurgence of the city after 1923. The concerns of the city had become modern, now, rather than before the quake, preoccupied literally with the new; the pace of production had so quickened that he was convinced that it was necessary to record the immense change of custom. With his friend Yoshida, he went into the streets of Ginza to investigate these customs first hand as they were being put into practice by passersby. Yet it was less the glitter of Ginza's shops, cafes, and restaurants that commanded his attention than the possibility for diversity. Kon looked at the place of the poor as well: the streets of the Fukugawa district, the conditions of neighborhoods around Waseda University, the households occupied by newly married couples, public parks, and so forth.[57]

Modernity, for Kon, constituted the moment of "civilized people." What drove him on this effusive and enthusiastic search for the modern was a conception of historical progress based on the evolution of custom. Authored first by the French sociologist of the late nineteenth and early twentieth centuries Gabriel Tarde (and restated in our times by the German social thinker Norbert Elias), this view of how custom evolved presented it as a civilizing force in the history of humankind. Tarde, whose major work was a treatise on imitation, argued against Emile Durkheim that as societies developed and became more refined, newer classes were integrated into the totality through the mechanism of imitation. As lower classes began to participate in society, they would invariably imitate the manners and customs of the upper classes. For Tarde, this operation represented a powerful challenge to the Durkheimian version of social solidarity based on the integrative capacity of the division of labor ("organic solidarity") to incorporate newer groups into the social order and thus avoid struggle and conflict. By contrast, Tarde's theory supplied a narrative of development in which the place of custom changed over time and became accessible to greater numbers of people. In this scheme, he identified custom, or, as Kon translated it, *kanshū*, predominating in the eighteenth century, popular fashion (*ryūkō*) succeeding it in the nineteenth century, and rationality dominating twentieth century (1:29–37). In Japan, Kon saw the co-existence of these three moments of customary usage, fashion, and rationality as stratified layers, piled on top of each other, struggling with each other within a common social order yet authorizing different styles of living and competing temporalities. Even the government, together with enthusiasts of what was called "cultural living," had after World War I promoted the importance of rationality in everyday life, which usually meant new products and economies (1:36–37).[58] Kon took this last and most recent stratum and divided it into four distinct categories of research: (1) things related to human conduct; (2) objects related to housing; (3) clothing; and (4) other. Each category, he believed, pointed to a vast diversity among people who live in the contemporary period (1:19–20). By merely walking in several circumstances to encounter a variety of people in the city, he wrote, it is possible to find an inexhaustible fund of objects for investigation, such as "customs of detail associated with the body," "the way the hips hung and sat," "the organization of strollers on the streets," "the arrangement of street shops together with roadside stands that appear as they walk," "walkers in public parks," "the spectacle of lecture halls," "a variety of processions," the exhibition of the national assembly," "sports plazas," "corner cafes and theater lobbies," "crowds at a festival," "conditions of physical exertion" and "the working manners of fisherman and farmers on the road and in the fields," "coolie laborers unloading and the activity road workers" (1:20). Kon's research agenda corresponded to a montage—the real organization of modern life in the city.

Previous research on and criticism of the history of custom, Kon complained, had proceeded no further than what the historian Nakamura Kōya referred to as "histories of daily life" that never managed to examine living conditions beyond the external forms and their transformations. To be sure, Yanagita Kunio was already in the process of demonstrating in classic studies like *Tōno monogatari* the thoughts and sentiments underlying these external forms of conduct and custom. Even in his later *Meiji Taishōshi, sesōhen,* where he inventoried the coexistence of received customs and new ones, he refrained from moving beyond the external properties of customs, convinced that description was adequate to meaning. Later, he would turn to a depth hermeneutics capable of penetrating the inner core of thought that only those who are part of the scene were capable of performing. Kon entertained no exceptionalist privilege for his ethnographic method, even though he was concerned with making his method responsive to examining the depths of thought and feeling not readily evident on the surface of customary life. He worked to develop a method that avoided objectifying life for a learning that would be situated within daily life itself. This meant that while the method would be rigorously and enthusiastically implicated in the particular, it would also aim to determine the social meaning of detail by referring to the whole environment in which the objects of investigation were situated. It was this combination of the particular and the whole he named as *kōgengaku,* which he translated as "modernologio" (GF, 5) and consciously juxtaposed to *kōkogaku,* which he translated as "archaeology" even though it actually meant the study of archaic custom (3). If the study of ancient remains and traces is realized in the discipline of archaeology, driven by the scientific method, the effort must be made to develop a methodology to study contemporary custom that can equally appeal to science, even though its facts are not scientific. Hesitant to say too much about *kōkogaku,* even though the very act of asking what it is impugned its veracity, Kon settled for the claim (following a certain Professor Hamada) that it was a discipline devoted to investigating the material vestiges of the human past that were still circulating in the contemporary present. "Archaeology," he wrote, "rather than being a science that possessed a coherent content, as such, was more properly a scientific investigatory method that treated material artifacts" (4). Owing to the newness of the field of contemporary study, he worried about *kōgengaku's* lack of coherence, even though he was convinced that it supplied an appropriate method for studying the object of contemporaneity. For this reason, it was important to approach things with a method based on the evaluation of material data, artifacts capable of yielding social meaning. Archaeology was related to the category of historical studies that validates it and through which it realizes its value. But this makes archaeology into a supplementary discipline, serving the needs of historical inquiry and helping to fill in the details of its narrative. The native ethnologist Orikuchi Shinobu proposed, at about the same time, that *minzokugaku* functioned as an "assisting discipline" to national literature.

What distinguished "modernologio" (I prefer simply modern studies for *kōgengaku*) was identification with the now, the immediate present. Because it was sharply contrasted to the old, the vestiges and ruins archaeology scooped up to examine, it focused on what was contemporary and appeared before the eye. The goal of the researcher is to study the contemporaneity of the human species (4). In fact, modern studies examined the world of "things" before they became history (and archeological remains) and resembled the method of native ethnology employed to understand the "unenlightened folk." With *kōgengaku*, method sought to "record and analyze contemporary custom before it passed into history." Both, it seems, were more concerned with preventing this passage into history and pledged their disciplines to maintaining the presence of the present and staving off the descent into the past. If they were sciences of custom, they were also knowledges that would be used to enhance the lives of the people. Accordingly, folkloric studies and modern studies were differentiated by objects of investigation but shared the same method that temporalized the present as the space/time of both the investigation and context of customs that were being observed. While archaeology appealed to history and narrative (the artifacts presumably were no longer living but dead survivals of what once was living), modern studies relied on sociology and thereby qualified as a supplement to it. But the method of *kōgengaku* was unique or original to Japan, Kon claimed; given his limited knowledge, he had not yet heard about a similar practice in the West (5). In this regard, he was correct, insofar as Japanese thinkers and writers had, throughout the 1920s, conceptualized modern life as an object and developed research agendas to examine and analyze it. In Europe, thinkers from Georg Simmel through Martin Heidegger had certainly identified the space of modern life and its everydayness (*alltag*) to show, as in the case of the former, the regime of the new and an endless present or, in the latter case, to warn against its negativity, mediocrity, its associations with the masses (*das Man*). There may have been important predecessors in Japan who had forged the way in the production of a variety of *Meishō zukai* during the Edo period, "Illustrated Guides to Important Places," such as Kitagawa Kamisada's famous "*Kinsei fūzokushi*" and countless other tour books. If these earlier studies appear similar to "our work," Kon remarked, it is still not possible to see in them an "analytic, scientific coloration" (5). It is interesting to note that Orikuchi Shinobu made a similar comparison between the discipline of Tokugawa native studies (*kokugaku*) as developed by Hirata Atsutane in the late eighteenth and early nineteenth centuries and the native ethnology of Yanagita Kunio and his followers (like himself) but divided by the difference of scientific analysis, which Hirata lacked, even though both nativism and folklore shared the same moral passion. Despite this apparent kinship with the past, Kon was more right than wrong to claim that the study of everyday life as an imaginary—the domain of modern customs—was perceived first by Japanese and constituted the sign of how they inflected their modern experience. Unlike his Tokugawa predecessors, Kon's interest in contemporary custom had more to do with laying hold of an experience mediated through the objects of modern life rather than reporting the customs of life. It was, in any case, precisely this grasp of a modern imaginary that ultimately prompted the production of its negative, the vast theorizing that "recalled" a timeless and essential culture and communal body capable of resisting the challenges posed by modern custom.

Kon's method of extracting the experience of lived contemporary life also resembled the method employed by anthropologists who made as their object of research the "primitive people of the present" (5). Where *kōgengaku* differed was in its desire to grasp the agent of this experience—the modern subject—and its rational conduct. The method of modern studies was itself the very sign of this subjectivity and rationality (just as establishing an incorporated "Cultural Dissemination Society" in 1922 was the sign of a modern organization for Morimoto Atsuyoshi). Kon's research agenda concentrated on observing the variety of rational subject positions people enacted "before the eye." Folklorists, like Yanagita, undoubtedly benefited from the same rationality but displaced the rational position they occupied as methodical observers by sliding it under the identity of the folk who presumably remained outside the boundaries of modern rationality and subjectivity. Because of this, *minzokugaku* never overcame the inherent tension between the pursuit of scientific rigor, Yanagita's obsessive search for facticity, and its hermeneutic effort to identify with the folk as a means of penetrating the inner core of sentiment. Folklorists pursued a collective subject, not an individual one, timeless and nonmodern, not contemporary, even though its traces still survived in the present. Yet Kon, as if to retain links to both native ethnology and anthropological ethnography, wanted to acknowledge that the work he and his collaborators carried out was more concerned with "principally a cultural modernology," as he called it. "Temporally," he proposed, "our modernology is opposed to archaeology; spatially it is opposed to native ethnology. It will study the everyday life of the modern man of culture (*bunkajin*)" (6).

I will return to this problem of everyday subjectivity in Kon's thinking below, but it should be said that much of this interest in subjectivity was inscribed in his method and object. Reminiscent of the Soviet filmmaker Dziga Vertov's "Man with a Movie Camera," he described his own work as "recording and composing (*sakusei*) continuously the manifestation of a Tokyo being made anew," bringing to it the same kind of enthusiasm he demonstrated when he produced reports in the "inconvenient country-side and mountain regions" (7). But, again, the difference now was the event of the earthquake. Down to 1923, the recording and composing of things in the "great city" was not difficult or complicated because its conditions seemed somewhat primitive. Rapid reconstruction of the city after the quake moved quickly and threw up virtually overnight "Tokyo-style" buildings that apparently bore little or no resemblance to what they had replaced. Hence, it was the space of this newly risen Tokyo that seized his ethnographic eye and supplied him with a field of investigation. Sponsored and assisted by the editorial board of the influential magazine *Fujin kōron*, he turned to interrogating life and customs on the streets of Ginza in 1925. Entrenched on a Ginza street corner, he explained,

> we were engaged in calculating statistically the customs of passersby, which amounted to ten items. From this, we tried, in succession, to investigate the customs of the streets among the poor and workers of Honjo-Fukugawa because we were interested in making manifest all of Tokyo. Therefore, we tried also to do the same thing in the outskirts of Yamanote where [life] could be objectified. . . . When we began to analyze and compare all these customs, a variety of meanings began to gush forth. We have tried to completely understand these first steps in the acquisition of knowledge that limited facts . . . but which made possible a small confidence toward the techniques of research related to the customs of contemporary men of culture and things we cannot get to do, things that are difficult to get at. (7–8)

Unlike either Tosaka or Hirabayashi, or even Gonda, Kon proceeded less from a conception of the whole, even though the totality remained on the horizon of his research on specific and particular customs. His concern, despite his enthusiasm for Tarde's narrative and his identification of the last stage as the new age of rationality, was in the particulars. This new age was still unformed, incomplete, still in the process of becoming. Kon's starting point was neither the social whole, as such, nor indeed structural or institutional analysis. In a report on a village in Saitama prefecture (1924), he reported that "he would like to see in fragments meanings that could shed light on the whole."[59] In brief, he gathered fragments that might be used in constructing a conception of the whole. It was from the perspective of fragments, the shards of contemporary life, its "relics" and "ruins," that he inaugurated his studies on modern life. This is what he meant when he announced that *kōgengaku* was not interested solely in an elucidation of surface forms but rather the interior life of contemporaries that are locked in them. Objectivity is determined not so much by a particular mode of viewing, even though it must be posited on the separation of subject and object, but by a new mode of experiencing a new social reality. Kon, like so many during the 1920s, was intent on finding ways to represent the experiencing of the new, which later cultural theorists and communitarians would dismiss in favor of recalling a space/time that had been once experienced and was now sealed in memory. Everything was fleeting ("moving before the eye," he never tired of saying), and no object could claim permanence, fixity or stability. Even the position of the researcher, like Vertov's camera, was moving, changing its perspective, ceaselessly shifting its location. If movement and change characterized the pace of modern life, crystallized in the identification of *supīdo*—speed as its description—only the fragments of this life could be seized, experienced. Above all else, the task of modern studies was to record the encounter with things, the very velocity marking this collision, and how people in different locations experienced them. Kon, like Gonda, imagined this vast spectacle as his field of investigation (*genzai*), both a heterogeneous temporality filled with the ever new mingling with the immediately past and a social space constantly shifting locations. "Visible existence," *genzai*, the now that could be seen, pointed to the temporality of the present as a form of historical totalization that commanded the relationship between the past and future. In Kon's thinking the present was eternal, like Simmel's endless present stretching out before contemporary society. The streets were like a "historical museum," one presumably without walls, living and alive with an exhibition of things reflecting the "commodities of the show windows." Unlike Benjamin, who also walked the streets of a great city like Berlin or Paris in his search for things and wanted to arrange everything by fixing it on a map, Kon was merely content to record everything that "passed before his eye" in its most minute detail. The poetics he envisaged saw the commodity as an allegory for modern life. His method demanded being there or, as he put it, "standing inside the household, the closet, wandering among the crowds of modern girls and making one's way in public meeting places we forget about the reality that orchestrates our everyday life" (9) Hence, nothing should be overlooked, not even the cigarette butts discarded on city streets. Even in the village (where he first applied this minimalist method in his classic *Nihon no minka*), his gaze fastened on the most trivial items, which, when he spotted them while walking, he would sketch. His sketch pad, pencils, and measuring tape were the equivalents of the entomologist's butterfly net and poison vial.[60] Everything that occupied a social space such as the household was inventoried and situated; the location determined and framed the placement. In his Saitama project, carried on after the earthquake, he both demonstrated this attention to detail and underscored the importance of describing precisely where things were supposed to fit. Toward the end of the report, he recorded the "living" tools and utensils, including agricultural implements and where these are placed in the farm house. Illustrating the scene allowed seeing exactly how these various things were scattered throughout the household and around its dirt floor. "Frequently," he confessed, "the traces of people are not recorded in this diagram. But in honesty these should also be included. We need to pay attention to the activities of people who are situated in the house—from the slightest scattered things. The diagram [which accompanies his report] draws out the relationship between the stage and the skills of men . . . by paying attention to their movements in a variety of situations." This method contrasted with architecture, which employed the sparest plan to simply denote the "idea of the human."[61] Attention to the place and the things that filled it suggested strongly that "humans are constructed unconsciously by the places in which they exist. Hurrying to pay attention . . . to the conditions as they are that clutter" this space ends in considerations of the psychological source of humans.[62] But Kon's observations on the countryside emphasized the status of temporality as well. The city, he explained, "is immersed in waves of global culture. Things are taken and progress daily . . . while the countryside takes in fewer things. . . . The city changes daily and . . . things that exist today are not there tomorrow; in the countryside, things don't get extinguished."[63] The city was linked to a distant place, a global culture and flow of things that changed daily, while the countryside remained locked in another temporality where nothing disappeared, because it was removed. In fact, Kon saw the Japanese city of Tokyo, especially after the earthquake, as the distinct site of a "double life," which for him meant a fusion between Western and Eastern motifs (KWZ 2:303–304).

Kon advised that research seeks to grasp people in their diverse performances, that is to say, as they occupy diverse subject positions and play them out in specific situations. "Even though it is possible to consider that the circumstances of rooms in which certain people reside and live out their daily lives reflected their characteristics, it is not unreasonable [to suppose] that different people with separate characters will arrange things differently."[64] What appeared on the surface and conditioned people was the "thing" (*mono*), the "dwelling place" (*sumai*), an early prefiguration of Pierre Bourdieu's *habitus*, without its appeal to simple reproduction serving the interest of maintaining social solidarity. Because he was persuaded that the "biter bit" (*miira toriga miira ni naru*) and the "liver ends by living" (*seikatsu tori ga seikatsu shite shimau*), Kon was concerned that the subjectivity of the researcher and the researched might dangerously share the same place and thus risk undermining the "objectivity" of the investigation.[65] To avoid this confusion of identities, one eagerly sought by Yanagita Kunio, he insisted upon seeing modern custom in a relationship between past and future and in a broader comparative framework. This explains why his research often concentrated on contrasting different zones of life-styles, what he called *fūzokuken*, such as Ginza, Fukugawa, and the salaryman's suburb in Koenji. But it also discloses how the researcher, separated from the scene of customs under investigation, is supposed to grasp the form of contemporary life objectively. This move required the researcher to possess a subjectivity enabling him/her to recognize and render a suitable judgment toward the particular object of research. Kon seemed to be driving toward a subjectivity associated with the researcher that would allow the identification of the individual's subjective practices in modern customs. What forestalled elision and the desired objectivity was the promise of distance offered by perspective. The best examples of this were his many diagrammatic indexes of "things investigated"; the most famous is from his Ginza study and portrays a man and woman standing, half their bodies clothed in Japanese style and the other half in Western style, with corresponding numbers denoting articles he explains in a legend (1:71). The establishment of subjectivity was the principal premise that enabled *kōgengaku* to lay claim to scientificity; experiencing what others experienced as the object of investigation meant exercising an "evaluation of values" authorized by the subjectivity of the researcher who was apparently in a position to know (1:17,43, 53). For Kon, the identification of this subjectivity constituted the basis for the new discipline of modern studies; even though the standard of evaluation reflected the "life attitude" (*lebensgefuhrung*) of the researcher, it did not necessarily conform to the everyday customs of the people who were the object of *kōgengaku*. If the results of research were to be socially significant, it was necessary to focus on precisely those practices of modern life that were capable of showing how customs either mediated or hindered the formation of subjectivity.

In making this move to identifying the determinations involved in forming subjectivity, Kon supplied his discipline with both a vocation and a recognizable content. Its vocation was to discern social meaning in the observed, external forms, grasping what they had come to mean to individuals who lived and experienced its customs; its content would be modern life as it was being lived and experienced in large cities like Tokyo (GF 17, 25). "Our study," he wrote "is principally the analysis of everyday life." The study of modernity became focused on the everyday, the local and most basic unit of modern society, and required concentrating on the "materiality, that is to say, the commodities contemporary people use" (11). But Kon considered shelter and clothes as part of "life within the house" belonging to an irreducible everyday, what he called the "beaten track" that he carefully differentiated from the streets, where people played and experienced an "emancipation from the everyday," where they were "free" (KWZ, 2:282). In a sense, this turn to the most basic unit of existence in everyday life, marked by the centrality of shelter and clothing, was a move away from the concerns he expressed earlier in his book on the Japanese farmhouse and which Yanagita had dramatized when he complained that a house was something more than a formal set of plans. "A house bought by a person," he said of Kon's *Nihon no minka*, "omits the humans who live there."[66] In Kon's revised understanding, it was now equally important to account for every aspect of a dwelling, not only its formal features, and how its inhabitants related to it. Clothes, like "canvas shoes with jumpers, close cropped heads, and shopping bags," were independent styles developed by individuals within everyday life. "As for conquering nothingness," he wrote, referring again to his youthful nihilism and sense of the meaninglessness of life, "restoring the complete human character is nothing other than situating the position of everyday life."[67]

Observation pointed to people's conduct, people walking, things relating to production, doing, to associations, people viewing things. "We must investigate the walking speed and manner in a variety of situations among a diversity of people in the city, the way their hips hang while sitting, the details of bodily habits, the organization of pedestrians on the streets," an inexhaustible number of scenes one found wherever one's eyes landed (GF, 12). Widening the perspective to include customs derived from the past, he was convinced that that he was in a position to clarify the differences between the social customs of antiquity and those of the present. While the problem of difference was already answered by the earthquake and the subsequent reconstruction of the city, its identity pointed to a recognition that saw modernity consisting of the intermingling of past and present, indeed how the past continued to exist in the present, and how modernity signaled the constant rhythm of the appearance and disappearance of customs, as if Japan had entered into the time of an eternal, never-ending present. In fact, this sense of an eternal present marks Kon's thinking and puts it proximally close to Tosaka's formulations, even though he never envisaged, as the philosopher had, the possibility of interrupting the now. The now he designated as the scene of observation was anchored by the domination of commodities which overdetermined the sense of an eternal present. The now, like the commodity it emulated, was without history and conditions of production. In this regard, Kon's subjective consumer was hardly distinguishable from the commodity it sought to consume.

When investigating clothes, Kon insisted on the importance of constructing a record of how these "commodities" are actually consumed in the streets, in meeting places, and so forth, how age and gender mediate fashions and their multiple usages. If research disclosed the social whole involved in consuming the objects colonizing everyday life, if modern life was riveted to the process of exchange, the act of consumption was driven by the desire of imitation. Like Tarde, Kon referred to "imitation" (mohō) as the "occurrence of a wave of custom" that stemmed from a desire to imitate the upper class (14). While he believed in the importance of accounting for the wave quantitatively, measuring precisely the ceaseless process of consumption driven by lower-class desires to imitate the upper classes, a desire that seemingly identified class with the commodity, he recognized that it had less to do with social solidarity, as such, than with the modern experience of encountering the "logic of economics," the confrontation of people and commodity culture. This collision was, he proposed, the "starting point" of the search for the "principles of everydayness" based on "use-values" in the unfolding struggle against the incessant demands of fashion. He hoped that his new discipline would actually foster a subjective attitude that would persuade people to avoid buying useless goods that entrapped them in the endless cycle of consumption and commodification and "economism" (KWZ, 5:434).[68] In this respect the discipline of kōgengaku was clearly seen as a more than adequate alternative to contemporary economic science. "When considering the relationship of the study of merchandising to our modern studies, which is concerned with the same commodities, it is opposed to the study of merchandising that seeks to grasp commodities that have been produced as things solely for exchange value. In modern studies, they are treated as use objects" (GF, 14–15). At the heart of this concern for use-value were the household environment and the things that occupied its space. Kon early distinguished between a fundamental everydayness associated with shelter and clothing and life on the streets and districts like Ginza, Shinjuku, places of play and liberation where an "anti-everyday attitude" was formed and prevailed.[69] While plenty of shops, department stores, cafes, restaurants, bars, etc. could be found in this zone, the activity they encouraged still contributed to the "everyday experience." What he meant was that people learned first in the household to identify useful things to buy and assigned one set of meanings to objects; in the streets, especially in shops and café, they learned to assign another set of meanings on the same thing. On the streets, he observed, people buy things "outside of necessity." Similarly, when one sits in a private tea room in a cafe, one is there to consume. The match that is used for one thing in the household is used differently on the small table of the cafe. The cafe was seen as an "oasis within the street experience," and its "spirit" was "opposed to the everyday life of the household."[70] Pleasure derived from the "height of foolishness" and increased to the extent things were wasted. But Kon was convinced that there must be a constant movement from the house and study to the streets and back. Even though the house and street are marked by different activities, they are nevertheless connected and necessary to each other. What was important was the placement of things everywhere commodities are used. This meant that that if the household constituted a basic unit of contemporary social organization, it was also the place where everyday life was managed.

Hence, it is the object and its circulation, he constantly advised, expanding and moving daily "before the eye," that *kōgengaku* must strive to grasp, in order to extract the social meaning locked in the mystery of the commodity (GF, 15). While we already know that a consideration of the commodity led him back to a preoccupation with finding ways to avoid conspicuous consumption and liberate people from the tyranny of fashion, Kon saw fashion as doubled edged. Even though it was associated with "wasteful living," it seemed also to possess the power to liberate people from the iron grip of tradition, custom, etiquette.[71] In feudal times, Japan was dominated by the rule of custom, which meant the absence of subjectivity and a "disregard for everyday life." A society ruled by custom was driven by a feudal unconscious composed of habit and tradition, "where things were always imparted on thought and life from above." Etiquette was the enemy of science and rationality; custom's hold on society was based on the need to "show to" and be "seen by" by others. Kon explained that this kind of society had been discarded with the call for the Meiji Restoration and the establishment of a society that would be founded less on habit and custom than on the rule of rationality and "flair for fashion." Feudal Japan was committed to the model of proprietary law, which determined the scope and size of house construction and dress codes to show one's social status, not to reveal anything about the routines of everyday life. Expenditure conformed to social hierarchy, and everybody was expected to play out in appropriate dress, conduct and housing the rank assigned to them on the social ladder. As a result of this rule of etiquette, there was no margin for the free expression of daily life, at least no possibility for officially sanctioned free expression. Social solidarity was secured by observing these rules of etiquette as if they were dictations from nature. Etiquette was the "cement" that sealed and sutured the seams of feudal social life into a harmonious order.

But a society based on the rule of etiquette simply excluded the possibility of everyday life. Such a society, according to Kon, was "unsubjective," "unreflexive," and, therefore, unself-conscious; its inhabitants were driven to perform in response to directives issued from on high. Consumption was ceremonial, ritualized, while clothing and homes were determined by an economy of ceremonial value and distinction rather than by actual use-value. Kon worried that feudal society, rooted in customary etiquette, lacked the necessary "freedom" to determine its own "form of everyday life" and the "shape of house structure" suitable for the needs of its occupants. Instead, it relied, often ruthlessly, on the implementation of abstract principles that referred to an imaginary that people internalized to constrain beauty. Utility, which meant for him the recognition of what was useful to everyday life, was the principle that should inform all art, not ritual or expenditure. Everyday conduct should not be separated from the concrete forms of daily happenings and occurrences, and it was this relationship that should motivate the design of architecture.

Customary life was based on waste, "using the useless"; clothes were worn for ritualistic purposes and stuffed into *tansu* to be brought out infrequently for special occasions; people occupied useless houses that served only ceremonial purposes and that marked one's social status. Life was lived not for human purposes but to satisfy the rules of etiquette. A life drained of actual human referentiality, directed by ritual and ceremony, was also one that actually consigned people to two distinct layers that separated the spiritual from the physical; where there was spirituality there was no flesh, where ethics prevailed there was no everyday life.[72] In this connection, Kon was calling to the fundamentally ideological separation between mental and manual labor Tokugawa rulership insisted on as a condition of political legitimacy. The bodily had no existence in the economy, the social, as it was lived. It should be pointed, here, that Kon was discussing feudal life precisely at the moment when writers and thinkers were seeking, especially after the earthquake, to resuscitate the traces of premodern life in Tokugawa Japan. During the 1920s and early 1930s, there was an inordinate impulse to recapture the image of a unified cultural order in Edo Japan and its spoliation by capitalism. We might call this move "Edoviewing." It was driven as much by a general dissatisfaction with modernity as it was by nostalgia. In the midst of Tokyo's reconstruction in the years after the earthquake, we can discern the construction of a "tale of two cities" that juxtaposes the vanishing Edo of the late eighteenth century and merchant material culture to the emerging Tokyo of the 1920s marked by the masses as an incipient political constituency, cheaply made consumer goods, new forms of entertainment (movies, dance, bars), new technologies and communications. In contrast to an ethical life removed from materiality, the appearance of the popular (*ryūkō*), fashion, the new, characterized nineteenth-century society. The pursuit of the popular came with capitalism, social and sexual competition powered by consumption of new commodities. While Kon condemned the popular for its excess, he still perceived in it a force capable of emancipating people from the grip of custom and etiquette. But because the rage for consumption was powered by the desire to imitate the upper classes, it could not lead to the development of life attitudes that could confer meaning. Kon, it is important to recall, was interested in "ethical studies of the self's life through everyday life" (KWZ, 5:515). This required constituting a conception of subjectivity that was unmediated by either custom or the desire for the fashionable but rather one where the position of the self represented an instance of meaning reflecting personal belief. Modern, everyday life, as he envisaged it, was the site where meaning was produced because it made available subject positions occupied and thus known by those who lived them (what he called "*seikatsujin*"), people who lived and produced meaning based on an ethics of everyday rationality. These people could never "disregard everyday life" dismissed by both custom and the popular. This embracing of a "theory of everyday life" was concerned less with economistic principles that valued mere efficiency and the maximization of profit than it was in pursuing "cultural values" and what he described as the "formation of an ethics of everyday rationality" that emphasized the necessity of connecting life to the everyday forms of shelter and clothing people lived and reproduced.[73] Subjective life emerged from a struggle against custom and the popular, from the necessity of reflecting on such conditions philosophically and constructing a science of living capable of freeing people from tradition.

Kon observed that few people in Japan had yet recognized or considered the centrality of modern, everyday life. Unlike the Western experience, Japan had realized only a political revolution in the Meiji Restoration but had failed, then, to move on to the achievement of a genuine "life revolution." Hence, Japan was never able to go beyond those external forms of imitations derived from Western life and stopped abruptly short of creating an everyday life inhabited by subjects who could act rationally and responsibly. The Restoration unfortunately produced no "living critique," no real criticism of custom, as such, but remained satisfied with incorporating only the form of a certain way of modern life without the possibility of experiencing it. What he was referring to was a process of capitalist modernization that would also equip people with an "attitude toward everyday life" based on actually experiencing it. Kon recognized that a "rationalistic everyday ethics" capable of promoting a progressive rationalization of life had not been widely disseminated among Japanese until the post–World War era. The rationalization of modern life, echoing Morimoto's inaugural enthusiasm for "cultural life," meant installing an ethical endowment that would combine spiritual and material (bodily) energy in the individual in his/her pursuit of a "living revolution." This conception of a "living revolution," suggestive of the cultural revolution first promoted by Chinese intellectuals, writers, and students streaming out of the May Fourth Movement of 1919, was nothing less than the construction of the subjective self, which had interiorized a rational ethics derived from everyday modern experience, as the basis of informed judgment and evaluation. Occasionally, Kon appealed to this everyday ethical stand as one of responsibility that determined how people would relate their lives to the "means of everyday life" consisting of housing, clothing, education, pleasure, and so forth. His idealization of a rational ethics later formed the basis of a discipline devoted to this "study of the everyday" (*seikatsugaku*) that would focus on the scientific analysis of household living, the existential grounding of his conception of subjectivity. While *kōgengaku* had originally been concerned with identifying and describing the subject of everyday life, the new discipline devoted to the "study of everyday life" constituted a transformation that focused on scientific planning for the widespread implementation of rational living. The model for society was thus the household and its twofold division of labor: production centered in the kitchen and consumption located in the living room, dining room, and bedroom. In this way the household became the privileged place for constituting the subject. The most important aspect of Kon's theory of modern life was to connect leisure to work and to dismiss the prevailing understanding that the two were fixed and separate. As far he was concerned, the household was connected to the streets, each opened up to the other. It should be pointed out that this theory challenged, by juxtaposition, the official idea of the "family state" ideology, entombed in the Civil Code; it prefigured, in yet another irony, the postwar desire to employ the model of the household for the firm and the rest of society, once the state association was discredited. But it is equally important to say that Kon saw the household as the site of a new form of subjectivity and thus the condition of emancipation from custom and the tyranny of popular fashion. He saw in pleasure the means to compensate for the fatigue caused by work, those tired in heart, as he described it. But he also recognized that where there was no work there was no leisure and pleasure, and thus advocated a scheme where the kind and amount of work would determine the "suitability" of recreation (KWZ, 5:200). Suitable labor and pleasure had to exist as a unity within everyday life.[74] The aim of this program was to avoid alienation and excess, even though he never quite put it in this way, and to secure the possibility of putting an end to the unconscious deformation of life. Like Gonda, he worried about the accelerated trend toward excessive play and consumption which, for men, invariably meant alcohol and food, and for women, the desire for clothing, both of which would weaken and undermine daily life. Life should be a harmony of "rational living" and "mental beauty," a symmetry of the proper material and spiritual forms of existence.

Consideration of the household ultimately brought Kon to think about a theory of design (*zōkeiron*) and the role played by the "industrial arts" in promoting forms of beauty in modern life. Designing, for Kon, became a problem when in the nineteenth and twentieth centuries the capitalist pursuit of profit forced society to abandon the concrete means of life—utility—and beauty. In a 1927 essay that concluded by discussing Frank Lloyd Wright's Imperial Hotel, "a building that is calm amid troubles" and that had an "Oriental feeling" about it, Kon wrote that "architecture is different from other pure arts and must always possess a healthy character as technology." What he seemed to mean was that beauty must be discovered by affirming the principle of "technological beauty," which "must always develop from this healthy character." Wright had paved the pay to demonstrate how functionality could satisfy aesthetic principles. Architecture was obliged to avoid ornamentation and instead seek its forms from "use-value," accompanying the "rationality of materials and structure" (9:25, 243). Elsewhere, he proposed that architecture aims at providing the people a pleasurable place to administer their lives. It should not seek to reflect the life of the artist, he advised, but rather the "lives of the people who are actually seen," to incorporate everyday life within buildings themselves. In short, the forms of life, always moving from the concrete to the abstract, must obey the coordinates of time and place. Everything, echoing Tosaka, returns to the experience of everyday life, which itself, as his first book on the Japanese house showed, started from life in the household, the microcosm of all subsequent social bodies and systems. For Kon, household life was the "hotbed of politics, the seedbed of national thought, and the source of true strength of the people" (*kokumin*).[75]

CHAPTER 4

The Persistence of Cultural Memory

THE PANIC OF THE EVERYDAY

Even as thinkers and researchers were seeking to uphold the completion of modern life as a future possibility, Japan was already being drawn into the crisis of the capitalist world in 1930 as the economic depression spread from the industrial and financial centers to the periphery. But the world depression was simply the most recent and certainly the most devastating of the economic episodes Japan experienced throughout the 1920s—episodes which, cumulatively, socialized the country into the cyclic ups and downs of capitalism and its capacity to produce periodic breakdowns. In Germany, Siegfried Kracauer had already alerted the country to the tenuous relationship between middle-class consumerist expectations and the consequences of capitalist crises in his *Die Angestellten*, an ethnographic report on the plight of the white-collar classes whose desperate search for a home coincided with the economic collapse of their world. Halfway around the globe in Japan, Aono Suekichi (1890–1961) was publishing his timely *Sararīman kyōfu jidai* in the same year. The title page of "The Salaryman's Panic Time" portrayed a drawing of a man falling to earth from a building. Whereas Kracauer sought to provide in-depth reportage of the living conditions, attitudes, pleasures, and aspirations of the German white-collar class—the petit bourgeoisie—as they sank deeper into the mire of economic despair and yearned for the safety of "shelter" and a "return to home," providing along the way a prescient example of urban ethnography, Aono's work looked more to analyze formally the social structure of the salaryman class (Japan's petit bourgeoisie) within the larger context of capitalist social relations in order to explain how and why they were fated to a life of continual unhappiness and psychological depression caused by the growing disparity between their consumerist aspirations and their incapacity to satisfy them. Unlike Kracauer, who supplied detailed ethnographic snapshots of the daily life of the German white-collar class adrift in spiritual homelessness, Aono interpellated his own life and class to dramatize the larger conditions lived by the Japanese petit bourgeoisie. If Kracauer seemed to privilege the status of white-collar lived experience in Weimar Germany, Aono portrayed the social and economic conditions during the 1920s that were driving the Japanese petit bourgeoisie into "panic" and which structured the experience of sagging expectations and growing dissatisfaction. But it is important to note that both thinkers concentrated on elucidating the category of modern everyday life and the conditions producing its experience.

Aono saw the petit bourgeoisie crushed by the weight of "big capital" especially, even though the social malaise he was reporting affected all groups in the present. He wanted to distinguish between "distress" (*kunō*) and "hardship/suffering" (*konnan*), whereby the former is on the "side of the life line," inasmuch as it is not a problem of having a place to live or enough to eat. In his view, hardship "exceeds life" because it is rooted in the problem of not having shelter or enough to eat.[1] Because the petit bourgeoisie stood between the upper middle class and large landowners, on the one hand, and the proletariat, small holders, and tenant farmers, on the other, they experience the worst of all possible "life lines." Although they shared with the proletariat and small farmers actual hardships as laborers and producers, they also, at the same time, participated with the wealthy in the experience of "distress" insofar as it is was on the side of "life" rather than on the side of "famine" (6). With the upper bourgeoisie, the Japanese salaryman had experienced a common political and cultural development, delayed in the proletariat and small farmers, and thus possessed a sharpened sense of "doubt" regarding their social problem, which was not yet raised to the level of consciousness among classes below them. "The struggle with hardship, the endeavor to overcome distress have different meanings from the standpoint of society's progress" for these laboring classes (7). A product of modern capitalism, the salaryman differs significantly in the way the class responds to the specter of hardship and distress. Aono was convinced that whereas the proletariat had not yet sufficiently developed politically and culturally to express doubt toward their conditions, the salaryman class was positioned to do so. The expression of doubt would lead to skepticism and agitation.

Salarymen were no more burdened by economic and political oppression than the proletariat and thus were "resigned" to this condition in the present; they were neither able to put together an organization that would defeat it nor yet in a position to produce a sign of struggle to show they had acknowledged the "dawn of emancipation." Today, Aono lamented, is the panic time of the salaryman, and the "valley of panic" must be understood within the larger framework of "hell" (*nanraku*). "The problem facing the salaryman recalls the problem of unpropertied intellectuals when the old revolutionary Klara Zetkin proclaimed: 'Today, the problem that confronts us . . . is one that affects hundreds of thousands of people on the verge of starvation and death. The problem we face emanates from the straightened circumstances of the spirit of hundreds of thousands of people' "(10). For Aono, the panic time of the salaryman was nothing less than the imminent prospect of mass starvation and the "impoverishment of the spirit." With this perception of a disastrous future, his purpose was to elucidate the circumstance of spiritual impoverishment, explaining how the salaryman has fallen into this "valley of panic," and how they might recover the "road to liberation" (11). At bottom, he was persuaded that the "contemporary custom of grief" among salarymen could be grasped as a trope—a "miniaturized and signifying value" characterizing a broader, socially shared fate. In fact, it is interesting to note how he identified "grief" with "contemporary custom," when others were intent on showing the introduction of new customs into the experience of modern life or recommending the preservation of customs from a timeless past. But today, he continued, the "living distances among various people have become marked as 'social classes' that reflect their positions, owing to either good fortune or contingency." What seemed important to the task of analyzing this sign of social grief—the custom of misery that had now become widespread practice—was the identity of social class which held meaning and value for all people. Aono, here, appealed to the signifying power of class to argue for the primacy of examining the "living experience itself" of people in order to ascertain the "reality" and "direction" of the particular social strata (13). While fear of job insecurity dogged the salaryman's everyday existence and contributed to the panic being collectively experienced, the principal custom of hardship lay in the "spiritual and psychological precinct," followed by the "insufficiencies of material life" (24). Spiritual distress emanated from specific psychological habits.

Although belonging to the bourgeoisie, salarymen could not hope to realize glory and honor in politics and society. Like the laboring classes, they were not capable of remaining satisfied with its frame of mind and material life. Speaking from the perspective of life-style, the petit bourgeoisie that formed the backbone of the salaryman strata aspired to living a tidy, correct, culturally peaceful existence; from the psychological view, they liked to present themselves as composed, optimistic, serene, cheerful, peaceful, and harmonious, habits that they hoped emblematized their social location, even though they were closer to bourgeois life. Among salarymen there was "living" and "separation," which referred to the existence of a certain kind of spiritual life (24). While they actively repudiated the reservoir of old morality, they sought to preserve the ethics informing kin relationships, neighbors, and customary friends. "Within the content of the salaryman's consciousness," Aono observed, "there was the nature of the fields and gardens, the true circumstances of the parent's home, the obligation of relatives, and the relations of friends." The calm, clear, and serene attitude they desired originated not only from their valuation of harmony but as much from the moral character of the class, according to scholars and intellectuals. In this way, the salaryman was both a progressive social stratum and an intellectual class. While they alone discovered the modern individualistic consciousness, they also, as an intelligentsia, were devoted to retaining some of the more solid values of feudal morality. Perceived as a clear contradiction, this double characteristic contributed to their hardship as it signaled alienation and psychological habit. "The social reality the salaryman lived fails to satisfy their habits of life and psychology." In every way, it continues to reinforce disillusionment. Although they aim to pursue a peaceful nature, what they get is a house barely in the suburbs with a garden that looks out only to the sky; while they pursue peace and harmony with relatives, they get the "icy separation of husband and wife, older brother and older sister"; and while seeking peaceful moral intercourse with friends and neighbors, they get only thoughtless opposition and competition (26). The quest for a moralistic and bright life has been "betrayed," and "disillusionment is followed by disillusionment." In the petit bourgeois household, the wife reinforced the "psychological distress," by virtue of making the husband rather than society at large the cause of the unhappiness. Hence, the wife would invariably avoid appealing to social ills and attitudes by attributing the husband's ill luck to individual adversity, which often meant incompetence and inadequate effort. The present was witnessing the first steps of a "familistic tragedy among the salarymen" (27).

The problem faced by the salaryman differed from that of both the bourgeoisie and the proletariat, each of which in their own way lacked the material and psychological bases to provoke family tragedy and the dissolution of familial affective ties (27–28). "Naturally, it goes without saying that both [classes] cannot exist without family and love, but there are only a few cases of tragedy among them." Only the salaryman sought to maintain the customary love between husband and wife as the spiritual basis of the family. The tragedy came with the salaryman's commitment to maintaining the "love between husband and wife in its traditional meaning as the spiritual basis of the family," when at the same time the bourgeoisie had in actuality collapsed and the proletarian had lost the real meaning of family life because of grinding poverty (28). Aono explained that the "close proximity" to the bourgeoisie as the object of desire and imitation contributed to increasing the plight of the salaryman. Yearning for this life style, driven by envy and imitation, they reached out psychologically for a livelihood well beyond their grasp. Even though the salaryman was produced by modern capitalism, the class paradoxically embraced values and attitudes often belonging to another time, alongside more modern forms of conduct and customs. What seems important in this observation is the recognition of unevenness and the coexistence of different values and customs signifying different temporalities within the class, what now clearly appeared as a contradiction. In this way, the "tragedy of the salaryman is completely a tragedy of self-contradiction," yoking the reality of a proletarianized life and bourgeois psychological ideal to feudal custom, "the contradiction between modern, individualistic pursuit and the harmonious, familistic quest" (30).

Aono attributed the unhappiness of unevenness (the "panic") to the "commodity form" (shōhin ikko) and the production of "knowledge" and the refining of "technical skills" under capitalism, that is to say, rationalization. He was convinced that the time had already passed when skills and knowledge were prized because they were received from "heaven" and thus could not be bought or sold. Contemporary capitalistic society, motored by a "completely erroneous idea," commodified all forms of knowledge and skills, as it does "shoes," "clocks," etc. Society was producing untold forms of knowledge and new skills that were being mastered by the salaryman; capitalism had established a regime of scientific rationality that managed to calculate production in units of quantity, without distinguishing between commodities as different as shoes and knowledge, both of which "fell into surplus production." To maintain market prices, it was frequently necessary to "burn" great quantities of commodities. "The matter is easily settled," he reported, when surplus commodities "are thrown into the sea." But when knowledge and skills become commodified, their surplus is a different and more difficult case to resolve. Salarymen who "embodied knowledge and skills like commodities, while sustaining the same operation of rules governing the conduct of commodities, are not lifeless objects like others but are living things that possess a red heart. It is a distressful situation without end" (32). The committed salaryman could neither be burned nor be thrown into the sea in order to maintain market prices. Above all else, the salaryman's distress was manifest in the scarcity of employment and job insecurity. At one level, new skills and knowledge accelerated surplus production to end the problem of scarcity, but overproduction devalued market prices, which undermined the stability of employment and diminished its real value. The universalization and equalization of "skills" and "intelligence" led rapidly to "internal competition" and chronic "conflict "among the social classes" scrambling for scarce resources like jobs and security (35). According to Aono, "internal competition" among the classes results in a dog-eat-dog struggle. Moreover, conflict produced anew the "oppression of regressive intellectual elements," disclosed in the reproduction of feudal practices that signified the deeply embedded "unevenness" of modern life. Finally, incessant conflict was caused by the appearance of "autonomous, individualistic activity among the social classes." What seemed most troubling to Aono in this inventory was the recognition that either a corrosive individualism or simple luck was the "doctrine" used to explain both the necessity of "internal competition" and the distribution of success and failure. The salaryman, in general, welcomed "discussions on success" and talk relating to the "skills of getting on" (37). But what spurred intense competition among the white-collar class was the panic it felt over the dim prospects of diminishing employment and the paralytic fear it now experienced over unfulfilled consumerist expectations (38). Increasing unemployment and the concomitant contest for jobs led to a process of "proletarianization" of the salaryman class, who "descended to the gate of hell and passed through to reappear on the other side as an intellectual proletariat" (39).

How was the panic manifested in the social and individual life of the salaryman class? On the surface, the panic could be found by investigating the "social customs" of the present, a tactic that corresponded closely to Tosaka Jun's call for an examination of what custom—a stand-in for the commodity form—concealed, Ōya Sōichi's denunciation of modern customs as the sign of cultural superficiality, and Yanagita Kunio's disciplinization of custom as the surviving trace of folkic authenticity and durability. In Aono's reckoning, what shaped the urban surface and fashionable social customs was neither the bourgeoisie nor the proletariat but the salaryman in their function as an intellectual class. The panic felt and dreaded by large sectors of society appeared in the form of "modern decadence," the "customs of *modan dekatan* circulating in the cities, its jazz joints, dance halls, cafes," and in the proliferation of new styles of sexuality, called collectively "nonsense eroticism," the world of frenzy (*kyōsō*) and bewilderment (*wakuran*), the scene that came to condense the meaning of the ultramodern. "The living things that danced furiously and madly were the hopeless petit bourgeoisie—the salarymen. Originally, modern dance seemed to offer endless variety." But the common psychological attraction that drew throngs of people to dance halls was its promise to satisfy the "quest to evade or overcome reality (*genjitsu kaihi* or *genjitsu chōetsu*), the demand for antireality." For Aono, this common thing was embedded in modern social customs—this vast, mysterious social hieroglyphic that now concealed a deeper reality and constituted the conventions that determined living in contemporary reality, even though they were symptoms of a deeper malaise agitating the social body. However unendurable the burden, the panic stemming from the "darkness of reality," or the "shivering" provoked by "reality," it was "hopeless to live contemporary life by trying to make it a stepping stone of reality within reality" (41). Everything was determined by social custom now disguising a psychological symptom, and there was no escaping it. The madness of dance, the paralysis produced by excessive alcohol consumption, the uproar of jazz, took from people both reason and the means with which to exercise control. Beneath these displacing customs was the malaise produced by panic, anxiety and unhappiness, the desire for shelter and home Kracauer perceived among the German white-collar class at the same moment.

While Aono detected the panic of the salaryman in their immersion in "mad clamor" and "boisterous dancing," recalling the St. Vitas dancing from another tradition, and in their inordinate appetite for the strange and the weird (Gonda used the term *henna* to describe it), he also recognized in this frenzied activity a "great cry," simmering rage, expressed in "silent endurance." If this silence was not one of the slave, it was neither that of the dead. It was premised on an "explosion" that verged on stoicism, massive passivity misrecognized as indifference but "filled with great discontent" (42). Far from possessing a content that was simply empty, the silence "bulged" with rage and anger. Aono was clearly referring to petit bourgeois resentment, precisely the accumulated rage stockpiled by the German petit bourgeoisie that Ernst Bloch observed in the early 1930s in *The Heritage of Our Times* and described as an internal and subjective "muffled nondesire for the Now . . . noncontemporaneous," "an impoverished center," "spiritually missed," and the subject of Kracauer's devastating portrayal of white-collar homelessness.

The tragedy of the Japanese salaryman class lay in its members' role as both intellectual producers whose skills and value were undermined by the market and custodians of culture who were losing their grip on cherished values. Hence, the ceaseless permeation of psychological despair that resulted from experiencing both a diminution of their social position and the disappearance of the culture they had once known (82ff). Because they occupied a subordinate position in the social economy, their "spiritual and psychological consciousness" was suborned to the ruling class, which meant that they had no strong, autonomous spiritual life. In this context, Aono's appeal to spiritual life carried with it the association of culture, which, in the 1920s, had already become identified with spirit, *seishin*, the world of nonmaterial values. Even though the class sank lower on the economic scale, it could not easily change the content of its psychology and consciousness. In his estimate, the members of the salaryman class embraced a conservatism that derived from their subordinate position and a liberalism produced by their peculiar psychology and consciousness. The former was expressed in promoting the maintenance of contemporary politics and society; the latter affirmed its "rationalistic reconstruction" (84). They were located in the "reservoir" of liberalism yet occupied the "stronghold" of conservatism. The plight of the petit bourgeoisie was generalized by the ruling class, even though it applied only to them and the "panic" that had "saturated" the scholarly strata recruited from the salaryman pool and was described as a "national crisis" (*kokunan*) (86). Aono identified the philosophical basis of the salaryman's "world view" in idealism and ambition, which it shared with the bourgeoisie. This view proposed that "spirit," "spiritualism," "consciousness," the "we" decided all things, that even "history, "society," the "state" and "this world" "were determined by the spiritual thing" (87). Although this idealistic view did not directly participate in the productive process, as it was the "philosophy of the leisure class," it was squarely at the heart of the salaryman's cultural and spiritual life and constituted the basis on which all things were judged. It provided the perspective of a "unitary spirit" that sought to explain everything. Idealist philosophy was marked by the absence of dialectic and thus privileged nonmovement, the stilling and fixing of things, upholding a consciousness that "saw nothing in the eye," like the "world," "society," and the "state" (88).

What is important to us is the way in which Aono located the spiritual world of the petit bourgeoisie in philosophy, one that already had been closely associated with the middle class in Japan and elsewhere. Philosophy authorized a conception of culture that was nonmaterial. Once it entered the salaryman's world view, it was immediately juxtaposed to the now time of the present, which was read as a contradiction. But the juxtaposition marked the moment culture was polarized into two registers, between a high spiritual level and a low, popular, and material one. In this new cultural economy, high meant fixed, still, unmoving, and eternal, while low referred to the popular, vulgar, the world of the ever new in the ever same, the world of the commodity consumed by the masses on the streets. Philosophy was given the task to grasp a true or truer experience, an authentic movement unaffected by history and change, as opposed to a life that increasingly was being lived and experienced by larger numbers of people in the industrialized cities. This was, of course, the life dominated by the commodity form, standardized, averaged, homogenized, a denaturing of human life in society. What philosophy sought to do was not analyze the social formation of capitalism but supply cultural consolation against the onslaught of the commodity. In this new vocation, it sought to realize this task by inverting the life of the masses for the poetic, mythic, even the natural—non-Being or the world of nothingness, where memory is less a product of lived experience in history than of "accumulated and frequently unconscious data."[2] The inversion thus worked to bypass the historical determination of memory completely by repressing the history that would in fact account for this move to make the appeal to a collective, accumulated, and unconscious experience appear natural. In other words, the condition for prompting this move to a truer, more authentic experience was the repression of actual facticity from which philosophy itself had evolved. Tosaka Jun had already recognized how philosophy had buried its own past and thus its origins in the materiality of everyday space. "In shutting out this experience," Benjamin wrote, describing the "inhospitable, blinding age of big-scale industrialism," "the eye perceives an experience of complementary nature in the form of an afterimage."[3] As we shall see, philosophy acquired the role of giving permanence to this "afterimage"—this original of what clearly was seen as mere copy—and promised, to both Benjamin, who was trying to construct a new historical materialism, and "philosophers of life," whose interest was to stay clear from experiencing modern life, to "wrest" from the "same" a different meaning that could be mobilized in the contemporary historical moment. If Benjamin grasped "historical understanding" (*verstehen*) as an "afterlife," an "afterimage" of that which was understood, Japanese philosophers saw it as a truer perception of "experience," what Miki Kiyoshi called the "fundamental experience" (*kisoteki keiken*). Japanese thinkers like Kobayashi Hideo, Kuki Shūzō, and Watsuji Tetsurō saw in this afterimage a truer perception of experience now cut off from the noisy and shocking mediations of modern life. What they privileged was poetics, art, and, ultimately, myth, all existing out of time and free from the domain of history and the social. The very modernity of everydayness that permitted thinkers to see in the same the possibility for renewal enabled others to recognize in it the mystery of involuntary memory once the mind's eye had shut out the experience of contemporaneity. The philosophic gesture pointed to the growing incapacity of people to "assimilate the data of the world around them" through the faculty of experience.[4] Newspapers and the explosion of modern mass media—magazines, movies, radio—daily bombarded people with information that could never be adequately digested, absorbed, incorporated as part of one's own experience, and that frequently worked to isolate or remove occurrences and events from the place they would affect the experience of their audiences. The impact of shock and speed was so jarring in the transformation of society that Japanese were forced to find a new word for it, *supīdo*.

According to Benjamin, it was often necessary to devise a program that would shield consciousness from the ravages of forgetting (Simmel had much earlier already noted this effect of metropolitan life on consciousness). Above all else, modernity was everywhere a form of forgetting at the level of social experience and the repressing of history into the cultural unconscious. Modernity, in fact, was the condition that forced the issue of memory and history/historiography and ultimately separated them under the sanction of a larger, authorizing division between experience and knowledge. Increasingly, history became historiography, historical knowledge, falling to the side of knowledge, while memory became identified with the sanctuary of true and authentic experience. The introduction of new forms of social experience colonizing everyday life, the ever present, the discontinuous interruptions of shock producing temporal amnesia, a life filled with constant starts and stops necessitated the move of consciousness to find a way to shield the self from shock, speed, and sensation by an operation that might manage to register these shattering data without actually recording them. The task was to protect the organism from being overloaded and thus removing the domain of memory from this world of over stimulation. The proliferation of data and new techniques for producing knowledge meant preserving the autonomy of experience by relocating the realm of memory outside of knowing. After World War I in Japan, and especially after the Tokyo earthquake and the subsequent reconstruction of the city, the line between what was experiencable and inexperiencable was beginning to blur. Experience laid claim to its own, other truth that knowledge simply could not elucidate.

Benjamin saw this process as a moment when older forms of communication and commemoration and narrative were replaced by "information," "of information by sensation" that signified the "increasing atrophy of experience."[5] The older forms of storytelling, the literature Kobayashi would recall as an alternative to the historical narrative of progress, were embedded not in information but in the experience of the life lived by the storyteller, whose "commonness" could be understood by listeners and readers to whom it was passed down from one generation to the next. Modernity in Japan, and undoubtedly elsewhere, scored this "tremendous shattering of tradition" and put into crisis the communication of experience. The ensuing discourses that sought to resolve this problem consisted of a struggle over the forms of memorative communication that would involve deciding who was to remember and what was to be recalled, in short, a contest over meaning and the forms capable of communicating what might be considered as significant experience.

Yet, at the heart of this struggle was the effort of the state to lay prior claim to what was to be remembered and to define the task of history— what Japanese called national history (*kokushi*). This activity moved from promoting the primacy of an official, public, voluntary memory enshrined in a variety of practices from days marked on the calendar commemorating national holidays to designating mnemonic sites strategically located to constantly remind the nation's subject of its narrative.[6] But when modernity continues to destroy the "chain of tradition," memory itself risks breaking down to precipitate a crisis in historiography.[7]

Thinkers like Watsuji Tetsurō and Kuki Shūzō in the late 1920s turned to "spiritual history" (*seishinshi*) to evade the constraints of progressive historical development in order to recall cultural moments that had been forgotten in public memory; Kobayashi Hideo proposed in the 1930s that the "I-Novel" (*shishōsetsu*) was a far more reliable form than historical narrative to convey the experience of living in modern Japan, and one that could claim links to a prior tradition of storytelling. The Japanese state, like all modern nation states, designated sites that would record the official narrative, and both national history and national literature (the canon) were pledged to enshrining its enduring values. Despite this desire to control voluntary memory, modernity proved to be far too elusive, open ended, and contingent, always in the process of opening up new positions or confounding official attempts to repress what the national narrative sought to stabilize as a single story line and a unitary memory. While this process has often been seen as an instance of how discourse, like language, can never fully suture the seams of the social into a smooth unity, it was less slippage that figured the crisis than, as Aono Suekichi and other contemporaries disclosed, a historical conjuncture marked by an overdetermination of social, political, and cultural unevenness. The crisis invited the recall of other memories that were revealed in flashes of prior folkic experiences that had been drowned out in the din of modernization, still inscribed in traces, in customs, material artifacts, and religious practices that would manage, through propinquity, to contest forms of memoration upheld by the state. Orikuchi Shinobu's attack on national literature and canonization, and Yanagita Kunio's dismissal of national history for folklore, as we shall see, pointed to the necessity of resuscitating even more prior forms of communication and experience that contemporary Japan had all but forgotten in the race to become modern. It is important to recognize that this immense effort to remember was directed not simply at preserving the truth of experience from immanent destruction but also at making accessible the experience of differing truths from different times which the singular and homogenous temporality of the national narrative had repressed as a condition for privileging its own time line. The quest for preserving experience by increasingly separating it from positive and scientific forms of knowledge based on data and the accumulation of information animated the desire for recollection and reminiscence; the experiential moment must be recaptured, unlocked, and released from its confinement to speak its truth in the present. But experience, in this sense, was reducible to difference that had been concealed by the regime of repetitive sameness and homogeneity demanded by the commodity form. If, then, the effort to unleash an auratic involuntary memory led to the production of theories of culture and community signifying identity, this practice also sought to rescue experience as difference in a society where everything was being leveled and flattened out into a homogenous sameness, where experience was atrophying at an alarming rate of speed, replaced by facts, information, and new forms of knowledge. But what appeared as a huge rescue operation to recall difference against the colonizing claims of the commodity form was inverted to become a discourse devoted to upholding a unique cultural identity rooted in the racial specificity of myth and the presumption of ethnic homogeneity. When the experiences unearthed by the desire to resituate involuntary memory were subjected to appropriation and put into the service of public memory, they risked slipping into the very process of reification they were supposed to counteract. Worse, they became the building blocks of an ideology of cultural exceptionalism and fascism.

If the identity of everyday modern life supplied the dialectical optic through which to read its "experience," appearing, according to Benjamin, as a "mystery only to the degree that we recognize it in the everyday" where the "impenetrable was discovered," the "impenetrable" was also the site of the everyday.[8] In this way, a generation of writers and thinkers would revisit modern life to locate the "mystery" of an as yet unenvisaged imaginary in an indeterminate future. By the same measure, modern everyday life possessed the power to invite a response to see in it the symptom of a prior memory and experience lost to the present—involuntary memory—and to inspire the opportunity to pursue it below the urbanizing stratigraphy in order to find an "existence" still capable of providing meaning to Japanese living in a bewildering time of speed, spectacle, and shock. But to make this move, it was necessary to have a "romantic turn of mind," impervious to the "dialectical intertwinement" demanded by the optic of modern life.[9] In response to the spectacle of modern everyday life in the cities and the "tragedy" Aono Suekichi so pointedly dramatized, writers and thinkers often remained content with simply emphasizing what remained as the "mysterious side of the mysterious," taking them no further. Yet the appeal to mystery exempted them from thinking about either history or the conditions of modern life, as such, without, as Benjamin has reminded us, the "profane illumination of reading about . . . phenomena." As a result, it was this strategy that inspired the production of a vast and complex discourse on the "mystery" of culture and community bent on displacing the materiality and historicity of modern life to the realm of ideality and spirituality: the world of the "afterlife" filled with eternal images, relationships, practices, beliefs, and artifacts that bespoke an indelible Japanese existence. It was that experience whose recall promised to anchor contemporary life in a fixed and authentic ground. While discussions concentrated on categories of culture and community, its proponents shared a common interpretative procedure that was loosely hermeneutic insofar as the desire was to get below the contemporary surface of things. Like any hermeneutic, it was concerned with finding immovable meaning. But because the purpose was to "get out of modernity," as Aono observed of the salaryman, the operation aimed to turn the traces of the modern inside out. Since time and mixed temporalities were already the problem requiring resolution, theorists of culture and community had to perform a topographical maneuver to produce an image of that which was more spatial than temporal. Instead of simply promoting differing temporalities juxtaposed to the homogenous time of the national narrative (by appealing to artifacts, practices, and experiences from different times of Japan's past), the proponents of the social discourse on culture and community released experience from time altogether, transforming culture and community into figures immune to the corrosions of change.

Claude LeFort has described this form of ideology as the "discourse on the social." By this he means the "disentangling of the social order and the order of the world," or, in other words, the process whereby the political is dissociated from the nonpolitical within the social. The purpose of this discourse is to dissimulate the very divisions instituted by historical society and transform relationships into natural determinations in order to reinstall the "dimension of society 'without history' at the heart of historical society."[10] Such a discourse, already trading in the "mysterious," refers now to a hidden reality that seeks to efface the status of a division of labor determined by productive relationships and its law of uneven and unequal development. Under these circumstances, it is a "secondary discourse" which, as it follows the lines of the instituting discourse, becomes a "folding over of social discourse on to itself."[11] For our purposes, this discourse on the social, culminating in the symposium on modernity in 1942, tried to overcome the spectacle of social division and observable unevenness between city and countryside, metropole and colony, and class and gender, manifest in dangerous "internal competition," by employing a folding operation that aimed to transform the negativity of unevenness produced in history into the positivity of cultural evenness, with its attending associations of authenticity and inauthenticity, respectively, marked by different spaces. By following the lines of the instituting discourse and tracing over them, the discourse on the social was able to momentarily transpose unevenness in the political economic realm, produced as a temporal phenomenon, into the image of cultural evenness and promote the superiority of authentic modes of existence produced in fixed spaces over inauthentic styles of life and fashion caused by historical change. Here, cultural and communitarian theorists figured a sense of unity within the context of changing and changeable social relations that managed to project an imaginary community or culture whereby "real" distinctions are transmuted into natural ones, the particular is disguised in the universal, necessity into contingency, and history effaced into the temporality of essence, that is to say, timelessness.[12]

The discourse on the social that envisaged an imaginary culture and community challenged the metropolitan interpretation of its own experience as universal. Despite the progressive urbanization of Japan between the wars, there were still large-scale reminders of other modes of existence in the villages of the countryside and mountains that supplied authoritative models to the imagination. The discourse on the social fastened onto all those traces that would reveal an existence prior to capitalism and modernity, what the neo-nativist Orikuchi described as early as 1916 as a "folk memory" that was intermittently revived in literature and customary religious practices to reveal the presence of a "prior knowledge." This prior knowledge was already locked in words that, when examined for their etymologies, would provide access to the original meaning and intent of archaic consciousness. In this way, the discourse on the social was primarily ideological inasmuch as its primary purpose was to remove, conceal divisions, naturalize historical relationships, and eternalize them in order to declare the recovery of a lost unity and coherence outside of time. An integral element in this strategy was to recall and thus posit a lost unity, which the modern division of labor had presumably destroyed. But loss was prompted by a desire to construct a narrative that defers experience in order to recover an origin beyond both time and space, what Susan Stewart has called a "desiring narrative."[13]

Much of this effort to recover a lost unity, however, was driven by the desire to bracket the experience of modern life, especially its particular temporality and its presentness, to restore a narrative capable of bringing together past and future, origin and end, completion and closure. This impulse informed Shimazaki Tōson's epic novel *Yoakemae* (1935), which sought to record recovery and loss, and it marked the program of the great folk narrative imagined by Yanagita Kunio and Orikuchi Shinobu. The solution to unevenness required incorporating the temporal process into place. And this necessitated a transaction that would separate place from what increasingly was seen as an abstract space, in order to refer it to a specific location. Returning to the primacy of a specific place as an effort to unify place with space, as had precapitalist society, Giddens has proposed that "The spatial dimensions of social life are, for most of the population, and in most respects, dominated by 'presence'—by localized activities."[14] Modern capitalism especially insists on separating space from place—locale—because it is driven by relations and operations that are not immediately present, such as the market or exchange. In this regard, the locale becomes subject to the movements of abstract space, distant forces, and faceless and nameless others. The effort to circumvent this problem of a concrete, immediate place and abstract space required, as Japanese showed, an almost heroic attempt to reconnect space to place and localize the pace of temporality, subordinating it to the spatio-place and the world of the immediate and always present localized activities. When Kuki Shūzō observed in 1929 upon his return to Japan after spending nearly a decade of study in Europe that everywhere he looked there were signs showing how Tokyo had come to resemble a colonial city like "Singapore and Colombo," he was already calling attention to how place had lost its distinctiveness and sense of familiar immediacy to the new regimes of abstract space and time of capitalism. For Japanese sensitive to the spectacle of unevenness and the modern separation of space from place, wherever the meeting between modern and its other took place, it produced what Bloch has described as "nonsynchronisms," a kind of dissonance in the modes of being whereby people were found occupying spaces and temporalities marked by differing modes of production that coexisted uneasily with capitalism in the Now.

It was, in any case, the transmutation of the dimension of time into space that explained how modern life is transported from its historical embeddedness to the timeless precincts of poetics, art, and myth. This was the strategy employed by the generation of thinkers like Kuki, Watsuji, Miki, and Yanagita, whose collective response to the challenges posed by "modern life" aimed at showing that what seemed to appear as the remains of degraded experience and custom in the speedy succession of events that were installing a new, more rational life for the masses was not the negative of modernization but rather the traces of a life once whole, coherent, unified, and authentic. Surviving traces of another way of life bore witness to its endurance and pointed to the relevance of its interest in modern society. Kuki's architectonic project to show the primacy of contingency over the claims of necessity, no-thing over being, Watsuji's stratigraphic history (*jūsōsei*), Yanagita's imaginary of the native place—"ones home"—and more all attested to the operation where the place of production was inverted into the production of place.

If, as I have already suggested, this interpretative operation appealed to the mystery of memory occasioned by the establishment of a new mode of existence that put older stabilities into crisis, it was also prompted by a recognition of the problem of social abstraction—capitalism's theory of exchange value—that was introduced into the center of modern, social life. The immense effort to reunite space and time (actually a doubling of precisely what capitalism had done with its conception of homogenous time everywhere) and to arrest the regime of linear, sequential time, always moving forward was in fact a response to the crisis produced by social abstraction and its production of abstract time and space. This recognition of the central role of social abstraction led to the familiar modernist preoccupation with the aporias of representation. At the same time, the acknowledgment of unequal development problematized further the status of social determinacy—the principles on which society is founded and held together—what Durkheim named as social solidarity—and how it might be represented in a context that had put the reliability and stability of representation into question. The distrust for representation under capitalism referred to the growing certainty that it was difficult to actually represent the concreteness of experience that was always changing with language and modes of expressibility that were suffused with abstraction. In this regard, representation was invariably reduced to an instrumental relationship to capitalism. Ultimately the uncertain status of representation required the attempt to get outside of capitalism in order to think the concrete. This meant finding a time and place whose existence had not yet been mediated by the structures of exchange value, the mediations of abstraction intervening between subject and object, self and the world, identities and distances which in modern society were increasingly collapsing and being reduced into object-things—mere abstractions. For modernist writers, artists and thinkers this crisis of representation would lead to a consequential search for new and concrete language and forms of communication capable of resisting social abstraction and retaining the identity between subject and object, that is to say, the autonomy of art and its nonidentity with capitalism.

If, as it has been said, "all fixed, fast-frozen relations, with their train of ancient and venerable prejudices and opinions, are swept away, all new formed ones become antiquated before they can ossify," it was equally important to grasp those relationships, objects, and things that were both fixed and concrete and were not simply abstractions disappearing in the ceaseless flow of temporal sequentiality. While capitalism and social abstraction undoubtedly led to the more familiar modernist anxiety about the stability of representation, the recognition of uneven development put into question the status of determinacy and raised the fearful specter of a society no longer assured of remaining solidary. The prospect of living with this kind of uncertainty and its consequences for social order in the 1920s and 1930s in the industrially peripheral world of industrialization and in the colonies fused with the question of representation to overdetermine the crisis by making it political as well as cultural. Social thinkers in Japan faced the daunting task of finding the proper principles capable of securing social solidarity, which meant searching for the most stable form of representing them in a society dominated by abstraction and ceaseless change. Both the question of social determinacy (the representation of the social) and the crisis of representation, the necessity of finding timeless principles guaranteeing social cohesion and ways of thinking and communicating the concrete, converged on the status of history and agency. During the 1930s, especially, writers and thinkers turned to assessing the representational claims of history and its presumed capacity to offer secure, stable, and enduring grounding to the social order and to identify the agent in question. Abandoning history's claim to representation, its custodianship of enduring principles, as spurious, and questioning the autonomy of the historical agent, modernist discourse looked for other forms of communication, expressibility, and agency. Tosaka, as we have see, shunted narrative altogether, while his contemporary and sometime adversary Kobayashi Hideo saw in history a fiction that lacked the power of real literature. What this revealed was a growing attempt to revive the status of agency in the autonomous artwork which, in the widest sense, included cultural artifacts, social practice, religious belief, or folk customs. For it was the autonomous artwork that held the promise of a "prior grounding in a pure practice of representation, one that enjoys a grant of autonomy from the object," thus avoiding an identity with capitalism.[15] At the heart of this move was a distrust of anything that had been submitted to representation because it had already been mediated by capitalist abstraction to constitute a kind of secondary revision (Adorno's "second nature") that removes the object from the immediate experiences of the subject. Owing to the progressive change demanded by capitalism and its great capacity "to melt everything solid into air," the artwork— cultural production itself—was increasingly seen as the stand-in for the lost historical agency, capable of resisting being swept into the ceaseless flow of history.

In Japan, this displacement entailed replacing the putative universal ground of capitalism as the source of all activity with the "seemingly concrete but historically indeterminate agency of the artwork." But in industrializing societies like Japan, where unevenness had become a trope for describing its position in relationship to the industrial West, the issue was complicated further by the widespread recognition that capitalism had not developed evenly to produce the much awaited universal terrain incorrectly identified with Western example. The specular image of unevenness put into question the "ground" on which to construct a historical subject unified with its object, affirming it but denying it. The question of representation was made to appear more urgent with the acknowledgment of a split dividing historical subject and object caused by the existence of an uneven ground that now needed to be mediated. Unevenness was particularly manifest in the spatiocultural realm and was symptomized in the conflict between abstraction and concreteness that dominated discourse in the 1930s. It was expressed in all those efforts to breech the gulf between art and life, materiality and spirituality. As Tanizaki Junichirō put it in his melancholic lament of the 1930s, In'ei raisan, the effort to reunite art and life, self and nonself, everydayness and cultural memory, indeed to dissolve the very antinomies modern life had foregrounded in Japan meant discounting the claims of historical representation and finding the modes of existence where temporality was incorporated in a fixed place.

The appeal to elements from a native tradition worked to privilege art and culture produced before and outside of capitalism to authorize its authenticity, superiority, and, ultimately, uniqueness. In this way, the call to tradition could be seen as both a critique of contemporary commodity culture and a resistance to it. And it was also in this way that the present constantly produced the past. Yet, it is important to remember that this appeal to the autonomy of culture and community stemmed from the commodity form itself and the attempt to escape its dominating network of production, distribution, and circulation. Both culture and community (the collective body) could lay claim to immunity against the commodity form that dominated the contemporary sociocultural order by identifying with concreteness and folkic customs (pure practice). Its appearance signaled the domination of commodity culture (and we need not fear referring to it as such because it is all around us, like the air) and thus the search for an autonomous outside that could supply a space in which to constitute a critical opposition to it. What the categories of culture and community both shared with the commodity form was its antipathy for history and the necessity of its erasure. It was able to make this move by invoking value and substituting it for exchange. The operation stemmed from "reflections on the forms of social life" that "take a course directly opposite to that of their actual historical development." The appeal to an indeterminate conception of culture and community, which marked intellectual production in the late 1920s and throughout the 1930s, to signify a "magnitude of values" meant that the "character that stamps products as commodities" has already acquired the "stability of natural, self-understood forms of social life." Hence, commodities require no intensive deciphering for their historical character, since they appear immutable "but for meaning."[16] In other words, the determination of value, and ultimately the price of the commodity in the exchange process, was analogous to the process leading to a decision on meaning. Nothing better characterized the discussions on both culture and community than their representations as value, which demanded not an accounting of their development in history but rather a determination of their meaning. It is not surprising to see in the discourse on the social a virtual privilege accorded to hermeneutics. In fact, it is interesting to note that the exercise of empathy linked both the commodity and its object (according to Benjamin reading Marx) and the recovery of culture and community and its interpreters which, in the end, limited the retrieval of meaning to only those who shared the horizon of experience, that is, those who actually lived it.[17] But it is well to recognize that despite the concretization of an auratic involuntary memory into culture and the elevation of folkic custom as pure practice, culture and community were never completely liberated from the regime of abstraction they were made to resist. Because they derived from the commodity form, they momentarily broke free to realize an illusion of autonomy only to come back, later, to reinforce the regime of commodity culture, a little like avant garde art once it became implicated in the market and exchange.

Whatever the case, as we shall see, the appeal to culture and community showed how urgent the problem of commemorative communication and memory appeared to contemporaries in the interwar period and the precariousness of enlisting modern memory to produce new constructions at the moment older conceptions of life were already in process of disappearing. In a certain sense, the call for total war and mass mobilization at the end of the decade was simply an outgrowth of the process of greater integration and impersonalization. While Tosaka had already seen that the problem was to think out of the concrete, most thinkers never exceeded going beyond the act of merely thinking about the concrete. Philosophers like Nishida Kitarō tried to forestall this process when he proposed that "spontaneous self-expansion was the form of 'self-consciousness,' " the moving "I," was where truth resided and authenticity existed, what he called "real existence." Yet this program, which tried to broaden the perimeters of experience under real existence or the movement of the ego's self-consciousness, never managed to exceed the subjectivism on which it was based. Thinkers like Tosaka held that categories such as the Japanese and the people were simply examples of abstraction, while Tanabe Hajime struggled against the abstraction produced by liberal conceptions of the individual and the subject and the folk of folkism. What this discourse revealed was an immense struggle to catch hold of an everydayness in its unavoidable primordiality, its concreteness, rather than in its contemporary phenomenal manifestation (since the objective world was already too reified to qualify as truly concrete). Instead, discourse moved to the place of creativity, where enduring ethical and cultural values were produced, what Tanabe once called "purposeful moral practice." Abandoning the empirical domain for an essentialized imaginary, a veritable archaeology was directed to unearthing the ground of authenticity, variously described as "the place of nothingness," "species and specificity" (shu), the "basic body," "the scene of speaking," "customary practice, "the lost home," "the other place," and so on. Watsuji Tetsurō blamed Meiji Enlightenment for introducing excessive abstraction into everyday life by recommending the dismissal of the various strata of the Japanese past because of its presentmindedness. "Those things that correspond to other layers [of the past] beyond the present," he wrote in his Zoku Nihon seishinshi kenkyū, "were not [considered as] reality but merely leftovers of the past (zanshi) that should be enlightened according to the program of Enlightenment."[18] "The abstract character of Enlightenment not only lacks a consideration of history, it captures only one occasion of concreteness," by which he meant its immense presentness. The special character of Japanese culture was its process of gradual growth and its punctual overcoming of that which had been an overcoming. Watsuji was certain that "no other folk like the Japanese existed, who take in the new sensitively while preserving the old faithfully." It is important to recognize that overcoming, in this connection, referred to the diverse layers of the past (history as palimpsest) that had been earlier overcome but were still accessible to the present, which, in its own time, would also be overcome.

Philosophy, the privileged form charged with the task of resolving this problem, worried about the status of "reality" (*jitsugen*) and how best to gain access to it. Real existence somehow survived in philosophical reflection, and vestiges were still available in remnants of older forms of existence in the present that had managed to avoid the constraints of representation. The real found its truth in memory and recall. This was surely the meaning of custom in Yanagita's thinking, not to forget his program promoting ancestor worship, literally remembering them, as it was of temple architecture in Watsuji and Buddhist sculpture in Kobayashi. Since the constraints of representation often expressed the form of a contradiction, the task, so it seemed, was how to reconstitute a unified totality, which now lay in dispersed fragments, and thus how best to integrate the particular into a lost totality, without relying on the abstracting mediations representation had made as a condition to realize its own interest.

CULTURAL ONTOLOGY

The Unavoidable Primordiality of Everydayness

If the "experience" of modernity raised questions that would provoke thinkers to consider the status of culture (wholeness and its ground), the category of culture itself would become the vocation of philosophic discourse. While neo-Kantians early (1920s) privileged the category of culture as a sign of the cultural sciences (*geisteswissenschaft*), the analogue to the claims of natural science, philosophic discourse concentrated on showing how culture embodied true and enduring values, the good, beautiful, and true, which transcended history and politics and was often juxtaposed to desire and consumption. But with the Heideggerian inflection, announced quite early in Tanabe Hajime's enthusiastic article of 1924 ("Genshōgaku ni okeru atarashiki tenkō"), philosophic speculation in Japan turned increasingly to the question of ontology and the conditions attending the temporality of Being's primordial existence which promised to fix the horizontal limits of culture. In *Sein und Zeit*, Heidegger's analysis of death opened the way for the existential structure of Dasein— "There-Being"—as the fundamental structure of interpretation in general. What he called "primordial temporalization," referring to the most basic form of everydayness lived by Being, required an "ontological

ground not only in external nature but also in some kind of primal socialization—some emergence of the human being out of its natural being."[19]
Kuki Shūzō (1888–1941), who studied with the German philosopher and
was one of his principal students in Japan, looked to non-Being and thus
to its source in the primacy of contingency, while Watsuji Tetsurō envisaged this ground as a specific geographic and climatic space, what he
called *fūdo*, that would explain all subsequent Japanese character and
culture. Kobayashi Hideo, who was not a philosopher but a literary critic,
looked to an essential commonness as the primordial condition that remained unchanged throughout Japan's history.

But it is important to acknowledge that for Heidegger, Dasein was individualized through the act of recognizing its own finiteness in death and
in the constitutive role played by "resoluteness." In the hands of his Japanese followers, Being was collectivized, because it was easily identified
with the Japanese folk and nation, exempted from death. Despite the difference, the appeal to ontology, at this time, sought to conceal a double
coding which posited a prior, nonphilosophic assumption that privileged
the folk/people. Even though human existence was futural, for Heidegger,
the future exists only as the projected horizon of a present defined by the
mode of its taking up of a specific past. Being anticipates its death, which
both constitutes it as a totality and permits the "temporalization of temporality." It is Being's futureness—its anticipation of death—which provides the possibility for a genuine experiencing of time. It is also in this
mode of experiencing time—past, present, future—that what has been
figured becomes refigured, interpretation follows the hermeneutic circle,
and history becomes repetition.[20] In Tanabe Hajime's earlier celebration,
what distinguished Heidegger from Husserl was a universal phenomenological ontology that supplied a concrete method to understand the
"Being of beings" as it is revealed: "a let[ting] that which shows itself be
seen from itself in the very way in which it shows itself from itself." In
other words, phenomenological ontology provided a method that promised to grasp Being in its concrete existence by taking into account a being
whose understanding of being is a "definite characteristic" of its own
being—thus its distinctive ontic nature.[21] By the same measure, Heidegger
(in *Being and Time*) claimed the superiority of hermeneutics as the form
of inquiry authorized by this questioning of Being that already asks the
"forgotten question of meaning."[22] Since this phenomenology starts from
a hermeneutic inquiry of being as "an analytic of existence," it has "made
fast the guiding line for all philosophic inquiry at the point where it *arises*
and to which it *returns*."[23] Heidegger called this plan everyday life, which
was the mode of Dasein's Being through which to approach its character.
Only through the medium of a primordial everydayness, characterizing
Being's originary existence, was it possible to envisage the determinate

world first inhabited by Dasein. First and foremost, it is also the least differentiated mode of Being's existence, familiar and near at hand, comprising, for Heidegger, "all existing, such as it is."[24]

Hence, everydayness became the enabling condition to reconfigure history as repetition and inauthentic life into authentic existence. It was Heidegger's purpose to relocate being's existence in a structure of temporality different from ordinary everyday life as it was being contemporaneously lived and its historiography which "endeavors to alienate Dasein from its authentic historicality" (448). This move required constructing what he called an "authentic historiology" that might deprive "today" of its character as "present" which becomes a way of painfully detaching oneself from the fallen publicness of " 'today' " (449). Authentic historicality must be discovered in Dasein's "primordial temporality," a mode of existence that would, according to Adorno, "immobilize history in the unhistorical realm" and sanction a freezing of culture as primordial existence for Japanese theorists in the 1930s.

"Being free for death," according to Heidegger, supplied Being with its goal and "pushes his existence into finitude" (435). Recognizing the anticipation of death and the finality of the individual existence disclosed Being's "primordial historicizing," rooted in an "authentic resoluteness" against the inconstancies of "distraction." It also opens the way to the "moment of vision of anticipating repetition" that will "deprive" the "today" of its character as mere "present." The moment "weans" one from all conventionalities associated with the "they" (443–444).[25] Kuki Shūzō, in his commentary on Heidegger's phenomenological existentialism, noted that in contemporary Japan this averaging of the "they" was reduced to the quest for novelty and idleness stemming from "vague understanding." Contemporary existence has "fallen" into the "world of the they," and this constitutes the da of Dasein's "everydayness" (KSZ, 80–88, 94–95). But authenticity (eigenlichkeit/genponteki e toku), the reverse side of the inauthentic life world of the they, required an act of appropriating one's own, which meant claiming and thus choosing one's fate in the face of one's own death. True historicality referred to the fateful repetition of "possibilities" as against the numerous distractions that produce "ambiguous" understanding, disconnectedness, dispersions lost in the world of the they.[26] In this world of the they that lacked sociological specificity but which clearly pointed to contemporary, modern life, choice is evaded and only the "actual" prevails, which is "information present at hand." Once lost in making present the "today," the past is "understood only in terms of the present—the staple of historicism and its promise to disclose progressive continuity and unfolding. Kuki observed that "contemporary existence falls into the anxious world of uncertainties, which, at the same time, appeared to be the collective existence of Others (*tasha*). Convinced that this social occurrence was not oneself, he wondered who took charge of a mutual collective existence of everydayness. Dasein exists under the subjective will of the other as an everyday, mutual, and collective existence and does not yet know existence through the self (*jiko*). "Others dominate its existence. . . . It is not that person or those; it is not even the totality. The who is the neuter person (*chūseisa*//*neutrum*); it is the average (*das Man*)" (3:212–213).

For Heidegger, this inauthentic understanding (and its history of misrecognition) is inscribed in the everyday and is weighted with the legacy of the "past," which "has become unrecognizable" as it seeks to realign the modern.[27] The "modern" was precisely the modern everyday life Japanese thinkers were in process of assessing, which was being lived by the masses or the they, depending upon how one felt about it, what Kuki called "Dasein's everyday" (*nichijōteki no gensonzai*) (3:213). If the "true self," according to Kuki, Heidegger's "I," had lost itself, it was imperative to return to the habitus of Dasein, the world of primordial identification. What Kuki wanted to emphasize in his text on Heidegger was a logic that demonstrated how averageness concealed from Being the possibilities it possessed, and how anxiety (*fuan*) would open the way for Being to realize its own possibilities for "authentic understanding" (3:22–223, 226–227, 230, 238, 240).

Kuki's reading of Heidegger dramatized the futural dimension of Being's anticipatory structure and the recognition of death and its own horizon. Yet this horizon was different from that fixed by "ordinary time." Exercising the decision for death is a phenomenon called *epoché* (*jikansei*/*zeitlichkeit*), which unifies as future that which exists immediately and appears before the eye. "The immediately given comes from the future. The future which exists immediately gives facticity to the present/now" (3:242). Insofar as Dasein is regulated by authentic temporality, the determinate choice is a possibility for it. In this way, time as *epoché* is the authentic whole existence of Being and "is thus experienced phenomenologically and originary in the phenomenon of primary determinateness." For determination to encounter the things it grasps while acting, it—determinateness—cannot do without the present (*genzai*/*gegenwart*) that is immediately before it (3:242). Being thrown to death, Kuki asserted, means that its true existence always ends. Hence, authentic future which regulates authentic time is finite (3:245). Originary time is also finite. But to make the decision means reflecting on "authentic, immediate existence." Dasein accepts the self of immediate existence and thereby repeats the self toward its most existential possibility (3:246). By contrast, inauthentic existing is "forgetfulness" (*bōkyaku*), blocking the recognition of true resoluteness, even though in the flash of an instant it is possible for Being to return to its true possibility. This instantaneous switch made possible the necessary moment of "recollection" (sōki) that would retrieve the memory of a lost cultural wholeness, which Kuki was later to use to justify his great work on the structure of aesthetic taste in the Edo period.[28] Above all else, "authentic understanding" is repetition—in an instant— to take the lead" (3:247). While Kuki acknowledged that inauthentic understanding is "forgetting—anticipating what is before the eye," "Dasein's movement in space is its personal history," which will disclose its involvement with distraction and its reunion with its own most authentic understanding. It was the purpose of existential philosophy to understand the structure of this personal history and clarify the conditions of its possibility for genuine historicality. The authentic personal history of Being is called destiny, which comes from the determinate decision to throw itself to death and thus realize resoluteness on this condition.

The importance of Kuki's recapitulation of Heidegger's argument is his decision to center the state of anxiety Being has fallen into. "Anxiety," he wrote, must be seen as a "situation" that "ends in failure" submitting to recuperating the Now. Those things that possess the structure called "this situation," "that occasion," "now" are anxious times. "Anxious time is an interpreted time because it's a time in which Dasein is forced into a situation with the collective existence of others and receives only an average interpretation" (3:252). But this is simply everyday anxiety, reflecting the world that is troubled. The time in which this anxiety is treated is not "his" time but the time that exists for the average person. Averageness conforms to public time, to publicness itself, worldliness. And publicness is related to the situation humans occupy on Earth—what Kuki referred to as the sedimented and fixed routines that regulated life in modern society (3:254). The argument proposed that whatever was called "ordinary time," "mundane time" was produced as "anxious time" (3:255). Centered on the Now, it discloses that it is nothing more than a point-by-point succession of events that manage to produce only a "continuous now" (3:255). The bridge between the now and its point by point succession is "clock time." The time known according to the watch becomes a variety of nows only, which exist just before, called now, now, now." For Kuki, the former (izen) is the "now that is not now," the later/hereafter (igo), the "now that is not yet." This was the customary conception of everyday time that locked people into the regime of averageness and sameness. (It was also the time of the commodity form.) What the hand of the watch calculates is always the now-here. But it is possible to say that the customary conception of time is a "now time" especially because of the flowing of the now (3:256). Clock time is first based on nature's watch according to the position of the Sun, which determines the time of work. "In such situations, we use the watch to speak of the now (ima) (3:255). Derived from the experience of "anxious time," it possesses a structure of worldliness, publicness, seriousness, and the possibility of "attachment to time." This sense of the "now" is always before us and puts Being immediately before one's eye. The now is ordinary time, what gets calculated by following the movement of a watch's hands; and ordinary time is simply a continuous now (*ima renzoku*).

Kuki pointed out that the ordinary time that produces "anxious time" is not space. "Ordinary time is brought forth from originary temporality as a derivative which is seen as inauthentic time" (3:257). Heidegger explained that Dasein was "spatial" in the meaning of its distance toward beings it encountered. By anticipating a "collective Being" that Dasein would encounter, by being in the world, Dasein would experience distancing and spatiality (3:269). Kuki was eager to establish this point, even though he acknowledged that because Dasein exists for the possibility of existence, it is only natural that temporality will be futural. But he also recognized the "authentic meaning" of spatiality outside of temporality, thereby adding weight to the relationship of the present toward the future. Moreover, Kuki proposed that contingency, his core concept, as a result, acquired greater power toward possibility (3:270). The character of contingency (*gūzen*) is nothing other than "meeting," "treating," and "receiving." The vision expressed in an "instant" in the present is an idea based on space (3:324). But this notion of the present derived from Kuki's reading of Bergson, even though he claimed to detect in Heidegger an acknowledgment of the importance of space. Heidegger rooted the "spatial thing" in the present, he argued, and called it "Dasein's actual space," which opened up to purposeful care. It was this idea of space that undergirded Kuki's understanding of contingency, and it was its link to the present that prompted Tosaka to rethink the now as space endowed with the possibility for critique and changing convention.

Kuki believed that existential analysis of Dasein is "made first in everyday life" (3:225). "Everydayness is between birth and death," he asserted, and "if Dasein is not seen from this perspective it lacks wholeness. The wholeness of Dasein must be first to last Dasein." While being was free to choose its "destiny" (authentic understanding) or not, interpretation until recently has ignored everydayness and sunk into inauthentic existence or understanding. Everydayness, in its primordiality, was simply an unavoidable category of analysis which, according to Kuki, meant the first and foremost familiar mode in which Being discloses itself to itself. Heidegger, it might be recalled, imagined everyday life as the least differentiated and determinate expression of Being's existence; this accounts for his own indifference to sociological (or historical) specificity.[29] "The undifferentiated character of Dasein's everydayness," he wrote, "is not nothing, but a phenomenal characteristic of this entity. Out of this kind of Being and back into it again—is all existing, such as it is."[30] Among

Japanese thinkers and philosophers who followed Heidegger, and even those who did not, this lack of a determinate character associated with everyday life proved to be the informing principle of phenomenological reflection, even if it often required thematicization and sociological and historical differentiation in the final analysis. If, as Peter Osborne has written, everyday life was an "unavoidable category because it was not originally thematicized, constituting its mode of presentation before reflection," this primordial account of Being's existence is also the starting point for all subsequent reflection.[31] But it is precisely later reflection—the "afterimage"—the "kind of Being" that flows back into all existence, reaching an endpoint that gives it significance that presumably opens the way for informing and transforming everydayness. Despite Heidegger's own, guarded effort to keep the conception of everydayness from sliding into sociological content, his views concerning the tyranny of the masses, his distrust for democracy (enthusiastically shared by Watsuji Tetsurō), and his contempt for modernity seeped through to disclose how much he depended upon nonphilosophic assumptions prior to philosophic reflection to construct his argument. The narrative from inauthentic back to authentic understanding (existence) itself opened the way to rethink, refigure, and recontextualize everydayness in historically specific forms "out of which and back into which, all existence goes."[32]

This was, perhaps, more the case among Japanese thinkers than it was among Heidegger's contemporaries in Germany. Japanese thinkers concentrated on demonstrating the primordial and determining character of Japan's culture, as Being's true and original condition, in contrast to foreign and Western cultures. The reasons for this difference are complex and steeped in the historical location and experience of each society. Germany was supplied with an official national narrative, based on an enduring "heritage," by the National Socialists; Heidegger provided its philosophic possibility. With Japan, the issue was complicated by the experience of accelerated modernization and exacerbated by the subsequent transformations inspired by adopting foreign models. Throughout the 1930s, the idea of a "historical crisis" gradually gained widespread acknowledgment as a description of Japan's modernity. Foreign affairs merely authorized this perception and agitated the urgency to resolve it, to "overcome" it, as it was widely advised. Kuki Shūzō might have spoken for his generation in the observations he made in a late essay "Nihonteki seikaku ni tsuite" (On Japanese character, 1936): "Since the early Meiji period down to the present," he wrote,

> our most direct reality is the circumstance whereby Japan's system of civilization, because it has taken in European things, has become worldly. Beyond such a reality, it is surely true that we Japanese have lived with the idea of

reverence toward Europe. We have everywhere learned that we must learn from Europe with humility and that we should be deeply thankful. But it has become a very different thing to make Western civilization as an object of blind reverence. We have taken in the system of Western culture but we cannot forget that in making use of this we are still Japanese. The army adopts Western organization and military drill but it is the Japanese spirit that is the power to move it. (KSZ, 3:376)

Complaining that the "proper respect" for the West had become "Western worship" that exceeded the boundaries of propriety, it is evident that "this attitude of thought is at the base of the belly and appears in a variety of forms as natural common sense in everyday life." Sometimes, he continued, foreign words from the West are used thoughtlessly and frequently we see also unnecessary words inserted within Japanese words. As a result, English words end up being written on signboards in front of Japanese shops catering to Japanese. "The national consciousness has become a vacant spot for Western culture to enter and occupy. We stand in a historical crisis that must bring the nation's people to an awareness that emphasizes the special character of Japan's culture and Japanese character toward this [importation]" (3:376; see also 3:273, "Nihonteki seikaku").

Other contemporaries thinkers, he explained, like Nishida and Watsuji, had already turned to considering the problem of Japanese culture and defining character in this moment of crisis. Kuki was clearly pointing to the widely shared concern with the culprit of commodity culture and its production of social disequilibrium. One solution, as already suggested, was to displace its effect by appealing to the priority of culture steeped in the unavoidable primordiality of everydayness as it was completed in archaic times. Thus Dasein's decision to choose, in an "instant," its destiny would bring to an end the regime of "forgetfulness" and deliver the full promise of the return to "heritage." This act of repetition, favored by a number of people in the 1930s, sought to bypass the endless continuity of now time and the fallenness of the they. In Kuki's meditations, it was important to strip the present of the baneful influence of presence. The present was seen as the site of modernity itself, a vastly different form of temporality that would require a strategy capable of structuring social practices as the specific objects of either memorative communication (Kuki, Watsuji, and Miki) or preservative rescue of the prior experience of the folk or as transformative intent (Kon, Tosaka, Gonda). Modernity, as Kuki recognized, construed a form of historical time that would valorize the new as the "product of a constantly self-regulating temporal dynamic" (3:376). But because it was first and foremost "an abstract temporal form," it remained open to competing articulations that would seek to concretize its presence.

For thinkers like Kuki, "crisis" was simply one of many markers associated with political modernity that called attention to the problem of time. His analysis aimed at revealing it and resolving it in the future. While clinging to a conservative politics no less modern than more progressive forms of Marxism and socialism, theorists like Kuki responded to the current situation by abandoning representational forms that favored developmental story lines and embracing new forms of communication and temporal experiences. The Heideggerian narrative, plotting the ascent from inauthenticity to authenticity and Being's resolute decision for death that would produce a desired, ecstatic unity of time—past, present, and future—provided a powerful model for new forms of representation and memorative communication that managed to avoid development, as such. The developmental form had simply lost its living relationship to the present—the place of *seikatsu*—as a stable form capable of expressing memory and recall. If some thinkers, as we have seen, resorted to a strategy guaranteeing distance from a memorative past, demand for narrating its historical conditions of existence in fixed periods would invite others to look to the past as the sanctuary of a primordial and originary condition of existence of the Japanese folk and race that was already completed. In such scenarios, politics meant rejecting social, cultural, and political modernity but not economic modernity (or, in some instances, technology) and encouraging the embracing of irrationalistic and nationalistic conceptions of culture and character. It was here that the discourse on the social made its pact with fascism and contributed the content of "involuntary memory" to the impoverished and recently constructed voluntary memory of the nation state. And it was here that "Being's personal history" became the stand-in for the history of the folk.

The Necessity of Contingency

While Kuki Shūzō was known as an aesthetician and for having written a celebrated text on style, he confronted the challenge of a degraded modern life and aporias of representation produced by the mediations of social abstraction that put the experience of reality beyond immediate grasp by trying to define the nature of the "conditions of existence." If his exposition of style in late eighteenth-century Edo material culture proposed the "conditions of existence" in concrete detail, the hermeneutic operation depended upon how cultural phenomena are grasped temporally. By the time he wrote his text in 1929, after spending nearly a decade in Europe, the category of culture as the sanctuary of eternal value was already a given of philosophical reflection. What distinguished the claim of culture as a "spiritual science" (as against the natural sciences) was its exemption from the historical process. Culture was the habitat of spirit whose trajectory could be traced in history but not fully explained by it. But its punctual manifestation in art, literature, and thought, corresponding to a realization of fundamental values like beauty, truth, and goodness, could never be exceeded or undermined by history. They could only be momentarily lost or forgotten.

If history was accidental to the production of culture, then culture would move according to a different rhythm of temporality. What particularly interested Kuki was the question of time in the construction of experience. Moved by a desire to show that eventfulness and experience were not driven by the force of necessity, which he identified with history, he was convinced that the primary principle was temporal contingency. The text that announced this interest—*Gūzensei no mondai* (The problem of contingency)—was written to fulfill requirements for a "doctorate" at Kyoto Imperial University and published after *Iki no kōzō*. There is ample evidence to show that he had been thinking about the question of time throughout the 1920s and that it was at the heart of his hermeneutic analysis of a historical moment.

Two considerations informed Kuki's conception of historical culture and will help in grasping his consuming interest in the question of temporal contingency. One was a lingering cosmopolitanism that derived from the postwar period and tradition of philosophic reflection initiated by thinkers like Abe Jirō, Soda Kiichirō, and Kuwaki Genyaku, who were preoccupied with the question of culturalism or personal cultivation (*kyōyōshugi*) and individualism. Concentrating on demonstrating the relationship between cultural value and the meaning of human existence, this intervention inflected prevailing forms of bourgeois liberal humanism and strenuously defended absolute cultural values in both personal and national life and led to rethinking the role or "part" played by Japan in the broader, universal chorus of humanity. Kuki may not have shared the class associations and political pieties of liberalism of this philosophic discourse, but he could easily sympathize with its desire to restructure Japan's culture as a representation of more fundamental human values within the wider context of a genuine cosmopolitan culture in which the constituent parts actively participated in universalism. His effort to show the maturation of cultural/aesthetic consciousness in the late eighteenth century as a distinct accomplishment of the Japanese folk echoed the earlier impulse to relate part to whole (synechdochally), whereby the whole could be grasped through the part and universality immediately revealed in particularity. The other consideration was a dissatisfaction with neo-Kantianism.

Like so many contemporaries, Kuki had tired of neo-Kantianism's formalism, its promise to valorize absolute values, and its incapacity to overcome a lifeless abstraction removed from actual existence and experience.[33] His colleague at Kyoto Tanabe Hajime, with others, was already calling for greater philosophic concreteness, a philosophy capable of engaging the "things themselves"—which meant uniting with everyday life—what Tosaka described as rescuing the original vocation of philosophy and resituating it in the world of common sense.[34] While Tosaka saw the separation of philosophy and everyday life in the use of language that marked class differences,[35] others, like Tanabe, believed that the process leading to an understanding of everydayness was indefinitely delayed by excessive abstraction that necessitated too much preparation of foundational essences. Ultimately, this consideration led to a contest over what constituted the concrete "real" (*genjitsu*) and the authority of existence and experience as the solution. That is to say, conceptions of value could avoid abstraction only if they were united to the "actual conditions of existence" which were located in "lived experiences." It was here, it is well worth recalling, that Heidegger's distinction between authentic and inauthentic understanding was so crucial to Dasein's liberation from constraints that have prevented it from realizing its true vocation or destiny. This choice of a true vocation was clearly at the heart of Kuki's program in *Iki no kōzō*, which it sought to make manifest in the folk's historicizing. Kuki's text concentrated on showing how the "reality" of an "inner experience" (*taiken/erlebnis*) was produced when, according to Benjamin, an "incident" is turned into a moment that has been lived. In Henri Bergson's hands, the very experience that prompted his speculations, that empirical domain in which it was embedded, "big-scale industrialism," was shut out in order to perceive an inner experience in a "spontaneous" and involuntary "afterimage," no longer mediated by history.[36] Capturing an instant in this way was retrieving an auratic moment. Kuki, we know, was profoundly indebted to Bergson's reflections on the concreteness of inner experience. "His principal role," he wrote, "was that of giving us a taste for metaphysics. Our spirit, desiccated by the critical formalism of German Neo-Kantianism," received cultural nourishment from the Bergsonian metaphysical intervention.[37]

But while Bergson disclosed the "inner life," Heidegger provided the impulse and means to historicize it. Retrieving a moment from the folk past was offered to show not its legacy, as such, which weighs the present down and forces it to seek the new, but rather an authentic historicality that reveals the recurrence of what is possible in the present. If *iki* (style) constituted the structure of existence, how Japanese appropriated what was their ownness, then its illumination would supply the present with the recurrence of possibility, by reminding the folk that it had once sought to make a decision on its destiny and that it must do so again resolutely for its future. Driven by the lure of the concrete, Kuki explained that since *iki* possessed a particular folk (or racial) character, it demanded a proper method for grasping its "cultural existence."[38] The best way to secure this concreteness is through the mediation of words, whose content stands in a direct relationship to folk existence. "We must start," he wrote, "from the concrete which has been given. The thing that has been given directly to us is ourselves (*wareware*). Still more, there is the folk (*minzoku*) that is considered the synthesis of ourselves." The conditions attending folk existence appear as a fixed "meaning," in circumstances that are central for the folk. This fixed meaning is opened through "words."[39] Persuaded that words were nothing more than the "self-manifestation" of a people's past and the conditions of the present, he projected the idea that this past self unfolded a particular culture that possesses history. Words signified the "concrete meaning" possessed by a folk capable of revealing the experience of their existence.

For Kuki, as Leslie Pincus has shown, the burden of having studied abroad for so long and returning to a Japan that looked like a colonial city marked the turn away from the everyday of his immediate present. While in Europe, he wrote a youthful poem entitled "Yellow Face" (*Kiiro kao*), which revealed a glimpse of the difference he must have felt as he studied philosophy with Europeans, who apparently saw representatives of the yellow race infrequently. "That being so," Kuki observed, "how does a yellow face become white?" If his own yellow face made him sensitive to his difference from whites, his experience of living in a "modern society" for so long and his awareness of Japan's desire to realize this status overdetermined his antipathy to modernity itself. The everydayness of modern life that installed regimes of sameness everywhere yet withheld full participation for nonwhites, insisting upon a relationship that resembled more one between colonizer and colonized, must have been particularly galling for him. Particularity reinforced this dread of modern life and undoubtedly prompted him to celebrate difference as a more than adequate alternative to the regime of identity. In a short essay written in French, "A Peasant He Is," Kuki approved of a Japanese proverb that held that "it is the peasant who boasts of his country."[40] He saw himself as a rustic among moderns (even though he was an aristocrat in Japan), and he recognized that living in Europe had necessitated speaking about his country, on which there was misunderstanding everywhere. But he was certain that the differences between Japan and Europe were vast. Even Europeans who have lived in Japan and speak passably good Japanese "do not generally know how to read the language." "How can the soul of a country be penetrated if one does not have access to its literature?" As an Asian living in the heartland of white civilization and navigating its modernity, he declared that Japan was his native land for which he had a deep and abiding affection. Because his entire "being" and "soul" belonged to it, he wanted to speak of his country, sing its praise, even at the risk of "being a peasant." "But," he warned, "it will not be a question of politics, nor of commerce, nor of the army and navy. Let us leave to the side superficial things."[41] Instead, Kuki wanted to speak of those things that lay beneath the surface, inhabiting the depths of cultural life, to speak of Japan's soul and spiritual culture. (The Japanese translation differs from both the French and English, which denote "moral civilization.") Despite his pride and affection for Japan's soul, and his desire to portray its depths to unknowing and uncaring Europeans, he disclosed, perhaps painfully, that his country was still countrified, not yet modern. In his later analysis of late Tokugawa culture, the figure of the rube, the rustic (*yabo*), who constantly misrecognized the rules and life-style of the Edo culture of play, contrasts vividly with the *tsūjin*, who has mastered all the moves and gestures to be a consummate "player." In this world, the *yabo* allegorizes the West which, in Kuki's time, looked upon Japan as not yet modern, rustic, backward, and countrified. Yet, Kuki's irony was not entirely lost since as a rustic and peasant, he had already mastered the rules of European culture.

If late Edo represented the moment Kuki sought to temporalize the being of the folk (the folk as a national, collective subject akin to Yanagita Kunio's own formulations), it was only one of several possibilities. Compared to other cultural moments, signified by the No, gardens, tea ceremony, Buddhist temple architecture, and so on, the culture of *iki* of late Edo was only one step in the spiritual history of the folk. After his return home and his resumption of duties at Kyoto Imperial University, he rarely talked about the world of style, as such. Instead, he returned to his earlier considerations on time and contingency that would provide the broader framework for thinking about the particularity of a cultural moment in the folk's appropriation of its conditions of existence. In a poem written in 1930, entitled "Contingency," the opening lines announced the following: "The axiom of parallel lines/as desired/is proof possible?" "Isn't it wondrous the mixing of parallel lines/this contingence/the confusion parallel with splendid virtue/with the approaching waves of causation, two men like gathered pearls." The kernel of this idea, he explained, went back to Heidegger, whose conception of "thrownness" and "destiny" has not overlooked the operation of contingency. But the existential meaning of contingence, in which spatial and communal existence accompany accumulation, manages to escape to the outside of the field of vision.[42] Contingence, in this regard, is not only the sentimental scene of chance that shows "two pearls" thrown together; it is the domain of substantial darkness contained in life and death. It is the unknown quotient, the accident that produces an occurrence and confounds the claim to identity by introducing difference. In Kuki's thinking, contingence was the "lining," as he put it, the backside of what is ordinarily considered as necessity, as conceived in Western theory. In this way, Japanese culture could have developed outside of the Western field of vision in an entirely different register, outside of the realms of coded necessity, and thereby it could pose a challenge to the claims of its causal logic. Yet, the logic of contingence paralleled necessity and reproduced its three modalities: categorical, hypothetical, and disjunctive. It constituted the other term of a binary and thus a complicity with necessity. Hence, the difference scored by the development of Japanese culture according to a logic of contingence failed to free it from the very necessity which it disclaimed and whose logic it recuperated.

The idea of contingence, prior to necessity, permitted Kuki to explore particularity in which concrete detail and difference, now liberated from the causal demands of necessity, derived not simply from Western philosophy but actually explained the development of the West. In his time, this sense of contingence was embodied best in Marxism, to be sure, and its theory of historical development. But it could include, as Kobayashi Hideo noted later, all developmental schemes driven by a self-present subject revealing its plan in a linear trajectory. It was this kind of historical representation, with its privileging of the sovereign self in the West, ceaselessly conquering nature with technology and science, establishing regions of imperial domination under the sign of a "universal ratio," that constituted the site of abstraction and contestation. Only an explanatory strategy based on the principle of contingence could sanction an interpretative program like *Iki no kōzō* and the elaboration of the particularistic culture of the Japanese folk before the "universalist" claims of instrumental reason. Contingence allowed Kuki to move from merely an accounting of the interior life of the Japanese race to the stage of world history.

Recognition of the role played by contingence in producing the lived experience of a people emboldened him to announce, early in *Iki no kōzō*, that he had "no trouble in thinking that *iki* is one of the most illustrious self-manifestations of the unique conditions of the life of the Yamato folk, nay in Oriental culture."[43] This confident boast came after an explanation of the word for *iki*, conveying its special associations which, he believed, can be found in European languages only through pale analogies resembling it. He was convinced that interpretation—the quest for meaning—should proceed at the level of the concrete rather than at the "ideational" plane. "We must," he confessed, "require the resolve of the heretic to decide the problem of 'universality' at the time of understanding '*iki*' in a nominalist direction. That is to say, grasping '*iki*' only as a species of an idea is not pursuing an 'essential intention' that confronts the abstracted universal of . . . an idea that contains it." The understanding of "*iki*" as a meaningful experience cannot do without a "concrete, real particular" perception of existence. Before asking about the "essential" of *iki*, it must first be asked about the "existentia" of the word. In brief, the study of *iki* is not formalistic.[44] Elsewhere in the text, Kuki warned that "nearly all people who try to illuminate the structure of '*iki*' by starting with objective representation fall into defeat and end in abstraction and formalism"[45] Here, he stayed close to the category of everydayness, which was based on lived experience rather than on the objective and abstract forms and representations that would lead only to further abstraction and formalism. Above all else, the study of style should be hermeneutic because the method promised to move from the part to the whole and back again.[46]

The argument from contingence sought to circumvent the tyranny of forms, which always imply the force of necessity. "The fundamental meaning of contingence," he reasoned,

> exists in the rejection of necessity. Necessity, nevertheless, means it possesses being. It is that existence, in other words, which grounds meaning in the self. Contingence is that existence or being, in the meaning of accidentally possessing being, that does not have sufficient grounding. That is to say, it is existence/being that is made possible by nothingness. . . . Contingence is the circumstance in which being is grounded in no-thing. . . In contingence, being/existence confronts nothingness . . . and goes to nothingness. It is the central meaning of metaphysics that it [Being/existence] transcends form and goes to that thing above form. (2:269; also 9–10)

In other words, metaphysics exceeds form, as such, derived from nothingness or non-Being and is therefore open to contingent possibilities from the very beginning. It is thus prior to the moment when form seeks to represent one thing over another. Under this circumstance form becomes a mere copy of an original formlessness and marks the distance between an original and its copy.

Contingence meant the groundlessness of Being or the inaugural presence of non-Being, nothingness, perhaps nature, whereas necessity claimed the ground of itself in Being. The logic of necessity made possible the primacy of identity, sameness, and the impossibility of nonidentity, difference, and opposition. In this scheme, causality originates in the presumption of a universal concept; what follows it—representation, image/sign (*chōhyō*)—exists within it, as a kind species bonded to a genus (2:11–13). When opposition (*hentai*) is excluded, Being possesses the reason of its existence within itself (2:271). It maintains the self that has been given as a self and self-maintenance, according to Kuki, held to the form of self-identity. Necessity, he asserted, anticipates identity and appears most significantly in theory, especially in the causal character of the experiential world, in the metaphysical absolute. For this reason contingence becomes its negative, its shadow opposed to the sovereignty of necessity. Because it is opposed to necessity, it acquires its modalities, which function to secure nonidentity. Kuki argued that this pairing of two terms was based on the conviction that contingence was actually the second term and could be understood only by "elucidating first the sense of necessity" (2:12). Since necessity is in Being an essence identical to itself (Hegel), there is a relationship to the absolute; there is the development of a process in which the relationship is elevated toward the absolute. The determination of identity and thus necessity is recognized in the conceptual, causal and totality, which meant "grasping the relationship of concept and thing, cause and effect, whole and part (2:13)

Kuki's defense of contingence was based upon a critique of representation. Specifically, he wanted to deconstruct the necessary link between "conceptuality" (*gainenteki*) and "representation" or "expression." This operation entailed putting into question any proposition where, say, A and B are said to share a mutual relationship. "The form that leads to a necessary recognition is the mutual relationship between A and B" (2:13). Worried that such a presumption claimed universal veracity, he reasoned that in universal judgments a (universal) concept A, as a genus, has to be produced a priori in order for B—its representation—to exist. Under this logic, representation can exist only within a universal concept A since it is held that B belongs to the class of species under genus A. It is thus the particular in relationship to the universal, reflecting its truth, not its own difference. Here is Kuki: "The structure of a concept is based on that which has witnessed some common universal identity in several representations. The constituent of the concept is the totality of the essential representation which, as identity, oneness, sameness, is abstracted. At the same time, its possible content is constituted by opening the way to nonessential representation, which is forced to be located outside of the sphere of identity through abstraction. . . . Moreover, the relation between an essential representation and its concept is necessary, insofar as it is prescribed by identity" (2:19). By contrast, he added, the relationship between a nonessential representation and concept lacks identity and is thus contingent. What is thereby seen as "essential representation" is called "necessary representation," while nonessential representation is classed as contingent. At yet another level, Kuki proposed that substance (*jittai*) conferred "existentiality" (*jitsuzaisei*) on concept, while its attribute related to the means of existence. "In this way," he explained, "the relation between substance and attribute is equivalent to the relation between concept and representation" (2:20–21).

The appeal to the groundlessness or nothingness of contingency established a "contact zone" between something and nothing. What this meant
was that something is grounded in nothing and possesses a "shape where
no-thing penetrates something" (ibid.). This formulation came close to
Miki Kiyoshi's argument concerning the role of *techné*, a kind of form
without form that makes present what was always already there. The
importance of Kuki's theory of the contingent, the "nonessential," is that
it discounted the claims that bound representation to its concept because
the concept, now, was held to be groundless, rooted in no-thing, where
something, whose representation depends upon a grounding in Being, has
been penetrated and formed by nothing. The logic of contingence, accordingly, could rightly put into question the presumption of "true Being"
problematized by metaphysics by claiming that it was, in reality, non-
Being. "Contingency," then, "meant that the distribution of the idea was
made incomplete by non-Being and therefore a difference must reside between the original [the concept] and the copy [representation]." Hence,
the "fullness" and completion claimed by "true Being," the presumed
stability of a seamless relationship between the idea and its representation, is undermined when non-Being is summoned.

Kuki's critique moved to evaluating the status of synthetic and analytic
judgments. A Kantian problem, analytic judgment related to necessity, everything logic claimed for it, and the demand of certainty, whereas synthetic judgment was associated with contingence and uncertainty. An analytic judgment corresponded to the subject (*shugo*) in an arrangement
where predicate B is immediately contained within idea A (2:10). But a
synthetic judgment is one where subject B is linked to subject A but remains outside idea A. This distinction acknowledged that in synthetic judgments the "I" must have a certain difference other than the identity of the
subject idea, which meant recognizing that the predicate is a subject itself
(2:13). For Kuki, the synthetic judgment, allied with "experiential intuition," or "pure intuition," "accompanies the necessary condition of synthetic unity of diverse contents of intuition in possible experience" (2:197).
Following Kant, he envisaged synthetic judgments as the fundamental
ground of human knowledge, which meant that he aimed to elucidate the
conditions of possibility and justifiability of their a prioristic claims.

By exploding the grounded claims of analytic knowledge and Being's
fullness, Kuki was enabled to mount a powerful critique of racism and
the claims of historical representation. Analytic judgments, based on
the necessary incorporation of the predicate into the subject, made possible a conception of social hegemony founded on excluding whatever was
considered nonessential, different. By contrast, synthetic judgments, authorized by the recognition of contingency, held that "yellow," for example, is contingent to the subject-concept human. In fact, it was a subject,

not a predicate to a white subject, a purely contingent, accidental fact which meant only that all humans are the same, regardless of race, analytically marked and differentiated by color. It should be pointed out, in this regard, that analytic judgments drew their force from universal judgments, whereas synthetic judgments—experiential—were classed as particularistic. Yet in Kuki's reckoning, the distinction should not appear unequal, with a first term dominating the second, but rather equal, complementary, with synthetic judgments becoming "expanded judgments" (2:25–30). Historical representation sought to express the identity of the concept as a universal judgment, but in his world of contingent synthetic judgments, based on particularistic experiences, there is only the possibility of "contingent representation" that remains outside of the sphere of concept's identity. There can never be an idea of history, as such, but only contingent facts that have occurred in the present of innumerable pasts and successive instances.

Since necessity insinuates that which Being possesses, it presumes the ground of itself; whereas contingency, as suggested, signifies a state of groundlessness of Being, negativity, non-Being, Plato's nonexistence, and Tanabe's "species." For Kuki, contingence constituted the ultimate condition that lies in the "contact zone" between something and nothing; it is the condition that something is grounded in nothing. When nothing penetrates, it is something. The real vocation of metaphysics is therefore a radical questioning of "true existence" that is possible only through a prior investigation of its relationship to "nothingness." Discounting the primacy of identity and its logic of causation, he was convinced that causal relationships and "purposeful stages" in development were authorized by identity. But under the regime of contingence, determination always comes from the future (2:60–63). The principal characteristic of the conduct of contingency in the experiential world is simultaneity, things occurring at the same time and within a specific space (2:135). Kuki imagined contingency as the occurrence of two events at the same time that are not necessarily related. The consequences for conceptions of received historical time are significant. When the "so-called historical" is grounded in simultaneous contingency that takes place here (*koko*), in space and the now (*ima*), history becomes the succession of simultaneous occurrences and takes the form of repetition (2:129). In this way, historical time is fundamentally spatial, inasmuch as it is located in a here or there (Heidegger's Da) and now. It is, in fact, a spatialization of the now.

By locating difference in the contingent and simultaneity and its repetition in the here and now, Kuki opened the way to speak of Japan's cultural endowment as both unique and equivalent to that of the West. He also undermined any effort to fix Japan in a temporal continuum based upon the necessity of Being grounded in itself. Throughout the text on contin-

gence, his favorite example of how it worked was the observation that
some humans are yellow, while others are white or black. Color differentiation was purely a contingent occurrence, an accident of place that implied no standard of valuation whatsoever. Yet, contingence could put
into place its own logic of necessity (2:259). The metaphysical wonder of
contingence, he wrote, is that it holds the form of a miracle toward fate,
destiny. When it possesses the whole man as a kernel for human existence,
it is called destiny (2:224). In this regard, contingence is a limit of possibility whose "kernel of meaning" holds a historically unrational form called
"a chance meeting in that place." Hence, it is phenomenological, as it
always depends upon the priority of the chance encounter in a specific
place, and because it takes place in the "instant of the present, like play
or sport." It appears as a "miracle" where nothing is seen in the background of the actualization of separate things (2:253). But contingence,
he acknowledged, always depends on the existence of an other, just as it
depends upon a relationship to necessity. The unity of experience was
originally based on grasping the contingency of an other and making it
the same as the self (2:256).

Kuki concluded this formalistic meditation on contingence by calling
attention to how experiential and empirical knowledge begins with contingence, which is the limit of understanding. Because the originary meaning of theoretical systems always aims at unifying experience, the contingence of an other was incorporated into the sameness of the self and
thereby internalized. "Identity, then, is at the heart of speculation and
thus is the founding principle of internalization." But it is also true that
identifying concretely the external "thou" with an internal self is a "judgment of an ideal," produced by desire, as it were. The thou—other—is
subordinated and incorporated in the identity of the self, its difference
effaced. In this way, identity becomes necessity, even though the process
of self-identification started with the contingence of the other's existence.
What Kuki wanted to press was the restoration of the primacy of contingence in a "narrative" dominated by the necessity of self-identity. Just as
Tosaka, as we saw, wanted to unearth the repressed primacy of materialism which had attended the inauguration of philosophic speculation in
the West, so Kuki wanted to recall how contingence was the source of all
necessity and thus difference (2:256–257). Any ideal that proposes to ar-
rive at theoretical knowledge, he asserted, cannot do so only with necessity. "There must be a contingent necessity or a necessity saturated by
contingency" (2:257). Significantly, Kuki rejected any effort to put contingence into the service of either a rational learning or one misled by the
claims of abstract universalism. This was especially true of ethics, which
he believed had to be individualized according to contingent occurrence
offered by the present. This emphasis upon the relationship between a

present and the exercise of contingence came close to Heidegger's formulation concerning the choice of possibility for the future that appears in the "instant of the present" and constituted for Kuki a principle he would reaffirm in his later essay on existence. The universal must always be concrete and limited to the particular according to the occasion of contingence (2:258). Indeed, the practical internalization of contingence "is nothing other than the awareness of the relationship of parts and all the parts [comprising] the concrete whole." For Kuki, contingence opened the way to futural possibility and the appropriate form of action. But, quoting Heiddeger, it was the possibility of contingence to realize a resolution from the perspective of the collectivity. What counted most for him was the always possible "chance encounter," which constitutes the contingency of the thou—other—accidentally meeting the I in any present moment (2:259, 317).

In his essays on existence and humanity, written in the 1930s, Kuki turned increasingly to emphasizing the importance of contingence, possibility and the present as forms of authentic understanding. Here, he proposed that "human history" existed only for the creation of an "historical humanity of others" and society (3:36). Even Heidegger believed that "Being in the world" was nothing other than "Being in the collective world." Dasein thus possesses the way of "collective, mutual existence," and society presupposes the other. In Kuki's formulation, this meant "grasping the special tendency of the I toward the other, the other toward the I, in order to make possible the chance meeting" (3:37–38). If, as some believed, the development of society is a necessity, it is still the nature of such a coming together of the I and thou through chance, circumstantial contingence. But "historical humanity" is individualized as a specific socius manifest in the form of speaking, knowledge/arts, technology, poetics, and religion as revealed in the founding myths (3:42). Intersubjective social values are nothing more than "cultural values" that show the objective productions of historical humanity. This meant that the social confronts the "problem of tradition" and discovers the structure of historical humanity in its particularistic meaning. Kuki wanted to emphasize that the discussion of how historical humanity develops never relates to "abstract humans" but rather inquires into the "tradition" and "history" as experienced by a group like the Japanese against the backdrop of a wider humanity. "Tradition," he wrote, "is the naturalization of freedom according to racial customs." Custom constitutes the sign of choices—the resolutions—a particular group has exercised under contingent conditions—chance encounters—what elsewhere he called "experience (*taiken*) of the particular" (3:43). Because this experience was produced by resolute choices under determinate conditions it represented an autarkic moment that memory would repetitively recall (*sōki*).

Kuki envisaged contingence as an interruption that always "imparts a surprise in the one-timeness of history" (2:115). At the same time, it opens the way to a "repetitious natural attitude of necessity through the practical mediation of possibility." While contingent existence is based on nothing, it still takes the form of Being as a reality. It is possibility that produces necessity through customization that establishes the law of repetition. Necessary existence exists within the temporal horizon of the past and is therefore a repetitive reality that exists from the perspective of an unlimited past. But, he cautioned, contingence always exists in the present since this is where the meeting takes place and where it can be known (2:116). It is opposed to carrying the burden of the past and thus lacks one in its essence. "Contingence spurts out in the instant of the present as a reality without a past. Even when speaking of contingence in the past, it is contingency in the present of the past." Pastness does not establish contingence in the past but the contemporaneity of the present in the past. The same is true of the future. Necessity presupposes continuity in history, and possibility always expresses the movement toward the future. But contingence means only an instantiation of the present. Because it is opposed to necessity, it is separated from identity (the idea), which in his favorite example demonstrates the truth that the "yellow race" is separated from an identity of the general idea called humanity. The skin color shows a differentiation of species and represents the truth of contingence. The force of the contingent also rejects the idea that there must be a necessary relationship between "reason" and "conclusion." Finally, it demands a separation from an identity that claims the whole as a totalization of the parts (3:144). In Kuki's opinion, contingence is found in the philosophers of Asia and pre-Socratic Greece but has no relationship to Christianity (3:164–165).

All of this thinking about the contingent aimed at presenting a supplement to the logic of necessity that never broke free from its hegemony. What Kuki produced was an image of difference that never rose above mere exceptionalism. Throughout his formal philosophic exposition there appeared a recurring concern for the "imperial" claims of identity—the self's absorption of the other—and the tyranny of that past that authorizes the privilege of necessity. Beyond these formal and philosophic categories lay the more concrete objects of analysis—the universalistic pretensions of completion announced by the West over the "incomplete" cultures of the Orient which could only attain completion by surrendering the "thou" to the "I." The assault on necessity was a revolt against a metaphysics of Being and the myth of self-presence, a prescient critique of this metaphysical history (actually deconstruction, as envisaged by Heidegger), and a disclosure of its spurious privileging of an identity and similitude. Behind Kuki's interrogation of contingence and necessity was nothingness and

Being; before it was the spectacle of civilizations and the division between universalism and particularism. The fullness and grounding of Being was, in fact, the justification for making the claim that Western civilization was complete, self-present, and thus universal. Incompletion, according to this standard of evaluation, meant lack that needed to be supplemented. Western culture, Kuki observed, is composed of a combination of Greek and Judaic (or Arabian) cultures that included Christianity, Judaism, and Islam, which he classified as "willful" and "intellectual" cultures. By comparison, it is commonly understood that Asia is an "emotional culture." "The willful and intellectual culture of the West is called a culture of Being (or existence, *yū*) that is opposed to the culture of Nothing expressed by the Orient's emotional culture" (3:377). Kuki's new division, an obvious transformation of an earlier East/West characterization promoted by writers like Okakura Tenshin, pointed to the metaphysical presumptions undergirding the respective cultural regions of the world. In this division he acknowledged that India showed a marked tendency for speculation and the acquisition of knowledge (resembling the West), while China reflected a practical utilitarian national character that clearly disclosed a penchant for willfulness. But Japan stood as a culture of emotionality that made life into an expression of pure heartedness (3:377–378). While he cited a number of writers like Nishida Kitarō and Watsuji Tetsurō who had already engaged the problem of a global division of cultural labor, he urged the additional recognition that the background of Japan's culture was Oriental culture in general. Its particularity had to be grasped within this broader context (3:378).

While Kuki's earlier exercise in cultural hermeneutics, *Iki no kōzō*, acknowledged the relationship between Japan and the Orient, the analysis itself focused primarily on the contours of a completed and self-possessed civilization, not yet affected by the West and confronted by the challenge of capitalism and its inexhaustible desire to destroy cultures of reference. In this study, Kuki sought to resituate the past of an everyday life within the horizon of a mature, historical society and the mundane life of contemporary reality. The purpose of the hermeneutic was to show those enduring characteristics of the race since its origins that reached mature perfection in the late eighteenth and early nineteenth centuries, just on the eve of the great transformation. By employing a strategy that juxtaposed cultural experience to contemporary life, he could dramatize what was being forfeited in the rush to imitate the West. The text pitted a concrete reality (*genjitsu*) of existence, timeless and enduring, against a present-day lived experience. For Kuki, the word *iki* was free from the instrumentalities of reason and utility and its interrogation promised to yield self-understanding and the experience of what it had meant to be Japanese.

The Edo of the Bunka/Bunsei era—the site of *iki*—appeared as the authentic original to the inauthentic copy of Tokyo life in the late 1920s. His choice was hardly accidental since the different moments shared the same space. Both cultures were "popular," inasmuch as they were fueled by money and consumption rather than simply the styles of aristocratic taste. But Tokyo was a culture of the masses, a diluted copy of real possibility without rules and constraints, while Edo was an intricate culture of play sponsored by wealthy urban townsfolk who made it their business to learn the rules of the game if they hoped to become serious participants. To be sure, Kuki's concentration on the everyday life of Edo, like the obsessional fixations of later Edoviewers, attested to the importance of everydayness in his present. *Iki* was an overdetermined text, inasmuch as the problem of the present drove him to resituate another, prior "experience" within the process of lived reality. Leslie Pincus points to the "allure" of the Japanese woman—the beauty of the Edo pleasure quarters and the splendor of its brocaded robes—and contrasts it to the figure of "modern girl," with all of her associations of coarseness, crassness, and commonness.[47]

Yet there is also Kuki's commitment to rescuing traces of what plainly was vanishing, and laying hold, perhaps for one last time, to an auratic memory that contemporary modern life was destroying. Like Heidegger, Kuki was persuaded that experience meant retaining and recalling what had been present to the self, and this pointed to both the possibility of repetition and retrieving the heritage of the past. Repetition promised to restore the possibility of recalling authentic understanding in the present, as it once had been secured in the past. It meant making resolutely a choice to overcome the inauthentic understanding dominated by the they, the average, a culture that has forgotten. Kuki wished to recall, through the experience of *iki*, the existence of a collective we—the Japanese race in a moment of cultural mastery and maturation. Convinced that history was founded on the experience of the race embodied in unique cultural forms, he argued that it also taught that these moments and their achievements outlast the immediate conditions of historical production. This was a view, shared by virtually every cultural theorist in the interwar period, that elevated culture to the level of ontological rather than mere ontic existence. But the manifestation of such forms attested to repetition, a characteristic Kuki linked to Oriental time and the instantiating powers of contingence and difference.

By the 1930s, Kuki's preoccupation with the hermeneutics of a self-possessed culture like Edo was replaced by a consideration of world cultures and their impending conflict. The allure of *iki* had all but disappeared from his reflections, apart from a lingering conviction that it had woven itself into the feminine culture of the Edo period as an enduring landmark of Japanese character. This identity of *iki* and a feminine culture echoed Hirabayashi Hatsunosuke's earlier pronouncement that the contemporary culture of the 1920s had become "feminized." But the problem of the present had grown to become larger than merely the transformation from Edo to Tokyo, from style to commodity form. Kuki now saw the conflict in the larger context marked by the clash of different cultures based on fundamentally different conceptions of apprehension and knowledge and the threat of inevitable struggle. The struggle was between a metaphysics of no-thing and a metaphysics of Being already prefigured in his text on contingence.

For Kuki, the real problem for contemporary Japanese was Western culture. "We stand in a historical crisis," he declared, "that necessitates understanding the structure of Japanese character that reveals the unique coloring of Japanese culture in the face of a decline of national awareness caused by the permeation of Western culture." Such an understanding, he continued, would, "in general, make the nation aware" (3:273, 376). He asked, rhetorically "why emphasize Japanese character or culture today?" It was important to "arouse" and "awaken" the nation, which had fallen into a torpor because of its worship of the West (3:375). Western worship derived from a sense of the superiority Western civilization possessed: (1) the demonstration of a tradition of geometric study, in contrast to the Indian proficiency in abstract mathematics (3:369) (this geometry made possible the conquest of the natural world through machine technology); and (2) the growth of scientific social theory in politics and economics. But the West also possessed a superiority in the spiritual realm. Since the Meiji period, Japan's cultural system had become "worldly," as the country had begun to take on European things in all sectors of life. While this cultural adaptation required expressing respect for Europe and the United States, blind worship of Western civilization was entirely different. The process of importing the Western system has led to forgetting that "we are Japanese" (3:376). What particularly was forgotten in this rush to incorporate Western life into Japan was the spiritual dimension of the national experience. Despite acknowledging the spiritual superiority of the West, Kuki fell back on an older argument that presupposed an identity between materiality and the West, spirituality and the East. This argument was first proposed by Okakura Tenshin at the turn of the century. Yet it flew in the face of a proposition that sought to establish the equivalence between particular cultures and the general, when the former is expressed in the latter or stands in for it, even though he believed that the particular is determined by and formed under contingent conditions that have been "historically and climatically individualized" (3:368, 370). Moreover, to make an argument that aimed to reinstate the spiritual over the material was one that already acknowledged a lack and a need for completion, even though Kuki was concerned with demonstrating how each particularized culture was complete in itself.

Recalling his earlier interest in Edo, Kuki asserted that the circumstances of Tokugawa Japan that prompted nativists to decry the excessive sinophilia of the times was vastly different from the conditions Japanese encountered in the present. The problem confronting Japan "today is the consideration of Japanese culture based on the Oriental totality (*zentai*) against the culture of the West." Compared to the West, Kuki's Orient was spiritual. It was this spirituality that formed the background heritage of Japan's culture. But it would be wrong to merely classify Japan as generally Oriental and leave it at that. It was equally important to examine this endowment for the "several occasions that have structured Japanese character." In doing so, he was confident that they would clarify the "signs of Japanese culture, catch hold of the true shape of the Japanese spirit," and supply a concrete foundation for "Japanism" (3:377).[48] The distinctiveness of Japanese culture lies in its capacity to adopt foreign material elements and complete them through a process of adaptation. This remarkable talent, based on the assimilative powers of the Japanese people, was revealed in the "double character" of culture, its propensity for "stratification" (*jūsōsei*). Remarkably, this was precisely the same historical concept expressed by Watsuji Tetsurō in his history of the Japanese spirit. With Kuki, however, the important point was not to boast about Japan's capacity to "receive influences" from foreign cultures in its own formation but rather to underscore the characteristic of doubling and stratification that guarantee the development of culture that has adapted imports to its own needs and marked them with its own individuality (3:274). Whatever genius of a people they demonstrate, stratification and doubling are merely formalistic principles, not those through which it is possible to "concretely grasp the content of Japan's culture." The content remains unfixed, ever changeable, reflecting the power of contingence in any present. In Kuki's thinking, Japanese culture/character was distinguished by three distinct modes: *shizen* (nature) *iki* (style), and *teinen* (which loosely referred to the heart that understands the truth).

Nature was clearly the most important element in the formation of Japanese character. Following the understanding of eighteenth-century nativists, nature appeared as things as they are, "corresponding to heaven and Earth" or "being at the mercy of the heart of heaven and Earth." Hence, nature points to the "natural Way" (*michi*) and was opposed to logic and reason (*kotowari*) (3:378–380). If life is not conducted naturally, morality will never be completed (3:381). What nature signifies most (for both Kuki and the eighteenth-century nativist Kamo Mabuchi) is "a dislike of the artificial and a reverence for a natural nature" (ibid.). By contrast, the West's view of nature is entirely different because it pits freedom of the self against the unfreedom of nature. In fact, freedom is freedom from nature. In Kuki's reformulation of nativism, nature requires unity, identity. In Japan, he pointed out, especially in the practice of landscape art and design and floral arrangements, there is the imperative to unify art with nature. The same identity is manifest in the unity of divine ceremony and the governance of humans—both are called *matsurigoto* (3:83). The import of nature in the formation of Japan's culture is its "profound relationship . . . to emotionality."

Next came style. This was the conception of style that had served as the object of his hermeneutic analysis of late Tokugawa culture, now recycled to become a decisive element in the formation of Japanese character. (Kuki's decontextualization and transformation of style was consistent with a strategy that made the part and whole infinitely interchangeable.) What had been summoned as a historical sign now became a timeless cultural characteristic that represented all historical experience, even though his explanation of the concept ("style does not feel or think about human style") could just as easily have come from any number of late eighteenth-century verbal fictions of writers like Santō Kyōden. The description of effortless style fitted the figure of the *tsūjin*, the master player of pleasure quarters who, more often than not, acted as both ethnographer and voyeur of the scene, monitoring and passing judgment on performance. In Kuki's revised understanding of *iki*, style became an unchanging durable. "In Japan," he wrote, *iki* "runs through the blood of our Japanese people through the spirit of bushidō." Even though the late seventeenth-century philosopher Yamaga Sokō spoke about "spirit and sentiment" (*shiki*), he was undoubtedly referring to *iki*. Yamaga pointed to how *shiki* demanded the utmost "spiritual control" in intending bravery and thus reinforced the desire for elevated ideals and their realization (3:383–384). Such acts always required "constancy," which "protects our principle" and the "heart/mind (*kokoro*) that never changes." The quality of constancy here resembled the Heideggerian conception of resoluteness. The ideal most valued was that which taught the warrior never to fear death, "never to dislike it," and to live every moment as if it were the last. "It is crystallized in the spirit of self-sacrifice born from a true and sincere intention" (3:384). A heritage handed down by warriors to townsfolk, narrated in war tales and puppet theater, the spirit of bushidō is reflected in both literature and drama and life itself. In time, Kuki observed, the principle of *iki*, as it was expressed in bushidō, was broadened to include women. Convinced that the spirit was not lost even in his degraded present, he pointed to Japan's recent military successes against the Chinese and Russians, as well as the even more recent "Shanghai Incident" and the seizure of Manchuria as proof of its living pulsation. The spirit of "style" is also inscribed in the arts of Japan which illuminate its nobility.

Finally, Kuki turned to *teinen*. The first part of the compound is the ideograph for *akirame*—resignation, abandonment. Like Watsuji, who had already established the primacy of resignation as a characteristic of monsoon Asia, Kuki proposed that resignation was a Japanese attitude and was expressed in the awareness of the powerlessness of the self (3:385). The spirit of resignation was represented best in the Japanese forms of Buddhism. Both Honen and Shinran, medieval Buddhist reformers, called attention to the saving powers of Amida Buddha—the other (*tasha*)—because of the helplessness of people to save themselves and recommended faith, not knowledge, in the face of the self's powerlessness. For Kuki, the value of resignation for Japanese exceeded this religious evaluation to become a founding block of Japanese culture and character, manifested in frankness, plainness, simplicity, and so forth. His example was the indifferent taste of Japanese food when compared to Chinese cuisine. Restraint is the mark of the "taste for black ink paintings and No." Its understated, quiet simplicity was ultimately expressed in the signifier *sabi*, which covered a diversity of qualities attesting to the force of resignation, acceptance, purity of heart, and simplicity.

Kuki explained that outwardly these three characteristics conformed to Shinto (nature), Confucianism (*iki*, decorum), and Buddhism (*teinen*); inwardly they were adapted to the self (Japan) and served as the mediations of "self-creation" (3:388). Although they constituted three separate moments or occasions, they formed a unity that reinforced both character and the form of culture Japanese produced. If nature is the natural Way, it is still to be walked on, like a path, and it is *iki*, formless style, that powers the journey. On this road, there is a starting point and a point of arrival. It is *teinen*, the heart that grasps truth, accepting things as they are, that is clearly a way of starting and a way of ending. Pushing further this triangulating movement, which hinted at a dialectic, Kuki proposed that this "fusion of forms" (3:394) was phenomenalized in the three sacred imperial regalia: the jewel (*tama*) appeared as benevolence (*jin*), the mirror as knowledge, and the sword as bravery. "The jewel signified nature, the sword *iki*, and the mirror the understanding heart." By materializing these three artifacts of imperial regalia, Kuki suggested the possibility of an identity between Japanese character (and culture) and the *kokutai* (3:395). But he quickly left it muted by considering how this conception of a unified Japanese character, on which Japanism was founded, related to cosmopolitanism (*sekaiteki seisaku*). He conceded that there might be contemporaries who declare a genuine concern for "pure Japanese things" such as jūdō, kendō or archery, a love for waka and haiku or indeed many of the things that inhabit everyday life like foods and the striped patterns of kimono. Each, however small a thing, "carries with it the trace of Japanese culture as a whole" (3:289). Confident that the smallest of traces would bring one to the most important thing, he clearly made this argument to concretize his prior conviction in the synechdocal relationship between the part (the world of experiential and synthetic judgment) and the whole. This argument between part and whole or the general (*ippan*) meant simply that part, which signified the experiential, was not incompatible with the general. Rather, the "general appeared in the part" and expressed it in a distinctive way (3:368). If cultural particulars are seen as the culture of one country, together they constitute a "general" (3:291). Cultural particulars, he wrote, recalling his more formalistic philosophic reflections, resemble the different views of the same city when seen from changing perspectives. "Even though it is the same city, it presents different shapes and feelings according to the place occupied by the person who is viewing it." In this way, the world as a whole (*zentai*) matches the space of the city; the cultural particulars of various countries are like the different views of the same city. Implied in this trope was the belief that these differing shapes and feelings could not be isolated from the diversity of views of the same city produced by changing perspectives. The city, he asserted, is "imparted synthetically," to appear as a composite, with a variety of differing shapes and feelings. Cultural particulars are fixed historically, culturally, and climatically. Hence, "world culture is disclosed within a synthesis of particular cultures" (3:368).

Although the general is illuminated by the part, the whole "radiating according to a strengthening of the part," the idea of culture of a worldly whole is, like a world state, an "abstraction," removed from "reality" (3:370). This world culture can only be discovered synthetically within the various cultures of different countries. Only the reality of the singular and exceptional culture, determined in its particularity by character and climate (*fūdo*), can claim the authority of reality. As suggested earlier, Kuki insisted that Japanese culture could only be grasped by referring to its Oriental background. Without this mediation, any consideration of it was doomed to fall into mere "abstraction." "Today," he announced, "an Orientalized Japanese culture has the opportunity to have all contact with the cultures of the West" (3:398). But it was worrisome that Western culture had already permeated the "whole body" with its influence through blind worship. Still, forfeiture of Japanese culture might be forestalled and its rescue still possible if it were made "absolute." What he meant by "absolute" was the end of imitation. Japanese must be made aware of the special nature of their culture and thus stand firm in a position of Japanism. Yet this required broadly surveying the cultures of the world and selecting only that which would enhance it. In a sense, Kuki wanted to restore the double promise of the Meiji Restoration's Charter Oath when it declared an intention to return to what was purely Japanese yet actualize a Japanism "founded on the universal Way of heaven and Earth." Clearly, he was, by 1937, more concerned with the primacy of the particular over the claims of the general, the force of contingence over the spurious claims of necessity. When discussing the form and content of Japan's culture, he acknowledged that some skeptics might argue that the content of Japanese culture possessed an unfixed form and remained open to change. This was plainly unsatisfactory and showed only that they had not looked at reality. "If this is the case, what in general is Japanese character?" he asked (3:379). To counter this claim of endless changeability, he appealed to the authority of his three cultural characteristics that had fused into a unity, but which had appeared in Japan's history as contingent events. Paradoxically, the elevation of these three characteristics became absolutes signifying necessity. To be sure, Kuki constantly recognized how history and *fūdo* qualified these characteristics, but their roles seemed only to reinforce the claim of constancy and exceptionalism, echoing the sentiments of his contemporary Orikuchi Shinobu, whose texts he probably never read.

In the end, Kuki's theory of contingence, advanced as a powerful critique of the universalistic presumptions of analytic judgment, representation, and the priority of identity (similitude and homogeneity), fell short of its purpose to replace the claims of "analytic judgment" with the authority of particular experience signifying difference. While it put into question universalism and identity, through a deconstruction of necessity, it risked sliding into an argument for necessary exceptionalism, even though he never went so far. With Kuki, there was still the residuum of a now discounted cosmopolitanism and its promise to link the particular to the general by showing how the latter could only be revealed in the former. Yet he went a long way to disavow the naked imperialism implicated in this position pledged to cultural exceptionalism, an imperialism Japan had already begun to implement in the 1930s. In his texts, imperialist events like the military seizure of Manchuria and the beginning of war in China are reduced to the status of "incidents" and used to demonstrate only instances of the Japanese cultural spirit rather than examples of precisely the kind of cultural imperialism he was trying to eliminate. Although the excesses of this position could still be contained by his abiding belief in the power of contingence that disclosed how a philosophy of subjectivity grounded in a Being present to itself merely masqueraded a culturally specific "universalism" projected as necessity, his contemporary Watsuji Tetsurō was not bound by such doubts and constraints. With Watsuji, the possible relationship between part and whole disappeared as he began to formulate a conception of cultural community excluding anybody who was not a member of it. In an early text called "Reconsideration of Contingence," he argued that contingence never went further than allowing for the existence of differences from "place to place" according to differing histories, culture, and climate.[49] For him, there was only difference according to "place to place," unconstrained by the lure and limit of a world culture. What Watsuji dramatized early was a rejection of a metaphysical structure that necessitated finding a complementary place for the operation of contingence. In his view, the primacy of a situational location determined difference, and while he was willing to call it contingence, it could just as easily qualify as a manifestation of necessity.

THE DOUBLE CHARACTER OF CULTURE

Stratigraphy of Everyday Life

The philosopher, cultural historian and ethicist Watsuji Tetsurō (1889–1960) expressed, in the description of his most severe contemporary critic Tosaka Jun, a "modern philosophy which, by linking European categories to those of Japanese spiritual essentialism, produced the most high collared aspect of Japanism in his day" (5:146). Tosaka went on to compare Watsuji with classically contemporary reactionaries like Gondō Seikyō and Kanoko Kajinobu and portrayed him as a tireless opponent of the "vulgar monotony of Japanese academic philosophy" who had, nevertheless, rejected the "new" less than the "general currents of the time.' (5:148). It is important to say of Watsuji that he was deeply affected by both Nietzsche and Kierkegaard, as his early essays on both Dōgen and the spiritual history of Japan clearly show. His own cultural analysis, drawing heavily on Nietzsche, especially, aimed at discounting the deceits of modern bourgeois society and its disturbing celebration of materiality and individualism. His unwavering solution was the predictable appeal to the "pathos" of aristocratic distance associated with older archaic values and culture heroes. If Kuki was genuinely an aristocrat by birth, Watsuji designated himself as the spokesman of this class by constructing a critique of mass society, the "general currents of the time," on the basis of recalling heroic ideals derived from an older aristocratic "experience" that had been forgotten and a philosophic anthropology (ningengaku) that would explain both the differences among social groups and Japan's unique endowment. Watsuji's theory of human relationships transformed Japanese into cultural aristocrats, from the homogenized masses and pointless materialism of capitalism to the truly human in a world that increasingly was becoming other to its nature. But his conception of "human" seemed to apply only to the Japanese. His "counterattack of reaction," as Tosaka put it, was driven by the discovery of an opposing methodology that represented a worthy adversary for Marxism. In this regard, Watsuji acknowledged that Marxism itself rejected abstraction identified with Enlightenment thought that had discounted the importance of historical understanding (4:305). When it came to Japan, however, this endorsement of historical concreteness slipped into the contradiction that ignored and even overlooked the special historical character of the country in favor of determining the intimate relationship between "historicality" (Heidegger's narrative of authentic understanding) and culture and climate. With this move, he risked falling into the same kind of abstraction he associated with Enlightenment thought (4:306).)

For Watsuji, Marxism signaled the advent of the modern consumer society—what he called "Americanism"—reflecting a destructive materialism promoting greed and desire that he feared was threatening to break up human relationships. At the same time, he was prompted by an awareness that Marxism by the 1930s, because of its suppression and near extermination, was an effective instrument of thought and action. In this context, he turned to the study of what he called human in-betweenness: a unique residue of antimaterialism now put into the service of elucidating form and formal relationships. Tosaka had observed that Watsuji's writings had always been more concerned with form than content and the distinctive mode through which culture and human conduct were structured (TJC, 5:148). But, ironically, just as Marx had denounced Feuerbach for promoting an idealist philosophical anthropology instead of one based on sensuous activity, Watsuji inverted a materialist anthropology for a return to ideal forms. To this end, he aimed at constructing a theory of ethics based on the study of human, social relationships. This ethics, as we shall see, was narrowly situational rather than globally common, inasmuch as it depended upon the diversity of conditions peculiar to each location and different human group as they are found from "place to place." The danger of this approach was that it would redefine what was truly human, according to criteria Watsuji wanted to privilege, and thus easily open the way to excluding peoples whose history and culture failed to satisfy the acid test of requirements. Watsuji's theory of ethics promoted not just exceptionalism but a notorious exclusivism with wide-ranging consequences. Owing to the situationality informing it, itself a good Heideggerian conceit, Watsuji was confident that one could find a characteristic ethical endowment in Japan by consulting the history and culture of place. His principal interest was in elucidating the experience of social relationships in Japan that sealed the group into an enduring human and solidary (and national) community. Why humans differed was the problem he hoped cultural study would resolve. But he discovered that culture alone could not provide an adequate accounting unless it was supplemented by a consideration of climate and environmental conditions, what he conceptualized as "climate and culture" (*fūdo*), which became the basis of a unique mode of analysis. The study of human relationality was prepared first by way of a method of cultural history that finally led to the discovery of climate.

In the 1935 edition of *Zoku Nihon seishinshi kenkyū*, published first a decade earlier, Watsuji added a new explanation to the meaning of cultural history he had practiced in the several studies within the book. He introduced the concept of stratification or stratigraphic history (*jūsōsei*) and its central importance for understanding Japan's modernity. The new preface rearticulated an anxiety about modern Japan's achievements and its effects for any consideration of Japanese culture. He had revealed a similar concern in the 1920s when he insisted, time and again, how creative individuals, free and unburdened by material things, produced culture. This was the central argument of his long essay on the Buddhist thinker of the fourteenth century Dōgen, whom he rescued from Zen sectarianism and represented as one of Japan's principal cultural heroes. What attracted Watsuji to Dōgen was Dōgen's great capacity to teach the masses a new doctrine yet remain separate from them. He also saw this creativity in the formation of Buddhist temple art and architecture in ancient Japan. On the occasion of a "sentimental journey" that professed to be a "pilgrimage" to ancient temples in Nara, Watsuji showed he was less a religious than an aesthetic pilgrim who visited these temples to admire and respect the aesthetic temperament they embodied. It is interesting to note that even at this early date (1918) he had already meditated on the comparison of Greek and Japanese aesthetic sensibilities and saw in both a shared commonality of climate, terrain, and human sentiment. In fact, he was surprised to see in ancient Japan how Greek sensibility found, for the first time, "a sympathetic reception."[50] The *Koji junrei*, which became a model for his later *Fūdo*, especially since it too was structured around a journey, disclosed how the ancients were able to give expression to indigenous ideals in sculpture and architecture, despite the obvious fact that they had learned these technologies from Chinese and Koreans. The temples of Nara represented for him a paradigmatic reminder of how Japanese idealism found lasting material expression.[51] While there are numerous anonymous artisans and artists who produced these temples, many of whom were Korean and Chinese, they were undoubtedly driven by ideals and belief that derived from the native soil to create beauty that has endured down to the present (317–318; see also 310). Watsuji was convinced that despite cultural borrowing, the work produced in Nara was no mere copy of an original but an authentic expression of "nature itself of this national soil." "The nature of the island country," he observed, "which embodies a bottomless mystery, is none other than kannon which appears in human shape" (375). Behind Watsuji's pilgrimage, according to Noriko Aso, was the anxiety he felt over a contemporary Japan that was already crowded with cultural imports and the example of Japan's inaugural cultural moment which also appeared to have been imported from the continent.[52] What rescued Nara art from the status of mere copy to achieve the level of genuine originality was the experience embedded in its production. If Nara was able to escape the limitations of imitation, so could modern Japan.

The problem posed by Japan's commitment to the Enlightenment in the Meiji period was its fatal embrace of abstraction. Watsuji, together with other contemporaries, worried that what increasingly appeared was the domination of abstraction over the concrete in life and thought (WTZ, 4:293; also 303–307 for his attack on Enlightenment and socialism). The abstraction introduced by the Meiji period's enthusiastic welcoming of Enlightenment thought lacked a concern for and consideration of history. It seized only upon the opportunity to realize the "concrete thing" without carrying through this program, tending rather to exchange history and culture for the whole (zentai) (WT, 377). Enlightenment trajectories of progress ignored actual historical development for imagined stages structured by the whole. The danger of such abstraction was particularly extreme when considering the problem of Japanese culture. In its eagerness to plot the march of progress according to a presumed goal, it ignores and overlooks the concrete specificity of a national experience. For Watsuji, Enlightenment conceptions of history failed to appreciate Japan's unique cultural inheritance which, he explained, stems from the "diverse moments that are piled on top of each other stratigraphically." What he wanted to reject was a view of history that moves to the next stage and thus leaves behind what it has just passed over because it is less advanced. A German, who did not understand Japan's unique culture, was correct when he called Japan a "country of coexistence" (Nebeneinander). Yet proponents of Enlightenment rationality fail to imagine that history constitutes a layering of past strata on top of each other. These stratigraphic accretions are the condition of Japan's culture and anything else is simply unrealistic. In fact, the Enlightenment view of history sees no further than those immediate residues that somehow contribute to the achievement of reason.

In Watsuji's conception of history, nothing is ever lost, forgotten, or left behind. What determines forgetfulness are those principles that promote an abstract theory of historical development. Diverse and different stratigraphic strata representing moments of the past never lose their authority and immediacy, which must be kept alive by the device of layering that resembles the form of a palimpsest allowing each layer to filter through to the surface. Different cultural layers laying on top of each other supplied the promise of "overcoming" (*chōkoku*). "Bringing to life through things that have also overcome other things and are overcome themselves is the remarkable uniqueness of Japanese culture." In his inflection of the idea of overcoming, widespread in the 1930s, he wanted to emphasize how the *jūsōsei* made possible a structure that housed all of the layers in the same space even though they signified different temporalities. If he implied the movement of temporal succession, it did not imply progressive sublation, where each new stage incorporates elements from its predecessor as it moves to a higher and improved stage. What he was pointing to was a characteristic of the folk, to whom he attributed this remarkable impulse to persevere yet move on. The agents of Japanese culture "are probably nothing more than folk, like Japanese, who have taken in the new sensitively, and folk like Japanese who preserve ancient things faithfully" (377). The disposition to preserve determines that all things are appropriate to make such a choice, from the diverse forms of eating, shelter, clothing through the historical changes that have taken place in society, religion, arts, thought, economics, and politics.

Watsuji's favorite example of cultural preservation was the survival of the aristocracy. When the warrior class seized leadership in medieval Japan, he explained, the court nobles were retained, not eliminated. They were now respected as cultured aristocrats, conservers and custodians of ancient traditions. The culture of the fifteenth century was aristocratic in meaning, even though political control fell to the military estates. While the aristocracy was rejected politically, they continued in a new register as cultural leaders. Watsuji was convinced that this was true also of the Meiji epoch, where there was yet another burst of aristocratic vitality; even though a new political leadership was established, the older aristocracy continued to exist. Even now, he declared, aristocrats are active in society everywhere. No other country has seen the survival of aristocracy for over seven hundred years after it had lost its position of political leadership (378). The tenacity of aristocratic survival differentiated Japan's history from others; it also disclosed the mark of character that reflected the superiority of Japanese social values. Watsuji remained silent on the real reason for the survival of the aristocracy which owed its retention to the strategic role of the imperial house. His primary interest was to promote the relationship between the aristocracy and the production of culture, which had already been prefigured in his youthful essay on Dōgen.

What caught Watsuji's attention were the residues of everyday life—food, shelter, clothing—those things that made the category both primordial and unavoidable. Anybody could have a thorough knowledge of the forms of shelter, clothing, and eating that formed the fundamental components of daily life. Forms dating from three hundred years ago are not only preserved, they "unify stratigraphically" in a single life the diverse items developed between the warrior and popular classes. In his day, the diffusion of Western garments could simply add another layer on top of this accumulation to thereby disclose a style of existence characterized by "diversifying different clothes that have wrapped up the body" (WTZ, 4:315). But, he cautioned, this jumbling together of different-style clothing did not lead to either "eclecticism" or a "jettisoning" of the old for the new. Instead, it paved the way to a unification of disparate levels in the totality of everyday life which is called "double life." Life in Japan was always a double-layered structure, not simply composed of what was most immediate and recent; it was also a mixing of the past in the present and the accumulation of different strata representing earlier moments of folk experience. In clothing and architecture, he observed, Japanese live on two different layers. But the Western-style homes and clothes they have imported are not quite the same as those in Europe and the United States. This double structure, whose existence was revealed early in his account of the formation of ancient temples in Nara in the wake of the continental cultural impact, was produced by Japan's encounter with the modern West and simply affirmed a continuity with the past. If the house, for example, employs the Western form of the window, outer walls, and flooring, there is the *genkan*—that sturdy Japanese vestibule (where one announces departure and return)—which immediately calls attention to the fact that the house is really not Western. For Watsuji, these new "culture" houses "unified the double structure of forms in a single life" (4:315). Japanese-Western eclecticism is not a new form, as imagined, but a doubling, unifying two separate forms. If an older form and design is succeeded in the construction of a new building, it is not abandoned, lost, or even repressed; it merges with the new in order to realize a new life in situational structure.

Watsuji believed that if the perspective changed from a consideration of mundane things of daily life to culture, the layering effect was even more conspicuous. In religion, the most original forms of belief have persisted down to the present alongside later beliefs promoted by Buddhism and Christianity. Archaic, native religious practices have continued uninterrupted for over a thousand years along with world religions like Buddhism. The importance of this layering of religious faiths and the tenacious survival of beliefs from the archaic experience meant that the Japanese folk had not abandoned the original *matsuri*—the union of ceremony and governance—that had represented its wholeness since the beginning of the race. Although the present is amply filled with people devoted to preserving the original forms of belief, and with it the solidarity of the folk community, the past showed that there had never been reason for the folk to feel inferior to other cultures. Buddhism tried to realize the hegemony of its Law but when this failed, its belief system, which had permeated the "depth of experience" (*taiken*), resurfaced to produce the reformist and faith sects of the Kamakura period. "Where the originary forms are never abandoned," he asserted, "there we can see the uniqueness of character" (4:316). While Buddhism, as a "universal religion," has "murdered" ancestor worship as a national religious practice, Japanese have been reluctant to forgo the archaic beliefs and have even given them new life (see 4:317).

Throughout this discussion, Watsuji was committed to showing how the doubling of belief forms derived from a past that might, on the face of it, seem to appear both distant and disconnected from the present. But he was certain that, like those sturdy Buddhist temples erected in the Tempyō period (729–749 C.E.) that still elicit admiration in the present, the double structure meant that past and present were never incompatible. This recognition, in part, was shared by other contemporaries, like the native ethnologist Yanagita Kunio, who called attention to Japan's "hybrid civilization" that was being lived in the present. For both Watsuji and Yanagita, this perception of a double structure constituted the distinct mark of modernity introduced by the encounter with Western capitalism. The appeal to a national talent for creating a double structure worked to lessen Japan's dependence on the West, as it revealed a way for "overcoming" it. It also diminished the temporal difference dramatized by modernity, whereby the new was easily made to coexist with the old to create new forms of life. Watsuji explained that despite Japan's commitment to a vast transformation in the Meiji era, Japanese culture has not been created merely in response to the new and its demand to abandon the old. After the Restoration, the nation's *matsuri* was reflected in the veneration of shrines, exemplified in the construction of a great national monument called the Meiji Shrine to commemorate both Meiji and Taishō emperors. Even the clumsiest Japanese who plan public parks created a "superior thing" in this shrine. "The prosperity of the Ise Shrine is not any less today than at any other period in history" (4:318). (But Ise was rebuilt every twenty years.) Both are expressions of the Japanese folk and remind people that the past continues to persist in the present, not simply as a ruin and a lingering residue heading for extinction but as a living trace of an originary experience that demands renewal. Zen, he noted, had permeated the daily life of common people during the feudal age, but it still lives powerfully in the present with contemporary Japanese. If its form has changed somewhat over the ages, it still appears in the character and temperament of the Japanese people. The Meiji effort to destroy Buddhism has simply provided the opportunity to make contact with those things that are deeply rooted in communal relationships and offered the occasion to revive folk life. By the same measure, the arts illuminate the existence of this double structure (4:319)

The discovery of a double structure informing Japanese life and culture pointed to wholeness—one, he charged, that had been rejected by the Meiji eagerness to indiscriminately adopt Western culture. What the new regime sought to reject stimulated a sensitivity to and an awareness of its "independent character." The double structure refused to be repressed and returned, like the uncanny, to haunt modern Japan, challenging it to recognize a presence that had accompanied the folk since the beginning. Moreover, because it appeared as the uncanny it disturbed precisely those boundaries between past and present that Enlightenment Japan tried to delineate. Watsuji was also sure that this historic capacity for stratifying moments of the past to preserve them in each present was unparalleled among the nations of the world. It was what distinguished Japan as unique from other cultures and would prove to be the only way to grasp the "Japanese spirit" (4:290).

Watsuji saw the modern social order, based on the "socialization of interest," as retrograde rather than progressive. If "national awareness" entails a consciousness of a "national, collective society," as he believed, a society singly devoted to the pursuit of interest leads to a "regressive ethics" in the "destruction of collective life" and the "isolation of humans." What qualifies as truly progressive is serving a mission that must avoid any occasion that seeks to deny the highest experience of the human collectivity. National awareness means being entrusted with this mission. Watsuji did not necessarily call for an eradication of capitalism, even though he despaired its social consequences. Like many conservative contemporaries, he wanted capitalism without its social effects, without conflict, struggle, mass consumption, homogeneity, and alienation. But he was aware that there was still a difference between capitalism in Japan and in the West. Until recently, he remarked, the intensity of a "capitalist interest society" was a unique phenomenon among Westerners. Oriental society had no other meaning for the West than the location of its colonies. Japan's drive to excel as a capitalist society was seen as hindrance to the continuing development of Western "capitalistic-interest society" (4:290). In response to the "oppression" imposed by the demands of an "interest society," the country was quickly aroused into national awareness of its own survival. "Under such conditions, Japan became the pioneer in the world in this awakening to a national communal society that would check the development of interest society." Japan, he continued, "without knowing it," actually paved the way for a new kind of capitalist order that somehow would avoid the excesses of interest and desire and the conflict it produced. In his thinking, capitalism inevitably led to imperialist domination, driven by interest, yet Japan, already committed to a capitalist mode of production, had escaped the temptation of interest because its transformation had been driven by the necessity to survive and the desire to maintain the integrity of the national community. Proponents of Enlightenment who had theorized the development of interest society could not understand this pioneering "denial of denial," this negation of the negation, which meant seizing the occasion to uphold the primacy of the national community in the face of the imperialism of interest.

Watsuji, it is worth remembering, was advancing this interpretation precisely at the moment Japan was becoming embroiled in an imperial war in China. What he seemed to be advising was the retention of capitalism but in a different form, one that resembled either the capitalism of the corporatist state or a folk or gemeinschaft capitalism (both of which, which were not mutually exclusive, were shared by contemporaries) that simply recommended that Japanese remain Japanese despite the "Europeanization of technology" (4:291). The subject that uses this technology, he declared, is not "Europeanized" (4:292).

Only Japan, then, was fully capable of challenging Western industrial capitalism promoted under the "banner" of liberalism and free trade and exemplified in the nineteenth century by Great Britain. But Japan appealed to an ideology that promised to overcome liberalism, one founded on proclaiming the promise of a "national community." In Watsuji's thinking, this ideology appeared as a "new formation" that Europeans had not sufficiently clarified. The meaning of the "Japanese spirit" unveiled the truth of Japan's capacity to develop a capitalist economic system yet retain its folkic character. Present-day Japan took precedence over other, advanced countries because it pointed to a new inflection of capitalism. Just as liberalism had toppled the "feudal tradition," so has it come to be itself viewed in the present as a force of "reaction" when compared to the "Japanese spirit." Both contemporary socialists and liberals, he acknowledged, considered invocations of the "Japanese spirit" reactionary and retrograde, especially its intensely nationalistic component. He was furthermore aware that many saw in it a staging platform for fascism that would "strengthen the stranglehold of the bourgeoisie" (4:293) and provide a powerful instrument to political movements of a decidedly "conservative and reactionary" bent (4:294). But all of these fears exposed only how insufficiently understood was the meaning of "national realization" summoned by the motto "Japanese spirit." The idea of the "Japanese spirit" had to be seen in its concrete "manifestation" and "expression." For this reason, it was unimportant to grasp the actions of the Japanese people in general as expressions of the spirit. The concrete criteria of manifest action were demonstrations of patriotic loyalty (*chūkun aikoku*), service to emperor and country (*kunkoku*) and self-sacrifice

(4:295). Any action that led to the realization of these principles illuminated the "Japanese spirit." Such displays of spirit were not limited merely to the classic forms of political loyalty and could be found throughout the life forms of the Japanese folk. Cultural producers like Dōgen and the No dramatist Zeami were just as effective as examples of spirit as a singular act of political loyalty serving the imperial cause. Watsuji was careful to make this distinction, which, while valorizing the individual culture hero, worked also to reinforce the importance of spectacular but single acts of heroism. The actor of all these actions disclosing the spirit was the Japanese folk. Even though the act might be committed by an individual, it constituted the performance of the folk, one that reflected "human relationality" (4:296). Just as Hegel's spirit employed outstanding individuals to further its purpose (usually left behind as mere "husks" once the deed was accomplished), so the act that disclosed the movements of the "Japanese spirit" was "a social act," one that was carried out only within a certain set of relationships (*nakama*), not in society (*seken*). If an act is to count, it must appear as the expression of folk life (4:297).

In the context of this discussion, Watsuji raised the question of Japan's involvement in imperial adventures in China and formulated the argument for its disavowal. Although this disavowal was made more explicit in his *Fūdo* (written before the publication of *Zoku Nihon seishinshi kenkyū*), he had no trouble linking, in this text, the so-called Shanghai Incident[53] to social acts expressing the working of the "Japanese spirit." It is important to see how Watsuji actually misrecognized Japanese imperial and colonial activity. If, as suggested earlier, he identified colonialism with Western "interest society," then he would have to find another explanation to account for Japan's long-standing involvement in Formosa, Korea, and, more recently, Manchuria and China. Convinced that these "incidents" had nothing to do with interest, he was equally persuaded that they represented relationships that were neither imperialistic nor colonizing. The various heroic deeds performed by Japanese to constitute the "incident" (enacted by the "Three Brave Bombers") "shouldered the phenomenal meaning of an expression of the Japanese spirit." The charge that Japanese committed "violating acts" against the Chinese could not be "seriously considered beyond this," by which he meant that the "incident," as Japanese officially called such imperial episodes, could not be seen as anything less than a disclosure of the folk spirit, not as an act of aggression against a sovereign people. In this account the Chinese were seen as faceless objects. "Since the manifestation of the Japanese spirit is nothing other than the expression of the folkic life of the Japanese, the Shanghai Incident itself must be acknowledged, here, as one expression of this great, folk life" (4:297–298). What is important to this misrecognition is how Watsuji sought to blur the distinction between acts committed against other peoples, like Chinese, and those inscribed in life and culture, so that both constituted moments of the "Japanese spirit." It did not seem to matter to him whether the folk produced an artifact for everyday life and a monument of culture or whether they performed abroad in violent acts against other people. The action of the Japanese people, he never tired of saying, was not limited to foreign affairs but reached all regions of life and culture. The route to the "Japanese spirit" was through the culture realized everywhere there was Japanese life (*seikatsu*) (4:298).

If the manifestation of spirit is grasped through "expression" of Japanese culture, its movement raises the question of the subject that has realized it in any given moment. "The subject that creates Japan's culture is none other than Japanese nation (*kokumin*)" or "folk" (4:298). To refer to the Japanese spirit is to refer to the Japanese folk as the subject. Watsuji agreed that if the idea of a Japanese spirit is premised on the opposition between "spirit" and "materiality," it would not be possible to identify the "subjective folk" as the "wholeness" of life. A position based on grasping only the Japanese spirit will instantiate the spirit in its material appearance. Originally, spirit was living, subjective matter (nature?), not yet separated from the "self-objectification of the subject." The "subjective flesh in the position of the individual" corresponded to the subjective climate, culture, and nature of the subjective folk. Spirit showed itself in this materiality, not as an object, as such, but as a manifestation of the folk subject through objects, transacted through the mediation of the "historical, climatic, and cultural structure of human existence." When human existence is merely grasped in general and separated from the conditions of folkic uniqueness, it will fail to see the important meaning of subjective climate and culture in the formation of communities and thus understand "historicality" (*rekishisei*) as an abstraction. Recalling Kuki's powerful argument linking contingence to exceptionalism, Watsuji declared that the circumstances of folk uniqueness were not "contingent, trifling things," but rather the most fundamental rules governing human existence, pointing to its primordial conditions where spirit first realized itself. In this respect, the Japanese spirit was similar to the spirits of Greece and Germany (4:300).

What is grasped is what is past, not something that has not yet been realized. Yet because culture and climate are at the heart of a specific human existence, it is impossible to understand the sense of the past in isolation, separated from the present and the future. The past is a moment that moves on to become included in the future. At the same time, the past places limits on what can be done in the future. Michelangelo, he explained, appealed to the sculpture of Greece and Rome as background to his own work, yet he recognized the impossibility of breaking the ground of new creativity by following the same path (4:302). The rejection of traditions, after they have been grasped, constitutes the sign of the most powerful continuity of traditions. Nowhere was this more true than in the relationship between the past and the cultural production of the folk. Moreover, the role of the past and tradition meant that those who come after not only will be constrained in what they do but will carry on the work of spirit even if it is not their intention to do so. Even a movement that rejects the label of the Japanese spirit, he insisted, will still manifest it if it is within the circumstances of a specific human existence. A Japanese who rejects the "Japanese thing" in any cultural endeavor is simply not able to create something that is not Japanese (4:321).

Watsuji was confident that Japanese, by the same token, would not be able to get outside of the Japanese thing, regardless of where they lived. Here, he exposed the unarticulated relationship between race and culture, which Kuki's theory of contingence tried to sidestep. The exceptional character of culture, deriving from history and climate, the most primordial conditions of human existence, necessitated the study of spiritual history and climate and culture (*fūdogaku*), a new discipline, contrasted to conventional social science and historiography, that promised to illuminate the self of Japanese spirit in all of its concreteness. The purpose of the new discipline would be to make up for what has been lacking in the received human sciences and to examine how climate (place) imbricated culture (race). It provided a method that would permit reading Japan's earliest experience as the formation of national community and nation. For, he was confident, self-realization must not be neglected if the Japanese folk is to carry out its "world historical destiny" (4:321, 300). The identity of Japan's "destiny" in world history urges upon the present a realization of "unprecedented importance."

Character Culturized

Watsuji's purpose was to establish a proper study of culture and climate that would be sensitive to the concrete, primordial conditions of Japanese existence. Even in 1935, he feared it was too late for the establishment of "this direction in the learning of Japan" as he "eagerly awaited the effort of superior young students who were physically strong enough" to carry on this project (4:321). He had already charted the course of such study in a series of articles written between 1927 and 1928 on the character of culture and climate, which he subsequently published as a book (*Fūdo*) in 1935. By the time the book appeared, Japan was embroiled in China, had seized Manchuria four years earlier, and was soon (1937) to become involved in the "Marco Polo Bridge Incident," which would plunge the country into full-scale war with China. The new discipline, an amalgam of philosophical anthropology, ontology, geography, and ethnographic reporting mixed with travel observations sought to formulate the principles governing the formation of human existence. Its focus was to elucidate the relationship of climate and culture in specific locations. Watsuji's book indulged in broad portrayals of national/racial character, similar to work being done elsewhere in the United States, Germany, and France, which too often employed culture and character as a stand-in for race. His initial articulation of principles ultimately led to a study of American character published during World II.

Watsuji's return voyage to Japan after a study tour in Europe in the late 1920s prefigured a national narrative for Japanese identity composed of an accumulated synthesis of "other climates, cultures, and peoples" he had viewed as moments "toward a final objective."[54] Clearly, his narrative was a doubling of his voyage back to Japan, inverting the Hegelian prototype, to change the direction of its movement along the East-West axis. While he journeyed by ship from west to east (reversing Spirit's course), the movement also took into consideration the status of the North-South axis, especially in the long chapter where he compared desert climate to meadow culture and tried to explain those vast regions Hegel had dismissed as unworthy of world history. But in Watsuji's meditations, this stood as a missed opportunity since the North-South axis appeared as little more than a caesura in a movement from west to east, a momentary dip or detour in the journey that led inexorably to home, Japan's identity, and its difference. It is interesting to note that he often re-expressed earlier Hegelian conceits about the various peoples and cultures his trip took him through. He was very self-conscious about his relationship to Hegel, and in a genealogy he supplied for his study of *fūdosei*, which ranged from the Greeks to the present, he acknowledged his debt to the Hegelian model (8:170–241, especially 226–227). Like Hegel, he was interested in identifying the world historical destiny of Japan through an analysis of its climatic conditions and cultural formation. Hegel taught Watsuji the importance of geographical place, the land, not simply as an "external region" but as the "natur typus" (*jikata no shizenkei*)—the natural type of location intimately connected to the folk who are the "children of the land." In this light, geography, in its broadest environmental climatic definition, constituted a source for understanding subject formation and subjectivity. What was important to his own program was Hegel's observation that " 'the character of the folk is nothing other than the way by which they secure the land there in order to enter world history.' " (Watsuji cited the quote from Hegel, 4:2:30). Acknowledging the elegance of a project pointing to the "climate and culture of spirit," he was persuaded that the "difference of nature" that accounts for the "unique possibility by which spirit develops" is never "contingent." The significance of Hegel was neither in what he had to say about the Orient, on which he had no reliable knowledge, nor in his identification of world history with the West. Rather, its importance lay in a method that established the geographical bases of cultures like China and India and permitted consideration of different types of nature outside of Europe (4:232).

In a related way, Watsuji was also interested in the status of Japan's world historical destiny in the present, like Hegel, who was riveted to his present and the importance of Prussia in the history of freedom. If his itinerary took him back to Japan, literally and metaphorically, it was, for him, a place that was unique yet beset by the problems introduced by modernity and its own strategies of splitting. The purpose of his long, characterological analysis in *Fūdo* appears in one of his last chapters, dealing with Japan's uniqueness, titled "Nihon mezurashiisa" (Japan's strangeness) (8:156–169). Upon his return to Japan, he encountered the strangeness of what he had left and believed to be a familiar place. This strangeness was as dramatic as anything he had observed in the Arabian desert and thus made Japan seem as unfamiliar and unique (*mezurashii-mono*) as anything in the world.[55] Etymologically, he reduced the meaning of the word to the "unusual," "unordinary," "rare" (8:157; CC, 157). What appeared odd and strange to him upon returning was the shock of recognizing that the familiar life he had lived in Japan for so many years had remained the same yet now faced him as a way of life that was fundamental but not fully understood, much less perceived, by him. In other words, he confronted his "home" and saw it for the first time. But it is important to emphasize that he was perceiving something that was "rare" that needed to be grasped, even though he had lived it. "We are used to seeing cars and tramways in everyday Japan," he wrote; "these are either imports from the West or copies [we have made]. But that we Japanese would feel a strangeness with these things would not be normal today. Traveling to Europe, we would not feel strange when encountering trains and cars. Rather we would be surprised by the dirtiness of the taxis and the smallness of the trains. . . . When I returned to Japan, I saw cars and trams on the streets and felt they were like wild boars rampaging through wheatfields." The electric trams dwarfed the houses lining the tracks and resembled commoners who prostrated themselves to appear "spiritless" as a *daimyō* retinue passed by them. The passing tram, taller than a single-story house and longer than its front, obliterates a view of the houses on the other side of the street. The sky above the roof of the tram can be seen. But even cars on Japanese streets, he reported, seemed to be large and outsized. "In smaller streets, the car stretches out like a whale in a canal and is higher than the eaves of a house" (8:158; CC, 158). By contrast, cars and trams appear smaller than houses in Europe and are seen primarily as instruments of communication and transportation, like retainers subordinated to humans or the towns. However, towns in Japan have become the "retainers" or tools of these modes of transport, which oppress humans, and towns.

There are a number of interesting implications in this observation. We must recognize how Watsuji recalls Tokugawa or feudal Japan as a trope. The disproportionate size of cars and trams makes them masters to towns and houses, who must serve in the capacity of "retainers." Moreover, the towns and houses cower, prostrated, as if the cars and trams were lordly masters in a procession. In Europe, by contrast, these modes of transportation are merely instruments. This retention of feudal servitude, now yoked to modern, technological instruments, suggests that Japanese had merely exchanged masters when they decided to become modern. Equally important for Watsuji was the relative scale and the differences it produced in Japan and Europe. He worried about the imbalance these outsized machines caused and how recognition of it stunned him upon return. The absence of balance appeared "strange," and this fact impressed upon him how much he had not seen before and how little he understood. In fact, the perception of "imbalance" (I think unevenness is a better marker) reflected the "complicated disunity of Japan's modern civilization we have felt for a long time" (8:159; CC, 159). What had been there all along, like Poe's purloined letter, was simply never seen, and this seemed to bother Watsuji as much as its eventual recognition.

Japanese widened roads and made communications easier to satisfy convenience, even though it aggravated the balance between town and house, car, tram, and road. By contrast, European roads showed an imbalance between densely packed streets, lined with large apartment buildings, whereas in Japan roads were spacious (after the earthquake), lined with low lying houses that, because of the climate, collected debris driven by the wind. "The wide roads were carried to the extreme of extravagance," he complained, "and opening up to a widening sky, they hold back the houses which are infinitely more meager than anything in Europe." Here, Watsuji lamented how the roads in Japan were not tools of transportation but extravagant commodities produced to make human life painful without knowing the reason. At the heart of these roads was the ceaseless process of widening and leveling the structure of Japan's cities. "If New York is the best example in the world of a city suffering from height, Tokyo is the best example in the world of a city suffering from width" (8:160; CC, 160). There was more horizontal sprawl than vertical lift. The land space covered by housing is far greater than that of Paris, thereby requiring facilities (drainage/sewer system, transport, etc.) in excess of those in any other modern city. Hence, the greater the city in Japan, the greater the inconvenience. While city life requires greater economic and psychological extravagance and waste, living (*seikatsu*) is less agreeable. Clothing, he observed, reflects the imbalance of city and house.

In the midst of these vast, slouching cities like Tokyo, the Japanese house becomes a "grotesquerie," whose smallness is devoured by the immense space of the city. Many contemporaries have proposed that the imbalance stemmed from economic factors since, it was believed, Japan was not as wealthy as many European countries and was thus incapable of putting up high-rise structures. If one considers the amount of time and money wasted on widening Japan's cities, the economic argument is difficult to accept.

In Watsuji's thinking, a more probable cause for the unevenness lay in the absence of "collective" and "cooperative" action in the cities, which, he was convinced, was a more convenient and agreeable method that demonstrated the real meaning of the cities. He explained that the absence of such cooperative action was caused by separating the house from the street and distancing what is within and without (8:161; CC, 161). On the outside, the house is detached from the street, and inside it is partitioned by *shōji* and *fusuma*, but not absolutely. Japanese within the house have no "independent rooms" (8:163; CC, 164), and this is the reason they do not feel the necessity of protecting the self against others, because "there was no separation of the self from others." Under this circumstance, there was no need for keys (8:164; CC, 165). Yet the European house was open to the outside world, reaching out to eventually include the whole town. Accordingly, this arrangement worked to diminish the meaning of the house, leaving only the "individual" and "society."

Hence, the Japanese house stands as the preserve of communal living, which accounts for the desire to maintain a firm separation from the outside world. But in Europe, this outside world constituted the social space where individuals constantly interact with each other. Where Europeans erected walls to separate the city from the surrounding countryside in the past, they have in modern times resorted to fixing national boundaries. Neither of these has existed in Japan. The difference could be explained by referring to the specific conditions of Japan's climate and culture, which prompted the development of a style of living constrained by close confinement within the house, while Europeans, experiencing a different climate, were disciplined by a practice of walling off their towns from others. Within these walled enclaves, the need for common protection led to cooperation—social life—which, in turn, further stimulated the growth of individuality, and with it the recognition of rights and obligations. For Japanese, the "small world" within the fence marking the property on which the house sits was not directed toward an enemy that might endanger life within but rather encouraged the shaping of a collectivity. This collective was "founded on natural affection that easily could draw out an attitude of self-sacrifice" (8:164; CC, 165). In this world the individual gladly effaced the personal self for others in order to feel more keenly the suffering of life. But if cooperation began only with the individual who realized its meaning, then it was natural that the individual who effaces himself/herself would not necessarily develop an ideal of cooperation in this small world. Affection and self-sacrifice could never have produced an idea of the social based on the recognition of mutual obligations and personal interests. "People did not advocate personal rights (*kenri*) nor develop an awareness of obligations in communal life" (8:165; CC, 166). In Europe, the symbols of life were the "castle wall" and the "key"; in Japan, affection and self-sacrifice. As a result, Japanese came to privilege feelings appropriate to their circumstances: sympathy, modesty, reserve, and considerateness. These sentiments were restricted to the small world of the house and never reached the "unaffectionate" world outside. In the world outside the house, Japanese would behave "unsociably," since the fence encircling the house was the limit of the social space. Watsuji envisaged the Japanese house as a microcosm of the European city.

The persistence of these small, enclosed houses in a world dominated by Europeanization and Americanization generated a "strange imbalance" (*mezurashii fuwariai*) that communicated the experience of a past from which Japanese can never be separated. Watsuji's projection of a perceivable imbalance was simply a recoding of the cultural and economic unevenness many contemporaries associated with the modernizing process. The survival of the Japanese house, and all its associations, merely meant that the past still existed in the present and that Japanese had made no disruptive break with it in their pursuit of capitalist modernization (8:166; CC, 167). People wear Western clothes, walk on asphalt roads in leather shoes, ride in cars and trams, and carry on business on any floor of a Western-style building. Is there anything left of Japan? he asked rhetorically. Even though the Japanese house was based on a newer Western design, the interiors still summon the past in the gate, the fence, the *genkan*, since the Japanese can never do without taking off their shoes once they enter the vestibule. Nothing essential to the Japanese house has been lost.

For Watsuji, unevenness called attention to the double structure of modern life. Although Japanese, even in a modern setting, often convey a sense of indifference toward the outside world—the world that belongs to others—this attitude is inscribed in indifference to politics and politicians, however corrupt and inept. Since "society does not belong to the self," "its life," the life of the ordinary Japanese, appears not to have been even slightly Europeanized (8:167; CC, 167–168). He dismissed both politics and political life as an activity monopolized by a few "specialists," and the proletarian movement, which was made up only of a group of leaders. All of this indifference to an outer world showed that Japanese cannot relate to anything outside of themselves and their immediate group, that despite whatever changes introduced from the outside, Japanese, owing to the dual compartmentalization of life, could remain uniquely as Japanese, like their ancestors since the beginning of the race. The double structure provided them with a perspective with which to contrast what was substantive, essential to what was merely superficial, just as it would compel them to constantly recognize cultural differences between themselves and others because of the specific experience of climate and culture.

At the heart of this unique double structure was a conception of climate and culture that would fix the primordial conditions of existence that formed the group into a distinct collective. Watsuji's appeal to *fūdosei* promised to demonstrate Japan's essential difference. So embedded is this primordial structure that Japanese are able to "see" their true selves in the flurry of modern, everyday activities, whether or not they are conscious of it. Following the powerful philosophic mediations of Nishida, he was convinced that nature was identified with nothingness (*mu*), non-Being. But rather than follow it to the place of "pure experience," or indeed to the articulation of a rationalistic view that saw nature as the object of domination, he proposed that it accompanies and deeply imbricates the construction of human relationships. The self was not outside of nature but was embraced within it. This move necessitated considering human relationships within nature and envisaging the role it played in producing those activities so necessary to the maintenance of daily life, such as customs, habit, and mores. For Watsuji, nature constituted an original habitus whose memory was inscribed in the specific form of human relationships a community would select that would continue to be accessible throughout history. This led to the Heideggerian "imperative" of returning to those primordial conditions attending the formation of the human community—its basic "ownness," which referred to its everydayness and its enabling conditions. While this pursuit resembled a philosophical anthropology, Watsuji actually rejected this category of reflection because it erred in concentrating excessively on the human species and thus risked "abstracting" "man" from specific human relationships. His primary concern was human relationships (*ningen*)—man within the world.[56]

Hence, his exposition of climate and culture, linked to his later theory of ethics, emphasized the centrality of relationality between people, which, he believed, would serve as a solution to the contemporary preoccupation with individuality and the status of the self. Its obvious purpose was to bring the person back to the totality, to the authorizing community, which had been the condition of original existence and experience. Watsuji wanted to remind his contemporaries that this experience was prior to and the source of any conception of the individual self. But to turn to the totality and community required reconsidering and resituating the relationship between space and time, which also was inflected into the climate, culture, and history that ultimately constituted the specific group. It was important for him to show that the originary condition of human existence was the totality, not the individual self or the sovereign subject; the relations between people, not their solitary isolation. Without ever saying so, this conviction also meant returning to a specific point of origin in the East and Japan. The relationships between people, which held them as a collectivity within nature, were superior to a dialectic between humans and nature propelled by a struggle of the former to dominate the latter. This difference reflected the intervention of differing climates and cultures that demanded an examination of human society within specific environments.[57]

Although the examination was undoubtedly inspired by Heidegger's *Sein und Zeit* (stemming from his study tour in Germany), Watsuji's reading constituted an important, critical supplement to Heidegger's emphasis on understanding Dasein's existence as a temporal experience. In fact, Watsuji's critique, which would remain unknown in the Western philosophic discourse on Heidegger until well after World War II (even its translation has been unread by philosophers), went a long way to rescuing Heidegger's formulation from the very subject-centeredness it was seeking to eliminate from metaphysics. Despite the ends his reading served, and they were comparable to the complaints of Heidegger's "political ontology," his own meditations represented an important intervention that sought to spare Heidegger from falling into the error he condemned Western metaphysic for having committed. Watsuji was quick to point out that Heidegger's account of human existence lacked sociological and historical specificity; he explained why the role of space, which was virtually ignored, was sacrificed to temporality as a determining factor. Although the German philosopher had not been insensitive to questions of space, its involvement virtually disappeared with the "strong illumination of temporality." "I saw the limitations of Heidegger's method. A temporality unconnected to spatiality was not true temporality. The reason Heidegger stopped there was because his Dasein persisted in never going beyond the individual. He grasped human existence by way of the existence of man. When this is seen from the standpoint of the double structure, social and individual, of human existence, it does not get beyond only an abstract single phase. When human existence there is grasped in its concrete double structure, temporality comes to correspond to spatiality. Historicality, which does not appear sufficiently concrete in Heidegger, is thus also directly presented in its true guise" (8:1; CC, v, vi). Even the Heideggerian "historicality" is connected to climate and culture.

If Heidegger had differentiated temporality from the space of nature, rooting Dasein's existence in it, Watsuji situated existence within nature and thereby privileged space (and place) over the domination of time, which now would conform to nature's clock. But nature, here, was simply climate and environment. This natural environment "enwraps" humans. Humans experience natural phenomena through the mediations of a relational structure that binds them to each other. When feeling the cold, he explained, it is not a subject (*shukan*)—we—that feels it. It is not outside, nor is it a thing (*mono*) or an object like "cold weather." When cold is felt, we ourselves are "lodged in the coldness of the outside air." Because humans come into a relationship with the cold means that they are outside. "That we ourselves are connected to the cold is nothing more than that we have gone out to the cold. Heidegger called this ex-sistere—being out there—or intentionality." "Moreover," he continued, "it is not only I who experiences this cold but we in common." This commonality is merely another way of referring to "relationality" (*aidagara*); feeling the cold in common is simply anticipating we "ourselves" as a relation of humans who are cold (TJC, 5:150). We, not the cold, are outside, not the "I," as such, but "we" (WTZ, 8:10; CC, 2–3, 4). The we exists in a mutual relationship that is discovered in the cold. There is no subject here who enjoys the flowers, who feels cold and hot. The experience does not belong to the subject. In a relationship to the cold or indeed any natural phenomenon, we put forth individually and socially various means to protect us against the cold (8:11; CC, 5). Hence, the we focuses not on the subject but rather on the particular natural phenomenon.

What Watsuji hoped to realize with this formulation was the identity of the collective (perhaps expanding upon Heidegger's *mitsein*—"being with"), being there in nature, rather than differentiating subject from phenomena. Climate is experienced in a relationship to the plain, topographical scenery of a region, that is, its *fūdo*. We discover ourselves, anticipate ourselves relationally. Climate and culture point to the one way that the relationality of human existence realizes itself (TJC, 5:151). The fixed form of the house that is constructed is the realization of human self-anticipation of climate and culture (WTZ, 8:13; CC, 6–7). *Fūdo* is neither subject nor object but the way humans express self-anticipation. Although the movement of self-anticipation is historical, it must, at the same time, correspond to climate and culture. Neither a separate history nor *fūdo* is possible. But as Tosaka observed, this relationship could not be explained from the "developmental historical relationship of nature and society" (TJC, 5:152). In fact, the idea of *fūdo* took on the role of a humanistic stand-in for nature; space was more important to it than time because *fūdo* was nothing more than place, which structures everything one desires, like certain foods when hungry (WTZ, 8:13; CC, 7). Watsuji called this the "space of living" (8:237–238), while Tosaka described it as "a subjectivized, humanized nature," naturalizing what, in fact, was not natural (TJC, 5:152). Yet the operation guaranteed the fixity of certain characteristics he considered essential to Japan's unchanging identity and its claims to uniqueness. The very "relationality" produced by a specific environment was seen as natural, fixed for all time, because it had developed under the original constants of climate and culture. But regardless of this immense effort to cloak the historical with vestments of nature, the idea of *fūdo* was as much a historical construct as it was an enduringly natural endowment, historical inasmuch as it belonged to a specific time (as against place) as a set of conditions.

Watsuji insisted that the formation of a collective attitude appeared only after the dispersion of individual entities, as if it represented an advanced stage in an evolutionary trajectory. Dispersions and union were "subjectivistic practices," self-generating and practical, but could not occur through the action of a "subjectivistic body." Accordingly, temporality and spatiality structure the movement from fragmentation to union, a movement that must always take place in a specific time and space. Paradoxically, he seemed to terminate this "movement" once the Japanese reached the stage of "relationality," at which point history gave in to nature. Temporality and spatiality are inseparable, leading to a "double life," he asserted, and any "intention" to grasp only the dimension of time as the structuring agency and structure of human existence will collapse into a view that detects human existence simply at the level of individual consciousness. "When the double structure is grasped as the essence of humanity, then it is immediately clear that spatiality must at the same time correspond to temporality" (8:15; CC, 9–10). Union and the collective attitude humans produce are systems that develop intrinsically into fixed orders; they are not static but active and moving. By the same measure, the double structure of temporality and spatiality are transformed into "climatic and cultural historicality." The inseparability of time and space is registered in the inseparable relationship between history and climate/culture. Social structure is impossible without a subjective humanity. "But a temporality not founded on social existence could never become [true] historicality" (8:16; CC, 9). It was important to demonstrate precisely the interdependent relationship between history and sociality and how they evolved in time. Although this orientation contrasted with Heidegger's theory of "repetition" by implying the possibility of some sort of developmental schema, it actually produced the same result since the double structure was a stratigraphic gesture that served as a retentional system.

The union of historicality (the decision on the group's destiny) and climate/culture supplies history with its flesh and body (*nikutai*). If spirit were opposed to matter, history would never have been able to embody its self-development. Spirit creates history only when it is a subject that objectifies itself, only when it includes the subjective flesh and body. In short, the subjective flesh and body, by which Watsuji was identifying the acting agent as against the passive, observing, and knowing subject (*shukan*), is climate and culture. Inverting the usual Hegelian order of things, Watsuji made *fūdosei* the creator of history, as against a disembodied spirit struggling to free itself from nature or its surrogates, individuals and class (8:16; CC, 10–11). Climate and culture has flesh, body, and the subjective power to generate self-activity. The fundamental meaning of the relationship between mind and body and its putative division is repaired in the relationship between body and mind of "humans" as it is grounded in their social relationships, which includes history and climate/culture (8:18; CC, 11–12). In this way, history and climate/culture are inscribed in the individual and social body/mind (*jishin*) relationship. Because humans must discover themselves in climate and culture, as individuals, they recognize immediately that they are not alone and act in concert in speaking, producing, constructing certain styles of building and creating the form of community. "Climate and culture, then, is the occasion *(keiki)* by which human existence objectifies itself . . . anticipates and discovers itself in climate and culture" (8:20; CC, 16). Humans stand outside, in climate, and are thus compelled to devise the means of protection against the elements, which means making tools "for doing something," recalling Heidegger's conception of the "nearest at hand" (8:19). But climate and culture is always "historical climate and culture" (8:16; CC, 8, 9).

To concretize the general role played by history and *fūdo* in shaping human existence, it was necessary to specify those climatic characteristics involved in the making of discrete human groups. This was a problem of typologizing climatic zones, as if they were powerful tropes (tropics) capable of condensing the fullness and complexity of different experiences into tidy summaries. Watsuji was correct in warning that grasping the ways of human life existentially would not lead directly, if at all, to understanding the diverse types of characteristic forms of existence, as Heidegger had implied. All ontology is capable of providing is "methodological guidance" to the existential comprehension as something that mediates understanding. Heidegger, as suggested earlier, was silent on the specific historical and sociological conditions Dasein encountered in its existence. Watsuji saw this lack as a crucial deficiency, as he did Dasein's "individuality," and offered his conception of "historical climate and culture" as a resolution. To comprehend existence in its distinctiveness, it was necessary to confront "existential understanding" directly, which required an "intimate understanding of historical and climatic phenomena" (8:22; CC, 16). Clearly, this was no Hegelian journey rolling over continents until it came to rest in Prussia. Rather, it was more the expression of how humans encountered their climate, resolved their destiny in response, and produced history.

This history, however, was locked in space, bound to a particular place, as formation was its destiny. The indelible characteristics a particular group develops come from the encounter with climate and mark them for all time to come. Since climate in a specific zone would always repeat itself, the historical response could never be other than what it had been in the inaugural moment the archaic group evolved those distinctive characteristics that permitted it to "exist on the outside" and reproduce itself indefinitely. Watsuji's appeal to "historical climate and culture" was meant to supply an alternative to the Hegelian stages that announced spirit's momentary progress to its final destination. Yet, in a curious but unintentional replication, "historical climate and culture" slipped rapidly into fast-frozen stereotypes rooted in the immobility of place; the stereotypes were as lifeless as the sublated stages. If, for Hegel, China was the land of "eternal standstill" or India a country mired in absolute subjectivity and negativity, they would remain chained to nature in Watsuji's philosophical anthropology by an unchanging climate and culture that could only repeat the original historical encounter and its characteristic response with the same forms imposed by "wind and water." Although he, unlike Hegel, hoped for a Chinese revival and a "return to the greatness of Han and Tang cultures," he acknowledged that the Chinese would have to look to the "culture Japan kept alive internally, which was the kernel of Chinese culture from the Jin to the end of the Han and Tang dynasties" (8:133–134; CC, 133). The fragmentation of contemporary Chinese society, which somehow must be overcome by the Chinese people themselves in the interest of restoring prior cultural greatness, was produced by a specific monsoon climate that made Chinese indifferent to any restraints other than those based on blood or regional association (8:124; CC, 123).

In the world there were three major climatic zones: monsoon (Asia, including Japan, in part), desert (North Africa, the Middle East), and meadow (Mediterranean Europe). By extension, the United States, given the character he ascribed to it, was an extension of European/meadow culture. The monsoon belt was clearly the most important climate zone, as it embraced most of East Asia, especially China and Japan (he had nothing to say about Korea). The various cultural formations of this region broadly shared common climatic features so as to differentiate the region with a distinctive way of life. Driven by a summertime wind, blowing landward from the Indian Ocean, monsoon Asia is characterized by a combination of intense heat and humidity. Owing to a fusion of extreme heat and moisture, the humanity that occupies the region spends most of its energy trying to resist the stifling atmosphere. Humidity produces weak resistance to an environment that is lush and enervating. Watsuji proposed that the relationship between humans and their world in this region is not one of resistance but rather of resignation. By contrast, the desert, which is just as harsh in its own way, produces opposite relationships. The sense of weakness dominating the monsoon region is reinforced by the violence of nature: powerful downpours, storms and floods, and periodic droughts that constitute part of the experience of everyday life and have continued since the beginning of the human community. Nature's power is so vast that people are cowed into passive resignation. Areas as different as Japan and South China, however, introduced variations to the characteristic of resignation and submissiveness. India and the countries of Southeast Asia represent true monsoon culture, with India being the most faithful example. Here, nature is most oppressive, creating a "fullness of feeling" that can never lead to unifying will power (8:30–31; CC, 27). Spiritual power was privileged over physical prowess; the warrior was also the priest. But in time, the priest became more important. Tribal humanity in India differed strikingly from its counterpart in the desert, which was warlike. The gods in India never belonged to a single tribe. The powers of nature that bless all equally do not "rouse" humans to resist, as does the monotheistic god of the desert monopolized by a single tribe. In this lethargic world, history is replaced by the repetitive movements of transmigration; only individuals have undergone transformations from present to present; and all exists in an eternal present. Watsuji interpreted this "conjuncture" of a sense of resignation linked to the idea that life was always full as the source of Indian receptivity. Hegel believed that together they created a dream world; Watsuji, a "fantasy world" greater than dreams. In fact, the linkage made the Indian a representation of oppression, even though the conditions of oppression are nowhere in sight. In Shanghai and Hong Kong, where Westerners flaunted their power, there was no sign of the Chinese shrinking before them in intimidation and oppression. They often appeared as the victors rather than vanquished. But the Indians immediately disclosed a lack of aggressiveness that cowed them into obsequious humans and stimulated the visitor to desire for them a struggle for independence. Watsuji appeared as the traveling subject or theory traveling, the observer who was in a position to judge the Indian as physically weak compared to Chinese and even Western workers (8:42–43; CC, 38). Although this spectacle inspires and even draws out "our own, aggressive character," his heart was nevertheless pained because of this submission to oppression. As the subject who knows, Watsuji believed that the character of a people cannot be changed overnight since it derives from climate and culture. Change, he announced, must depend upon the conquest of *fūdo*, which required recognizing the importance of climate in character formation. Only when humans become aware of the force of *fūdo* will they be able to leave the grip of climate and culture. Yet, it is important to note that he was disclosing a privileged knowledge (which he never explained) that will free some societies from the enslavement of *fūdo* they have known since the beginning of the race. How this knowledge is secured he never said, any more than why Japanese are exempted from the charge of imperialism.

Improving on Hegel, Watsuji felt obliged to include some of those neglected peoples and regions like the Arabs and the Middle East. Despite the desire to include this vast part of the world in his inventory, it is a place where nothing manages to live. It is empty, barren, infertile, harsh, and even abstract, even though it does not lack history and society. Those who live in the desert might understand its character least. "The awakening of humanity is usually realized through an other" (8:45; CC, 41). It is the traveler, not the man of the desert, who is in a better position to understand the "concreteness" of its life forms. Specifically, "the "tourist" will recognize the historical and social reality of the desert in which he plays no part as he passes through. Ironically, Watsuji seemed to suspend the hermeneutic privilege that demanded immersion, which had characterized so much of his writing on Japanese culture. In this new guise, he resorted to a conception of subjectivity that placed him in a position to know what others could not grasp. His traveler to the desert was a specialist in character and climate, just as the purveyor of Europe, India, and China would immediately understand the relationship between a specific habitus and climate. Dryness is the backbone of desert climate and produces all of its characteristics: the absence of people, vitality, gentleness. Humans, here, expend all in the search for water, roaming the desert endlessly, fighting others ceaselessly for this scarce resource. Nature is ungiving, unyielding, yet its very harshness often provokes people to band together and unify in order to carry out the immense struggle (8:49–50; CC, 50). Humans stand outside of nature, differentiated; labor and production depend on nomadism. Since life is far from full, there is no reason to wait for nature's blessings, which come in monsoon Asia in staggering abundance. Instead, the desert demands activity searching to snatch what little a niggardly nature will offer. Struggle for nature's meager gifts leads to conflict among men. The formation of associational life was based on the recognition of scarcity and the necessity of struggle; life constrained by strict regulations governing customs, morals, and laws. Everything serves the necessity of defense. In this world, individualism is difficult to sustain, as it is the fate of the single person to depend upon the group (8:54; CC, 50). What Watsuji pointed to in this vast emptiness was the possibility of still discerning a characteristic historical experience and social formation. "It is not only land," he wrote, "that keeps people in place" (8:55; CC, 50). Even if they are able to leave the desert as land in the spatial sense, they are not able to leave it socially, as a historical reality.

Finally, there was "meadow" (*makiba*) culture: the Mediterranean world and its benign, gentle climate. If one moves with the sun from East to West, he observed, departing from Japan, one will experience (*taiken*) first the intense humidity of monsoon lands and next the aridity of the desert. But when Europe is finally reached, there is neither humidity or aridity. "Nay, there is both moistness and dryness. . . . Experientially, there is the union of both" (8:64; CC, 61). If this comes close to resembling a dialectical operation, it was not based on historical development, but rather, according to Watsuji, existed in the traveler's experience. Europe and its meadow climate marked the place of a permanent synthesis of climatic experience and cultural typologies reflected in social and histori-cal forms (8:65; CC, 61). It is interesting to note how Watsuji left his own trajectory when contrasting Europe to Japan. In his account of monsoon and desert climates, there is little cross-comparison, and when there is, it is between zones, not national cultures. With Europe, however, he refers to Japan to sharpen the contrast between distinctive characteristics, even though Japan is simply a member of the monsoon zone. His comparative perspective, in other words, is based on a comparison between a national culture—Japan—and a climatic zone—Europe. (This strange pairing re-sembled the contemporary Marxist strategy to concentrate on the devel-opment of capitalism in Japan, focusing on the race-nation, thus accepting the givenness of the general development of capitalism.) Was Watsuji struck by Japan's capacity to incorporate the characteristics of meadow climate, even though it was located outside of it? Japan, unlike other Asian societies, had been able to modernize sooner and more successfully and thus maintain its independence aggressively by becoming an imperial com-petitor. He explained that even though he had tried to understand Eu-rope's culture by looking at its climate, he acknowledged that climate and character are not the only determinants of culture. "In culture," he wrote, "historicality and climate and culture (*fūdosei*) are two sides of the shield, and one cannot be separated from the other. When there is no historical formative substance that doesn't possess its climatic character, there is no climatic phenomenon without its historical character. If we are able to detect the climate within the substance of historical formation, we will be able to read the history within climatic phenomena." Nevertheless, reason and feeling are products of meadow and monsoon climates, respectively, yet each will make its inhabitants aware of what it lacks most and what it must learn from the other (8:119; CC, 116–117).

In Watsuji's comparative framework, the placement of the West, whose development was driven by meadow climate, had it far easier than a Japan constantly reeling under a capricious but ferocious nature. In his narrative, Japan's achievement appears heroic: it was able to overcome a cruel nature and remain strong and independent, unlike others in the monsoon neighborhood. Only Japan was able to master and learn from others what it lacked. The character it had forged in the experience of weathering monsoons, typhoons, and earthquakes stimulated a self-realization that would lead to the adaptation of cultural traits from the others. Hence, he managed to bypass conventional historiography and the practice of seeing human action as the agency of event-driven movement. In fact, eventfulness was meaningless in his historical scheme and belonged to those strategies that preached the development of progress and needed a device to chart it. Plainly, he was targeting contemporary Marxian historiography when he proposed that the purpose of history was not to explain the present, as Heidegger had advised, but to reveal the conditions of possibility for the future. Human agency was replaced by *fūdosei*, which forced groups to respond in order to survive and reproduce their social conditions of existence. History was the sign of this human response, which reduced epoch-making events to decisions on destiny that were determined by the exigencies of climate. Watsuji was convinced that *fūdosei* as agency meant that the self-realization of the group and the choice of action were provoked by the force of climate and the limitations it would impose. He constantly reminded his readers that groups cannot change the climate, but self-awareness of the necessity of climate would enable them to supplement what they lacked in their own environment. There is nothing contingent about this move since climate enforced a terrible necessity upon each and every group that needed an appropriate response (8:120; CC, 117–118).

In this respect, Japanese, endowed with the vast intuitive powers characterizing typhoon climates, enhanced their culture by acquiring "the light of reason which shined most brightly in a meadow climate" (8:119; CC, 117). Although it was not possible to turn Japan into a meadow climate, he declared, it was possible to "acquire its characteristics." At this time, "our typhoon characteristics will open up to new and fresh aspects. When we discover Greek clarity within ourselves and sufficiently nourish reason itself, the meaning of our 'perception' and 'temper' will become revived" (8:120; CC, 118). This "super rational reason" will sweep over Japan like a typhoon, as Japan's adoption of European science represented a "craving" and "longing" for the characteristics meadow climate offered and Japan lacked. By the same measure, we must recall Watsuji's own dismissal of the enlightenmentism Meiji Japan had so enthusiastically and uncritically embraced, and its baneful effects on Japan's received culture.

Meadow climate, known for its benign nature—called "mother nature"—led to calculability, control, and individualism, all qualities characterizing capitalism and its impulse for aggressive expansion. Nature, he observed, shows no violence, no real unpredictability, and presents itself in logical and rational forms capable of being condensed in laws and principles. It was no surprise that science was produced in such circumstances. The Mediterranean, unlike the seas surrounding Japan, has always served as a means of communication, travel, and trade, not as a source of food or even defense. With the Greeks, humans first learned that they could seize control of a docile nature. Identifying closely with nature, they humanized it by putting man at the center of it, as subject and agent. The struggle with nature observed in other climate zones was recoded into a struggle between men, which Watsuji attributed to a desire for power and competition, the increase of creative powers, a thirst for knowledge and artistic production. Hence, a docile nature, the place of "green meadows," spurred an attitude of competition and aggressive behavior manifest first in Greek expansion. Competition subsequently divided the population into warriors, godlike citizens, and the rest—slaves—who were seen as part of nature that demanded domination. Slavery and leisure encouraged unrestricted "observation," which, accordingly, was linked to discovery and creativity, not, as in China, the mirroring of what was already in place (8:88; CC, 85). The landscape was bright and clear, and everything appeared distinct and could be measured precisely. Northern Europe, lacking the sunshine of the South, had contributed the dimension of gloominess and the disposition of brutality to character and culture. In time, Western Europe avoided sinking into permanent gloom by resorting to the light of reason, which accounted for its stunning success in wordly cultural progress.

In this connection, Watsuji saw America as an inflection of this combination of rationality and brutality. Like the later participants of the symposium on modernity, he envisaged American culture—Americanism—as an extension of Europe, but distinctive for its shallowness and superficiality. Europe was still the home of high culture while America, as the experience of Japan in the 1920s reminded him, was a dilution that exaggerated the cultural balance of the original. In a revealing essay on American character ("Amerika kokuminsei"), actually written during wartime (probably 1942), he saw Anglo-Saxon character (northern) as the basis of American national character. In this essay, Watsuji brought together his theory of *fūdosei* with his longstanding antipathy for mass consumer culture, which he associated with "Americanism." British expansion to North America, driven by the necessities of defense, trade, and manufacturing, was the representative philosophy of the age in which America was colonized.[58] The two philosophers who best exemplified this national spirit that led to the defeat of the Spanish Empire and the subsequent hegemony of England in the seventeenth century were Francis Bacon and Thomas Hobbes. Both functioned in Watsuji's account as tropes for the authority of experience. Bacon was the spiritual embodiment of this age of discovery and invention by making both the vocation of philosophic inquiry (40–41). The aim of learning was to discover those qualities that direct men to "govern nature; it resulted in the production of enlightenment." In Bacon's thinking, however, this idea referred to "material enlightenment," which Watsuji associated with the character of Anglo-Saxon culture and its American transformation into "materialism" and "utilitarianism," the plaint most often heard in denunciations of Americanism in the late 1920s. Experience and induction, used in daily affairs, distinguished this approach. Parliamentary politics, developed in England, signaled the effort to enter into calculation countertheories insofar as they were based on fact. On his part, Hobbes promoted the power of natural law in human society. Although he conceived of the existence of a state of nature where all share equally and the differentiation between physical and mental powers is small, two persons with equal rights would find themselves struggling over the same resources. In this world, described as the war of all against all, there is no injustice, and virtue belongs to those who are strongest and most fraudulent (45). To prevent a complete collapse into disorder, Hobbes advised the establishment of rules aimed at prohibiting conduct injurious to life that led to fixing obligations binding the conduct of all. Even though Hobbes seemed to favor peace as the principal law of nature, the way was opened to employing war to attain it. "The pursuit of peace," Watsuji explained, "was also the determination for carrying out a heartless war"—an apt description of how American policy led to war (46). If men exercised their natural right to behave freely toward others, they would by necessity fall into the conditions of warfare and slip into cruel unrest. Under these circumstances, Hobbes explained the necessity of a binding social contract capable of constraining men from going so far in the pursuit of their personal interest, but which Watsuji described simply as "English-like good conscience in the plunder of settler lands."

The "migration" of the philosophy of Bacon and Hobbes to America was expressed early in the colonial expansion into the interior of the continent and the destruction of native life. The Hobbesian effect appeared in the contradiction between the Quaker opposition to the war and the colonists' need to open up land for further settlement. Because North American Indians, Watsuji noted, did not possess a culture comparable to the Indians of Peru and Mexico, the colonists rejected using them as laborers to clear off the land. Convinced that "there was no good Indian other than a dead Indian," the Anglo-Saxons, from the beginning, resorted to mass extermination of the native population. Watsuji argued that the Hobbesian conception of nature supplied powerful justification, if not outright inducement, to this act of genocide. Since humans have natural rights to all things, even the settlers could lay claim to clearing the forests for cultivable land, like the Indians who claimed the right to gather and harvest in the forest. Both groups possess the right to promote their interest in the same forest and thus must fight it out. It is not a moral problem that the weak in such a struggle are killed, but rather a natural principle that the conflict is resolved through force. Violation of a peace treaty between colonists and Indians was always the means to resort to "unpeaceful means and massacre the natives" (55).

In Watsuji's eyes, Benjamin Franklin best represented this frontier spirit and the practical application of Hobbesian principles. For the Indians, who possessed no conception of private property and landownership, treaties were meaningless; but for settlers, a violation of the "contract" was cause for massacre. "While brandishing the equality of rights, they [Anglo-Saxons] coolly murdered natives" (66). Calling attention to this contradiction in American life, Watsuji pointed out how, in a Hobbesian world, murder and slavery in the name of justice were always possible when relationships were governed by "contracts" that produced the "law." What he wished to dramatize was how the "law" was employed against other people and found lasting enthronement in American foreign policy. "We can't forget that Commodore Perry threatened Edo with his cannons and imposed a threat of trade. . . . Japan, at that time, could not but submit to the stipulations of the treaty." Recognizing that force always backs up treaties, Japanese, like the Indians, were not strong enough to resist. Yet when the country later (during World War I) signed a treaty with China, it was considered an ineffective reason that was done under the pressure of military coercion. After the "Manchurian Incident," America "persecuted" Japan for "treaty violations" and condemned the country for acting in self-defense (68–69). While Watsuji's grasp of the Manchurian seizure avoided raising the spectacle of Japan's own Hobbesian treatment of "natives," it captured the logic of capitalist society in the interwar period and demonstrated the importance of understanding how the Hobbesian character masqueraded in appeals to "peace" and "justice."

If America was a Hobbesian nature where the strong always prevail, Bacon's influence was crystallized in the establishment of a materialist and utilitarian civilization. For Watsuji, "machine civilization" and "American character" were fundamentally linked (72). Franklin was the hero of invention, calculation, and discovery. But his greatest achievement was the publication of his newspaper, which "became the workshop for American public opinion" (74, 77). Newspapers in American life imparted only "emotionality," "sensation," and "passion" to the people, not "thought." After 150 years of constantly prodding the population, the people of America have lost the ability to think and understand. From the standpoint of culture, the objective of the newspaper has not been to advance progress but rather to induce the "barbarization" of life. Echoing Japanese complaints concerning the importation of American material culture in the 1920s, Watsuji accused the newspaper of invading every nook and cranny of modern life to convey the baleful influence of "Americanism" everywhere. Even in his day, he observed that the newspaper and its emphasis on the written word was coming to an end, swiftly being replaced by the noise of the radio and the primacy of the ear, revealing only the "mastery of the machine," not the power of thought. The machine had enslaved people in contemporary Japan, made people passive, superficial, culturally regressive. "America, today, stands at the vanguard of a 'machine civilization' " that prevents it from advancing morally and refining itself aesthetically. For Americans, there seems to be no civilization without machines, but in the slavery of the machine, there is no culture. The machine has eliminated the moral meaning found in work. "Americans are taught that each individual is a master, not a follower, and is thus entitled to enjoy the fruits of technology, like cars, radio, newspapers, refrigerators, and electric stoves, which they employed as 'several slaves' to permit management of life like a king." Unhappily, they have lost the feeling for anything but the new, the luxurious, which transforms them into slaves of the machine. A world dominated by technology is one where everything is quantified (78, 79) and expressed in numbers. Numbers are the spirit of America.

The Anglo-Saxons penetrated the very heart of the continent with an awful energy in less than two hundred years. Having come this far so rapidly, there was no reason to stop at the Pacific. Three years after linking the west coast to the rest of the country, Perry showed up at Uragu, demanding the opening up of the country and the exchange of embassies. By the end of the century, Americans were in Hawaii and the Philippine Islands. America transformed the Anglo-Saxon settlers and extended the aggressive, cruel, and calculating climatic endowment already formed in northern and western Europe. Watsuji worried that this spirit, embodied in the machine, was already beginning to exert its mastery over the Japanese. The problem he perceived was the disappearance of moral meaning, precisely the kind of national ethics Japanese had developed in response to the challenge posed by monsoon climate. The only meaning the machine offered was the instrumental means to defeat the enemy (84). Persuaded that America's aspirations for world dominion came from neither lofty moral ideals nor the demands of national existence, the historical experience of sweeping over the natives and destroying the environment behind the surety of the contract and superior technology had become a fixed "disposition" in its character. The destiny of the peoples of Asia was already prefigured in the destruction of native America. Driven by neither necessity nor reason, Watsuji observed, Americans would merely repeat this action. Plainly, America lacked morality. Firm in the belief that numbers and "quantity" will protect them, they will fight to the end to preserve this "civilizational superstition," even though the true reserve of a people's strength lies in its moral and spiritual strength rather than in the power of quantity.

The superiority of Japan's moral endowment, articulated almost hysterically in the companion piece "Nihon no Shintō," was the national character produced in the encounter with monsoon climate. Yet, Watsuji had to clarify why Japan, which belonged to the monsoon region like other countries, differed from China or even India. China, he explained from an observation of the Yangtze River plain, conformed to the climatic characteristics of receptivity and passivity, like Japan, but in a way strikingly different from the Indian experience. Owing to the immense length of the river and the width of the plain it snaked through, he concluded that the Yangtze and its surroundings encapsulated the whole of the monsoon environment. People who live there, in contrast to Japanese, never see themselves outside the limitation of sameness, referring to an endlessly expanding plain that repeats itself and whose scope cannot be measured by the eye. Hence, the monotony and seeming timelessness of the landscape produce a tenacity of will and the abandonment of emotion. Here, there is a "flourishing of a persistent historical sensation of tradition," which is diametrically opposed to India (WTZ, 8:123; CC, 122). If India experiences an "overflowing of feeling," China is known for its lack of emotionality, its emptiness of feeling. This characteristic caused anarchic tendencies and a sense of submissiveness linked to the absence of affect. Although it was not his intention to rob Chinese of emotional life, what he seemed to be saying was that they came with an outlook that saw no cause for change demanding response or a show of feeling. The importance of this observation was that it accounted for China's incapacity to unify nationally and supplied Japan with a mission to restore the cultural grandeur that Japan had long ago absorbed but China had lost. Watsuji saw this as the occasion for a restoration of China's greatness under Japanese tutelage. But it was a benign cultural program thinly disguising Japanese imperial interest and the conceits of racism that sustained the relationship between colonizer and colonized. Worse, his theory of climate and character could not explain why one monsoon culture was able to do what another was prevented from doing while facing the same environmental challenge.

Accordingly, Japan's uniqueness derived from the presence of heavy rain and heavy snowfall, even though it belonged to monsoon climate (8:135; CC, 134–135). The symbol of this doubling of tropical and frigid weather was the bamboo covered with snow. In addition, the punctual recurrence of violent typhoons that carried destructive winds and dumped flood-making rains contributed to making Japan's climate unique in the monsoon belt. The climate consisted of hot and cold temperatures, the seasonal and the sudden. While the country showed the monsoon region's appetite for passivity and resignation, Japan also knew strenuousness and exhilarating emotionality. The Japanese experience with seasonal yet sudden typhoons produced what Watsuji believed was the destructive cast of mind that elevates emotionality while abhorring persistence to frequently unleash historically momentous social change accompanied by tenacious struggle. Violent winds and downpours enforced resignation and passivity but could also periodically inspire resistance and struggle. Through this combination, Japan replicated the characteristic associated with meadow climate, even though he never went so far as to say that the country represented the best in East and West.

House-ing Human Relationships

For Watsuji, this combination of emotional will and abandonment imprinted itself on Japan's history through a distinctive form of sociality that figured the national collective. Uniquely concrete forms of life were always manifest in specific social relations and "associational attitudes" developed in the groups' formative experience. Male-female relationships are based on associational attitudes of the family; the functions of relationships like mother/father are first developed within the family unit rather than through the association of man and woman. Family structure in monsoon societies like China and Japan, in contrast to those found in meadow culture, placed great importance on community life. Whereas family life in ancient Greece was reducible to husband and wife, tracing descent back only to the father, the desert family assumed the weight of the whole lineage group going back to the first ancestors, the tribe taking precedence; social organization in the monsoon belt kept the whole lineage within the family unit. The "house" or "household" (*ie*) was synonymous with the "whole" (*zentaisei*) of the family (*kazoku*). Although it was represented by the head (*kachō*), it was still the whole that authorized the head of the family to be its head. In this world, the family does not exist according to the will of the head, but rather the will of the head depends upon the authority of the whole. The priority of the "house" signified that the whole took precedence over the individual members of the family (8:141; CC, 141–142).

Watsuji loaded the Japanese family with such importance that its survival would constitute the guarantee of Japan's continuing identity in a world marred by sameness, while its disappearance would mark the end of what it meant to be Japanese. Not to leave things to chance, he also proposed that the relationality associated with the family constituted the foundation of an ethics claiming normative value. This overdetermined emphasis on the singular uniqueness of a form of relationality and its consequences for a normative ethics revealed a genuine concern, if not panic, about the problem of social solidarity which, in the late 1920s and 1930s, began to show signs of buckling under the weight of new relationships and the threat of social conflict. Linking the primacy of the family to the imperatives of ethics reinforced an ideological representation, inscribed earlier in the Civil Code but seriously under threat, that the state and the family were interchangeable.

In the Japanese household, the relationship is not one between merely man and woman but between husband and wife, parent and child. What Watsuji wanted to center in this arrangement was the relation of "inbetweenness" (*nakama*), which signaled an affection binding a union that never separates (8:142; CC, 141–142). The house (*ie*) referred to the space of relationality, the place where *nakama* prevailed to structure and guide the relationships among the individual members of the family. Archaic history confirmed the existence of this "inseparable" family unit informed and enhanced by mutual affection. "The way of human existence in Japan through the house," he asserted, "is none other than realizing in the family Japanized relationships (*aidagara*) such as quiet but emotional and martial selflessness" (8:143; CC, 143). This unique form of relationality has become the basis for the development of the house. Values like "quiet violent emotionality" prevented the contemporary habit of viewing people abstractly, artificially, and excluded as inappropriate any consideration of a larger community founded on the consciousness of the individual. The house in Japan took on the uniquely important meaning of the community within the community, a sentiment that his contemporary Yanagita Kunio had already made as the subject of folkloric investigation. Clearly, Watsuji's conception of the house/household challenged the claims of contemporary social organization and its privileging of associational relationships—society, *gesellschaft*. As if fearful of the charge of ideologizing the idea of the family state, which the Meiji Civil Code had already authorized as an official representation of the imperial order, he was convinced that the *ie* and the relationships it housed uniquely characterized the Japanese way of living since the beginning of the race and possessed a much "deeper foundational layer" than an ideology referring to the family system (8:147–148; CC, 148). Yet, he was plainly replacing the ideology of the family state with a more deeply implicated form of social organization and its distinguishing relationship that claimed exemption from ideological taint by appealing to its "naturalness"—precisely the quality that would make it ideological. Regardless, he consecrated the house as the site of primordial everydayness that derived from Japan's most remote experience with *fūdosei*.

Watsuji was persuaded that despite the importation of capitalism, the Japanese way of life continued to exist, even if its scope was diminished since the Tokugawa period. What was still intact in the present was the form of the *ie*—the heart of the system. Modern European capitalism, he observed, tries to see humans as individuals. Even its family system is understood as a union of individuals who pursue their own economic interests. But Japanese who have adopted capitalism cannot be seen as merely interest-driven individuals since, for them, the idea of "house" was like a second skin. "Japanese grasp house as the most [basic] everyday phenomenon, as 'inside.' (*uchi*) The world (*seken*) beyond the household is the 'outside' (*soto*). Within this inside, the distinction between individuals disappears." For the wife, the husband is the "inside," "man inside," the "house" (*taku*); for the husband, the wife is "inside the house" (*kanai*), the term he uses to refer to his spouse. The family is described also as "people within," denoting differentiation from people outside. But distinction among family members within is disregarded. Hence, the whole of the family is grasped as inside, as an "inseparable relationship." Watsuji believed that such distinctions between inside and outside were not found in European languages. Even though it is possible to speak of being *in* and *out* of a room or the house, one never speaks of being in and out of the family to the extent that its meaning corresponds to words like *uchi* and *soto*. (8:144; CC, 144).

Since the house, therefore, structures relationships within, its interior is a union without distinction even as it is differentiated from the outside. It is for this reason that Japanese who return home from the outside leave their *geta* in the *genkan*, a room that serves to separate the inside from the outside and prepares those inside to exit to the outside.[59] Despite the massive transformations inflicted on this house, its form still persisted, not merely as an artifact but as a living fixture. Again, its uniqueness appears obvious when compared to the European house, where the rooms are partitioned into individual and autonomous units separated by doors and thick windows (8:146; CC, 146). In Japan the wholeness and unity expressed by the house inflected the larger, archaic unity of the religious community represented by an emperor descended from the gods. Like the house, the archaic unification of the nation within a single, whole religious grouping reflected the union of the emotional yet calm, martial yet selfless abandon. The unique character of the Japanese in archaic times was thus based on originary beliefs that produced a union through the religious collective. What the distant past had firmly established became the cultural formation of later periods. Even after the penetration of a strong consciousness of individualism, it was still possible to discern this insepa-rable union of the people. An examination of subsequent historical ages affirms the persistence of this truth and the continuity of Japan's unique, moral endowment based on quiet emotionality and selfless abandon.

Unique to Japan, an ethics of relationality differentiated the nation's moral history from all others and supplied a lasting emblem of identity. Because it represented what was most essential to Japanese, it occupied a commanding purpose in his investigations. In his thinking it was not mo-rality itself that claimed uniqueness but the form Japanese had evolved in their long history. At the heart of this concern was the conviction that ethical relationships had been founded on the recognition of "in-betweenness." If social relationships in Japan derived from the interaction with a specific climate, the individualism and egoism that had accompa-nied the importation of capitalism could only lead to a further undermin-ing of the received endowment. Watsuji, it is important to note, saw in the principle of historical upheavals from archaic times to the Meiji Resto-ration a confirmation of the persistence and continuity of this ethical sub-structure, not its evolutionary unfolding. In this respect, the temporality of the past was linked to that of the present and markedly different from the modernity of the West. Since time affirmed what was always already there, space, embodied in the social relationships of in-betweenness, the inside and outside, and the specificity of place—the country—remained primary and fixed as nothing was lost to time in this world. Tosaka, it should be recalled, prompted by the power of spatiality disclosed by Wa-tsuji, configured it as the place of the now where established conventions could be changed rather than as the site of the past and unchanging moral relationships. In fact, his critique of morality as the product of a specific practice that had effaced its history was an assault on ethical theories that aimed to repress the presence of the present in order to stabilize everyday life in timeless social relationships and custom.[60]

Watsuji saw the materiality of the house as an "everyday phenome-non," its stolidity and continuity of internal organization constituting a sign of the persistence of the most fundamental space of the Japanese form of life. But if the primordial conditions of existence were grounded in the house and household, the corresponding social relationships it fos-tered—housed—were the foundations for a national ethics. The identifi-cation of a prior ethical endowment that was still manifest in social orga-nization and conduct permitted Watsuji to read the nation back into the most archaic moments. Behind this passion for an unchanging set of social relationships recoded as ethics was a response to the visible signs of indi-vidualism and egoism that had grown in Japanese society since the late Meiji period . By the 1930s, in the wake of mass consumer society, such individualism was perceived as a problem of immense proportions for the question of social order. In contemporary discourse, class conflict and gender autonomy were seen as merely an inflection of individualism, inasmuch as both produced antagonism and struggle capable of uprooting the moral basis of collective existence. On his part, Watsuji was persuaded that the prevalence of individuality in his time represented the "misconception of the modern world which takes ethics merely as a problem of individual consciousness."[61] Watsuji argued that because ethics (*rinri*) originally meant "betweenness" (*nakama*), it was completely inappropriate to use it to describe an "individualistic subjectivistic ethical consciousness." With this move, he came close to identifying ethics, as such, with relationality, excluding all considerations that failed to satisfy the requirements of conduct within the group. Individual consciousness, which has abandoned the figure of communality, has no connection to the word denoting "ethics." In-betweenness, summoned by *nakama*, attested to the fact that humans (*ningen*, between men) originally lived their social life as a collective. Society (*seken*)—referred to the whole, while subjective human existence pointed to relationality and communality. Grasping a subjective existence bonded to community in words, things, and deeds (relationality as practical action) demanded finding the routes to its understanding. Kant, for example, believed that the practical self-affirmation of the subject was the reality of direct consciousness through a practical philosophy. Even though this was a transcendental subject, that is to say, a self-affirmation of the original self, the place (*basho*) where this "provision" was directly found was in the individualistic consciousness. It was known directly by the subject (*shukan*), and there was no necessity for other mediation (WT, 102). But Watsuji complained that this form of comprehension referred only to the individual and reduced the understanding of human existence to human subjectivity. What this formulation seemed to grasp was not subjective action but knowledge as the subjection of action by a knowing subject. Rejecting any attempt to start from the consciousness of the knowing subject, he recommended beginning with "practical, active connections." Since the standpoint of the existence of *ningen* is objective, the act of comprehension can never be reached through the reality of the individual's direct consciousness. It must always be pursued through the mediation of the reality humans have produced, which is both historical and social.

Among neo-Kantians, reality was invariably grasped through the mediation of social science, not through ethical study. Hence the privilege accorded to the basic disciplines of "special sciences" like economics, law, education, and pedagogy, which problematized the "unity of intentionality among humans" as a basic premise. Yet despite its putative capacity to locate the problem for study, social science never went beyond the representation of experience, organized scientifically. "The idea of experience means experience organized according to the procedures of natural science. . . . Even though it manages to reach the figure of communality, it is still an idea, not human existence." In other words, social science fell into the same kind of trap of abstract representation that was already plaguing writers and artists. To eliminate this misrecognition, Watsuji called for an approach leading to "actual" comprehension of the "reality of experience" in exchange for the "reality of study" (103). This meant, simply, that experience was not only the consciousness of an intuited or contemplated object but rather one that "imparted within itself, practical and active contact." There, he announced, is found the expression of human existence.

> We experience commodities immediately when buying things daily. But if these commodities were only object things, there would be the idea of economics. However, these are things that express a variety of moments in human existence, through clothing, shelter, and food and are treated as such; they are sold in diverse shops or department stores. Food items are characterized as daily necessities, restaurant consumer goods, presents or congratulatory gifts. Similarly, stores sell clothing, evening dress, and apparel for visitations, uniforms, children's clothes, baby outfits, and so forth. Even house utensils disclose the forms of life. That is to say, they are not [only] things that express human existence as a commodity. Therefore, we are connected to commodities that conform to these expressions [of life forms]; we do not treat things without representation as commodities. If that is the case, we will be able to understand the expression of human existence immediately in the experience of the commodities and undoubtedly reach it through experience. (103–104)

In this observation on the commodity and commodity form, Watsuji apparently recognized its commanding position in contemporary society and how even the most basic necessities of life had become commodified. Although life was already heavily mediated by the process of commodification, it was not yet reducible to it. Behind the commodity form was still the experience of real human existence, which could be reached by employing the proper method of investigation. The variety of experiences organized by the social science disciplines offered an incomplete route mired in representation. Reaching experience had to be secured by gathering the "experience of everyday humans" in their concrete existence. It was possible, he stated confidently, to detail the "rich meaning" of these experiences by returning to their everydayness (104). While he congratulated the social sciences for inaugurating an approach for studying human existence, he also condemned it for having failed to overcome its reliance on a conception of knowledge based on the reality of the individualistic consciousness and for not having "selected" the everyday experience of humans in their practical and active contact as the primary route to understanding human existence. Informing this particular formulation was the figure of Watsuji's "double life" again, and his obvious belief that commodification, like modernization, simply represented an overlay of a more fundamental native existence that continued to persist and recall a primordial experience. This experience was immune to complete commodification, even though it remained buried within the process and represented for him the kernel of concreteness in contemporary social abstraction. Yet the reverse was even more true, since he appealed to the persistence of unchanging culture (experience determined by relationality) to displace the effect of commodification, which, far from shaking off the taint of abstraction, was inseparably tied to it. For his conception of culture, despite invoking the sign of historicality, repressed the conditions of its own historicity as conclusively as the commodity effaced the circumstances of its production. Watsuji's attempt to resituate the category of culture as the trace of historical concreteness, as if it had remained unaffected by the commodity, disclosed only the effect of the commodity form to induce a misrecognition that saw timeless relationality (*aidagara*) for the social relations of production, the abstract for the historically concrete. By locating the timeless relationships within the materiality of the house, whose form was still present when he was writing, he believed he had found a way to avoid the encroaching commodification of life. But this would offer, at best, only the temporary refuge of the inside, not a response to the alienating world of the outside, a timeless sanctuary of withdrawal where Japanese could, only momentarily, live the other half of their double life and remain Japanese. Even more illusory was the promise of the form of the house and its materiality. Despite the claims that the internal organization of the house corresponded to the relationality of the family, the rooms had no natural defense against bringing in the outside world, where Japanese were spending most of their time, and being made to take on other functions.

It was in this connection that Watsuji criticized Heidegger for having not understood the implications of his own insight that "Being in the world," linked to other things, authorized a view that saw human existence as fundamentally communal and relational. Heidegger had apparently overlooked that Being—humans—exists within the world (*seken*), inasmuch as it was the existence of man, which is a relational and communal, and not merely human existence (105, 107). Heidegger never raised the question of relationality that required the "oppositional unity of self and other" (107). "We cannot do without clarifying the 'Being in the world' first through relationality. Before we are connected to 'things' (*mono*), we are connected to 'men.' Although it is said that other men are discovered through the medium of tools, it is a speculation that tries to reach the other by starting from the 'I,' and is thus not the reality of a practical and active human existence" (108). When humans discover tools in reality, there is a relationship to the other. Without living in family life, he continued, there would be no connection with the tools the family must employ; without laboring in a social context, the hand would not be able to make a hammer. Watsuji, recalling Heidegger's views on the importance of tool making, insisted that tools manifested relationality, not "things in one's hand." As if to resituate the primordial conditions of human existence to its central philosophical position, he proposed that the "route" to human existence required sensitivity to diverse material manifestations signifying everyday relationships, such as expressions like meeting together and working together. "Our everydayness," he stated, "is formed in the comprehension of these manifestations." Starting from those things that "correspond to reality," Watsuji acclaimed the collective nature of life forms. Practical and active relationality are prior to observation, reflection, logic, and theory that get transformed into "facts." Once submitted to comprehension and representation, they are sorted out into a classification of "true things" and "untrue things." But the diversity of human experience presented an almost insurmountable complex spectacle for comprehension. To resolve this problem he advised that it was permissible to rely on condensed human portraits imagined by writers who had a sharp grasp of everyday experience. "Writers," he remarked, "always represented anew the manifestation of everyday existence" (109).

Here, Watsuji shared a sentiment with the critic Kobayashi Hideo, who had already seen in the *shi shōsetsu* both a content that located experience in the mundane and a form of unsurpassable comprehension. On his part, Watsuji also wanted to emphasize how an understanding of human existence had to take into account an understanding of the double character of humans as collective and individual beings. Taking as an example the act of eating rice, something that is everybody's experience of the mundane, he pointed to the obvious fact that it occurred within the household. This household is not only a pile of logs and timber and earth; it also expresses the immediacy of human existence as a "dwelling' " (*jūkyo*) (109). Such rooms as the living room (*ima*), the tokunoma, guest room, kitchen, genkan, and so forth all show the form of familistic, communal existence. In circumstances where the house serves as an inn or boarding house, there are still rooms that maintain these fixed functions. Wherever people congregate, it is possible to see how they immediately understand the forms of family existence. Even though these rooms are partitioned by sliding doors, their forms are "a manifestation of the historical, climatic limitations of a definite society." When a person regards another inside sliding doors that open and shut freely, he or she will lower the lock in order to see. This represents the act of "relationality" to the other. But if there is distrust for the other person, nothing will happen there because there is no desire to see what is beyond the *fusuma*. By the same token, the other person will not try to open the sliding door without permission. There is, in this example, the lesson of a fixed way to open the sliding door, which discloses a more fundamental form of life. We wash our faces, he continued, and eat rice daily. The tableware, dining table, food, and etiquette governing the conduct of eating all express the forms of a definite existence that has its roots in a prior experience with *fūdosei*. "We are able to eat rice only in the comprehension of these forms" (110). Words and countless gestures are exchanged within the family in the house, and dining becomes a collective act. Taste is only partially a personal response, as food is also tasted communally. Without knowing that taste is relational, people would probably not be able to taste anything. All these, and more, are understood immediately as manifestations of relationality directing the conduct of members of the groups in their mutual interaction.

Watsuji's account of enduring forms of human existence was propelled by an interpretative or hermeneutic strategy. His examples show how each participant in the fixed forms of life must actually be in a position to understand the proper codes of conduct that go without saying because they come without saying. "The expressions of everyday life and their comprehension are a problem of understanding expressions." At the same time, the space of the mundane was a "sea of expressions" (113). Anxious about the immanent prospect of "drowning in this sea of expressions" without any effort to grasp human existence, it was necessary to move beyond the representations produced by disciplines that have "organized everyday experience under fixed viewpoints." (The program of extracting meaning from things that express existence from the narrow standpoint of scholarly expertise results in treating experience as things. What is missed is not the phenomenality of everyday existence but its bases. A corrective to this approach, then, is the experience of living these forms, which is tantamount to understanding them. It is for this reason that the idea of commodification, he never tired of saying, has no reality or meaning outside of economics, which means it has no relationship to the fundamental basis of human existence. "But for us," he added, "this hidden grounding (*jiban*) is the important thing" (111). Moreover, it is vital that the "subjective human existence" is transformed into a "sense of things," that practical and active contact constitute the "melting furnace" that transmutes experience into meaning. By grasping what was "there," it was possible to return to the origins of human existence; what was being lived in the present supplied access to the past, as an interpretative gesture accompanying the lived experience. For Watsuji, living a specific life form, and being aware of its specificity, was to understand it.

Despite the "inundation of expressions" invading the precincts of everyday life, these would all lead to affirming "relationality" as the fundamental expression of human existence. The major error of modernity was the misrecognition of man for society, inspired by Enlightenment philosophies of individualism that mistakenly separated one from the other. A study of society that failed to properly study "humans" was worthless; although man is an "individual," he is also, at the same time, a communal figure. In this misreading of the Enlightenment, Watsuji condemned sociology, especially, for having pulled apart the social as a representational form of human existence from its expressive meaning (113). His target was Marxism, to be sure, but also a phenomenological social science that seemed content with surface descriptions. What bothered him most was the incapacity of sociology to discern within the social a subject (*shutai*) of action rather than a mere object of investigation. But, he advised, this "subject" is not simply the individual subject who is in a position to know (*shukan*) but "humans" living and acting relationally and communally. This sense of an acting subject/agent was his reply to the challenge of class promoted by Marxism. Unless sociology makes this distinction, it will never become an ethics. Understanding the gestures between two people discloses what has been comprehended between them, the practical and active contact between two persons grasped as an instance of exchanging gestures. Hermeneutics supplied the "objective" means of understanding, even though, as Tosaka observed in his critique of Watsuji, it risked producing an "abstract" yet too general conception of human existence.[62] Although hermeneutics was expended energetically to tap life forms through artistic expression, as Dilthey had recommended, Watsuji cautioned that despite the utility of his advice that "man must start from life," his program fell short of recognizing the role played by everyday life expressions and its comprehension in mediating philosophical understanding. Echoing Tosaka's meditations on the relationship between philosophy and everydayness, Watsuji revised Dilthey's injunction to mean that "life" referred originally to living within human relationships, which "started from the expressions of the most daily human existence, humans relating to humans." Why this was so important was because this state was prior to consciousness itself, what he called "immediate subjective contact" (120–121).

Though Watsuji returned to the Heideggerian problematic of everydayness as the world of the "they," it was at a different level. We must recall that Heidegger proposed that when phenomenology starts from everydayness, it soon becomes complicated in a hidden realm. Phenomena only show themselves to phenomenology, not to everyday life. What ordinarily reveals itself in the everyday are the phenomena of common and vulgar meaning, which refers to things where they are and as they are.

For Heidegger, everydayness invariably took on a pejorative association, where Dasein got lost in the world of the "they," the average, cut off from authentic understanding. But it was also the place where being would discover its destiny. In Watsuji's inflection, everydayness marked the site of real human existence, where the experience of living relationally supplied both the condition for comprehending the meaning of life and for privileging authentic understanding of those who experienced the "practical and active contact" in the everyday. Yet, as we know now, this conception of the everyday was rooted in the house, which was produced by a unique historical and climatic environment. For Watsuji, returning home to Japan was literally returning to the shelter of the house that structured the most fundamental "human relationships" and provided the place within which to put into practice an ethical life restricted to Japanese.

CHAPTER 5.

The Communal Body

THE MNEMONICS OF THE COMMUNAL BODY

If the pursuit of a "living culture," where intellect was embedded in nature, provided the prospect of concreteness to a world dominated by social abstraction and "nonrelationships," the communal body formed by the folk was seen as an even more promising defense against the uncertainties and destructions of modern life. Even before Miki Kiyoshi called for the establishment of a "new gemeinschaft," as we shall see in the following chapter, native ethnologists, self-proclaimed folklorists, and other communitarians had already turned to the task of refiguring the folk and resuscitating their beliefs, customs, and practices in order to preserve the last but lingering traces of a prior existence and to reactivate in the present the kernel of community life needed to negotiate the troubling presence of modernity. If some saw in the nation the figure of an artwork, the community was its body and flesh, the organum and physis that supplied the malleable material, which had existed before the formation of the nation state and made a space of identity available to it. That is to say, the communal body, called in Japanese *kyōdōtai*, a kind of beautiful corporeality, was the organ of expression. As the matter of nature, physis, the body was transformed through work into a national artwork. In fact, it was the presumption of the organicity of both the community (gemeinschaft) that already embodies the later form of the nation and the folk that enabled national formation to be a natural or "physical determination." This organic conception of the political finds its meaning in what Jean Luc Nancy has called "immanentism," or "being in common." According to Nancy, the force of this immanentism empowered the community of beings to "produce their own essence" as their work and thereby shape it as a "communal body."[1] It is the "fusion of community," the "happening" of coming together under a variety of conditions at a moment in the archaic experience, that seals its members into lasting union for all times to come. Native ethnologists located this process of self-formation in the most archaic practices and religious beliefs of the Japanese folk. But the truth of the process lay in the "fusion of community," in Nancy's explanation, in "ecstatic identification" with a place or a leader [in Japan, the emperor and his system (*tennōsei*)], who did not represent any form of transcendence, even though he was seen as a "manifest deity," but the "incarnation, in immanent fashion, the immanentism of the community." This truth would also be found, as both Yanagita Kunio (1875–1962) and Orikuchi Shinobu (1887–1953) disclosed in their own ways, in an identification with the ancestors and national deities. In the formation of a communitarian discourse in modern Japan, the real conflict came with the clash of claims over which "deity" best represented the immanence with which the community could identify. Yanagita's ancestors, far from claiming transcendence, occupied earthly sites like the precincts of cemeteries and mountains and were "like our parents." In the hands of folkists like Takada Yasuma, this communal body itself became the absolute object of ecstatic identification and veneration, inflecting a distorted Durkheimian obsession with community self-worship as the primary condition of social solidarity and thus transmuting the communal body into an ideology of the (collective) subject. Yet, at the same time, appeal to the folk body fetishized "natural" social relationships in the paradoxical effort to find an alternative to the commodity form and its propensity to "objectify" social life. It should be pointed out that the appeal to organicity, like the valorization of myth (Miki) as the first expression of techné and fashioning through language, need not necessarily imply racism. But once physis is reinterpreted into bios, once culture is identified with the ethnic specificity of race, they both slip easily into racism, as an effect and consequence of seeking to envisage the organic as political. The logic of immanentism and its will to immediate "effectuation" (Nancy's term) undergirds the national aesthetic and is capable of driving the community to the extremes of exterminating the other (as the experience of German national socialism constantly reminds) but also to less systematic genocidal episodes like the massacre of Nanjing by Japanese soldiers. Yet, for our purposes, the logic of immanence fusing the communal body can also lead to "suicide" of the community in its most extreme scenario and to a deadening and life-denying conformism in its more benign form, something postwar Japan produced with depressing but consequential effectiveness under the sign of the good Japanese.

In the interwar period, the appeal to the communal body promoted by the native ethnological goal of preserving the traces of a prior life of the folk easily satisfied the same kind of purpose informing the construction of cultural imaginaries. Both were seen as solutions to the domination of the commodity and the circulation and permeation of its form in everyday life, with all of its attending associations and consequences for social relationships and customary conduct; both were also seen as the best defense against the ceaseless commodification of cultural life. The call for communal fusion seemed to promise even greater protection than culture, insofar as it was based upon rescuing concrete social relationships and modes of organization, restoring older practices now threatened with extinction and fundamental beliefs that had become attenuated, even though their observance went back to the time of origins, where they had been employed to suture the original fusion into a coherent community. Unlike theorizing about culture, the authority of communalism lay in its grounding in cognitive elements. Communitarian thinking could immediately point to the organic/natural basis underlying folk customs, practices, and beliefs—not simply as past lived experience but as still living, coexisting with the new and modern in the present. On the face of it, these cognitive traces were able to command greater authority for the idea of community because they are outside (and prior to) the social abstraction that was installing a new kind of life in the cities. But, as we shall see, they possessed no more immunity from the circulation of the commodity form than culture itself, sharing with it a virulent allergy to history. Yanagita, Orikuchi, and Takada, not to mention fellow travelers like Kobayashi Hideo and the linguist Tokieda Motoki, all showed this in their own ways. Even the communitarian valorization of concrete social relations illustrated only the absence of history or the effacement of the conditions under which practices and beliefs had once been formed. If culture demanded an assessment of meaning—value—community announced its value in the meaning of practice and custom. Native ethnologists rarely specified the production of artifacts and beliefs in terms of determinate historical periods but rather remained content only to cite them as examples of natural/organic determinations. Yanagita momentarily recognized economic causes in the perceived unevenness between city and countryside, but when it came to recommending a solution to this problem, he discounted economics for the restitution of older religious practices which he believed would reveal an answer to the plight of the farmer. Unfortunately, the putative answer offered only consolation and continued resignation. Orikuchi rarely, if ever, turned his sights on the contemporary problem of the countryside, since the aura of originary belief found in the rituals of the archaic community beseeching the gods for good fortune would return the folk back to communal life. And Takada, a modern social scientist who eschewed history for the primacy of empirical phenomena, located communal harmony in blood ties as the surest way to secure a "new gemeinschaft" within a historical and historicizing society. We will conclude with a brief examination of Takada's theory of the communal body because it brought folk into a direct alignment with race—blood—and culture. Once confronted with collapse of the rural economy in the wake of the depression, Takada looked to Manchuria to solve the problem of too many people and too little land for cultivation in order to maintain the solidarity of the communal body. But the paucity of land, the specter of rural poverty, and a surplus population were simply alibis to deflect the real cause of colonial expropriation, which was driven by the logic of immanentism that demanded the expansion of the communal body. Like the expansion of capital, which is limited only by capital, the expansion of the folk was limited only by the folk. Where the communitarian discourse departed from contemporary culturalists was in its own claim to authority in history. The organicist conception of community had sunk its roots in the historical experience of the folk long before the Meiji Restoration of 1868 and could proclaim kinship with the self-conscious efforts of earlier thinkers (*kokugakusha*) to uphold the primacy of natural determination in work and practice and the organic coherence of the village community: close to nature, the ancestors, and tutelary deities.

More than the commemorative ceremonies invented and orchestrated by the Meiji state, the continuing survival of social forms, customs, and practices in villages in the countryside presented a more cognitively concrete and authentic reminder of pasts before there was a nation. They were simply older than the mapping out of the sites of memory and the invention of various practices of observance centered on the emperor, designed to link people in the present to a national past stretching back to origins. Familiar to those who lived in villages and to most who could claim relatives in the countryside, these artifacts and practices needed to be defamiliarized in order to be seen in the new light of native ethnology, so that they could actually be seen for the first time rather than numbly recognized. But what is important about these practices is that they belonged to the community and thus attested to its identity. Hence, performance of rituals, for example, that managed to utter a collective "we," thereby acquiring a definitive form, constituted a liturgical community or what Tokieda called the "scene of speaking." Orikuchi saw in the first rituals, performed by female chanters, the formation of a community bonded by their call to the gods, and the place where it recalls to itself this "experience." It was for this reason that he looked to literature as the place where community, through performative utterances, would recall for Japanese the constitution of themselves as a community, what he called the "mother-country."

Native ethnologists like Orikuchi lived with the immense paradox of a modernity driven by the desire to wipe out what came earlier, in the hope of at last reaching a point that could be called a true present, all the while recalling what had, in fact, been deliberately forgotten.[2] If the present marked a new departure, the lapsed past would signal for them a new beginning. They were caught in the interplay between forgetting and being drawn to what modernity had negated. This undoubtedly led to a greater dependence on the past in a present that had done its utmost to eliminate. But, as we have seen, this interplay between the past and a present trying to wipe clean the slate of memory was, in fact, what distinguished modernity. Among communitarian thinkers, this forgetting coaxed people to imaginatively envisage a form of life and a way of thinking about life that was clearly the polar opposite of the modern experience. According to Frank Connerton, commenting upon Thomas Mann's "Freud and the Future," "we are to envisage the ego, less sharply defined and less exclusive than we commonly conceive of it, as being so to speak 'open behind': open to the resources of myth which are to be understood as existing for the individual not just as a grid of categories but as a set of possibilities which can become subjective, which can be lived consciously."[3] Connerton is describing those instances of an "archacizing attitude" whereby life is momentarily lived as a "sacred repetition of prototypes." In Japan during the interwar period, such prototypes were authenticated by surviving traces that stood as monuments to the pasts that the present was rapidly "forgetting." In social life, there was much for celebrants to "imitate" and enact and perform as a sign of continuing vitality. Yanagita, for example, was always pointing to the making of certain artifacts by contemporaries with methods that had not changed in a thousand years. When native ethnologists turned to collecting and preserving practices and beliefs from diverse regions of the country, many of which were still being lived, they were laying claim to the possibility for celebrants to form "prescribed procedures" belonging to a different version of the national narrative, one that they proclaimed was closer to the folk and their experience. If they failed to make available a "strong sense of imitation as mythical identification," which the state was bent on monopolizing with its control of the calendar and the necessary resources with which it could mobilize the population, native ethnology managed, nevertheless, to produce a desire for the communal body and thus a wish to repeat the past of the folk consciously.[4]

It must be recognized that despite its capacity to generate compensatory rituals, capitalist modernization strikes at the heart and uproots those conditions that encourage the performance of "ritual enactment" and "recapitulative imitation" in one form or another. The pursuit of capital accumulation and the ceaseless expansion and dissemination of the commodity form through the market inevitably demanded the constant revolutionizing of the means of production. What this entailed was the construction of a temporality of the market and of commodities that circulate through it to generate an experience of time as quantitative and as flowing in a single direction: "an experience in which the moment is different from the other by virtue of it coming next, situated in a chronological succession of old and new, early and later."[5] This means that the temporality associated with the market and the process of exchange inhibits the possibility that there might coexist qualitatively distinguishable times, temporalities that represented different registers of time like profane and sacred separate from each other and corresponding to different orders that cannot comingle and be reduced to each other. To be sure, we have seen the coexistence of different historical temporalities embodied in practices stemming from differing modes of production and ways of life that belonged to quantitatively different times. But these were considered only as signs of earlier or older moments which would, according to the logic of capitalism, disappear in the wave of progressive modernization and even development. Thinkers like Yanagita and Orikuchi, especially, struggled with the conviction that there might just exist forms of life that were exemplary because they were "prototypical" or, better yet, archetypal since they derived from an indeterminate but archaic folkic experience which had managed to endure because it was complete and whole. Capitalism denies the disposition "to imagine life as a structure of exemplary recurrences" or even a space marked by the coexistence of different temporalities that connect with each other in a relationship of unevenness.[6] But that was precisely what native ethnologists and communitarian theorists sought to redeem, envisaging a poetics of everydayness in its primordiality, in its changeless archaic aspect. Their discourse consisted of the "imaginative persuasiveness" of this perception which they re-presented through and as a "rhetoric of reenactment." In a certain sense they took the promise of hermeneutics much further than did the culturalists, who had employed it merely as a method of interpretation. The neo-nativists stretched it to become a scenario for performance and reenactment. Accordingly, this rhetorical performance was employed in three modes of articulation: verbal, celebratory, and gestural reenactments which frequently imbricated each other. What held these modes together in discourse was the belief that the act of re-presenting meant making the exemplary life reappear, making visible the invisible realm, much like their Tokugawa progenitors—nativists—had sought to do in their effort to ground everyday life and practices of peasants with an authority denied by prevailing structures of knowledge and power. In the 1930s, these articulations of reenactment, dramatized most by Orikuchi but inscribed in Yanagita's conception of custom and practice, easily authorized the performance of folkic rhetoric in the construction of a new communal order.

This operation of identifying re-presention and reenactment with making the past present, making it appear, was supplemented by the communal body itself. What I mean here is that though native ethnologists looked to utterance and gestures that found their way into a discourse that signaled the return of the past under the guise of re-presentation, the idea of a communal body, authenticated daily in the survival of artifacts, practices, and beliefs, in the materiality of the village itself, and language maintained the past as memory in effective form, inasmuch as these practices and beliefs were still being lived and continued as habitual skills and performance and the "scene of speaking" still appealed to a commonly shared referent. Connerton, in this connection, has remarked: "We may not remember how or when we first learned to swim but we can keep on swimming successfully, remembering how to do it, without any representational activity on our part at all; we consult a mental picture of what we should do when our capacity to execute spontaneously the bodily movements in question is defective. Many forms of habitual skilled remembering illustrate a keeping of the past in mind that, without ever adverting to its historical origin, nevertheless reenacts the past in our present."[7] Native ethnology, whose conception of the past was historically indeterminate, a conflation of different moments, saw remembering much in the same light, insofar as it was the communal body that never forgot movements and habits which were like second nature. It upheld an image of the collective body that spoke, moved, and acted habitually, with necessary conscious intent, which the ancients had first formulated in response to their world but since that time had been incorporated and internalized as a reflex. Second nature was precisely the description of what they hoped to make present, because it pointed to a doubling of first nature, the folk's original abode. Habitual memory of the past, kept alive in numerous surviving practices centered in rural and mountain villages ethnologists tirelessly visited to record its knowledge, was sedimented in the communal body. But their organicism was made all the more real by the materiality of the existing village life and folk artifacts—precisely those things that became the object of a desire for collecting and preserving. Folklorists, especially, wished to maintain the identity of the communal body because of its capacity to embody sedimented memory from innumerable pasts. Layered much like Watsuji Tetsurō's *jūsōsei*, it became identical with memory itself.

But it was memory of a certain kind. For Yanagita, memory was found in practices and custom, while Orikuchi looked to words for traces of the folk experience now forgotten. Others located it in the village itself, or even in something called the "folk spirit." Regardless of where it was found or made manifest, culturally specific performances imprinted in corporate and inscriptional practices, linked to the poetics of primordial everyday life, supplied a mnemonics of the communal body. Orikuchi particularly was attracted to the search for an archaic experience derived from an oral tradition of punctual, ritual chanters that subsequent writing and state building nearly obliterated. He discerned archaic experience in patterns of rhyming repetition that could be transmitted to successive traditions. In this way, he could argue that literature, though inscriptional, still disclosed flashes of the folk memory and experience. If the folk, through the operation of techné, gave shape to the body in the form of a national community (itself an artwork), the communal body was performed through particular movements and expressiveness that transparently revealed the qualities that distinguished it. These bodily movements, tropes for custom, practices, and beliefs, manifesting the folk at that point "least susceptible to willful modification," announced its habitual nature. Habit was not merely a sign but rather an embodied experience, a knowledge and memory of it, interpreted in the sinews of the organism, in the body and its various parts which "knew" how to move. Custom and habit, in their way, were the body's knowledge, and through cultivation the communal body would come to understand itself.

The program of native ethnology aimed to restore a prior tradition, just as Kobayashi and Tokieda sought to recall a community of speakers and the shared sense of a speaking a language shaped by common referents. Prompted by the conviction that the Restoration's spiritual impulse was obliged to promise the reinstatement of the tradition of an organic and natural village community presided over by the ancestors and gods, it was early evident that this dream would be rapidly abandoned in the drive to achieve "wealth," "power," and a modern and rational political identity. The novelist Shimazaki Tōson eulogized this loss in his epic novel *Yoakemae* (1935). In this text, he recounts the collapse of the nativist ideals and the willful sacrifice of its most intensely committed adherents, those who believed that the Restoration would not only return the emperor to direct political rule but also recall the natural organic community of archaic Japan. Where Shimazaki plotted a story of shattered ideals, broken promises, and irretrievable loss, native ethnology tried mightily to evoke a changeless existence as a living form in order to prevent its ultimate disappearance.

Hence, from its explosive beginnings, Japan's modern history has oscillated ambiguously between the cultural determination of political arrangements to establish a viable human order and the political necessity of the moment to determine the use of culture to mobilize the masses. It is well known that the Meiji Restoration immediately announced the aim of returning to the events of antiquity—the time of state founding by the legendary emperor Jimmu Tennō—and origins, as if they had been lost in the humus of history, and therefore back to a time before Japan had been corrupted by continental civilization and Buddhism. The purpose of this call to origins, formulated earlier by late Tokugawa nativist scholars like Hirata Atsutane and Ōkuni Takamasa in their recommendation to "adhere to origin," was to reach an unalloyed native experience which, presumably, still remained accessible in traces.[8] Language, as nativist scholars in the eighteenth century had already concluded, offered the necessary reminder testifying to this prior life and could, it was believed, animate memory to recollect such a time. The ever-present imperial institution, however truncated or concealed by "cloud cover" (noted by the *bakumatsu* activist Shintō priest Maki Izumi), could also inspire people to dream once more of remote antiquity. After all, the event of 1868 was nominally devoted to restoring the ancient authority of the emperor, and adherents of this cause would continue to lament this unfulfilled ideal when, long after the Restoration, it became evident that the emperor was no closer to exercising direct authority than he had been in remote antiquity. At the same time the government appealed to antiquity, it declared its determination to "search for new knowledge throughout the world" and to "eliminate old customs and abuses," as if to immediately announce its intention to inaugurate a genuinely new beginning rather than a repetition. But the act of summoning the most archaic and inaugural moment of national formation by invoking the mythic achievement of Jimmu Tennō was consistent with the nativist conviction, articulated in the last days of the Tokugawa order, that reproducing the archetypal achievement of the deities constituted both an assault on representation (long enthralled to Confucianism and Buddhism) and a valorization of practice.

By itself, the Restoration represented one of those moments in which a society appeals to figures outside of time to manage an epochal historical event or experience. Indeed, it was seen as a time most to be imagined that would break free from the eventfulness that had produced the Restoration, a utopia unfettered by history. In a sense, the very ambiguity of the political arrangements accomplished by the Restoration resembled most what Antonio Gramsci, writing about Italy in the nineteenth century, described as a "passive revolution," a revolution/restoration that combined social forces in such a way as to install the contradictory impulses of both revolution and restoration. Even before the Restoration, Tokugawa nativists had already developed the idea of a political poetics they believed capable of recruiting timeless forms from a historically indeterminate experience to control contemporary eventfulness. When Motoori Norinaga subjected the world of things (*koto*) to the mediation of words *(kotoba)* and made its "recitation" (or representation) a supremely poetic act, rousing the poet to produce-sing the world into existence after having been "deeply moved" by empathic sympathy and sensations (*mono no aware*), he was, in effect, demonstrating how "figuration" (*aya*) "shapes" events and thereby orders them. Here, we can also discern a prefiguration of the later folklorist valorization of performance and reenactment as forms of practice that escaped the constraints of mere representation. Among late Tokugawa nativists, it was Hirata who reinforced this belief in the power of practice to evade the distortions of representation with a conception of repetition that derived from his formulations concerning the necessity of reproducing the conditions of creation. His follower Ōkuni Takamasa went further with a theory of restoration that sought to secure the effect of difference in the act of repeating the same. And this was, I believe, the informing principle behind all those attempts in the 1920s and 1930s to resituate a timeless and eternal everyday life, usually modeled after the village, within the space of a modernizing society. Such efforts were seen as fulfilling the original intention motivating the Meiji Restoration to manage a momentous historical experience by reinstating a figure enlisted from outside of time in the historical world of capitalist modernization. This might be the perpetual domain of the folk, the village, the shrine, or even an original aesthetic sensibility attesting to genuine cognitive difference that distinguished Japanese from others.

What Meiji statesmen failed to notice, or misrecognized, was the coexistence of two differing and contradictory visions for national history that could, in the years to come, provide authority for competing claims to national identity. This is what animated native ethnologists, early in the century, to begin their immense project of collecting and preserving the remainders of folk life in order to construct a version of national history decidedly different from the one promoted by the state. Both of these versions were free from binding associations since one projected an imaginary but necessarily mythic past that had already been completed but was now lost, while the other envisioned an imagined future that was still to be found on the basis of a national history that linked emperor and people. Nonetheless, the creation of a modern ideology of national formation in Japan depended on the state's capacity to naturalize the contradiction of restoration/revolution as a unique accomplishment of the Japanese endowment. What this meant, on the one hand, was embracing an image of an evolutionary, progressive history which the Meiji state had launched (proclaimed by the publicist Fukuzawa Yukichi when he declared that Japan had no history until 1868, only political regimes), driven by a linear narrative that demonstrated the development of new productive forces, technologies, and institutions. Once development came up against the limits posed by the relations of production, the choice was either to accommodate them in new adaptations (the Spencerian, and later Parsonian, conception of evolution) or to dissolve them (the Marxian plot line.) But, on the other hand, the autonomy granted to this developmental narrative was early challenged by the idea (promoted first by nativists and then later by their folklorist successors) that production remains subordinate to socionatural conditions, to the existence of the community which always mediates the relationship to the land. This relationship plainly privileged an alternate conception of history based on the possibility and necessity of repetition. Whereas the former version was capable of setting forth the breaking up of relationships and instituting of a principle of self-transformation, the latter merely seeks to set free a cumulative history; in the former scheme, the forms of human existence are altered, changed periodically, while in the latter they remain fundamentally intact. (The changes that take place mean that humans will not perceive themselves as separate from the land and from each other and were at the heart of the Tokugawa nativist conception of history and society but reappropriated by native ethnologists in the twentieth century as the context of the communal body.) Repetitive, collective history called for "constancy," a principle celebrated by Orikuchi as one of the principal values of the archaic endowment, and the image of a communal body that seeks to eliminate externality in its desire to expand imminence.[9]

For nativists who developed this idea of repetitive history before 1868, and saw in the event of the Restoration the opportunity for positioning the principle of commonality in a place of primacy, an identity was posited among individual, community, and the land as the dwelling place, as raw materials or as supply of tools that generated the "play of reciprocal embodiments."[10] This view prevailed for only a few years after 1868, expressing the unity of politics and religious ceremony (*saisei itchi*), and was soon abandoned for central control, new institutions of governance, bureaucratic management, rational planning of national policy, and the separation of state and religion. But a view that was concerned with projecting an identity between the inaugural moment and the communal body, and imagining a repetitive history that emphasized the causal force of irreducible cultural elements and the subordination of production to the socionatural community, would continue to supply resources for all those alternative efforts to contest the state's claim to fix the content of "ecstatic identification." So powerful was this appeal to an organic community that the state eventually sought to appropriate it as its own. What better ideology for the continuing expansion of capitalism in its imperialist stage than an ideology of the communal body whose immanentism promised to incorporate other Asians into the community? In this way, it was an easy step to envision something like a gemeinschaft capitalism, as Žižek more recently has proposed, that seeks to retain capitalism's emphasis on private property yet eliminate its baleful social consequences like class conflict and civil disorder. In Japan's East Asian empire, as imagined (we shall see later) later by theorists like Miki Kiyoshi, "cooperativism" putatively meant a community occupied by all Asians. But, as I have already suggested, this worked, as it did in domestic society, to transmute Asians into an economic category vital to the empire but at the same time lacking any political identity. At work was a logic of inclusion and exclusion, where Asians, like workers, were included because of their role in the productive process but excluded politically because they constituted a serious challenge to the conception of social order that kept them oppressed. The paradox of this situation lay in the recognition that workers and the colonized were produced by capitalism yet never completely controlled by it, never completely assimilated to it even though enabled by its mode of production. Even partial exclusion kept both worker and especially colonized on the outside and thus in a position to develop strategies of political resistance. In the world of the late 1930s, this fusion of communitarianism and capitalism became the basis of fascist regimes in Japan and elsewhere and constituted the solution to the crisis of accumulation provoked by the world depression and its social consequence of conflict and struggle. Although war, itself, ultimately resolved the economic problem of accumulation, the appeal to community, where all divisions have been dissolved, aimed to rid society of the specter of conflict. But even with this solution, the colonies still remained outside, by virtue of ethnic differentiation, which played out in racist distancing, as Koreans experienced first in Korea and then as migrant, marginal laborers in the metropole.

The idea of a repetitive history was thus posited on the recognition of loss or a fetishization of a lost origin and the desire to recover it in the present. Fueled also by the fear of losing those primordial forms of everyday life and practices believed to be directly linked to origins, this narrative was, by necessity, dedicated to reproducing over and over the essential social conditions of existence in each generation. Recovery was possible if the necessary move made to return to the origin replaced a regime based on merely representing it. Practice, not representation, was seen as the surest means of actualizing the pure presence of origin in the present. In this regard, Motoori Norinaga was, perhaps, the first nativist to systematically call into question the status of representation as a condition for envisaging a practice of poetics that was deeply implicated in daily life, while Hirata abandoned poetry altogether for the practice of religious devotion and work.[11] If, in any case, Tokugawa nativists pinned their own program of recovery on the necessity of practice, their direct genealogical descendants in twentieth-century Japan, native ethnologists, agrarian reformers, communitarian theorists, and even aestheticians, would justify their own calls for recovery by appealing to a second loss that occurred when the Meiji Restoration abandoned the project of returning to a founding origin for the promise of modern transformation. Specifically, this meant rejecting the nativist insistence on an imperial polity based on the unity of ceremony and governance and, more importantly, implementing the promised communitarian order, fashioned after the archaic, agricultural community. Ultimately, this "loss" led to the dispersal of nativism, driving its message back to the margins of society, again, to make it a vision of marginality—a loss poignantly recounted in Shimazaki Tōson's novel but also in the activity of native ethnologists who constructed a different version of the national narrative based upon the centrality of the folk, their customs and ancestors, rather than the imperial house. Hence, the call for repetition in the folkloric program would rely not on the practice of reproduction, as Tokugawa nativists had urged, but on re-presenting practice as a repetitive event. The central element of this repetitive gesture was fixing, by which I mean inventing the communal body of the folk as a national subjectivity devoid of gender, class, and even regional location (apart from the recognition that the place of the communal body was first seen to be the countryside and then, later, all of Japan). In this communitarian discourse, the earlier preoccupation with recovering a lost origin was cathected onto a new effort to regain the ground of an authentic and originary experience, which could claim for itself identification with origin and provide protection against the alienating changes demanded by capitalist modernization. Among neo-nativists, the lived experience of modern life was dismissed as "unnatural" and "unreal" for a "remembered" experience of the concrete existence of the folk, marked by a sense of the "ordinary," "the common," built on historical fragments and residues, Yanagita's "vestiges" and "survivals," that had been able to remain outside of the temporality of modernity and the new.

Thus, beneath new constituencies circulating in modern discourse, like the "people" (minshū), the "masses" (taishū), new subject positions produced by class affiliations and the acknowledgment of gender-based and sexual distinctions, was Yanagita's "ordinary and abiding folk." Their unseen ancestors watched over and still directed the living (jōmin), an invented term that was a transformation of the Tokugawa nativists' aohi-tokusa, the "blue grass–like people." Underneath a millennial tradition of written narratives and, now, modern novels were Orikuchi's women chanters, who in punctually beckoning the gods to provide good fortune to the archaic agricultural community established the origin of art. Lodged deeply within a modern society based on voluntary associations was the folk gemeinschaft—the native place (kyōdo)—of thinkers like Takada Yasuma, founded on involuntary association and kinship relationships authorized by blood ties. Even seemingly modern economic problems like tenancy were seen, by a sociologist like Aruga Kizaemon, as merely manifestations of older social relationships, just as the modern scientific and rational outlook of the Japanese was undergirded by an archaic cognitive and perceptual endowment which the nativist Motoori had identified as mono no aware. But all of these were simply constructions that came into existence at the moment when older conceptions of life were beginning to disappear. Yet what native ethnologists, especially, sought to offer to contemporaries struggling to account for the speed of modernization was the prospect of erecting a palimpsistic imaginary where the earlier (and essential) layers of national life still shined through the modern overlays to illuminate the present and provide it with a map.[12]

Finally it should be recalled that the program of native ethnology in the twentieth century signified a double loss: the loss that came first when the Restoration turned to renovation (*ishin*) and forgot about restoring origin; and the loss of seeing the demise of the nativist program in national politics and its subsequent integration into state-controlled Shinto. This second loss (dramatized by Shimazaki) merely overdetermined the modern memory of loss and the necessity for searching for an auratic experience to such an extent that it would be difficult, even today, to dissociate the nativist idiom in modern Japan from any discussion concerned with what it means to be Japanese. But, in the interwar period, the impulse to imagine a pure and essentialized communitarian culture must be seen as a continuing effort to fill the place of loss experienced by nativism. The act of forgetting a lived experience for a "remembered" existence was like one of the characters of Orikuchi's *Shisha no sho* (Book of the dead), who comes back to life through the immense task of remembering a woman.

FIGURING THE FOLK

As formulated by Yanagita Kunio, Orikuchi Shinobu, and their followers, the project of native ethnology (*minzokugaku*) provided the prospect of realizing a repetitive history exempt from modernity's temporalizing regime. Steeped in the recurrence of a punctual, rhythmic cycle of a socionatural order, lived by an (imaginary) folk, complete, coherent, and unchanging under the Sign of immutable custom, native ethnology believed it had found a challenge to the presumption of an evolutionary, progressive schemata and a grant of immunity from abstraction and the instabilities caused by constant change. What this means is that Yanagita, especially, located in custom (*fūzoku*) an alternative to the world of reified object commodities that had come to dominate life by the 1930s. A venerated term employed in the Tokugawa period to denote folk life, *fūzoku* was used by native ethnologists as an example of what was still living in everyday life—practices, beliefs, stories, and observances—that derived from long histories and continued to play a role in people's lives. Custom was deployed to offset the baleful effects of the commodity—the world of things—and the persistence of social abstraction, which signified death more than the living. In the thinking of native ethnologists, it also offered the momentary promise of difference against the circulation of the ever new in the ever same, the sign of an identity rooted in a living culture from a distant past. It extended the prospect of relief, if not refuge, against the ceaseless claims of an alienating process of leveling and homogenization. But where Tokugawa Confucianists employed the idea of custom to differentiate between civilized and barbarian, and nativists to distinguish between Japanese and Chinese, the modern ethnological appropriation was neither able to free itself from the commodity form which had prompted the search to find a new function for it nor capable of repressing its racial/racist associations when marking difference.

In the writings of Yanagita, especially, and Orikuchi, we find the construction of an epic narrative of an essential folk that has successfully remained unaffected by the ravages of capitalist change and outside of history itself. In many ways this narrative must be read in relationship to Shimazaki's *Yoakemae*, which sought to chronicle the history of loss and unfulfilled expectation experienced by nativism and the folk they spoke for in the early Meiji period. Specifically, I am concerned with showing how an image of the folk furnished both the reservoir of authentic meaning in an environment where it was always in danger of vanishing and the resources for attacking a "modern life" that seemed to be always escaping because it lacked a true subject. Native ethnologists, with others, sought to redefine daily life in its unchanging primordiality and give form and lasting meaning to it in order to overcome an indeterminate public space—the streets of the great metropolitan centers—where alienation, fetishism, and reification were producing their effects.

Even though enduring essentials were figured in the discourse of native ethnologists simply as constructions to ward off problems fostered by capitalist modernization, it should not be supposed that their deployment aimed at either contesting the state or advocating the overthrow of capitalism. Despite an original antipathy toward the state, practitioners of native ethnology usually supported the state and imagined a communal realm compatible with capitalism. For it should be remembered that the state made available the space of the nation the folk occupied once they were constructed and was, therefore, prior to both the nation and the folk. The state constituted the *referent* for whatever was designated as the sign of an enduring and ineluctable national existence that lay below the surface of contemporary life, waiting to be recalled. Early in Yanagita's career, he had ratified the boundaries set by the state when he tried to describe its constituent parts. In the *Nōgyō seisakugaku*, he wrote that the national state was organized on the basis of the people (*jimmin*) and native territory (*kyōdo*). Territory, which conveyed the sense of "native place, "was separate from people," who do not actually possess it but simply occupy it. Boundaries delineating a territory "clarify the place where sovereignty has reached." The realm was composed of both the people and the idea of sovereignty as it is reflected in the conception of territory. But because people first inhabit the land, they form collectivities, since it is inadvisable for these groups to merely congregate as "swarms." (The term "swarm" was often used by Tokugawa nativists to describe peasant uprisings.) For this reason, it is necessary for people and land to be linked together by "fastening" the human community to the bounded extension of sovereignty. Hence, people rooted in the land, he proposed, are a primary element in the existence of the state, and this fundamental connection represents the beginning of the modern nation state.[13] In this way, his new discipline would seek to compensate for the double loss experienced in modern memory by filling the new national space with the timeless life of the folk, which was, in his thinking, coterminous with origin itself.

In Yanagita's texts the folk became simply an epistemic subject (the progenitor of today's national subject represented as the "broad middle stratum"), rather than a subject of practice, whose existence was realized in discourse, in the very act of representation he had disclaimed. This move to representation was apparent throughout Yanagita's writings and was made explicit when he declared in the early 1930s that Japan was "one's native place," implying a place-bound identity as against a more flexible, place-based one. Because the state fixed both the boundaries and space of national community, thinkers like Yanagita were given only the choice of envisaging a place-bound identity, one that would chain culture, community, and even ethnicity to a specific, fixed place. To have otherwise imagined a placed-based program would have required a political strategy that took seriously the identity of different interests associated with localities, with relationship to the claims of the center, and thus see through the original promise of the Meiji Restoration. Whatever may have been the original impulse behind the communitarian discourse, it slid rapidly into an effort to fill out a space already made accessible to it by the state. Yanagita early on made a move to envisage what he called "One Japan," comprised of the emperor and the *jōmin*, unified in the practices of everyday life since the time of remote antiquity.[14] What his version of the national narrative sought to realize was merely a supplement to the state-driven account, which already was centered in the emperor. Yanagita paired the "abiding folk" with the emperor as the twin pillars of a unified Japan that had existed since the archaic period, continuing without interruption until the modern era when the growth of the cities undermined the unity of everyday life. The task he undertook was to reconstruct this unity, whose memory glimmered through vestiges and surviving practice of the folk, in their stories, beliefs, and artifacts, that would provide a map for the present to recover the location of the "real," the "true Japan," and the meaning of "Japanese." In his thinking, "Japan," like the *jōmin*, was everywhere and nowhere, bound by a place that was fixed and immovable. Because the native place never managed to exceed the boundaries established by the nation state, the folkloric and communitarian discourse was never able to articulate a sufficiently different national narrative that might, as a place-based program, be mobilized against the center. Even the periphery, according to Mitsuru Hashimoto, was rethought and transmuted onto the larger stage of the world. For Yanagita, since the folk were everywhere and nowhere, there was no periphery in Japan, as such, but Japan became the periphery to the global modern world centered elsewhere.[15] Hence, place carried with it the sense of boundedness, the place where one lives, produces customs and repeats timeless practices, and has ancestral roots; it is the final abode of the ancestral spirits, who continue to look down upon the community and protect it. Yet, despite its desire, the "new nativism" (as Yanagita renamed it in 1935) was never able to generate the utopian aspiration of a no-place that late Tokugawa nativism began to envision in its theory of community autonomy as a stand-in for the center. Rather than a no-place (one that was genuinely neither here nor there), it was still Japan of the capitalist nation state that late Meiji reforms ultimately formed in a final effort to solve the problem of late Tokugawa Japan and the diverse sectionalism it had generated, leading to the Meiji Restoration itself. Never far from the very capitalism that had undermined the unity of folkic life, Yanagita and his followers resorted to constructing representations of the folk that managed only to fill in the space assigned by the state, not reshape it—thus their fundamental compatibility with capitalism. In this respect, Japanese theorists merely confirmed Marx's earlier observations about the supposed compatibility of capitalism and romanticism when, in *Grundrisse*, he explained that "it is as ridiculous to yearn for a return to the original fullness as it is to believe that with this complete emptiness history has come to a standstill. The bourgeois viewpoint has never advanced beyond this antithesis between itself and this romantic viewpoint, and therefore the latter [the 'childish world of antiquity') will accompany it as legitimate antithesis up to its blessed end."[16]

Yanagita Kunio's program stemmed originally from the community studies movement started by people like Nitobe Inazo before World War I and was devoted to supplying relief to the rural poor. It resembled the precepts of the Tokugawa theory of *keisei saimin*, but Yanagita began to shift his attention away from relief to re-presenting the image of a timeless, essential communal order marking the place of the folk and their *seikatsu*—what he described as "returning to the community in the community." As early as 1910 (in *Jidai to nōsei*), he confessed that he had been mistaken in his earlier view concerning the necessity of "agricultural management" and the role played by the state.[17] Years later, with the publication of *Toshi to nōson* (1929), he called for a "communal management of the land" (*tochi no kōkyō o kanri*) and advocated the implementation of a program that would lead to the "public production of a previous age."[18] Faced with the spectacle of enormous unevenness between city and countryside (which this text documents), Yanagita promoted not a new rural policy designed to improve the lot of Japan's farming classes but rather a return to older precedents and spiritual exemplars. His intention to return to the "community in the community" placed an emphasis on the continuity of certain social forms like the family and the larger structure guaranteeing cooperation and communitarianism. In *Jidai to nōsei* (1910) he acknowledged the fundamental importance of the continuity of the household (*ie*) in Japan's history. The "awareness of the connection of each person to their ancestors, that is to say, the existence of the household, forms a chain (*rensa*) of individual and state at the same time in the national character of Japan." The awareness, he continued, that these ancestors have multiplied and served under the imperial court for one hundred generations has produced the most unmistakable foundations for a spirit of loyalty and patriotism. Hence, it is "harmful for individuals to slight the continuity of the household" and to advocate "an individualism that has come to be carried out prosperously and sees the history of our country and the history of foreign countries through the same eyes."[19] This argument was re-expressed in the later *Meiji Taishōshi*, where he valorized the "favor of household permanence" and the necessity of "a spirit that prays for the continuity of the household" embraced by the ancestors since antiquity for the maintenance of peace and harmony of society.[20] In these earlier texts, he argued that terms like *ōya*, used in a restricted sense in the present to denote blood ties, encompassed the larger leader/follower relationship that organized labor and would thus locate servants within the extended family. The social unit of the larger household was thus based on the presumption of fictive relationships that bound workers to the core group. In the later *Toshi to nōson* (1929), he announced that the "servants of the ancient agricultural villages were primarily a single clan (*zoku*)." It was the cooperative form of work that necessitated a peculiar, indeed "unique" organization, centered in the figure of the *ōya*, that has marked the "parents of today" and the "household of offspring" since the beginning.[21] But, as we shall see, Yanagita's attention turned increasingly toward developing a discipline based on narrating the "everyday experience of the folk" and always from the more detailed analyses of social units like the "natural village" and the "extended group"; these analyses were continued by rural sociologists like Aruga Kizaemon, who saw the persistence of traditional lineage systems despite historical changes, and sociologists like Suzuki Eitarō, who envisaged these folkic life forms as a manifestation of a "folk spirit." This is not to say that Yanagita's interest in social organizations like the household and village diminished but rather to suggest that he began to consider the broader implications and consequences of communitarian life as it confronted the devastating erosions inflicted by modernity.

Moreover, this shift was accompanied by a move that would emphasize those practices and beliefs, derived from the ancient past, that were capable (because of their survival) of binding the group together in collective solidarity. Yanagita fused his conception of household continuity to the larger religious dimension of ancestor veneration. In his thinking, this religious practice undergirded social organization and the methods of co-operative work and communitarian interest informing Japan's long history. Simply put, the religious authority of the head of the household derived from his direct, lineal descent of the *ie*. The argument represents his mature identification with the nativism of Hirata Atsutane and the theory of spirit migration after death. In Yanagita's reinterpretation, the spirits do not travel very far from their household and village and usually take up residence in nearby hills in order to watch over their descendants. (Hirata believed they resided in sites around cemeteries, even though they now "lived" in the invisible realm.) The enormous respect associated with the head of the household was based upon a prior respect of the ancestors; the head of the household constitutes a link in the great chain between the living and the dead, the invisible and visible realms, the dead and their descendants. On their part, he insisted that the head of the household must serve the ancestors by continuing to participate in festivals, integrating the household (maintaining its solidarity), and seeking to enhance the property of the *ie*, which represented signs of respect.[22] Failure to do so registered as disrespect and an abdication of responsibility. By 1935, when Yanagita published his major text on the methodology of the native place, his commitment had solidified into a resolution dedicated to concentrating not on community, as such, but rather on what he would identify as "certain aspects of the life of the community," especially those practices and beliefs that had constituted the enduring life of the folk.

After 1935, Yanagita moved to implementing a strategy aimed at representing folk life rather than engaging it as an ongoing practice as in his earlier agricultural writings. This involved projecting a conception of subjectivity that identified the people with the "folk" and society with nature. It also revealed the immense stakes in upholding an imaginary in which subject/agent reproduced social relationships and customs in a timeless socionatural productive order that remained outside of history. To realize this program Yanagita turned to traveling and collecting tales and stories produced by the folk over the long duration.

Collecting tales preserved the voice of the folk and, presumably, allowed them to speak for themselves. Presenting stories in an authentic voice avoided ethnographic reporting which, for him, risked falling into representation. But Yanagita was never able to sufficiently differentiate the native place from the boundaries fixed by the state; his communitarian discourse was never able to articulate a sufficiently different narrative from that other place—the outside—that might lastingly challenge the state's capacity to appropriate whatever version it wished to project as its own. Place was where one was bound to live, as suggested above, to produce custom, repeat timeless practices constituting a cyclical and unchanging daily life, and where one died to become a resident ancestor. Although this place was originally rooted in the countryside and its villages, it eventually came to signify Japan as a whole. Because it was place-based, Japan as a whole came to easily replace the countryside; the contest between city and the countryside was transposed to a struggle between Japan and the West. Once acknowledging that the question of modernity was no longer limited to the countryside, which could not remain unaffected by the forces of capitalist modernization, he discovered values still existing in the village—condensed in custom—that would stand in for all of Japan in its struggle to maintain difference against the West. This conception of an enduring folk life invariably functioned like an invisible realm that coexisted with the visible world of power and change and recalled an earlier nativist division of labor between things seen and unseen. What differed in modern Japan were the temporalities; the two realms—a double structure—occupied the same place.

The discipline of native ethnology could only seek to compensate for the loss experienced in modern life by recalling the memory of a prior form of existence whose traces, presumably, still remained available in the countryside. The immediate impulse prompting the formation of a new discipline, inflecting the broader modernist project, was the perception of unevenness Yanagita recognized early and shared with others.[23] Uneven development was paradigmatically illustrated by the vast division between city and countryside that Yanagita and others quickly recognized as an effect of Japan's capitalist transformation. As a champion of the importance of the countryside and well aware of how urbanization and industrialization were eroding its social basis and economic viability, Yanagita saw in this process the deterioration of the periphery—the *chihō*—which he would later identify with Japan in relationship to the world centers. Uneven development emphasized the coexistence and combination of quite different forms of social relationships and the ways by which capitalist growth continued to rely on the existence of the noncapitalist periphery. According to Yanagita, the periphery was being bled dry by the cities, emptied of labor and drained of its distinctive mode of existence. (This is the gist of the book *Toshi to nōson*.) Thus, primitive forms of "accumulation" remain as continuing aspects of capitalist development rather than leftovers that will soon disappear with the establishment of an even ground, "confined to a once and for all transition between precapitalism to capitalism."[24] This observation was reformulated by Louis Althusser, in this connection, when he proposed that each site or sphere of activity in the social formation is marked by a diversity of social practices and natural processes that moves each according to its own logic. Overdetermination and contradiction indicate how each semi-autonomous sphere (economy, society, religion, culture, ideology, etc.) exists with relationship to others, while unevenness points to the mechanism that induces change. But this recognition entailed exploring and identifying more specific consequences of unevenness. In time, the unevenness Yanagita perceived on the political-economic level was recoded in things and objects on the spatial and cultural level to produce the image of different temporalities. It was at this spatio-cultural level that historical differences are both lived and observed in everyday life and where differential rhythms produced noncontemporaneous and nonsynchronous contrasts. In this respect, the observation of cultural/spatial unevenness conformed to Marx's earlier perception that "alongside the modern evils, we are oppressed by a whole series of inherited evils, arising from the passive survival of archaic and outmoded modes of production with their accompanying train of anachronistic and political relations." Where Marx looked to their eventual disappearance, Yanagita and others saw in them the hopeful signs of a more authentic life still available in trace in the countryside. In combination with the new, they offered an alternative to modern life. Hence, in the crevices of unevenness lay the real possibility for antagonism and social conflict that would demand change and transformation. Yanagita saw this possibility early and, fearing its excesses, sought to transmute unevenness into a theory of hybridity, as we shall see, that was made to reflect Japan's uniqueness. As part of this project, he invented the *jōmin* in the hope of erasing the various social relationships and class differences generated and exacerbated by the experience of unevenness.

Within sight of the immense commercial and political power of metropolitan Tokyo—the spectacle of modernity—was the vast population of depleted human beings who lived within its widening shadow. Materially, there were sharp contrasts between the newer metropolitan centers and the countryside where center and periphery met to form temporal and spatial boundaries and where the contradictions of capitalism were often greatest. Yet behind this figure of unevenness was the lived experience of unequal development that marked the relationship between colonizer and colonized. This display of contrasts, so vividly portrayed by Yanagita and systematically analyzed by sociologists like Takada Yasuma, threw into question the relationship between representation and experience and problematized the status of agency. It might be recalled that in Marx's narrative of nineteenth-century modernization, capital appeared in its real abstraction, to break free from certain political representations, relations, and structures. In this respect, the condition of capitalism insisted upon autonomy and arrogated to itself the attributes of a superordinate social agency with no fixed political or cultural subjectivity. Under these circumstances, events would show that the traditional heroes of history had been supplemented by the anonymous forces of capitalism. With Yanagita, we can see how both the agency of capitalism and the figure of the traditional hero were replaced by the ordinary folk and their customs. In describing the purpose of his *Meiji Taishōshi*, he declared how it fails to "display fixed nouns and proper names willfully, effects that are insufficient for received historical narrative. Accordingly, a history of contemporary custom doesn't explain the thoughts of heroes. If one keeps eye and ear open, insofar as one is attentive to the ordinary people who inhabit the country, one thus relates only opinions of things they have come to feel, even if they—the people—slightly conceal their minds."[25] In Yanagita's thinking, a history of custom was an expansion of "natural history."

Early in his career, Yanagita discounted literary naturalism and its program of privileging surface description (what was called *shaseibun*, or "sketching from nature") for a form of reporting where the voice of the folk would speak through him, the "listener" of their tales. In time he abandoned the promise of direct description pretending to a photographic recording of reality because it failed to account for a vast diversity of experience that seemed always to escape its vision. In its place he installed what we might call a depth hermeneutics (what Orikuchi called *jikkan*), that posited an inside and outside, a surface and depth, whose operation he first revealed in *Tōno no monogatari* (1910). With this inaugural collection of folktales he made the gesture to move beyond merely retelling the stories recounted to him by Sasaki Kiyoseki and ethnographic reporting to the more complex operation of penetrating the essence of the experience and returning to give it expression. During his encounter with the teller of the tales, Yanagita tells us that Kiyoseki was "sincere and honest, even though he was not skilled in recounting the stories. I added no word or sentence [to these tales] and wrote [them] down as I *felt* them" (*kanjitaru mama o kakitaru*) (TYKZ, 4:5; my italics). Yanagita placed himself in the position of the traveler, not the teller of the tale but its patient listener, to secure the effect of being witness to the self-presence and timelessness of the folk experience. (He even made a trip to Tōno to give further authority to the role of witness and the effect of presence.) He "prayed" that by relaying the tales he would make plain people "shudder," and he noted that it was his desire to "present this book to all people who live in foreign lands" (4, 5). This self-conscious preamble attesting to innocence and an intention to familiarize the strange found in the midst of Japanese society shows that from the beginning he was interested not in simply describing but rather in expressing things as they moved him. Understanding meant getting inside and beneath the surface. It was for this reason that he and his followers dismissed ethnography, which, because it consisted of reporting from the perspective of an outside, could never hope to reach the interior of folk experience derived from an inaugural moment that could only be ascertained in memory and trace, in "vestiges" and "survivals" (25, 355). But it is important to recall that

Yanagita, despite his "hermeneutic," and his distrust for photographic reporting or indeed even newspapers, still valorized the importance of "seeing" and "listening" as the first step in grasping the complexity of custom as "trace" and illuminating the totality of ordinary life (MTS, 19–22). The importance of Yanagita's program was its capacity to replace capitalism as the source of all activity with the seemingly concrete but historically indeterminate agency of the unchanging life of the folk in their native place. Thus a fixed and static cultural space could be substituted for the changes in temporality necessitated by political economy.

This theme was expressed first in earlier works like *Jidai to nōsei*. Here he reported that the "splendor" of the cities was simply outpacing the "glory of the villages" which were being sacrificed to the development of the former (16:26). Owing to the massive migration from the farmlands to the cities, the rural population was being emptied out from the countryside and the demographic shift was creating everywhere an uneven distribution between capital and labor (31:40). "The savings from the agricultural sector," he wrote, "is gathered by the center and before capital accumulation becomes substantial, the center uses it up for enterprises in Korea and Manchuria." Depleting the countryside of resources for modernization in the cities meant also that the farm population was paying for Japanese colonialism. Two decades later, the subject of unevenness was submitted to thorough analysis in *Toshi to nōson*. In this text, he sought to account for the deepening disparities between city and countryside and the "loneliness it caused by separating people from production on the land, making them suddenly sensitive and uneasy" (250). (This was as good a description of alienation for an avowed non-Marxist as I have seen.) Convinced that continued unevenness would inflict incalculable damage on the country before too long, he worried about the alienation caused by a process that removed people from the land, where they had for so long produced by hand their own food, clothing, and shelter and had been anchored by stable social relations that had defined daily life (241–242).[26] (Ibid.) Over the past sixty years, he declared in 1929, the cities of Japan, "resembling a waterfall pushing out the pool of water below in all directions," have displaced large numbers of peoples and areas with a constant stream of newcomers (253). Peasants are starving and the invasion of city capitalism into the countryside has denuded mountains and thus eliminated "spare lands for continued living in forested regions" (261). Publicly owned fields and forests have been "bathed" up to their "shoulders" in the "blessings of capital from the cities." The great symbol of this unevenness has been the centralization of culture and an imbalance that has produced a "despotism of the urban arts" (272). "Eternal things" like the village are no more (264).

If the policy of sacrificing the countryside for "the splendors of the city" and its resulting economic and ecological consequences was the task of a proper agricultural economics to resolve, as Yanagita once believed, the spectacle of cultural unevenness escaped the capacity of prevailing disciplines to either identify it as a problem or comprehend it. It was this recognition of a cultural unevenness more complex than the material division between city and countryside that prompted Yanagita to move away from the "science" of agricultural economics to formulate a method that might more adequately account for the incidence of unequal development and thus delay the conquest of capital over the surviving forms of received social life. The new discipline would also alter the way he viewed the question of rural relief. The spectacle of capitalism speedily eliminating remaining traces of an older form of life in the countryside persuaded him that neither the historical method, with its reliance on narrative form, nor the new social sciences like anthropology and sociology could supply guidance in explaining this new phenomenon. Moreover, the task was particularly urgent as capital would accumulate in "every nook and cranny of the country" and the struggle for power to sustain the quality of rural life would cease (274). The growth of these vast contradictions had occurred in a scant twelve years, since World War I.

To freeze-dry the moment of cultural unevenness, it was necessary to create an image of a timeless folk that continued to exist in custom and religious observances within the vortex of modernizing changes. Hence the desire for discourse was to stave off death, which could only be sustained by producing an epistemic subject—the folk—and a narrative of eternality centered on the native place, Japan.[27] Yanagita's new discipline sought to resituate a timeless communal order following the rhythms of a repetitive socionatural process, within a linear, evolutionary, and progressive historical schemata driven ceaselessly by the laws of capitalist motion. Native ethnology aimed at implanting an image of an unmoving social order at the heart of a society in constant motion, a historyless and classless community within the historical epoch of capitalism dominated by class relationships. The result was gemeinschaft capitalism, a vision of capitalism without the divisive effects of class conflict: a prefiguration of the "gathering of fascism." By making this move, Yanagita was able to offer his contemporaries a picture of a world that had always existed and transcended class and gender divisions and social conflict precisely at the moment an industrial workforce was being created. Equally as important, this was the moment when a consciousness of new gender relationships was being forged and represented in overdetermined figures like the "modern girl," "kissing girl," cafe waitress, and so forth. Furthermore he managed to project a conception of regional diversity and marginality at the moment when centralization of economic and political power was taking place in the expansion of metropolitan cities.

While Yanagita wanted to challenge the metropolitan interpretation of its own experience as universal, it would be wrong to assume that the new discipline of *minzokugaku* was a critique of capitalism. To be sure, he was acutely aware of the predominance of imperial metropolitan centers of production, exchange, distribution, and consumption that had literally swept up migrants from the countryside to make them internal migrants and exiles in their own land. In Japan thinkers like Takada, Yanagita, and Suzuki Eitarō grasped how this metropolitan perspective concealed the reality of unevenness, owing to capital and its propensity for controlling representation and deterritorializing fixed relationships. In response they sought to articulate a microhistorical experience of the local as a counter-explanation and necessary supplement to the universalizing claims of global capitalism. The reality they wished to disclose, invariably excluded in universalizing macrohistorical representations like H. G. Wells's *Outline of World History* that Yanagita dismissed, was one exposed primarily at the periphery, the margins where the modern and its other met, producing "nonsynchronisms" caused by dissonant forms of being.

If Yanagita failed to sanction a critique against capitalism, he was able to call attention to its problematic and to the way in which its production of unevenness could become the purpose of a research program. The task of re-presenting this fading world, what Marilyn Ivy has properly called a "discourse of the vanishing," [28] was clearly epic and must have required, as in the opening passages of *Yama no jinsei* (1925), immense personal resources to avoid slipping into a bitter condemnation of the very forces that had caused the lamentable circumstances of the mountain villages he was describing.[29]

> There is nobody, apart from myself, who remembers this today. In the last thirty years, during a time of harsh social depression, a man of about fifty years who burned charcoal in West Mino murdered two of his children with a broadax. What were the conditions of this place? The woman [the man's wife] had died and he was raising . . . two children of about the same age, nourishing them in the small cottage of a charcoal maker. I can't even remember their names now. In any case, they couldn't sell any charcoal and when they went down to the village they returned with empty hands, without rice. With bitterness I see the face of these starving children. . . . Even now, that great record of human suffering remains hidden at the bottom of an oblong chest.[30]

In the story, Yanagita further recounted how the children begged their father to kill them and even handed him the broadax. Again, he was describing a condition where the women all died young, where men, who eke out a living, must also raise children. But as the text makes clear, he has recovered this episode with an immense act of recall, seeking to go beyond the mere description of the fact of harshness and brutality in order to express an experience that lay buried in his memory. His emotions had already worked over the scene he was describing. Now, through an act of writing that exceeded ethnographic reporting, he hoped to bring back to life the world of mountain folk, the people of the original Japan, before it disappeared forever. Yanagita recognized that the charcoal makers of this region had lived a spiritual and social life in the same place and way from time immemorial. But in recent years they were being driven out, living desperate and hidden lives in the shadows of Japan's mountains. Pursuing a livelihood derived from the mountains, which had been adequate to provide for his needs, the charcoal maker (and Yanagita) knew that everyday life was now meshed with capitalism and the force of the market.[31] The act of writing, he recognized, could defeat the goal of actually rescuing this hidden world and drive the true life of the Japanese to the outside. History, which he early equated with writing, had already banished the life of the folk to memory. But, he was confident, the erasure of history might be salvaged in the records of people, accounts of their experience, that came in the form of legends and tales (densho). For the "legends that have been transmitted by families explain [these] households themselves."[32] In the *Yama no jinsei*, he observed that traditional folk beliefs "flowed silently," from family to family, generation to generation, so long as there was no real interruption to discontinue them. The episode he recounted of the father killing his two children would signal the condition of a traumatic interruption that would end the record of everyday life lived by mountain folk. In this respect, the earlier *Tōno monogatari* dwelled on the intermingling of mountain folk beliefs and practices and recounted the incidents of ordinary people in their everyday encounter with tutelary deities, ancestors, household, and friends. Yet we must note how Yanagita had placed himself at the end of these tales and legends, at the end of the signifying chain that had produced them without interruption.

　Far from contesting official pieties and the state's version of a national narrative, the tales, with others Yanagita collected, disclose the details of the experience of the everyday lives of the folk and its diversity. Concentrating on those aspects like daily practices and religious beliefs that official narratives invariably excluded, they acted as supplements, whose very diversity would testify to the basic and essential similarity of Japanese beliefs, not their heterogeneity. His interest in collecting folk details for what they disclosed about the experience of the folk's everyday life undoubtedly resembled Hirata Atsutane's earlier *Senkyō ibun* (1809): an

"interview" of the boy hermit Kiyoshi, who traveled regularly between Edo and the otherworld, the mountain dwelling place of spirits and ghosts and thus the domain of "unseen things." But both Hirata's text and Yanagita's later recounting of legends depended upon an original teller of tales and a willing listener; both emphasized the natural relationship between everyday life and the world of spirits and deities of creation; and each, in its own way, showed a bonding between the visible and invisible worlds. With Hirata, as it was with Yanagita, the world of invisible things was eventually identified with the domain of the folk, those who remained unseen and hidden from the glare of the visible world of power. But where Yanagita differed from his great, nativist predecessor was in his commitment to scientific rigor. Throughout his writings he frequently reminded his readers of the necessity of rigorous scientific practices. Owing, perhaps, to his earlier career as an agricultural economist, he retained a passion for positivistic science and was devoted to collecting data that would ultimately "speak" (a piety Orikuchi did not share)—thus his reluctance to interpret and his distrust for mere representation, as well as his desire to allow the facts—tales, legends, and customs—to speak for themselves. To be sure, this commitment to positivistic rigor was consistent with a strategy that constantly tried to capture the immediacy and presence of experience rather than merely representing it, even though he was never able to realize such a heroic program. According to Orikuchi Shinobu, Yanagita's new spirit of folk studies promised to complete the nativist program by introducing the element of "doubt" into inquiry—an element remarkably absent in the "moral certainty" associated with *kokugaku*. By linking the quest for knowledge to the dimension of doubt, Yanagita felt assured that his research program would guarantee a more complete understanding of a contemporary life still coterminous with folkic past. Scientific skepticism was therefore the entry point to investigating the "extremely interesting materials" offered by folk life, and these should always be approached "rigorously." By appealing to nativist methods yet seeking to detach himself from this genealogical past, Yanagita, inadvertently perhaps, ideologized *kokugaku* by drawing attention to its moral certainty.

Yanagita's discipline sought to make manifest what hitherto had remained hidden as an act of preserving endangered life-forms. At the heart of Yanagita's effort to construct a discipline capable of understanding the folk and their life in a modern society was a critique of history and historical representation in narrative form. In fact, the act of constructing a new "science" of community studies (*kyōdogaku*) was supposed to make up for the deficits of a historical method that suppressed knowledge about the folk and remained silent on the details of their everyday life. Historical narratives have "obscured the role of the ordinary folk by concentrating

on wars and heroes." Even those records that manage to disclose aspects of farming life in the past have invariably been written down by government and village officials—people who were outside of the daily life of the folk. A three-thousand-year-old genealogy of the folk has been scarcely transmitted in writing (25:266).[33] Concentrating only on "great events narrating the story of politicians and military struggles," history was invariably limited to representing the past rather than accounting for how it constantly interacted with the present and lived within its precincts. Moreover, "history has not been able to explain such things as the profundity of concerns that affect [people] most, how households flourish today in contemporary *yashiki*, and the ways diverse policies are formulated on the everyday life of the rich and the poor" (25:264). In fact, Japan "has no history of the ordinary people" who have been treated with "little respect," coldly, by history, even though they constitute the backbone of the country (27:16–77).[34] But the study of the native place must aim at securing a "knowledge of the past of the common folk in order to understand the doubts in "real life confronting society today" (25:264).

History failed principally because it was based upon the presumption of a single, nonrecurring event instead of taking into consideration the ceaseless rhythms of repetition.[35] "Because many people are resigned to the fate that history is limited to a reality or facts that occur only once rather than over again . . . it is confusing to know that there are so many types of the same tales and legends throughout the country" (15:313). The availability of a vast hoard of tales testified to how historical representation worked to put different and alternative modes of existence "into the shadows," excluding them from the public record. Even so, their presence in history illustrates incontrovertibly their capacity to escape concealment and endure down to the present (25:267). Since culture is continuous, the daily life of earlier times is still contained within the present. This discovery of the principle of historical repetition, suppressed by conventional historiographical practices, constitutes the "great strength" that has renewed the study of the folk in the native place. Hence, the "history with which we have become accustomed," he declared, "is repetitive" and appears as the great unbroken record of everyday life that has been repeated over and again since the beginning of the race. "The footprints of the people's past have never stopped," and concrete material practices employed to gather and produce food, make shelters and clothing, and the performance of yearly and seasonal rituals constitute enduring life forms immune to historical change and epochal events. "Although straw raincoats (*mino*) are repeatedly made anew every year," he remarked, "it is still the same raincoat made in the past."[36] Even those practices and material artifacts that have originated in a distant past now appear as new manifestations when contemporaries embrace them in their everyday

lives. Yet this doubling or fold (*repli*) resulting from repetition invariably produced a difference and represented an encounter with the realm of the uncanny: the same but yet the not-same, the past that was still present, the modern and its other. When "repetitive deeds are gathered and piled on top of each other, we will certainly [find] there the immediacy of national existence." "For us," he continued, "the realities of everyday life narrate the past that existed before the present. We name those things that have been left behind [for future generations] survival. In calling these things continuing vestiges, an excessively large amount of archaic custom surrounds and enwraps us and lies concealed within us. Even the most cultivated among us finds it impossible to live without being conscious of the past within us. In many circumstances, the act of reflecting [on this] leads to collecting, and where there has accumulated an assortment and classification of materials there is also comparison. It is not possible to desire, in any other country, (the availability) of such conditions for consolidating material to understand the past so easily to this extent" (25:297–298). This search for knowledge from "a variety of real facts that exist before us," he wrote elsewhere, will result in "supplementing common sense."[37]

Only by living the experience of cultural unevenness was it possible to grasp it. Yanagita's method entailed travel, spending time on the road, as if he were continually returning to a home he would reach only in the last, lonely instance, in order to collect tales and legends of ancestral life forms. Contrasting this procedure to the practices of the "white man" who inevitably stands at a distance to observe and judge the life histories of natives they have put under observation, he explained that a method that produced only ethnographic reports inseparable from the act of representing and interpreting could never get any farther than scratching the surface of a culture. Collecting what had been produced by the folk in the process of returning home was a far more accurate method than recording observations. Relying on ethnographic reporting of field observers was like looking at or taking photographs: both operations placed the viewer outside of the picture.

Yanagita's strategy put the investigator inside the scene of investigation, the precinct of the uncanny where modern Japan confronts its double, where the present encounters a past that in all respects is similar but is now out of time.[38] In modern society this is precisely how the appeal to memory works against the claims of history. For Yanagita, the ethnographic method was not capable of performing the difficult task of engaging the very cultural unevenness that signified the historical watermark of this uncanny experience and which now marked the native place. "Among scholars of Europe and the United States," he wrote, there are many who believe that old and new customs exist separately from each other, like fresh and salt water. Even people like Levy-Bruhl, the renown author of *The Primitive Mind*, believes this to be true. But if one looks at the conditions of Japan as they are today, he will see that they seem to resemble more the ebb and flow of the tide of a river. If one is a scholar of conscience, he will not be too greatly attached to the presumption [that separates spheres of existence]. Civilizational hybridity (*ainoko bunmei*) exists not only in Japan but can be respectively seen in the harbors and ports throughout East Asia. In mixed cultures, there are no fixed forms. If one [cultural form] is not rejected, the other may still find a place for itself. As for considering the ways of thinking or modes of deportment that do not always seem to harmonize with the general currents of the times, it is only a situation in which one [cultural form] leans to one side or the other, advances or retreats. When such circumstances are seen with a cold eye from an external perspective [i.e., ethnographically,] it will be judged to be a contradiction, but in the reality of the people's daily life, such things are being lived (*kurashite ikeru*) all the time without any concern whatsoever. There is the so-called countryside in the capital; a variety of archaisms enter into and mix with the modern. (25:279)

Yanagita named this experience of unevenness "the treasure island of scholarship," and he was convinced that it was Japan's good fortune and his happy destiny to have witnessed and lived it. In fact, the appearance of his *Meiji Taishōshi*, which aimed at examining customs that "exist before the eye," disclosed how modern Japanese life in the cities, especially, represented a hybridization of life forms in the mixing of old and new customs and the adoptions and adaptations the ordinary folk had made. Yet this was possible because the folk (as Hani Gorō acerbically pointed out at the same time) had left the villages for the cities, farming for new urban occupations. In this sense, Japan was no longer restricted to the countryside and the village but rather referred to anywhere where traces of folk life were embedded. In large cities like Tokyo and Osaka, Yanagita proposed, the spirit of folk life still prevailed in the fusion of customs and in the capacity to reconstruct the life of "one's native place," in process of vanishing, from the perspective of an "other place" (*ikyō*).[39] "People without the special experience of this ["living in a village"] today are still able to explain the attitudes of our villages. We understand our villages because we see them from other villages. The result permits us to compare things that are not adjacent to each other. The changes in one's native place appear to accompany an increase of interest in other places."[40]

Foreigners, he charged, were always limited to constrained circumstances of research both "laughable" and "appalling" and were compelled to speculate on and embellish the "gleanings" they are able to skim off from secondary reports rather than relying on firsthand experience. Understanding the folk required not interpretation but the exercise of empathizing with their experience. The investigator had to be in a position to recognize what constituted the fund of spiritual beliefs the folk took as second nature—beliefs forever beyond the powers of the outsider to grasp. "It is difficult to grasp what is behind an interlocutors' words without possessing considerable skill," he warned, and the investigator must make every effort to avoid a "regrettable imitation" that "chases after the footprints stamped by the white man" (25:355). In the *Minkan denshō*, the final step in a research agenda, and clearly the most important, was collecting materials relating to the heart (*kokoro*) and consciousness of everyday life, that is to say, the "essentials," which most foreigners are "excluded" from reaching (25:337).

In England, Yanagita noted, the old style of daily life derived from a remote age had become indistinct. Because of its disappearance, a community studies program dedicated to examining the native place is simply impossible to carry out. Scholars who usually congregate in London, he continued, resort to employing the technique of collecting materials by going everywhere else outside of the country (25:292). In other words ethnographers collected materials from abroad to speak about an everyday life in England that no longer was accessible to them, even in trace. Their procedure reinforced even greater specular distance by establishing a division between those who investigate and those who are investigated. A perspective that posited an outside to investigation was already mediated and forever prevented the investigator from gaining direct access to the object of inquiry. Ethnography could have no surety that the information it was collecting from abroad would have any direct relevance to understanding daily life at home. Unlike folk ethnology, it was simply an encounter with the strange and unfamiliar, not a confrontation with the uncanny, the recognizable repetition of the same with difference, the return of the repressed of the collective experience of the native place, one's home. Yanagita was insistent that custom constituted referents for the scene under examination and had meaning only for those who lived them and belonged to the cultural configuration in which they had been produced. In this restricted sense he saw folk studies, like Tokugawa nativists, as a discipline (*gakumon*) committed to revealing self-knowledge and understanding (25:325–328). To avoid slavish dependence upon faulty foreign methods of investigation, he reclassified the levels of research to demonstrate how differing objects of inquiry corresponded to deeper layers of experience: (1) the first level of material related to travelers' collections that reported external forms of daily life secured through observation; (2) next came collections and reports that commented on daily life and required a knowledge of the language; and (3) finally there existed collections that revealed "essential" information about the spirit and everyday consciousness of the folk (25:336–337). We already know that among the three layers, the third was the most important and "excluded foreigners, with few exceptions." But the first and second levels ultimately depended upon the operation of the third and constituted the stages of an itinerary that led from the surface to the heart of things, promising disclosure of "the inner secrets of the heart of the native that can never be realized" by the act of "viewing and listening from the outside." As he explained in the earlier *Meiji Taishōshi, sesōhen*—listening and viewing—had to be carried out from an inside perspective. "Our collecting," he claimed, "is *also*, at the same time, a consideration of the inner live of the native" (25:270, italics added). It supplied the means to "return to the community within the community." With this move Yanagita supplied native ethnology, if not the modern Japanese consciousness, with a structure of desire for an origin that could never be reached and opened the way for a nostalgia driven by irretrievable loss.

Yanagita's apparent slippage into exceptionalism, a gesture shared by most of his contemporaries in the 1930s, was linked to the conviction that the purpose of inquiry was to attain self-knowledge that might yield "good fortune" in the future. This argument was already articulated by Orikuchi Shinobu in the theory that national literature derived from the chanters of yearly rituals in archaic times who summoned the deities to continue abundance and good fortune for the community. Never entirely abandoning his first interest in rural relief, Yanagita believed, by the 1930s, that relief meant identifying those principles and collective experiences that guaranteed social solidarity. Knowledge of the inner, spiritual life of the native and social utility converged to constitute what he called a "new nativism" (*shinkokugaku*) in the early 1930s. This new nativism was reinforced by his "discovery of Okinawa" after making his first trip in 1921—what he later described as an "epoch-making event in our studies." Okinawa offered a treasure trove of unchanging religious beliefs and practices that were fundamental to the figure of an enduring Japanese daily life. Viewing Okinawa as a freeze-dried reminder of what Japanese life supposedly looked like in archaic times (it was more of a misrecognition than an actual sighting), what Orikuchi deemed a vast, living replica or even laboratory of seventh-century Japan in the present, Yanagita ironically risked recuperating the very same misrecognition he had condemned foreign ethnography for making. But this easy and seemingly unproblematic assimilation of Okinawa and its own claims to difference (claims being made in Korea at the same time with far less success) constituted the sign of a colonial unconscious that stalked the cultural sciences in Japan during the interwar period. It was shared by others as diverse as Orikuchi, who saw in the island ancient Nara; Miki Kiyoshi, as we shall

see, whose formulation of "cooperativism" based on communal brotherhood easily overlooked differences among East Asian peoples; and Watsuji Tetsurō, whose philosophical anthropology authorized assimilative
concepts like "relationality" (*aidagara*) and the determination of Being by
spatiality rather than temporality and the Heideggerian "historicality."[41]
Yanagita rhapsodized Okinawa as a singularly important source that was
capable of providing inexhaustible possibilities for the continuing study
of the folk because of the antiquity of life still existing there (its ruling
house was contemporary with the Kamakura bakufu), an antiquity he
attributed to the relative isolation of the island from foreign contact.[42]
Even the presence and influence of Buddhism was negligible and had
failed to affect deeper rooted and more remote native beliefs and practices. If Okinawa did not provide a complete template for understanding
an authentic and unchanging Japan, it nevertheless offered an important
interpretative target of opportunity. "Today," he wrote, [Okinawa] preserves unconscious archaic customs that cannot be seen and compared"
elsewhere and "imparts a key to understanding our own doubts"
(25:217). The restoration of the foundational beliefs that were still being
observed in Okinawa and that had once configured the organization of
the ancient collectivity would serve the present in its search for finding
principles of social determinacy and the appropriate forms for binding
the folk into a socially cohesive unit. Observing the present as a time when
concern for religion was waning, he advised that the moment was thus
propitious for resuscitating foundational beliefs that still lay buried
through the operation of a proper discipline of folk studies (25:322–323).

Yanagita came around to believing that an explanation of rural distress
and a policy of reconstruction aimed at preserving families on the land,
so much in the air in the 1920s, could not rely exclusively, if at all, on an
appeal to material factors. The solution, he was persuaded, was not political and economic but rather cultural, specifically religious and spiritual.
The problem of rural distress derived, in great measure, from the weaken-
ing of religious consciousness in the countryside and, by extension, in the
nation as a whole. The task of the new nativism was "archaeological,"
therefore, directed to restoring archaic religious practices to the center of
national life. And this could not be accomplished without acknowledging
the existence of "remains" of ancient beliefs existing within the depths of
contemporary rural "agitation" and "suffering," without, in fact, recognizing the presence of the repressed real of religious consciousness. To
fully grasp the crisis, he proposed, and to "know the processes we have
passed through, we cannot set aside the problem of ancient beliefs"
(25:327). Folk studies became "useful" once it recognized the importance
of religion and its function in the modern society.

Yet an equally compelling argument for utility lay in the conviction that the study of the folk must also contribute to "self-understanding" and thereby to "relieving the people." Yanagita saw the contemporary crisis as one caused by capitalism, which undermined all settled relationships and fixed beliefs. It was especially manifest in unemployment and the chronic distress experienced by the farming classes. The movement for social reconstruction (*kaizō*) announced in the 1920s was a response to a "beehive of problems." Although there was observably widespread unemployment throughout the country and an equally large number of people were committed to finding solutions, much of it was simply talk. Many proposals advanced were "unsuitable to the current of the times" (25:326). What he meant by employing the richly laden term of an earlier era, *jisei*, referred to all those solutions that were produced by human labor and were thus counted as natural; the various proposals for reconstruction enthusiastically promoted in his day went against nature. Here Yanagita was plainly pointing to left-wing political ideologies and programs that had been imported to Japan. By returning to both an earlier commitment to a program leading to practice and the utility of knowledge, he refracted the modernist assault on abstraction and its search for the concrete. "If slipping into a theory of abstraction is avoided," he advised, "people will be firmly rooted at the source where they will be able to extract from the state of affairs those things that need to be reformed; they will come to the necessity of seeing and carefully scrutinizing the causes of the distress that need to be discarded" (25:326). Knowledge of the native place taught him that rural distress and the necessity to preserve families on the land could not, in the end, rely on appealing to material—economic—solutions (25:327). While he was willing to acknowledge the existence of widespread rural poverty, he refused to support any scheme that failed to account for the way things were before the contemporary crisis. If contemporaries refused to recognize the existence of "remains" (*nagori*) of archaic beliefs underlying rural "agitation" and "suffering," he warned, there would be no chance for reconstructing the everyday life of the folk. People had to work for a reunion with what was their true self, even though it would appear uncannily other and strange to them. In this inflection Yanagita came close to aping the moralistic palliatives that were being peddled by contemporary agrarianists. But where he differed from more strident rural fascists was in his deep concern for resituating religious beliefs at the heart of a modernizing society as the surest solution to preventing the occurrence of an even greater threat that now promised to disrupt the bonds of social cohesion and tear society apart. The new nativism he imagined in this historical conjuncture also promised to answer his "prayer that man will understand himself."

At this point, Yanagita's construction of the folk converged with the ideologization of its figure that was being formulated in the 1930s by social thinkers like Takada Yasuma, who called for a transformation of "anthropologism" to "folkism" (*minzokushugi*); Suzuki Eitarō, who celebrated the communalism signified by the "folk spirit"; and Aruga Kizaemon, who located hierarchical relationships like *oyakata/kokata* in the folk substrate of the extended family (*dōzoku*). This ideologization, as we shall see, named "folkism" and condemned as "archaism," eventually resulted in employing the figure of the folk and their unchanging social order as a stand-in for the state itself. Yet it was also in this historical conjuncture that thinkers like Hani Gorō and Tosaka Jun began to call into question the claims of native ethnology and community studies and its representation of the folk as a fantasy, and its longing for a lost origin that never existed. What Hani called for in a searing critique of community studies ("nine in ten people no longer live in a community," he roared) was a new subject of action—not the epistemic subject embraced by folklorists captured in and controlled by representation, but rather a subject of praxis capable of making history in the act of liberating the community for the masses instead of the folk. If Hani never acknowledged the immense consequences of unevenness, even between city and countryside, he was, nevertheless, committed to establishing a proper community science that would "emancipate the people from illusions and deceptions." When Tosaka Jun discounted as a fiction the lavish claims of "Japanists" (*Nihonshugisha*) who upheld the family system as continuous since antiquity, he was also trying to liberate the Japanese from a desire for loss and the nostalgia it produced.

The program of Yanagita, among others, was principally concerned with demonstrating how the "natural community" worked to produce its own essence in the customs of everyday life. In their hands, the image of community acquired a preeminently immanentist representation to appear as an organized, living totality, one that is always self-present. Yet the fashioning of the folk was produced by an interpretative framework that already promoted orality, spatiality (the synchronic picture of a system with no history), alterity (especially the difference a cultural break signifies), and unconsciousness (the status of collective phenomena and the averaging of those elements that were believed to have permeated the ordinary life of the people). All these were held up against concepts like writing, temporality, that is, the succession of historical moments marked by events, identity, and consciousness. Moreover, the appeal to a "natural, organic community" and its timeless folk was deployed to displace the threat of social dispersion and the agency of historical classes. By the end of the 1930s the folkic group had become the basis for a larger, more encompassing identity called the East Asian folk and supplied ideological support to a variety of imperial and colonial policies that were demanding regional integration and incorporation. Finally, the discourse devoted to figuring the folk and their natural community often slid under a larger discourse on culture, just as earlier discussions on community were assimilated to considerations of culture. The implications of this triumph of the epistemic subject for the practices of social science and thought in Japan are difficult to gauge, even though we can detect its ghostly presence in all those shrill discussions about the Japanese that are regularly mobilized to dramatize the hoary binary that insistently differentiates "we Japanese" from "Them" (the outside world)—thus recalling in yet another register Heidegger's distinction between authenticity and inauthenticity. We can say that it ultimately authorized the formation of a discipline called Japanology that made folk, community, and culture (a synonym for race) interchangeable subjects of knowledge representing a completed history and the presentation of an accomplished essence.

ART, AURA, AND REPETITION

For Japanese who lived the reality of capitalist modernization and experienced the penetration of instrumental rationality in their lives during the interwar years, the image of the Meiji Restoration as a repetition of what Walter Benjamin once called an original "fore-history" offered the promise of relief to all those seekers of the authentic who were convinced that something essential had been lost in the commitment to modernity. Throughout the period there were punctual calls for a Taishō Restoration, a Shōwa Restoration, and even a "return to Japan" (*Nihon kaiki*) in the effort to endow it—repetition revealed by the Restoration—with the meaning of a " 'will of have been' as an event, a past which comes from the future."[43] Before World War II, many people in Japan, and elsewhere, seemed willing to act on the belief that repetition, not the endless chain of temporal linearity, revealed the only possible meaning history could offer and thus supplied the mechanism for suspending the narrative of continuous progress, for contesting the official national storyline by dramatizing the double gesture of sacrifice and destruction. But the apparent slippage of the national narrative and its incapacity to suture the difference between the claims of an empty, homogenous time, on the one hand, and a strategy of repetitious performance demanded by "now-time," on the other, was undoubtedly exacerbated by experiencing life in a Japan marked by different but coexisting temporalities—in other words, by experiencing the unevenness that was the principal condition of capitalist modernization. Not everyone in the interwar years was as confident as Yanagita Kunio in the happy coincidence of hybridization which, in its own way, worked as effectively to efface difference as did capitalism itself. We have seen, already, that recognizing this experience persistently prompted the production of cultural theory that sought stability and the hope of security in the figure of repetition that was made to promise the relocation of a privileged moment or even place. Japanese in the interwar period, like contemporaries elsewhere (Walter Benjamin), aimed to fill the present with the past, or at least to call attention to how the past still commingled with the present, by inserting a moment of repetition, a memory, a "trace" of another life and place that would recall a "fore-history" and its meaning of difference in a world dominated by homogeneity, continuous time (as against continuous structures), and the leveling effect of sameness. Yanagita, we have seen, exulted in discovering an original Japanese life in Okinawa after his trip to the island in 1921, and Orikuchi Shinobu went even further to announce that the island had preserved, almost perfectly, life as it had existed in the Nara period (seventh/eighth centuries). But, as we shall see, Orikuchi seemed to have a greater penchant for empathetic identification with the archaic past and indeed other genders and subject positions, a greater desire to relive these identities, than did Yanagita, whose single-minded commitment to positivist rigor prevented the excesses of imagination. (We must recognize that Orikuchi's passion for cross-dressing at the very least revealed a desire for other identities and occupying other subject positions.) Benjamin, for his part, identified this world of nonsynchronous temporalities and spaces as the state of "historical apocatastasis," which yielded glimpses and images that flared up of another form of existence and even utopian aspiration.

The means of reaching this "other place" was frequently through the exercise of hermeneutics or some comparable form of empathetic understanding, which more often than not resembled Benjamin's conception of "construction," even though it avoided acknowledging such a kinship. For Orikuchi, it became the privileged route of entry into the time of modernity's distant prehistory, and to an earlier way of life that could still be remembered by the collectivity, not in historical narrative but in surviving traces, lingering customs, and artisanal skills that were in danger of disappearing. The aim of native ethnologists was to redeem commodified existence phenomena from their "degraded immediate state"— drawn, that is, from their givenness. While Yanagita Kunio devoted his immense efforts to revivify custom and tutelary worship as the source for revealing the original life of the Japanese, and Yanagi Soetsu single-mindedly attempted to resuscitate folk arts and crafts in the 1930s, Orikuchi Shinobu, a self-styled follower of Yanagita, summoned folk memory itself. This was memory that flashed up in literature to reveal the preliterate origins of art and the auratic moment in which archaic folk first gave utterance in expressions of thanks to the gods for the continuing good fortune and well-being of the agricultural community. But it was the repetition of these utterances in punctual rituals that marked the nature of folk life. In an age of "mechanical reproduction," it was precisely the identity of endlessly repeatable processes, like Yanagita's conception of custom and Orikuchi's celebration of religious ritual, that signaled both authenticity and a historical testimony of practices and beliefs that have been experienced. Yet it was a testimony that had to bracket history, as such, for the enduring recurrence of the originary and auratic moment. When Yanagita and Orikuchi rejected the practice of historiography for native ethnology, what the latter called a "prior knowledge" (*sendai no chishiki*), they were upholding the claims of a primordial (and archaic) folk everyday life whose authenticity was based on all that is transmissible from the beginning. To perform this act of retrieval implied a reclamation of utopian expectations from the discredited vestiges of earlier forms of life which, when contrasted to the present, might still prove their superiority and thus satisfy Benjamin's "secret agreement" between the past and present that animated modernists everywhere. It might also offer the possibility of a "reconciled existence," as Yanagita demonstrated in his powerful account of contemporary custom, *Meiji Taishōshi, sesōhen*, between a capitalist and reified present and the aura of prehistory that still managed to illuminate sectors of Japanese society. In actuality, such a condition of existence might ultimately supply the occasion for experiencing past in the present and thus the opportunity of laying hold to the auratic— what Benjamin described as the "unique manifestation of distance"—that both modernity and capitalist modernization were busily eliminating. Among seekers of the auratic distance none dramatized more the urgency of restoring the figure of repetition in contemporary life than Orikuchi, who saw in the recovery of timeless custom and affect the key to finding both the authentic life of the folk and its immense difference from the homogenous world of the present.

Orikuchi was born in 1882, the same year that the last, great Tokugawa nativist, Yano Harumichi, died.[44] Not long before Yano died, he lamented the loss of those utopian possibilities nativism had momentarily offered its most intense adherents in the halcyon days immediately before the Meiji Restoration. In an exciting moment after the epochal event, the reinstatement of the dreamed archaic arcadia seemed to be within reach. But in less than a decade, the Restoration had turned into a renovation as a growing chorus of vocal dissenters began to see in it deception and the deathblow to their most cherished aspirations. Before the writer Shimazaki Tōson recounted this experience in *Yoakemae*, Yano Harumichi recorded in a short poem his own vast disappointment and sounded an elegiac lament for the vanished glories of Kashiwara and the promise of returning to its enchanted time for a fresh start in the new, uncharted present of Meiji Japan. All that was left was a "dream that will never be." The unintended irony of this solemn judgment, mourning the abandonment of the nativist restorationist ideal, was that it would enable subsequent thinkers and writers to constitute the figure of return and repetition outside of time, and activists to recruit it regularly to challenge the unfinished business of the Restoration. With the collapse of the nativist ideal, the Restoration was seen as an incomplete event that still required fulfillment. Yet the defeat of the nativist ideal marked the beginnings of a conception of nationhood that would constantly utilize the literary and spiritual resources of the archaic Japanese experience which earlier nativists had established as a condition of their own practice. In Orikuchi, a discredited nativism would find its most ardent champion, who with tireless energy would seek to show, time and again, that the very practice of national literature (*kokubungaku*), which had been institutionalized to define the new nation, could not be considered an effect of modern state formation but its enabling condition. By making this dramatic move, Orikuchi changed the nature of what a Japanese national literature and, by extension, a nation might be. He also redefined the vocation of folklore as the study of national literature.[45] The upshot of his intervention was not only to redefine national literature as the purpose of folk studies, but to locate its inaugural moment in the archaic experience and thus at the origins of art itself.

Orikuchi intervened first in a discussion on national literature in the early 1920s and then turned his sights on native ethnology, constantly returning to it in the postwar period, when he completed his essays on the "Production of Japanese Literature" ("Nihon bungaku no hassei"). At one level, his discourse represented an inflection of a larger purpose to rescue nativism from its degraded state as the source of an alternative knowledge whose claims to authority derived from modes of knowing unconstrained by rational utility. By the same measure, his program reflected one of the several attempts during the interwar period by modernists to find—literally in his case—a ground of existence, or the "mother country" (*higakuni*). But even before he turned to perform a systematic assessment of the status of national literature and its meaning for the Japanese, he constructed a critique of the Meiji bureaucratic state that sought to explain how imagination was forfeited in the commitment to Enlightenment. In an article of 1921, titled "Higakuni e, Tokoyo e" (To the mother country, to the far-off land), he complained that the "light of Enlightenment" had transformed "our hearts" into a "wretched, dry beech." "We have become tired of looking at the chief councilors of the august Meiji who are bewildered about the spirits of the numerous ancestors." What troubled Orikuchi was the sacrifice of imagination and a tradition of beliefs for the utility of rational instrumentality. He feared that the stories the ancestors had transmitted from antiquity when they began to "dream of a native place under a blue sky and white clouds" had almost disappeared in the present. Yet, it was a "feeling" that undulated over the centuries, like the "furrows of waves of the folk spirit." What bothered him most was how little people understood of their own beliefs, what was actually "our *kokoro*" (heart). Even if it is a good thing to talk about bringing back into contemporary view considerations of the ancestors from times unseen, it has not yet become a reality. The "light of the Enlightenment" fell short of illuminating older beliefs derived from the folk spirit and had not entered into contemporary discussion. There is only the world of the heart, he proclaimed, and thus only a knowledge produced by feeling and emotion and nothing else. Among those who have achieved "extraordinary careers," he remarked, the acquisition of new forms of knowledge have prevented them from understanding that the "heart," like the "sound and long sleep of moss," should not be disturbed. Here, Orikuchi was referring to how the acquisition of new instrumental knowledge had become the criterion for bureaucratic recruitment. In this complaint he was expressing a characteristic dissent that he articulated later in his critique of the custodians of national literature. Careerism was identified with certain forms of knowledge and a neglect of others, especially those that were closest to the Japanese spiritual experience and which were based on a different kind of logic. Examples of this exclusionary modern practice abounded everywhere but were particularly evident in language usage, where certain designated means repress other, older associations. "The example of ancient terminology," he explained, "also shows how an experience beyond expression was made into an object." The ancients considered as the "other place" (*ikyō*) lands on which they had no firsthand knowledge or simply countries other than Japan. But not all these places and lands that could be found on maps today qualified as the other place, however strange and different they may have appeared. Even among those countries that actually exist, they cannot be classified under the name of *ikyō*, since the other place is woven into the "woof" of imagination." The world view of "our ancestors" has dissipated in our times, he deplored, and contemporaries who now lived in the "latter days" had to take notice of deceased ancestors which, accordingly, meant "attaining the dreams we have not considered, constructing accounts of countries that have illuminated the spirits of men who have dreamed." Orikuchi was convinced that through the "movement of art" it was possible to "anticipate" and "imitate" the yearning for the "other place." Scholars of ancient history and archaeology, he explained, never move beyond presenting evidence. Vast contradictions existed between the literature of prayers and divination transmitted by the teller of tales (*kataribe*) and subsequent historiographical interpretation. "There is a crossing of swords of reflection between the reality of the past and the historical content that comes after it. There has occurred a temporal mistake there. There are many contradictions in Japanese literature between knowing that something is a fact of the past and feeling that it is a fact of the present. Japanese literature calmly recognizes the mixing of temporality." While this particular characteristic was nothing to boast about, he continued, "its real, historical meaning pointed to a spatial, geographic mixing." While prayers and divination were produced in a specific locale, in other words, their transmission over time opened them up to additions, especially by storytellers, that required paying special attention to thought, periodicity, and geography in any subsequent consideration of them. But what has been immediately "forgotten" has been the remains that have survived which revealed the "heart that yearns for connection with the original country recorded from the mouths of the ancestors. I believe that the strength that has moved the ancestors two thousand years before still lives within our heart today." In the text on the "mother country," he recalls how ten years before writing it, he had made a trip to Kumano. "When I stood at the extreme edge of Daioka promontory, which jutted out into the sea on a bright afternoon . . . , I didn't feel that it was the native abode (*furusato*) of our spirit. Because of the sentimentality of affected poets who pass over this, it has not come down to the present. Will this not appear as 'nostalgia' and an intermittent legacy that agitated the breast of our ancestors?"[46]

Orikuchi was referring to an experience of longing that was all but lost to history and even memory. The experience of the ancestors, who first expressed it was itself already a nostalgic longing for the "mother-country" existing beyond the "crest of waves": the "native place that shook the spirit adored by our ancestors."[47] Though the ancients did not cry out the name of "mother country" for this land, he was, nevertheless, convinced that it was produced by the archaic imagination. Its first manifestations could be traced in the faintest "shadow" of an age of "matriarchal authority," at the moment when the young were separated from their "mother households" and came north, to these islands, which ultimately stimulated powerful nostalgia for the land they had left. But today, Orikuchi added, it is important to consider even more strongly a "second imaginary" that related to the "tragic conclusion seen in exogamous marriage." Because this longing was deeply imprinted on the heart of the young, it provoked "sympathy with the villages of other families who wanted to return to their mother." It is natural to think of the name of the mother when thinking of a land to which they had not returned.

In this interpretation, Orikuchi was pointing to how poets and ultimately literature had simply repressed the memory of this yearning for an other place that informed the spirit of the ancestors. Yet he was also suggesting that this sentiment was driven by an archaic imagination that tried to envisage the mother country beyond the sea as the place they had left for the islands. The memory he constructed resembles the kind of memory Proust unveiled in volume four ("Sodom and Gomorrah") of *In Search of Lost Time*. Proust was talking about the effect of soporifics on the memory and the way it puts "out of action . . . the power to act in little things, in everything that demands exertion in order to recapture at the right moment to grasp some memory of everyday life." But Proust then went on to ask the question, surely implied in so much of Orikuchi's own desire to recall a folk memory, "What, then, is a memory which we do not recall?" What Proust was concerned with was the mechanism of recalling a distant memory. He was certain that it was possible to recover memories that are not remembered, which are invisible and unknown, but "if I do not have the faculty of calling them to me, how do I know whether . . . there may not be some that extend much further than my human existence?"[48] I am not saying Orikuchi had read Proust, and I personally think he was probably unaware of the French writer's texts. But it is interesting to note the parallel thinking about memory between the two and how Proust's desire to find ways to "recall" what is not immediately available to the senses illuminates Orikuchi's effort to resuscitate a folk memory that originates with the beginning of the race but which, in his present, has been lost. I shall return to this problem below when considering the identity of this "distant land," as he called it, and the "gods who come rarely" (*marebito*).

To this end, Orikuchi aimed to forge a conception of custom and belief rooted in prior modes of knowing, a knowledge that was all but forgotten in the present, but that still brought to light the archaic daily life as it was lived by the ancestors since the beginning of the race. Orikuchi called this knowledge, founded on nonrational principles, the "logic of the gods," in contrast to the "logic of the Greeks." The "logic of the gods" called for a method of empathic entry into a collective folk experience that still lived in the heart of contemporaries. But Orikuchi was also proposing that modern, rational knowledge and its logic foreclosed dreaming and inhibited the exercise of imagination in the production of knowledge. With this goal, he undertook the immense project of reassessing the purpose of national literature in seminal texts like *Kokubungaku no hassei* (The production of national literature), published in 1926, and *Kokubungaku gairon no seiritsu no nōto* (Notes on the introduction of Japanese literature), compiled in 1933. These texts targeted and challenged the wisdom of received institutional practices and the teaching of literature at universities like Tokyo Imperial University. Regardless of motive (and it is difficult to dissociate critique from personal pique against elitism), the effect was to contest the "rational" principles on which a proper study of national literature had been undertaken and its assigned function in the new national pedagogy. He managed to project a conception of national literature that was indistinguishable from folk studies (*minzokugaku*) and the life of the folk as it was inaugurally imaged as an archaic agrarian order. To make this argument, he equated fundamental religious beliefs formulated and practiced by the ancient community with the first production of national literature and its lasting principle (KG, 24–25). What the modern conception of national literature threatened to efface from memory through the agency of canonization and exclusion was in fact the memory of this inaugural experience. His program specifically resituated the political state at the end of what might be called the signifying chain rather than at its beginning, and thus it risked removing its necessity when he decided to shift the discussion of literature and art to the time of origins, to a preliterate and oral culture, to a "literature before literature" (6, 30). Despite the possible critique of the modern state implied by this performative (and it should be recalled that folk studies originated in an antipathy for the modern state—witness the more than passing resemblance to Kamo Mabuchi's earlier (eighteenth-century) dismissal of the machinery of the state because it was made possible by the adoption of Chinese ideographs—writing), Orikuchi's effort to read folk memory for its traces resulted in rethinking nationalism not in sociopolitical terms but in a religiocultural idiom that expressed an enduring anxiety about death and an insurmountable desire for continuity fueled by a nostalgia for origins.[49] But it should not be supposed, again, that this fear of death was only an anxiety inspired by modernity. Orikuchi's concerns for death and continuity also owed much to the precedent of Hirata Atsutane who, in the early nineteenth century, constructed a vast cosmological system to console people against the fear of death by demonstrating that the spirits of the dead do not migrate to the dreaded and foul underworld of permanent pollution but rather take up residence in the "invisible realm" where they watch over the living, their descendants.

Nonetheless, it was Orikuchi's principal purpose to locate the symbolic origins of art (*geijutsu*), "art before it was aestheticized" (49), in the archaic and inaugural moment of Japanese life, which, he believed, first disclosed those sturdy "religious" ideals that had guided the folk throughout history and would now secure in an uncertain present what Regis Debray once called the "two anti-death processes." The double process imagined by Debray combined an irreversible loss of time and the dissolution of the solidary community, the destruction of both time and place. (There are echoes of Bergson's conception of *durée* in this formulation in which the elimination of death isolates it from the historical order, as well.) By identifying the death-defying gestures in the reenactment of "congratulatory" performances, commemorative performances, and the "ritualization of memory," Orikuchi was convinced he had discovered the necessary mechanism of recall and the forms of activity devoted to redeeming time and community and returning life against death.[50] Like Yanagita, he designated a place as part of this founding gesture, which was, of course, the space marked off by the archaic agricultural community—*Yu*. This was also the place of art and literature, where ritual practices were punctually performed to persuade the gods to grant continuing good fortune. In time, Orikuchi concluded, these places of the past community became Japan—continually present—because it was a bounded space where "divination is still undertaken."[51]

The immediate object of Orikuchi's intervention was the formation of the discipline of national literature and its domination by scholars like Haga Yaichi, who, ironically, shared many of his nativist sympathies. Undoubtedly a translation of the German, the term for national literature—*kokubungaku*—came into usage in the Meiji period and first appeared in 1891 in the eponymous journal *Kokubungaku*, edited by Ueda Mannen, and the book edited by Haga and Tachibana Senzaburō, *Kokubungaku tokuhon*. Soon after, a number of important handbooks on national literature appeared under the editorship of Haga (1892), Fujioka Sakutarō (1909), and Igarashi Chikara (1911). Organizationally, the discipline of "classical short study courses" was implemented in the 1880s and differentiated Chinese from the "national" classics; in 1886, a formal division between a discipline of Japanese literature (*wabun*) and Chinese literature came into being. Four years later, Japanese literary studies was reformulated into a curriculum of national literature at Tokyo Imperial University. This transformation also marked the growing presence of nationalism since the late 1880s and an expanding consciousness of what Japanese increasingly were calling the "principle of national essence" (*kokusuishugi*). In this early stage, the study of national literature was still removed from the science envisaged later by people like Haga. Moreover, its curriculum apparently covered a broad area of concern, which included national language, literature, and history (*kokugo, kokubungaku, kokushi*). But once national literature as a discipline was able to differentiate its content from national history and language (but ultimately remain linked to both in some deep and enduring manner), it would open the way for its practitioners to rethink it as a modern scientific discipline. This division occurred in 1901 at Tokyo Imperial University when the institution went over to a lecture system.

Yet the really important event in this narrative of nation building and formulating a proper national literature was Haga's trip to Germany in 1901. Sent by the Ministry of Education to spend a year and a half in Germany, Haga was to see through a Monbushō program dedicated to studying the research methods of literary history. Upon his return, he immediately presented a set of lectures at the imperial university on the "Method and Outline of Literary Studies" that sought to show how the study of national literature must be a modern, scientific discipline. What Haga brought back to Japan was German philology, which at that time was considered a scientific discipline, as it had been developed by scholars like August Boeckh throughout the nineteenth century. German philology could be easily assimilated to an earlier nativist penchant for the etymology of words, syntactical construction, and sound of archaic Japanese before the incorporation of a Chinese writing system. In doing so, Haga reinforced the connection between national literature and national language and introduced an interpretative strategy that was more hemeneutic than simply linguistic. At the same time, he began to reorganize the literary curriculum into the study of Japanese literature. Although he has often been seen as the formulator of a scientific discipline by combining nativism and German philology, the nativism remained somewhat recessive in his program, a reminder of a nonscientific precursor that could only be overcome with a proper methodology. A critical philology not only would permit Haga and others to distance themselves from a nonscientific nativism but would offer them a historical perspective from which to understand the development of literary production which older methods had entirely lacked. His preoccupation with philology and its Japanese counterpart—*bunkengaku*—supplied the study of national literature with a crucial historical supplement, which, according to Orikuchi commenting later, had become its primary vocation.

In Orikuchi's subsequent critique of *kokubungaku* and its study, this privileging of literary history as a scientific discipline reflected both the domination of an Enlightenment rationality that would determine the purpose of a proper national literature and a discourse that managed to exclude large areas of "literary experience," what he often called "nonliterature," because it lacked a location in the developmental trajectory of literary history (KG, 30). More often than not, the study of national literature was devoted to the "classics," owing to the "exegetics" (*kunkoshugi*) demanded by philological analysis (18). Specifically, it would eliminate oral discourse, which predated inscription, as well as writing that failed to conform to an ideal of literature characterized by a conception of aesthetic appreciation (values). It was these very productions, as Orikuchi would seek to demonstrate, that constituted the enabling condition for generating a national literature.

Haga identified ten national characteristics he found in Japanese literature expressed before and after the Nara period that, nevertheless, transcend the diverse periods in which they were produced and continue down to later ages. For Orikuchi this desire for condensing characteristics for all times to come expresses only a modern Japanese taste for such things.

Contrary to expectations, such characteristics are not even manifest in antiquity. "Literature before the Nara period, a nonliterature, a literature before literature, an age without literature broadens the limits of literature" (29–30). If writing with ideographs and producing sentences are the criteria, then the definition of the literary is too narrow and will conceal what should be seen. Orikuchi privileged Haga's "Ten Lectures on National Literary History" (an expansion of his better known "Ten Lectures on National Character") as the most systematic representation of how national literature had been institutionalized to exclude both literary experiences that did not conform to scientific definitions of literature and the enduring characteristics of the Japanese people which a proper study of national literature unveiled. Haga was convinced that history offered the key to understanding those elements like aesthetics and emotionality that comprised a "true literary history"—a proper historical study that had not yet gotten beyond the introductory stage in Japan. The history of national literature, he proposed, omits only those things that emphasize utility in works, since it is concerned with the communication of ideals. What he wished to contest was a too narrow definition of the canonical and the possibility of recognizing the admission of both poetic and scientific works into official literary history. This flexible attitude opened up the possibility to see in national literature a reflection of Japanese character (kifū), morality, and emotionality, which, he was convinced, could be grasped directly by historical study. An investigation of those texts that express the thought of the people will reveal the changes that have taken place in national thought and emotional life. Although political history disclosed only the outside forms (a view shared by Yanagita Kunio), it was still important to penetrate those experiences that will manifest the kind of life the Japanese people have led and the kind of environment attending it, the best way is to know the history of literature. There are moods (kokoromochi) that reside in certain periods that manage to gain entry into the hearts of men. Since the civilization of a country is created by its people (kokumin), the inner recesses of literary history reveal changes in national thought and emotionality and as such disclose also a history of Japanese uniqueness in the world. This recognition of national uniqueness has no other rationale than the necessity of literary history. Moreover, historical study imposes a developmental order that serves to both inhibit the act of reinventing earlier forms from the past and induce the creation of new works. Literary history must show the route of developmental changes in such a way as to clearly define the circumstances of its regions. Condemning contemporaries for their failure to study ancient literature (a challenge accepted by Orikuchi), Haga's disappointment stemmed from the conviction that literary production constituted a causal factor capable of "moving" periods, influencing thought and changing society. If national history was the record of a nation's progress, national literature was the principle generating it. Hence, the true objective of literary study must be the explanation of circumstances that clarify the relationship between literary heroes molded by specific periods and the appearance of new literary principles. The essence of Japanese literature was thus its ceaseless commitment to elegance, refinement, and beauty, which could be explained only partially by appealing to "outer form," the language used to shape it. Only history and the chronologizing of its development would supply an adequate explanation of this essence and uncover the interiority of national life as it made its passage to the present. Haga's essay "Kokugaku to wa nazo ya?" (What is national studies?) demonstrated how Tokugawa nativism had prefigured modern philology because of its disposition to study Japanese language before it incorporated Chinese ideograms and locutions: in it he proposed that a proper study of this accomplishment would provide the "basis" of new research. At the same time, he insisted that this research agenda should be "rational" and "scientific," carried on by the "nativists of Meiji today."

What concerned Orikuchi most about Haga's scheme was how national literature had been resituated within a historically developmental chronology that implied the possibility of change—a change that would, supposedly, foreclose reproducing earlier forms, as well as creativity and innovation. The developmental scheme followed by the canonization of national literature reflected the development narrative of the nation. Instead of employing a critical history promising to define developmental stages in the life of literature, Orikuchi sought to get behind and beyond history itself. The program he envisaged aimed to rework the ground of national literature, relieving it of its developmental desire and scientific pretensions, and fixing its origins in a place before there was a written literature. Implied as well was a critique of what hitherto counted as criteria for canonicity. Beyond this goal was the even more ambitious project of discovering the means to recall what had been completely forgotten: resituating an archaic presence in his present and restoring an identity between contemporary Japanese and the origin of belief and art. His preferred method was plainly hermeneutic and philological and inspired by the conviction that it was the task of a proper native ethnology to read the traces of oral utterances through the encrusted mediations of folkic remembrance and, later, written evidence. Hence, his method was both transhistorical (even though it sought to recapture history and historicity) and regressive, empowered to conflate temporal and spatial distances, history and geography, yet discretely specify them. Orikuchi's great program was to return to and enter the place of unreason, a precinct that lay beyond the capacity of rationality to reach or even recall. Neither philosophy nor historical studies was adequate to understanding the remote facts of antiquity. He condemned historians for their "unfortunate endeavor" of "slicing up time according to months and years." The past he wished to find could not be identified by political markers and temporal delimitation. Antiquity was spirit as it acquired manifestation in the survival of artistic forms and skills. Although he acknowledged the difficulties encountered in distinguishing between history and legend, he doubted the veracity of the so-called historical method to actualize the "logic of antiquity." "Since the results of historical discourses (*shiron*) are supposed to be realized in the concrete," he remarked, "I think that the novel must be advanced anew in order to discover the shape of the [human] drama. In this, I have used the form of the novel as the expressive means to study tradition and legend."[52] Because of literature's capacity to "excavate the theories of social life" inscribed in folk legends, native ethnology has the same goals and must be seen as a "classic of life," a "prior knowledge." But, he advised, ethnology so constituted to resuscitate the traces of older forms of life could never be limited to mere study and research. "Its actualization is not realized as knowledge alone but reached through the content of one's life."[53] In this sense, native ethnology could only be known as an enactment, in fact, an enunciation, a performative, a way of living.

Orikuchi called this method *jikkan* (actual feeling, realization, experience) and believed it was the proper approach for illuminating the "logic of the gods" because it could deliver the observing/perceiving subject to actively relive and experience the past in the present by penetrating the "heart of matters to view correctly the relationship between all kinds of things."[54] Orikuchi recognized the vast differences separating contemporaries from the ancients and the necessity of knowing how to "read ancient books" as had the ancients rather than through the mediations of modern morality and interpretation (KG, 27–29). If he understood that the present would never become the past, he was convinced, nonetheless, that the past would have to be grasped on its own terms. Even though the method he employed resembled Motoori Norinaga's theory of cognition ("knowing *mono no aware*"), which presumably had grown out of earlier practices of reading/writing derived from the everyday experience of Heian courtiers, Orikuchi's conception of *jikkan* also had a passing resemblance to Heidegger's own decision to chart a detour around conventional historiographical narratives—the domain of the inauthentic—to reach an authentic "understanding" of being in the world through an etymological examination. What he shared with Heidegger, however, was the conviction that an identity between contemporaries and ancients was possible and necessary for understanding because both shared the same cultural horizon of expectations. Persuaded that classics actually existed but were difficult to understand, he felt it was imperative to grasp their meaning, which modern interpretation had all but effaced. This was a principal reason why exegetics must be employed in approaching the meaning of classics, which invariably produced doubt and disagreement over correct understanding.[55] Genuine understanding proceeded not simply from doubt toward the whole but was rather prompted by a grasp of the part. But "true interpretation," he advised, "must grasp the meaning of the whole first"; only then will the part in question be subsequently illuminated (32). For Orikuchi, this relationship between the whole and the part, the universal and particular, justified privileging the act of interpretation (*kaishaku*) and authorized paying close attention to the elements of a composition. In fact, hermeneutics had already demonstrated its broad applicability and was currently employed in the study of the law. As a form that has permeated the interpretation of national literature, many have considered the study of national literature as an interpretative discipline embedded in daily "living" (*kurashiku*). "My attitude," he acknowledged, "is close to this [approach] and reflects it. In a word, it is a primitive method of doing things. There is no difference in the meaning that interpretative hermeneutics is useful to national literature" (33). Orikuchi was identifying hermeneutics with the way the ancients lived their lives and proposing a harmony between life and national literature. What was essential to its operation was the part, particularity, which ultimately is universalized by the presumption of understanding the whole that gives it meaning (34).

This interpretative program targeted the Meiji emphasis on the act of appreciation (*kanshō*) and the dissemination of aesthetic values attributed to works of literature that classified their place in the economy of inclusion—the canon—at the expense of determining meaning (34–36). Although the act of appreciation had a long and venerable history since the Heian period, when court noblewomen turned from reading and listening to narratives to "reading them silently," transforming "explanation" into acts of "appreciation" and thus narrative into literature (OSZ, 1:172), the term appreciation in the late Meiji period meant only "appreciating literary history." Orikuchi worried that since a confusion had been introduced that eliminated the distinction between a national history produced in Japan and the study of national history, the real problem was the desire to know how an "enlightened peoples" might directly read this literature in the modern age. Moreover, the serious effect of this effort to establish a national literature was to project a conception of a unitary subject authorized by the state as the only site of meaning. (This is not to suggest that Orikuchi was actually challenging the state; rather, he was calling attention to a different site of meaning that would authenticate a different kind of national subject.)

In Orikuchi's reckoning, the discipline of national literature as it had become institutionalized in universities was driven by an unrelieved positivism (in keeping with the promise of the Enlightenment) that saw in the accumulation of parts the eventual disclosure of the whole, rather than the reverse: empathetic understanding that grasped the parts as the key to the existence and meaning of the whole. It was this methodological conviction that set him apart from Haga and the presumption of fixed and enduring characteristics illuminated by the history of literature, and encouraged him to propose that any proper understanding of the whole would require an investigation of origins which, he believed, was coterminous with it. Like Yanagita, he accepted the prior existence of a whole as the guarantee of authentic understanding which "research" would inevitably elucidate. In this regard, he saw "folk studies" as a more than adequate substitute for literary history because it was committed to explaining the nature of what was called "folkloric literature": what had developed from practices of belief and was continually nourished by them, even though it would be eventually separated from its generating sources and seek to "forget its origins" (OSZ, 7:489; KG, 15–16). Native ethnology, he said on so many occasions, was "an assisting discipline." Received conceptions of literature always imagined that literary practice was steeped in emotionality, aesthetics, and even pleasure (kyōraku) rather than basic religious beliefs that had motivated Japanese life since antiquity (KG, 40–41; OSZ, 1:24–25).

In fact, national literature had ignored the time in which such beliefs were produced and practiced. It began with a study of texts from the Heian period and was eventually pushed back to the literatures of prior periods before and after the founding of the Nara court. Moreover, it retained a strong dependence on poetry and linked verse and its "appreciation." In this way, the literature that was produced in the Heian period was privileged as a standard for studying and evaluating what came before and after, thereby defining the boundaries of what counted as literature. This convention was normalized by scholars of the Tokugawa period and completed the effacement of archaic Japan as the source for Japanese literature. Nativists of the Edo period plainly favored the Heian period as the marker of a golden age, which began with the Manyō poems and ended with the Tale of Genji. Orikuchi argued that this particular perspective resulted in a view that continued to uphold emotionality and aesthetic pleasure as the source generating Japanese literature and lyricism as its principal expressive form. By the same measure, it cast a pall over the archaic age as a time that was said to have no worthwhile literature (KG, 4–5). His complaint was double-barreled: (1) the study of national literature since the Meiji period had easily become identified with a method of literary history and its subsequent academic institutionalization; and (2) institutionalization inordinately emphasized education in the national language (18–19). In his thinking, the turn toward literary history, stemming from the Meiji Enlightenment and showing the "influence of the West," dominated not only imperial universities but how national literature was to be understood as well (8). Acknowledging how the move to a critical literary history introduced "deep methodological meaning" to the study of national literature, Orikuchi insisted that the approach forfeited a renewed interest in commentary and interpretation which increasingly was being displaced by an interest in the values of appreciation (*kanshō*) (17–18). Appreciation, steeped in the valorization of both aesthetic values and pleasure, summoned the trope of the mirror and its power for reflecting moral lessons and exemplars. As an interest, it accompanied the transformation of *monogatari*—telling of tales—into a full-bodied narrative (OSZ, 1:172). But in Meiji Japan, appreciation came to mean only "appreciating literary history," which inhibited access to literature (KG, 18). Orikuchi agreed that an emphasis on the standard of appreciation, which resulted in judging the value of a work as literature, signaled an enlightening and worthwhile attitude but was meaningless since it has more to do with the promotion of taste and sociologizing students in it than understanding (18–19). In this educational sociolization of appreciation, an interest in interpretation and the means of actually determining meaning was being abandoned for the task of classifying texts according to their literary and aesthetic qualities. Among contemporaries, there appeared a "common consent" that interpretation was "unnecessary," and this began to look like a conspiracy of "cooperation" and "harmony" against interpretation and the search for meaning. The failure to emphasize the function of interpretation, beginning with the nativist scholar Keichū in the seventeenth century, would sacrifice the realization of all understanding. And because the reading of any text required knowing the forms of prose employed, Orikuchi worried that the means for attaining interpretation and understanding—exegeses and commentary—would soon disappear (20).

The role occupied by Heian literature in the history of national literature and its heavy predilection for pessimism constituted a misrecognition of the whole. Under the tyranny of this perspective, Japanese literature has been grasped from a single and self-limiting viewpoint, which may have been a useful description for literary production in the Heian and Kamakura periods but fell far short of representing all of literary history (24). Specifically, he objected to Buddhist conceptions that encouraged a "pessimistic despairing of the world," frequently inspired by political disorder and uncertainty, whose simplicity was limited to the experience of these historical moments. But the power of this view was that it persuaded critics to disregard earlier periods of literary production that did not conform to the medieval perspective and even dismissed them as historical ages that had no literature at all. The chronology authorized by the discourse on national literary history excluded the inaugural gesture of literary production, its enabling experience, which he named as "nonliterature" or as a "literature other than literature" to risk completely overlooking the importance of native ethnology as an "assisting discipline" (OSZ, 7:488). Orikuchi envisaged *minzokugaku*—native ethnology—as a more than adequate substitute for literary history precisely because it was devoted to explaining oral cultures—"folkic literature"—that had originated in beliefs and religious practices. Only native ethnology, not literary history, committed to searching out the traces of lost belief and religious practices in the archaic moment, was equipped to grasp the first utterances of Japanese literature before the implementation of settled inscription, before there were "works" (*sakuhin*) (7:489). However, this was not to say that he failed to recognize the immense good fortune for having available "histories" and "documents" from later ages that "transmitted forms before there were [generic] works" (7:490).

Plainly, Orikuchi had altered the object of study of national literature. National literature was less literary history, as such, classifying works according to their conformity to principles of aesthetics and appreciation, and more native ethnology pledged to unearthing the beliefs that had organized and motivated Japanese life from the beginning. "Among the Japanese, there is one principle of life since antiquity, and this has been Shintō. It has fixed folk life since the beginning of the cosmos" (KG, 24–25). It is important to recognize, in this connection, Orikuchi's desire to explain the original and essential unity of Japanese life, embedded in the first religious practices of the community, and continued down to the present. Religion, which produced and defined the nature of Japanese culture, formed the group into a community and collective subject, while the Japanese maintained their identity as a communal subject through the practice and performance of culture. Orikuchi believed that this endowment constituted a form of religiocultural unconscious that continued to manifest itself "intermittently" in art, even after religious ceremony was historically separated from its performance and making. Without saying so, his effort to reach back to origins in order to historicize Japanese collective identity in the first religious rituals hinted at a solution to both the division of contemporary life caused by instrumental knowledge and the new regime of commodification. But instead of actually historicizing the conditions of producing community and religious ceremony, he mythologized them and even reinforced culture's illusory claim to autonomy in its struggle with the commodity form.

In the *Nihon bungaku hassei*, he proposed further that what had become included among the literary arts (literature, music, dance, theater, etc.) invariably favored forms that sought to "approximate" religion

(OSZ, 7:491). In fact, this constant mixing of religious practice and art inspired the "blooming of the flower of a literature that was other than literature." Even though the cluster of beliefs classified under Shintō have changed since antiquity, their core still accounts for the "spirit of the Japanese people." Despite the powerful role played by Shintō in shaping the arts of Japan, Orikuchi was persuaded that few people had actually considered it as the basis of art and learning. The reason for this was that Japanese literature was still seen to be solely concerned with emotional life, pleasure, or entertainment. When this description was viewed from the standpoint of literary history and its system of classification, it failed completely to "touch on values," which have moved to the center of contemporary discussion and now require even greater attention. "Although there has been love literature in the nation's [history], it has not been the spirit that informs Japanese literature" (KG, 25). Value was created by an enduring spirit that emerged early in the life of the people, continuing to manifest its force throughout history, and has become a principal consideration in constructing an agenda for the present.

Hence, Orikuchi's refiguring of national literature moved its locus from medieval Japan to the archaic agrarian community, a time before writing and formal literature, from affect and aesthetics to spiritual values, from appreciation to hermeneutic interpretation based on philological rescue and empathetic understanding of meaning, from literary history to native ethnology. Behind this vast reordering of priorities was the desire to show how archaic, agricultural life, whose daily life rhythm steeped in spirituality rather than sentimentality and aesthetics, had generated archetypal literary forms. Yet he was just as passionately concerned with demonstrating how traces of the inaugural moment were still available in folk practices and words in the Japanese countryside during the 1920s, not to mention Okinawa, which he considered a showcase of antiquity, a living laboratory of the preliterate society that Shintō had shaped (OSZ, 1:19; 6:10–11; 3:146). "Even today," he wrote in an article on the religion of the Ryukyus, "going to Okinawa, one can see realistically the life of the ancient Japanese before the Nara period, but in that place there is deep yearning, as well as sections of filth and squalor." Literature won its status as art once it was separated from its enabling religious impulse. Yet, as he never tired of reminding his readers, it would continue to disclose traces of its inspiration.

The sign of this archaic literary production was speech and utterance derived from everyday usage, orality and gesture rather than writing. Although prose came early in the life of the folk as an "authoritative expression," it had no reason to exist outside of spoken conversation, even though it had become a familiar practice (1:63). The constraints posed by the spoken language seemed to closely match or parallel the confinements of a stateless society loosely composed of widely scattered agricultural communities. Just as language was used only in the circumstances of everyday communication and thereby limited the capacity of memory and retention in a number of matters, so the decentralized organization of communities had little need of settled representation and modes of recall. Reliance on oral exchange and the "natural incapacity to depend upon written records" meant forfeiting the forms of prose in all cases but everyday speech. As an instrument for remembrance (*kioku*) it was inadequate for important matters and events. Since composition in antiquity was not bedeviled by memory but held the form of prose writing, it never had to consider temporal continuity. It was used only in the circumstances of everyday speech and limited to compositions that had no need of repetition. Yet, everyday language was driven by the force of repetition, by the production of repetitive utterances, patterns, and locutions that constituted a storehouse of memory when contrasted to prose, which appeared to have no need for its operation. Speech, he declared, is "haunted" by repetition and often produced the same effects as written composition (*seibun*) (1:64). This exercise of repetition may well have supplied the force to prompt the development of the rules of poetic composition but was not its only condition. Instead, a more natural "impulse stimulated the emergence of poetry," which was the "words of the deities" (*kamigoto*). According to contemporary rationalist arguments, lyric poetry was seen to have developed prior to the formation of narrative (or epic) poetry. The reason for this order of development lay in the conviction that lyric was employed to "capture the love of the opposite sex"—an explanation that valorized the naturalness of sexual feeling and emotionality and identified poetry with voice and gender difference. Dismissing this approach as "commonsensical," even "primitive," Orikuchi argued that the theory was based on the assumption that some sort of psychological purpose for literature existed before its formal development. But, he continued, the production of oral, lyric poetry marked by repetition of patterns of utterances, cadences, and rhythm derived from the development of narrative or epic poetry (see 7:220ff). The epic or narrative poem was, he said, the earliest form of oral composition "repeated in our country" (1:65). At about the time of the Asuka court (593-610), "when there was a clarification of "national consciousness among the Japanese folk," all the poetic forms represented in the Manyō were identified and fixed. However, he warned, these finished forms that appear in later poetic composition fail to betray their conditions of production from an earlier time, often repressing them as naturalist creations. Orikuchi extended this observation to the first histories like the *Kojiki* and *Nihonshoki*, which have recorded only the "life forms that have materialized after our ancestors began the realm (*kunitsuchi*)" (1:64). If it is easy to have assumed that this description represents a unified narrative, it is only because the interest of the

histories has been to efface and even repress the "mixed conditions involved in the true founding of this land." These forms today transcend
philology and conceal the diverse circumstances and places implicated in
the foundation of the realm: "which times?" "which places?" and "which
clans?" (1:65).

The turn to epic immediately necessitated a consideration of voice. Orikuchi believed that even though later histories like *Kojiki* and portions of
Nihonshoki resembled oral transmissions of the *kataribe* (the tellers of
tales), the frequent use of the third-person voice approximated a naturalist narrative description. The passage of time, he proposed, invariably
confused and mixed, thereby effacing, the first-person voice that actually
uttered the archaic poem by substituting a third person in the presentation. This later insertion "implied a fossilization of the first person description that had been omitted in [subsequent] translations of voice" as
a result of misunderstanding its significance. The confusion was imprinted
in the progression of the narrative poem. But despite the confusion and
the elision of voices that apparently characterize the early narratives, the
"narrative poem expressed in the form of a first voice was a monologue
of the gods," who, from time to time, seized possession of humans (*kami-
gakari*) in order to have the history of the kami, the species and the various
clan lineages related. These first narrators were sorceresses (*miko*), whose
accounts never exceeded their imagination at the time of ecstatic trance.
Nevertheless, it was an "imagination" that rested on the "intention" of
the species; the accumulation of the memories of the tribe was "unexpectedly regenerated" at the time the *miko* underwent a trance and ecstatically
identified herself with the gods. The composition, which told the story of
the "main relationships," was an oral utterance delivered from the mouth
of the sorceress, who undoubtedly added "sufficient poetic elements"
(1:66). "My consideration on the archaic scene is that the source of Japanese literature is in the oracles of mediums," he wrote in *Nihon bungaku
no hassei*, and many of these sorceresses were regarded as spouses of the
deities who frequently mixed their own deeds with the acts of the kami
(7:26). These *miko* served the court by reporting narratives, poems, and
incantations, which were transmitted to regional and provincial households to become later the basis of court literature. Although the content
of these narratives undoubtedly derived from the intervention of the mediums themselves and was shaped by their mediation, Orikuchi conjectured
that it must have accorded with the intention of the race, as if to suggest
that a racial unconscious employed the body of woman as a vehicle for
periodic pronouncements (1:66). Nevertheless, the connection with the
narratives of the later Heian court, dominated by women, was evident,
as these archaic sorceresses "became the origins for the development of
court literature" (1:28). It should be pointed out in this regard that in

many attempts to show the relationship between gender and the formation of literary form, lyric poetry is invariably identified with women,
while narrative, and probably narrative or epic poetry, has been associated with men. Orikuchi was rarely comparative, dismissing it as another
technique similar to literary history. But he seemed certain that this practice was found nowhere else as the mediums served the imperial court by
conveying to all corners of the realm their incantatory recitations and
methods for constructing narrative poems which "became the origins that
caused the development of court literature" (7:28). This tradition was
bestowed to the later Heian court, whereas the educational role of the
miko to "receive the spirits residing in the incantations" and reveal the
exemplarity of "superior manhood and womanhood that lay in these
poems" gave birth to a self-knowledge that was ultimately taken over by
court noblewomen. If antiquity illustrated the gradual unification of court
and the life-style of the village communities, he was also convinced by a
revisionary opinion that most of the "tellers of tales" were women (1:28–
29). What this meant was that the archaic village communities produced
the first tales through the medium of sorceresses—in other words, from
the periphery—and later merged with the center to become a national
style. The incantatory utterances were cast in colloquial language—"everyday words"—and were invariably rhythmic because they were the
product of the medium's repetitive, frenzied, possessed state. But because
the sorceresses were speaking the tales of the gods, the everyday language
they employed changed into a sacred language during these performances;
and because they were "unitary portraits seen from the [perspective of
the] gods themselves, they were unnatural, as well as incomplete. But
expression accorded to the first person voice." After a time, the mediums
would add musical elements to their recitations, and the event could become a performance—a dance of bodily movements that corresponded to
the pitch of chanting. There was also confusion of memories that came
on the occasion of reciting utterances. Marked by a performative strategy
of "syllabic repetition to indicate plurals" (*jōgo*), "couplets," and
"changes in the meaning of passages," these forms constantly favored
repetition to produce an instantaneous impression. In spite of the variety
of stories about the kami and the high probability that many simply disappeared, others, deeply embedded in folk life, were fixed through the exercise of constant repetition. Embellished over time, these stories remained
the authentic "voice of the gods." The important thing about this narrative poetry was the addition of "unconscious figures of speech" (1:66).
"More than being rhythmic elements in language," he continued, "the
direction of these musical elements as voice, in reality, worked profoundly
on these kami words." Transmitted by the "mouths of the medium," they
became used as common idiom in appropriate ceremonies, rituals, and

rites. But what solidified their placement and ritualized their memory was the formation of corporate life which increasingly emphasized their importance as permanent custom. This bonding between the performance of religious ceremonies and the corporatization of the group into a permanent communal collective (thereby forming a concrete identity long before there was a nation state) was the great historical endowment of archaic Japan the present had forgotten. The division and subsequent differentiation of villages of people who belonged to the same clan has, in fact, caused later generations to "forget the history before the divergence took place" (1:67).

The consolidation of archaic agricultural communities into large political units resembling a proto-state was brought about through the "rational" unification of religious practices and the reconciliation of beliefs. In the most remote times, Orikuchi declared, these communities may have fostered some form of "village consciousness," but no one ever thought of them as a nation. But in fact the world of the village was the nation. What seemed to exist were scattered agricultural sites which remained divided from each other, even though it was entirely probable that the reason for the divisions separating members of villages who belonged to the same clan prompted the effacement of a memory of conditions before the break. Their beliefs derived from a fundamental and widely shared agricultural experience and constituted the basis of community life. Before the period of the Asuka court, they often assumed the form of rituals devoted to solar cults and observances that gradually prepared the diverse villages for sharing common religious characteristics. This process of rationalization and consolidation yoked an older concern for protecting the kami and a newly emerging impulse to rely on their intercession (1:67). At this conjuncture, the occupational group called *kataribe*—tellers of tales—was gradually formed and assumed the task of unifying the diverse set of village beliefs into a commonly shared system. What had started as the work of sorceresses, whose appeal to the authority of kami possession allowed them on occasion to recite the "words of the gods," was gradually transformed into a profession of storytellers distanced as a hereditary group from service because of greater involvement in reciting verse from memory and the necessity of retaining a control over the circulation of musical elements(1:68). Thus, the history of the clans was not transmitted through history but rather was "known according to the kami words." The gods themselves personalized narratives in order to explain how belief must be carried out. Even though the "tellers of tales" were not implicated in conducting ceremonies, everything they sang referred to the gods. Before the compilation of historical records, it was impossible to understand the conditions of village life outside of any reference to belief. Moreover, these villages were called "countries" (*kuni*), and their inhabitants adhered to the "music of the *kuni*." Countries that became territories were called *kunizukuri* in later ages, but they were limited to those things left by priests. The important families of villages ruled over people according to their role in serving the gods. Even though these *kunizukuri* were "gradually distanced from service to the gods, they were not able to escape the great godly affairs because of the priests" (1:70). In time, villages were unified to become "our Yamato court." For Orikuchi, then, the narrative showed how the "life of one village grew into one country," as villages gradually expanded into numerous *kuni* that formed into a state (*kokka*). Although the life of these newly founded countries or territories broadened, they were the same as consolidated villages, inasmuch as they did not abandon "godly affairs." "In a period like the present," he advised, "we must repeat this life through the agency of Shinto priests." Specifically, the lesson for his present was the example of ancient ancestor worship, which had been linked to the customs of the archaic villages (1:71). Accepting the vast changes that had taken place since archaic times, Orikuchi admitted that it was not easy to substitute the original life of the village for the subsequent changes that had "actualized the ideal of decoupling the important families from the gods" and the villages. But there was the reminder of how archaic villages had sought to protect the life of the individual household and how this had led to the establishment of diverse occupational groups that "fixed the family system." Regardless of change, Orikuchi still believed that the "words of the gods," celebrations beseeching the gods, represented "one direction for the present."

For Orikuchi, a possible purpose in recounting this archaic narrative was to show that the gods descended at fixed times during the year on a regular basis to utter godly words that would confer blessings and good fortune on the village's agricultural production. These gods, "who came rarely" (*marebito*), would customarily visit households and have the folk hear the words celebrating the destiny of the household, home, and production. Yet, this punctual visitation was nothing more than a repetition of the "primitive drama" that instructed villagers of the kami's return and the relationship among the gods, the earth, and the community. The gods "fix time," "drop down to the villages," and "relate words that bless the village's yearly production." It is natural that they would call on households and listen to the lives of these families and the commemorations of house and production. This never went beyond the "primitive drama that taught the advent of the gods." The form these ceremonies and commemorative occasions took was incantatory, the repeating of sounds and patterns and cadences—the rhythms of life itself that were supposed to cast spells and ward off the spirits of the earth. If Orikuchi previously envisaged a completely different relationship between incantation and the formation of narrative, it was because he had failed to "relate the oracles of deities who came to bless production" and how the actual process of giving blessings that used kami words changed to utterances employing human speech. Not only did this explain the intimate and causal link between the incantatory and magical utterances enunciated in regular performances and narrative poems, it managed also to persist in a transformed form down to the present in "congratulatory" forms (hokai, manzai, monoyoshi) which still convey in human words the idea of the advent of the gods (1:74). What apparently secured longevity was the operation of repetition of both verbal utterances celebrating the power of the deities and requesting their intercession in the human cycle and the performance itself; incantations at the beginning of spring (manzai) that "praise the supports" (the house), the garden, and the well could still be found in the villages of the Tokugawa period and even in his own time (1:75). "In these words of praise," Orikuchi remarked, "there is the effort to induce favor from the gods of the house." In the use of words like hōmu and hōgu, whose meaning is anticipatory prayers, there is praise for the future as well.

The crucial element in this narrative construction was, as suggested above, the appearance of god/men (marebito)who came regularly in the spring to initiate the blessings and ward off the evil spirits of the earth. Yanagita Kunio condemned this problematic concept as lacking evidence, but Orikuchi embraced it early (as found in his Kokubungaku no hassei) and stayed with it until the end of his life, by which time it had acquired associations of marginality, as articulated in the functionalist schemes of the anthropologist Yamaguchi Masao, and native authenticity against foreign importation, as in the thinker Tsurumi Shunsuke. But for Orikuchi the god/men who come rarely from beyond the sea come from the land of tokoyo, as it was called: the "mother country" to which the ancients had dreamed of returning.[56] Tokoyo was an imaginary, to be sure, but still the "basic land" conjured from folk prayers, and the marebito constituted the central agents in plotting the archaic drama of origin and production. In Kokubungaku no hassei, he explained, the word meant "welcome guest," acquiring over time associations that called forth the "only," the "one," and conveying respect and esteem (1:3). But it also came to denote "stranger," men who came from the distant "other place." Because these god/men came yearly to make their incantations, the sense of "rarely" came to mean "cyclic," implying, again, the rhythm of repetition, a rare performance taking place once a year. Above all else, the rarity of the event signified the necessity of repetition. Archaic folk knew only that the god/men came "rarely," in spring, and this recognition led to developing a method of treating honored guests who visited infrequently the same as if they were the gods. "Even in the Tokugawa period," Orikuchi wrote, "the reception of an honored guest was the same as that shown toward the gods. Because the *marebito* came and were considered honored guests, it is probably correct to say that the style employed for kami was used toward honored guests" (1:35). More than simply referring to an honored guest, *marebito* called forth the status of the "temporary visitor." Although many may have been deities impersonating priests or priests impersonating gods, they were still seen as visitors who came once a year from a land of good fortune and abundance. The rituals that accompanied their advent have become deeply embedded in folk traditions and memory. The *yokoza*, which, even in the contemporary countryside, was the seat occupied by the village head, had at its side the *kyakuza*, guest seat (1:6). Orikuchi believed it was still possible to observe a variety of examples in Okinawa of the custom of visitation and calling upon households and villages that have derived from this inaugural agricultural experience (1:19).

The purpose of the visit coincided with the beginning of the yearly cultivation in early spring. The arrival of the god/men was supposed to bring good fortune to the community, health to the household, and abundant harvest.[57] Through the exercise of pledges and various congratulatory incantations, these god/men sought to provide protection against household calamity and fend off the evil spirits of the earth, who always seemed to gather punctually every year. These incantations, as we have seen, casting magical spells, were directed at birds and insects, not humans. The god/men, it was believed, came from a land beyond the sea, a place of wealth and eternal life that was marked by "constancy" and "absoluteness" and "continuity" (1:56). In fact, Orikuchi proposed that in *tokoyo*, time and space were measured differently. The standard of time and space was such that they were without measure.[58] The term *yo* of the word *tokoyo* inspired a series of associations that transformed this place of darkness into a country of immortality. Moreover, the word *yo*, since remote antiquity, has referred to cereals and grains and their ripeness; it has also "accompanied an association of ideas relating to a country of wealth and abundance" (1:60). In Orikuchi's reckoning, the important operation in this narrative was the enunciation of magical and spell-bound incantations at certain moments in the year. Archaic folk believed that such expressions possessed the power to summon good fortune or ill luck, "to recite *yogoto* (good things) and simultaneously to deploy disease and grain worms to lay waste of life and cereals" (1:106). Nevertheless, these incantations constituted the source for the subsequent development of epic narratives, literature, and art itself in Japan. Despite his own efforts to exceptionalize his explanations and show its embeddedness in a specific religioracial experience, his account of the relationship among religious belief, literary form, and artistic production shares more than a passing resemblance to Frazer's *The Golden Bough*, while the constant performance of a drama celebrating communal life was clearly inspired by Durkheim. Orikuchi wanted to dismiss rationalistic arguments that located art and literature in emotionality. "Even though the inspiration of love, joy, and sorrow have organized an emotional poetry," he observed, "it has not formed the types and modes of composition, sentences, of language. . . . The reason poetry and prose was sustained for so long until a literary consciousness developed and a writing system was adopted was that it was related to belief" (1:124). For him, "unwritten expression" relied on nothing more than voice and sound and was preserved in folk memory down to the present. What survived the archaic experience in which communal religious practices produced art after the separation of the latter from the former was, in fact, the aura of the moment of production.

Nothing was more crucial than belief in securing continuity in the long preliterate duration of archaic Japan. "I have placed the starting point of Japanese literature in the incantations—which were believed to have been a divine gift." Convinced that "archaic forms" could be traced down to the present, he insisted that it was possible to detect the echo of ancient voice and, hence, presence in the "distant hints of chants" and the rhythms of conversations, in the language of narratives. Poetic and prose utterances, coming from the inaugural circumstances of sorceresses possessed by the gods and "resulting in repetition time and again took hold of determined form that transmitted the life of the agricultural community from past to present" (1:125). The god/men who came yearly narrated the story of creation, explaining to villagers the origins and generation of seeds, the beginnings of the "national soil," the making of the mountains, rivers, grass, and trees, the birth of the sun and moon, daylight and darkness; they recounted the principal storyline when hunger and thirst were remembered to produce the first foodstuffs. Moreover, they recounted the beginnings of purification ceremonies, which derived from the death of humans and whose practices resulted from contact with the gods. Accordingly, these agriculturally produced things were divine. Because of this, people who committed acts against godly things would have difficulty removing the "stains" of *tsumi* (transgression). The narratives, here, explained the beginnings of *harae* (purification) and the final repose of the spirits.

It was, of course, the image of *tokoyo*, the other world, the mother country, from which the *marebito* punctually came and to which they returned, that captured the archaic imagination. It also supplied Orikuchi with that sense of difference he wished to contrast with a contemporary Japan already committed to the model of modern sameness. In his reading, the visitations were accompanied by exhausting banquets in return for the godly blessings. Fearing but esteeming these visitors at the same time, the villagers believed that the spells the incantations cast overpowered the spirits of the earth. But the god/men brought the sign of genuine difference associated with *tokoyo*, a utopian imaginary symbolizing eternity, abundance, and continuity, time and space without limitation, that folk memory would continue to recall intermittently in dream and religious ritual. If it marked the origins of art, now coterminous with the beginning of community life and beliefs that came from another place, it also signified the place of difference. No real distinction occurred between the act of explaining a history that was the background of godly affairs and the dramatic poetic effects that repeated the story of kami affairs each time as a condition of realizing them in the present. The incantations did not actually narrate the past but were utterances that aimed to realize past in present through performance. The great change came later when past and present were differentiated into distinct times and it became necessary to explain the new relationship between the two moments. Hence, the principal purpose of the epic narratives was to explain the "historical basis of reality," precisely what Orikuchi believed he was doing in the present, which meant locating it in "kami affairs." Moreover, the incantations completely lost the power to cast spells and manipulate the spirit world as a result of the momentous transformation in antiquity. Art, in Orikuchi's thinking, emerged as "art" precisely at that moment when magic and its power to manage the world disappeared, when the world became disenchanted (*entzauberung*). "Art," in this sense, coincided with both the development of a Sinified bureaucratic state and a writing system that made possible the dissemination of Buddhism. The loss of archaic aura accompanied this transformation of community into a centralized state, orality into inscription (noted first in the eighteenth century by Kamo Mabuchi), and may very well have caused it. When narrative lost its living contact with the power of incantations, when the oracular utterances promising to cast a spell over the spirits of the earth were separated from the religious beliefs that authorized such a practice and necessitated performance, ritualized memory, chanting and repetition, and invocation praising the future, art appeared in the form of written narratives and poetry (1:74). But the ancient precedent was never far from contemporary political society. When the magic of incantations prevailed, spirits even resided in words, which, it was believed, possessed the power to animate things by the act of referring to them (*kotodama*). Once the *kataribe* "left the shrine for the world," as they were separated from the land because of a political transformation in antiquity, their relationship to the gods was severed, and they were no longer bonded to the task of maintaining in narrative the relationship among the gods, the household, and the land (1:73, 72). Writing alone does not account for the decline of this group of storytellers. As the diminution of their religious function was linked to losing their powerful, landed patrons, who themselves experienced a wrenching transformation that separated them from the land, the "tellers of tales" became "wandering minstrels," singers of song (1:73). The content of their stories no longer conformed to the "current of the times."

But the beliefs enabling art reappeared in folk memory, despite the momentous separation of religion and culture. Today, Orikuchi remarked, there has developed a variety of literatures from this occupation on the side of the tradition of incantations. What had been seen as art linked to place now became the place of art itself, that is to say the place of culture, capable of serving the modern state, timeless in its promise of good fortune, abundance, and continuity. But to return to this place of art meant rescuing those religious principles that unified Japanese life since the beginning and reexperiencing a forgotten sense of wholeness that state and social formation had disrupted. In the *Nihon bungaku no hassei*, he argued that the life of archaic Japan could not simply be discussed from the perspective of the court, which was the "place of a primary life style. It was possible to see a similarly styled life, a lesser one, in several of the agricultural communities. What must be emphasized is that even though the life of the clans in the countryside was completely different, they came around to imitating life at the top" (7:7, 8–9). But life at the top was constantly nourished by its contact with the periphery. The negotiation between center and periphery, in time, made it possible for each to stand in for the other (7:9). In this yearning for wholeness, first experienced by the archaic society, Orikuchi's conception of culture converged with a utopian fascism which was already seeking refuge in the fantasy of wholeness and timelessness by invoking the model of the *gemeinschaft*—the corporate group—that first appeared in the archaic agricultural community. Genuine life had already been completed in archaic times and could be reanimated in the present. As suggested earlier, Orikuchi's identification of the place of art constituted a struggle against the irreversibility of time and the disappearance of the solidary community. This irreversibility of time is that which never returns, the opposite, therefore, of the repetition of the primitive drama that always punctually returns, while the loss of principles that once guaranteed social solidarity leads to the "disaggregation of community by mere probability."[59] Orikuchi, like so many contemporaries, recognized in the immense spectacle of industrial transformation taking place a crisis of social and cultural indeterminacy and the unbearable truth that the principles that were said to bind societies were simply arbitrary, "probabilistic," and transitory assumptions that could offer neither grounded guarantees nor permanence. The turn to origins, the "delimitation of time," promised to free society from the "infinite regression of cause and effect." If times passes and never returns, the process could be stopped by fixing origins and the inaugural gesture of the gods who came rarely, once every year to reassure the community of its continuing survival and good fortune through the act of repeating rituals. In this way, the fixed moment in origins overcomes the "irreversibility of time," which is to say history, and allows the regular and punctual ritualization of memory, celebration, and commemoration. Only a folk memory of the "mother country" that recalled the unity of the group and the wholeness of life could reunite the present with the distant past. Yet, it is important to pause on his identification of the origin of art, women, and the dream of the "mother country," which, combined, were seen to embody a timelessness against history. Although this identification seemed to support a contemporary reassessment of the role of independent women and may have seemed to register an exceptional difference, it was little more than a rearticulation of an older nativist conception (Motoori) that the Japanese language was feminine. With Orikuchi, it resulted in reaffirming a cultural division of labor by actually dehistoricizing the role women played in social reproduction.

When time is "defeated" by repetition enacted through remembrance and commemoration, it is place (and space) that appears as the primary staging arena for performance and portrayal. Orikuchi saw the performance of these yearly rituals, much like Yanagi Sōetsu imagined repeated gestures of folk crafts, taking place within a sacred precinct, whether the shrine or the village or, ultimately, Japan itself. Place, in this instance, was the marked off and bounded space that delimited the community and interpellated them as subjects of the collectivity of the godly offerings, just as making a pot or straw sandals constituted use-value in the economy of the village and defined the boundaries of everyday life lived by the inhabitants. The performance defined the space for carrying out the incantations and the management of magic and divination. In Orikuchi's thinking, this bounded space was indistinguishable from the act of divination, the place of *jugon*, the enunciation of utterances casting their spells and, therefore, limiting the borders of community itself. We know that he saw a fundamental transformation occurring in antiquity when the teller of tales left the shrine for the world, when upper-ranking families (*gōzoku*) were removed from the land. Until that time, he wrote, the *kataribe*'s "meaning for existence" was to "narrate the relationship of deity, household and land" (1:72; also 7:8–35). Despite their capacity to survive this epochal change into the Heian period, the separation from religious reenactment—living culture—found expression in new narrative forms down to the present day. With the promotion of this poetics, the figure of an archaic imaginary in which the folk dreamed of the "mother country" and requested the kami to confer good fortune on the community and the blessing of continuity was transformed into a discourse on native ethnology that sought to offer the space of an authentic sanctuary or "shel-

teredness." After all, what was the "mother country" but a distant and
lost home, the place so many before the war longed for? Orikuchi's poetics supplied a map that charted the route back to finding this lost home
that lay beyond the sea. Such a home, it was believed, was capable of
guaranteeing the security and solidarity of the national community and
preventing its disaggregation into the innumerable fragments and the indeterminate sameness of modern society.

Just before the war, Orikuchi, a self-styled follower of the Tokugawa
nativist Hirata Atsutane, returned to this theme in an essay. In this article,
he proclaimed that Hirata was, above all else, a scholar devoted to integrity who possessed a broad learning that was always informed by moral
intensity and a deep and abiding love for scholarship (20:331). More than
any other thinker of the day, Hirata single-handedly liberated learning
from a reliance on Chinese knowledge and its methods. In his exploration
of religiosity, nativism came to constitute a "backbone" discipline that
successfully was able to uncover the authentic image of ancient history
and its moral structure. "A nativism without this dimension," he asserted,
"cannot exist." The development of a new style of learning "must be
passionate," even sensuous. For "it is not sufficient merely to acquire
knowledge [and contemplate it] meditatively, because it must also be endowed with elements of activity." Nativism, he believed, had been the
learning of active and practical belief. "Today," he urged, "the time has
arrived to act according to [this] exercise of moral passion. While we must
always aim for the accomplishment of this goal [practice], the time is ripe
for us to act" (20:318). "Japan, since antiquity, has been at a standstill,"
which must be overcome if the folk is to be reunited with its original
purpose. Yet, the "history of Japan is filled with examples of believing in
miracles" (20:319). The miracle he apparently was referring to was the
necessity to recall the basic belief system disclosed first to the archaic
community and which the present must rescue for renewed inspiration
and reunion with the inaugural gestures of the race. In his "fictionalized"
narrative Shisha no sho (Book of the dead, 1939), a work self-consciously
seeking to contest the conception of a unified subject (the individual self)
inhabiting modern novels, Orikuchi constantly interrupts temporality by
employing memory and the powers of recall that, for him, raise the dead
and constitute meaning and life itself. For Orikuchi, recalling the difference of the archaic imaginary was reaffirming life against death.

CHAPTER 6

History's Actuality

EXISTENCE, EXPERIENCE, AND THE PRESENT

If Heidegger, as Watsuji believed, erred too much on the side of phenomenology—separating humans from everydayness—Watsuji erred too much on the side of a hermeneutics that mandated living a specific life as a condition of comprehending it. While he exceptionalized culture, differentiating it from others, he turned around to make its understanding inaccessible to all but those who lived and experienced it. But his discourse undoubtedly persuaded others to attempt a reunification of a changeless everyday life and the claims of an exceptional culture in order to meet the assault of modernity. In practical terms, this meant retaining the spatiocultural unevenness created by modern capitalism as the means of maintaining capitalism without keeping its devastating social consequences. This arrangement was already implied in Watsuji's acclamation of Japan's unique civilization, based on climate and character, and his conception of a "double life" and its capacious powers of accommodation. It was even more explicit in his expressed conviction that Japan was developing a different kind of capitalism in keeping with this special cultural endowment. Toward the end of the decade of the 1930s Miki Kiyoshi (1897–1945), who was a member of Konoe Fumimaro's think tank, the Shōwa Kenkyūkai, turned to this problem and its solution in his consideration of the status of culture. The double life he envisaged sought to resolve the agonistic ambiguity between folkic community and cultural production—what he increasingly called *techné*—between memory and the performance of the folk body by appealing to the actualization of history.

In many ways, Miki was the consummate modernist thinker and resembled in philosophy and thought the writer Yokomitsu Riichi whose own career traversed a dizzying course of literary innovations, only to exhaust himself in the end. Yokomitsu died before he was able to complete his epic novel, *Ryoshū*, dedicated to the theme of "returning to Japan." Its not clear that he would have been able to finish this novel, any more so than Miki would have been able to complete his last text on the medieval religious thinker Shinran before he died. But Miki was imprisoned by the state, while Yokomitsu was eulogized by his friend Kawabata Yasunari as a pioneer of Asianism. Regardless, it is easy to imagine Miki as exhausted at the end, not only from imprisonment, but also from having traveled an intellectual itinerary in which he tried to master all of the principal philosophic and intellectual perspectives of the twentieth century. His principal philosophic principle, the "theory of conceptual power" (kōsō ryoku no riron), attempted to bring the vast diversity of ideas into concourse with each other, almost as if this immense orchestrating itself possessed the power of an amulet.[1] Just as he sought to absorb as much philosophy as he could in the three years he studied in Germany, echoing Max Weber's earlier effort to see how much he could bear, Miki's intellectual adventure visited all of the major venues: neo-Kantianism, phenomenology, existentialism, Marxism, pragmatism, and their variants and hybrids. Like Yokomitsu, whose unfinished novel tried to supply a narrative structure to the idea of "returning to Japan" (Nihon kaiki), which in reality showed only how he could not find his way, Miki tried also to return to the tradition of religious thinking and action of Shinran and the text of sayings, Tannisho, and never quite got there.

For Miki, the logic of conceptual power, capable of pulling together diverse intellectual threads like the dialectic but claiming to include it also, was a "philosophy of action." Because action (kōi) was understood as production in its broadest sense, the theory of conceptual power, he wrote, is thus a theory of production. The thing that has been made is accompanied by form. To act is to work on a thing, to transform it and produce a new form. The form is a historical thing by way of having been made; it changes historically. Form, in this way, is not only objective but a unity of subjective and objective, a unity of idea and reality, existence and living, time and space. The theory of conceptual power is, therefore, an urlogik that also includes formalism and Hegel's dialectic.[2] His procedure strangely prefigured Louis Althusser, inasmuch as he was concerned with the production of thought through action on things. He shared with Althusser a theory of knowledge that claimed the power to understand the "current situation" that would reveal the design of a proper theory of acting upon it. But unlike Althusser, Miki was deeply implicated in both Heidegger and policy making for empire and war. According to some, he joined, without fear of contradiction, a discourse that sustained the idea of "total war" and "colonial outside" to the kernel of his own thinking devoted to analyzing the contemporary condition through a theory of conceptual power.[3] Despite the hostility he registered in response to Heidegger's Rector address and his decision to join the Nazi party in 1933, there was simply no way of bridging Miki's two sides: the philosopher analyzing the "current situation" (Marxism) and the thinker promoting the space of Asia (fascism). Far from being only an essayist on contemporary affairs, he always disclosed in his writing an understanding of politics based on the articulation of grounding principles. Philosophy was a vocation for

[handwritten marginalia] J place = imperialism, not fascism

understanding contemporary reality and envisaging the proper course of action. In this sense, he remained true to the Marxian analytic, even though his theory of action promising a solution bordered on fascism.

The theory of conceptual power was both a logic of forms and technique (*techné*), making and shaping and changing. Without ever saying so, Miki envisaged an identity between conceptual power with culture itself, especially its capacity to incorporate diverse traditions and patterns of expressability. The importance of conceptual power was its relationship to action. Even though it represented an expansion of "artistic activity," where form is completely locked within the position of observation, action does not stem from an abstract intention, as envisaged by certain idealisms, but from understanding something by making it. "All action," he remarked, "makes things in the widest meaning and thus possesses the meaning of production." In this way, a theory of conceptual power is really a theory of production which underlies all cultural activity. What else is culture if not making? Originally, "conceptual power" was limited to understanding perceptual and aesthetic problems, which were constructed as a theory of action through "poises" that then became a theory of creative production.[4] The position of production was grasped according to the "mold" called "production" (which referred to poises) and technique (techné/*gijutsu*). Once liberated from the realm of aesthetic production, production became a theory of the representational world in general. But it was important that it was made into a philosophical principle that stipulated the action of technological productivity through a constant reinterpreting of the representational world. In other words, interpretation became the necessity of production. Form, in this connection, became the problem of making form as techné, but it was also capable of transcending form to become the unformed.

Miki's theory of conceptual power claimed no transcendent reason, even in its analytic capacity. It occupied a position of "active intuition" without being only intuitionist. Rather, it appeared to him as a theory of realistic action mediated by science and technology. Modern science, he urged, was form derived from technological necessity; the logic of culture, obtaining an orientation in the conception of form (meaning that the idea of techné is basically form) and technology, is universalistic insofar as it is grounded in science. Moreover, the logic of conceptual power imparts a philosophic basis to the creation of a new culture capable of transcending modernity. In this operation, he proposed that form unites the history of nature to the history of humans, nature to culture, and thus lays the foundation for a "narrative science related to culture and nature."[5] In the "Bunka no chikara," culture becomes a stand-in for the logic of conceptual power because it was able to unite the folk. It was the place where both humans produced things, by working on the raw material offered

homo faber

by nature, and things acquired forms that constantly mediated the continuous process of making culture.

Like many of his contemporaries, Miki was interested in finding the foundation of a proper philosophical anthropology. It is in this context that we must situate his Marxian interlude and the production of two texts of lasting importance, "Ningengaku Marukusuteki keitai" (1927) and Marukusushugi to yuibutsuron" (1928). These texts introduced such durable concepts as the "basic experience" (*kisoteki keiken*), anthropology, and ideology as a theory of mutual interaction. Why the former essay is so important for his later meditations on the "power of culture" is that it is here that he articulated first the profound adhesion of experience to "real life" and "everydayness." Despite the overt appeal to Marx in these essays, it is possible to detect the prominent shadow of Heidegger, especially in his powerful concern for the primordial conditions of Being's existence. According to one of Miki's principal interpreters, Arakawa Kazuo, this tendency to see the everyday as the founding source of knowledge and truth was dramatized first in a youthful confession written in 1919 when he was twenty-three years old. Like Walter Benjamin, who in his essay "One Way Street" argued the importance of "concrete living" over religious thinking, Miki wanted to "feel" within the depths of the self "trivial occurrences of the everyday that have been abandoned to ordinary inattention and unconsciousness. Men who truly know that the important things in life are not what is experienced but how 'this' is experienced are blessed philosophically." He yearned for diverse and deep experiences, but he knew that these become necessarily reflective. "The philosophy I have recounted," he continued, "is not one that lives but rather one that tries to revolve around thought quietly with respect to living well, beautiful, correctly. . . . This emphasizes the importance of everyday life rather than knowing. It . . . seeks . . . truth that secures knowledge related to true principle only according to living."[6] Miki early abandoned the *bildungs* philosophy, which his generation had been nourished on and which he acknowledged in an early autobiographical account. By 1920 he had already turned to a philosophic perspective based on the concreteness of "real existence," which, he believed, was philosophy's real vocation. This did not mean abandoning reflection, which was central to examining a life ordinarily abandoned to "inattention and unconsciousness," but only envisioned an "untiring quest for a concrete philosophy" capable of understanding it. This change lay behind his subsequent effort to design a proper philosophical anthropology.

If a philosophical anthropology is to claim concreteness, he proposed, it "must be first linked to human knowledge." We must note the contrast to Watsuji, whose anthropology was steeped in the primacy and thus exceptionality of climate, which determined culture and character. In his essay on the Marxist concept of humanism, Miki pointed to the role of "originary concrete intercourse in existence" as the source of anthropology (MKZ, 3:9). In his thinking, human knowledge referred to understanding and judging those conditions of society and human feeling that "ordinarily accompany real everydayness," and is located in a "position of real action" that flows back to join a process of producing "human knowledge." Miki believed that this conception of anthropology was based on "human self-interpretation" (*Selbstauslegung/jiko kaishaku*), which confronted "ideology," self-understanding, which accordingly was always a mediation supplied either by philosophy or the diverse disciplines (3:9–10). But human understanding was produced by *logos*, whereby the "experience of everyday life" is "guided by words," "relieved by them"(ibid., 5). Miki, here, pointed to the primacy of something he called the "fundamental experience": that which was not directly accessible to human consciousness and understanding, free from words, but which invariably employed them. Logos fixes experience, often transmuting it into "publicity" and idle chatter, hence catching it in its "uneasy movement," which is the "most basic stipulation of basic experience," bringing "light" to what most probably will be "dark" (3:6; also 40). But the "basic experience" is the dark side of the experience of reality. Human self-understanding also expressed "pathos," which referred to a recognition that "internal necessity," fate, was often beyond the control of will (*Rekishi tetsugaku*, MKZ, 6:39–41). Anthropology, in short, was "logos made directly from the originary, concrete intercourse of existence" (3:9). But since it is mediation, it is also interpretation, hermeneutics, an "evaluation" of the "expressions of our existence" (3:10). Miki acknowledged that logos, under certain conditions, tended to oppress or "restrain existence" because it occupied an "absolutely, despotic position" in mediating experience. Once that happens, it is necessary to "search for a new logos" and oppose the old. This was the work of the dialectic, which pitted logos and basic experience as a necessary contradiction that required a transformation of anthropology, that is to say, a way of interpreting and thus understanding the world.

Miki saw anthropology, directed by logos, as a first stage. The second register of logos was called ideology, and it referred to the historical and social sciences. Ideology differed from anthropology inasmuch as the latter aspired to represent basic experience in its directness even as it relied on words, while the latter openly and publicly grasped it through mediations of a philosophic nature, whose claims to objectivity were limited by these very, self-conscious disciplines. Yet the structure of ideology derived from the prior structure of anthropology, even though the former was not revealed directly (3:13). Miki argued that ideology, as he conceived it, penetrated all aspects of life and seemed to reduce existence to its requirements. This was, as we shall see, precisely the role he assigned to the commodity form. When the development of experience reaches a fixed stage, its intervention tends to restrict its originary development and becomes harmful. Under these circumstances, "ideology has been transformed from the developmental form of experience into fetters." (3:16). Miki saw this moment as the "second transformation of logos," when the movement of ideological change completes itself as a result of the dialectical relationship between word and experience. Much of this view was marshaled to show that the "basic proletarian experience" would ultimately act on the world, rather than remain content to continue interpreting it. For a Marxist, the basic experience conformed to the proletarian conception of the world. Accordingly, this proletarian "basic experience," for Marx, had less to do with the experience of poverty than with "interpreting the essence of humanity as sensuousness," armed with a practical orientation toward the world. History supplied the account of this form of existence in the processes and development of its growth. Hence, Marx's anthropology as logos was formed immediately from within this basic experience of the propertyless class to constitute a practical, sensuous activity and the original philosophy of labor. It was also seen as the original philosophy of the historicity of existence. It should be noted, in this connection, that Miki, in his second essay on Marx's materialism, rendered this conception of a "basic proletarian experience" even more concrete. In this text he referred to the "ground of reality," where the "basic experience" of the proletarian could be found and which consisted of the whole structure of contemporary existence (3:44). Consciousness becomes a reality for the first time in the movement of this basic experience, specified by Miki as "labor" that structures the totality of existence. The basic experience of the proletariat supplied both the mode of society's organization and its structure of existence.

Action was propelled by the body in its subjective meaning to become the agent of acts and the maker of history. For Miki, the body was "mine" and constituted the person's environment, which meant that the world was always grasped by the body through action, which would supply the basis of knowledge. He was aware that while the body was limited to the individual, the I, it enters society at the same time to encounter others, the Thou, which thus constitutes the basis of human existence. The most important dimension of this observation on the role played by the body was its capacity, indeed its necessity, to interact with others, where action must be seen as a relationship between an I and a Thou. In his essay on Marx's materialism, he had already demonstrated that the solitary I could not exist without a relationship to the Thou since the starting point of society was production. Humans have to mutually interact in order to produce and make things. Hence the I becomes Thou and vice versa. In this way the I is both subject and object, depending upon the perspective (3:50–51). This relationality, he explained in his *Rekishi tetsugaku*, transformed the individual body into a social body and even a historical body. Society is both internal to the I and external to it, immanent and transcendent. Action becomes possible when it aims at an idea that is outside of the immediate concerns of the body. Further, action and production were virtually interchangeable. and all human action, therefore, possessed the meaning of formation and working.

Humans are in the world; they make the world, that is, they express and represent it; and they are the world, which points to sociality. Because humans act, produce, and make things, they are expressive, representational. Humans and nature are connected as a singular "representational world." Productivity undertaken by humans is first conditioned by its bodily organization and the primacy of the hand, which grasps and manipulates tools. In this way, it is immediately connected to the making and using of tools and the development of skills, which Miki designated as techné. As a sign of human expressibility, tools represented the objectification of knowledge. Yet it is techné, in the final analysis, that signifies the human capacity for expressibility and representability, since it makes tools, not discovers them. Technology discloses the expressive character of human existence. Because it was linked to the body of individual artists, it was more art and expression than mere technology. Similarly, words function to facilitate human expressibility and the capacity to submit experience to representation. Words, accordingly, unify the outer and inner, connecting body to spirit in the self as an autonomous entity. Rhetoric was the techné of words since it allowed humans to use language as if it were a tool to do something and secure a specific effect. "Humans not only represent things, they, themselves, are representational."[7] The expressibility signified by tools opened the way to the representation of experience offered by words. But as Miki recognized in his discussions of anthropology and logos, experience was never fully expressed in the presentation of words. That basic experience, despite its shadowing of reality, remained hidden in its uneasy movements, harboring a surplus that constantly escaped the snares of expression. That uneasy fit between an unspecified basic experience that served as the foundation for all subsequent expression and representation was precisely the ground that most modernists wanted to resuscitate. For some, and especially Miki, this would be the site of an authentic ground that could only be caught on the wing, so to speak, as logos tried mightily to discipline and constrain it with the despotism of words. In Miki's thinking, logos aspired to representing the fundamental experience of "everyday life" directly, repressing its own mediating purpose by calling attention to the defects of "self-understanding." By the same measure, he was convinced that an originary existence—signified by a "basic experience"—continued to remain as surplus, outside of representation, capable of generating changes in a present fraught with danger and in need of fundamental changes. It was never outside of the totality of existence, as it "moved" and thus "possessed several opportunities to develop and regulate the existential character of the self mutually." What organized existence and structured it was the mode of intercourse (kōshō) governing human life. For Miki this mode of relating was historically and socially specific, and "proletarianization" represented a historical type. But it was the "historical character of actual existence that has been regulated according to it[s mode of relations]" (3:45). In other words, the present was dominated by the proletariat, and its conception of relating characterized by "sensuous praxis" (3:46).

It was precisely the contradiction between the "basic experience" and its subsequent manacling that claimed Miki's interest in the contemporary scene and prompted him to resituate the present as the site of history and its transformation. During his Marxian phase (which, in a certain sense, remained with him until the end), he specified the nature of this contradiction when he showed how the "basic proletarian experience," founded originally in the ownership of one's labor power, had "hardened" into an abstraction, as Marx had exemplified in his condemnation of Feuerbach (3:36–37). Despite Feuerbach's own desire to rid anthropology of its religious taint, he succeeded only in recuperating the very abstraction he was trying to overcome because of his failure to acknowledge the original sensuous and practical nature of human existence, because "he had failed to grasp historical and actual humans." Marx, by contrast, advised exchanging the "reverence for abstraction that produces the kernel of a new religion in Feuerbach for a learning related to actual human beings and their historical development" (3:35). For this reason, Marx's anthropology was necessarily transformative. To pass beyond the "abstraction of Feuerbach" to human beings who have actually lived, it is imperative to consider them as beings "who act in history" (3:36). Even though the controversy between Marx and Feuerbach took place in the last century, it still spoke with meaning and relevance to contemporary circumstances in Japanese society. Marx's anthropology, according to Miki, an "anthropology of logos born directly from the proletarian basic experience," qualified as a mode of consciousness that is singularly actual, the only consciousness capable of grasping the contemporary moment (3:37). Since it consists of an "originary practice" (or praxis), it is primarily aimed at changing "existence" (3:39).

In Miki's analysis, the present already revealed the signs of the growing contradiction between logos and basic experience and clearly provided the occasion for embarking on the "first process of transformation." The purpose of such a transformation was, in his idiom, to return existence to the "actuality" of "human interactions" (3:7) and recover the most basic and originary condition of humanity. But it would involve "grasping nature in its historicality" (*rekishisei*), which meant in the "sensuousness, practical relationships of humans" (3:34). Any philosophy that lacks a relationship to the "proletarian basic experience," which dominated modern life, is simply an "abstraction for contemporary consciousness" (3:37). Reading off Marx's "revolutionary theory" was a necessity for the present because the proletarian basic experience is capable of discovering the essence of the self in the act of transforming "things of the present." Hence, the basic experience requires a logos that expresses the self in its natural growth. "But logos," he explained, "clearly is other (*ta no mono*) in relation to the basic experience. Hence, basic experience necessitates an ideology, that is to say, the other, in order to develop the self" (3:40). By the same token, the other must embody a concrete ground in the basic experience of its self-actualization. Consequently, the basic experience emerges from the self and changes into an other, but this other, through the act of grasping the self, is changed and returns to the self. Lenin, he added by way of explanation, liked to use the example of how the relationship of two ideas like natural growth and purposeful consciousness should be grasped dialectically. The dialectical unity of basic experience and ideology—its other—cannot be pursued without analyzing the actual phases of experience. Miki announced that the development of experience and ideology is mutually implicated and self-limiting.

When he sought to concretize this revolutionary situation, he turned to describing the process whereby the "so-called logos has become the universalized category of the commodity" (3:65). Logos, in other words, chained to the domination of the commodity, had been "abstracted from life and, accordingly, separated from the actuality of conditions" (3:65–66). In this way, logos, which once claimed direct or immediate access to basic experience, had become ideology in the bad sense of the word, restricting and even oppressing the development of human character. Miki's conception of the commodity and the power of the commodity form to transform all relationships was a genuinely sophisticated reading of the first volume of Marx's *Das Kapital*; it echoed Lukacs's earlier theorization of reification and some of the formulations on ideology promoted by members of the Frankfort School without in any way being dependent on either. Though it was the most originally forceful analysis of the current situation of Japanese capitalist society at the time (excepting perhaps Tosaka's own application of it), it fell on deaf ears among contemporary Marxists, who dismissed the domain of consciousness and ideology as mere reflection, and among postwar intellectuals, who failed to explore its utility for their own society. The theory was based upon an account of language usage that itself was original inasmuch as it situated words in the social interaction between humans. Existence, Miki argued, is always mediated first by words; things that have to be talked about must be submitted to "this structure of words" and are things I speak of or things of a "he" who listens or a "who." "They are," he continued, "public in their meaning" (3:57). Consciousness, insofar as it is social, can only exist in logos, in words, in representation. The consciousness of the individual who "lives socially" is thus "buried within words which have a public existence." On their part, individuals are obliged to bury their own subjectivity in words by representing the consciousness of the self with words. Without making words "public," "there is no chance for social intercourse" and for the realization of cooperation among people. This was the meaning of Marx's observation (in *The German Ideology*) that "words are as old as consciousness itself," as they are "practical" and "exist for other humans." Words, for Miki, resembled consciousness, beginning from the "desire" and "necessity" for "communication with other human beings." But a "pure consciousness that mystifies things can never be sensuous" (3:56). Existence, represented by words, is "social," and when words manage to permeate the world in established categories like "man," they carry the weight of "marked characteristics." When words achieve this level of utility, they are named the "commonplace" (*bonyo*), or its neutral character. What he wanted to convey with this reminder of the social instrumentality of words, especially those words that have acquired the status of sufficient generality, was the condition for communication and exchange that constituted the ground of commonness, a commonsense signifying of sociality and the possibility of mutual understanding. "Social practice in us," he wrote, "becomes possible according to an existence that occupies a common place." If words are originally a practice [they were also original tools] rather than mere theory, nothing shows this truth better than the "phenomenon of commonplace existence" (3:58). Miki advised that words be completely free from the sense of a universal idea, which, he believed, always risks distorting the possibility of communication. Only words in their concreteness will satisfy the desire to a buy a practical thing like a table. The commonplace, life's mutuality, cannot therefore be based upon particularity or uniqueness, nor the abstract or universal idea. Rather, they must be independent, concrete, capable of facilitating negotiation without compromising the usage of another's claims. "Actual existence everywhere has meaning according to the commonplace." Words are initially practical, and where this practice is substantially social, there is the original location of the commonplace of existence (3:59). Because everything we love, despise, yearn for in existence, all of our internal thoughts and feelings, are buried and concealed, this interiorization of words constituted the realm of subjectivity. (At about the same moment in the Soviet Union, Bakhtin and

Voloshinov had put forth their views on a Marxian philosophy of language that introduced this interiorization of words as "inner speech" and sought to replace the Freudian unconscious with it.) Yet the common place of existence that has been so useful to human sociality is eventually transformed into a "fetter" that forestalls further development. When such alterations take place, the great transformation in the structure of actual existence must have been completed. The principle dominating the commonplace of modern existence is plainly the commodity. "The commodity gradually becomes the leading category and finally becomes a universal category; the common place restricts the development of human sociality to the extent that it obstructs it" (3:60). Under the ideological constraint of the commodity form, which has permeated all sectors of society to become dominant, the common place of existence must collapse into contradiction. Logos must also fall into the same contradiction. A common place that had once engendered sociality is now inverted into a common sense that effaces the relationship between people into one between things and objects.

Miki was persuaded that the analysis of the commodity, along with the role of history, was one of Marx's two greatest insights, because it disclosed the structural basis of the totality of capitalist society. Modern society, he urged, is a "society of commodity production," which, rather than serving merely as a special question or even a central concern for economics, constitutes the whole problem of capitalist society. "The structure of the commodity is the prototypical form of the object character of so-called existence in this society" (3:61). The tendency of commonplace existence is to comply with it and submit completely to the requirements of the commodity form. Consciousness is thus removed from real life, as the greater materialization of existence becomes dominant. Here, human labor, the most interiorized of human possessions, becomes nothing more than a single commodity and is subsequently prevented from having spiritual meaning. Emptying both life and labor of meaning, the commodity swiftly acts to bury both consciousness and the social relationships governing human interaction. For the essence of the commodity demands that the relationship between humans acquire the character of materiality, an objectivity that conceals what truly links them and effaces all trace of the relationship between man and man to assume a "ghostly apparition" (yōkaiteki taishōsei). "In our society," he wrote, "the social relationships between humans, which are exerted in the service of mutuality, are thus conducted in a form that conceals this [relationship] to our eyes. In the world of capitalism, one does not see the labor binding humans together. . . . Things embody only the form of all commodities, moving in the market, which humans do not manage rationally but are managed by it with its pricing structure." Under these conditions, the relationship between humans appears simply as one between commodities. Marx called this extraordinary transformation the "fetish character of the commodity" (*Fetisch charakter der Ware, shōhin no majutsusei*), where exchange value has transformed every product of labor into a "social hieroglyphic" that discloses its "secret." In Marx, "the complete secrecy of the commodity form reflects the social character of labor among humans . . . as a socially natural disposition of these things. In this way, the commodity comes to reflect the social relations of production toward all labor as the social relations of objects that exist outside humans. The quid pro quo is that labor, which produces things, becomes commodities, transsensible or social things." The fetish character of this world of "fantastic appearances," according to Miki, is produced by laborers in the form of object relationships. Human labor is thus administered as the movement and circulation of commodities, according to norms that have no connection to it; "humans are dominated by the very things they themselves make" (3:63). But here, he observed, was the completion of the site of "self-alienation" (*ningen sogai*). The special nature of capitalism manages to perfect the universal common place of existence in self-estrangement, which confronts both producer and proletariat in contemporary Japan. Although producers feel a certain happiness in this self-estrangement, however illusory, knowing they possess the "semblance" of human existence, proletarians feel in their powerlessness that they have been rejected. Eventually, all classes will lose themselves in the conditions experienced first by the proletariat, owing to the progressive process of social abstraction propelled by the commodification of social relationships. Miki's gloss on this narrative of the future proposed that the producers, if they are to affirm their own existence in the self-alienation of Japanese society, will have to separate its phenomenal form from its capitalist ground, from its historicality, and thus risk the further illusion of "eternalizing." As objects of fetishization and its alienating effect, commodities disclosed two features: one was self-sufficiency or independence from their processes of production, and the other was the privilege of the present and the appearance of novelty and the constant need to make available the new. With Miki, the first, which Marx had already perceived, meant that the constitutive power of labor, driven by social relations of dependence, was simply disavowed by fetishistic mystification of the processes of production. In the case of the second, the concern for the centrality of the present was the way he envisaged modernity and rethought the problem of history. Although fetishistic disavowal led to alienation, it also produced, among the bourgeoisie, a genuinely antihistorical view (see 6:40–41, 47). Hence, the relationship between humans, now structured according to the commodity form, appeared both as autonomous and as the timeless model of possibility for all subsequent relationships. "If that is the case, the structure of the commodity today has reached the point where it assumes a universal meaning as the prototype of the object character of social existence in general" (3:65).

To erect an "eternalizing ideology," it is necessary to realize the claim of "eternality" in existence by constructing a theory based on the presumption of "universal appropriateness." Miki attributed the power of this conception of eternality to the ceaseless process of "self-abstracting" that reflected human self-alienation steeped in the commodity. What worried him most was that the logos, the word, had become "universalized in the category of the commodity" (3:66). The theory of eternality and the repression of history were the inevitable consequences of capitalism, which claimed the authority of its own timelessness and "universal appropriateness," associated with the circulation of the commodity. Yet this set of circumstances offered the occasion for criticism in the present, which represents the "starting point" of any consideration of "actuality." The "present" implied the place of novelty and ever repeating newness; it was the appointed moment to begin the difficult task of constructing a criticism leading to an emancipation not simply from "material desire" but rather from the "totality of material life" (3:76).

Five years later, Miki turned to the question of the present, which, he believed, must be the location of emancipation, and which he renamed "history as actuality." The importance of his decision to analyze the structure of the commodity form as the key to understanding capitalist society everywhere fastened his attention on the present and its meaning for history. From the perspective of the commodity, in other words, there was only the present. Like Tosaka, Miki was correct in believing that Marx's great contribution to social theory was a method aimed at analyzing capitalism as a contemporary social formation in order to assess and evaluate the requirements of the "current situation." In part, this is what an investigation of the commodity offered, but it would remain incomplete without an additional examination of the status of the present. Concentrating on the present, as such, did not mean forgetting about the past or history, as many contemporaries—historians—believed he was promoting. Leading Marxian historians like Hattori Shisō and cultural critics like Kurahara Korehito mercilessly denounced Miki's presentism and condemned his Marxism as "showy idealism," "vagrant dialectics," and the "criticism of camouflaged disclosure" while he was serving time in a detention prison in 1930 for having made illegal contributions to the Communist party. What seemed to be at stake was a developmental narrative that already dominated historiographical practice and aimed to show that the social contradictions leading to emperor system absolutism derived from the Tokugawa past. During the late 1920s and 1930s, the controversy over the nature of Japanese capitalism dominated historical production, and while it sought to explain conditions leading to fascism and imperialism, it focused almost entirely on the eighteenth and early nineteenth centuries. Tosaka, it should be recalled, also remained silent on this historiographical controversy, even though he specifically rejected a developmental narrative as the plot for history in a number of his philosophical texts. Miki's essays on Marxism earned him both savage criticism and involuntary separation from a number of left-wing journals on whose editorial boards he had served and in which he had published articles. For his analysis of the contemporary social formation through the optic of the commodity form was clearly at odds with a narrative of development centered on the Japanese nation state, whereas its identity of the present as a social hieroglyphic demanding to be read for its history was inconsistent with a conception of historiography whose storyline was already known. Far from banishing considerations of history, Miki's powerful conception of the commodity form called into question those forms of emplotment that charted a linear trajectory of a fictionalized object called the past. What was needed was a historical practice that started from the present, that is, the "current situation."

While it is tempting to argue that the text he produced after his release from confinement, *Rekishi tetsugaku* (Philosophical history), written in 1931 and published a year later, reflected in his thinking changes he had recently experienced (what Japanese confidently have called "conversion" [*tenkō*]), the matter was not so simple. Miki had already acknowledged the importance of examining history for any proper philosophical anthropology and declared his intention to forge a new path of the self according to a unique method that "hopes to name philosophy as a historically destructive method"(3:53). If all existence was historical, it was necessary to a find a method capable of understanding the historically necessary contradiction between emancipation and oppression in order to eliminate effects it produces. Far from demonstrating a change of mind, Miki's "Philosophical History" was both a continuation and deepening of a program that concentrated on the role of history in the "basic experience" of humans. Since he had already designated the commodity as the key to the structure of capitalist society, he had now to think through the relationship of history to the present, to the current situation. This meant starting not from a prescribed story line that began in the past and moved inexorably to the present, but beginning in the present to look at both past and future. In this regard, he was forced to abandon the developmental emplotment associated with received historiographical practice for what Foucault much later described as an "history of the present."

To envisage such a program, Miki had to show first that received historical practice was actually authorized by an unacknowledged assumption that the past always comes from the future (which, of course, is the present in which history is being written). For this move, he made a crucial distinction between history as existence and history as logos; the former was the starting point for the latter (I3:6, 7). But if seen from the perspective of historical narrative, history as existence is not the starting point but the point of arrival. With this distinction, he perceived an apparent distance between word—historical materials—and historical existence, which, he conceded, might completely escape the means with which to keep a full record and even write a partial history. (Without saying so, folklorists like Yanagita Kunio and Orikuchi Shinobu were already pushing this conception.) Although history as existence passed for experience, it invariably fell far short of actually representing the historical record. Because of this "inequality," a virtual asymmetry, a history as logos is still "less than history," while "a history as existence is more than history" (3:10). Regardless of changes in historical writing and interpretation necessitated by the discovery of new materials, prompting the recurring practice of rewriting history, it was never enough as it could never be complete. In his view, the now, as he put it, not only becomes the past, but the past, as such, is always in the now. The fact that antiquity is in the now means that it is never past and that its influence still extends into the present and moves it (3:11). Grasping a past still pulsating in the present in this way defined Miki's conception of the modern, what he called *gendai*; at any given moment, the modern contained the history of past experiences that still co-mingled with new. The starting point of history is not in the past but in the present of the past, where the historical project takes shape. Since the present (*genzai*) is the source of historical writing, the necessity for rewriting is internal to it (3:13–14). What this meant is that no real difference existed between writing and rewriting history, as they shared the same point of departure in the present. As a result, it was possible to write history only from the "perspective of contemporary temporality" because the present was able to unite the beginning and end of history according to the perceivable fact that it supplied a starting point. The reason for this arrangement came from seeing the present as the moment that constituted the fullness of time and therefore gave it shape, even as it was always changing, into a completed whole (3:17). Under this circumstance, the present cannot lack historical consciousness in the act of shaping a totality; as presents change, new totalities are formed. Paradoxically, the present both unifies history as logos and history as existence, word and experience, yet also keeps them "estranged," separated. "History moves according to the present. People who fail to understand this adhere only to historical materials and fall into the mistake of thinking that it is the same as history as existence or history as logos" (3:17–18).

Although the present is called "modern" or "contemporary" in the order of history, this classification derived from the convention practiced by historians of dividing chronology into discrete periods—ancient, medieval, early modern, modern—all occupying a fixed but different place in a shared continuum of time. But the present is vastly different from the "modern" (*gendai*), which constitutes the present in the order of history. It is not possible, he insisted, to conflate *genzai* and *gendai*, as if they meant the same thing, in the order of history. One referred to the modern era in a successive, linear continuum and was linked to the periodization of history, while the other related not to a period, but to a moment of time. While the modern belonged to the order of history and represented a period in the process of history as existence, the present corresponded to an entirely different order as it was linked to what he called "history as actuality," or the not yet (3:19). For Miki, the starting point of history is locked into the present and the past represents a transmission, "something that has been handed down" (3:20). But the order signified from the now of the present back to antiquity is clearly opposite to the progress inscribed in history as existence where the modern comes last, not first. In this way, he reasoned, modern or even contemporary cannot be the present, which is the starting point of history and must, therefore, belong to a different order. This is the order of history as actuality. In this scheme, there was no necessary continuity between "existence" and "actuality," since they belonged to different orders. It is important to recognize, like Marx, that it is mistaken to "see later forms, the several forms of the past, as stages toward self-realization, to grasp them on a single level." Later, as we shall see, Miki discounted developmental schemes inherent in any move to collapse different orders of the past in the interest of identifying later forms as completions of earlier moments. Citing Marx, again, he advised that it would be difficult to escape the trap of falling into the "error of economists who erase all historical differences and see the form of civil society in all social forms" (3:92). The present provides the perspective from which to acknowledge the basic differences and diversity of characteristics produced in past periods. Precisely because it is not the modern and not part of the seriality of chronology which leads from antiquity to the modern, it belongs to an order of succession that demands both conflation of differences and the continuity of forms. In his thinking, the modern was only part of a whole, whereas the present shapes the whole. If there is ever to be a true historical consciousness, he maintained, it can only be bestowed in and by the present. For Miki, only the proletariat possessed a true historical consciousness in the present because it originated in history as actuality. Later he was to change his mind and endow true historical consciousness on the folk (3:47).

The present is an "instant" whose temporality cannot be measured in the order of time. Although history as existence is seen as something that has already passed and is now the past, the modern, as such, belongs to the same order. What distinguishes history as existence is its measurability, its capacity for being dated and chronologized. But only *genzai*, not the modern that has already passed, can be opposed to the past since it is clearly different from it. In fact, Miki's conception of the present suggested not simply a difference from history as existence but rather the space of difference itself that challenges the claims of the latter, which were marked by sameness and identity. But the now is the place of history as actuality, precisely because it has not yet happened and passed into the past, like *gendai*. Yet history as actuality, like the now, is atemporal, the not yet but still possible. "History as actuality," he explained, "surely has a historical character since it drives the history of the past. But, at the same time, as it buries the past, it is unhistorical" (3:23). In his thinking, history as actuality was life itself, the living, the reverse of history as existence, which represented dead, commodified forms that had once been alive even though they were still being lived. The two forms of history represented different kinds of existence. But what characterized history as actuality was its capacity "to realize the self in history as an oppositional one" (3:94). In his last, unfinished text on the fifteenth-century Buddhist reformer Shinran, Miki returned to this theme to show how Shinran's greatness stemmed from this conception of an oppositional self. Hence, history as actuality was the means to promote the necessary transformation of logos one, while history as existence had sunk into logos two, the form of "fettering," and collapsed into an ideology that signaled both a "moment of danger" (Benjamin) and a time for change that would "blast" the continuum of blank seriality.

In this regard, Miki, whose understanding of the historical derived from a reading of Heidegger but whose conception of a "philosophic history" often resembled Walter Benjamin, envisioned history as actuality as a revolutionary force capable of tapping into the "basic experience" that history of existence had turned into mere ideology. "But "actuality" was in fact prior to "existence" and took precedence over it, offering the possibility of transcending lived existence and grasping the immediacy of "basic experience" (3:24–25). "It might be good," he avowed, "to call history as actuality an *Ur-Geschicte—genshi rekishi*—as something that overcomes existence. . . . But this does not mean that it is unchanging and unmoving . . . it is true movement." By contrast, lived existence is fixed in its determined rejection of actuality. History as actuality, from the first, signifies the "historicality of actuality," echoing Heidegger's powerful dismissal of mere historiography for a conception of historical destiny. What Miki was plainly seeking was a history based on action and production that reflected the human capacity to constantly make and remake history (3:26). The problem posed by a history as existence, like the commodity, was that it had effaced this dimension of human intervention and production to project existence as finished and complete and as such clearly vastly different from one that was yet to be made. Since the temporality of the now requires a relationship to the future, action must always be oriented toward it. In this scenario, the future is the privileged moment of time, since the present that orients action toward it is only an "instant." Here, the characteristic of time is "anticipation," which means only that time is originally "anticipatory time." But the future is not eternality, which as its opposite projects a transhistorical program that is never a "historical thing." Although the present is an instant, it is the moment that demands resolute action for the future. And since the "future is a denial of the now or death, the present that anticipates this future can only be a moment prompting one to act for the living." The instantaneity of the present contains both past and future, timefulness and timelessness, providing both the potential for denial and rejection and the occasion for action for an unenvisaged future.

If the present constituted a moment of difference and real existence aspired to historicity, the "historical thing" must first be essentially contingent (3:63). Miki supplied his conception of the present with a complex argument on contingence that often resembled Kuki Shūzō's formulations. Its importance lay in its capacity to reinforce the identity of the present as the site of genuine difference. Although it was undeniably true that history contained the contingent that corresponds to "our basic experience," it has not always been discerned in its true light. What seemed vital to an understanding of its role was the distinction between "real existence" and its "reason." Contingence has a reason outside of the self; it possesses no essence even though it exists and appears in reality as something that is already there (*sude ni*), as an occurrence, a "matter of fact" that is "an actual thing" (3:65). But the matter of fact does not refer to a "true *genzai*," even though it is characteristic of actual existence to take the contingent as its basic condition. The now (*ima*) is never a true "present" but only a "matter of fact" that contains the meaning of the "already." For Miki, it was important to show that the contingent was the moment of possibility at the same time that it was "everywhere the actual." Since the actual everywhere is nothing more than something that possesses only the "value of possibility," "it is not a true present" because it has already occurred. This meant that the basic condition underlying history as existence was contingence, inasmuch as the fact of the already, the matter of fact was rooted in history as actuality. Yet they appeared as products of necessity (3:68). Again, Miki was suggesting that history of existence fell into the trap of ideology which effaced the contingent nature of things and occurrences to make them appear as necessary. This is not to say that he rejected the operation of a necessity of a high order, which he identified in a relationship between the part and whole that corresponds to a "concrete whole" revealed to the self, rather than "abstract, totalistic universals" (3:85). Even though existence appears to adhere to a conception of "causal necessity," things as they are and must remain so, it is basically contingent when considered from the position of actuality which aims to destroy it. Causal necessity has no authority other than appearance. The "causal problem" belongs to an entirely different order because of the distinction between "real existence" and the "basis of existence"; these constitute separate orders that relate to each other through the dialectic. Actuality (*genjitsuteki namono*), from this perspective, was not planar (single leveled) but rather dimensional, "doubled layered," since "existence" and its "basis" not only were differentiated, but did not belong to the same order.

Despite the appearance of this false necessity, Miki was convinced that there existed a "higher order" of necessity that was capable of "forming an actual totality," one that is "living." In this sense, this higher order of necessity resembled Louis Althusser's conception of "determination in the last instance" by the economy, while recognizing the semi-autonomy of other realms within the social formation. Though Miki, of course, never specified what this higher order of necessity was, it was marked by a sense of a "living totality" which he tried to define later when he discussed the character of "living culture" (*seikatsu bunka*). Nevertheless, the historical process was profuse with moments from the past that exemplified how actuality supplied existence with a conception of a living totality that eventually had lost contact with its true and immediate foundation. History as actuality represents the unenvisaged totality that constructs history as existence and establishes the relationship of the part to the whole that signifies the larger relationship of the whole to the part. In other words, history as existence appears to stand in for an unseen totality—history as actuality—and it is ideology that provides the specular illusion that the part is adequate or identical to the whole. In spite of Miki's eccentric language, we can recognize the presence of a Hegelian Marxist orchestration of a vast dialectical drama of opposites and the process by which history as existence is constantly sublated by history as actuality. But where he seemed to depart from the Hegelian model was that each "true present" that scored a transformation of existence represented a "living" or "concrete totality," not necessarily a moment in a process leading to an aggregate whole ending history (or prehistory) altogether. Without this totalization, Miki's several presents would risk simply looking like an elaborate game of musical chairs and his history as actuality appearing as another manifestation of the commodity form serving any master who had the power to invoke its authority.

Finally, Miki saw history as existence as the developmental form of history as actuality, its representation of experience (3:94). But he also recognized that existence would inevitably seek representation in what had already occurred, bonding the experience of the present and self to a representation of "certain things that have already happened" and ignoring those areas that had escaped the word (3:93). Hinting at a contemporary practice that had already placed so much confidence in developmental schema, he pointed to how representation always fell short of the experience it was seeking to capture. In this way, he added, history as existence is, by nature, opposed to history as actuality; the former is constantly transformed into a "fetter" of the latter. Still, he accepted the destiny of "all actuality" as one that must crash into a contradiction between experience and representation. In spite of this inevitably fatal stain, history as actuality must seek to "destroy the form of the old existence at this time and move forward to a new form of existence" (3:95). If "actuality" aligns with "nothingness" (*mu*) and existence with being, the latter constantly "oppressing the former," the binding of actuality and nothingness will not produce but will disclose a more originary form of existence rooted in the basic experience. At another level, history as existence reflects culture, which promotes its own norms and theory of the self but ultimately is helpless against the development of a new life. Life, he persisted, will never develop a self without retaining a connection to the culture of the past. Yet a culture is not only a "congealing," a kind of curdling into a fixed and static figure, but also movement following the pursuit of a developing self. The culture of the past can be recalled in this effort since it already coexists with the present in the now. What Miki seemed to be struggling with was the recognition that if the form of culture that accompanies the development of society fails to avoid falling into "congealed nonrelationships" and "atomization," if it gets no further than becoming the "husk" of creative life, society will never possess history. Hence, history as existence represented a "clotted life," solidifying all custom and habit into lifeless routine. What better description of the process of commodification foreclosing any imagination of the possible and existing only for the endless repetition of the ever new in the already same? Without ever saying so explicitly, Miki saw commodification as the model for history as existence, just as revolution mirrored the realm of the possible offered by history as actuality.

It is important to recognize, however, that he was calling for a mode of cultural production rooted in history, one that promised to offer immunity against "coagulation" and the sure prospect of being merely a shell of creativity. He assigned to culture the vital role opposite the one played by the commodity and the process of social abstraction. Even culture could easily slide into hardened forms and abstraction and forfeit its true purpose. As he came to understand this category, culture offered life, living, creativity, true relationships between people, whereas the commodified structure of capitalism signified death, nonrelationships, objectification, and self-estrangement, a world of monotonous sameness. But culture was still only an inversion of commodification, a further reification that projected the illusion of a noncommodified life, a space still exempt from the processes of capitalism. The evidence for this inversion of commodity into culture was, as it still is, the disappearance of history. In spite of the claims to ground culture in history, it was, as Watsuji and so many others showed, a history that had already been completed in the remote past. The category of culture, as it was articulated between the wars by people like Miki (and as it still appears in cultural studies), was never able to free itself from the ahistoricality that marked the commodity form and its relentless desire to efface and repress the conditions of its own production. Miki's conception of history as actuality never succeeded in overcoming this constraint. Presciently and dangerously, he bonded cultural creativity to the commodity, where the former signified the supposed overcoming of the latter, without accounting for either the dependent relationship between the two or thinking through a strategy aimed at moving beyond it. Inadvertently, perhaps, he posited a necessary relationship between the commodity form and the category of culture and preemptorily closed off any further attempt to think through one without referring to the other. His effort to envisage what he called a "living culture," as we shall see next, was no more unrestrained by this fatal relationship than other contemporary projects designed to imagine a culture that could supply a genuinely autonomous alternative to capitalism and the commodity form.

"LIVING CULTURE"

It was Miki's almost obsessive concern for the status of the present and the historical conjuncture it seemed to signify that drove his desire to figure the immediate experience of the self within history.[8] Although contemporary events in China, especially, commanded his attention in the mid- to late 1930s, Miki's passion for understanding the meaning of the "current situation," signaled by his essay "Jimu no riron," referred to both domestic and foreign societies. His vision of a larger East Asian communal and cooperative brotherhood was probably not so different from what he envisaged as a new "living culture" in Japan in the late 1930s.

The principal difference, of course, was that the space of Asia was really "outside" for him and marked as a colonial sphere that he simply could not deny, however elastic his conception of community and cooperation. When he went to the Philippines in 1942 as an official, he recorded the observation that immediately put him on the outside: "If the Spanish brought religion, and the Americans education, the Japanese will bring agriculture to the Philippines." Japan would teach the subject peoples of the island the techniques of modern agricultural production which—it goes without saying—would produce foodstuffs and raw materials for he metropolitan country.

Miki turned to the question of "living culture" (*bunka seikatsu*) in 1940 and 1941. The text must be read alongside others composed during the decade that dealt with national culture, culture and politics, new technology and new world views. But the theme of "living culture" or "everyday culture" (the word *seikatsu* was used interchangeably with *nichijōsei* and *kurashii* throughout the 1930s) had become a compelling issue for popular discourse in magazines and newspapers and the subject of a research discipline devoted to measuring daily life quantitatively and introducing new rational techniques into it to facilitate its routines. The idea was an inversion of the concept—"cultural living"—envisaged earlier by people like Morimoto Atsuyoshi, Gonda Yasunosuke, and Kon Wajirō, with its own built-in disposition for the program of rationalizing life, making it more efficient, cheaper, and speedier. Cultural living referred to the importation of Western-made consumer goods and techniques in the 1920s and was monumentalized in the "cultural house" inhabited by the nuclear family of the new, urban salaryman. What originally was associated with the life-style of the middle class soon became a description of modern, urban living among all classes. A discussion staged by the *Fujin kōron* in the mid-1930s, titled "On Living Culture," already revealed the extent to which modern everyday life in the cities and beyond had been transformed. The discussion problematized the relationship between what distinctively appeared as Japanese and what was Western in the household and the consumer goods occupying it. Concentrating on how contemporary Japan had effectively developed a double-tiered life, one participant, Ito Shigehira, proclaimed that the present age continued to show the implantation of doubling everywhere. Recalling our discussion of Watsuji, we see again the coexistence of different elements in Japanese life and their fusion. Another participant, Tanigawa Tetsuzō, saw the "culture house" as the classic model of "double living," since it combined Japanese house architecture with Western interiors, "detestable," in his view, even though he confessed he once lived in one. (Tanizaki Junichirō had already put this house into question in his cultural lament of 1931, *In'ei raisan*.) Tanigawa was convinced that culture houses showed classically the "foolishness of double living among Japanese." Ito went further to cite an "undigested Western civilization" as the height of foolishness. The discussants worried about the effects of these houses on the individuals and families who live in them and other practices that clearly worked against the "discipline of communal living"[9] Forgetting the discipline, especially in the cities, would cause "unusual defects." Notwithstanding the charge of foolishness, which most seemed to share, and the fears it prompted, the doubleness was acknowledged as a fact of life, particularly in circumstances women found themselves in "modern" Japan. Not many years later, Tanigawa wrote a book called *Seikatsu to bunka* (Living and culture) that contrasted the "cultural living" of the 1920s with the "Westernization of life" and the "living culture" that appeared in the early 1930s, complete with "an understanding that sought to respect traditional things within the way of thinking about 'living' or everyday culture."[10] Miki, it should be recalled, believed in the possibility of recalling older cultural elements of the past in configuring a new culture and turned to this theme of a "living culture" in his *Seikatsu bunka to seikatsu gijutsu*.

In order to not miss the "essence" of "living culture," he wrote, it is necessary to differentiate it from "cultural living" (14:387). Until recently, the word for culture (*bunka*) had been restricted to considerations of literature and art. Something like "living culture" was not even a problem; culture simply "reflected different civilizations" and the realm of the "spirit" (3:384). What seemed to distinguish living culture most was its positive and progressive attitude toward life. Appealing to the German *kultur* and the English culture, implying the meaning of cultivation, he hoped to demonstrate that culture actually refers to the act of working on nature and human production. "Living culture, as production," encompasses the transformation of life, and not simply the process of importing things. There must be, Miki demanded, a "will to culture." On closer inspection, "living culture" was nothing other than his conception of history as actuality.

Because everyday life in Japan was cultural from the beginning, rather than natural, it was shot through with traditions from the past in both its content and form. "There are words we are unable to neglect in our everyday lives. These are not things we produce for the first time but are transmitted to us from the distant past of the folk. And we are born within these traditions. It is the same with other cultures. Cultural living is also traditional" (3:385). By the same token, traditions are not left in the past but are "living, moving things." Miki pointed out, in this connection, that the doubling that characterized life in Japan was first formed by the late Tokugawa thinker and activist Sakuma Shōzan, who came up with the formula "Tōyō no dōtoku, seiyō no gakugei"—"science" and "traditional philosophy." If they are combined, Miki explained, Japanese must still acquire a new philosophy to make up for the moral lassitude of contemporary people for whom the older morality is no longer adequate (Kokuminteki seikaku no keisei, 14:351). Moreover, the producers of the past—its traditions—are the folk who, frequently in his texts, are interchangeable with the "people" or even the "masses." Elsewhere, he proposed an identity between the "folkic character of intelligence," similar to Orikuchi's "prior knowledge" and "Japanese intelligence" (Tetsugaku to chisei, 14:83–85). Tradition (*dentō*) was distinguished from the "remains" (*yuimotsu/ibutsu*) because the latter were simply "traces" that were completely dead even though they had been left behind while the former continued to live. For Miki, tradition meant things from the past still living in the present. The past must "unceasingly penetrate humanity by being grasped by it"—that is, it must "enter into the symbolic domain of humans." Tradition is understood subjectively and is counter to surviving remains that are only objective things that have no life. The act of transmission that realizes the past can only take place in the present. In the present, tradition is activated and brought to life, but it is important to recognize that the action of the present implies a relationship to the future. The past serves to link the present to the future (14:308).

Observing a distinction between tradition, which derived from purposeful action, and traditionalism, which simply apprehended tradition only as a "continuing thing," Miki faulted would-be traditionalists for overlooking the role played by active agency and for neglecting to explain how creativity is produced. This move was already prefigured in his conception of the present as an instant and his decision to remove it from the series of succession in order to make it the point of what precedes it as past. But these pasts, as we saw, were also in their time presents and the center of a particular perspective that founded a totality, with its retentions and protentions.[11] In these past presents, there is action that intends to realize production. "Where there is no action," he warned, "tradition is not able to truly live as tradition" (14:310). In other words, the creation of living culture was already tradition that would be bestowed to the future. Traditionalism fails to ground itself in the authority of tradition steeped in hope. If tradition were continuously interior, it could have no authority for people, who would not be able express their responsibility toward it. Miki's attack on the spurious claims of traditionalism showed the operation of what he earlier called history as existence, the congealing of culture into frozen forms that foreclosed the possibility of acting and creating culture anew. It also resembled Tosaka Jun's more studied attack on "restorationism" and "Japanism," which sought to freeze history in

timeless achievements derived from the remote past. Both Miki and Tosaka perceived that what was lacking in these articulations of traditionalism was the perspective of the present, what was present at hand. With
Miki, traditionalism represented an extreme form of antirationalist denial
that he described as "intellectually conscious deterioration."

Tradition is not only something people created in their presents but
also what lives in the future. What traditionalists ultimately forget is that
tradition has been actively produced from the perspective of their present
(14:310). Without this activation, there is no chance for history. History,
he explained, is the location of cultural production, and producing, with
difference, the intentions of an earlier time. For this reason, it can never
be understood from the perspective of the individual. What is produced
historically possesses determinate forms. History, in this sense, is the process of form production, which embodies experience; form unifies the
subjective and objective domains to shape a historical subject that constitutes a subject/object identity. But, by the same measure, these historically
produced forms are transcendent, insofar as they outlive the moment in
which they were produced as heritage transmitted to the future (14:313).
It is possible to discover what continues to live in the form of another life
and experience by looking at a self that has been "sacrificed." Quoting
T. S. Eliot approvingly, in this connection, Miki was persuaded that "poetry is not the emancipation of emotions but rather a taking leave of the
emotions; this is not the representation of a personality but a taking leave
from it" (14:313). In other words, what is produced is independent of the
producer as form, leaving the personality behind as it embarks on its journey into the future as part of a collective bestowal of tradition. If tradition
always signifies a heritage of forms, it also stands to restrict experience
through the exercise of these forms that will act as cultural restraints.
With Miki, this meant that production—making—which he increasingly
associated with techné, required the constant process of working on forms
that were present at hand but had been transmitted from earlier times.
Reproduction always required production, repetition demanded difference (14:386).

Miki thus identified culture and tradition with active life and production. Yet, a living culture was the product not of a handful of "geniuses"
or *bunkajin*, but of the human group as a whole. If it is "living," then "it
must be culture" (14:386). "Like the artist who makes art objects, we,
ourselves, are living producers." Although only a few people ever truly
create great art or understand science and philosophy, this limitation was
not relevant to "living culture." Women, he observed, have been seen to
have no relationship to cultural activity but have enormous importance
for "cultural living," an importance linked to their capacity for consumption and appreciation. Miki looked back to the 1920s as a time when

the "beauty of traditional things" nearly vanished from view. Moreover, Japanese, at the time, had failed singularly to grasp the "deeper essence" of the things they were so enthusiastically embracing. In the midst of society, "there appeared a colonized culture under the name of 'cultural living' " (14:387). Kuki Shūzō, it should be recalled, registered the same complaint upon returning to Japan after spending years abroad. Miki's conception of cultural colonization, shared widely, accused "cultural living" of causing shock among thoughtful people, who felt that its content was "frivolous" and dangerous. What seemed particularly noxious about this episode was its embrace of the "external," the "surface," while abandoning "true living culture," "interiority," and "substance." Cultural living was "tainted" in the dye of "Europeanism" and "Americanism" and dramatized the truism that a new, living culture in the present must be produced from the perspective of Japanese autonomy. Cautioning against concluding that such a strategy endorsed the highly narrow "self-complacent antiforeignism" that was beginning to emerge, Miki recommended that much could be learned from the West but only through the mediations of tradition and heritage. In the end, Japan had to shape its own living culture. The problem confronting Japan had always been one of excessive and abusive imitation induced by a lack of understanding foreign cultures. The present was the appointed moment for Japan to undertake an adequate understanding of the limitations of foreign cultures as a condition for envisaging a new living culture that would, by necessity, look back and survey deeply the country's traditions.

For Miki, individualism and liberalism were at the heart of "cultural life" in the 1920s. "People who yearn for 'living culture' pursue the free life of individuals, emancipated from a variety of feudal fetters. . . . The forms of cultural life are liberalistic and individualistic. Insofar as it is important for the development of a national 'living culture' to conquer feudal remains, individualism and liberalism retain a significance" (14:388–389). The example he cited was women who "yearned" for cultural living because they were even more tied to feudal fetters than men. As important as this was, cultural life must be seen as merely a stage in a larger development aimed at establishing a "living culture." In other words, liberalism and individualism were useful means to achieve goals that were not necessarily liberal or individualistic. To be convinced that a living spirit would not terminate in liberalism did not mean a reversal back to feudalism but rather a move forward to the accomplishment of "cooperativism," which would be the foundation for a new living culture.

The idea of cooperativism had appeared earlier in Miki's writings on the "China Incident," as he called it, and the possibility of forming a new Asian community. In his thinking, it signified a new mode of social organization that would advance society to the next stage beyond class.

Although he believed that liberalism spawned cooperativism, Tosaka was proposing that it produced its own self-negation in accommodating new and dangerous forms of "Japanism," restorationism, and fascism. But Tosaka was driven by the desire to mount a critique that would link liberalism's espousal of affirmative culture to capitalism's struggle to survive in the inhospitable world of the 1930s and thus explain the evolution of fascist forms that promised to resolve social and economic crisis. By contrast, Miki believed that the "life forms of cooperativism" must be shaped toward contemporary "individualistic life forms," not as a solution to the problems they have raised but as an evolved, next stage. His purpose was to salvage liberalism, which Tosaka had already demonstrated to be complicit with fascism, and to affirm capitalism in a new register rather than call for its rejection. Hence, the importance of cooperativism lay in its promise of "social discipline" more than its necessity for the formation of a new, living culture (14:389). Contemporary society was deadlocked in the "abuses" of individualism, "liberalism," and "rationalism," which all lacked a sense of the whole, the totality (*zentaishugi*) (Zentai to rōjin, 14:270). Culture, itself, is either "cooperative," "public," or simply cannot exist (Bunka seikatsu, 14:366). In his thinking, culture was always identified with folk production, the people, masses, which constituted its strength; it was always collective and communal (Kokumin bunka no keisei, 14:338). Modernity lacked a system of control capable of bringing people together in a united effort. Contemporaries appealed to a "restoration of feudal things" to secure control while liberalism undermined any conception of "social discipline" among the nation's people (14:348). Cooperativism promised both the prospect of wholeness and social discipline that would unite people in the common effort to move beyond the superficial and dangerous content of "cultural living." "A new living culture," he demanded, "must create a diversity of forms of cooperative life, like the example of neighborhood associations, but at the same time should not ignore reverence for the particular in the life forms of each person" (Seikatsu bunka, 14:389–90). But cooperation and uniformity were not the same thing. Even though Japanese acquired an "elegant state," it was still inferior because it had not developed historically, as the rapid evolution of liberalism had proved to be inadequate to the country's needs. Japan lacked an ethic that would manage to "control" the population without recourse to the threat of coercion, state-initiated violence, a kind of ideological state apparatus that would be able to interpellate subjects (*shutai* not *shinmin*) to perform voluntarily and acceptably. Liberalism's great defect was that it had not gone far enough (Tosaka believed it had gone too far) because of its failure to "consider the social completely." Cooperativism promised to fill this vacuum to become the necessary social cement that would bind all in what he called the "space of Asia"—that is, the Japanese Empire.

Conformism, he admitted, always produces an impoverished culture and can be no model for a "living culture." The true individual is "formed" as a synthesis of the unique and general. For this reason, "living culture" in Japan must start from the particular when striking out for improvement. Equally important, a living culture should not be limited to the artifacts of high culture, like music, art, and literature. In Japan, "cultural living" had aggressively imported these new cultural practices but "lacked an idea that there is a culture that is still completely everyday" (14:390). Miki here seemed to be pointing to how imported artifacts were implanted in a received, everyday culture without recognizing its prior existence. When speaking of words, culinary matters, ordinary discourse, customs, all these and more are important and fundamental to a culture made by humans. But people seem to be principally concerned in cultural life with listening to the radio, playing records, reading books, and looking at pictures—in short consuming new commodities for entertainment. These things, he confessed, are not, in themselves, harmful and are significant additions for the advancement of "cultural living." Regardless, they are capable of inflicting a variety of injuries. If the word "culture" in "cultural life" were adequately interrogated with the long view in mind, without pursuing it within this narrow framework, it would show the extent to which the rush for new commodities undermines the received everyday life transmitted from the past. Aware of the consumerist dimension of cultural living, driven by money, he feared that cultural life in general would be reduced to the sole concern for luxury, entertainment, and consumption (14:391). Accordingly, culture has to be found outside of family life rather than within it, since consumption appeared to be bonded to the household and thus separated from life, setting off the concern for culture, now read as consumption, from the experience of living. Like Tanizaki Junichirō in his *In'ei raisan*, Miki recognized that the separation of culture and life had been overdetermined by "cultural living" that now necessitated an effort to repair the division. The experience of a unified culture and life was a "tradition of Oriental antiquity" that should supply the model for unification. As he envisaged it, the idea of a "living culture" starts from the presumption that life and culture are identical and that any differentiation signifies decline and danger. The progression toward the achievement of a "living culture" comes from "below," whereas recent experience has shown that "cultural living" starts from the top down. The unity between life and culture was a transformation of an earlier conviction that politics and culture should be unified (Bunka no chikara, 14:318, 326). The strength of Japan's culture, he wrote in another text, stems from the movement from "bottom to top, center to countryside" (14:326; Kokumin bunka no keisei, 14:337). In East Asia, it is commonly accepted as its special characteristic since its strength has spread among all peoples. Similarly, Japan's culture is East Asian, even though this space of Asia, as he conceptualized it, would also be a "colonial outside" (Bunka no chikara, 14:330). It was impossible to imagine the status of culture without considering its "foundation in the masses," who supply the energy for its formation and cultural renovation and serve as its custodians, (14:338). In another register, Miki's quest for unity was propelled by his earlier desire to realign logos and pathos, subject and object (see Shinsekaikan e no yōkyū, 14:69).

Fearing the contemporary domination of "abstraction," signified by vast divisions of labor and knowledge domains, Miki called for a proper "cultural policy" capable of enforcing formation from within the "cultural environment" whose goal must be "public welfare." By synthesizing science, education, and religion, the wholeness he identified with "living culture" would be reestablished. Such a policy would also reflect the unification of politics and culture and thus "connect to the body," securing "embodiment" where logos and pathos are one (Atarashiki chisei, 14:96). Earlier culturalism, so dominant in the intellectual circles of the 1920s, had forfeited concreteness for abstraction in privileging lasting and enduring values like the good, beautiful, and true, while the craze for "cultural living" had estranged people from each other because of their desire to consume new commodities. Their lives, he remarked, were dominated by the abstraction of objects. Instead, Miki's cultural policy "recognized the meaning of culture embedded in everyday things," recalling, at the same time, an archaic tradition that "culture enlivened" (bunka wa seikatsuteki ni suru) and "respected everyday things" (nichijōteki namono) (14:390, 359). Cultural purpose must strive to produce a whole living culture rather than merely art, literature, and music, which only the few ever understand and appreciate.

At bottom, the problem of "living culture" was production, which "cultural living" had repressed in the interest of promoting consumption. It is important to work creatively, he wrote, "productively in national life, in the individual's life, in the household, in everyday life." Living culture is a national problem, and its greatest priority is to produce the spirit that represents the folk. Instead of seeing culture as discretely divided practices, estranged from each other, they must be brought together, "enlivened," made to be living. The process of making such a culture requires mapping out a "broad, fertile ground" for the development of diverse practices connected to the lives of the folk. Forming such a living culture means that it is informed by a "love of life and humanism as its basis" (14:392). But we must recall, again, that Miki's conception for a new living culture was linked to the larger arena of empire. Humanism, as we shall see, was implicated in the program of cooperativism to constitute the foundation of a new order in Asia, not just domestic Japan. A new living culture is born from the "spirit of humanism which seeks to advance life" and avoids the desire for luxury; it must valorize what is "healthy" and "efficient." Although the most important element in the new living culture is the necessities of daily life, it is not limited to it. Pleasure was necessary for both cultural health and efficiency, he confessed, and represented a "form of life," even though its immediate goal was not always apparent. It functioned like a "joint" or "seam" that sutured life together and designated a different kind of power. In this regard, pleasure resembled art (*gijutsu*) and belonged to its domain. Art, in the wider sense, was vital for the formation of living culture and national life because it provided the model for making, producing (techné), which ultimately opened the way for technological development and the establishment of greater rationality. In this regard, Miki went back to his earlier views concerning the operation of techné, which the Greeks had associated with *poises*, the work of the word—logos—, constructing poetic myth. But techné, as he saw it in its larger dimension, was "form," or a "form without form," which was empowered to make present of what is embedded in physis. Under this charge, even the political belonged to the sphere of techné, which Miki, following through its logic, would see in the accomplishment of the "space of Asia" as a spontaneous formulation that has sprung from the intelligence of the folk identified with nature. Here, techné was *mimesis*, not actual representation in the sense of a secondary revision or presentation, but in the sense of making present what is already a subject, even though it is still plastic and malleable. This view, as we shall see, would have profound consequences for the relationship between culture and politics, the former incorporating the latter, and the formation of a political or communal body that claimed its authority in nature.[12] What he feared most was the formation of a "technism" separated from the authority of techné; technology must be "living techné," devoted neither to "hurrying around to resolve a money problem" or simply making life more comfortable. Rather techné, exemplified in art, making, production, and technology, must be employed to establish a new, living culture. Because technology is "born from distress," such as making commodities from scarce resources, it is imperative to pursue a living technology from the perspective of straitened circumstances of life (14:397). This means that its purpose is to "impart clarity on life where there is darkness, negativity," but techné can exist only if there is adequate scientific knowledge, not the hardened custom and morality that had characterized the past but was no longer useful in the present (14:90). Techné, for Miki, leading to "technological reason", originated in the unity of subject/object, a "synthesis of objective laws and subjective desire" (Rekishi no risei, 14:257). In his thinking, techné referred to producing things for everyday life, but it also meant basing "living culture" on science. "Today," he wrote in the *Bunka seisakuron*, "the great necessity is the dissemination of science," and this must be a knowledge that does not serve only its own interest. To avoid this, he called for an "enlivening of science" which was realizable not through the accumulation of scientific knowledge but by introducing techné and machine into the "everyday life of the people." This program of enlivening would stimulate both a "scientizing of life" (by which he meant rationalization) and "making science a living thing" (14:366). But he warned of the importance of differentiating the new living culture, founded on a science for the folk, from "mechanical technology." Technology must be humanized and even individualized before it completely enslaved humans.

Modernity represented the "period of machine" whose appearance has not only transformed humans into the "slaves of machines," but created a profusion of "nonhuman things" in the midst of human society. Although it is hard to know what Miki had in mind, it undoubtedly included the diverse forms of alienation and estrangement he had perceived earlier, excessive (possessive) individualism and, worse, degradation of workers. The development of machines has "destroyed humanity," even though its effect derives from the establishment of scientific knowledge. "In order to protect humanness, some people have considered rejecting the machine and censoring its reason—its basis in science." While this appeared to be an impossible solution, it riveted attention to those conditions that encourage denunciations of reason from a humanistic perspective devoted to defending humans. Nevertheless, pure, unreflective denunciations of science and knowledge were pointless unless informed by a genuine effort to protect humans from further alienation and debasement. Miki called this approach "humanistic" and represented it as a "new thing" stimulated by the establishment of "new intelligence." But he also easily recognized the paradox in defending humans by attacking intelligence and reason, which were precisely the faculties that differentiated them from animals. Human intelligence, he conceded, had actually reached the point where it was beginning to work against humans rather than enhance their lives. Returning to an older argument that insisted on the presence of pathos, he now argued that instinct promotes the human character, as it is impulse, feeling, emotion, and "pathos" that motivates (14:89).

Intelligence, expressed through the mediation of logos, words, separates humans from their nature and leads them to destruction. Yet intelligence is also part of this very human nature rather than being merely its opposite. Isn't it possible, he asked, to see even instinct as an "idea of nature," as an "intellectual" construct shaped by words (14:90)? Intellect has separated humans from nature, to be sure, objectifying it, submitting it to human domination, but the time has now come to reverse this course and to seek a reunion of mind and nature. Contemporary scientific technology had claimed autonomy from human instincts and declared the machine independent of human intervention. "Intelligence was nothing more than the sign of this impulse, and the words of intelligence never more than the words and sign of this impulse" (14:92). Humans know things according to what they make, and they make according to what they know. In this way, techné is implicated in productive action, and the modern excesses attributed to both science and technology stem from social systems that utilize them. Machines will make it possible to "massify" spiritual and "cultural treasures," making them more available to larger numbers of people. The further development of the machine must therefore be constrained by a "new humanism" capable of reintroducing the genuinely human into a culture devoted technology for its own sake.

Miki insisted that the "intelligence" of this new age must be a social intelligence, unlike the relationship of intelligence to nature. Behind this program to rehumanize science and technology lay the conviction that the new humanism was possible only if pathos, now associated with the folk, and logos, expressed in "tradition," are unified. "What is customary," he asserted, "is the intellect that remains submerged in nature. Folkic intelligence is this traditional intelligence. To understand either tradition or folkic intelligence, it is necessary to . . . link pathos and logos, nature and intellect, as in technological intellect" (14:94). With one sweeping move, he denied the claim of scientific autonomy, identified the folk with nature, and demanded the establishment of an identity between nature (folk) and intelligence. The unification of pathos and logos would therefore succeed in producing a culture that was "bodily," "materialized" in its pursuit of the human. For Miki, humanism was the guarantee of catching hold of a knowledge and intellect that was always concrete (14:96). If the older humanism of Descartes emphasized intuition, the present demands one founded on active intention; and while modern humanism has insisted on the centrality of individualism and the subject who is in a position to perceive, the new humanism, yoked to action, avoids abstracting humans from the bodily and proceeds from the recognition that it is the basis of real existence (14:97). What he was contesting was the subject-centered humanism that emphasized the separation of mind and body, mental and manual labor, which, in liberalism, was reflected in the privilege claimed for the "critical intelligence." Despite liberalism's original celebration of the creative self, it has forfeited this "guiding principle" for an empty, critical intelligence, "abstract," separated intuition, the body's emotions. However, the intelligence of the new age was creative, not critical, precisely because it is united to pathos. Intelligence must be submerged in the pathos of the folk, tradition, heritage; when it is weak in pathos, it will not be creative (14:98). "To secure creativity," he explained, "it is necessary to pursue how pathos becomes logos, an idea born from nature." In this sense, creation is produced not by intellect but by feeling. Hence, living culture must, above all else, be "emotional," "beautiful," "tasteful" at the same time it is "rational" and "efficient" (14:399). Confident that the beautiful leads not always to the merely luxurious but rather to the "rational," "even the machine, to the extent it is efficient, possesses a beautiful form." Although living culture must be technological through and through, he feared the commonplace excess of people "using it unconsciously." "We are always in process of forming life," he declared, "and there is techné in all forms." Yet, the important thing about "living techné" is not intelligence but wisdom, an Oriental wisdom close to nature now pitted against a "Western intelligence," which can claim for itself an understanding of "living technology" because it was based on doing, making, and acting. "The so-called Way is not only like an ethical law but in reality a technological one" (14:399–400).

"THE POWER OF TECHNÉ"

At the heart of Miki's meditations on modern society was the problem of politics and culture and the aporia of their seeming polarization into discrete spheres. In the separation, politics, he believed, had taken precedence over culture, confirming his worst fears about the crisis of "technism" manifest in contemporary societies like the Soviet Union. Just as importantly, the division reinforced the perception of the increasing abstraction of culture itself, its visible removal from the "living," principally through the agency of a science devoted to abstract laws (Rekishi no risei, 14:258, 259). During the late 1930s, Miki produced a number of texts (in his "journalistic" and would-be-policy maker incarnation) that either problematized this splitting or sought to repair it in a new relationship. Yet this concern surely constituted a sign of a global historical conjuncture where fascism increasingly was the political strategy employed to save capitalism, while communism was the movement that overdetermined the challenge to capitalism's continuing survival. Miki's intense commitment to resolving the problem of capitalism by rethinking the relationship between politics and culture would take him on an itinerary from envisaging "living culture" as an expression of a new humanism to defending lamely Japanese imperialism as both the space for this humanity—called cooperativism—and the final resolution of capitalism. The one thing Miki failed to do was call for the replacement of capitalism itself. But this attempt to realign politics and culture, where the latter would supply the symbolic boundaries containing the vision of order of the latter, showed clearly the linking of fascism and imperialism that Takada Yasuma and others would see as a natural manifestation of the expansion of the communal body.

Surveying world conditions in a text he wrote near the end of the 1930s, *Sekai bunka no genjitsu*, Miki could have been mimicking, in a reverse way, Walter Benjamin's own contemporary fear that "politics had become increasingly aestheticized" in a present that urgently demanded a "politicization of aesthetics." For Miki, the problem was that there was not enough art and culture in the political process. "When speaking about what is most distinctive," he wrote, "it is the management of culture by politics. We are not able to separate what is called either the crisis or the confusion of culture discussed so frequently in recent days, which is connected to the special circumstances in world culture today and refers to the political management of culture." But today, philosophy, as well as culture, has become the "servant of politics" (14:3). This essay addressed those instances that restrained and even banned intellectual freedom. Under such conditions, it was ultimately impossible to defend intellectual freedom when it was implicated in politics. Contemporary history reinforced this particular judgment because most people saw the present marked by a sharp polarization between the claims of fascism and communism and a political world no longer held together by "unifying principles." The current situation, it seemed, no longer recognized liberalism as the "principle of world politics." If a Marxist like Tosaka Jun could condemn liberalism for its easy accommodation of fascist ideology, fascism in turn long ago disclaimed any kinship with it and denounced it as bankrupt. In fascist and communist states, there was only absolutism, and no third, neutral way of thinking that could substitute for liberalism. For, as the Nazi theorist Carl Schmitt put it most starkly, in politics the most fundamental categories are "win" or "lose" (14:8). War, then, represented the great possibility of politics since it aimed to resolve the question of politics. A world without this basic differentiation between winning and losing is one without politics.

Moreover, the contemporary world has witnessed the "religionization" or "sacralization" of politics. "Politics," Miki declared in this connection, "appears now as a new religion, substituting for the older religions." Because modern science is incapable of supplying "beliefs" in life so that people can continue to exist, it has found other, spiritual representation and political ideologies in the form of one such belief. Significantly, this "sacralizing" of politics led directly to its hegemony, even in the Soviet Union, which has preferred to call its politics "scientific." The more serious consequence of this process was the "conquest of politics over culture." The "politicization of culture" in the present is nothing more than a "theologizing of culture" that constitutes contemporary culture's greatest danger. Quoting the German cultural sociologist Edward Spranger, who warned the present of the peril it confronts with the absence of intellectual freedom, he predicted that culture itself would face the "danger of death" (14:17, 19). Although he appeared ambivalent toward contemporary (Japanese) politics, he nevertheless advised that politics might well turn its attention to the "danger in thinking that culture is a problem." Projecting the problem into the future risks obliterating the meaning the present possesses as present. There are, of course, people who oppose the "hegemony of politics" today, but they are scorned as culturalists. Miki wanted here to distinguish his conception of "culturalism" from the older brand as one that does not stall in the contemplation of abstract values but rather possesses a political meaning within it. "If politics for us today is a 'new destiny,' then it will be necessary to ask what kind of reason (risei) we should pursue toward this new fate, still more, our culture" (14:20, 21).

The answer to this question was provided by reenvisaging Japan as part of the Orient and Asia as a space for a new humanity. Toward this end, he called for a "culturing" of politics. But if politics accords with culture, this program will have to be grasped from the perspective of techné. "The dearth of cultural character means a scarcity of techné in politics" (Bunka seisakuron, 14:362). Both culturalists and politicians will have to make an effort to understand each other's domain. Miki proposed that the reason bureaucrats lose the cultural picture is that they do not respect specialists in culture. Culture's importance is its power to synthesize, its vast capacity to form as it makes, realized through the "cooperation of true specialists." For Miki, culture, it is well to remember, is common, public, folkic; even though it is often produced by the solitary artist, the work is detached to become public. It was an object of self-realization precisely because it intervened directly into the lives of the people (14:325, 337). "All culture is rooted in a mass base and its tradition becomes fixed" (14:338, 390, 391). The strength of the masses lay in their desire to preserve culture yet change it substantially. The folk supply the common base of departure shared by both politics and culture that ultimately unifies the two realms. Hence, "it is correct to say that world views are born from myths that exist among the people. Nay! The people themselves appear as the great myth of the present" (14:77–78). By the same measure, the "Asiatic stagnation" most marked in Chinese society stems from the experience that culture never reached the people. Although Japan benefited immensely from China's superior culture, the strength of culture meant its dissemination among the people (14:328). China, Miki noted elsewhere, had privileged politics over culture, with its incessant emphasis on moral education that appeared as nothing more than the ethical dimension of politicized culture.

As culture unifies people, linking them together in commonality, it also mediates between humans. Words—language—signifying the publicity of culture, shaped national culture.[13] For this reason it was meaningful to see the publicity of culture as the instrument of mediation that established the terms of "true cooperation." Culture's essence, in short, was its "cooperativeness." Breaking down barriers eased the path to opening up to the publicness of culture, which increasingly came to resemble the "openness of techné" in his thinking, which was the true task of cultural policy. Miki here proposed that the accomplishment of "true cooperation based on culture's publicness" marked the dissolution of "feudalistic isolation, "cliqueism" that had persisted in national culture until recently. A culture that lacked cooperativeness inevitably presented a weak facade that signaled immediately the necessity for reorganizing it into a "cooperative system" (14:364, 365). Cultural policy that relies on the publicness and cooperativism of culture brings out the "brightness" in politics and humanizes it. Overwhelmingly convinced that cultural cooperativeness and publicness distinguished all national cultures in the pursuit of nationhood, the dissemination of science will enhance policy in a present aimed at forming a genuine national culture.

Miki was devoted to the idea of a public culture and the work of the collectivity; even the contributions of the solitary artist depended upon that art's diffusion among the people. In this light, the cultural producer must exist like a foreigner among the people. Words must still pass between them (14:368). Yet it was essential for culture to reach all regions of the country if was to make good its national claim. As such, it was not a happy occurrence that culture's production and its consumption were concentrated in the large cities like Tokyo and Osaka. Cultural policy, he explained, echoing Yanagita Kunio's earlier complaint, is compelled to measure the development of regional culture and adduce what needs to be done in order to redress the imbalance between city and countryside. But it is not enough for the growth of regional culture to merely "sprinkle" the culture of the great cities throughout the country. What was required was a program designed to stimulate diverse development in different regions, emphasizing the growth of particularity, in order to offset the "maldistribution" (henzai) between city and countryside and discourage the danger that was reducing culture to the consumption of commodities. Like others, he was describing the scene of unevenness and unequal distribution in the cultural domain and demanding its correction before it undermined national culture itself. As suggested earlier, Miki believed that the formation of national culture cannot occur one-way through the flow of culture from "top to bottom," "center to periphery" (14:369). It had to move also from the bottom to the top and the regional localities to the cities. In this particular connection, he urged an indivisible relationship between the promotion of cultural policy and one aimed at reorganizing the continent, by which he meant China (14:374). This linkage, he explained, stemmed less from the "special standpoint" of Chinese cultural policy than from a perspective sensitive to the "future trends of world culture." Solving the problem of cultural unevenness in Japan was allied to a cultural policy for all of Asia; resolving the cultural problem in Japan relied on its resolution in Asia, since unevenness marked the space he had envisaged all Asians would occupy.

In pursuit of this program, Miki insisted upon the ironclad relationship between Japan and China, for both political and cultural reasons (14:330). Japan resembles China but is still completely different. Like so many of his contemporaries, Miki recognized the cultural kinship with China and East Asia as historical, if not ontological, yet clearly contended that Japan, once having absorbed China's earlier civilization, was still different in the present. Contemporary culture in China had stagnated for a variety of reasons: dogmatism, conservatism, the ceaseless polarization of culture between center and periphery, the separation of people from culture, and a historical legacy that exempted the country from the law of history that shows how countries must borrow from others. This, it seems, was China's greatest conceit. Because China had been surrounded by what were considered lesser cultures, it had no need to borrow, and thus risked sliding into a reflex of self-satisfaction that automatically inhibited the Chinese from overcoming their self-image of centrality and taking the West seriously when it arrived in modern times (14:341–342). But Japan had avoided this conceit and turned itself around to assume responsibility for the highest task, which was to "sublate" (shiyō) the "spirit of folkic selfishness" and "arrogance" to produce a culture in the true meaning of the Orient (Bunka henbō, 14:109). In this emerging drama, Japan would take the lead to induce other countries to overcome arrogance and selfishness to build a new culture. Japanese writers would create works of art that would portray the life of the Chinese that "Chinese would love": works directed at winning their assent and inspiring a joyful response. Although Japan and China were currently involved in war, Miki advised that it should be seen from the perspective of "political reality" that would, in a "roundabout way," provide great insight. It would reveal that war was really about "life" and the "power of culture" rather than territorial and economic domination. For Japan's intellectuals, the task at hand was to produce a culture that would truly contribute "toward the ultimate aims of this incident," which are "Sino-Japanese good-neighborliness and cooperation" (14:108).

The "incident" to which he was referring was, of course, Japan's invasion of North China and the subsequent military occupation of substantial portions of the country in a long, drawn-out war that could not be won. Imperial adventure and open war were thus reduced to the status of an "incident." For his part, Miki, ensconced in Konoe Fumimaro's "brain trust," the Shōwa Kenkyūkai, seized upon the conflict to envisage it as possessing world historical meaning and providing the opportunity to establish a "new culture." The war was transmuted into an instrument of cultural policy. The war, he explained, was related to both Japan and China and represented an "Oriental *sturm und drang*" (14:66). The question that surfaced was how Japan would seek to erect culture anew in the "raging bellows." What principles should inform the foundation of this new world view? The basis for such a world view must be the folk, but it should not stop there. Instead, this new view must be driven by science, which now "stands with the folk" and is capable of transcending them (14:71). If the world depends only on the folk, the union between Japan and China will have no foundation. War showed the central role played by the folk and their culture, now bonded to science and technology—techné—that would motor the necessary changes to bring about a new culture. "It is important for Japan," he wrote, "to be kind toward the cultures of East Asian peoples," to recognize and respect their customs and sympathetically accommodate them. With reference to China, Japan must acknowledge its enormous cultural debt. This was all possible because Japan shared a culture with Asians and was, despite some differences, part of Asia, a common community that remained in a plastic state that techné would make present (14:330). Although it was currently vital for Japan to recognize and even assimilate foreign cultures, it was equally necessary for East Asian societies to learn this lesson from the Japanese example. Foreigners have seen only the foreign, imported elements in Japan's culture and not its whole, which is Japanese and Asian. The accomplishment of a real synthesis and union of elements is never realized in a simple mixture of adopted assets but rather through a combination carefully shaped by the "fixed cultural power" of the folk. This kind of folkism, observed in Japan and throughout East Asia, differed from the volkisch ideology of national socialism and was not necessarily incompatible with "globalism" (14:332). Miki emphasized that the construction of an East Asian new order was a "moral obligation of the folkic destiny of Japan," and that the starting point for such an adventure that would lead to an "East Asian cooperative system" lay in affirming the historical necessity and historical meaning of Chinese folkism. "Depending upon the power of culture to unite independent folk to folk is a great thing," he announced, but the "thing that possesses such power must be a culture that contains a global essence" (14:331). "Worldly," a good Heideggerian word, was not the same thing as "Western," despite the claims of a Eurocentrism that had always identified the West with the world.

Hence, the world historical meaning of the "incident" points to the "unity of the Orient," which, in his thinking, was simply another word for true "worldliness." "Beyond speaking of the East Asian cooperative body, the unity of the Orient does not reject regional principles. That Japan's culture has become worldly doesn't mean that it is completely Western. Rather, it goes without saying that we should be awakened to the Orient" (14:332). Ever the rationalist, Miki seemed to want it both ways. If he found it difficult to express unqualified praise for regionalism, it was because East Asian culture had already adopted the strength of the West. Yet the purpose of constructing a new culture in East Asia, through public cooperation among the folk, "was to resolve the world problem of the day which is capitalism riven with abuses" (14:333). What he wanted to dramatize was the unevenness that existed between the industrial societies of the center and the periphery, composed of colonies and countries like Japan who were seen as latecomers and not as advanced as the societies of the industrial West. In 1940, in a text produced under the auspices of the Shōwa Kenkyūkai, *Tōa shinchitsujo kensetsu no riron to hōsaku*, he turned to the problem confronting the achievement of a new order: how to resolve the several domestic contradictions and move toward the construction of an Asian cooperative society. "Spiritually, we must organize a folkist movement within the limitations and maintenance of the new order. . . . Materially, press for the new organization of a folk productive structure whose basis is economic, or to put it another way, urge the accumulation of folk capital."[14] Referring to still another text, which he apparently had had a hand in composing, the *Shin Nihon no shisō genri*, Miki in his "Bunka no chikara" explained that the world historical meaning of the "China Incident" existed "spatially in the unity of the Orient, temporally in the revolution of capitalism." As for the spatial, it was identical with the region, that is to say, the Japanese Empire, which he depicted now as the space of publicity and cooperativeness. The problems of the space of Asia and the temporality of folk capitalism were momentarily interrelated, since the resolution of the former would solve the question of the latter. But, he warned, failing to resolve the problem of capitalism, both its political economic unevenness, manifest in the question of folk accumulation, and its cultural unevenness, which already was unleashing social conflict in class struggle and the colonial enslavement of Asians, "the true unity of Asia will never be realized." Throughout this otherwise prescient discussion concerning the space and temporality of capitalism, Miki refused to recognize either Japan's own role in inciting class conflict and colonial disaffection or the obvious fact that however much he tried to press for cooperativism, the space of Asia was still the colonial outside. Miki acknowledged the existence of capitalism in the West and Asia and the vast differences in development between Japan and China. "To disregard this differentiation," he cautioned, "would make it impossible to create an East Asian economic cooperative body" (14:333). The intellectual principles of the East Asian cooperative body must be realized first in Japan and then spread to Asia. This explains, he noted, why there is manifest in the present a theory of a "National Cooperative Body: without domestic reform there would be no chance for the construction of East Asia."

The clue to the new order was in the "philosophy of Oriental gemeinschaft": the traditional social philosophy of the Orient that had privileged form, thus grasping materiality in its true shape, in the form of a thing, subjectively. Whereas Western philosophy viewed things objectively, Miki, in this regard, equated form with the Idea (eidos), but it had to be formless, capable of escaping, like pathos, all representation because it was already a subject. He was returning to his earlier conception of techné and mimesis and the power to create and produce, which meant making present what already was embedded in plastic matter. This was also the source of nothingness, as against the Western veneration of Being. Following Nishida, who was at the same time trying to describe Eastern thought in the same idiom, Miki argued that nothingness "contains all form, it unifies" (14:262). In the West, form is grasped from the objective side, while in the East it is understood from a subjective perspective. For this reason, even though techné existed in the East, it never developed science. The point to this comparison was to show how the idea of a new culture in Japan and Asia must correspond to the logic of techné, which derived from art, authorized "making" and "producing," and thereby disclosed the way to fashion and fictionalize—in the good sense—of community. The appeal to techné enabled the unification of culture and politics precisely because the act of shaping and giving form constituted the work of art, applicable even to the political realm. In Miki's reasoning, the idea of social order that the present required was one that "had to transcend modern gesellschaft to conform to a new gemeinschaft" (14:263). This new gemeinschaft was to be seen not as a throwback to a primitive or feudal community (here, his fascism was both modern and rational), but rather as one that now was capable of sublating (shiyō) modern society within itself, overcoming it, to be sure, but retaining something of it in the communitarian configuration. What he was recommending was an order based on the operation of techné and science. Techné, he was confident, would transform the laws of science into form, not just form in general but forms that were both general and specific that possessed the power to unify the objective and subjective. Similarly, the creation of the new culture must be "connected to the tradition of Oriental culture," in which Japan had historically participated. Miki identified the central trope of Oriental culture as a "philosophy of form in the thrall of its peculiarity" (14:264). But this valorization of the specificity of form had already been prefigured in his meditation on "living culture," which aimed at "enlivening" culture, unifying life and culture. The very society this program envisaged for Asia, not just Japan alone, was "public," "co-operative," and "technological." Given the logic of techné and its capacity to make present what was always already there in formless inertness and malleable plasticity was the folk community. The essence of Oriental culture, he asserted, was the fusion of "life" and "culture," the unity of "nature" and "culture," bonded to the idea of making and producing. "Techné," he proposed, "is culture fused to life" (14:265). Intellect returns to nature, again, by way of techné, which meant customizing what technology had produced. Despite the war in China, the "reason of history" will permit the necessary overcoming of the event that will enable the present generation to discover and grasp what it really meant.

In this sense, the essence of culture and politics was organic. Since the state was too abstract a conception, it was not always possible to see this organism as a "living totality" or as an artwork, even though these images were forcefully implied. The organicity implied by Miki's conception of fashioning a community was "infrapolitical, if not infrasocial," an organic totality identified with the folk, designating a socionatural or, better yet, "physical determination of the community which can only be revealed to the people" through the work of techné, art, and language.[15] The logic of techné operated as the "surplus of physis," that is, the material body, through which it decodes and presents itself. In Miki, this organicism led to political totalitarianism since techné and physis shared a common origin.

Finally, Miki's program, driven by the power of techné, demanded a defense of difference. His argument was based on a conviction that form depended upon environment, context. If nature, for example, makes different forms for the bird and fish, the techné of humans continues the work of nature. Yet the relevance of specific forms is mediated by certain historical environments and moments whose meaning can only be assessed later. For this purpose it is imperative to determine the reason of history when confronted with themes like the "construction of an order in Asia" or the "creation of a new culture" (14:268). Paradoxically, Miki had already made this determination of history's reason with his conception of the "space of Asia" as the site of a new culture (already envisaged in outline in Japan) and a conception of capitalist temporality that would induce folk accumulation. He often sought to distance himself from historic fascisms even as his analysis of Japan's modernity and his defense of imperialism led him to imagine an order that was just as fascistic, inasmuch as it sought to salvage capitalism and the folk which had been estranged from it in its original form as an organic community. A "modern gemeinschaft" propelled by technological rationality and an organicist folk cooperativeness was simply another name for fascist political totalism.

FOLKISM AND THE SPECTER OF FASCISM

If Orikuchi Shinobu and Yanagita Kunio stopped short of becoming full-fledged ideologues of fascism, their effort to replace the masses with the folk, history for native ethnology, unbounded space for bounded place, meant trading in an idiom that could easily slip into reinforcing calls for both the establishment of gemeinschaft in the midst of a historical society and the ideological naturalization of social relationships. By the same measure, Miki Kiyoshi, as we have seen, envisaged a vast folkic space coterminus with East Asia, occupied by the folk who would cooperate to bring about a lasting resolution to spatial and temporal problems posed by capitalism. In fact, he insisted on representing the folk at this crucial moment in history as the part that would call attention to the whole and unify the special and exceptional with the general (13:167, 168). Miki condemned both Japanists, who simply reduced culture to an exceptional endowment, and intellectual-producers, who had failed to exercise their responsibility toward the folk by spreading culture and making it more accessible (13:220, 222). The space he envisioned for an East Asian brotherhood was none other than a cultural one, in the broadest sense, absorbing politics even though it never rose above being the colonial space of the East Asia Co-Prosperity Sphere directed by imperial Japan.

Between the two world wars, Japanese thinkers could easily agree with the German philosopher Max Scheler's dim description, before the rise of national socialism, of the concept of society as "only the *remnant*, the *rubbish* left by the inner decomposition of communities," and applaud his unequivocal denunciation of contractual arrangements that signify the end of communal life and the unleashing of a "completely unorganized 'mass' portending worse things to come." But they might also have drawn reassurance for their own critical programs in this authoritative insistence that "society" is not the inclusive concept, designating all the "communities" that are united by blood, tradition, and history.[16] Yanagita envisaged custom, stories, and legends as the experience that sustained the corporate identity of the group and even extended this communalism to include the dead ancestors; remembering them was remembering Japan. Orikuchi located in the founding beliefs the social cement that unified the group, bonding it to punctual commemorations and rituals requesting continued good fortune from the gods. Although neither actually referred to the binding ties of blood, as such (though Yanagita emphasized the importance of fictive kin relationships), the racially specific nature of the groups' stories and legends could not have but helped imply the importance of both blood and the "national soil." To this end, both sought, each in his own way, to rob the social of its commanding role as a principle (and principal) of determinacy, promoting voluntary associations, division of labor, contractual arrangements as the basis of modern capitalist social life, by appealing, instead, to an undifferentiated folk (without class, gender, sexual, or regional identity) and to elucidating the meaning of their enduring customs—precisely those aspects of life that had not been assimilated to modern society. In this effort, they, like so many of their contemporaries, were driven by the problem of locating the concrete in an increasingly abstracted culture dominated by the commodity form. Yanagita looked to the survival of premodern and precapitalist customs to secure the effect of concreteness, whereas Orikuchi, leaping over history, believed it was possible to reenact ceremonies and rituals and thus recapture the inaugural gestures of the archaic community. Native ethnology, Orikuchi's "prior knowledge" and "classic of life," was formulated to challenge a conception of society, and thus culture, based upon exchange, by summoning a social imaginary that had prevailed prior to the organization of contemporary society and whose fundamental elements continued to persist uneasily in the present. The social imaginary native ethnology projected was condensed in the figure of the folk, its candidate in the competition to determine which subject positions would prevail in modern Japan, the individual or collective. As a collective subject, the folk body was presented as an unmarked, smooth surface figure, showing no differentiations, seams, or divisions; it constituted the sign of corporate and communal life (kyōdōtai). But precisely because native ethnology identified its discipline with rescuing the "seductions," as Orikuchi put it, of older forms of life associated with the folk and reinstating them as practices in the present, it risked sliding into a process of ideologization that sought to impose its timeless social imaginary on a historically driven capitalist society based on the division of labor. In other words, native ethnology's privileging of the folk could not help but supply fascism with its most powerful trope, an object of fantasy and political desire, and thus could not, itself, avoid complicity with the "gathering" of fascism as it was increasingly articulated in promises to remove both unevenness and conflict and eliminate cultural abstraction in programs proclaiming the establishment of folkism. Even more important, the linking of the communal body to forms of practice and performance in a language charged with rhetorical force went a long way to fulfilling fascism's own vocation for enactment and action. In fact, the very language used to critique the modern and provide an image of loss possessed vast rhetorical powers to persuade and animate. What had been deployed as critique could be made to perform for the construction of a new order pledged to resolving the aporias of modernity, retaining essence, guaranteeing the sanctity of spirit's realm and the folk's community against the divisions and corrosions of modern life. Implicit in native ethnology's valorization of making custom and the repetitious performing of archaic gestures was the desire to enact a new community, to bring it into existence by acting it out.

The urgency of this project was undoubtedly provoked by the perception of fragmentation, disunity, and even the appearance of conflict that threatened to tear apart the social fabric in the late 1920s and 1930s. As a replacement, folklorists looked to the unity and coherence of archaic community, held together by common custom and practices of belief. But Marxists too, in the same years, were providing their own critique of capitalist exchange value and social abstraction; they too saw the "inevitable" decomposition of the social order in cataclysmic revolution. If thinkers like Yanagita and Orikuchi offered their version of a primordial everyday life recruited from the "poetry of the past" as a resolution of contemporary social problems, Marxists offered their own image of daily life drawn from a future not yet envisioned. Both Yanagita and Orikuchi employed a hermeneutic (even though the former believed he was only unearthing factual evidence) they believed capable of extracting meaning from the moment when discourse fixed in narrative a relationship between bounded place and folk (and their ancestors and gods). In so doing they could demonstrate how their experience and custom had remained immune from the caprices of historical chance or the laws of necessity. While Yanagita situated ethnology in the contemporary scene to combat the dissolution of the native endowment by offering the prospect of stability in enduring folk customs and remembering all the ancestors, Orikuchi moved to exhume the lost, dead meaning of folk *mentalities* for the present. This difference was further sharpened by the contrast provided by Yanagita's concern for the ancestral spirits and Orikuchi's articulation of the *marebito*. Yet the disparity was not nearly as great as it appeared (especially to Yanagita), since the category of the social, society itself (which Yanagita continued to call *sesō*, a term used in the Tokugawa period, while Orikuchi favored employing *yo*, which evoked archaic associations of the agrarian community) seemed to vanish altogether in their respective programs as a result of the narrative identification of place, folk, and the gods. In fact, Orikuchi's conception of the "gods who rarely come" behaved as a supplement to Yanagita's image of the communal body authorized by an appeal to the ancestors. For it should be noted that the archetype of the social group worshipping and thus remembering its ancestors was ultimately expressed in the form of familistic community—the *kyōdōtai*—that is indistinguishable from place. Immediately after the war, Yanagita identified the space of the village with the space of the (tutelary) deities. Worshipping the clan or guardian god was really making observances to place and its inhabitants, the "ordinary and abiding folk." "When referring to the *kamisama*, the gods, in the language of our commoners, and speaking of temples and shrines, these mean our villages and households. They are the same words for mother and father."[17] By contrast, the *marebito*, since they belonged to the other place (*ikyō*), another community and place called *tokoyo*, or even the "mother country," were not in a position to have founded the original community. What characterized the group that celebrates these god/men is therefore not identical with the clan or family unit that offers respect to its departed ancestors. They were visitors who were called upon by the community not to supply abundance to any particular family group but rather to offer "good fortune" to humans who organize themselves into a communal unit devoted to work and worship. As a result, the texts of Yanagita and Orikuchi provided an account of social origins that was present to itself in the repetition of practices. Moreover, they imagined a conception of community whose existence persisted in the repetition of practices associated with a specific place whose memory performance could always recall. In this way, society as an object was exiled to an absent existence in the subsequent articulation of an ideology that would privilege presence, space, and atemporality, to live a fugitive life as a negative image of all those declarations that have shrilly insisted upon the irreducible communalism of the Japanese.

At this point, the project of native ethnology to construct a communal body of the folk converged with its ideologization that was taking place in the 1930s by social thinkers like Takada Yasuma, Shimmi Masamichi, Suzuki Eitarō, Aruga Kizaemon, Matsunaga Motoki, and others too numerous to mention. The powerful meditations of Miki Kiyoshi to locate the folk at the basis of a new cultural configuration for all of Asia provided the philosophical grounding for this ideologization. This ideologization, named "folkism" and condemned as "archaism," eventually employed the figure of the folk and their unchanging social order as a stand-in for the state itself. But what is important about this ideological move to folkism is how it inflected the work of native ethnology. That work was devoted to figuring an imaginary principally characterized as a "natural community" that worked to produce its own essence in the customs of everyday life. In the hands of native ethnologists, the image of community acquired a preeminently immanentist representation, appearing as an organized, living, organic totality that was always present. The fashioning of the folk was produced by an interpretative framework that emphasized orality, spatiality (a synchronic picture of a system with no history), and alterity (especially the difference which a cultural break signifies). It also promoted a sense of cultural unconscious that blended collective phenomena and averaged or stockpiled those elements believed to have permeated the folk's daily lives, as against concepts like writing and temporality, which signified the succession of historical moments marked by events, identity, and succession. This appeal to a "natural organic community," the priority of the whole over its parts, and its timeless folk was easily appropriated and transmuted into an ideology of folkism that was deployed to displace the threat of social dispersion, the agency of historical classes, and to provide an alibi for imperialism and colonialism. By the end of the 1930s, folkic Japan had become the basis for a larger, more encompassing identity called the East Asian folk, signaling the implementation of policies demanding regional integration and incorporation through the agency of "cooperativism."

The ideologeme of folkism that bonded folk to place and dominated discourse in the 1930s was employed to directly counter the challenge of Marxism as it was dramatized in the powerful debate over the nature of Japanese capitalism. It was this contest over different claims that drove non-Marxian social thinkers like Takada Yasuma (1883–1956) to shift the emphasis on interactionist sociology toward forms of essentialism and organic community, from Simmel to Tonnies. This thinking conformed to the native ethnological program of Yanagita and Orikuchi, not to mention others, insofar as it shared their fear and distrust of society as a core unit of social science for one that now proposed harmony and solidarity (*ketsugō*). In Takada's thinking, the apparent reason for this intensification of an essentialist social science was the growing influence of Marxian modes of social inquiry, especially its explanation of social conflict and the volatile nature of social relationships in the late 1920s. It is, in fact, for this reason that I have decided to conclude these studies with an assessment of Takada's contribution to the specter of fascism in Japan. Not only was he one of the most articulate critics of Marxism during the 1920s, prefiguring a widespread identification between anti-Marxism and fascism found throughout the industrialized world, he was also the theorist who took the idea of an organic communal body furthest by emphasizing its immanentism, its molecular permeation of the entire society.[18] Furthermore, he linked it to the necessity of colonial expansion in Manchuria. In Takada's conception of the folkic body, blood and culture were finally fused into the principles of a new, communal order for Japan and all of East Asia. Once this was accomplished, there was little to distinguish his version of folkism from the more strident pronouncements of "Japanists" like Matsunaga Motoki, Kawai Hiromichi, and Seki Sakayoshi and others

who clearly were envisaging a "Japanized wholism that was a true wholism" rather than merely a "particular thing."[19]

Although Takada's interest in sociology derived from a prior interest
in socialism and the belief that the new social science was the way to
satisfy the requirements of the latter, his intellectual and methodological
orientation early abandoned the promise of explanatory strategies based
on evolutionary theories of development for the pursuit of "universal laws
of society."[20] "I want to reject completely, in whatever form, the theory
of social progress as an aspect of sociology." In fact, he early expressed a
desire to rid "universal laws" in sociology of theories of historical development because he was convinced that they were "contained within the
transtemporal sections" of the discipline. Sociology offered the prospect
of directly engaging "concrete social phenomena" and a "universalistic
science" and elucidating as an object of scientific inquiry the "union of
sentient beings." It is interesting to note that despite this penchant for
formalism, his sociology was always concerned with a specific "historical
and social reality" which ultimately was represented by the experience
of contemporary Japan and its capitalist transformation. But instead of
grasping society historically, he wanted to examine and understand it psychologically, without bothering to know how the present came into existence but only to sort out its characteristics. "With relation to a sociology
that is a learning that grasps the social [society]," he wrote, "the sociology
of today or sociology as a bourgeois science was abstract and lacked a
historical character, and has come down to a criticism that claims that it
does not understand the meaning of the present."[21] But Takada's obsession with a formal sociology and his distrust of theories of historical development were aimed at Marxism which had, already, condemned "bourgeois social science" for its neglect of history and its valorization of a
present reality isolated from specific historical contexts. Far from caving
in to the lure of historical analysis, he proclaimed that history had no
place in a proper sociology and that those who insisted on the relationship
misrecognized the fact that history and theory or laws moved in completely different directions.[22] In this way, the "several laws of the stages
of economic development" were "an idea of historical reality" but not
the "laws of a universalistic science." Although he was willing to acknowledge the movement from the model of military society to industrial
society, from status to contract, from mechanical solidarity to organic
solidarity, these represented "intersectional laws" that appeared in the
general movement of social development. Because they were the fulfillment of universal laws, they were unchanging and unchangeable, more
in accord with a "natural history" than a social history.

It was, in any case, this effort to implant a universal science of society,
based on laws that aped the laws of nature, that became the basis of his

critique of Marxism and his articulation of what he called the "third view of history." It is interesting to note that Takada's "third view of history" aimed to discount both an idealistic conception of history that emphasized the agency of the spirit and a materialistic view (Marxism) that privileged the relations of production (as well as the forces of production)— the economy—as the motor of development and change. In its place, he wanted to offer a third candidate that was free from the determinisms of both metaphysics and materialism—both of which reflected a particular social, cultural, and political endowment—for a view more in keeping with Japan's particular experience. Takada's third view of history was probably the first attempt to express a specifically third world view on the question of social development that tried to account for the particular experience encountered in the process of capitalist modernization. Even though he sought to distance himself from both, because of their inapplicability to the Japanese scene, it is evident that his long and informed critique of the "economic view of history" (Marxism), based fully on an account of the role played by productive relationships, mediated his own, third view which emphasized conscious social relations rather than productive and economic ones.[23] According to Kawamura Nozomu, Takada's decision to privilege mental social relations as the primary constituent of society stemmed from his reading of Georg Simmel, especially those observations that tried to chart the relationship between metropolitan urban life and the individual, apart from state and household.[24] But where he differed from Simmel, and this difference reflected Takada's reading of the specific Japanese experience in the 1920s, was in his move to emphasize the force of unity or bonding between individuals rather than on their mutual interaction—in short, the means of securing social solidarity in a society undergoing cataclysmic changes and beginning to show the signs of disorder and disintegration. In his revision of Simmel, society was an aggregate far more complex than the image produced by the mental interaction between the material forces of city life and individual conduct. Rather, it was how people, living in a complex division of labor, are able to establish the forms of conscious unity, which meant how they would have agreed to live cooperatively within society, despite the mental interactions they experienced in everyday modern life. Accordingly, the inhabitants that occupy a society must have the will to live together even though they interact with each other as individuals. In this respect, he was convinced that the forms regulating the unity of social relationships were objective facts, undoubtedly part of a society's endowment, and thus the sign of its capacity for endurance. But to make this move meant identifying the essence of society in this will to unity, this agreement among its several members to love each other in cooperation, rather than merely interact, which conformed more to the model of an "interest society."[25]

Before he worked out the "third view of history," Takada envisaged two fundamental laws of social change that would explain the nature of the movement of societal forms: the movement from gemeinschaft to gesellschaft, famously mapped out by Ferdinand Tonnies, that differentiated between a primitive communal society based on the primacy of blood ties and involuntary association (what Durkheim referred to as "mechanical solidarity") and secondarily on cultural ties; the other was a law pertaining to the "quantitative framework of society" (*shakai no ryōshitsuteki kumitate*) which proposed that the social bond remains constant, according to the population. The more individuals come into contact with each other in society, the more the possibility for less dense interaction and vice versa. The smaller the society, the better chance there is for more intense, emotional ties binding its members. This was an observation made by Yanagita, who observed that people in villages do not need to make eye contact with members of a village because they know who they are, whereas in the cities, interaction and encounter strain the capacity of the senses to decode the immediate surroundings. In his later, folkist incarnation, Takada proclaimed that the spiritual strength of Japan was embedded in the social and affective ties of the village, and in its youth, who were leaving for the cities in hordes.

The third view of history represents a principal stage in an itinerary that led back to the folk and the village community. According to his account, it represented a "sociological historical view" (KDS, 299, 306), which emphasized the "quantitative framework of society." For Takada, this meant a historical view that took into account the number and character of people who entered into social relations (308) Under this conception, the form of social organization would depend upon identifying the extent of the population and how members of a society were differentiated. "The sociological historical view," he explained, "establishes the quantitative composition of society as an initial explanation. This [factor] refers to the quality and quantity of charter members of society who enter into social relationships. In a word, it is the form of social structure seen from the perspective of population density and the heterogeneity of society, and it becomes the basis on which to determine the relations of mutuality among humans, relations of union and division. These social relations also determine the content and change of all other social phenomena."[26]

Hence, this principle, he insisted, determines the "mutual relations between humans," the relations of union and separation (309). If Marx designated productive relationships as the determining agent in a society's make-up, the "quantitative framework of society" must be acknowledged as an even greater determinant of social relations because it is able to account for the formation of social relations between the members of a social group according to the place they occupy in the arrangement of social power. What this meant is that economic life alone was not sufficient to explain social interaction but rather the social power one exercised. The problem posed by Marxism was how to assimilate social relations to production when, in fact, they must be grasped as outside the productive process, even though it might mediate the relations and interactions between people. Takada saw these material social relations as independent from the consciousness of people, which was determined by how each related to the other. The social was simply the "union of people," their decision to live with each other. The trouble with a view that defined social relationships according to production was that it emphasized the quantitative dimension of these relationships, their content, which, in his thinking, was always secondary to their form. Both the first and second views of history, ideal (spirit) and economy, he wrote, "surround such relationships with materiality" when in fact they are formal categories apparently obeying some universal imperative (316). It is interesting to see that while Takada relied on Marxism for privileging social relations, he smuggled back into his system the idealism of the first view history with his appeal to the priority of form. In other words, the formalism of a bourgeois social science persisted in his effort to find a third way that would be more accountable to Japan's transformation from community to society. The social relations that governed the nature of human action thus acted as a "backbone," as he put it, that often closely rivaled the infrastructural role played by productive relations and the mode of production in Marx (319). And like the base, they act causatively to determine the specific form of superstructural phenomena like the political system and legal structure.

What interested Takada with this concept was its capacity to show how society was produced as a result of some sort of consensus that was already prefigured by the decision of its members to agree to live together (321). It seemed to provide him with a powerful critique against the agency of class and the agenda of revolutionary change, which now were assimilated to prior social relations based upon the nature of demography in shaping society's mode of interaction. In a sense, Takada was proposing that the determination of historical development is society itself, that is, society's capacity to constantly produce itself according to the nature of its population and the degree of density affecting social interaction, and how they combined to bind people together (an idea that was put forth by the French sociologist Alain Touraine not too many years ago, even though there is no question of his having read Takada). Where he differed from Marxism was in his tireless promotion of a conception of "social power" as the force and agent, if not subject itself, of history that always determines human interaction and accounts for the forms of sociation.

Through the mediation of this conception, which itself acted as mediation, he was able to explain that class, or any form of social differentiation, originated not in productive forces, which were too limited and limiting a criteria, but from fundamental divisions between the powerful and powerless based on the acquisition of talent and ability. Like Yanagita and Orikuchi, Takada sought to separate production—economic activity—from the social order in order to argue that the relations between people constituted an independent variable. But by making this move, he had taken a long step in the direction of effacing the social itself for a more communal set of arrangements that resembled the model of a gemeinschaft in almost every respect, except in his effort to assimilate status to talent and ability rather than to the capitalist society his formal sociology was pledged to uphold. With this scheme, the third view of history already revealed the outline of a modern gemeinschaft society, complete with capitalism but without the necessary differences and divisions that inevitably cause social conflict. If modern social science had relentlessly sought to pursue the subjectivity of class as a sign of capitalist modernity, Takada turned back to the agency of the folk and the communal body as the solution to contemporary conflict and disorder. Even though the "third view of history" was "betrayed as a 'bourgeois social science,'" observes Kawamura Nozomu, it opened up to a "theory of social power" rooted in a "desire for power" and signaled the beginning of a change toward envisaging a "theory of the folk." It is important to note that even when he was promoting a rigorous but formal social science based on universalistic laws, he saw its utility and application in particularistic situations. Takada did not turn or even return to Japan, which he had never left in his social theorizing, but rather transferred his obsession with class in the 1920s to the figure of the folk, which consumed his intellectual energies in the 1930s and 1940s. "I am not able to believe like many people today," he remarked, "that communism is a religion. But at the same time I am determined that we must destroy it at the level of Marxian studies in order to protect the Japanese folk." In 1934 he confessed in *Hinja hisshō* that when he wrote his major work, *The Principles of Sociology*, there was nothing more in his head than class. As a person governed by the cosmopolitanism of the 1920s, the folk meant nothing to him. "But after that, I have spoken of the folk from the bottom of my heart and held up this great reality in my head. . . . I believe we must consider the future of class together with the future of the folk."[27] Although he acknowledged the importance of the development of an "interest society along the route of social progress," he was, in spite of this, "a child of nostalgia in spirit, a child of the village. I yearn only for the communal social form, for the fresh, emotional life of the village. While my life is in the city that escapes the eye, my heart ceaselessly pursues gemeinschaft. Isn't this a feeling that makes one think about Japan, the ancestral country as a broad native place?"[28] During the halcyon days of the 1930s, beset by a sense of crisis, he acknowledged that "the time will come when we must clear away the despotic politics that has occurred from uncertainty and the profound opposition to the folk," but "history has not yet entered into a new age of folk struggle."[29] Takada worried about the "future of the folk" in this moment of crisis and confessed that he himself was a "child of spiritual homesickness" that made him think about the folk. What caught his attention most were the conquest of capital over village life and the necessity of formulating policy aimed at "returning the folk to their home."[30] The spiritual strength of Japan was the villages; to protect the integrity of village communal life meant protecting Japan itself. For in the Japanese folk there are unique conditions that attest to the superiority of communal life founded on the intimacy of union (ketsugō).

Under the sanction of this third view of history, Takada was emboldened, in the early 1930s, to call for the construction of a "Japanized" social science. Such a social science, consistent with the growing claims of "Japanism," aimed to emphasize the special characteristics of "Japaneseness" (Nihontekina mono) and to counter the hidden injuries inflicted by a mistaken acceptance of class and productive social relations as viable principles of social determinacy. Worse, he wanted to eliminate the misrecognitions that had already substituted class for folk. As he saw it, the task before his generation was to find a way to implement a transformation of "anthropologism" to "folkism," as he put it, in order to explain the unity of the folk, what held society together, and its capacity for "self-defense."[31] But by this time, Takada had turned his attention to the "folk problem," which he believed had been provoked by concerns over the future of the folk and the rural crisis (especially in the years immediately after the world depression and the Japanese seizure of Manchuria) caused by the process of subordinating villages to the necessities of urban industrialization. Yet this concern was informed by a prior conviction that only the folk, dwelling in a place for a long time, constituted the "unbreakable" bond of solidarity that would reveal the essence of society. In contrast to modern society, which was constantly being threatened by imminent "breaking up," since the nature of interaction was less dense and the bonds insuring solidarity too weak, nothing is more resistant to social dissolution than the community of land ties that originated in the remote past. Here he appealed to Max Scheler who, as we have seen, had rejected the claims associated with society for the more enduring forms of community based on land and blood. Society was based on the "ideal of production," which is not the basis of a "real union," but must rather be founded on a "sense of one body, one flesh in life, if I can borrow an expression from Scheler" (TMS, 62). Scheler was pointing to the "communal life and soul" which produced an "affective union connected to blood and land relationships" (2). What he seemed to fear, above all else, was the rampant individualism that interest society spawned and its devastating consequences for social solidarity, undermining any possibility for lasting union (14). At the same time, he expressed anxious concern about the effects of the "atomization" of social arrangements he perceived in societies like China, which had been grazed by capitalism through the medium of European imperialism but whose disintegration into swirling fragments was no less a problem than the effects of alienation of modern capitalist orders.

Behind this valorization of the folk community and its powerful sense of "union" was an analysis based on a reconsideration of the relationship between the part and whole. Throughout so much of Takada's social thought, this problem continually appeared to figure his conception of social order. The folk idea of the present is not founded on the relationship of ruler and ruled but rather on the reverse, the guide and follower. "The thing that guides and leads," he wrote, "is grasped as the embodiment of the folk spirit and is the highest value for its folk." It is the folk spirit that "guides" the folk, which means that the "individual follows the wholeness of the folk." Assured that the individual emerged within the whole, lived according to its requirements, and acted to satisfy its imperatives, the individual is not a "symbol of the whole, subordinating other individuals as individuals." Instead, the individual stands simply in a master/serf relationship to the folk whole. The highest characteristic of the "whole," he asserted, which is what "wholism" consists of, is "respect" and "subordination to it," showing the "union" of those "atomized, equal, individuals" (20). Takada saw the idea of the folk that elevated their "wholeness" as the principle that guided the contemporary state. It was a reality, he insisted, that the idea of an East Asian cooperative body and the East Asian folk, expressed in particular form in Japan, promoted the sense of a "communal whole." In other words, the whole represented by the folk was not simply immanent but infinitely expandable to incorporate the folk of East Asia. The philosophy that emphasized this whole was already found in those forms previously developed, like Japanism, Japanese nationalism, and Sino-Japanese cooperation, that signified the ultimate arrival at the idea of the folk in the present and sealing the "relationship between folkism and wholism" (21). Wholism starts not from the part but from the whole; because the part exists in the whole, it is the whole (24). Whole and part were interchangeable, but Takada was insistent on establishing the primacy of the whole, so as not to suggest that the whole was simply an accumulation of its constituent parts. The importance of this all encompassing whole was that it provided the means by which the folk could relate to other folk and thus secure harmony. In Takada's thinking, this elision of different folk identities made it possible to envision one great East Asian folk—the perfect expression of the expanded communal body. The large organism was held together by an identity of blood, soil, and culture (43).

Rejecting the claim that an East Asian folk was simply an "idealist abstraction" or an "empty abstraction," Takada argued that the category of race was an essential condition of the existence of the folk. While he was willing to acknowledge the existence of diverse cultures, land ties, and lineage groups throughout East Asia, they were still united as an East Asian folk. What unified the folk was "folkism," that is, its sense of autonomy, the existence of a "natural union" opposed to the "self-centered" individualism associated with interest society. In other words, folkism was signified by both autonomy and union. Union referred to the pursuit of unity, based on a "natural bonding" connected by racial ties. "The pursuit of union and autonomy," he wrote, "was the pursuit of the self-completion of this folk. It is, moreover, the natural destiny of communal society to not pursue selfishness" (51). Takada was convinced that the "essence of the Japanese spirit pulsating in the Japanese folk" had already disclosed this idea of folkism. "When we think about expanding the folk we must acknowledge the East Asian folk." The idea of an East Asian folkism was simply an enlargement of the experience of the Japanese folk in their destiny driven effort to achieve self-completion through union and autonomy. In other words, the experience of the Japanese folk in the maelstrom of capitalist modernization to secure the identity of communal relations yet maintain a distance from interest and individualism would now be applied to the larger arena of East Asia. But Takada believed that achieving this greater goal was possible because internally the East Asian folk was tied by common bonds of land, blood lineage and culture. The purpose of this great crusade was only to eliminate the self but more important to "maintain the peace of the whole." "If one family is not peaceful, there will be no peace in the village; if one village is not peaceful, there will be no peace in the region; without peace within the diverse peoples there will be no world peace." For East Asian peoples, therefore, the accomplishment of "union" is not only to pursue the folk's "innermost feelings," as if it were a natural impulse, but also a "duty" that must be shouldered by one segment of the human species. Takada related Japan's experience of "Americanization" as a form of colonialism to the history of East Asia which had been dominated by "white man's despotism for over 400 years." East Asianism did not propose to exchange the white man's despotism with an equally yellow despotism. Rather it aimed to liberate the East Asian folk from the yoke of the white race on the basis of a program proclaiming Asia for Asians (52).

While this program was to be carried out under the sanction of emancipation and autonomy, he was convinced that its achievement constituted a natural conclusion of those principles shared by East Asian folk that guaranteed "mutuality." Despite the apparent fragmentation experienced by this communal body in recent history, undoubtedly provoked by the introduction of capital and new technologies, the various divisions must be overcome in order to establish a system capable of advancing the development of the whole (53). In dramatic contrast to later claims celebrating Japan's racial homogeneity, Takada proposed that Asians were related to each other through a long history of a mixing of races to constitute not a pure species but a mixed one. It was for this reason that Japanese could look upon other Asians as relatives and upon the Asian continent as a home to which the folk could return. Hence the declared aim was not colonial expansion in China and Manchuria but rather the folk returning to their ancestral home. Because of Asia the Asian folk has become a single body. Undergirding this spatial identity was, of course, the presumption of commonly shared blood ties and culture, race and the lifeworld that transcended the differences in local custom to constitute the unshakable foundation for pursuing autonomy (58). What Takada was advocating behind the mask of imperialism and colonialism, was the equality of all races, which could be realized only when white man's domination and Asian submission were eliminated. The present, he remarked, is the appointed historical moment for a reconciliation of the folk with their true destiny—autonomy and union—that required the destruction of white man's despotism. The yellow race has never fully realized an existence reflecting the "solidarity of wholeness" (67) and must, now, turn to a policy promoting the "self-defense of the folk." The folk possesses the necessary power to prevent the further socialization of interest and individualism since it constitutes the heart of group solidarity; the center of folk consciousness resides in the "traditional thing," which reflects the folk's status as original "charter members" of communal life. As a result, the folk possess the "requirement for self-expansion." In fact, folkism is nothing more than this capacity of the folk to "expand the group self which has been called the folk," that is to say, to expand the folk body (221). Even though this expansion of the folk appears to resemble imperialism, it has nothing to do with the capitalism that has been the driving force behind recent imperial seizures. But Takada's conception of folkism and its right to pursue "self-defense" and "self-expansion" recognized the necessity of war and conflict to achieve the imperative of the folkic body, which corresponded to fascism's vocation to make war an unlimited movement with no other end than itself, despite the rhetoric of folk expansion. When Takada acknowledged that for the Japanese folk the state was all, he was already envisaging the performance of a total state seized by a "war machine" that exceeds the very apparatus that had initiated it. In the late 1930s, this was the meaning that had settled around the concept of "total war," so forcefully articulated by philosophers of the Kyoto School as the goal of Japan's world historical mission. In Takada's thinking, folkism, with its powerful desire for "self-defense" and "self-expansion," demanded enactment and performance on the stage of world history because such imperatives could only be realized in the folk body's necessity to wage war.[32] For war was the only way the folk would finally free itself from the abstractions of enlightenment thought, which, as we have seen, estranged the Japanese from their own history, from their own essence—the "historical whole"—which still remained intact within the folk, waiting to be recovered for enactment and performance.

By the time Takada was pronouncing on the necessity of "self-defense" of the folk and expansion, the folk had come to occupy the space of the commodity form, even though it was supposed to supply a living alternative to its regime of social abstraction. Nothing, in fact, was more abstract than an appeal to a historically indeterminate folk, despite Takada's desire to invest in it the power of a "historical whole" capable of inducing enactment and performance on the stage of world history. Years earlier, Tosaka Jun had already identified the idea of the folk with a process that had executed "thoughtlessly" and "abstractly" the so-called concretization of the "self" or "ego" (jiga) so dear to contemporary bourgeois literature (TJZ, 4:206; also 203–204). Tosaka worried that such abstractions like the folk and the people were made to appear concrete when linked to the "Japanese thing" (Nihonteki naru mono). Too often, he reasoned, it was simply the operation of making these terms stand in for each other. Invocation of the folk automatically called attention to the "Japanese thing" or the people and vice versa. "When looking at how people search for the Japanese thing," he observed, "whether it is the intuitive, rich purity of the Manyō, the mono no aware of the Genji, the bushidō of the middle ages, or the feeling of obligation of the Tokugawa, none of these are connected to contemporary people" (4:206). The farmer should not be expected to live according to the warrior's code, and while the townspeople of Tokyo might feel mono no aware, they are not thinking about working. What Tosaka objected to most was the move to "draw out this or that folk from cultural characteristics." In this light, the "Japanese thing" could never be unified (4:207). But as representatives of the Japanese thing, the folk's character is made into a problem; it makes no difference whether the figure of the folk is either derived from folkist theory or incorporated in it. Whatever the case, folkism traded in a counterfeit currency based on the claims of blood and lineage, authorized by a spurious and abstract conception of subjectivity that was supposed to provide the necessary concreteness to a life already imperiled by objectification and the tyranny of things. In Tosaka's reckoning, this conception of the subject, expressed first in the form of the sovereign self, ego in literature, was "abstractly educed" from the individual and testified only to the domination of the bourgeoisie since the Meiji period. But the problem of the folk, which in folkist theory now shares the form of this subjectivity (even though it is unclassed), cannot be separated from the task of resolving the question of everyday life of the Japanese people and cannot be forgotten by declarations of blood and culture.

What is important about this critique is the way Tosaka was able to locate the abstract in its disguised concreteness. Yet, this was true of all those discussions that masked abstraction by appeals to the "real" (*genjitsu*). It is well to remember that modernism's vocation to avoid abstraction for concrete and stable meaning turned on itself when the move was made to supply culture and community with embodiment and life. The key to this operation was to employ the figure of an indeterminate folk which, according to native ethnologists and folkist ideologues, not to mention those writers and critics Tosaka called "gentlemen," could lay claim to the stable meaning of all history yet one empowered never to exceed itself that could be recalled in moments of crisis, both a fixed representation and a presentation where the folk produces itself as community.

Hence, both modernism and fascism attacked the problems raised by capitalism at the level of representation, each, in its own way, trying to find a stable ground and referent capable of guaranteeing the possibility of representation. Both, in other words, tried to resolve the aporias of representation raised by capitalism rather than call into question the structural conditions that produced these doubts. In this way both, despite their seeming critique of what they called modern life, actually affirmed its capitalist grounding. In fact, the appeal to "modern life" was simply a strategic and ideological misrecognition at the representational level of a system driven by the reproduction of capital accumulation. Each, in their way, would also find in the industrial and decolonized world of the postwar new tactics of accommodating the representational aporias first encountered before World War II to show how modernism and fascism, far from belonging to a dead past that has passed, are still part of what Jean Luc Nancy once described as "our history." Yet we must see in this bonding of modernism and fascism and the shared desire to escape the ruinous regime of social capitalistic abstraction both the flight from history and a quest for meaning that ended in a national fantasy. If the folk was employed as a stand-in for the artwork, which itself was seen as a stand-in for the lost historical agency the anonymous forces of capitalism erased, the artwork nevertheless could claim a concreteness denied the folk. All of this merely pointed to how modernism and fascism sought the impossible task of re-enchanting the world and thereby restoring the auratic to a life where only its dimmest and fading traces still managed to survive for the moment.

Abbreviations

AK	Watsuji Tetsurō, *Nihon no Shintō, Amerika no kokuminsei* (Tokyo: Chikuma Shobō, 1944).
Aono	Aono Suekichi, *Sararīman, kyōfu jidai* (Tokyo: Senshinsha,1930).
CC	Watsuji Tetsurō, *Climate and Culture*, trans. Geoffrey Bownas (Tokyo: Ministry of Education, 1961).
GF	Nakamura Kōya, ed., *Nihon fūzokushi* (Tokyo: Yūsankaku, 1929), vol. 3.
GKKG	Kurihara Yukio, ed., *Geijutsu no kakumei to kakumei no geijutsu* (Tokyo: Shakai Hyōronsha, 1990), vol. 14.
GYC	*Gonda Yasunosuke chōsakushū* (Tokyo: Bunwa Shobō, 1974–1975), 4 vols.
HHBHZ	*Hirabayashi Hatsunosuke bungei hyōron zenshū* (Tokyo: Kyōbundo, 1975), 3 vols.
KDK	Takada Yasuma, *Kaikyū oyobi Daisan shikan* (Tokyo: Kaizōsha, 1927).
KGN	Orikuchi Shinobu, *Kokubungaku gairon nōto* (Tokyo: Chūō Kōronsha, 1958).
KHS	*Kobayashi Hideoshū*, ed. Yoshimoto Takaaki, in *Kindai Nihon shisō taikei* (Tokyo: Chikuma Shobō, 1977), vol. 29.
KNC	Kawakami Tetsutarō and Takeuchi Yoshimi, eds., *Kindai no chōkoku* (Tokyo: Fuzanbō, 1979).
KSZ	*Kuki Shūzō zenshū* (Tokyo: Iwanami Shōten, 1981), 12, vols.
KWS	*Kon Wajirō shū* (Tokyo: Domesu, 1986), 9 vols.
MKZ	*Miki Kiyoshi zenshū* (Tokyo: Iwanami Shōten, 1966–1967).
MT	Takada Yasuma, *Minzoku taibō* (Tokyo and Kyoto: Kocho, 1943).
MTS	Yanagita Kunio, *Meiji Taishōshi sesōhen* (Tokyo: Kodansha,1993).
NPBH	*Nihon puroretaria bungaku hyōronshū, Hirabayashi Hatsunosuke, Aono Suekichi* (Tokyo: Shin Nihon Shuppansha, 1990), vol. 3.
OSS	*Orikuchi Shinobu shū*, ed. Hirose Tamotsu, in *Kindai Nihon shisō taikei* (Tokyo: Chikuma Shobō, 1975), vol. 22.
OSZ	*Orikuchi Shinobu zenshū* (Tokyo: Chūō Kōronsha, 1965–1968), 32 vols.
TJS	*Tosaka Jun sakushū* (Tokyo: Itō Shōten, 1948), 5 vols.
TJZ	*Tosaka Jun zenshū* (Tokyo: Keikusa Shobō, 1977), 5 vols.
TMS	Takada Yasuma, *Tōa minzokuron* (Tokyo: Iwanami Shōten, 1939).
TYKZ	*Teihon Yanagita Kunio zenshū* (Tokyo: Chikuma Shobō, 1962–1971).
YK	*Yanagita Kunio*, ed. Masuda Katsumi, in *Gendai Nihon shisō taikei* (Tokyo: Chikuma Shobō, 1965), vol. 29.
WT	*Watsuji Tetsurō*, ed. Karaki Junzō, in *Gendai Nihon shisō taikei* (Tokyo: Chikuma Shobō, 1963), vol. 28.
WTZ	*Watsuji Tetsurō zenshū* (Tokyo: Iwanami Shōten, 1961–1963).

Notes

Preface

1. Gianni Vattimo, *The End of Modernity* (Baltimore: The Johns Hopkins Press, 1988), p. 165.
2. Kristin Ross, "Watching the Detective," in *Postmodernism and the Rereading of Modernity*, ed. F. Barker, P. Hulme, and H. Iverson (Manchester: Manchester University Press, 1992), pp. 49–50.
3. Vattimo, *End of Modernity*, p. 165.
4. Karl Marx, *Eighteenth Century Brumaire of Louis Napoleno* (New York: International Publishers, 1969), p. 15.
5. Nihon Gendai Bungaku Zenshū, *Saitō Riyoku, Ishibashi Ningetsu, Takayama Chogyū, Uchida Roan* (Tokyo: Kodansha, 1967), vol. 8, pp. 286–291.
6. Sawada Ken, "Toshi to hangyaku," in *Taishō shisōshu*, II, *Kindai shisō taikei*, ed. Kano Masanao (Tokyo: Chikuma Shobō, 1977), vol. 34, pp. 270–289.
7. Mabel Berezin, *Making the Fascist Self* (Ithaca: Cornell University Press, 1995), p. 13. No political term has inspired more historiographical anxiety than fascism, or produced more declarations announcing the impossibility of agreement over definition and meaning. Readers should consult Stanley Payne, *A History of Fascism, 1914–1945* (Madison: University of Wisconsin Press, 1995), for the most recent, exhaustive treatment of fascism, which seeks to include fascisms outside of Europe as well, like Japan's experience. This work is both detailed in coverage but somewhat hesitant in its willingness to generalize the phenomenon, as if to suggest that specificity of experience shows only the necessary impossibility of reaching a workable definition. Yet the danger in this historically cautious reluctance to generalize is that it permits the easy presumption that what has been taken as fascism was mistaken for something else, that its historically specific appearance means it could not have occurred elsewhere and that it will not reoccur again (unintentionally reinforcing the exceptionalist claims fascisms usually employ to explain the superiority of their own agendas). We can discern this argument in the texts of Miki Kiyoshi, who, as we shall see, sought to supply a critique of fascism of the German and Italian varieties in order to distance his own conception of political and social order, which strikingly resembled what he was discounting. One wonders, in any case, why so much industry has been expended on a subject that is virtually invisible.
8. Nikos Poulantzas, *Fascism and Dictatorship* (London, Verso, 1979), pp. 17–19.
9. Ibid., pp. 19–20.
10. Ibid., p. 67.
11. Ibid., p. 252.
12. We might call this the Parsons' effect, as it was once persuasively conceptualized by Robert Bellah, Clifford Geertz, and others.

13. I am indebted to Arno Mayer's brilliant and provocatively applicable book, *The Persistence of the Old Regime, Europe to the Great War* (New York: Pantheon, 1981), for this idea, which certainly characterizes Japan's political and social history until World War II.

14. Slavoj Žižek, *Tarrying with the Negative* (Durham: Duke University Press, 1993), p. 209.

15. See Fredric Jameson, *Postmodernism or the Cultural Logic of Late Capitalism* (Durham: Duke University Press, 1991), p. 204, where Jameson calls for a broader "comparative sociology of modernism and its cultures," resembling Weber's earlier efforts to survey the relationship between capitalism and world religions, that might "measure . . . the extraordinary impact of capitalism on hitherto traditional cultures, the social and psychic damage done to now irrevocable forms of human life and perception" (304). Frantz Fanon earlier pointed to how colonialism and capitalism had virtually destroyed the older "systems of reference," "sacking cultural patterns," "flaunting" values, "crushing" and "emptying" them. F. Fanon, "Racism and Culture," in *Toward and African Revolution* (New York: Grove Press, 1967), p. 33.

16. Ernst Bloch, *Heritage of Our Times*, trans. Neville and Stephen Plaice (Berkeley and Los Angeles: University of California Press, 1991), pp. 37–185. In this work, written in the early 1930s and published in Zurich first in 1935, Bloch introduced the concept *Gleichzeitigkeit des Ungleichzeitigen*—the "simultaneity of the noncontemporaneous"—as a means of explaining the appeal of Nazi ideology and its reliance on the co-existence of elements derived from a distant, even mythic, past and the industrial present. See also Ernst Bloch, "Nonsynchronism and the Obligation to Its Dialectics," *New German Critique*, no. 11 (Spring, 1977): 22–38, for a shorter version explaining this important idea.

17. Nakamura Takafusa, *Lectures on Modern Japanese Economy* (Tokyo: LTCB International Library Foundation, 1994), pp. 1–128.

18. Perry Anderson, "Modernity and Revolution," in *Marxism and the Interpretation of Culture*, ed. C. Nelson and L. Grossberg (Urbana: University of Illinois Press, 1988), p. 324.

19. Ibid., pp. 324–326.

20. Theodore Adorno, *Critical Models*, trans. Henry Pickford (New York: Columbia University Press, 1987), pp. 41–49.

21. Tosaka Jun, *Nihon ideorogiron* (Tokyo: Iwanami Bunko, 1977), p. 99.

22. Alice Kaplan, *The Reproduction of Banality* (Minneapolis: University of Minnesota Press, 1987).

23. Mayer, *Persistence of the Old Regime*, p. 192.

24. See Nakamura, *Lectures*, pp. 3–50.

25. Jameson, *Postmodernism*, p. 310.

26. Yanagita Kunio, *Meiji Taishōshi, sesōhen* (Tokyo: Kodansha, 1993), pp. 187–190.

27. Ibid., pp. 19–22. See also Fredric Jameson, *Fables of Aggression: Wyndham Lewis, the Modernist as Fascist* (Berkeley and Los Angeles: University of California Press, 1979), p. 14.

28. Jameson, *Postmodernim*, p. 311.

29. See Matsuyama Iwao, *Rampo to Tokyo* (Tokyo: Parko, 1984).

30. In Yamamoto Akira, "Shakai seikatsu no henka to taishū Bunka," in Iwanami Kōza, *Nihon rekishi* (Tokyo: Iwanami Shōten, 1976), vol. 19, p. 306.

31. Peter Nicholls, *Modernisms* (Berkeley and Los Angeles: University of California Press, 1995), p. 7; W. Benjamin, "Central Park," trans. Lloyd Spencer, *New German Critique* 34 (Winter, 1985): 46.

32. Kawamura Nozomu, *Nihon shakaigakushi kenkyū* (Tokyo: Ningen no Kagakusha, 1973), vol. 2, p. 231.

33. Ibid.

34. Giles DeLeuze and Felix Guattari, *A Thousand Plateaus*, trans. Brian Massumi (Minneapolis: University of Minnesota Press, 1998), pp. 214–215.

35. Gilbert Allardyce, "What Fascism Is Not:Thoughts on the Deflation of a Concept," *American Historical Review* 84 (April 1979): 367–388.

36. Perry Anderson, *The Origins of Postmodernity* (London: Verso, 1998), p. 112.

37. Slavoj Žižek, *They Know Not What They Do* (London:Verso, 1991), p. 186.

Chapter 1

1. E. Sydney Crawcour, "Industrialization and Technological Change," in *Cambridge History of Japan*, ed. Peter Duus (Cambridge: Cambridge University Press, 1988), vol. 6, pp. 385–450; also Takafusa Nakamura, "Depression, Recovery, and War," in ibid., pp. 451–467; and Koji Taira, "Economic Development, Labor markets and Industrial Relations, 1905–1955," in ibid., pp. 606–653, especially 619–629.

2. Ibid., pp. 385–421.

3. Nakamura, *Lectures*, p. 14.

4. Takemura Tamio, *Taishō Bunka* (Tokyo: Chūō Kōronsha, 1980), p. 40.

5. Ibid., p. 43.

6. Ibid., p. 45.

7. Sawada, "Toshi to hangyaku," p. 281.

8. Ibid.

9. Ibid., p. 282.

10. Yanagita, *Meiji Taishōshi, sesōhen*, p. 172.

11. Quoted in Matsuyama Iwao, *Rampo to Tokyo*, p. 13.

12. Ibid., pp. 82–83.

13. *Hirabayshi Hatsunosuke bungei hyōronshū zenshū* (Tokyo: Kyōbundo, 1975), vol. 3, pp. 776–778 (hereafter, *HHBHZ*).

14. Yamamoto, "Shakai seikatsu no henka to taishū bunka," p. 331.

15. Ibid.

16. Taira, *Cambridge History of Japan*, p. 619.

17. Ibid., pp. 619–629.

18. See Minami Hiroshi, ed., *Taishō Bunka* (Tokyo: Keikusa, 1965), pp. 246–247.

19. Ibid., p. 247.

20. Ibid., p. 249.

21. Ibid., p. 253.

22. Morimoto Atsuyoshi, *Bunka seikatsu kenkyu* (1920), quoted in Yamamoto, "Shakai seikatsu," p. 303.

23. Sano Riki, *Jūtakuron*, quoted in ibid.

24. See ibid., pp. 257–258.

25. In ibid., p. 364.

26. Yamamoto, "Shakai seikatsu," p. 305.

27. In Minami Hiroshi, ed., *Shōwa Bunka* (Tokyo: Keisei Shobō, 1987), p. 62.

28. Ibid., p. 65.

29. Wada Hirofumi, *Tekusūto no modan toshi* (Nagoya: Fubaisha, 1999), pp. 219–247. Many writers, like Aono Suekichi, as we shall see, saw the proliferation of dance halls and the throngs of people who congregated in them as a sign of social pathology, unhappiness, and escape from the harsh disciplines and disappointments of modern, urban life.

30. Yamamoto, "Shakai seikatsu," p. 308, who sees this as its ideological meaning.

31. In Minami Hiroshi, ed., *Nihon modanizumu no kenkyū* (Tokyo: Buren, 1982), p. 24. Also in a special issue of *Chuō kōron*, September 1918.

32. See Minami, *Shōwa Bunka*, p. 66.

33. *HHBHZ*, vol. 2. pp. 412–413; Minami, *Shōwa Bunka*, p. 209.

34. In Minami, *Shōwa Bunka*, p. 66.

35. Ibid.

36. Minami, *Nihon modanizumu*, p. 24.

37. Ibid.

38. Ibid.

39. Ibid.

40. Žižek, *Tarrying with the Negative*, p. 216.

41. Minami, *Nihon modanizumu*, p. 26.

42. Minami, *Shōwa Bunka*, p. 216.

43. Ibid.

44. Ibid., p. 217.

45. *HHBHZ*, vol. 2, p. 385; Minami, *Shōwa Bunka*, p. 218.

46. *HHBHZ*, vol. 2, p. 385.

47. Ueda Toshio, "Josei Zasshi ga Mita Modanizumu," in Minami, *Nihon modanizumi*, p. 127.

48. In Yamamoto, "Shakai seikatsu," p. 328.

49. Ibid., p. 330.

50. Ibid.

51. See Minami, *Shōwa Bunka*, "Sei," pp. 126–157.

52. Claude LeFort, *The Political Forms of Modern Society* (Cambridge: MIT Press, 1988), pp. 149–151.

53. Minami, *Shōwa Bunka*, p. 159.

54. Ibid., pp. 165–171.

55. Maurice Blanchot, "Everyday Speech," in *Everyday Life, Yale French Studies*, no. 74, ed. Alice Kaplan and Kristin Ross (New Haven: Yale University Press, 1987), p. 19.

Chapter 2

1. The prevailing literature has, effectively, followed the lead of Takeuchi Yoshimi in his pioneer postwar essay "Kindai no chōkoku," which concentrated on sorting out the intellectual genealogies of the various participants, historicizing their affiliations without, at the same time, analyzing the content of the symposium's proceedings, however wordy and repetitive. Takeuchi dismissed much of the discussions as empty and vacuous, appearing as an empty "ideological sign," even though he was sympathetic to the general concern that Japan's modernity had been bought at too high a price that resulted in unresolved aporias. The essay was published first in *Kindai Nihon shisōshi kōza* (Tokyo: Chikuma Shobō, 1959), vol. 7, pp. 225–281. It also appears in Kawakami Tetsutarō and Takeuchi Yoshimi, eds., *Kindai no chōkoku* (Tokyo: Fuzanbō, 1979).

2. Kawakami and Takeuchi, eds., *Kindai no chōkoku*, p. 166. Hereafter, references to this work are indicated within the chapter by page numbers in parentheses.

3. Also Takeuchi, in ibid., p. 294.

4. The term *genjitsu* was used widely in philosophic discourse in the interwar period to denote a sense of the real, reality, the actual, even though it often failed to conceal its kinship with abstraction and appearance. For some critics the term signified "false reality."

5. Vattimo, *End of Modernity*, p. 165.

6. Ibid.

7. From *"Kindai no chōkoku" oboegaki*, in Hiromatsu Wataru, *Kindai no chōkoku* (Tokyo: Asahi Shuppansha, 1980), pp. 18, 231–235.

8. Ibid., p. 18.

9. Ibid., p. 19.

10. For chronological narratives of the interwar period, especially the decade of the 1930s, see Gordon Berger, "Politics and Mobilization in Japan, 1911–1945," pp. 97–153; Mark R. Peattie, "The Japanese Colonial Empire," pp. 217–270; and Ikuhiko Hata, "Continental Expansion, 1905–1941," pp. 271–314, in *Cambridge History of Japan*. For a more interpretative account, see Andrew Gordon, *Labor and Imperial Democracy in Imperial Japan* (Berkeley and Los Angeles: University of California Press, 1991), pp. 123–342.

11. In Hiromatsu, *Kindai no chōkoku*, p. 229.

12. Ibid., p. 231.

13. Ibid., pp. 131–135.

14. Ibid., pp. 136, 145.

15. Ibid., p. 86. But also see Horio Tsutomu, "The Chūō Kōron Discussions, Their Background and Meaning," in *Rude Awakening*, ed. James Helsig and John Maraldo (Honolulu: University of Hawaii Press, 1994), pp. 289–315, for a thinly disguised whitewash of this symposium, whose major orientation was philosophic fascism.

16. Hiromatsu, *Kindai no chōkoku*, p. 86.

17. The term *kokutai* was variously translated as "national body" (connoting a mystical body), "national polity," etc., and referred to an essentialized conception of Japan's imperial, sacral, and ethical endowment which it simultaneously

evoked. It was claimed that this endowment was first formulated with the beginning of the race and has remained unchanged continuously since foundations. The term was used as an empty signifier in the late Tokugawa period by different groups to criticize the bakufu. In the late 1930s the state sponsored the compilation of a "textbook" titled *Kokutai no hongi* (Fundamentals of national polity) that aimed to supply an ideology steeped in hoary myths for national mobilization.

18. Vattimo, *End of Modernity*, p. 165.

19. It should be noted that Suzuki Shigetaka wanted to separate the formation of American culture from Europe and see it as a different manifestation from the perspective of world historical meaning. See Ryōen Minamoto, "The Symposium on 'Overcoming Modernity,' " in *Rude Awakening*, ed. Helsig and Maraldo, pp. 227–228.

20. Louise Young, *Japan's Total Empire* (Berkeley and Los Angeles: University of California Press, 1998), pp. 55–114.

21. Neil Larsen, *Modernism and Hegemony* (Minneapolis: University of Minnesota Press, 1990), p. xxiv.

22. Ibid.

23. Tosaka Jun looked upon Kobayashi as "a paradoxical talker" who was frightened of the "objective material world." See Yoshida Masato, *Gendai Nihon no shisō* (Tokyo: Azusa Shuppansha, 1988), p. 125.

24. See Yoshida Masato, *Sengō shisōron* (Tokyo: Aoki Shōten, 1984), pp. 110–112.

25. Kobayashi explicitly dismissed history because of its putative repetition. But despite his rejection of historiography, his own notion of the endurance of the common closely resembles Yanagita's understanding of the timeless and repetitive.

26. Years later, immediately after the war, the Kyoto philosopher Tanabe Hajime invested this attribute of nonpossession in the emperor, who was thus made to appear as the only true subject.

27. According to Walter Benjamin, Baudelaire looked to the endurance of classic forms within the changing present as an anchor and sign of the eternal.

28. One of the awful ironies of this history is that while the world, especially the West, was not prepared to hear these criticisms at that time, it would have been unable to do so since so few people on the outside knew either Japan or its language. Perhaps lack of genuine interest in Japan at that time, melancholically noted by Kuki Shūzō when he was in Europe during the 1920s, and reproduced in our day, constitutes the most disturbing sign of a historical conjuncture that had "imprisoned" Japan and driven its "inmates" to find an "escape," an overcoming that promised the impossible illusion of reuniting them with themselves and their difference. In this regard, contemporary postcolonial discourse is simply a repetition of the Japanese experience in a different historical register, where the outside, Europe's unacknowledged shadow, returns to take reprisals for the injuries inflicted on it by colonialism and imperialism, which Japanese were the first to recognize and put into question.

Chapter 3

1. See Leo Trotsky, *Problems of Everyday Life* (New York: Monad Press, 1979). Gramsci, who was also concerned with defining the space of everydayness, showed keen interest in the concept of *byt*—one of the terms Trotsky and Boris

Arvatov used to denote everyday life. This interest in everyday life was linked to a complementary concern for the phenomenon of "Americanism," which appeared as a ubiquitous trope and elastic signifier throughout the industrializing world in the 1920s. See also Boris Arvatov, "Everyday Life and the Culture of the Thing," trans. Christina Kiaer, *October* 81 (Summer 1997): 119–128. Bakhtin's theory of "carnivelsque," worked out in the Soviet Union in the 1920s, can be read as an analogue of the commodity that objectifies social relationships but which still might yield a new possibility, or, put in another way, an image of everyuayness constituted by hierarchical power and routine that is momentarily capable of exploding into its obverse. This obverse is, in fact, the difference of everydayness that remains hidden by modernity—capitalism as the reproduction of accumulation—but is ready to be actualized, as both Benjamin and Tosaka, in their own ways, recognized.

2. Shibata Shuji, *Seikatsu kenkyū josetsu* (Kyotoshi: Nakanishiya Shuppan, 1995), p. 11.

3. Terade Koji, *Seikatsu bunkaron e no shōtai* (Tokyo: Kyōbundo, 1994), pp. 92–93.

4. Omuka Toshiharu, *Taishōki shinkō bijutsu undō no kenkyū* (Tokyo: Sukaidōa Shobō, 1995), pp. 443–704.

5. Murayama Tomoyoshi, *Kōseiha kenkyū*, p. 56, in *Geijutsu no kakumei to kakumei no geijutsu*, ed. Kurihara Yukio (Tokyo: Shakai Hyōronsha, 1990), vol. 14; hereafter, GKKG.

6. *Nihon puroretaria bungaku hyōronshū* (Tokyo: Shin Nihon Shuppansha, 1990), 3:18 (hereafter, NPBH); HHBHZ, 1:17.

7. GKKG, p. 71.

8. NPBH, 3:21; HHBHZ, 1:18.

9. NPBH, 3:26; HHBHZ, 1:20.

10. NPBH, 3:27; HHBHZ, 1:21.

11. NPBH, 3:28; HHBHZ, 1:22.

12. GKKG, p. 72.

13. Washita Koyata, *Shōwa shisō zenshi* (Tokyo: Sanichi Shobō, 1991), p. 32.

14. Ibid., p. 33.

15. Ibid., p. 30.

16. Ibid., p. 35.

17. HHBHZ, 3:222.

18. Ibid.; see also NPBH, 3:113–116.

19. HHBHZ, 3:221, 222–223, 224.

20. Ishiyama, *Rampo*, p. 207.

21. Washita, *Shōwa shisō zenshi*, p. 76.

22. Eugene Soviak, "Tsuchida Kyōson," in *Culture and Identity*, ed. Thomas Rimer (Princeton: Princeton University Press, 1990), pp. 83–98, especially 86.

23. *Tosaka Jun sakushū* (Tokyo: Itō Shōten, 1948), 4:1–16 (hereafter, TJS).

24. Martin Heidegger, *Being and Time*, trans. John Macquarrie and Edward Robinson (New York: Harper San Francisco, 1962), p. 442.

25. See also "Fūzoku to shite no shakai jikyo," 53–61, in TZS, 4 (1948).

26. See, for example, Tosaka Jun, *Nihon ideorogiron*, pp. 62–92; H. Harootunian, "The Postwar Genealogy of Fascism and Tosaka Jun's Prewar Critique of Liberalism," *The Journal of Pacific Asia* 2 (1994): 95–112.

27. V. N. Voloshinov, *Marxism and the Philosophy of Language*, trans. Ladislav Matejka and I. R. Titunik (New and London: Seminar Press, 1973), p. 23.

28. Yoshimi Shunya, *Toshi no doramatourgi* (Tokyo: Kyōbundo, 1995), pp. 45–52.

29. Ibid., p. 42.

30. Ibid., p. 43.

31. Ibid., pp. 48–49.

32. See Siegfried Kracauer, *The Mass Ornament*, trans. and ed. Thomas Levine (Cambridge: Harvard University Press, 1995), pp. 323–328.

33. See 2:295, where Gonda supplies the example of the piano player who plays for a living but does so "lightheartedly in the heat of having fun" and thus experiences pleasure while working. Marx suggested this example.

34. Yasuda Tsuneo, *Kurashi no shakai shisō* (Tokyo: Keisō Shobō, 1991), p. 64; also GYC, 1:316.

35. Yasuda, *Kurashi no shakai shisō*, p. 70.

36. Ibid., p. 72.

37. Quoted in ibid., p. 74.

38. See ibid., p. 75; GYC, 2:124.

39. See Inoue Shin, *Kaisetsu*, GYC, 2:402; also 240.

40. Yasuda, *Kurashi no shakai shisō*, p. 76.

41. GYC, 4:237. See "1930 nen to kaikō 'eiga,' " GYC, 4:231–233, for films *and ero guro nansensu* and how the film preference for the erotic replaced action films.

42. See Yasuda, *Kurashi no shakai shisō*, pp. 83–84; GYC, 3:23.

43. Yasuda, *Kurashi no shakai shisō*, pp. 80–82.

44. Ibid., p. 83; GYC, 3:13.

45. Yasuda, *Kurashi no shakai shisō*, p. 83.

46. Nakamura Kōya, ed., *Nihon fūzokushi* (Tokyo: Yūsankaku, 1929), 3:30 (hereafter, GF).

47. KWS, 1:36–37 (hereafter, KWS).

48. See Peter Osborne, *The Politics of Time* (London: Verso, 1995), pp. 116; 114–115. Writing in *Politics of Time* about Benjamin's conception of modernity and critique of historicism, Osborne called this urge to establish the continuity of the historical "bad modernity."

49. Ibid., pp. 116, 114.

50. Kawazoe Noboru, *Kon Wajirō*, in *Nihon minzoku bunka taikei* (Tokyo: Kodansha, 1978), 7:245.

51. Yoshimi, *Toshi no doramatourgi*, p. 62.

52. "Kōgengaku to wa nanika," KWS, 1:17.

53. KWS, 1:16–17; Shibata Shuji, "Kon Wajirō no shutairon," in *Seikatsu Genron*, in *Kōza Gendai Seikatsu Kenkyū*, ed. Sonoda Kyoichi and Tanabe Shuichi (Tokyo: Domesu Shuppan, 1971), vol. 2. p. 31.

54. KWS, 1:15;GF, 6.

55. KWS, 1:1; GF, 7.

56. KWS, 1:42–43.

57. Kawazoe, *Kon Wajirō*, p. 246.

58. Shibata, *Seikatsu*, p. 31.

59. Quoted in Kawazoe, *Kon Wajirō*, p. 252.

60. See ibid., p. 248.

61. Ibid., pp. 248–249. See Kon Wajirō, *Nihon no minka* (Tokyo: Iwanami Bunko, 1989), pp. 20, 288–307.

62. Kon, *Nihon no minka*, p. 34.

63. Ibid., p. 32. Also KWZ, 2:310–312.

64. Quoted in Kawazoe, *Kon Wajirō*, p. 248.

65. Quoted in Shibata, *Seikatsu*, p. 24.

66. Quoted in ibid., p. 25.

67. Ibid.

68. Shibata, "Kon Wajirō no Seikatsu Kenkyū," p. 34.

69. Kawazoe, *Kon Wajirō*, p. 281.

70. Ibid., pp. 282, 283.

71. KWZ, 5:13, 14, 161, 432; 6:104, 131; 9: 395. Also Shibata, *Seikatsu*, pp. 28–29, and "Kon Wajirō," in Seikatsu Kenkyū," p. 36.

72. Shibata, *Seikatsu*, p. 28.

73. Ibid., pp. 22, 30–31.

74. Ibid., p. 33.

75. Quoted in ibid., p. 41. Also KWZ, 6:25.

Chapter 4

1. Aono Suekichi, *Sararīman, kyōfu jidai* (Tokyo: Senshinsha, 1930), 6–7.

2. Walter Benjamin, *Charles Baudelaire, a Lyric Poet in the Era of High Capitalism*, trans. Harry Zohn (London: Verso, 1983), pp. 110–111.

3. Ibid.

4. Ibid., p. 112.

5. Ibid., p. 113.

6. See Takashi Fujitani, *Splendid Monarchy* (Berkeley and Los Angeles: University of California Press, 1996).

7. See Osborne, *Politics of Time*, p. 135; Walter Benjamin, *Illuminations*, trans. Harry Zohn (New York: Schocken Press, 1968), p. 98.

8. Walter Benjamin, *Selected Works*, ed. Marcus Bullock and Michael Jennings (Cambridge: Harvard University Press, 1999), vol. 2, p. 209.

9. Ibid.

10. LeFort, *The Political Forms*, pp. 187, 201.

11. Ibid., pp. 202–203.

12. Ibid., p. 191.

13. Susan Stewart, *On Longing* (Durham: Duke University Press, 1995), p. x.

14. Anthony Giddens, *The Consequences of Modernity* (Stanford: Stanford University Press, 1990), p. 18.

15. Larsen, *Modernism and Hegemony*, p. xxiv.

16. Karl Marx, *Capital* (New York: International Publishers, 1972), vol. 1, p. 75.

17. Benjamin, *Charles Baudelaire*, p. 55; Marx, *Capital*, vol. 1, pp. 84–85.

18. *Watsuji Tetsurō zenshū* (Tokyo: Iwanami Shōten, 1961–1963), 4:315 (hereafter, WTZ).

19. See Osborne, *Politics of Time*, p. 67.

20. *Tanabe Hajime zenshū* (Tokyo: Chikuma Shobō, 1963–1964), vol. 4, pp. 31–32.

21. Heidegger, *Being and Time*, p. 32.

22. Osborne, *Politics of Time*, p. 186.

23. Heidegger, *Being and Time*, p. 62.

24. See *Kuki Shūzō zenshū* (Tokyo: Iwanami Shōten, 1981), 10:105 (hereafter, KSZ).

25. Also KSZ, 10:80–81, "Heidegger no genshōgakuteki sonzairon."

26. Heidegger, *Being and Time*, p. 442.

27. Ibid., p. 444.

28. Kuki Shūzō, *Iki no kōzō* (Tokyo: Iwanami Shōten, 1972), p. 149.

29. Osborne, *Politics of Time*, pp. 186–187.

30. Heidegger, *Being and Time*, p. 30.

31. Osborne, *Politics of Time*, p. 187.

32. Heidegger, *Being and Time*, p. 69.

33. Leslie Pincus, *Authenticating Culture* (Berkeley and Los Angeles: University of California Press, 1996), p. 70.

34. *Tosaka Jun zenshū* (Tokyo: Keikusa Shobō, 1977), 4:162 (hereafter, TJZ).

35. Ibid., 4:166–168.

36. Benjamin, *Charles Baudelaire*, pp. 117, 111.

37. Stephen Light, *Shūzō Kuki and Jean-Paul Sartre* (Carbondale: Southern Illinois University Press, 1987), pp. 71–72, "Propos on Japan."

38. Kuki, *Iki*, p. 2.

39. Ibid., pp. 2–3.

40. In Light, *Shūzō Kuki*, p. 77, "A Peasant He Is."

41. Ibid.

42. KSZ, 3:270.

43. Kuki, *Iki*, p. 12.

44. Ibid., pp. 14–15.

45. Ibid., p. 140.

46. Ibid., pp. 14–15, 137.

47. Leslie Pincus, "In a Labyrinth of Western Desire: Kuki Shuzo and the Discovery of Japanese Being," in *Japan in the World*, ed. M. Miyoshi and H. Harootunian (Durham: Duke University Press, 1993), pp. 222–236; also Pincus, *Authenticating Culture*, pp. 98–208.

48. Kuki's views were widely at odds with those articulated by Tosaka in his *Nihon ideorogiron*; see KSZ, 3:367–371.

49. See TJC, 5:146–156, for a penetrating, contemporary critique of Watsuji's *Fūdo*.

50. Quoted in Noriko Aso, "New Illusions: The Emergence of a New Discourse on Traditional Arts and Crafts, 1868–1945," Ph.D. dissertation, University of Chicago, 1997), p. 144.

51. *Watsuji Tetsurō*, ed. Karaki Junzō, in *Gendai Nihon shisō taikei* (Tokyo: Chikuma Shobō, 1963), 28:300–301 (hereafter, WT).

52. Aso, "New Illusions," p. 145.

53. The Shanghai Incident refers to the action of the Japanese Special Naval Landing Party, a paramilitary group whose purpose was to defend Japanese residents and interests. Joined by the Imperial Reservists Association in 1932, they moved against the Chinese Nationalist forces encamped outside of the city of Shanghai. The act constituted a violation of the Settlement's traditional policy of neutrality.

54. Naoki Sakai, "Cultural Difference, Subjectivity and Watsuji Tetsuro," *Discours social/Social Discourse* 6, 1–2 (1994): 93.

55. Watsuji Tetsurō, *Climate and Culture*, trans. Geoffrey Bownas (Tokyo: Ministry of Education, 1961), p. 156 (hereafter, CC), translates the word as unique and strange.

56. "Ningen no gaku to shite rinrigaku," in WT, 67–68.

57. Tetsuo Najita and H. D. Harootunian, "Japan's Revolt against the West" in *Cambridge History of Japan*, ed. Duus, pp. 745–746.

58. Watsuji Tetsurō, *Nihon no Shintō, Amerika no kokuminsei* (Tokyo: Chikuma Shobō, 1944), p. 38 (hereafter, AK).

59. The Japanese greeting upon returning home, *tadaima*, uttered in the vestibule, meaning "I'm back," always struck me as a signal of assurance that one had returned from the outside again, as if it were possible that one might not!

60. See TJC, 5:156, where Tosaka argues that "original nature is diversely expressed through history objectively" and this was "none other than national character."

61. Watsuji Tetsurō, "The Significance of the Study of Ethics," trans. David Dilworth, *Monumenta Nipponica* 25, 3–4 (1971):395.

62. Tosaka, *Nihon ideorogiron*, p. 170.

Chapter 5

1. Phillipe Lacoue-Labarthe, *Heidegger, Art and Politics*, trans. Chris Turner (Oxford: Blackwell, 1990), pp. 66, 70. A more precise term than totalitarianism, immanentism is an effective replacement because it manages to describe the political experiments before the war. While the concept is articulated in Nancy's *Inoperative Community*, I have relied on Lacoue-Labarthe's application.

2. Paul Connerton, *How Societies Remember* (Cambridge: Cambridge University Press, 1989), p. 61.

3. Ibid., p. 62.

4. Ibid., pp. 63, 64. Connerton proposes that the "celebration of recurrence can never be more than a compensatory strategy, because the very principle of modernity itself denies the idea of life as a structure of celebrated occurrences." Yet we know that despite the claims of modernity, the ever new and changing is also the already the same, that simple reproduction and repetition mark the rhythm of life more than movement from one stance of difference to another.

5. Ibid., p. 64.

6. Ibid., p. 65.

7. Ibid., p. 72.

8. See H. D. Harootunian, *Things Seen and Unseen* (Chicago: University of Chicago Press, 1988).

9. LeFort, *The Political Forms*, p. 149.

10. Ibid., p. 151.

11. See Harootunian,*Things Seen*, pp. 76–175.

12. See Maruyama Masao, "Rekishi ishiki no kosō," in *Nihon no shisō, rekishi shisō*, ed. Maruyama Masao (Tokyo: Chikuma Shobō, 1973), pp. 3–46. A similar tactic, as we have seen, was developed by Watsuji Tetsuro with his conception of *jūsōsei*, which strangely resembles Maruyama's postwar idea of *kosō*, reinforcing the suspicion that the palimpsistic effect is one of the distinguishing markers of capitalist modernization.

13. *Teihon Yanagita Kunio zenshū* (Tokyo: Chikuma Shobō, 1962–1971), 30:345–577 (hereafter, TYKZ).

14. Mitsuru Hashimoto, "Chihō: Yanagita Kunio's 'Japan,' " in *Mirror of Modernity*, ed. Stephen Vlastos (Berkeley and Los Angeles: University of California Press, 1998), p. 140.

15. Ibid., pp. 142–143.

16. Karl Marx, *Grundrisse* (London: Penguin, 1973), p. 162.

17. Kawamura, *Nozomu Nihon Shakaigaku shi kenkyū* (Tokyo: Ningen no Kagakusha, 1975), 2:159–160.

18. Ibid., p. 163; TYKZ, 16:355–357.

19. Kawamura, *Nihon Shakaigaku shi*, 2:160; TYKZ, 16:355–357.

20. Yanagita Kunio, *Meiji Taishōshi sesōhen* (Tokyo: Kodansha, 1993), p. 277 (hereafter, MTS).

21. TYKZ, 16:321.

22. Nozomu Kawamura, *Society and Sociology of Japan* (London: Kegan Paul, 1994), p. 67.

23. See MTS, 3–8.

24. Richard McIntyre, "Mode of Production, Social Formation and Uneven Development," in *Postmodern Materialism and the Future of Marxist Theory in the Althusserian Tradition*, ed. Antonio Callari and David Ruccio (Middleton: Wesleyan University Press, 1996), pp. 234–235.

25. MTS, 7.

26. It is interesting to note that at almost the same time Yanagita was expressing his fears concerning the alienation and removal of people from the land to the cities, the writer of detective stories Edogawa Rampo was making the subject of many of his stories the loneliness and estrangement people experienced when coming to cities like Tokyo from the countryside, as well as the difficulties they faced in their new social relationships and sexual roles.

27. Michel DeCerteau, *Heterologies*, trans. Brian Massumi (Minneapolis: University of Minnesota Press, 1986), pp. 119–136. DeCerteau has described the formation of a discipline of popular culture—folklore—in Third Republic France and the conditions attending it. There have been some attempts to link up the tradition of Japanese folkore and "people's history" to the formation of the *Annales* historiography in France, but the fit is a poor one since the former is based upon the presumptions of an irreducible and unchanging experience and an exceptionalist, authentic ground, while the latter is simply concerned with eliminating the agency of events for long durational structures.

28. Marilyn Ivy, *Discourses of the Vanishing* (Chicago: University of Chicago Press, 1995).

29. TYKZ, 4:59–60.

30. Ibid.; Hashimoto, "Chihō," p. 133.

31. Hashimoto, "Chihō," p. 134.

32. TKYZ, 4:44.

33. Writing in 1929–1930, Yanagita called for the study of custom based on "seeing" and "listening." See MTS, 21.

34. Hashimoto, "Chihō," p. 39.

35. It is instructive to contrast Yanagita's dismissal of history because it was not repetitive with Kobayashi Hideo's discounting of history a few years later because it seemed to repeat itself.

36. *Yanagita Kunio*, ed. Masuda Katsumi, in *Gendai Nihon shisō taikei* (Tokyo: Chikuma Shobō, 1965), 29:283 (hereafter, YK).

37. Ibid., 19.

38. Ivy, *Discourses of the Vanishing*, pp. 84–85.

39. MTS, 182–187.

40. Ibid., 183.

41. See Naoki Sakai, "Return to the West/Return to the East: Watsuji Tetsurō's Anthropology and Discussion of Authenticity," *Boundary 2*, 18, 3 (1991), for an assessment of the dangers created by Watsuji's anthropology.

42. Yanagita was making virtually the same arguments for the reversion of Okinawa after World War II.

43. Slavoj Žižek, *The Sublime Object of Ideology* (London: Verso, 1989), p. 141.

44. On Yano Harumichi, see Harootunian, *Things Seen*, pp. 393–402.

45. Orikuchi Shinobu, *Kokubungaku gairon nōto* (Tokyo: Chūō Kōronsha, 1958), 3 (hereafter, KGN).

46. Orikuchi Shinobu, "Higakuni e, Tokoyo e," *Kokugakuin zasshi* 26, 5 (1921): 3–5; *Orikuchi Shinobu zenshū* (Tokyo: Chūō Kōronsha, 1965–1968), 7:33–34 (hereafter, OSZ).

47. Orikuchi, "Higakuni e, Tokoyo e," p. 6.

48. Marcel Proust, *In Search of Lost Time*, trans. C. K. Scott Moncrieff and Terence Kilmartin, rev. D. J. Enright (London: Vintage, 1996), vol. 4, p. 444.

49. Timothy Brennan, "The National Longing for Form," in, *Nation and Narrative*, ed. Homi K. Bhabha (London: Routledge, 1990), p. 51.

50. Ibid.; OSZ, 7:64–65.

51. Orikuchi Shinobu, "Kokubungaku no Hassei," *Nikkō* 1, 1 (1925): 67; see also OSZ, 7:7–10.

52. Quoted in Hasegawa Masaharu, "Orikuchi Shinobu no 'gaku' no kozo," in *Orikuchi Shinobu o yomu*, ed. Takahashi Tetsu (Tokyo: Gendai Kikakushitsu, 1981), p. 90.

53. OSZ, 16:491; also see *Orikuchi Shinobu shū*, ed. Hirose Tamotsu, in *Kindai Nihon shisō taikei* (Tokyo: Chikuma Shobō, 1975), 22:386–389 (hereafter, OSS), for his argument for realizing the past in the present from the "perspective of one's heart" and his conception of a transhistorical antiquity.

54. Also in *Okina no Hassei*, OSS, 77, 79, 92.

55. "Kokubungaku no seiritsu," 18.
56. Orikuchi, "Hahaga kuni," p. 7.
57. Ibid., pp. 9, 11.
58. Ibid., pp. 10–11.
59. Regis Debray, "Marxism and the National Question," *New Left Review*, no. 105 (September–October 1977): 27.

Chapter 6

1. Arakawa Kazuo, *Miki Kiyoshi* (Tokyo: Kinokuniya, 1968), p. 7.
2. Ibid., p. 10.
3. Iwasaki Minoru, "Miki Kiyoshi ni okeru "gijitsu,' Dōin, Kūkan," *Hihyō kūkan* 2, 5 (1995): 145.
4. Ibid., p. 151; *Miki Kiyoshi zenshū* (Tokyo: Iwanami Shōten, 1966–1967), 8:6 (hereafter, MKZ).
5. Arakawa, *Miki Kiyoshi*, p. 10.
6. Quoted in ibid., p. 42.
7. Ibid., p. 110.
8. Ibid., p. 143.
9. "Seikatsu bunka ni tsuite," zadankai, *Fujin kōron* 22 (March 1937): 416–435.
10. In Ikimatsu Keizō, *Nihon bunka e no isshikaku* (Tokyo: Miraisha, 1976), p. 78.
11. Osborne, *Politics of Time*, p. 51.
12. See Lacoue-Labarthe, *Heidegger, Art and Politics*, p. 66.
13. Though he recommended "introducing the Japanese language into native languages" to serve as a kind of lingua franca for the East Co-Prosperity Sphere, he apparently never went so far as to propose eliminating the native tongue, as colonial policy in Korea was seeking to accomplish at the same time. See MKZ, 15:556.
14. Quoted in Arakawa, *Miki Kiyoshi*, p. 181.
15. Lacoue-Labarthe, *Heidegger, Art and Politics*, pp. 68–69.
16. Max Scheler, *Problems of a Sociology of Knowledge*, trans. M. S. Frings (London: Routledge and Kegan Paul, 1980), p. 8.
17. Quoted in Haga Noboru, "Yanagita Kunio to Orikuchi Shinobu," in *Nihon Shisōshi Kōza*, ed. Furukawa Tetsu (Tokyo: Yuzankaku, 1977), vol. 8, p. 225.
18. Deleuze and Guattari, *A Thousand Plateaus*, pp. 208–231. What I have in mind is the conception of fascism articulated in that book. "What makes fascism dangerous," write Deleuze and Guattari, "is its molecular or micropolitical power, for it is a mass movement: a cancerous body rather than a totalitarianism" (215). It is precisely for this reason that fascism's capacity to spread indefinitely makes it impossible to simply consign it to a historical moment and declare that it is now in the past. This idea is marked by the wholism and immanence of the communal body and comes very close to the view proposed by Takeuchi Yoshimi, who after the war saw the emperor system in "every blade of grass, in every leaf of a tree."

In this sense fascism in prewar Japan was a mass movement, despite the apparent absence of a mass party. Moreover, this is the only way to grasp the emperor system, usually identified with prewar fascism, as a component in the construction of a fascist social order. Instead of simply appealing automatically to *tennōsei* as if its enunciation immediately summoned the image of a fascist regime, it must be situated within the larger process of immanence and the communalization of the folk body.

19. From Kawamura, *Nihon shakaigaku*, p. 265.
20. Ibid., p. 23; Kawamura, *Sociology and Society*, p. 55.
21. Kawamura, *Sociology and Society*, p. 29.
22. Ibid., p. 30.
23. KDS, 217–306.
24. Kawamura, *Sociology and Society*, p. 55.
25. Ibid., p. 37.
26. Odo Yasujirō, *Takada shakaigaku* (Tokyo: Yuikaku, 1953), p. 161.
27. Kawamura, *Nihon shakaigaku*, p. 39.
28. Ibid., p. 33, from *Shikyōki* (Record of remembering home, 1941, p. 2).
29. Ibid., pp. 244–245.
30. Takada, *Minzoku taibō*, 253ff.
31. See Takada, TMS, 61–82.
32. Kawamura, *Nihon shakaigaku*, p. 248.